Who's Who in the Age of Alexander the Great

For Anneli, who was usually on the podium before I ever caught sight of the finish line, and who kept raising the bar – so that I could get under it.

Who's Who in the Age of Alexander the Great

Prosopography of Alexander's Empire

Waldemar Heckel

A John Wiley & Sons, Ltd., Publication

This paperback edition first published 2009

Edition history: Blackwell Publishing Ltd (hardback, 2006)

Blackwell Publishing was acquired by John Wiley & Sons in February 2007. Blackwell's publishing program has been merged with Wiley's global Scientific, Technical, and Medical business to form Wiley-Blackwell.

Registered Office
John Wiley & Sons Ltd, The Atrium, Southern Gate, Chichester, West Sussex, PO19 8SQ, United Kingdom

Editorial Offices
350 Main Street, Malden, MA 02148-5020, USA
9600 Garsington Road, Oxford, OX4 2DQ, UK
The Atrium, Southern Gate, Chichester, West Sussex, PO19 8SQ, UK

For details of our global editorial offices, for customer services, and for information about how to apply for permission to reuse the copyright material in this book please see our website at www.wiley.com/wiley-blackwell.

Library of Congress Cataloging-in-Publication Data

Heckel, Waldemar, 1949–
Who's who in the age of Alexander the Great / Waldemar Heckel.
p. cm.
Includes bibliographical references and index.
ISBN: 978-1-4051-1210-9 (hard cover: alk. paper); 978-1-4051-8839-5 (paperback: alk. paper)
1. Greece—History—Macedonian Expansion, 359–323 BC—Biography—Dictionaries.
2. Iran—History—Macedonian Conquest, 334–325 BC—Biography—Dictionaries.
3. Alexander, the Great, 356–323 BC—Friends and associates. I. Title.

DF234.2.H39 2005
938'.07'0922—dc22 2005010995

A catalogue record for this book is available from the British Library.

Set in 9/11.5 Stone Serif by Graphicraft Limited, Hong Kong
Printed in Singapore by C.O.S. Printers Pte Ltd

01 2009

Contents

Introduction

In 1926 Helmut Berve published *Das Alexanderreich auf prosopographischer Grundlage,* a two-volume study of the individuals, the administration, and the military organization of Alexander's army and empire. The second volume deals with all individuals of whom it could be shown that they came into contact with Alexander ("Personen, welche mit Alexander nachweislich in Berührung gekommen sind"). Of course, Berve used the word *Berührung* ("contact") loosely, and I have followed a similar principle by restricting the individuals in my collection to people who are attested as involved in events that pertained to the *History* of Alexander, that is, primarily the literary texts. In some cases, famous persons made only brief appearances on Alexander's stage, and I have found it impractical to include all the details of their lives beyond the roles they played in the Alexander history. Hence, in the case of major figures like Aristotle, Demosthenes, and Theopompus, I have provided brief summaries of their careers while giving detailed information concerning their dealings with Alexander or those closely connected with him. I have also included non-historical figures, like Thalestris the Amazon queen, whose relationships with the Macedonian conqueror, although fictitious, are featured in the major historical accounts. On the other hand, historical individuals, who appear only in the most unreliable sources like the Alexander Romance and whose connections with Alexander cannot otherwise be substantiated, are omitted. Others still, like those Athenian orators and politicians, whose only connection with the history of Alexander is that they are named as prosecutors in the Harpalus affair, are given very brief treatment.

Berve, in his prosopography, omitted both Philip II and Alexander the Great, and the reasons for this are clear enough: the work was intended to facilitate the study of the Macedonian kingdom, and of Alexander in particular, by shedding light on the individuals around the King. I would have followed this practice, but for the comments of the readers whose opinions were solicited by the publisher. One remarked that a *Who's Who in the Age of Alexander* without Alexander himself was "like Hamlet without the Prince." Although I rather doubt that my *Who's Who* will be required reading in literature courses five hundred years from now, I have taken the advice of my readers and added entries on father and son. The entry on Alexander (**Alexander** [2]) covers the basics of the conqueror's life, without further elucidation; that on Philip II gives a brief outline of the man's career and provides more detail on his relationship with Alexander.

The greatest difficulty is to do justice to those men who began their careers under Philip or Alexander and became even more influential in the age of the Successors. Complete biographies of these men have been published in various modern languages, and particularly in recent years in English. Hence, for Antigonus the One-Eyed, Cassander, Eumenes of Cardia, Lysimachus, Ptolemy son of Lagus, and Seleucus, I have chosen in most cases (and, I admit, somewhat arbitrarily) to end with the settlement at Triparadeisus (which I date to 320) or the death of Antipater and the power-struggle between Polyperchon and Cassander. For some of the lesser lights, I have included complete biographies, especially if their careers do not extend beyond the year of Ipsus (301). On the other hand, I have also included brief notices of individuals who do not, strictly speaking, belong to the age of Alexander but who are closely connected with prominent individuals or royal families, and I have included them in my stemmata.

After much consideration and on the advice of numerous friends and colleagues, I have decided to adopt Latinized spellings of names, despite the fact that this practice requires me to "invent" unattested Latin forms. The majority of Alexander scholars writing in English use the Latinized spellings and the most popular biographies do so as well. I have therefore considered it more useful to readers – especially laymen, students, and scholars in other fields – to employ the more recognizable forms. There is in the transliteration of Greek no consistency amongst scholars, and I myself have difficulty with some of the spellings favored by the "purists." But, even with the Latin forms, there are problems. I have chosen to convert "ou" to "u" (that is, Aristobulus rather than Aristoboulus) but have retained "ei" instead of "i" (as in Cleitus and Cleitarchus instead of Clitus, Clitarchus). Certain names have been anglicized: Ptolemy instead of Ptolemaeus; Philip instead of Philippus; but Heracles is preferred to Hercules, Rhoxane to Roxane (indeed, all names beginning with the Greek letter *rho* are written Rh-). Names ending in -on in Greek but in -o in Latin remain in the Greek form: Damon, Parmenion, Platon. Of course, the catalogue follows English rather than Greek alphabetical order. Variant forms are provided in parentheses at the beginning of each entry, and a concordance of forms is supplied at the end of the book.

The citation of works is equally idiosyncratic, but employs a logic of sorts. Standard works (Abbreviations II) are provided as follows: Beloch iii^2 2.126; *SEG* xiv.24; *IG* ii^2 461; Tarn ii.115; Berve ii.32 etc. Single-volume works that are cited frequently (Abbreviations III) are given by author's last name and page number (e.g. Carney 204 or Billows 414 no. 86). Other works, listed in the Bibliography at the end of the book, are cited in the "Harvard" or "Social Sciences" style. I have also adopted a set of convenient abbreviations for the ancient sources, although in the case of some less familiar authors and texts – especially those that are cited infrequently – I have given the full names of authors and works, the latter often in English (e.g. Lucian, *How to Write History*). But even here there will be a certain amount of unavoidable inconsistency, and I ask the reader to keep in mind that my aim is to make the work as useful as possible to a wider audience. Some of the more detailed arguments or references to details that are not essential to the basic understanding of an individual's career have been relegated to endnotes.

I have also included a list of 138 anonymous individuals (out of a collection of well over 200), most of whom are certainly historical and, in fact, prominent persons, especially the women.[1] The names of some of these individuals may yet become known (through the discovery of new documents) or their relationships to known persons verified. In some cases, I have included nameless individuals who are the subject of stories both real and fictitious. But I have left out the nameless agents of various actions (for example, "a messenger was sent," "a bugler sounded the alarm," "an archer wounded someone") since this would mean including thousands of unnamed soldiers and civilians. For a similar reason, I have omitted the ten Gymnosophists who were said to have debated Alexander and other "groups" of persons who are doubtless historical, even if the stories about them are untrue. Anonymous females are listed as **F** and males as **M**.

Several individuals in my collection have left behind published works, either extant or known only from fragments. Berve, in many cases, discussed the nature of these works in detail. I have omitted such discussions, since a great deal of literature is available on most orators, philosophers, and historians, and have referred the reader to the most important or accessible modern works. Although it was my intention, when I began my prosopographic work in the 1970s, to provide an updated, English-language *Who's Who* of the Alexander period, this work does not claim to be the English equivalent of Berve's fundamental work – comparisons will inevitably be made and I am afraid that my efforts must fall short of the master's – or even "Son of Berve," as many of my colleagues have jokingly called it. My inspiration in recent years – though, again, I do not pretend to have produced its equal – has been the splendid *Who's Who of the Conquistadors* by Hugh Thomas (London: Cassell, 2000), which attempts to reach a wider audience without sacrificing scholarly content. Occasionally, I have retained, with the permission of the Taylor and Francis Group, the original wording of entries, or portions thereof, in *The Marshals of Alexander's Empire* (London, 1992); for there were places where I could hardly do otherwise. The major biographies contained there are, however, compressed and somewhat truncated in this version. My editor, Al Bertrand, kindly agreed to accept a typescript that far exceeded the originally contracted length. Nevertheless, in most places I have written much less than I intended. Lord Thomas calls his work "a labor of love," and so is mine, though there have been many times in the final stages of composition when I have questioned the depth of my devotion. Nevertheless, I am sure that the layman will complain that the book contains more than he needs and the scholar that it does not have everything he wants. But, if I have done something to make the work of others – amateurs, students, scholars – easier and more enjoyable, then I shall feel that the labor has not been in vain.

It is impossible to produce a work of this kind without the help, friendship, and encouragement of numerous individuals. No words can adequately express my indebtedness and my thanks, and I apologize in advance if I have omitted anyone from the following, alphabetically ordered list: Lindsay Adams, Ed Anson, John Atkinson, Barry Baldwin, Elizabeth Baynham, Richard Billows, Gene Borza, Pierre Briant, Stan Burstein, Jack Cargill, Beth Carney, Bob Develin, Albert Devine, Boris Dreyer, Erin Garvin, Tom Goud, Kirk Grayson, Peter Green, Bill Greenwalt, Erich Gruen, Christian Habicht, Charlie Hamilton, Phillip Harding, Konrad Kinzl, Holger Koch, Brian Lavelle, Leo Mildenberg, Bill Mills, Jeanne Reames-Zimmerman, Jennifer Roberts, Yossi Roisman, Klaus Rosen, Catherine Rubincam, Cynthia Schwenk, Sam Scully, Andy Sherwood, Graham Shipley, Gordon Shrimpton, Ralph Siferd, Richard Stoneman, Carol Thomas, Michael Walbank, Gerhard Wirth, Julia Wong, and Ian Worthington. I am particularly grateful to the late Miguel Alonso-Nuñez, who urged me to complete this work after seeing an unfinished script collecting dust in my study, and to Brian Bosworth, Frank Holt, and Daniel Ogden, who helped to persuade Blackwell Publishing to undertake this project; to my friend and colleague, John Vanderspoel, for help with the stemmata; to Liz Hardy, Pat Wheatley, and Michael Leventhal for support and understanding in the most difficult times; and to Larry Tritle and John Yardley for doing what friends do – and for telling me to "get a life." Al Bertrand and Angela Cohen at Blackwell demonstrated their usual patience and goodwill as I moved from one missed deadline to the next. I can't thank them enough for sticking with me. I especially thank Brigitte Lee for her careful reading of a difficult and confusing typescript, and Carole Schwab of the Tamarindonet Internet café in Tamarindo, Costa Rica, for helping me keep in touch with the outside world. And, of course, as always, I could not have done any of this without the help and support of my wife, Lois, and my children, Julia and Darren. I wanted to dedicate the book to my cat, Subedei ("Sweet Subi Blue-Eyes"), who was my faithful and untiring companion on those long and late nights when I finished this book, but I thought that my sister, my oldest friend, deserved it more.

Chronological Table

383/2	Birth of Philip II of Macedon.
360/59	Defeat of Perdiccas III by the Illyrians. Accession of Philip (either as king or regent).
358/7	Births of Cynnane and Arrhidaeus (Philip III).
357	Philip marries Olympias of Epirus.
356	Birth of Alexander the Great (July 20). Philip's chariot successful in Olympic games.
ca. 353	Birth of Cleopatra [2].
352	Battle of the Crocus Field.
346	Peace of Philocrates.
345	Birth of Thessalonice?
343–340	Alexander educated by Aristotle.
340	Alexander "regency." Campaign against the Maedians.
338	Battle of Chaeronea. Defeat of Athens and Thebes; destruction of the Sacred Band.
337	Marriage of Philip II and Cleopatra-Eurydice. Rift between Philip and his Epirote family.
336	Pixodarus affair (see s.vv. **Ada** [2], **Pixodarus**); exile of Ptolemy, Harpalus, Erigyius, Laomedon, and Nearchus; forces under Parmenion and Attalus sent to Asia Minor; marriage of Alexander of Epirus to Cleopatra [2]. Death of Philip II. Accession of Alexander III.
336/5	Deaths of Amyntas son of Perdiccas and Attalus. Triballian and Danubian campaign.
335	Illyrian campaign against Glaucias and Cleitus. Destruction of Thebes.
334	Alexander crosses the Hellespont; battle at the Granicus; surrender of Sardis by Mithrenes; capture of Miletus; siege of Halicarnassus and Alexander's "adoption" by Ada [1].
334/3	Winter. Arrest of Alexander Lyncestes (see also s.vv. **Sisines** [1], **Amphoterus**). The newly-weds (*neogamoi*) winter in Macedonia. Death of Memnon [1].
333	Capture of Celaenae (Antigonus installed as satrap of Phrygia); cutting of Gordian Knot; death of Charidemus. Battle of Issus; capture of Damascus by Parmenion.
333/2	Surrender of Phoenician cities; Abdalonymus installed as King of Sidon.
332	January–August: siege of Tyre; September–October: siege of Gaza; death of Batis. Alexander enters Egypt.
332/1	Visit to oracle of Amun at Siwah.

331	Founding of Alexandria in Egypt; battle of Megalopolis; battle of Gaugamela; fall of Babylon and Susa; Uxian campaign (see s.v. **Madates**); passage of the Persian Gates.
330	January–May: Alexander at Persepolis. July: death of Darius III. Alexander moves into Afghanistan. Deaths of Philotas, Parmenion, Demetrius the Bodyguard.
330/329	Revolt and death of Satibarzanes. Surrender of Bessus.
329	Summer: Alexander at the Iaxartes (Syr-darya). Revolt of Spitamenes. Polytimetus disaster.
329/8	Winter quarters at Bactra.
328	Spring: capture of the Rock of Ariamazes (Rock of Sogdiana). Summer: death of Cleitus [2]. Autumn: capture of Rock of Sisimithres (Chorienes). Winter: wedding of Alexander and Rhoxane.
327	Introduction of *proskynesis*. Conspiracy of Hermolaus. Beginning of the Indian campaign.
327/6	Swat campaign and capture of Aornus.
326	Alexander at Taxila; battle of the Hydaspes; mutiny at the Hyphasis; death of Coenus.
326/5	November 326–July 325: descent of the Indus.
325	Return to the west. Gedrosian campaign.
325/4	Winter in Carmania.
324	Punishment of the satraps (see also s.vv. **Cleander**, **Heracon**, **Sitalces**); flight of Harpalus; mutiny at Opis. Proclamation of the "Exiles' Decree" at Olympia. Death of Hephaestion.
324/3	Cossaean campaign.
323	Death of Alexander. Arrhidaeus becomes King Philip III; settlement in Babylon. Birth of Alexander IV. Outbreak of Lamian War.
323/2	Antipater in Lamia.
322	Antipater relieved by Leonnatus. Craterus arrives, defeat of the Greeks at Crannon. Peace settlements; peace with Athens. Peithon deals with rebellious Greeks in Upper Satrapies. Deaths of Demosthenes and Hypereides.
322/1	Craterus and Antipater in Macedonia. Marriage of Craterus and Phila. Perdiccas in Asia Minor.
321	War with the Aetolians. Death of Cynnane; marriage of Adea and Philip III.
321/0	Craterus, Antipater, and Antigonus prepare to wage war on Perdiccas. Theft of Alexander's corpse by Ptolemy and Arrhidaeus [2].
320	Death of Craterus against Eumenes. Perdiccas defeated and murdered near Memphis. Settlement of Triparadeisus. Marriage of Phila and Demetrius Poliorcetes.
319	Death of Antipater. Polyperchon appointed guardian of the Kings; Cassander appointed chiliarch.
318	Polyperchon declares "Freedom of the Greeks" in the name of Philip III. Nicanor installed as commandant of Munychia. Death of Phocion.
317–307	Cassander controls Athens through the agency of Demetrius of Phalerum.
317	Battles of Euia (Olympias vs. Adea-Eurydice); deaths of Philip III and Adea-Eurydice; siege of Pydna.
317/16	Battles of Paraetacene and Gabiene. Death of Eumenes.
316	Death of Olympias. Flight of Seleucus from Babylon (dated by some to 315).

315	Cassander restores Thebes, marries Thessalonice.
312	Battle of Gaza. Seleucus returns to Babylonia.
311	Peace arranged by Antigonus (and Demetrius) with Cassander, Lysimachus, Seleucus, and Ptolemy.
310/309	Death of Alexander IV and Rhoxane (date uncertain).
309/308	Death of Heracles, son of Barsine and Alexander the Great (date uncertain).
307–301	Demetrius Poliorcetes controls Athens.
306	Battle of Salamis. Antigonus and Demetrius proclaimed "Kings."
305–304	Siege of Rhodes.
301	Battle of Ipsus. Death of Antigonus the One-Eyed.
297	Death of Cassander.
285–283	Joint rule of Ptolemy I Soter and Ptolemy II Philadelphus.
283	Death of Demetrius; death of Ptolemy I Soter.
281	Battle of Corupedium. Death of Lysimachus. Seleucus killed by Ptolemy Ceraunus.

Abbreviations I: Ancient Authors

A	Arrian, *Anabasis*
A*Ind*	Arrian, *Indica*
A*Succ*	Arrian, *Successors* (*Events after Alexander*)
Ael*NA*	Aelian, *Nature of Animals*
Ael*VH*	Aelian, *Varia Historia*
Aen Tact	Aeneas the Tactician
Aes	Aeschines
AP	*Anthologia Palatina* (*The Palatine Anthology*)
App*BC*	Appian, *Bella Civilia* (*The Civil Wars*)
App*Mithr*	Appian, *Mithridatic Wars*
App*Syr*	Appian, *Syrian Wars*
Apul*Apol*	Apuleius, *Apology*
Apul*Flor*	Apuleius, *Florida*
Arist*Pol*	Aristotle, *Politics*
Arist*Rhet*	Aristotle, *Rhetoric*
[Arist]*Oecon*	Pseudo-Aristotle, *Oeconomicus*
Ath	Athenaeus, *Deipnosophistae*
Ath Mec	Athenaeus Mechanicus, *On Machines*
C	Curtius (Quintus Curtius Rufus)
Cic	Cicero
D	Diodorus of Sicily
Dem	Demosthenes
Dem*Ep*	Demosthenes, *Letters*
[Dem]	Pseudo-Demosthenes
Din	Dinarchus
Dio Chr	Dio Chrysostom
Dion Hal	Dionysius of Halicarnassus
DL	Diogenes Laertius
Euseb	Eusebius, *Chronicle*
Euseb Arm	Eusebius, *Chronicle* (Armenian version)
Fr*Strat*	Frontinus, *Stratagemata*
Gell	Aulus Gellius
Harp	Harpocration
Hdt	Herodotus
HE	*Heidelberg Epitome* = Jacoby, *FGrH* 155
Hyp	Hypereides
Isoc*Ep*	Isocrates, *Epistles* (*Letters*)
Isoc*Phil*	Isocrates, *Philippus*

IA	*Itinerarium Alexandri* (*Itinerary of Alexander*)
J	Justin
Jos*AJ*	Josephus, *Jewish Antiquities*
Jul Val	Julius Valerius (Latin *Alexander Romance*)
L*Cal*	Lucian, *Calumniae non temere credendum*
L*DM*	Lucian, *Dialogi Mortuorum*
[L]*Macrob*	Pseudo-Lucian, *Macrobii*
LatAlex	*Laterculi Alexandrini*
Lib	Libanius
LM	*Liber de Morte*
Lyc	Lycurgus
Macr*Sat*	Macrobius, *Saturnalia*
ME	*Metz Epitome*
MP	*Marmor Parium* (*Parian Marble*)
N*Eum*	Nepos, *Eumenes*
N*Iph*	Nepos, *Iphicrates*
N*Ph*	Nepos, *Phocion*
N*Timoth*	Nepos, *Timotheus*
Oros	Orosius
P*A*	Plutarch, *Alexander*
P*Ages*	Plutarch, *Agesilaus*
P*Agis*	Plutarch, *Agis*
P*Art*	Plutarch, *Artoxerxes* (*Artaxerxes*)
P*Cam*	Plutarch, *Camillus*
P*Cleom*	Plutarch, *Cleomenes*
P*Dem*	Plutarch, *Demosthenes*
P*Demetr*	Plutarch, *Demetrius*
P*Dion*	Plutarch, *Dion*
P*Eum*	Plutarch, *Eumenes*
P*Galba*	Plutarch, *Galba*
P*M*	Plutarch, *Moralia*
[P]*M*	Pseudo-Plutarch, *Moralia*
P*Pel*	Plutarch, *Pelopidas*
P*Ph*	Plutarch, *Phocion*
P*Pyr*	Plutarch, *Pyrrhus*
P*Ser*	Plutarch, *Sertorius*
P*Sulla*	Plutarch, *Sulla*
P*Tim*	Plutarch, *Timoleon*
Paus	Pausanias
Philostr*VS*	Philostratus, *Lives of the Sophists*
Phot*Bibl*	Photius, *Bibliotheke*
Pl*NH*	Pliny, *Natural History*
Plb	Polybius
Pol*Strat*	Polyaenus, *Stratagemata*
Ps-Call	Pseudo-Callisthenes, *Alexander Romance*
Pt*Geog*	Ptolemy, *Geography*
Quint	Quintilian
Sen*Ep*	Seneca, *Letters*
Sen*de Ira*	Seneca, *de Ira*
Sil	Silius Italicus
StByz	Stephanus of Byzantium
Str	Strabo, *Geography*

Tatian *ad Gr*	Tatian, *Oratio ad Graecos*
Them*Or*	Themistius, *Orations*
Theophr*HP*	Theophrastus, *Historia plantarum* (*History of Plants*)
Thuc	Thucydides
Tr*Prol*	Pompeius Trogus, *Prologues*
Tzetz*Chil*	Tzetzes, *Chiliades*
Xen*Anab*	Xenophon, *Anabasis*
Xen*Cyr*	Xenophon, *Cyropaedia*
Xen*HG*	Xenophon, *Historia Graeca* (= *Hellenica*)
Val Max	Valerius Maximus
Vell Pat	Velleius Paterculus
Vitr	Vitruvius, *De Architectura* (*On Architecture*)

Abbreviations II: Multi-Volume Reference Works

ABC	A. K. Grayson, *Assyrian and Babylonian Chronicles* (Locust Valley, NY, 1975)
ADRTB	A. J. Sachs and H. Hunger, *Astronomical Diaries and Related Texts from Babylonia*, vol. 1 (Vienna, 1988)
Anspach i–ii	A. E. Anspach, *De Alexandri Magni expeditione Indica* (Leipzig, 1903)
Atkinson i–ii	J. E. Atkinson, *A Commentary on Q. Curtius Rufus' Historia Alexandri Magni* (Amsterdam, 1980, 1994)
Beloch i–iv^2	K. J. Beloch, *Griechischen Geschichte*, 2nd edition (Berlin and Leipzig, 1912–17)
Bengtson i–iii	H. Bengtson, *Die Strategie in der hellenistischen Zeit* (Munich, 1937)
Berve i–ii	H. Berve, *Das Alexanderreich auf prosopographischer Grundlage*, 2 vols. (Munich, 1926)
Bevan i–ii	E. R. Bevan, *The House of Seleucus*, 2 vols. (London, 1902)
BHLT	A. K. Grayson, *Babylonian Historical-Literary Texts* (Toronto, 1975)
Blaβ i–iii^2	F. Blaβ, *Die attische Beredsamkeit*, 2nd edition, 3 vols. (Leipzig, 1887–98)
Bosworth i–ii	A. B. Bosworth, *A Historical Commentary on Arrian's History of Alexander* (Oxford, 1980, 1995)
Brunt i–ii	P. A. Brunt, *Arrian: The History of Alexander and the Indica*, 2 vols. Loeb Classical Library (Cambridge, MA, 1976, 1983)
CAH^2	*Cambridge Ancient History*, 2nd edition
CHIndia	*Cambridge History of India*
CHIran	*Cambridge History of Iran*
CIS	*Corpus Inscriptionum Semiticarum*
Cook i–iii	J. M. Cook, *Zeus: A Study in Ancient Religion*, 3 vols. (Cambridge, 1914–40)
Droysen i–iii^3	J. G. Droysen, *Geschichte des Hellenismus*, 3rd edition, E. Bayer (ed.) (Darmstadt, 1980)
FGrH	F. Jacoby, *Die Fragmente der griechischen Historiker* (Berlin and Leiden, 1923–)
FHG	C. and Th. Müller, *Fragmenta Historicorum Graecorum*, 5 vols. (Paris, 1841–70)
Goukowsky i–ii	P. Goukowsky, *Essai sur les origines du mythe d'Alexandre*, 2 vols. (Nancy, 1978–81)
Gow i–ii	A. S. F. Gow, *Theocritus*, 2 vols. (Oxford, 1950)

Griffith, *HMac* ii	G. T. Griffith in N. G. L. Hammond and G. T. Griffith, *History of Macedonia*, vol. 2 (Oxford, 1979)
Hammond, *HMac* i	N. G. L. Hammond, *History of Macedonia*, vol. 1 (Oxford, 1972)
Hammond, *HMac* ii	N. G. L. Hammond in N. G. L. Hammond and G. T. Griffith, *History of Macedonia*, vol. 2 (Oxford, 1979)
Hammond, *HMac* iii	N. G. L. Hammond in N. G. L. Hammond and F. W. Walbank, *History of Macedonia*, vol. 3 (Oxford, 1988)
Head, *HN*^{2}	B. V. Head, *Historia Numorum*, 2nd edition (London, 1963)
IG	*Inscriptiones Graecae*
Kaerst i–ii	J. Kaerst, *Geschichte des Hellenismus* (Leipzig, 1926–7)
Kl. Pauly	*Der Kleine Pauly*
Lassen i–iv	C. Lassen, *Indische Altertumskunde*, 4 vols. (Leipzig, 1861–74)
Launey	M. Launey, *Recherches sur les armées hellénistiques*, 2 vols. (Paris, 1949–50)
LGPN	*Lexicon of Greek Personal Names*
Niese i–ii	B. Niese, *Geschichte der griechischen und makedonischen Staaten seit der Schlacht bei Chaeronea*, 2 vols. (Gotha, 1893; repr. Darmstadt, 1963)
OCD^3	*Oxford Classical Dictionary*, 3rd edition, Hornblower and Spawforth (eds.)
OGIS	W. Dittenberger, *Orientis Graeci Inscriptiones Selectae* (Leipzig, 1903–5)
Osborne i–iv	M. J. Osborne, *Naturalization in Athens*, 4 vols. in 3 (Brussels, 1981–3)
POxy	*Oxyrhynchus Papyri*, B. P. Grenfell and A. S. Hunt (eds.) (London, 1898–)
Pros Ptol	W. Peremans, E. van 't Dack et al., *Prosopographia Ptolemaica* (Louvain, 1950–)
PSI	*Papiri greci e latini* (Pubblicazioni della Società Italiana per la ricerca dei papiri greci e latini in Egitto)
RE	*Realencyclopädie der classischen Altertumswissenschaft*, Pauly, Wissowa, Kroll (eds.)
Robinson i–ii	C. A. Robinson, Jr., *The History of Alexander the Great*, 2 vols. (Providence, RI, 1953)
Schaefer i–iii^2	A. Schaefer, *Demosthenes und seine Zeit*, 2nd edition, 3 vols. (Leipzig, 1885–7)
SEG	*Supplementum Epigraphicum Graecum*
SIG^3	W. Dittenberger, *Sylloge Inscriptionum Graecarum*, 3rd edition (Leipzig, 1915–24)
Staatsv iii	H. H. Schmitt, *Die Staatsverträge des Altertums*, vol. 3 (Munich, 1969)
Tarn i–ii	W. W. Tarn, *Alexander the Great*, 2 vols. (Cambridge, 1948)
Tod i–ii	M. N. Tod, *Greek Historical Inscriptions*, 2 vols. (Oxford, 1948)
Walbank, *HMac* iii	F. W. Walbank in N. G. L. Hammond and F. W. Walbank, *History of Macedonia*, vol. 3 (Oxford, 1988)
Welles, *RC*	C. Bradford Welles, *Royal Correspondence in the Hellenistic Period* (London, 1934)

Abbreviations III: Modern Works

Anson	E. M. Anson, *Eumenes of Cardia: A Greek Among Macedonians* (Leiden, 2004)
Austin	M. M. Austin, *The Hellenistic World from Alexander to the Roman Conquest* (Cambridge, 1985)
Bagnall	R. Bagnall, *The Administration of Ptolemaic Possessions Outside Egypt* (Leiden, 1976)
Bagnall & Derow	R. Bagnall and P. Derow (eds.), *Historical Sources in Translation: The Hellenistic Period* (Oxford, 2004)
Baumbach	A. Baumbach, *Kleinasien unter Alexander dem Grossen* (Weida i. Th., 1911)
Bengtson	H. Bengtson, *Die Diadochen. Die Nachfolger Alexanders des Grossen* (Munich, 1975)
Benveniste	E. Benveniste, *Titres et noms propres en iranien ancien* (Paris, 1966)
Besevliev	V. Besevliev, *Personennamen bei den Thrakern* (Amsterdam, 1970)
Billows	Richard A. Billows, *Antigonos the One-Eyed and the Creation of the Hellenistic State* (Berkeley and Los Angeles, 1990)
Blackwell	C. W. Blackwell, *In the Absence of Alexander: Harpalus and the Failure of Macedonian Authority* (New York, 1999)
Blass	Friedrich Wilhelm Blass, *Die griechische Beredsamkeit in dem Zeitraum von Alexander bis auf Augustus* (Hildesheim, 1977)
Boerma	R. N. H. Boerma, *Justinus' Boeken over de Diadochen, een historisch Commentaar. Boek 13–15 cap. 2* (Amsterdam, 1979)
Briant	P. Briant, *From Cyrus to Alexander: A History of the Persian Empire*, trans. Peter T. Daniels (Winnona Lake, Indiana, 2002)
Brosius	Maria Brosius, *Women in Ancient Persia (559–331 BC)* (Oxford, 1996)
Brown	T. S. Brown, *Onesicritus: A Study in Hellenistic Historiography* (Berkeley and Los Angeles, 1949)
Buckler	J. Buckler, *Aegean Greece in the Fourth Century BC* (Leiden, 2003)
Buraselis	K. Buraselis, *Das hellenistische Makedonien und die Ägäis*, Münchener Beiträge zur Papyrusforschung und antiken Rechtsgeschichte, Heft 73 (Munich, 1982)
Burstein	S. M. Burstein, *Outpost of Hellenism: The Emergence of Heraclea on the Black Sea* (Berkeley, 1974)
Carney	Elizabeth D. Carney, *Women and Monarchy in Macedonia* (Norman, Oklahoma, 2000)
Caroe	O. Caroe, *The Pathans* (London, 1962)

Cross	G. N. Cross, *Epirus: A Study in Greek Constitutional Development* (Cambridge, 1932)
Davies	J. K. Davies, *Athenian Propertied Families* (Oxford, 1971)
Develin	R. Develin, *Athenian Officials: 684–321 BC* (Cambridge, 1989)
Düring	I. Düring, *Aristotle in the Ancient Biographical Tradition* (Göteborg, 1957)
Eggermont	P. H. L. Eggermont, *Alexander's Campaigns in Sind and Baluchistan and the Siege of the Brahmin Town of Harmatelia* (Leuven, 1975)
Ellis	J. R. Ellis, *Philip II and Macedonian Imperialism* (London, 1976)
Engel	R. Engel, *Untersuchungen zum Machaufstieg des Antigonos I. Monophthalmos. Ein Beitrag zur Geschichte der frühen Diadochenzeit* (Kallmunz, 1976)
Engels	D. W. Engels, *Alexander the Great and the Logistics of the Macedonian Army* (Berkeley and Los Angeles, 1978)
Ferguson	W. S. Ferguson, *Hellenistic Athens: An Historical Essay* (London, 1911)
Fleming	W. B. Fleming, *The History of Tyre* (New York, 1915)
Fortina	M. Fortina, *Cassandro, Re di Macedonia* (Turin, 1965)
Fränkel	A. Fränkel, *Die Quellen der Alexanderhistoriker* (Breslau, 1883)
Fraser	P. M. Fraser, *Cities of Alexander the Great* (Oxford, 1996)
Fuller	J. F. C. Fuller, *The Generalship of Alexander the Great* (New Brunswick, NJ, 1960)
Gehrke	H.-J. Gehrke, *Phokion. Studien zur Erfassung seiner historischen Gestalt.* Zetemata, Heft 64 (Munich, 1976)
Ghiron-Bistagne	P. Ghiron-Bistagne, *Recherches sur les acteurs dans la Grèce antique* (Paris 1976)
Goldstein	J. A. Goldstein, *The Letters of Demosthenes* (New York, 1968)
Goukowsky	P. Goukowsky (ed.), *Diodore de Sicile, Livre XVII* (Paris, 1976)
Grainger	J. D. Grainger, *Seleukos Nikator: Constructing a Hellenistic Kingdom* (London, 1990)
Green	P. Green, *Alexander of Macedon* (London, 1974)
Griffin	A. Griffin, *Sicyon* (Oxford, 1982)
Griffith	G. T. Griffith, *The Mercenaries of the Hellenistic World* (Cambridge, 1935)
Gude	M. Gude, *A History of Olynthus* (Baltimore, 1933)
Guthrie	W. K. C. Guthrie, *Aristotle: An Encounter = A History of Greek Philosophy*, vol. 6 (Cambridge, 1981)
Habicht[2]	C. Habicht, *Gottmenschentum und griechische Städte.* Zetemata, Heft 14, 2nd edition (Munich, 1970)
Hamel	D. Hamel, *Athenian Generals: Military Authority in the Classical Period* (Leiden, 1998)
Hamilton	J. R. Hamilton, *Plutarch, Alexander: A Commentary* (Oxford, 1969)
Harding	P. Harding, *From the End of the Peloponnesian War to the Battle of Ipsos*, Translated Documents of Greece and Rome, no. 2 (Cambridge, 1984)
Harris	Edward M. Harris, *Aeschines and Athenian Politics* (Oxford, 1995)
Hauben	H. Hauben, *Het Vlootbevelhebberschap in de vroege Diadochentijd (323–301 vóór Christus). Een prosopografisch en institutioneel Onderzoek* (Brussels, 1975)
Heckel	Waldemar Heckel, *The Marshals of Alexander's Empire* (London, 1992)

Heisserer	A. J. Heisserer, *Alexander the Great and the Greeks: The Epigraphic Evidence* (Norman, Oklahoma, 1980)
Hoffmann	O. Hoffmann, *Die Makedonen: ihre Sprache und ihr Volkstum* (Göttingen, 1906)
Hofstetter	J. Hofstetter, *Die Griechen in Persien. Prosopographie der Griechen im persischen Reich vor Alexander.* Archäologische Mitteilungen aus Iran, Ergänzungsband 5 (Berlin, 1978)
Hölbl	G. Höelbl, *History of the Ptolemaic Empire* (London, 2001)
Holt	Frank L. Holt, *Alexander the Great and Bactria* (Leiden, 1988)
Hünerwadel	W. Hünerwadel, *Forschungen zur Geschichte des Königs Lysimachus von Thrakien* (Zürich, 1900)
Instinsky	H. U. Instinsky, *Alexander der Grosse am Hellespont* (Godesberg, 1949)
Jacobs	Bruno Jacobs, *Die Satrapienverwaltung im Perserreich zur Zeit Darius' III* (Wiesbaden, 1994)
Jaschinski	S. Jaschinski, *Alexander und Griechenland unter dem Eindruck der Flucht des Harpalos* (Bonn, 1981)
Judeich	W. Judeich, *Kleinasiatische Studien* (Marburg, 1892)
Julien	P. Julien, *Zur Verwaltung der Satrapien unter Alexander dem Grossen* (Weida i. Th., 1914)
Justi	F. Justi, *Iranisches Namenbuch* (Marburg, 1895)
Kirchner	J. Kirchner, *Prosopographia Attica*
Klinkott	H. Klinkott, *Die Satrapienregister der Alexander- und Diadochenzeit.* Historia Einzelschriften, Heft 145 (Stuttgart, 2000)
Kornemann	E. Kornemann, *Die Alexandergeschichte des Königs Ptolemaios I. von Aegypten* (Leipzig, 1935)
Krumbholz	P. Krumbholz, *De Asiae Minoris Satrapis Persicis* (Leipzig, 1883)
Landucci Gattinoni	Franca Landucci Gattinoni, *L'arte del potere. Vita e opere di Cassandro di Macedonia.* Historia Einzelschriften, Heft 171 (Stuttgart, 2003)
Lane Fox	R. Lane Fox, *Alexander the Great* (London, 1973)
Lauffer	S. Lauffer, *Die Bergwerkssklaven von Laureion*, I (Akad. der Wiss. in Mainz, Abh. der geisteswiss. Kl. 1955, no. 12) (Wiesbaden, 1956) and II (ibid. 1956, no. 11) (Wiesbaden, 1957)
Lehmann-Haupt	F. Lehmann-Haupt, "Satrap," *RE* IIA.1 (1921): 82–188
Leuze	O. Leuze, *Die Satrapienteilung in Syrien und im Zweistromlande von 520–320* (Halle, 1935)
Lund	Helen S. Lund, *Lysimachus: A Study in Early Hellenistic Kingship* (London, 1992)
McCrindle	J. W. McCrindle, *The Invasion of India by Alexander the Great* (London, 1896; repr. 1969)
Macurdy	G. H. Macurdy, *Hellenistic Queens: A Study of Woman Power in Ancient Macedonia, Seleucid Syria and Ptolemaic Egypt* (Baltimore, 1932)
Marquart	J. Marquart, "Untersuchungen zur Geschichte von Eran, II," *Philologus*. Supplbd. 10 (Leipzig, 1907): 1–258
Mehl	A. Mehl, *Seleukos Nikator und sein Reich* (Leuven, 1986)
Milns	R. D. Milns, *Alexander the Great* (London, 1968)
Mørkholm	O. Mørkholm, *Early Hellenistic Coinage from the Accession of Alexander to the Peace of Apamea (336–188 BC)* (Cambridge, 1991)

Müller	Sabine Müller, *Maßnahmen der Herrschaftssicherung gegenüber der makedonischen Opposition bei Alexander dem Großen* (Frankfurt a.M., 2003)
O'Connor	John B. O'Connor, *Chapters in the History of Actors and Acting in Ancient Greece: Together with a Prosopographia Histrionum Graecorum* (Haskell, 1966)
Ogden	Daniel Ogden, *Polygamy, Prostitutes and Death: The Hellenistic Dynasties* (London, 1999)
Olmstead	A. T. Olmstead, *History of the Persian Empire* (Chicago, 1948)
Olshausen	E. Olshausen, *Prosopographie der hellenistischen Königsgesandten. Vol. 1: Von Triparadeisus bis Pydna* (Leuven, 1974)
Papastavru	J. Papastavru, *Amphipolis. Geschichte und Prosopographie.* Klio Beiheft 37 (Leipzig, 1936)
Pape & Benseler	W. Pape and G. Benseler, *Wörterbuch der griechischen. Eigennamen* (Braunschweig, 1911)
Parke	H. W. Parke, *Greek Mercenary Soldiers from the Earliest Times to the Battle of Ipsus* (Oxford, 1933)
Pearson	L. Pearson, *The Lost Histories of Alexander the Great* (Philadelphia, 1960)
Pédech	P. Pédech, *Historiens Compagnons d'Alexandre* (Paris, 1984)
Pollitt	J. J. Pollitt, *The Art of Ancient Greece: Sources and Documents* (Cambridge, 1990)
Poralla	Paul Poralla, *Prosopographie der Lakedaimonier bis auf die Zeit Alexanders des Grossen*, 2nd edition, with Introduction, Corrigenda, and Addenda by A. S. Bradford (Chicago, 1985)
Powell	J. E. Powell, *A Lexicon to Herodotus* (Cambridge, 1938)
Prandi	Luisa Prandi, *Fortuna e realtà dell'opera di Clitarco.* Historia Einzelschriften, Heft 104 (Stuttgart, 1996)
Reuss	F. Reuss, *Hieronymus von Kardia* (Berlin, 1876)
Rhodes & Osborne	P. J. Rhodes and R. Osborne, *Greek Historical Inscriptions 404–323 BC* (Oxford, 2003)
Sandberger	F. Sandberger, *Prosopographie zur Geschichte des Pyrrhos* (Stuttgart, 1970)
Schachermeyr	Fritz Schachermeyr, *Alexander der Grosse. Das Problem seiner Persönlichkeit und seines Wirkens* (Vienna, 1973)
Schober	L. Schober, *Untersuchungen zur Geschichte Babyloniens und der Oberen Satrapien von 323–303 v. Chr.* (Frankfurt, 1981)
Schubert	R. Schubert, *Die Quellen zur Geschichte der Diadochenzeit* (Leipzig, 1914)
Schwarz	F. v. Schwarz, *Alexanders des Grossen Feldzüge in Turkestan* (Munich, 1893; 2nd edition, Stuttgart, 1906)
Schwenk	C. Schwenk, *Athens in the Age of Alexander: The Dated Laws and Decrees of the "Lykourgan Era" 338–322 B.C.* (Chicago, 1985)
Sealey	R. Sealey, *Demosthenes and his Times* (Oxford, 1993)
Seibert	J. Seibert, *Untersuchungen zur Geschichte des Ptolemaios' I.* (Munich, 1969)
Seibt	G. F. Seibt, *Griechische Söldner im Achaimenidenreich* (Bonn, 1977)
Skalet	Charles H. Skalet, *Ancient Sicyon with a Prosopographia Sicyonia* (Baltimore, 1928)
Smith[3]	Vincent Smith, *The Early History of India*, 3rd edition (Oxford, 1914)
Stein	A. Stein, *Alexander's Path to the Indus* (London, 1929)

Stewart	A. Stewart, *Faces of Power: Alexander's Image and Hellenistic Politics* (Berkeley and Los Angeles, 1993)
Strasburger	H. Strasburger, *Ptolemaios und Alexander* (Leipzig, 1934)
Tataki	A. Tataki, *The Macedonians Abroad: A Contribution to the Prosopography of Ancient Macedonia* (Athens, 1998)
Tomaschek	W. Tomaschek, "Topographische Erläuterung der Küstenfahrt Nearchs vom Indus bis zum Euphrat," *SB Wien* 121 (1890), Abhandlung 8: 31–88
Tritle	Lawrence A. Tritle, *Phocion the Good* (London, 1988)
Vezin	A. Vezin, *Eumenes von Kardia* (Münster, 1907)
Welles	C. Bradford Welles, *Diodorus of Sicily*, vol. 8, Loeb Classical Library (Cambridge, MA, 1964)
Westlake	H. D. Westlake, "Eumenes of Cardia," *Bulletin of the John Rylands Library* 37: 309–27; reprinted in *Essays on the Greek Historians and Greek History* (New York, 1969): 313–30
Whitehead & Blyth	David Whitehead and P. H. Blyth, *Athenaeus Mechanicus, On Machines* (*Περὶ μηχανημάτων*), translated with Introduction and Commentary. Historia Einzelschriften, Heft 182 (Stuttgart, 2004)
Whitehorne	J. Whitehorne, *Cleopatras* (London, 1994)
Wilcken	U. Wilcken, *Alexander the Great*, trans. G. C. Richards (New York, 1967)
Will	W. Will, *Athen und Alexander. Untersuchungen zur Geschichte der Stadt von 338 bis 322 v. Chr.* (Munich, 1983)
Worthington	I. Worthington, *A Historical Commentary on Dinarchus: Rhetoric and Conspiracy in Later Fourth-Century Athens* (Ann Arbor, 1992)
Yardley & Heckel	J. C. Yardley and Waldemar Heckel, *Justin: Epitome of the Philippic History of Pompeius Trogus*. Vol. 1: *Books 11–12. Alexander the Great* (Oxford, 1997)

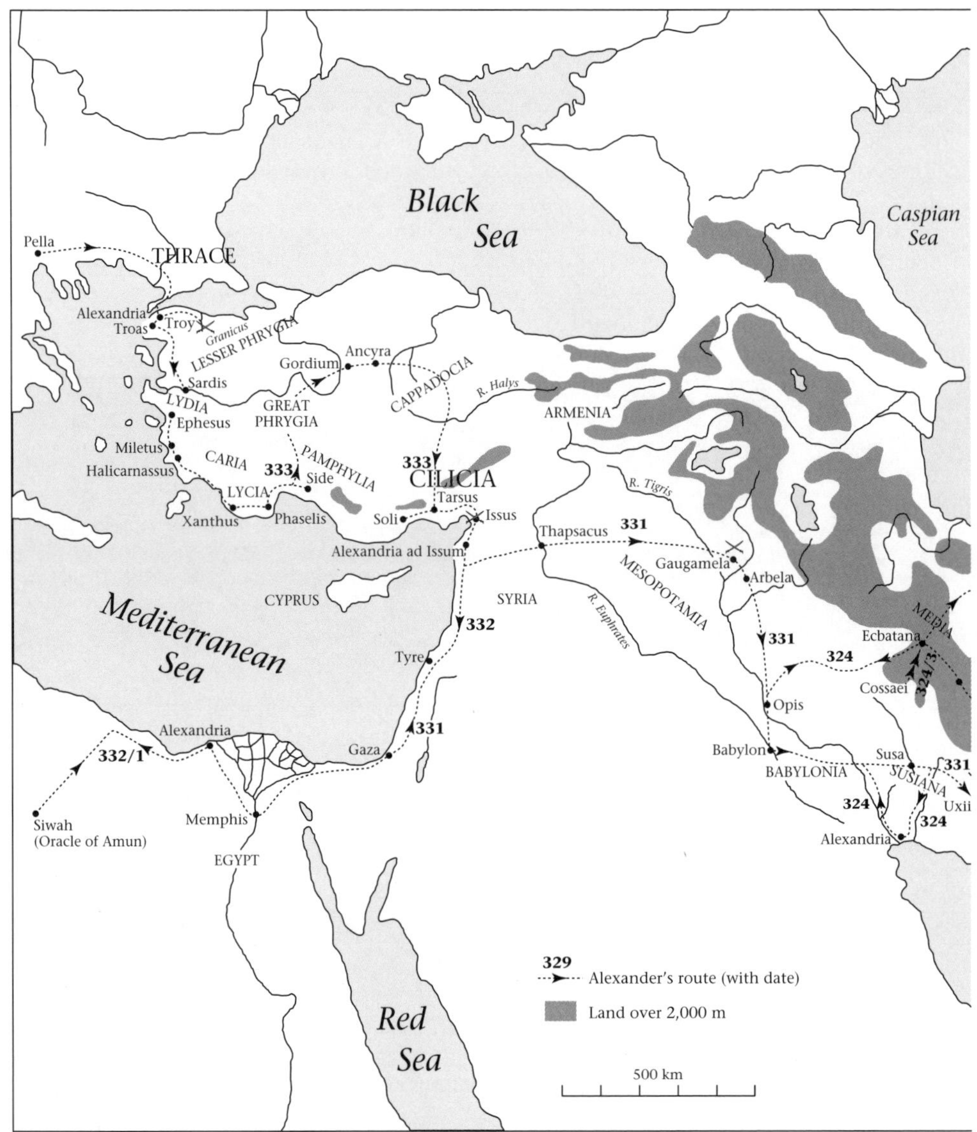

Alexander's campaigns, 334–323 BC

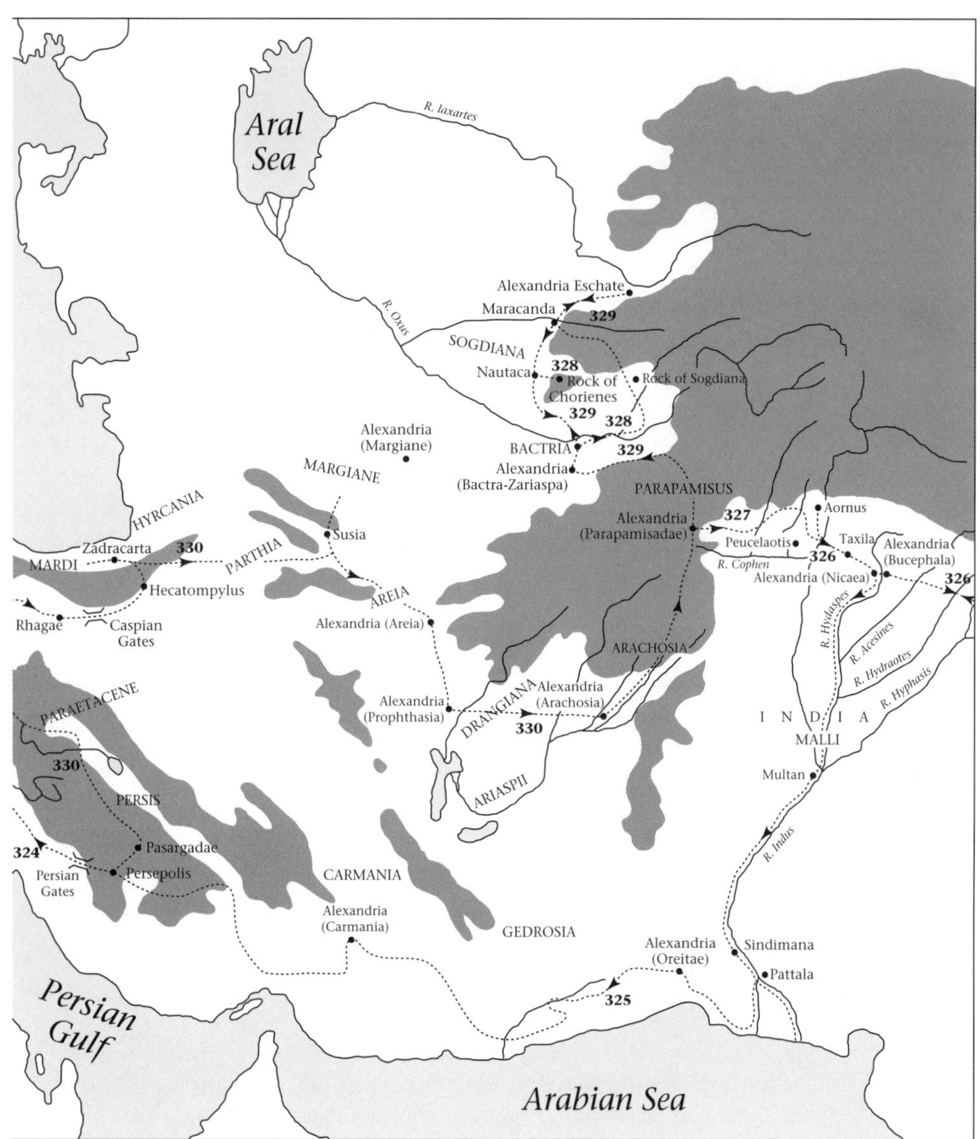

Aral Sea
R. Iaxartes
Alexandria Eschate
Maracanda
329
R. Oxus
SOGDIANA
328
Nautaca
Rock of Chorienes
Rock of Sogdiana
329
328
Alexandria (Margiane)
BACTRIA
329
Alexandria (Bactra-Zariaspa)
MARGIANE
PARAPAMISUS
HYRCANIA
Alexandria (Parapamisadae)
327
Aornus
Susia
Peucelaotis
Taxila
Alexandria (Bucephala)
Zadracarta
330
PARTHIA
R. Cophen
326
Alexandria (Nicaea)
326
MARDI
Hecatompylus
AREIA
Rhagae
Caspian Gates
Alexandria (Areia)
R. Hydaspes
R. Acesines
ARACHOSIA
R. Hydraotes
PARAETACENE
Alexandria (Prophthasia)
DRANGIANA
Alexandria (Arachosia)
R. Hyphasis
330
I N D I A
MALLI
330
Multan
PERSIS
ARIASPII
Pasargadae
324
Persepolis
R. Indus
Persian Gates
CARMANIA
Alexandria (Carmania)
GEDROSIA
Alexandria (Oreitae)
Sindimana
Pattala
325
Persian Gulf
Arabian Sea

A

Abdalonymus (Abdalonymos; Abd-elonim = "servant of the gods"; D 17.46.6: "Ballonymos"). An impoverished scion of the Sidonian royal house,[2] Abdalonymus was appointed king of Sidon in December 333 or January 332 in place of the deposed Straton (Abdastart) son of Tennes, who although he submitted to Alexander, was considered loyal to Darius III (D 17.47.1; cf. C 4.1.16). Abdalonymus was selected for the kingship by Hephaestion because of his exceptional nature and lifestyle, although he was constrained by poverty to work as a gardener; the man was found at his work, unperturbed by the war going on around him (J 11.10.9; D 17.47.1–6; C 4.1.17–26).[3] Despite its dramatic and cynic touches, the vulgate does give us some insight into the factional strife in Sidon, which was bound to accompany the defeat of Darius and the arrival of foreign troops. Abdalonymus was favored by the popular party (D 17.47.6), which may indeed have played some part in securing the deposition of Straton (cf. C 4.1.16); but opposition to the appointment came from the wealthy, who sought to influence Alexander's decision by lobbying his Companions (C 4.1.19, 24). According to P*M* 340d, Abdalonymus was enrolled in Alexander's *hetairoi* (cf. D 17.47.6), a privilege which he appears to have extended to at least some of the kings of Cyprus as well: cf. Nithaphon and Nicocreon, A*Ind* 18.8. A bilingual inscription from Cos (*SEG* 36.748) shows that Abd-elonim's name was not Graecized into Apollodorus and that he was not the father of Philocles as was previously thought (Merker 1970; cf. Atkinson i.218).

On his activities during Alexander's lifetime, we hear only that Abdalonymus sent Alexander a gift of perfume from henna and lilies (Pollux 6.105), Sidon being famed in antiquity for the former (Ath 15.688f). He was succeeded in the kingship by a son whose name ended in [. . .]timus, but the length of his reign cannot be determined. The accession of Philocles son of Apollodorus would, however, signal the end of Abdalonymus' line (see Grainger 1991: 63 and Billows 444–5 no. 129). That he was the occupant of the so-called "Alexander sarcophagus," as is almost universally believed,[4] is unlikely, since the occupant appears to have been a Persian and to have fought in two major battles against Alexander. Neither of which suits Abdalonymus.

Kaerst, *RE* s.v.; Berve ii.3 no. 1; Billows 444–5 no. 129; Merker 1970; Stewart 294–306; Bosworth 2003a: 181–6.

Abisares [1]. (Embisares, Sasibisares). Indian dynast of Abhisara, the hill-country between the Hydaspes and the Acesines;[5] according to Indian custom, he took his name from the territory he ruled (cf. **Assacenus** and **Taxiles**). Abisares had known of Alexander's advance since at least winter 327/6: he sent troops to Ora (Udegram) in a futile attempt to bolster its defenses (A 4.27.7). After the fall of Aornus in 326, natives from the region between Dyrta and the Indus fled to him

(A 4.30.7), and he renewed his alliance with Porus, with whom he had earlier conducted a rather ineffectual expedition against the Oxydracae (A 5.22.2). Although somewhat inferior in authority (C 8.12.13), Abisares could muster an army comparable in size to that of Porus (D 17.87.2); hence Alexander planned to attack the latter before Abisares could join forces with him (D 17.87.3). Abisares did not, in fact, act in time to aid Porus, who looked in vain for his reinforcements (C 8.14.1). Instead, he made (token?) submission to Alexander, content to await the outcome of events (C 8.13.1; A 5.8.3; *ME* 55). After the defeat of Porus, he sent a second delegation to Alexander (C 9.1.7; D 17.90.4; A 5.20.5).[6]

Abisares nevertheless ignored Alexander's demand that he come in person (C 9.1.7–8; A 5.20.6; cf. *ME* 65): instead he sent his brother (**M21**), in concert with Arsaces (who ruled the territory adjacent to his, i.e., Urasa = Hazara; Berve ii.81 no. 147) and the envoys whom Alexander had sent to Abhisara (*ME* 55 names a certain Nicocles), bringing a further thirty elephants and offering the excuse that Abisares himself was too ill to present himself to Alexander, a fact verified by Alexander's own agents. The King allowed Abisares to retain his kingdom and included in his administrative sphere the hyparchy of Arsaces. This was, in fact, a confirmation of Abisares' authority over Urasa (or Hazara), since the fugitives from Aornus sought refuge with him, i.e., across the Indus (A 4.30.7; cf. Stein 123; *CHIndia* i.335). Abisares was, however, assessed an annual tribute, which was probably due to the satrap of India between the Hydaspes and the Indus, Philip son of Machatas (A 5.29.4–5). Although Abisares is referred to as "satrap" by Arrian (5.29.5), his son doubtless followed an independent course of action after Alexander's return to the west. Unlike Porus and Taxiles, there is no reference to an Abisares in the satrapal allotments of 323 or 320 BC (cf. Brunt ii.474). In 325, Alexander received word that the elder Abisares had died of (the above-mentioned?) illness, and he approved the accession of his son, who also took the dynastic name (C 10.1.20–1).[7]

Kaerst, *RE* s.v.; Berve ii.3–4 no. 2; Anspach ii.5 n. 132.

Abisares [2]. Son of the former ally of Porus, that Abisares whose death from illness was reported to Alexander in Carmania (325 BC); the son inherited the father's kingdom – apparently with the approval of Alexander, who was scarcely in a strong position to deny it – and the royal name of Abisares (C 10.1.20–1). He appears to have pursued an independent policy after Alexander's departure from the East and into the time of the Diadochoi. Nothing else is known about him.

Berve ii.4–5 no. 3.

Abistamenes. See s.v. **Sabictas**.

Abulites (Aboulites; also Abouletes). A high-ranking Persian,[8] Abulites was born not later than the 370s; the fact that his son, Oxathres, commanded the Uxians and Susani at Gaugamela (A 3.8.5) may indicate that Abulites was considerably older. As satrap of Susiana under Darius III, Abulites surrendered the city of Susa and himself to Philoxenus (A 3.16.6),[9] whom Alexander had sent to him after the battle of Gaugamela. Sending his son ahead to confirm the arrangement (C 5.2.8–9; A 3.16.6), Abulites made his official surrender in person to Alexander on his arrival (C 5.2.9–10),[10] and was allowed to retain his satrapy (C 5.2.17), which he later enlarged at the expense of Madates (C 5.3.16, giving him authority over the Uxians of the mountains); Alexander, nevertheless, established a military garrison in the city (A 3.16.9; D 17.65.5; C 5.2.17).[11] But Abulites fell into disfavor when he failed to send Alexander supplies which he had requested, probably during the Gedrosian campaign (P*A* 68.7), and, when Alexander returned to Susa, he sought to buy his forgiveness with three thousand talents but was executed along with his son, Oxathres (A 7.4.1; cf. P*A* 68.7, claiming that

Alexander ran Oxathres through with his *sarissa*).[12]

Kaerst, *RE* s.v. "Aboulites"; Berve ii.5 no. 5.

Achilles (Achilleus). Athenian of unknown family. Achilles and Diophantus were sent by the Athenians to Alexander to negotiate the release of their countrymen, who had been captured at the Granicus River and sentenced to hard labor in Macedonia. They met Alexander near Tyre as he returned from Egypt in 331 and achieved their purpose (A 3.6.2; cf. C 4.8.12–13).

Berve ii.98 no. 192; Kirchner no. 2796; Develin 388.

Acuphis (Akouphis).[13] Indian dynast. The foremost (P*A* 58.7 says "eldest") of the thirty ambassadors sent by the Nysaeans[14] to Alexander to ask for peace and independence (A 5.1.3). Alexander demanded 300 horsemen to serve with him in India (A 5.2.2, 4; cf. 6.2.3 for their return). Alexander entrusted him with the rule of Nysa (as *hyparchos*), which had previously been ruled by 300 leading citizens. The story goes that, when Alexander appointed him as ruler and demanded 100 of his best men as hostages, Acuphis replied that he would serve him better by taking 200 of the worst (A 5.2.3; *ME* 37–8; cf. P*A* 58.9). Although the king relented on the demand for 100 hostages, he did take the son and grandson of Acuphis instead (A 5.2.4; **M28, M29**).[15] See also **F59**.

Anspach i.20ff.; Berve ii.17 no. 36; Bosworth ii.203; Yardley & Heckel 238–40.

Ada [1]. Daughter of the Carian dynast Hecatomnus (A 1.23.7; Str 14.2.17 [656]; Tod no. 161B) and possibly Abas (Hornblower 1982: 36 and 37 n. 9); Ada was both sister and widow of Idrieus (Hidrieus in A 1.23.7), and also the sister of Mausolus and his sister-wife, Artemisia (D 16.45.7; cf. Hornblower 1982: 366, M7), and of Pixodarus. Ada was presumably born in the 390s – the *terminus ante quem* is 377, the year of Hecatomnus' death and the beginning of Mausolus' reign – since it is likely that she died of old age no later than 324 BC.[16] After Idrieus' death she ruled alone (A 1.23.7; cf. D 17.24.2) for a period of four years (from 344/3 to 340/39: D 16.69.2), until she was ousted by the youngest of Hecatomnus' sons, Pixodarus (D 16.74.2). By the time Alexander arrived in Asia Minor, Pixodarus had died (D 16.74.2; cf. Str 14.2.17 [657]), leaving Orontopates (his son-in-law: A 1.23.8) in charge of Caria and the elder Ada living in Alinda (Str 14.2.17). Ada met Alexander as he marched into Caria (D 17.24.2–3), seeking reinstatement and promising to help him win over those areas of the satrapy that continued to resist. Alexander's troops confined Orontopates to the citadel of Halicarnassus, and Asander and Ptolemy (see s.v. **Ptolemy** [5]) captured it in 333 (A 2.5.7). Although Ada recovered the satrapy of Caria, the adjacent territory of Lycia, which had been under Hecatomnid control (Keen 1998: 172–4), was detached and given to Nearchus to administer (see s.v. **Nearchus**). Alexander allowed himself to be adopted by Ada (A 1.23.8), and the story goes that his adoptive mother sent him delicacies and even a cook for his meals, though Alexander declined the latter, preferring to adhere to a more "Spartan" regimen imposed upon him early in life by his tutor Leonidas (P*A* 22.7–10; cf. P*M* 180a, 127b, 1099c). Abramenko's argument (1992) that the mother of the king who warned him to beware of Alexander Lyncestes (D 17.32.1) was Ada and not Olympias is not compelling. Nothing further is known about Ada's life or reign in Caria. She must have died no later than 324; for in 323 we find a certain Philoxenus in Babylonia with troops from his satrapy of Caria (A 7.23.1, 24.1; cf. [Arist]*Oecon* 2.31.1531). Tests intended to identify the physical remains of the queen have been inconclusive (Özet 1994).

For the Hecatomnid dynasty see Beloch iii[2] 2.141–5; Hornblower 1982: 34–51. Aspects of Ada's career: Judeich, *RE* s.v.; Berve ii.11–12 no. 20; Lehmann-Haupt 140–1; Abramenko 1992. See Stemma XVI.

Ada [2]. Eldest daughter (*PA* 10.1) of Pixodarus and Aphneis, a Cappadocian woman (Str 14.2.17 [656–7]). Ada II was apparently the bride offered to Arrhidaeus in spring 336, though these plans were disrupted by the intervention of Alexander (*PA* 10.1–2). Soon thereafter Pixodarus reverted to a pro-Persian policy and arranged her marriage to Orontopates (Str 14.2.17; cf. A 1.23.8).[17] This marriage took place very soon after Pixodarus' failure to gain an alliance with Philip II. The arrival of Pixodarus' messenger (Aristocritus) in Macedonia occurred soon after the crossing of Parmenion, Attalus, and Amyntas into Asia in the spring of 336 (Heckel 1981c: 55; cf. Olmstead 490). When Ada's father died, some time before the summer of 335 (D 16.74.2), she may have ruled Caria briefly with her husband (cf. Hornblower 1982: 49–50) until her aunt, Ada I, was reinstated by Alexander in the summer of 334. What became of her we do not know.

Berve ii.12 no. 21; Hornblower 1982: 49–50. See Stemma XVI.

Adaeus (Adaios). Macedonian of unknown family background, though possibly related to Adaeus Alectryon ("the Cock"), a mercenary captain of Philip II who died fighting Chares in 353 (Ath 12.532e). Adaeus appears as a chiliarch – apparently of hypaspists, although the term is anachronistic (cf. Berve ii.12) – during the siege of Halicarnassus in 334. Here he served under the command of Ptolemy the *somatophylax* (see below s.v. **Ptolemy** [1]), along with Timander (A 1.22.4), and was killed in a skirmish with enemy troops who sallied forth from the Tripylon (A 1.22.7).

Kirchner, *RE* s.v. "Adaios"; Berve ii.12 no. 22; Heckel 303.

Adea (Adeia). Daughter of Cynnane (Cynna) – who trained her in the Macedonian art of war (Duris, *FGrH* 76 F52 = Ath 13.560f; cf. Pol*Strat* 8.60, also from Duris; Heckel 1983–4) – and Amyntas IV, son of Perdiccas III (A*Succ* 1.23; Ael*VH* 13.36 wrongly calls her daughter of Philip II). Born not later than 335, for Amyntas was known to have been dead by the spring of that year (A 1.5.4). She was of marriageable age in 322/1, when her mother led her to Asia to arrange a union with Philip III Arrhidaeus, a plan that was fulfilled only after the death of Cynnane on the orders of Alcetas (Pol*Strat* 8.60; A*Succ* 1.22–3). Upon marrying the King, Adea assumed the name Eurydice (A*Succ* 1.23), by which she is known in all subsequent references.

After the death of Perdiccas son of Orontes in Egypt, Adea began to agitate for greater political power, in the name of her husband: hence she wreaked havoc for the elected guardians of the "Kings," Arrhidaeus and Peithon (D 18.39.2; A*Succ* 1.30–1), who resigned at Triparadeisus. In the turbulent events that followed, her ambitions were further inflamed by the arrival of Attalus son of Andromenes, and she was aided by the *grammateus* Asclepiodorus (A*Succ* 1.33). But he soon departed and Antipater, to whom the *epimeleia* was entrusted, managed to subdue the strong-willed queen (D 18.39.3–4). Once back in Europe, Adea, threatened by Polyperchon's summoning of Olympias to serve as *epimeletes* of her grandson Alexander IV, formed an alliance with Cassander (J 14.5.2–4) and brought an armed force against Olympias and Aeacides of Epirus at Euia (Duris *ap.* Ath 13.560f; D 19.11.1–2; J 14.5.9). Here her troops defected to the old queen mother (D 19.11.2; J 14.5.10) and Adea was captured as she fled toward Amphipolis with her advisor Polycles (D 19.11.3). Upon the death of her husband, and after tending to his body, she committed suicide, shunning the instruments of death (dagger, rope, poison) sent to her by the vindictive Olympias in favor of her girdle (D 19.11.6–7; but Ael*VH* 13.36 says she used the rope; cf. D 19.35.1, news of death reaches Cassander).[18] Her body, along with that of Philip III Arrhidaeus, and her mother Cynnane, was buried by Cassander in 315 (D 19.52.5; Diyllus, *FGrH* 73 F1 = Ath 4.155a).[19]

Kaerst, *RE* s.v. "Adea (13)"; Berve ii.12–13 no. 23; Heckel 1983 and 1983–4; Carney 132–7. See Stemma I.

Admetus (Admetos). Macedonian officer, perhaps commander of the *agema* of the hypaspists, and a man of great bodily strength (D 17.45.6), Admetus commanded the ship carrying the hypaspists in the naval assault on Tyre (A 2.23.2). He displayed great courage, fighting as he did in full view of Alexander, and, although he was the first to scale the wall, he was killed by a spear (A 2.23.5) or perhaps by an axe (D 17.45.6).

Kaerst, *RE* s.v. "Admetos (5)"; Berve ii.13 no. 24; Heckel 253.

Aeacides (Aiakides). The name reflects the claims of the Molossian royal house to be descended from the mythical Aeacus (P*A* 2.1; Paus 1.11.2 cf. Heckel 1981a: 80–2). Son of Arybbas and Troas (P*Pyr* 1.5; D 16.72.1; Paus 1.11.1; cf. J 7.6.11 for the marriage of Arybbas and Troas), thus also a nephew of Alexander I of Epirus (cf. J 17.3.16). Born no later than 341, but perhaps as early as 357 (Sandberger 17). Husband of Phthia, daughter of Menon of Pharsalus (P*Pyr* 1.6), and father of Pyrrhus (Paus 3.6.3; D 16.72.1; P*Pyr* 1.7), Deidameia, and the younger Troas (P*Pyr* 1.7; J 14.6.3; D 19.35.5). In 317/6 he supported Polyperchon and Olympias against Adea-Eurydice and Philip III Arrhidaeus (D 19.11.2), thereby alienating many of his followers (Paus 1.11.3–4; J 14.5.9, 17.3.16) and incurring the enmity of Cassander (P*Pyr* 3.2). His attempt to relieve Olympias, who was besieged in Pydna, was foiled by Cassander's general Atarrhias, who held the passes between Epirus and Macedonia against him. Distrustful of his army, he allowed those who did not support him to leave, thus weakening his forces and dooming them to failure. He was expelled in 317 by the Molossians, who installed the "sons of Neoptolemus," killed many of Aeacides' supporters (P*Pyr* 2.1), and made an alliance with Cassander (D 19.36.2–4). After the defeat of Olympias by Cassander, Aeacides and his supporters accompanied Polyperchon to Aetolia (D 19.52.6). He was eventually forgiven by the Epirotes (Paus 1.11.4) but opposed by Philip, the brother of Cassander, who had marched on Aetolia in 313 only to find Aeacides re-entrenched in Epirus (D 19.74.3). In a battle at Oeniadae Aeacides was wounded; he died shortly afterwards (Paus 1.11.4; D 19.74.4–5 says he died in the battle). The throne now devolved upon Alcetas II (D 19.88.1), apparently a half-brother (Paus 1.11.5).

Cross 43–7; Sandberger 17–19 no. 5. See Stemma II.

Aëropus (Aëropos). Macedonian commander (*hegemon*) in the army of Philip II at the time of the battle of Chaeronea (338 BC). Aëropus, together with another officer, Damasippus, was banished from Macedonia for bringing a female harpist, whom they had hired at a local inn, into the camp (Pol*Strat* 4.2.3). The punishment is clearly too harsh for the crime, and one suspects that Philip regarded the actions of Aëropus as a deliberate flouting of his authority. Hence it may be that the incident became a pretext for removing from Macedonia a political rival. If Aëropus can be identified as a member of the Lyncestian royal house, perhaps even the father of Arrhabaeus and Heromenes, the Lyncestian involvement in the murder of Philip takes on a new dimension. Damasippus may have been a close friend of Aëropus. This identification of Aëropus is speculative but ought not to be dismissed out of hand.[20]

Kirchner, *RE* s.v. "Aeropos (3)"; Hoffmann 206; Tataki 223 no. 36.

Aeschines (Aischines). Athenian orator from the deme Cothodicae (ca. 390/89–322 BC).[21] Most famous for his political opposition to Demosthenes. Son of Atrometus, who had been exiled in the time of the Thirty, and Glaucothea ([P]*M*

840a), but details about his family background are invented and distorted by his political enemies.[22] He had two brothers, Aphobetus and Philochares (Dem 19.237), of whom the former was a commissioner of the Theoric Fund. Aeschines himself was a supporter of Aristophon and Eubulus. He appears to have come to oratory and a public career late, and it is doubtful that he actually studied with Isocrates, Plato, and others ([P]*M* 840b). What we know of his military career comes from Aeschines himself: he fought at Nemea, Mantineia, and twice on Euboea (Aes 2.168–70). In the period leading up to the Peace of Philocrates (346), Aeschines supported Eubulus' attempts to bring about a Common Peace as a means of preempting the expansion of Macedon under Philip II. He was sent on two embassies to Philip, which resulted in the conclusion of the Peace of Philocrates and represented in fact the failure of Eubulus' initiative. Unlike Demosthenes, however, Aeschines came to accept the fact of Macedonian hegemony and his pro-Macedonian stance was attacked by Demosthenes, especially in his speeches *On the Peace* and *On the False Legation*. Aeschines is most famous for his indictment of Ctesiphon for proposing illegal honors for Demosthenes (Aes 3 = *Against Ctesiphon*, answered by Dem 18 = *On the Crown*). The charge was made originally in 336, before the death of Philip II, but was postponed until 330, no doubt in part because of the changing political climate (Harris 140). Aeschines failed to gain a conviction – or even one-fifth of the vote – and was forced into exile, going perhaps to Ephesus ([P]*M* 840c–d) and then to Rhodes (P*Dem* 24.2–3; cf. Quint 11.3.7; 12.10.19; Pl*NH* 7.110), where he set up a school. Eventually he moved to Samos, where he died soon after Alexander's death ([P]*M* 840d–e).[23] Three speeches of his have survived: 1. *Against Timarchus*, 2. *On the Embassy*, and 3. *Against Ctesiphon*.

Thalheim, *RE* s.v. "Aischines (15)"; Berve ii.15–16 no. 33; Kirchner no. 354; cf. Davies 544–7; Harris; Cawkwell, *OCD*³ 25–6.

Aeschrion (Aischrion). Cf. Pape & Benseler 41. Mytilenaean (Tzetz*Chil* 8.398). An epic poet who, on the recommendation of his friend, Aristotle, accompanied Alexander in order to commemorate his achievements (Nicander *ap. Suda* s.v. "Aischrion"). Nothing else is known about him.[24]

Knaak, *RE* s.v. "Aischrion (7)"; Berve ii.16 no. 34.

Aeschylus (Aischylos). Rhodian. At Memphis in 332/1, Alexander appointed him and Ephippus (son of Chalcideus) as *episkopoi* of the mercenaries left behind in Egypt (A 3.5.3; C 4.8.4, omitting Ephippus). Aeschylus is apparently identical with the admiral of 319 BC, who was conveying 600 talents of silver to Macedonia from Cilicia (D 18.52.7) – hence a supporter of Polyperchon. Aeschylus' cargo was confiscated by Antigonus, who claimed he needed it to pay his mercenaries, and Aeschylus himself appears to have entered Antigonus' service at that time. He is next attested as an agent of Antigonus, sent with Demarchus, to negotiate first with Cassander and then with Ptolemy (cf. Olshausen 88). The result of these negotiations was the "Peace of 311" (*OGIS* i.5.5, 48 = Welles, *RC* no. 1). Billows 365 suggests, on the basis of *IG* ii² 569, that Aeschylus the Rhodian may have been the Antigonid commander of Lemnos between 310 and 307.[25]

Kaerst, *RE* s.v. "Aischylos (12)"; Berve ii.17 no. 35; Billows 364–5 no. 4; Hauben 7–9; Olshausen 88 no. 63.

Agathocles (Agathokles). Samian *taxiarches* in Alexander's army (presumably a commander of allied infantry, perhaps mercenaries), Agathocles had been held in high esteem by the King, but he narrowly missed being exposed to a lion because he wept when passing Hephaestion's grave, thereby regarding him as dead rather than divine. The story, found only in L*Cal* 18, continues that Agathocles was saved through the intervention of Perdiccas, who observed that Agathocles wept not because he considered Hephaestion dead but because he remembered his former friendship.[26]

Berve ii.6 no. 7.

Agathon [1]. Son of Tyrimmas (A 3.12.4), apparently of Macedonian origin. Commander of the Thracian cavalry between 334 and 330.[27] Agathon is attested at the Granicus (A 1.14.3) and Gaugamela (A 3.12.4; he was stationed on the left wing with Sitalces and Coeranus [Caranus?]). Although in the latter case Agathon's troops are described as "Odrysians," he will have been the commander of the entire Thracian cavalry (so Berve ii.6; cf. Brunt i.263 n. 7). In mid-330, he remained behind at Ecbatana, with his cavalry unit and in the company of Parmenion, Cleander, Heracon, and Sitalces (A 3.19.7). He soon played a role in the elimination of Parmenion (C 10.1.1). But in 325/4, Agathon was charged with maladministration when Alexander returned from India. Together with Heracon, Cleander, and Sitalces, he met the King in Carmania, where he was arrested and presumably executed (C 10.1.1–8; cf. A 6.27.3–4).

Kaerst, *RE* s.v. "Agathon (7)"; Berve ii.6–7 no. 8; Heckel 361; Marsden 1964: 71–3.

Agathon [2]. Prominent Macedonian from Pydna, though his family background is unknown. Agathon first appears as the commander of 700 Macedonian troops garrisoning the citadel of Babylon (D 17.64.5; C 5.1.43 gives him an additional 300 mercenaries; his appointment is not mentioned by A 3.16.4). Nothing else is known about him.

Kaerst, *RE* s.v. "Agathon (8)"; Berve ii.7 no. 9.

Agesilaus (Agesilaos). A member of the Eurypontid house of Sparta, Agesilaus was the son of Archidamus III and brother of Agis III and Eudamidas I. In 333/2, Agis sent to Agesilaus ten triremes, which he had secured from Autophradates at Siphnos; these ships and thirty talents of silver were conveyed to Taenarum by Hippias, with instructions that he should pay the wages of the crews and sail to Crete to set affairs in order there (A 2.13.6), that is, to secure Crete as a base for the Persian fleet (cf. Bosworth i.224). Nothing else is known about him. Bosworth believes that he may have died before the battle of Megalopolis, since after Agis' death Eudamidas succeeded to the kingship (P*Agis* 3.3); Berve may be correct in assuming that Agesilaus was the youngest of the brothers. Plutarch speaks of only two sons of Archidamus, but he is merely recounting the lineage of Agis IV and may have overlooked Agesilaus because he did not rule.

Niese, *RE* s.v. "Agesilaos (5)"; Berve ii.7 no. 11; Poralla 9 no. 11.

Agesimenes. Son of Hermesideius, hence grandson of Hermus, who shared the tyranny of Eresus in the 340s with his brothers Heraeus and Apollodorus. Agesimenes was banished after the fall of the tyrants (cf. s.v. **Herodas**); in 332 he joined Alexander and sought restitution. The King left the matter to the Eresians, who voted to uphold the banishment of the tyrants and their descendants (Heisserer 38–9; Harding no. 112; *OGIS* i.8, II).

Berve ii.7 no. 12; Berve 1967 i.337–8; Heisserer 27–78; Lott 1996.

Agesipolis. Berve ii.8 no. 13 (cf. Poralla 9–10 no. 15). See discussion s.v. **Cleomenes** [3].

Agis [1]. Agis III of Sparta. A member of the Eurypontid house, Agis was the eldest son of Archidamus III (P*Agis* 3.3; Paus 3.10.4) and brother of Agesilaus (A 2.13.6). Succeeded to the Spartan throne upon the death of his father, who was killed in Italy on the very day of the battle of Chaeronea (D 16.63.2, 88.3–4). From 338 to 331/0 he ruled Sparta, which rejected the Macedonian alliance and failed to join the League of Corinth (A 1.1.2, 7.4), and spearheaded the anti-Macedonian movement in the Peloponnese. An early attempt at rebellion was suppressed in 336/5 by the speedy action of the new king (D 17.3.5;[28] cf. J 11.2.7, with Yardley & Heckel 86). In late 333, after the battle of Issus, Agis sailed with a single trireme to Siphnos, where he met Pharnabazus and Autophradates and requested money and ships (A 2.13.5). Autophradates gave him thirty talents of silver and ten triremes, which Agis sent to his brother Agesilaus at Taenarum through the agency of a certain Hippias (A 2.13.6), ordering the former to pay the wages of the crews and sail to Crete to set affairs in order there, that is, to secure Crete as a base for the Persian fleet (cf. Bosworth i.224). D 17.48.1 and C 4.1.39 record that after Issus, 8,000 Greek mercenaries[29] took service with Agis. He himself remained briefly at Siphnos and then joined Autophradates at Halicarnassus (A 2.13.6), but nothing further is known of his activities in Asia Minor.

On his return to Greece, Agis fashioned a dangerous uprising against Macedonian authority in 332/1 (Aes 3.165, 167; Din 1.34; [Dem] 17.15; D 17.62.6–63.4; C 6.1.1–20). His cause was hampered by the failure of the Athenians to participate in a general rebellion. Agis had the support of Sparta's traditional Peloponnesian allies (excluding the Messenians), the Eleans, the Arcadians except for the Megalopolitans, and all Achaea except Pellene (cf. Din 1.34; C 6.1.20; Paus 7.27.7; [Dem] 17.7.10; for the background see McQueen 1978). He defeated the Macedonian *strategos* Corrhagus, but was eventually defeated and killed in the battle of Megalopolis in summer 331 (D 17.63; C 6.1.1–16; J 12.1.4–11; cf. Paus 1.13.6; P*Agis* 3.3).

Niese, *RE* s.v. "Agis (3)"; Badian 1967a; Berve ii.8–9 no. 15; Brunt ii.480–5; Hofstetter 5–6 no. 5; Poralla 13 no. 27; Wirth 1971a: 617–20.

Agis [2]. Greek from Argos, Agis was an epic poet and flatterer of Alexander (P*M* 60b; C 8.5.8; A 4.9.9), found in the King's entourage in 328/7 BC. Whether he wrote an epic poem about Alexander himself (Berve ii.9), as did Choerilus, who alone surpassed him in the writing of bad verse, is uncertain. He is named also by P*M* 65d as one of the notorious flatterers of the King.

Wissowa, *RE* s.v. "Agis (8)"; Berve ii.9 no. 16 = ii.7 no. 10 "Agesias."

Agonippus (Agonippos). Greek from Eresus, patronymic unknown. Installed, along with Eurysilaus, as tyrant when Memnon recaptured most of Lesbos in 333 (A 2.1.1; D 17.29.2). The previous tyranny of Apollodorus and his brothers had been reinstated in 335/4 only to be driven out in 334 (see Rhodes & Osborne 417), probably through the efforts of Alcimachus son of Agathocles, whom Alexander had sent to establish democracies in the area (A 1.18.1–2). Agonippus and Eurysilaus exercised the tyranny in a most cruel fashion (*OGIS* i.8a). Hegelochus' "liberation" of Lesbos in 332 led to the overthrow of the tyrants, who were handed over to the Macedonian admiral (A 3.2.5) and, in turn, to Alexander in Egypt (winter 332/1: A 3.2.7; cf. *OGIS* i.8a, 13–15). Agonippus and Eurysilaus were sent back to Eresus to stand trial, sentenced to death and executed (*OGIS* i.8b, lines 60–9).

Kirchner, *RE* s.v. "Agonippos"; Baumbach 33 n. 1; Berve ii.10–11 no. 19; Berve 1967: i.338, ii.691; Habicht[2] 14ff.; Heisserer 27–78; Hofstetter 6–7 no. 6; Harding no. 112 B and F; Lott 1996; Rhodes & Osborne no. 83.

Alcetas (Alketas). Younger brother of Perdiccas (J 13.6.15; D 18.29.2; A*Succ* 1.21), hence probably also a son of Orontes of Orestes (cf. A 3.11.9; 6.28.4; A*Ind* 18.5); possibly of Argead descent (C 10.7.8).[30] Born ca. 355, he succeeded Perdiccas as taxiarch of the Lyncestians and Orestians, perhaps as early as 331/0, though Perdiccas retained nominal command of the *taxis* (cf. A 3.18.5). In 327 he campaigned with Craterus, Polyperchon, and Attalus in Paraetacene (A 4.22.1; cf. C 8.5.2), receiving the news of the abortive attempt to introduce *proskynesis* and the conspiracy of Hermolaus in a letter from Alexander (P*A* 55.6). During the Swat campaign of 327,

Alcetas, Attalus, and Demetrius the hipparch attacked the town of Ora, while Coenus was besieging Bazira = Bir-Kot (A 4.27.5–6); the honor of taking the town appears to have been reserved for the King himself (A 4.27.9).[31] At the Hydaspes Alcetas' battalion, along with that of Polyperchon, remained in the main camp under the direct command of Craterus, with orders to engage Porus only if he moved to deal with Alexander's circumventing force or had turned in flight (A 5.11.3–4).

Between 323 and 319, Alcetas served as Perdiccas' lieutenant, urging him to marry Antipater's daughter, Nicaea, and remain on friendly terms with the regent (A*Succ* 1.21). This advice won out, at least temporarily, though Perdiccas' negotiations with Cleopatra, conducted through the agency of Eumenes, raised suspicions amongst his political enemies. Otherwise, Alcetas did little to help his brother's cause. He foolishly put to death Cynnane and caused the army to mutiny and demand that Adea be taken to Perdiccas, where she could marry Philip III Arrhidaeus in accordance with her mother's wishes (A*Succ* 1.22–3; Pol*Strat* 8.60; cf. D 19.52.5). Furthermore, he disregarded orders to serve Eumenes in the defense of Asia Minor against the forces of Craterus and Antipater (D 18.29.2; J 13.6.15; P*Eum* 5.2), claiming that his Macedonian troops would not fight against Antipater and were favorably disposed toward Craterus (P*Eum* 5.3).

Alcetas and some fifty other leaders of the Perdiccan faction were outlawed by the Macedonian assembly at Triparadeisus and condemned to death (D 18.37.2; cf. 18.39.7; J 13.8.10; A*Succ* 1.30, 39). Although he was in contact with Eumenes in Phrygia (P*Eum* 8.7–8 implies that they were both at Celaenae), the two would not reconcile their differences (A*Succ* 1.41; P*Eum* 8.8) and Alcetas, together with Docimus and Polemon son of Andromenes, moved south into Caria, where he was soon joined by his brother-in-law Attalus and by Laomedon (App*Syr* 52 [265]). In Caria, they defeated the satrap Asander, whom Antipater had sent against them (A*Succ* 1.41), and then withdrew into Pisidia.

Alcetas took up a position in the so-called Pisidic Aulon (in the vicinity of Cretopolis; for the battle see D 18.44–5, 50.1; cf. Pol*Strat* 4.6.7; Engel 1972a; Ramsay 1923: 1–10) with forces vastly inferior in numbers to those of Antigonus, who made short work of the enemy infantry. Hemmed in by the advancing elephants and the cavalry on all sides, Alcetas escaped from the battlefield with his hypaspists and the Pisidians, reaching Termessus in safety (D 18.45.2–3). There, he fell victim to the treachery of the city's elders and committed suicide; his body was handed over to Antigonus, who maltreated it for three days and then left it unburied (D 18.47.3). The younger Pisidians, however, recovered the body and buried it with appropriate honors (D 18.47.3).

Kaerst, *RE* s.v. "Alketas (5)"; Berve ii.22–3 no. 45; Heckel 171–5. For Alcetas' tomb see Kleiner 1963: 71ff.; Picard 1964; Rice 1993: 234–5; Pekridou 1986; Fedak 1990: 94–6. See Stemma XII.

Alcias (Alkias). Greek from Elis. Alcias brought 150 cavalrymen from his homeland to Alexander at Gordium (A 1.29.4). Presumably he remained with them and shared in Alexander's conquests until at least 330. He is, however, not mentioned again by the sources.

Kirchner, *RE* s.v. "Alkias (1)"; Berve ii.23 no. 46.

Alcimachus [1]. (Alkimachos). Son of Agathocles, Alcimachus is generally identified as the brother of Lysimachus, Philip, and Autodicus (Beloch iv^2 2.131 adds a word of caution). This may be correct, but there is no explicit evidence to support the identification beyond the patronymic and the existence of a certain Philip son of Alcimachus (Hoffmann 224: *IG* vii.316.2). After the battle of Chaeronea, Alcimachus and Antipater were sent by Philip II to Athens, where they were made *proxenoi* (Hyp frg. B 19.2 Burtt = 77 Jensen;

cf. *IG* ii^2 239 = Tod ii.180; Anaximenes, *FGrH* 72 F16 = Harpocration s.v. "Alkimachos").[32] Alcimachus served in Asia Minor with Alexander in 334 and was sent to establish democracies in the Aeolian and Ionian cities (A 1.18.1–2). He may be the Alcimachus named in the *Second Letter to the Chians* (*SEG* xxii.506; cf. Heisserer 96–116). If so, then Alexander will have voiced some displeasure with Alcimachus' handling of affairs there.[33] *IG* xii.2.1001, an inscription from Ios, honors Lysippus son of Alcimachus and refers to the *eunoia* of his father toward the state. This may very well refer to the son and grandson of Agathocles.

Kirchner, *RE* s.v. "Alkimachos (5)"; Berve ii.23 no. 47; Bosworth i.134; Lenschau 1940: 201; Wilhelm 1943; Forrest 1969: 204–5; cf. Tod ii.267. See Stemma IX.

Alcimachus [2]. (Alkimachos). Chian. Friend (*philos*) of Alexander. His existence and relationship with the King depends on the restoration of line 10 of Alexander's *Second Letter to the Chians* (*SEG* xxii.506); see above.

Alexander [1]. (Alexandros). Alexander I of Epirus. Son of Neoptolemus I (cf. Head, *HN*^{2} 322; brother of Olympias and Troas; nephew of Arybbas (J 8.6.5; cf. 7.6.10–11; 12.2.1; Livy 8.3.7). Born ca. 362 BC (J 8.6.7), Alexander came to the Macedonian court at some point after 357 and remained there until 342; the charge that he was Philip II's catamite was doubtless fabricated (J 8.6.6, 8). In 342, Philip II deposed Arybbas and placed the 20-year-old Alexander on the throne (J 8.6.7–8, 17.3.14–15; Tr*Prol* 8; D 16.72.1; [Dem] 7.32; cf. Errington 1975). Fr*Strat* 2.5.10 reports a stratagem against the Illyrians that must date to the early years of Alexander's reign,[34] and it appears that Alexander aided Philip in the establishment of a garrison in Ambracia (D 17.3.3; cf. Theopompus, *FGrH* 115 F229). In 336, in the aftermath of the family quarrel that accompanied his marriage to Cleopatra-Eurydice and the flight of Olympias to her brother's court, Philip II arranged the marriage of Alexander to his daughter, Cleopatra, the bridegroom's niece (J 9.6.1, 7.7; cf. 13.6.4; D 16.91.4–93.2). Alexander and Cleopatra produced two children: the first, Cadmeia, appears to have been born in 335, after the sack of Thebes by her uncle, Alexander the Great (P*Pyr* 5.11); the second was a son named Neoptolemus, who ruled Epirus after the expulsion of Pyrrhus (P*Pyr* 5). Alexander himself soon accepted the invitation of the Tarentines to act as their champion against the Lucanians of southern Italy (Str 6.3.4 [280]).[35] After several victories against the Bruttians and Lucanians, he took Heraclea, Sipontum, Consentia, and Terina, as well as other towns of the Messapians and Lucanians; he sent 300 nobles as hostages to Epirus (Livy 8.24.4). But he was fated to die in Lucania (Livy 9.17.17; cf. Paus 1.11.3, 7; according to Pl*NH* 3.98 = Theopompus, *FGrH* 115 F318, he died in the Lucanian town of Mardonia or Mandonia).[36] His death in winter 331/0 (Aes 3.242; cf. Bosworth i.284) is said to have been foreshadowed by the oracle of Dodona (Livy 8.24.1–3; J 12.2.3–4; Str 6.1.5 [256]). It was during the campaign near Pandosia, where he was attended by some two hundred Lucanian exiles, that he was cut off by the enemy and in danger of being handed over to the Lucanians by these exiles, who asked in return to be restored to their homes. Alexander broke away, killed the Lucanian general in hand-to-hand combat, but finally was killed by a javelin hurled by an unnamed Lucanian exile (Livy 8.24.5–13). His body was mutilated and cut into two parts; half the body was buried by a woman in Consentia who sent the bones to Cleopatra and Olympias in Epirus, hoping to gain the release of her husband and children who had been captured by the enemy (Livy 8.24.14–17).[37]

Kaerst, *RE* s.v. "Alexandros (6)"; Berve ii.19–21 no. 38. See Stemma II.

Alexander [2]. (Alexandros). Alexander III, the Great. 356–323 BC (*regn.* 336–323). Son of Philip II of Macedon and Olympias (see s.v. **Olympias**); born on the 6th day of Hecatombaeon (the Macedonian month Loüs) = July 20, 356 (*PA* 3.5), but it may be that his birthdate was deliberately misrepresented to make it coincide with Philip's chariot victory at Olympia. Cleopatra [2] was his full-blooded sister, born ca. 353. A precocious youth, he was educated in his early years by Lysimachus of Acarnania and Leonidas the Epirote (see s.vv.), a kinsman of Olympias. Stories of his questioning of Persian ambassadors and his breaking of Bucephalas (*PA* 5–6) illustrate the intelligence, daring, and disregard for physical dangers that were to become his trademark. He was educated by Aristotle between 343 and 340 (*PA* 7–8) and would remain in correspondence with him until the end of his life, though their relationship had doubtless suffered as a result of the disgrace and execution of Callisthenes [1]. At the age of 16 he was left by Philip as regent though under the watchful eye of Antipater. He campaigned against the Maedians and founded a city, which he named Alexandropolis (*PA* 9.1). Two years later, he commanded the Macedonian left at Chaeronea and destroyed the Sacred Band (*PA* 9.2–3). But his relationship with his father soured when Philip married Cleopatra [1], the niece of Attalus [1], in 337. The quarrel between father and son was precipitated by Attalus' drunken toast, praying for *legitimate* heirs from the new union and thus insulting Alexander and challenging his rights to the throne (*PA* 9.7–10; Satyrus *ap.* Ath 13.557d; cf. J 9.7.3–4). Alexander fled first to Epirus, where he deposited his mother with her brother, Alexander I, and then to Illyria (*PA* 9.11; J 9.7.5). Summoned back to Macedonia through the agency of Demaratus of Corinth, Alexander returned but viewed his father's actions with suspicion. Whether he participated in Philip's punitive campaign against the Illyrian King Pleurias (D 16.93.6) in the winter of 337/6 is unknown. But he did misinterpret Philip's plan to marry Arrhidaeus (Alexander's mentally deficient half-brother) to Ada [2], daughter of the Carian Pixodarus. Encouraged by his mother and his *hetairoi*, Harpalus, Erigyius, Laomedon, Ptolemy, and Nearchus (see s.vv.), to regard this as a threat to his right of inheritance, Alexander sent Thessalus to Pixodarus, informing him of Arrhidaeus' mental state and offering Alexander instead as a groom. Philip responded by banishing these *hetairoi* from Macedonia for the remainder of his reign (*PA* 10.1–5; A 3.6.5).

In October 336, after celebrating the marriage of his daughter Cleopatra to Alexander I of Epirus, Philip was murdered by one of the hypaspist guard as he entered the theater in Aegae (Vergina), where he planned to witness his own statue carried in procession behind those of the twelve Olympian gods (see s.v. **Pausanias** [3]). Alexander's role in the murder of Philip II was the subject of speculation in antiquity (esp. J 9.7.1–6), just as it is today. Those who see him as a regicide undermine their arguments by emphasizing the weakness of Alexander's own position (Hamilton 1965; Badian 1963; Green 108–10). Olympias too has been singled out as a plausible candidate (Develin 1981; Heckel 1981c), but the case against her cannot be proved either. Nor does it necessarily follow that he who benefited the most was behind the murder; for many who stood to gain were caught entirely off guard by the act. The assassin himself was quickly despatched – some say too quickly – and a number of political rivals were eliminated on the mere suspicion of favoring and instigating the murder (see also Bosworth 1971a; Ellis 1971; Fears 1975). Hence, the new King, who gained the throne with the help of Antipater and Alexander the Lyncestian, purged the court and the army of dissidents: Heromenes and Arrhabaeus (A 1.25.1); Attalus (D 17.2.3–6); and Amyntas IV (A 1.5.4). Secure at home, he turned his attention to the kingdom's borders and establishing his right to succeed Philip as *archon* of Thessaly, *hegemon* of the League of Corinth (D 17.4.1–2; J 11.3.1–2; Westlake 1935: 217–20), and director of

Greek affairs. In conjunction with this he inherited the expedition against Persia, which was destined to bring him undying fame, but at the predictable cost.

The year 336/5 was preoccupied with preemptive expeditions, putting to rest any thoughts the Greeks might have of throwing off the Macedonian yoke and securing the borderlands of the northeast and northwest (P*A* 11.1–6). First Alexander confronted the so-called "autonomous" Thracians and the Triballians in a campaign that took him over Mt. Haemus and to the Danube, where he also made a brief demonstration against the Getae across the river; at Pellium he demonstrated his power by overcoming Glaucias and Cleitus, while his ally Langarus, king of the Agrianes, dealt with the Autariatae (A 1.1–6; Fuller 219–26). But a more dangerous uprising occurred when the Thebans, incited by their Athenian "allies," besieged the Macedonian garrison on the Cadmeia and called upon their fellow Greeks to join forces with the Great King against the true enemy of Greece. Encouraged by promises of Athenian aid and rumors of Alexander's death in Illyria, the Thebans found themselves suddenly confronted by a Macedonian army 30,000 strong. The Athenians melted away and Alexander's army made short work of the Thebans, who paid the ultimate price: their men were slaughtered, their women and children sold into slavery, and their city razed to the ground (A 1.7–9; D 17.8.2–14.4; P*A* 11.6–13.5; J 11.3.6–4.8). At the time it was an effective lesson to any others who contemplated defection, but it appears that as the campaign progressed, Alexander had reason to regret the harshness of the measure (see, for example, s.vv. **Dionysodorus**, **Thessaliscus**). Alexander's provisions for the restoration of Thebes in the forged *Last Days and Testament* (*LM* 109) may indicate that he had actually considered the idea in his lifetime.

In 334, he was free to launch the Persian expedition, moving via Amphipolis to the Hellespont and crossing to Asian soil, which he claimed as "Spear-won Land" (D 17.17.2; J 11.5.10; cf. A 1.11.7). His army at this point comprised 32,000 infantry and 5,100 cavalry (D 17.17.3–4; cf. P*A* 15.1, between 34,000 and 48,000 in total; Fr*Strat* 4.2.4: 40,000). Alexander also exploited the full arsenal of panhellenic propaganda, linking himself and the Graeco-Macedonian forces with the heroes of the Trojan War. At Troy he is said to have crowned the tomb of Achilles, his mythical ancestor, but the stories of Alexander's imitation and emulation of Achilles (and, by extension, Hephaestion's role as a second Patroclus) were all later inventions inspired by the early deaths of the King and his dearest friend (D 17.17.3; P*A* 15.8–9; A 1.12.1–2; Ael*VH* 12.7; Perrin 1895). Having dispensed with the formalities of propagandizing, Alexander confronted a coalition of satraps of Asia Minor at the Granicus River. Their army contained a large body of Greek mercenaries, led by Memnon of Rhodes, but the deployment of Persian troops and the overall battle plan were defective. The Persian cavalry and lightly armed were quickly routed and the Greek mercenaries subjected to butchery or enslavement (A 1.13–16; D 17.19–21; P*A* 16; J 11.6.8–13). Again Alexander played the panhellenism card, proclaiming the Greek mercenaries who fought for pay against their countrymen as traitors and sentencing them to hard labor in Macedonia. In the aftermath of the Granicus battle, Sardis was surrendered by its Persian garrison commander, Mithrenes (A 1.17.3; C 3.12.6; D 17.21.7; P*A* 17.1), and various Greek cities welcomed Alexander as liberator. The belief that he showed genuine enthusiasm for contrived war of vengeance is naïve; for the apparent strengthening of Persian power under Memnon a few months later brought the liberated back into the fold of their oppressors, arguing then, as they would later when Alexander repeated the conquest, that they had no choice but to yield to overwhelming force. Miletus (A 1.19; D 17.22.1–23.3; P*A* 17.2) and Halicarnassus were defended by Memnon, Orontopates, and those loyal to Darius, but fell to the Macedonian war-machine. Alexander established Ada [1] as ruler of Caria, strengthening and legitimizing his own claims to the area by becoming her adoptive son (A 1.23.8). Winter 334/3 saw Alexander in Lycia and Pamphylia.

In a move designed to boost the morale of his troops, spread the word of his successes in Asia, and garner new recruits, Alexander sent those who had recently married back to Macedonia to spend the winter with their wives (A 1.24.1, 29.4). But in their absence, disturbing news came to his attention: Alexander [4] the Lyncestian, who, since the promotion of Calas son of Harpalus to the satrapy of Hellespontine Phrygia, commanded the Thessalian cavalry, was implicated in a plot to murder the King. The negotiations between Alexander and Darius came to light when the messenger, Sisines, was captured and interrogated by Parmenion and then sent to the King at Phaselis. Alexander sent Amphoterus, brother of Craterus, to arrest the Lyncestian (A 1.25; cf. D 17.32.1–2; J 11.7.1–2), who was kept in chains until he was finally executed in 330 in the aftermath of the Philotas affair (C 7.1.5–10; 8.8.6; D 17.80.2). The spring saw the reuniting of the armies, the return of the *neogamoi* with reinforcements, and the capture of Celaenae and the undoing of the Gordian Knot by Alexander (A 2.3; C 3.1.14–18; *PA* 18.2–3; J 11.7.2–16; Str 12.5.3 [568]). When the army pushed on into Cilicia, which it entered after frightening the defenders of the Cilician Gates into abandoning their positions, Alexander was stricken with illness as he bathed in the cold waters of the Cydnus River (C 3.6.1–17; D 17.31; *PA* 19.4–10; J 11.8.3–9; Val Max 3.8 ext 6). It has been suggested that he was suffering from malaria (Engels 1978), and this may be true; the sudden onset of the symptoms suggests that he had contracted the disease earlier and not in mosquito-infested regions of Cilicia itself. The illness threatened to cut short the expedition, and Darius himself mistook Alexander's delay for cowardice (C 3.8.10–11). This induced him to enter Cilicia from the northeast and to abandon the spacious plains of Mesopotamia near Sochi. It was a major miscalculation, pointed out to him by his advisors, and the result was a crushing defeat at Issus in November 333 (A 2.8–11; C 3.9–11; D 17.33–4; *PA* 20.5–10; J 11.9.1–10; *FGrH* 148). Victorious on the battlefield, Alexander captured the Persian camp (and with it the family of Darius: C 3.11.24–12.26) and also the Persian treasures which had been deposited and now left undefended at Damascus; these were secured by Parmenion (C 3.13; A 2.15.1; Ath 13.607f–608a; cf. J 11.10.2; *PA* 21.8).

The stunning success at Issus and the temporary confusion of Darius' affairs allowed Alexander to turn his attention to the Phoenician coast. Some cities surrendered at his approach – Aradus, Marathus, Byblos, and Sidon (C 4.1.5–6, 15–16; cf. D 17.40.2) – but Tyre held out against the enemy, confident in its seemingly impregnable position and the King's apparent lack of naval power. But the latter was quickly remedied, when the ships of the newly surrendered Phoenician towns, and those of the Greeks of Cyprus, defected to Alexander. After a siege of seven months (January–August 332), in which the causeway, which survives to this day, was built to link the island city to the mainland, Tyre fell to troops attacking the weaker walls from the sea (A 2.16.1–24.5; C 4.2–4; D 17.40.2–46.5; *PA* 24–5; J 11.10.10–14; Pol*Strat* 4.3.3–4; 4.13). From Tyre, Alexander advanced to Gaza, which he also captured after a siege of two months (see s.v. **Batis**). After securing the Levantine coast, Alexander entered Egypt, where he met no resistance: the Egyptian satrap had been killed at Issus (see s.v. **Sauaces**) and his lieutenant, Mazaces, had recently defeated a mercenary force under Amyntas son of Antiochus. Whether he was crowned as "Pharaoh" in Memphis is debated; in 332/1 he marched to the Oasis of Siwah, where he was greeted by the high priest as son of Amun. Probably on his return from Siwah he founded Alexandria at the mouth of the Nile (for the Egyptian sojourn see A 3.4–5; C 4.7.8–8.9; D 17.49.2–52.7; *IA* 48–50; P*A* 26.3–27.11; J 11.11.1–13; Str 17.1.43 [814]).

Alexander's return from Egypt in 331 took him back through Phoenicia; he crossed the Euphrates at Thapsacus and proceeded to cross the Tigris before confronting Darius for a second time at Gaugamela. Greatly outnumbered on terrain that favored the enemy, he nevertheless put Darius to flight and won an overwhelming victory (A 3.11–15; C 4.13–16; D 17.57–61; P*A* 31.6–33.11; J 11.13.1–14.7; Pol*Strat* 4.3.6, 17; Marsden 1964). As a consequence, Babylon was surrendered to him by Mazaeus, and Susa by its satrap Abulites. Next he subdued the Uxians, a hill-tribe that had retained a measure of independence under the Achaemenids, charging payment for safe passage through their territory, an ancient equivalent of the *hongo* demanded by African tribes in the nineteenth century. On the route to Persepolis, Alexander was briefly held up at the Persian Gates, but he was able to circumvent the position held by the satrap of Persis (A 3.18.1–9; C 5.3.16–4.34; D 17.68; P*A* 37.1–2; Pol*Strat* 4.3.27; cf. Speck 2002; see s.v. **Ariobarzanes**). The clearing of the Persian Gates left the road open to Persepolis, which was surrendered to him by Tiridates; the palace at Persepolis was burned as a symbolic gesture: Alexander was, after all, still leader of the panhellenic war of vengeance (for the capture of the Persian capitals see A 3.16.3–18.12; C 5.1.17–7.11; D 17.64.3–72.6; P*A* 35–8; J 11.14.7–12). In May 330, the pursuit of Darius continued; for the Great King had been in Ecbatana awaiting reinforcements from the Upper Satrapies. Forced to flee again, Darius was finally arrested and killed by his own subordinates; his corpse was found by Alexander by the roadside just to the east of the Caspian Gates (for details see s.v. **Darius**).

The death of Darius saw a stream of defections, and Alexander received the prominent Persians with clemency, even allowing some to remain in office. One such was Satibarzanes, who repaid the King's kindness by rebelling again and killing the Macedonian forces under Anaxippus. Alexander was thus diverted from the direct route to Bactria via the Merv Oasis (Margiana) and forced to march into Areia. At Phrada (modern Farah) he dealt with the conspiracy of Dimnus, which raised doubts about the loyalty of Philotas (A 3.26; D 17.79–80; C 6.7–7.2; P*A* 48.1–49.13; Str 15.2.10 [724]; J 12.5.1–8). Philotas and his father Parmenion were executed as a consequence. Alexander followed the Helmand river valley upstream, founding Alexandria in Arachosia (modern Kandahar), and then crossing the Hindu Kush near Kunduz, he made his way to Bactra (Balkh). Under the pressure of Alexander's pursuit, Bessus fled across the Oxus River (Amu-darya), but was arrested by his colleagues, most notably Spitamenes, and surrendered to Alexander (see s.v. **Bessus**). But the punishment of Bessus did not end the resistance to Macedonian arms in Bactria and Sogdiana (see esp. Holt 2005). When the King proceeded to the Iaxartes River (Syr-darya), a smaller force left behind at Maracanda (Samarcand) was ambushed and destroyed by Spitamenes at the Polytimetus River (see s.vv. **Menedemus**, **Pharnuches**). It was only after the capture of two mountain fortresses – the Rocks of Sogdiana and Chorienes (Bosworth 1981; Heckel 1986a) – and a political marriage to Rhoxane, daughter of Oxyartes, that peace was established (see s.vv. **Oxyartes**, **Rhoxane**).

In 327, Alexander proceeded to India through the Swat and Buner regions, defeating en route the Aspasians and Assacenians (see s.vv. **Assacenus**, **Cleophis**), and finally reaching the Indus (A 4.22.3–30.7; C 8.9.1–12.3), which had been bridged by an advance force under Hephaestion and Perdiccas [1] (A 4.30.9; C 8.12.4). From there he advanced into the kingdom of Taxiles, who submitted to him voluntarily (C 8.12; *ME* 49–54), and by May 326 reached the Hydaspes (Jhelum). Defeating the rajah Porus in a difficult struggle at the

Hydaspes (A 4.8.4–18.5; C 8.13–14; D 17.87–8; J 12.8.1–8; PA 60; Pol*Strat* 4.3.9, 22; Fr*Strat* 1.4.9; *ME* 58–60), he founded a city on either side of the river (Nicaea and Bucephala). But it appears that Alexander's decision to turn back had already been made after a settlement with Porus was reached; for a shipbuilding program was initiated on the Hydaspes for the purpose of moving to the mouth of the Indus. His eastward advance to Hyphasis was an attempt to create a buffer on the edge of the empire. It is doubtful that he really expected the troops to show enthusiasm for a campaign to the Ganges (A 5.25.1–29.1; C 9.2.1–3.19; D 17.93.2–95.2; P*A* 62; *ME* 68–9; J 12.8.9–17). During the descent of the Indus river system, Alexander received a near fatal wound in the town of the Mallians (near modern Multan; A 6.6–11; C 9.4.15–5.21; D 17.98–9; J 12.9.1–10.1; P*A* 63; P*M* 327b, 341c, 343d–3, 344c–d), but was rescued by his bodyguard (see s.vv. **Habreas**, **Limnaeus**, **Peucestas**). The army secured Sind and reconnoitered the Indus Delta (and the island of Patala), and after sacrificing in the Indian Ocean, Alexander made his return to the West. On the return, Alexander found that the need to maintain contact with the Ocean fleet took the land army through inhospitable terrain. Particularly difficult was the Gedrosian march (A 6.22–3; C 9.10.5–18; D 17.104.4–106.1; P*A* 66.4–7; J 12.10.7). If Alexander had requested supplies in advance, they did not materialize, and the governors of surrounding satrapies were held responsible and punished. Whether he needed scapegoats or not, Alexander found a disturbing pattern of malfeasance in these areas; for it appears that few expected him to return from India (Badian 1961; Higgins 1980). At any rate, it was an embittered and suspicious King who returned to Babylon in 323, especially after the death of his closest friend, Hephaestion, in Ecbatana in October 324 (A 7.14; D 17.110.8; P*A* 72; J 12.12.11–12).

Like his father, Philip II, Alexander blended military success with diplomacy and propaganda – but often this created dissension among his own troops. Although he exploited panhellenic symbols and ideology in his dealings with the Greeks (for example, the sacrifices at Ilium and the punishment of mercenaries who fought for Persia), he soon forged alliances with the defeated Persians: he kept Mithrenes in his entourage and later appointed him satrap of Armenia (see s.v. **Mithrenes**); he allowed Ada [1] to recover her kingdom and was pleased to be recognized publicly as her adopted son (A 1.23.8); he treated the captive members of Darius' family with respect (A 2.12.6–7; C 3.12.15–26; D 17.37.5–6, 114.2; P*A* 21; *IA* 37); and he accepted the surrender of prominent Persians in Egypt (see s.vv. **Amminapes**, **Mazaces**). After Gaugamela, he accelerated this program of "inclusion," allowing Mazaeus to rule in Babylon and retaining Abulites and Oxathres in Susa and Paraetacene; Tiridates was rewarded for surrendering Persepolis, and large numbers of prominent Persians entered his entourage at the time of Darius III's death (notably the family of Artabazus). In Sogdiana he gave new meaning to this "partnership" – whether Alexander regarded it as anything more than political expediency is a matter of debate – by marrying Rhoxane, daughter of Oxyartes. Not all his experiments with "orientalism" were successful: the army objected to his adoption of Persian dress, even in a toned-down form (P*A* 45.1–4; *ME* 2; C 6.6.2–10; A 4.7.4; Val Max 9.5 ext 1), rejected outright the introduction of *proskynesis* (A 4.9.7ff.; C 8.5.5–22; P*A* 54.3–6), and grumbled about the integration of barbarians into the army. But the King persisted and, at Susa, conducted a mass-marriage of some 10,000 average Macedonians to their common-law barbarian wives and wedded almost a hundred prominent *hetairoi* to the daughters of Iranian nobles (A 7.4.4–8; D 17.107.6; P*A* 70; P*Eum* 1.6–7; Ath 12.538b–539a; Ael*VH* 8.7; cf. C 10.3.11–12; Bosworth 1980). This was followed by the infiltration of large numbers of barbarian troops into the Royal

Army (A 7.23.1–4). The reaction to this was strongly negative, as one might expect, but the implementation of the program was suspended by the King's sudden death in 323. Nevertheless, the Diadochoi had their share of foreign troops and could scarcely have survived without them.

In matters of religion, Alexander showed great tolerance, with the result that the indigenous populations had little cause for complaint. Uprisings came instead from members of the Persian aristocracy – in some cases descendants of the Seven (in the case of Orzines it is difficult to determine if he was villain or victim) – who would have been equally perfidious under Achaemenid rule, or from Greek mercenaries who found themselves planted in colonies far from home (C 9.7.1–11; D 17.99.5; 18.7), and conspiracies arose from internal conflicts that touched, in many cases, on Alexander's enlightened views. His acceptance of Zeus-Amun as his divine father was, undoubtedly, for political advantage and there are numerous indicators that he was not taken in by his new status (at least not in the early years; see s.vv. **Anaxarchus**, **Dioxippus**), but the King's divine pretensions did not sit well with the *hetairoi* for whom the Macedonian King had always been *primus inter pares*. This only helped to fuel existing political rivalries amongst the Macedonian factions: those whose support for Alexander had been lukewarm in 336 were now more open in their criticisms, and the great confrontations with Philotas (A 3.26; C 6.7–7.2; D 17.79–80; J 12.5.1–8; P*A* 48–9; Str 15.2.10 [724]), Cleitus (A 4.8.1–9.6; C 8.1.19–2.12; P*A* 50.1–52.2; P*M* 71c; J 12.6.1–18), and the Pages all had resentment of the King's aloofness and orientalisms as a unifying theme. On two significant occasions, at the Hyphasis in 326 and at Opis in 324 (C 10.2.8–4.3; D 17.108–10; P*A* 70–2; J 12.11.4–12.6), the army voiced its displeasure, but these were objections to policy rather than to the person of the King. Though these episodes, which required brutal countermeasures, stained Alexander's reputation, one must remember that, in comparison with other rulers who enjoyed less success but wielded similar power, Alexander remained relatively safe in his own camp and continued to be adored by the common soldier (for opposing views see Badian 2000a; Heckel 2003). They had followed him to the ends of the earth, and the possibility that he would not be present to lead them home constituted one of their greatest fears.

In the course of the expedition Alexander founded numerous cities, most of them named Alexandria. PM 328e speaks of seventy, which is perhaps no exaggeration if one takes military foundations and the rebuilding of older towns into consideration; StByz s.v. "Alexandreiai" names eighteen famous Alexandrias, and Ps-Call 3.35 mentions nine; J 12.5.12–13 names Alexandria-on-the-Tanais (Syr-darya) and mentions twelve cities in Bactria and Sogdiana alone (Str 11.11.4, only eight). Not only did many of these survive to become influential centers in the Hellenistic age, but also the program of military settlements and synoecisms was imitated by the Diadochoi and their descendants. For full discussion see Tarn ii.232–59 and Fraser.

Alexander's true appearance is another matter of uncertainty. He appears to have been of average or slightly less than average stature: certainly his friend Hehaestion was physically more imposing (C 3.12.16–17); his feet did not reach to the footstool when he seated himself on the Persian throne at Susa (D 17.66.3); and the Amazon Queen thought that his physical presence did not do justice to his reputation (C 6.5.29). But the claim of the *Alexander Romance* that he was less than 3 cubits in height, that is, 4.5 ft (Ps-Call 3.4), must be dismissed as absurd. Portraits of the King were certainly stylized, emphasizing the tilt of his head, his flowing locks, and the upward-turned eyes; for he permitted only certain artists to represent him in the various media (P*A* 4; see s.vv. **Apelles**, **Lysippus**, **Pyrgoteles**); coin-portraits too are idealized (for a full discussion see

Stewart, with images and testimonia). His sexual appetites seem not to have been very strong: his parents are alleged to have introduced him to a courtesan in the hope of stimulating his interest in women (Ath 10.435a; see s.v. **Callixeina**), and despite the now popular view that he and Hephaestion had a homoerotic relationship (PA 39.8; Ael*VH* 7.8, 12.7; Val Max 4.7 ext 2; A 7.14.4; Reames-Zimmerman 1999), a number of liaisons with women are attested (Ael*VH* 12.34; J 11.10.2–3; see s.vv. **Barsine**, **Pancaste**) – one must leave aside the fictitious relations with the Amazon Queen and the Assacenian Cleophis. His rejection of boys (P*A* 22.1–3), if not a deliberate attempt to counter rumors about his relationship with Bagoas, may reflect a lack of enthusiasm for pederasty, which had had dire consequences for his father (see s.v. **Pausanias** [2, 3]). In the case of Bagoas, it ought to be stressed that those writers who depicted him as "vile" were reacting to the fact that Bagoas was a eunuch (and an eastern one at that), and they were not finding fault with him as the King's *eromenos*. Attempts to see Olympias as the cause of Alexander's alleged sexual insecurities have met with only limited success, but the modern scholar will interpret these personal details in accordance with his or her own predilections, and the reader will believe whatever he or she chooses, often with little regard for cultural context. He is known to have fathered three children (the illegitimate Heracles, son of Barsine; a child by Rhoxane who died in India (*ME* 70); and Alexander IV, who would be the legitimate King of Macedon, though he never exercised any power). Whether his royal Persian brides conceived is unknown: Stateira was killed, as a precaution by Rhoxane (P*A* 77.6), and Parysatis may have met a similar fate.

The combined effects of campaigning and the hard Macedonian lifestyle took their toll on the King's body. His documented wounds include minor wounds from clubs and arrows against the Illyrians, a blow to the head and a grazing of the scalp at the Granicus, a thigh injury at Issus, an arrow to the ankle and a blow to the shoulder at Gaza, three more arrow wounds in India, including the near fatal one to the chest at the town of the Mallians (P*M* 327a–b); at the Iaxartes an arrow broke his tibia (P*A* 45.5–6); and he suffered from a variety of diseases during the course of the expedition. To this we may add a penchant for drinking which, although exaggerated by hostile sources (e.g., Ephippus of Olynthus), cannot be explained away or put down to "social drinking." Perhaps his drinking accounted for his relatively low sex drive; and certainly the argument with Cleitus that led the King to murder him was fueled by alcohol (but see also Tritle 2003); at worst, it may even have caused his death (O'Brien 1992).

Alexander died in Babylon on June 11, 323 (Depuydt 1997; cf. Koch 2000), after a lengthy illness, the exact nature of which continues to baffle scholars, though there is no shortage of speculation (typhus, malaria, alcoholism, pancreatitis, perforated bowel, even West Nile Virus or bereavement). Rumors of poisoning were fabricated by the party hostile to the adherents of Antipater and Antigonus, and it appears that a forged pamphlet on the *Last Days and Testament of Alexander* was published in the early years of the Successors: 321 (Ausfeld 1895, 1901; Merkelbach 1954, 1977), 318 (Tarn 1921; Pfister 1961; Heckel 1988), and 308 (Bosworth 2000) have all been proposed as dates for its publication with Perdiccas, Polyperchon, and Ptolemy respectively regarded as the instigator of the propaganda; though one recent book actually argues that Ptolemy was the "assassin" (Doherty 2004: 141–86). After a brief period of indecision regarding the succession, it was agreed that Arrhidaeus would succeed immediately, as Philip III, and that a share of the kingship would be reserved for Rhoxane's child, if it turned out to be a boy. See s.v. **Alexander** [3]. The arrangements were neither unanimous nor enforceable. Instead they triggered a series of coalitions and war, which ended in the extermination of the male members of the Argead house, the assumption of the title of "King" by some of Alexander's former marshals, and the eventual formation of the Hellenistic Kingdoms. Relatives of Alexander's generals ruled in the East until the death of Cleopatra VII of Egypt in 30 BC. For the impact of Alexander's conquests see Green 1990; Erskine 2003; and for his image in Rome see Spencer 2002; cf. Weippert 1972.

Contemporary sources are lost or survive in second-hand fragments. The most important of the writers who accompanied the expedition and knew the King personally deserve mention. Eumenes of Caria and Diodotus of Erythrae were said to have been the authors of the Royal Journals or *Ephemerides*, but the authenticity and nature of the Journals are hotly disputed. Chares of Mytilene was the court chamberlain and an eyewitness source for some of what went on "behind the scenes." Callisthenes of Olynthus accompanied Alexander as the "official historian" and sent reports back to Greece at the end of each campaigning season, serving thus as both propagandist and war correspondent. Onesicritus and Nearchus described the progress of the fleet from the Hydaspes to the Tigris and their fragments deal with India, but the former may have written a work on Alexander closely modeled on Xenophon's *Cyropaedia* (Brown). Ptolemy and Aristobulus, who were regarded by Arrian of Nicomedia as the most reliable (perhaps because the least critical) sources, still enjoy inflated reputations (Strasburger, Kornemann; but see Errington 1969; Roisman 1984). Others in Alexander's entourage wrote memoirs and scurrilous gossip (Medius of Larissa, Polycleitus, and Ephippus), while the bematists kept records that were used by contemporaries. Marsyas of Pella, a *syntrophos* of the King and a half-brother of Antigonus the One-Eyed, contributed little to the history of events after 333; for he remained with Antigonus in Phrygia. Cleitarchus of Alexandria appears not to have participated in the expedition, though he did have access to important written work and eyewitness reports (Schachermeyr 658–62; Prandi). The fragments of their works are collected in volume IIB of Jacoby, *FGrH*; translations into English in the first volume of Robinson, into French in Auberger 2001; discussion by Pearson. The extant sources are listed at the beginning of this *Who's Who* and cited throughout.

See, particularly, Tarn i–ii; Fuller; Wilcken; Schachermeyr; Milns; Green; Lane Fox; Seibert 1985; Badian, *CHIran* ii.420–501; Bosworth 1988a; *CAH*[2] vi 791–875; *OCD*[3] 57–9; and for a different perspective, Lendering 2005.

Alexander [3]. (Alexandros). Alexander IV of Macedon (*regn.* 323/2–310 BC). Son of Alexander and Rhoxane (Paus 9.7.2), born not later than September 323 (Rhoxane was 6 or 8 months pregnant when Alexander died at the beginning of June; cf. A*Succ* 1.1, 8; App*Syr* 52, 54). Upon his birth he was recognized (by prearrangement) as *symbasileus* with Philip III Arrhidaeus (A*Succ* 1.1, 8; J 13.4.3). His birth appears to have provided Perdiccas with the opportunity to assume the *prostasia*, since Craterus did not exercise his claim, which at any rate pertained only to Philip III Arrhidaeus (cf. D 18.23.2). Perdiccas took Alexander IV with him to Cappadocia and Pisidia (J 13.6.10), and eventually to Egypt (Paus 1.6.3). From there Alexander was taken to Triparadeisus in northern Syria and, at first, entrusted to Antigonus the One-Eyed (A*Succ* 1.38). But when Cassander became suspicious of Antigonus' intentions, Alexander IV and Philip III were taken by Antipater to Macedonia (A*Succ* 1.42, 44; *HE* 3.2). After Antipater's death, Polyperchon assumed the guardianship of Alexander and summoned Olympias to Macedonia to exercise the *epimeleia* and see to the boy's upbringing (D 18.49.4; cf. D 19.23.2). It was, no doubt, Olympias who arranged to the betrothal of Alexander to Deidameia, the daughter of Aeacides and sister of Pyrrhus (P*Pyr* 4.3). Alexander was in the company of Olympias when she was besieged at

Pydna by Cassander's forces (D 19.35.5; J 14.6.2, confusing Alexander and Heracles), and eventually he and his mother were sent to Amphipolis, where they were kept under guard (D 19.52.4; J 14.6.13; 15.1.3). Although an agreement made with Antigonus, Ptolemy, and Lysimachus spelled out that Cassander should be *strategos* of Europe until Alexander came of age (D 19.105.1), a certain Glaucias, who commanded the guard over Alexander, murdered Alexander and his mother Rhoxane in 310 and concealed their bodies (D 19.105.2; J 15.2.5, cf. 16.1.15; *HE* 2.3; Paus 9.7.2 says Alexander was poisoned).[38]

Kaerst, *RE* s.v. "Alexandros (11)"; Wirth, *Kl. Pauly* i.250 no. 7. See Stemma I.

Alexander [4]. (Alexandros). A son of Aëropus (A 1.7.6, 17.8) of Lyncestis (D 17.32.1, 80.2; C 7.1.5; 8.8.6; J 11.2.2, 7.1), Alexander was probably an adherent of that canton's royal house. His brothers, Heromenes and Arrhabaeus (A 1.25.1), were both executed for their alleged complicity in the "plot" to assassinate Philip II (cf. J 11.2.2); Alexander himself had married a daughter of Antipater (C 7.1.7; J 11.7.1; 12.14.1; D 17.80.2 wrongly calls his father-in-law "Antigonus").[39]

Although his brothers were executed for complicity in the murder of Philip (A 1.25.1; J 11.2.1–2; cf. D 17.2.1; P*A* 10.8), Alexander was spared on account of his connections with Antipater and because he was the first to hail his namesake as "King" (A 1.25.2; J 11.2.2). He was promptly appointed *strategos* of Thrace (A 1.25.2): in 335 it was rumored in Thebes that the approaching Macedonian army was led by Alexander Lyncestes, coming from Thrace; for certain politicians had encouraged a false report that Alexander the Great was dead (A 1.7.6). In 334, Alexander accompanied the King, who clearly did not trust him with the *strategia* of Thrace in his absence. Nevertheless, he received Calas' command of the Thessalian cavalry, when the son of Harpalus became satrap of Hellespontine Phrygia (A 1.25.2).[40]

Alexander was hipparch for only a few months, in which time he helped Calas establish himself in the Troad (A 1.17.8; cf. Pol*Strat* 4.3.15). In 334/3 Parmenion informed the King that a Persian named Sisines had been arrested, bearing a letter from Darius III to Alexander Lyncestes, which offered him 1,000 talents of gold if he assassinated his king (A 1.25.3; the offer may have come from Nabarzanes, C 3.7.12). The Lyncestian was arrested, through the agency of Amphoterus, whom Alexander sent from Phaselis to Parmenion's camp (A 1.25.9–10; D 17.32.1–2 places the arrest shortly before Issus). Deposed from office and kept under guard until 330, he was eliminated in the aftermath of the Philotas affair (C 7.1.5–9; D 17.80.2; J 12.14.1). C 7.1.6 speaks of two informants against Alexander Lyncestes, gives a radically different version of the arrest of Sisines (3.7.11–15; cf. Atkinson i.183ff.), and appears to have discussed him in the lost second book of his *History* (cf. Heckel 1991: 125). But C 7.1.6 follows a primary source (Cleitarchus?) dating the arrest of Alexander to autumn 333 (i.e., not long before Issus); in this context, most sources describe Parmenion's suspicions that Philip of Acarnania had been bribed by Darius to poison Alexander (C 3.6.1–17; P*A* 19.4–10; Val Max 3.8 ext 6; Ps-Call 2.8.4–11; Jul Val 2.24; Sen *de Ira* 2.23.2; also A 2.4.8–11).

Kaerst, *RE* s.v. "Alexandros (12)"; Beloch iii^2 2.77, and *passim*; Berve ii.17–19 no. 37; Bosworth 1971a; Carney 1980; Heckel 357–8; Badian 2000a: 56–60; Heckel 2003: 210–13. See Stemma XV.

Alexander [5]. (Alexandros). A member of Alexander's cohort (C 8.11.9–10) but apparently not a Page. Together with Charus, Alexander led a band of thirty young men selected from the Royal Hypaspists for the assault on Aornus. Alexander was killed in a valiant assault on Aornus (C 8.11.15). Curtius' description of their deaths recalls Virgil's account of Nisus and Euryalus (*Aeneid* 9.176ff.), but the historicity of the event (cf. P*A* 58.5) and of

Alexander and Charus themselves need not be questioned.

Berve ii.21 no. 40; Heckel 295–6.

Alexander [6]. (Alexandros). Macedonian from Tymphaea, son of Polyperchon. Alexander was born before 334 and, in the light of his appointment as Somatophylax of Philip III at Triparadeisus in 320 (A*Succ* 1.38), most likely in the 340s. His appointment as Somatophylax was undoubtedly intended to give Polyperchon some input into the management of affairs. Conversely, it may be seen as a way for Antipater the Regent to keep at his court the relatives of prominent men, who might serve as hostages. At some point he married Cratesipolis (D 19.67.1; cf. P*Demetr* 9.5), a Macedonian woman who was to prove herself a formidable force in the struggles of the Successors. Alexander arrived with an army in Attica in 318 to back up demands for the liberation of Athens, but he was soon persuaded by Phocion and others who had been of the pro-Macedonian party to retain Munychia and Piraeus for himself; hence Alexander conferred in secret with Nicanor (D 18.65.3–5). The party which had favored Antipater was deposed and they, including Phocion, took refuge with Alexander, who sent favorable letters on their behalf to his father Polyperchon (D 18.66.1). His negotiations with Nicanor came to naught, and soon Cassander sailed into Piraeus to relieve the city. Polyperchon took the bulk of the army to the Peloponnese, leaving Alexander with a portion in Attica (D 18.68.3). What he did in the interval, we are not told, but it appears that Alexander was either near or in the Peloponnese when Cassander directed his attentions to Macedonia in 317 (D 19.35.1). In 316, Aristonus, in control of Amphipolis, looked in vain for relief from Polyperchon and his son (D 19.50.8). After the collapse of the Polyperchon–Olympias faction in Macedonia, Cassander turned his attention back to the Peloponnese and Alexander (D 19.53.1), who now occupied the Isthmus but stood idly by when Cassander ferried his troops to the Argolid and began to recapture the Peloponnesian cities (D 19.54.3–4). In 315, when Ptolemy, Lysimachus, and Cassander had formed a dangerous alliance against him, Antigonus sent Aristodemus of Miletus to attempt to win Alexander and Polyperchon to his side (D 19.57.5). The attempt met with initial success, with Polyperchon supporting Antigonus' cause in the Peloponnese, while Alexander sailed to Asia to meet Antigonus himself (D 19.60.1), with whom he established a pact (D 19.61.1). Antigonus gave him 500 talents and sent him back to Greece filled with greater expectations (D 19.61.5). Ptolemy responded by sending Polycleitus with fifty ships to the Peloponnese to attack Alexander who, with his father, was now cooperating with Antigonus' agent, Aristodemus (D 19.62.5). Alexander wasted an opportunity to seize Argos in the absence of Cassander's general Apollonides (D 19.63.2). Cassander himself now turned his attentions to Corinth and captured Alexander's garrisons there (D 19.63.4–5) before directing his army to Orchomenus. This action Cassander followed up by sending Prepelaus to Alexander and persuading him to desert Antigonus (and Polyperchon) by accepting the position of *strategos* of the Peloponnese (D 19.64.2–5; cf. 19.66.2). As Cassander's lieutenant, Alexander suppressed an uprising by the Dymaeans, only to lose the city soon after his departure (D 19.66.5–6). Setting out from Sicyon in 314 he was murdered by Alexion, a Sicyonian who had pretended friendship (19.67.1). Alexander's wife Cratesipolis was successful at keeping the army together and retaining some control over the Peloponnese (D 19.67.1, 74.2).

Kaerst, *RE* s.v. "Alexandros (13)"; Berve ii.21 no. 39; Heckel 283; Wirth, *Kl. Pauly* i.250 no. 9. See Stemma XII.

Alexander [7]. (Alexandros). Son of Cleophis (and Alexander?). His existence is questionable; certainly his paternity might be doubted (see s.v. **Cleophis**). But it may just be that Cleophis named a son

Alexander after the Macedonian conqueror (C 8.10.36; J 12.7.9–10).

Seel 1972: 181.

Alexander [8]. (Alexandros). Macedonian. Namesake of the King (Aristobulus, *FGrH* 139 F2b = P*M* 259e).[41] The leader of a band of Thracians who burst into the home of Timocleia during the sack of Thebes (335), he raped the woman but was fatally deceived by her. Timocleia pretended to have hidden gold and silver in a well, into which she pushed Alexander to his death (P*A* 12). According to Pol*Strat* 8.40, he went into the well looking for plunder, whereafter Timocleia threw rocks down upon him. See further s.v. **Timocleia**.

Griffith, *HMac* ii.433 n. 4.

Alexander (Alexandros). Seer, according to D 17.17.6. Probably a manuscript error. See s.v. **Aristander**.

Alexippus (Alexippos). Physician who healed a wound sustained by Peucestas during a bear hunt and received a letter of thanks from Alexander (P*A* 41.6). Berve ii.22 suggests that the incident occurred after Peucestas assumed the satrapy of Persis in 325/4. This is rendered more likely by the fact of Alexander's letter, which implies that Peucestas and Alexippus were not in the King's camp. Alexippus is otherwise unknown.

Wellmann, *RE* s.v. "Alexippos (6)"; Berve ii.21–2 no. 43.

Alexis. Tarentine rhapsode; performed at the mass-marriage ceremony in Susa in 324 (Chares of Mytilene, in the tenth book of his *History of Alexander*, *FGrH* 125 F4 = Ath 12.538e). Nothing else is known about him.

Kirchner, *RE* s.v. "Alexis (8)"; Berve ii.22 no. 44.

Amadas. J 12.12.8. See s.v. **Polydamas**.

Amastris (Amestris, Amastrine). Persian princess, daughter of Oxyathres (A 7.4.5; D 20.109.7; Str 12.3.10 [544]; Memnon, *FGrH* 434 F1 §4.4; StByz s.v. "Amastris") and thus niece of Darius III. Amastris and her cousin Stateira were of similar age and raised together (Memnon 4.4); she appears to have accompanied the royal family westward during the Issus campaign and was captured at Damascus after the battle (C 3.13.13). Hence, she too may have remained in Alexander's camp until the army reached Susa in 331; there she married Craterus in 324 BC (A 7.4.5; Memnon 4.4; D 20.109.7). In 322/1, she married Dionysius of Heraclea Pontica (Str 12.3.10; StByz s.v. "Amastris"), with Craterus' consent, and bore him three children: a daughter, also named Amastris, and two sons, Clearchus and Oxyathres (Memnon 4.8); after Dionysius' death in 306/5, she ruled as regent for her underaged children, supported by Antigonus the One-Eyed. But in 302 Amastris married Lysimachus, with whom she resided as queen in Sardis (D 20.109.7; Memnon 4.9; Pol*Strat* 6.12).[42] The marriage was, however, terminated amicably in 300 or 299 BC when Lysimachus married Arsinoë, the daughter of Ptolemy I Soter (Memnon 4.9, incorrectly identifying Arsinoë as daughter of Philadelphus). Amastris founded a city that bore her name in Paphlagonia by synoecizing the four settlements of Sesamus, Cytorum, Cromma, and Tieum, though the last revolted from the united city (Str 12.3.10; Memnon 4.9).[43] She may have taken up residence in her city, where she minted coins proclaiming herself "Queen Amastris" (Head, *HN*² 505–6). Amastris was murdered (by drowning) by her own sons (ca. 284; thus Burstein 85, cf. 93–4), and her death was avenged by Lysimachus to his own political advantage (Memnon 5.2–3).

Wilcken, *RE* s.v. "Amastris (7)"; Berve ii.24 no. 50; Burstein 75–86; Lund 75, 82, 88, 188; Brosius 78, with n. 70. See Stemma III.

Amedines. *Scriba regis*, that is, secretary of Darius III, Amedines had presumably surrendered to Alexander after the Great King's death; he was appointed satrap of the Ariaspians (or Euergetae; on whom see Str 15.2.10 [724]; A 3.27.4; D 17.81.1–2) in autumn 330 (C 7.3.4). The appointment is difficult to reconcile with two other notices: A 3.27.5 says that Ariaspians remained free (but this may simply refer to an extension of the grant of *ateleia*; cf. D 17.81.1; Bosworth i.366 notes that their autonomy could only have been nominal), and D 17.81.2 says that Tiridates was appointed satrap of the Gedrosians and the Euergetae. Berve's suggestion (ii.25) that Amedines was a native of the region points to a possible solution, but the same would then have to apply to Tiridates, if he was Amedines' successor.

Berve ii.24–5 no. 51.

Amminais. Brother of the Indian dynast Assacenus and (apparently) a son of Cleophis (*ME* 39), Amminais brought into the city of Massaga 9,000 mercenaries (*ME* 39), who were later treacherously massacred by Alexander (D 17.84; *ME* 43–4; Pol*Strat* 4.3.20; A 4.27.2–4 is apologetic). He may have been in charge of the operations against the Macedonians, since his brother had recently died and Cleophis herself ruled the kingdom (C 8.10.22). Perhaps he was the *hegemon* of the place, whose death precipitated the surrender of the Assacenians (A 4.27.2; wrongly identified by some as Assacenus himself). Berve ii.26, however, thinks that Amminais is that brother of Assacenus who opposed Alexander in the Buner region after the fall of Aornus (A 4.30.5), but Eggermont 183 is perhaps correct in identifying this "brother" with Aphrices (D 17.86.2; Erices in C 8.12.1, thus Anspach i.32 n. 92, emends Diodorus to "Aerices"; Ariplex in *ME* 42).

Berve ii.25–6 no. 54; Eggermont 183–4.

Amminapes (Manapis). Prominent Parthian who had come to the court of Philip II as an exile during the reign of Artaxerxes III Ochus (C 6.4.25) and later, together with Mazaces, surrendered Egypt to Alexander (A 3.22.1). Amminapes remained in Alexander's entourage until the surrender of Phrataphernes in 330 (C 6.4.23; A 3.23.4), when he was appointed satrap of Hyrcania and Parthia (A 3.22.1; cf. C 6.4.25, naming only Hyrcania). Alexander left Tlepolemus as *episkopos* to keep an eye on Amminapes' activities. Although the satrapies were soon returned to Phrataphernes (A 3.28.2; 5.20.7; cf. C 8.3.17), there is no indication of Amminapes' death or misconduct on his part. What became of him is unknown.

Berve ii.26 no. 55.

Amphimachus (Amphimachos). A*Succ* 1.35 calls Amphimachus "brother of the king": hence Berve ii.32, followed by Bosworth 2002: 113 with n. 60 and Carney 61 with 276 n. 45, identifies him as a son of Philine of Larissa from an earlier union. He is probably the brother of Arrhidaeus the satrap of Hellespontine Phrygia (thus, rightly, Jacoby, iiD, 563; following Beloch iv^2 2.316), who was sometimes confused with Philip III Arrhidaeus (cf. J 13.4.6), and thus perhaps the son of Alexander (cf. Billows 1993). Satrap of Mesopotamia and Arbelitis in the settlement of Triparadeisus in 320 (A*Succ* 1.35; D 18.39.6). In 317 BC he supported Eumenes against Antigonus the One-Eyed at Paraetacene, bringing 600 horsemen who were stationed between the troops of Stasander and Cephalon (D 19.27.4). He may have been killed at Gabiene, or executed afterwards (cf. D 19.44.1), or simply deposed. At any rate, there is no further trace of him.

Kaerst, *RE* s.v. "Amphimachos (9)"; Berve ii.32 no. 66.

Amphistratus (Amphistratos). Sculptor. Amphistratus produced a statue of the historian Callisthenes of Olynthus (Pl*NH* 36.36). The date of this work is uncertain, as is whether Amphistratus had any personal connection with Alexander.

Robert, *RE* s.v. "Amphistratos (3)"; Berve ii.32 no. 67.

Amphoterus (Amphoteros). Macedonian from Orestis (cf. A*Ind* 18.5), Amphoterus was the son of Alexander (A 1.25.9; cf. A*Ind* 18.5) and, perhaps, Aristopatra (cf. Str 15.1.35 [702] = *FGrH* 153 F2), and the brother of Craterus (A 1.25.9). The generally accepted view that Amphoterus was the younger brother (Berve ii.32) is not compelling. Craterus' achievements outshine those of his brother, but do not impute seniority. The fact that Alexander used Amphoterus for some rather delicate missions (A 1.25.9–10; 3.6.3; C 4.8.15; cf. Bosworth 1975), and even appointed him navarch of the Aegean fleet (C 3.1.19), suggests that he was a man of some experience. During the winter of 334/3 he was sent by Alexander from Phaselis to Parmenion in Gordium with orders that the latter arrest Alexander Lyncestes on a charge of treason (A 1.25.9–10). Amphoterus traveled in native dress, accompanied by guides from Perge, in order to avoid recognition (A 1.25.9). From there, in the spring of 333, he proceeded to the coast to share the command of the reconstituted Aegean fleet with Hegelochus (C 3.1.19; cf. A 2.2.3). Together they secured control of Tenedos, Chios, and Mytilene (A 3.2.3–5; C 4.5.14–22), and Amphoterus captured Cos with a separate force of sixty ships (A 3.2.6). Both appear to have rejoined Alexander in Egypt (A 3.2.3; cf. Bosworth 1975: 31 n. 20), whence Amphoterus was sent to the Peloponnese in 331 to aid those who remained loyal to Macedon at the time of Agis' revolt (A 3.6.3); C 4.8.15, however, claims that Amphoterus was sent to liberate Crete and that he left not from Egypt but when Alexander made his return visit to Tyre. Although the departure point is confused, both authors may refer to an expedition against Crete, since Str 10.4.1 [474] includes Crete in the Peloponnese (cf. Bosworth 1975: 34–5). What became of Amphoterus is unknown, but since Alexander had moved rapidly into the heart of the Persian empire in 331 it appears that, unless some mishap occurred at sea, he remained in the west under the authority of Antipater.

Kaerst, *RE* s.v. "Amphoteros (4)"; Berve ii.32–3 no. 68; Bosworth 1975; Hauben 1972: 57 and 1976: 79–105, esp. 82–7; Heckel 107–8 n. 231. See Stemma VI.

Amyntas [1]. Son of Perdiccas III (A*Succ* 1.22), and thus nephew of Philip II. Amyntas was born ca. 365 BC and the rightful heir to the kingdom at the time of his father's death (360/59), but, on account of his youth, he yielded the throne to Philip II, who served either as regent (J 7.5.9–10; Satyrus *ap.* Ath 13.557b) or as king (D 16.1.3, 2.1).[44] He grew up at the court of his uncle and could claim several important members of the Macedonian aristocracy as his *syntrophoi* (cf. C 6.9.17, 10.24). Philip later married him to his daughter Cynnane; their daughter Adea later married Philip III Arrhidaeus (A*Succ* 1.22; cf. Pol*Strat* 8.60). The honors for Amyntas son of Perdiccas at Lebedeia (*IG* vii.3055, 9) and Oropus (*SIG*[3] 258; Rhodes & Osborne no. 75), the former calling him *basileus*, may belong to the turmoil after the death of Philip II, but it must be stressed that by spring 335 Amyntas had already been executed by his cousin (J 12.6.14), Alexander; for A 1.5.4 makes it clear that Cynnane was already a widow at that time and was offered as bride to Langarus, king of the Agrianes. Clearly there was a faction in Macedonia that favored him over Alexander (*PM* 327c), whether he himself sought the kingship or not.[45]

Kaerst, *RE* s.v. "Amyntas (15)"; Berve ii.30–1 no. 61. See Stemma I.

Amyntas [2]. Son of Antiochus (A 1.17.9; *SIG*[3] 258, 2, 4; Rhodes & Osborne no. 75). He and Amyntas son of Perdiccas were awarded proxenies by the Oropians at some point before 338 BC (cf. Ellis 1971). After the death of Philip II, Amyntas fled from Macedonia (D 17.48.2; C 3.11.18) and is found in 334 at Ephesus, which he and the Greek garrison there deserted after the news of Alexander's victory at the Granicus (A 1.17.9). Amyntas appears to have joined Darius at Sochi, shortly before the battle of Issus, in the company of Thymondas (cf. C 3.8.1; certainly he was there advising the Persian King not to abandon that position: *PA* 20.1–4; A 2.6.3; cf. C 3.8.2). At some point in 334, he appears to have acted as the agent of Alexander Lyncestes in his treasonous dealings with the Persians (A 1.25.3). Amyntas fought at Issus, whence he fled to Egypt, via Tripolis in Phoenicia, with 4,000 mercenaries (D 17.48.2). At Tripolis he took enough ships to transport his troops and, burning the remaining ships, he sailed to Cyprus. There he augmented his forces and fleet and continued to Pelusium, which he seized, claiming that Darius had sent him there as *strategos* in place of Sauaces, the satrap who had fallen at Issus. At first Amyntas was greeted with some enthusiasm (C 4.7.1–2), but, in an attack on Memphis, he and his troops were slaughtered after they had turned to careless plundering (D 17.48.3–5; C 4.1.27–33; A 2.13.2–3).

Kaerst, *RE* s.v. "Amyntas (16)"; Berve ii.28–9 no. 58; Ellis 1971; Hofstetter 13–14 no. 15.

Amyntas [3]. Son of Arrhabaeus (A 1.12.7, 14.1, 6; 1.28.4) and brother of the defector Neoptolemus (A 1.20.10).[46] Thus probably the grandson of Aëropus and nephew of Alexander Lyncestes. Berve ii.29 identifies him tentatively with the envoy sent (with Clearchus) by Philip to Thebes in 338 BC (Marsyas, *FGrH* 135/6 F20 = *PDem* 18.1–2). Given the frequency of the name in Macedonia, this is far from certain.[47] He may have been one of the commanders of the advance force in Asia Minor in 336–334 (J 9.5.8), along with Parmenion and Attalus. In 334, he led the scouting party – four *ilai* of *hippeis prodromoi* (i.e., *sarissophoroi*), and the squadron of Socrates son of Sathon – from Hermotus toward the Granicus (A 1.12.7), and in the battle, his squadrons (*sarissophoroi* and Paeonians: A 1.14.1) occupied the right wing and initiated the assault on the Persian forces on the opposite riverbank (A 1.14.6–15.1; cf. 1.16.1). In winter 334/3, Amyntas commanded the entire left at Sagalassus (A 1.28.4).[48] All three attested commands show that the son of Arrhabaeus was an officer of high standing, militarily competent, and trusted by the King. This makes his disappearance from history all the more intriguing, as Berve ii.29–30 rightly notes. Had he died – in battle or from illness – in the first year of the campaign, the sources would almost certainly have recorded the fact.[49] Probably, his disappearance is a consequence of the arrest of his uncle Alexander. His successor was probably Protomachus. Identification with Amyntas Lyncestes (C 5.2.5), the infantry commander, is impossible given the ranks of the two individuals (cf. Heckel 247 n. 32, for the obscurity of the commanders appointed in Sittacene).

Berve ii.29–30 no. 59; Bosworth i.109; Heckel 352–3. See Stemma XV.

Amyntas [4]. Eldest of four attested sons of Andromenes (A 1.8.2, 14.2; D 17.45.7) and one of Alexander's *hetairoi* (*philoi*, D 17.45.7), Amyntas was a close friend of Philotas son of Parmenion. He was perhaps born soon after 365 and brought up at the court of Philip II as a *syntrophos* of Amyntas son of Perdiccas (C 7.1.11). He first appears as a taxiarch of *pezhetairoi* in the Theban campaign (335 BC), where his unit was teamed with that of Perdiccas, whom they followed in the assault on the city (A 1.8.2). Of his role at the Granicus, we know only that he was stationed to the right of center (A 1.14.2); after the battle he was sent to accept the surrender of Sardis to secure the city from its commander, Mithrenes, but he remained there only until Pausanias had been placed in charge of the citadel (A 1.17.4, 7). Perhaps his was one of the three battalions assigned to Philotas at Miletus (A 1.19.8); he reappears in the unsuccessful attack on Myndus, together with the Companion cavalry and the battalions of Perdiccas and Coenus (A 1.20.5–7). At Issus, Amyntas' battalion is found next to that of Ptolemaeus son of

Seleucus, but again his participation in the battle is not otherwise documented (A 2.8.4; C 3.9.7). That he shared Alexander's determination not to break off the siege of Tyre (thus D 17.45.7) is plausible but incapable of proof. Soon after the capture of Gaza (late 332), Alexander sent Amyntas to Macedonia with ten triremes for the purpose of enlisting reinforcements (D 17.49.1); he rejoined the King near Sittacene in late 331, bringing 6,000 Macedonian infantry and 500 cavalry, along with 3,500 Thracian foot and 600 horse, 4,000 Peloponnesian mercenary foot and 380 cavalry, as well as fifty Pages (C 5.1.42; cf. D 17.65.1).[50] Upon his return, Amyntas resumed the command of his battalion, which formed part of the contingent sent to bridge the Araxes River while Alexander dealt with Ariobarzanes at the Persian Gates (A 3.18.6; C 5.4.20, 30). In the Mardian campaign, his battalion and Coenus' accompanied the King (A 3.24.1); the same force was led by Alexander against Satibarzanes at Artacoana (A 3.25.6).

The loyalty of the sons of Andromenes was called into question as a result of the Dimnus affair (A 3.27.1).[51] The case against Amyntas did not amount to much: he had been arrogant in his dealings with Antiphanes, the *scriba equitum* (C 7.1.15); during a recruiting mission to Macedonia, he had pressed into service some young men from Olympias' court (C 7.1.37–8), and indeed Olympias had written damaging letters about him and his brothers to her son (C 7.1.12); but, most of all, he had close ties of friendship with Philotas (C 7.1.11; cf. A 3.27.1); like Philotas, he must have been on friendly terms with Amyntas son of Perdiccas and Amyntas son of Antiochus. Convicting him was undesirable, if not impossible: fully one-third of the Macedonian infantry could be expected to stand by him – his own battalion and that of Polyperchon; and his brother Attalus had been raised at the court with Alexander himself. Not long after the acquittal of the sons of Andromenes, Amyntas was killed during the siege of a small town (A 3.27.3).

Kaerst, *RE* s.v. "Amyntas (17)"; Berve ii.26–7 no. 57; Heckel 176–8. See Stemma XII.

Amyntas [5]. A 1.7.1 describes Amyntas as a member of the occupying force on the Cadmea in Thebes in 335 BC. He and Timolaus were murdered by a group of Theban exiles who had slipped into the city during the night, and the action was followed by the rebellion of the Thebans. There is a strong likelihood that Amyntas is identical with Anemoetas, whom Demosthenes in the *de Corona* names as a traitor to the Theban cause, along with Timolaus and Theogeiton (Dem 18.295; cf. Schaefer iii^2 107 n. 2). Hence Amyntas and Timolaus were not garrison troops but rather leaders of the pro-Macedonian party; for their own security, they doubtless resided on the Cadmea.[52]

Berve ii.31 no. 62; A 1. 7. 1; Beloch iii^2 1.615 n. 2.

Amyntas [6]. Macedonian of unknown origin. In the contest of valor in Sittacene, Amyntas won fourth place and was appointed *chiliarches* or *pentakosiarches*, presumably of the hypaspists or of some battalion of light infantry (C 5.2.5).[53] Nothing else is known about this Amyntas, nor is it possible to identify him with any of his namesakes.

Heckel 305.

Amyntas [7]. "Amyntas Lyncestes." An infantry commander of Lyncestian origin, Amyntas finished sixth in the contest of valor in Sittacene and was appointed *chiliarches* or *pentakosiarches*, presumably in the hypaspists (C 5.2.5). Nothing else is known about him. Identification with the son of Arrhabaeus is all but impossible.

Berve ii.31 no. 63; Heckel 305.

Amyntas [8]. Macedonian. C 6.7.15 lists him amongst the conspirators who had joined with Dimnus against Alexander; he was executed with the other conspirators (C 6.11.38). The name is too common to make identification with any known Amyntas certain. But, since he is mentioned together with Demetrius the Somatophylax, whose involvement in the conspiracy is also suspect (see s.v. **Demetrius** [2]), Amyntas' inclusion in the list may be the result of the trial of Amyntas son of Andromenes (Heckel 1975: 394–5; cf. Badian 1960a: 334 n. 30; rejected by Bosworth i.360).

Berve ii.31 no. 64.

Amyntas [9]. Son of Nicolaus (A 4.17.3); perhaps the brother of Pantauchus, and thus from Alorus (*AInd* 18.6). When Artabazus asked to be excused from his satrapy of Bactria on account of old age (summer 328), Alexander at first designated Black Cleitus as his replacement (C 8.1.19); but after the latter's death, the satrapy was given to Amyntas (C 8.2.14; A 4.17.3; *IA* 103), who appears to have taken office in the autumn of 328. Because of the unrest in the satrapy, Alexander left the battalions of Coenus and Meleager, 400 Companions and all the *hippakontistai*, as well as the loyal native troops, with Amyntas at Bactra, all under Coenus' command (A 4.17.3). These were presumably the troops that defeated after a stubborn fight the 2,500 Bactrian rebels who had left Xenippa at Alexander's approach (C 8.2.15) – they lost some 700 men, while the Macedonian casualties numbered eighty dead and 350 wounded (C 8.2.16–17). When Alexander departed for India (spring/summer 327), he left 3,500 cavalry and 10,000 infantry with Amyntas in Bactria (A 4.22.3), most of these Greeks, who rebelled in 325 on the false report that Alexander had died in India (C 9.7.1–11; D 17.99.5–6; cf. D 18.7.1). It appears that Amyntas was killed during this uprising, for in 323 the satrap of Bactria and Sogdiana is Philip (D 18.3.3; Dexippus, *FGrH* 100 F8 §6), who (as is implied by C 10.10.4) was the ruler at the time of the King's death. J 13.4.23 assigns the satrapy to Amyntas in error.

Kaerst, *RE* s.v. "Amyntas (18)"; Beloch iii[1] 2.243 §110; Berve ii.30 no. 60; Holt 81ff.; Julien 43; Lehmann-Haupt 147 §120; Klinkott 22, with nn. 58, 62.

Amyntas [10]. Bematist or, at least, author of a work on the *Stages* (*Stathmoi*) of Alexander's expedition (eight fragments of his work survive). Whether he was contemporary with the events he describes and a participant in the expedition is unknown. His presence in Alexander's camp cannot, however, be ruled out. Nothing is known about his origins or his life.

Berve Abschn. II no. 4; Jacoby, *FGrH* 122.

Amyntas [11]. Macedonian. Son of Alexander from Mieza (cf. *AInd* 18.6), brother of the Somatophylax Peucestas; Amyntas was appointed Somatophylax of Philip III Arrhidaeus at Triparadeisus in 320 BC (*ASucc* 1.38). Otherwise nothing is known about him unless he can be identified with the hipparch of Perdiccas' expedition against Cyprus in 321/0 (*ASucc* 24.6, ll. 26–7). If this is the case, then the entire force will have gone over to Antigonus and received favorable treatment from Antipater: Medius of Larissa, the *xenagos* of this expedition, is found in the camp of Antigonus. Antipater may have found Peucestas a useful ally in the east, to keep both Eumenes and Antigonus in check; for it is perhaps significant that Antipater did not appoint Peithon's brother Eudamus (or another, if one existed) in place of Amyntas son of Alexander. The appointment of the latter suggests that Antipater trusted Peucestas more than he did Peithon.

Kaerst, *RE* s.v. "Amyntas (20)"; Berve ii.26 no. 56; Heckel 282–3.

Amyntas. Berve ii.31–2 no. 65; C 6.9.28: *regius praetor*. Possibly the hypaspist commander [6] or [7] or Amyntas son of Andromenes [4].

Anaxagoras. Ephesian, son of Echeanax. Together with his brothers Codrus and

Diodorus, he murdered the tyrant of Ephesus, Hegesias. Philoxenus forced the Ephesians to surrender Anaxagoras and his brothers and imprisoned them "for a long time" in Sardis. From here Anaxagoras and Codrus escaped to Athens, but Diodorus was injured in the escape, recaptured, and sent to Alexander in Babylon. After Alexander's death, when Perdiccas sent Diodorus back to Ephesus to be tried, Anaxagoras and Codrus intervened to save him (Pol*Strat* 6.49). The events seem to have spanned the years 325 (or 324) to 323 BC.

Berve ii.33 no. 69.

Anaxarchus (Anaxarchos). Abderite philosopher of the school of Democritus, born ca. 380 BC (DL 9.58 gives his *floruit* as the 110th Olympiad, 340–337); a student of Diogenes of Smyrna. Anaxarchus accompanied Alexander on his campaigns. He alienated Nicocreon of Cyprus by saying to Alexander at a feast, that all that was missing was the head of some satrap (*sic*), meaning Nicocreon (DL 9.58; cf. P*A* 28.4). Anaxarchus is depicted as a flatterer of Alexander (Ath 6.250f–251a) – especially in the aftermath of the Cleitus affair (P*A* 52.4–7) – and an opponent of Callisthenes of Olynthus (A 4.10.5–11.9; P*A* 52.8–9), but several of the anecdotes concerning Anaxarchus are elsewhere told of other individuals or reported in different ways.[54] Hence there is little that can be considered certain. He was said to have consulted and annotated the so-called "Casket Copy" of the *Iliad*, which Alexander carried with him (Str 13.1.27 [594]). In 323, he persuaded Alexander to ignore the warnings of the Chaldeans (who predicted Alexander's death) and enter the city of Babylon (J 12.13.5; D 17.112.4–5). Anaxarchus accumulated great wealth and lived in luxury (Clearchus *ap.* Ath 12.548b–c). After Alexander's death, he was driven ashore on Cyprus, and captured by Nicocreon who ordered him put to death. When he made light of his sentence, Nicocreon ordered his tongue to be cut out, but Anaxarchus, it was said, bit it off and spat it out (DL 9.59; Val Max 3.3 ext 4).

Kaerst, *RE* s.v. "Anaxarchos (1)"; Berve ii.33–5 no. 70; Borza 1981; Bernard 1984.

Anaximenes. Son of Aristocles (*Suda* A 1989; cf. Ps-Call 1.13; Jul Val 1.7), he was a famous orator and sophist from Lampsacus (Str 13.1.19 [589]; D 15.76.4 shows that Ephorus considered Anaximenes one of the leading lights of his era) and an enemy of Theopompus of Chios.[55] He was a student of Diogenes the Cynic and Zoilus (DL 6.57; *Suda*); that he was a teacher of Alexander is, however, chronologically impossible and derives from the *Alexander Romance* (cf. Berve ii.35). The author of a history that included the exploits of Philip II and Alexander, Anaximenes accompanied the latter on his Asiatic expedition and saved the Lampsacenes, who had supported the Persian cause, from condign punishment by means of a simplistic trick (Paus 6.18.2–4; Val Max 7.3 ext 4; *Suda*).[56] Nothing certain is known about Anaximenes' relationship with Alexander, and various anecdotes confuse him with others at the King's court (Choerilus, Anaxarchus). Anaximenes published a work, *Ta peri Alexandron*, which seems to have formed the last of a trilogy of historical studies that began with the *Hellenica* (D 15.89.3) and *Philippica*. For his historical works see Jacoby, *FGrH* 72; Pearson 243–5.

Brzoska, *RE* s.v. "Anaximenes (3)"; Berve ii.35–7 no. 71.

Anaxippus (Anaxippos). Macedonian; family background unknown. Anaxippus is described as one of Alexander's *hetairoi* (A 3.25.2). In 330, he was sent with forty *hippakontistai* (Berve ii.37, incorrectly sixty) from Susia (Tus, near modern Meshed) in Areia to accompany the reinstated satrap, Satibarzanes, back to his capital and prevent the plundering of Areia (A 3.25.2). Anaxippus' position is hardly clear: Arrian claims that he was to establish a guard in advance of the Macedonian army to prevent it from plundering Areia as it passed through, but the number of men assigned for this alleged purpose is ridiculously small (cf. Bosworth i.355, who suspects "a lacuna either in the text or in Arrian's excerpting"). Berve ii.37 n. 3 suggests that Anaxippus was to be the Macedonian *episkopos* (cf. Neiloxenus, A 3.28.4). Soon after Alexander's departure from the satrapy, Satibarzanes murdered Anaxippus and his men (A 3.25.5).

Kirchner, *RE* s.v. "Anaxippos (2)"; Berve ii.37 no. 72; Heckel 361.

Androcles (Androkles). The ruler of Amathus on Cyprus (D 19.62.6: *dynastes*, perhaps used only for variation), Androcles appears to have joined the other Cypriot and Phoenician kings, who sailed with the Aegean fleet of Pharnabazus and Autophradates in 334, but soon defected after the battle of Issus and joined Alexander at Sidon in 332 (A 2.20.3). Thereafter, he took part in the final assault on Tyre, though his own quinquereme was destroyed (along with those of Pnytagoras of Salamis and Pasicrates of Curium) by a Tyrian attack as it lay at anchor in the harbor (A 2.22.2). He remained in control of Amathus, and in 321 (320) he joined Nicocreon, Pasicrates, and Nicocles in allying himself with Ptolemy against Perdiccas, who sent Aristonus and Sosigenes against the Cypriot cities (A*Succ* 24.6). We have no details of this campaign, though Antigonus appears to have come to the aid of the Cyprians. From that point on, Androcles appears to have taken a pro-Antigonid stance until 315 BC (unless he was only temporarily won over by Agesilaus in that year), when he was forced by Seleucus into giving a guarantee of neutrality(?), or of cooperation with the Ptolemaic forces (D 19.61.6, where the dynast is apparently still Androcles; see also s.v. **Agesilaus**). Hill 1949: 149 n. 6 suggests that a Delian inscription (*IG* xi.2.135), which names "King Androcles" as the dedicator of a gold crown ca. 313 BC, shows that Androcles did not assume the kingship until after 315; but this demands too much precision from Diodorus, who uses the term *dynastes* loosely.

Berve ii.37 no. 73; Hill 1904: xxv.

Androcydes (Androkydes). Greek physician who was supposed to have written to Alexander urging him to be more moderate in his drinking (Pl*NH* 14.58);[57] Clearchus *ap.* Ath 6.258b cites Androcydes for the etymology of the word *kolax* ("flatterer"), which may suggest that he had some experience of Alexander's court.

Wellmann, *RE* s.v. "Androkydes (1)"; Berve ii.37–8 no. 74.

Andromachus [1]. (Andromachos). Son of Hieron (A 3.12.5), first attested commanding the mercenary horse at Gaugamela (A 3.12.5). In 330 he remained briefly in Ecbatana, rejoining the King in Areia in the company of Philip son of Menelaus (A 3.25.4). In 329, Andromachus led sixty Companions – in the company of Caranus (who commanded 800 mercenary horse; A 4.3.7), Pharnuches, and Menedemus – at the Polytimetus (Zeravshan) River, where the Macedonian forces were ambushed by Spitamenes (A 4.3.7; 4.5.5–6.2). A 4.6.2 says that forty cavalrymen and 300 infantry escaped the slaughter. If Andromachus had been among them we should expect Arrian to have mentioned the fact. Curtius' account of the Polytimetus disaster omits Andromachus entirely (7.6.24, 7.7.31–9).

Kaerst, *RE* s.v. "Andromachos (6)"; Berve ii.38 no. 75; Heckel 364.

Andromachus [2]. (Andromachos). Macedonian. Possibly identical with Alexander's *nauarchos* at Tyre (see below). In 332, presumably on Alexander's instructions, Parmenion left him in charge of Coele-Syria (C 4.5.9), apparently as the *strategos* assigned to Sanballat (see s.v.) in Samaria (he was not satrap of southern Syria, as Bosworth 1974: 50–1 suggests). He was, however, killed during a local uprising (C 4.8.9).

Kaerst, *RE* s.v. "Andromachos (7)"; Berve ii.38–9 no. 76.

Andromachus [3]. (Andromachos). *Nauarchos* at the siege of Tyre in 332, where he commanded the Cypriot contingent which blockaded the northern harbor (A 2.20.10). There is a strong temptation to identify him with the officer assigned to Sanballat in Samaria (see above). Identification with the son of Hieron is much less likely.

Kaerst, *RE* s.v. "Andromachos (5)"; Berve ii.39 no. 77.

Andron. See s.v. **Hagnon**.

Andronicus [1]. (Andronikos). Noble Macedonian, son of Agerrus (A 3.23.9). Father of Proteas (and perhaps also Theodorus: Berve ii.176 no. 362; cf. Carney 1981: 152, with n. 10) and in all likelihood the husband of Lanice, daughter of Dropidas and sister of Black Cleitus. If this identification is correct, then Andronicus will also have been the father of the two unnamed sons who died at Miletus in 334 (C 8.2.8; cf. A 4.9.4; **M41–42**). Andronicus is first attested in 330 as the officer sent by Alexander (in accordance with their request) to the 1,500 Greek mercenaries who had served with Darius III. These, after his death, were prepared to surrender to Alexander (A 3.23.9; Artabazus went with him, presumably as a guide). He returned with these men and interceded on their behalf with the King, who spared their lives and installed Andronicus as their commander (A 3.24.5). Not long afterwards, Alexander sent Andronicus, along with Caranus, Erigyius, and Artabazus against the rebel Satibarzanes (C 7.3.2; A 3.28.2–3 does not mention him, perhaps because he was subordinate to Erigyius and Caranus). There is no record of Andronicus' death in the campaign, in which Erigyius is said to have slain Satibarzanes with his own hand (A 3.28.3; cf. C 7.4.32–8), and it appears that he retained his command.[58]

Berve ii.39 no. 78; Carney 1981: 153ff.; Heckel 341–2. See Stemma VIII.

Andronicus [2]. (Andronikos). Macedonian from Olynthus (D 19.69.1). Andronicus had accompanied Alexander on the entire expedition – though nothing is known of his activities before 314, when he conducted the siege of Tyre briefly in Antigonus' absence (D 19.59.2) – and was already advanced in years in 314 BC, when he became an advisor of the young Demetrius Poliorcetes (D 19.69.1); hence he was born at least ca. 370 BC. He commanded 1,500 cavalry on the right wing in the battle of Gaza (D 19.82.4). Antigonus left him as *phrourarchos* of Tyre, in which capacity he refused to surrender the city to Ptolemy, to whom he responded in abusive terms. But, when his troops mutinied and expelled him from Tyre, Andronicus fell into Ptolemy's hands, only to receive kind treatment from him; he appears to have ended his career as one of Ptolemy's *philoi* (D 19.86.1–2).

Wilcken, *RE* s.v. "Andronikos (11)"; Berve ii.39–40 no. 79; Gude no. 4; Billows 367–8 no. 9; Launey 301–4, 1170.

Androsthenes. Son of Callistratus (A*Ind* 18.4 = Nearchus, *FGrH* 133 F1), was a Greek from Thasos (Str 16.3.2 [766]) who had been settled in Amphipolis, and presumably had received Macedonian citizenship (A*Ind* 18.4, 6). He is named as one of Alexander's trierarchs of the Hydaspes fleet in 326 (A*Ind* 18.4); later he accompanied Nearchus on his ocean voyage (Str 16.3.2 [766]). Of this voyage, Androsthenes also wrote his own account (Str ibid., citing Eratosthenes; Ath 3.93b), which included also his Arabian expedition and appeared soon after Alexander's death (it was used by Theophrastus). In 324/3, Alexander sent Androsthenes down the Euphrates to explore the Arabian coast (see also s.vv. **Archias** [1], **Hieron**); he skirted the coast of Arabia in a triakontor, sailing farther than Archias, who had reached Tylus (Manamah), but not as far as Hieron (A 7.20.7). Nothing else is known about him.

Berger, *RE* s.v. "Androsthenes (9)"; Berve ii.40 no. 80; Papastavru 60–81 no. 8.

Anemoetas (Anemoitas). See s.v. **Amyntas** [5].

Antibelus (Antibelos). Son of Mazaeus and, perhaps, a Babylonian wife. A 3.21.1 says that he surrendered, in the company of Bagisthanes, to Alexander as he was passing through the Caspian Gates. C 5.13.11 records the surrender of a son of Mazaeus named Brochubelus in a slightly later context, but it is virtually certain that the sources refer to the same individual. Brochubelus may be the correct form (see s.v. **Brochubelus**) and Arrian may have confused this son with Artiboles, who was later enrolled in Alexander's cavalry.[59]

Berve ii.40 no. 82; Bosworth i.340–1.

Anticles (Antikles). Son of Theocritus (A 4.13.4). One of the *paides basilikoi*, Anticles was persuaded by Hermolaus and Sostratus to join the so-called "conspiracy of the Pages" in 327 (A 4.13.4; C 8.6.9). He was later arrested, tortured, and executed (A 4.13.7, 14.3; C 8.8.20; cf. P*A* 55.7; J 12.7.2).

Berve ii.44 no. 88; Heckel 289; Hoffmann 180.

Antigenes [1a]. Macedonian, patronymic unknown. Born ca. 380 BC, he was among the commanders of those veterans, who must have included the Argyraspids, discharged at Opis in 324 (J 12.12.8). Antigenes appears to have been with the expedition from the start, and in late 331 in Sittacene received second prize in a military contest; with it, the rank of chiliarch of the hypaspists (C 5.2.5). Antigenes is not heard of again until the Hydaspes battle: together with Tauron and Seleucus he commands infantry, though clearly not *pezhetairoi* (A 5.16.3; cf. C 8.14.15), hence probably the hypaspists.[60] Antigenes left India with Craterus and the *apomachoi*, patrolling Drangiana and Arachosia and rejoining Alexander in Carmania (A 6.17.3). In 324 he was sent from Opis to Macedonia, in the company of Craterus, Polyperchon, Gorgias, Polydamas, White Cleitus, and 10,000 veterans (J 12.12.8; cf. A 7.12.4; C 10.10.15).[61] Antigenes, however, must have remained in Cilicia, since in 320 he was in Egypt, where he played a leading role in Perdiccas' assassination (A*Succ* 1.35; D 18.39.6).[62] The Argyraspids thus protected Philotas' satrapy and the treasury at Tarsus. In 321/0 Perdiccas moved through Cilicia *en route* to Egypt, picking up Antigenes' troops, which he now led against Ptolemy (A*Succ* 24.2; J 13.6.16). But Antigenes soon turned against Perdiccas, and, together with Peithon and Seleucus, murdered him (A*Succ* 1.35; D 18.39.6; N*Eum* 5.1; cf. D 18.36.5).

It appears that the Argyraspids were formed in India (cf. C 8.5.4), took the northern route to Carmania in 325, and set out for Macedonia in 324: Antigenes was thus their original commander. Despite being awarded the satrapy of Susiane in the settlement of Triparadeisus, Antigenes appears to have seen Susa on only two occasions between 320 and his death in 315: first in 320, when he conveyed some of the treasure from there to Cyinda (Quinda) in Cilicia, and again in 317, when he accompanied Eumenes to the east. Nor do we know who administered Susiane in Antigenes' absence, though Xenophilus is the most likely candidate (C 5.2.16; cf. D 19.17.3; 19.18.1, 48.6). Antigenes' satrapal rank may, however, be reflected by the fact that, in the battle of Paraetacene, he and Peucestas shared an *agema* of 300 horse (D 19.28.3), that is, two *agemata* of 150 horsemen (cf. D 19.27.2, where Eudamus has an *agema* of 150 cavalry, which Devine 1985a: 76 aptly refers to as "his satrapal *agema*").

Polyperchon, writing on behalf of the Kings, required the Argyraspids to serve Eumenes (D 18.58.1, 59.3; P*Eum* 13.3), and Antigenes with some reluctance obeyed (N*Eum* 7.1). A compromise saw the theoretical command of their forces retained by the spirit of Alexander, in whose tent the commanders met to decide policy (D 18.60.1–61.3; P*Eum* 13.7–8; Pol*Strat* 4.8.2; N*Eum* 7.1–2). Entreaties and bribes from both Ptolemy (D 18.62.1–2) and Antigonus' agents (Philotas and thirty others: D 18.62.3–63.6) were rejected – though Antigenes found his colleague Teutamus wavering in his loyalty (D 18.62.5–6). Antigenes served Eumenes on the written orders of the Kings and resisted Peucestas' bid for supreme command. Instead he asserted the right of the Makedones to select a leader (D 19.15.1–2), and Antigenes appears, as the army moved toward the Tigris, to have exercised some kind of joint command with Eumenes (cf. D 19.17.4).[63] But, with Antigonus' forces threatening and the oriental element inclining toward Peucestas, the Macedonians opted for Eumenes (P*Eum* 14.8–11). At Paraetacene, Antigenes' subordinate role is clearly spelled out: together with Teutamus, he leads the Argyraspids and the hypaspists (6,000 men in all), and he shares an *agema* (300 horse) with Peucestas (D 19.28.1, 3); Eumenes has a squadron of 300 to himself.[64] The battle was at best indecisive, but at Gabiene, distressed because their baggage and the camp-followers had fallen into Antigonus' hands, the Silver Shields delivered up Eumenes to the enemy (D 19.43.7–9; P*Eum* 17; cf. N*Eum* 10.1–2). Antigonus handed some 1,000 of them to Sibyrtius, satrap of Arachosia, ordering him to wear them out and destroy them (D 19.48.3; P*Eum* 19.3; Pol*Strat* 4.6.15). Antigenes himself was thrown into a pit and burned alive (D 19.44.1). This barbaric act does not appear to be justified.[65]

Kaerst, *RE* s.v. "Antigenes (9)"; Berve ii.41–2 nos. 83–4; Heckel 308–16; Hammond 1984; Hammond 1989: 64–5.

Antigenes [1b]. P*M* 339b claims that a certain Antigenes Pellenaeus (or possibly Pellaeus, as Berve ii.41 suggests, perhaps rightly) was invincible in war but a slave to pleasure and vice; that he tried to enroll himself amongst the sick in order to return home with Telesippa, the woman he loved (P*M* 339c–d; cf. 181a); and that a certain Antigenes, a one-eyed man, tried to defraud Alexander, when he was paying the debts of his veterans (P*A* 70.4–6). In the *Moralia* (339c), Plutarch calls the one-eyed man Tarrhias (almost certainly, Atarrhias) son of Deinomenes. And this leads to a virtually insoluble problem: since the man who lost one eye at Perinthus (in 340/39) is described as still young at the time, and since both Antigenes, the commander of the Silver Shields, and Atarrhias (who distinguished himself at Halicarnassus) were well advanced in years at the time of Alexander's death, we must suppose that there was a younger, one-eyed, man whose name was either Antigenes or Atarrhias. Are we to prefer the evidence of the *Life* to that of the *Moralia*? Or did the error occur in the *Life* because Plutarch confused Antigenes with Antigonus "the One-Eyed"? We must stop short of identifying, as Billows (27–9) does, Antigenes of Pallene with Antigonus the One-Eyed (Tarn ii.314 n. 1): there is uncertainty about whether this is really Antigenes or Atarrhias; Antigonus himself could not have been present in Susa or Opis when the episode with Antigenes (or Atarrhias) occurred; and we are dealing in this episode with a relatively low-ranking officer or soldier, which would suit either of the hypaspist commanders but not Antigonus (cf. also Hamilton 196). If Plutarch is mistaken in calling him young (*neos*) in 340/39, it is still somewhat unusual to find no other source mentioning that the leader of the Silver Shields had lost an eye. Berve's entry (ii.41–2 no. 84) obscures the problem. Nor do I see any reason for identifying the Antigenes of C 5.2.5 with the man from Pallene.

Berve ii.41–2 no. 84; Hamilton 196; Billows 27–9.

Antigenidas. Son of Simulus. Cavalryman from Orchomenus, who served with Alexander's allied cavalry until the expedition reached Ecbatana in 330. There he and his compatriots were discharged. On their return (ca. 329), they made a dedication to Zeus Soter in Orchomenus (*IG* vii.3206).

Berve ii.42 no. 85.

Antigone (Antigona). Pydnaean (P*A* 48.4) or Pellaean (P*M* 339e) by birth, Antigone had been captured, after sailing to Samothrace to celebrate the mysteries, by the Persian admiral Autophradates (P*M* 339d–f). The year of her capture is uncertain, but Hamilton 133 rightly rejects Burn's suggestion that she was sold into slavery after Philip's capture of Pydna in 356. Hamilton's suggestion that she was captured earlier in 333 leaves little time for her to have found her way to Damascus, where she was taken by Parmenion in late 333. Hamilton rejects Berve's (ii.42) observation that she was captured at sea, on the basis of P*M* 339e. The use of the word *gynaion* in both Plutarchean passages implies that she was of low birth. She soon became Philotas' mistress and the sounding-board for his complaints about the King. Philotas' comments were related by Antigone, innocently we may assume, to her friends, and eventually the gossip reached Craterus' ears (P*A* 48–9). What became of her we do not know.

Wilcken, *RE* s.v. "Antigone (7)"; Berve ii.42 no. 86; Hofstetter 16–17 no. 19a. See Stemma VII.

Antigonus [1]. (Antigonos). Nicknamed "the One-Eyed": *monophthalmus*, *heterophthalmos*, or Cyclops (Ael*VH* 12.43; P*Ser* 1.8; Pl*NH* 35.90).[66] Antigonus was born ca. 382 BC (Hieronymus *ap.* [L]*Macrob* 11 = *FGrH* 154 F8; App*Syr* 55 [279]; cf. P*Demetr* 19.4, who says that in 306 he was "a little short of 80 years old"; Porphyry of Tyre, *FGrH* 260 F32, says he was 86 at the time of his death!), the son of a certain Philip (A 1.29.3; *SIG*[3] 278, 5; Str 12.4.7 [565]; J 13.4.14; Ael*VH* 12.43; P*Demetr* 2.1; Hieronymus *ap.* [L]*Macrob* 11 = *FGrH* 154 F8). The name of his mother is not recorded, but we do know that she was remarried at some time after the birth of Antigonus and his brothers, this time to Periander (otherwise unknown), to whom she bore a son named Marsyas (*Suda* M 227; see below s.v. **Marsyas**). Since Marsyas was born ca. 356 – he was a *syntrophos* of Alexander the Great (*Suda*) – we may assume that the mother was still very young when she bore Antigonus, Demetrius, and, apparently, a third son of Philip, Polemaeus (father of Antigonus' nephew of the same name who was active in the early age of the Successors). Billows' assumption (17) that she married "an important noble from Pella" is unnecessary: the ethnic "Pellaeus," often used of young men raised at the court, tells us nothing about their fathers' origins.

That Antigonus began his career as a common laborer is hostile propaganda, characteristic of the Diadochic period (cf. Ael*VH* 12.43; *Suda* M 227). Philip V's later claim of kinship with Philip II and Alexander (Plb 5.10.10), if not outright invention, may suggest that Stratonice, the daughter of Corrhagus and wife of Antigonus, may well have been related to Philip II; for the name is attested in the Argead house (cf. Thuc 2.101.6). Antigonus himself was an *hetairos* of Alexander (Ael*VH* 14.47a; cf. J 16.1.12).

In 334, Antigonus commanded 7,000 allied Greek hoplites, when the expedition crossed into Asia (D 17.17.3; Briant 1973: 27–41; Billows 36–41). Nothing is recorded about his role in the battle at the Granicus; at some time before August 334 he was sent to win over Priene to the Macedonian cause. The initial arrangements with Priene were confirmed, in terms favorable to the city, by Alexander himself (cf. Tod nos. 184–5). Priene, appreciative of Antigonus' efforts (Tod ii.245–6), honored him, bestowing *proxenia*, citizenship, and exemption from taxation (*SIG*[3] 278 = *I. Priene* no. 2 = Tod no. 186; Harding no. 103). Arrian says nothing of Antigonus' mission, perhaps a deliberate omission by Ptolemy the historian. Antigonus seems to have remained with Alexander until early spring 333, when he was appointed satrap of Phrygia (capital: Celaenae; A 1.29.3; C 4.1.35 wrongly says "Lydia"), which he ruled until his death in 301. At the time of his appointment, Celaenae had not yet surrendered to the Macedonians, though the inhabitants had promised to do so at the end of the second month, if no help arrived from Darius III before that time. The garrison of 1,000 Carians probably continued to serve Antigonus upon the surrender of the city; the 100 Greek mercenaries may, however, have been handed over to Alexander or shipped to Macedonia for punishment.

As the satrap of Phrygia, which controlled the main lines of communication in Asia Minor, Antigonus became responsible for the suppression of any remnants of Persian resistance in the area (see Anson 1988: 471). After the battle of Issus (November 333), a substantial force, loyal to the Persian King, escaped from the battlefield and prepared for a counter-strike by enlisting troops in Cappadocia and Paphlagonia (C 4.1.35). These forces were, however, crushed in three separate battles in 332: Antigonus himself was victorious in Lycaonia, Calas in Paphlagonia (an area which had been added to his satrapy of Hellespontine Phrygia, although it had not been adequately subdued [C 3.1.22–4]), and Balacrus expelled the Persians from Miletus (C 4.5.13).[67] It appears that, after the departure of Nearchus in 331/0 BC, Antigonus assumed control of Pamphylia and Lycia (cf. D 18.3.1; C 10.10.2; cf. Baumbach 57). Stratonice, Antigonus' wife, joined him in Celaenae (ca. 330), along with their sons Demetrius and Philip.

Confirmed as satrap of Greater Phrygia in 323 (D 18.3.1, 39.6; J 13.4.14; A*Succ* 1.6; Dexippus, *FGrH* 100 F8 §2), he was nevertheless ordered by Perdiccas to aid Eumenes in the conquest of Cappadocia, and his refusal to obey these instructions placed him in jeopardy when Perdiccas called him to account (P*Eum* 3.4–5; D 18.23.3–4; cf. A*Succ* 1.20; D 18.23.4). Antigonus fled to Europe, bringing with him reports of Perdiccas' duplicity and aspirations (D 18.23.3–4; A*Succ* 1.20, 24). Having persuaded them to terminate the war against the Aetolians and prepare for war in Asia, he crossed the Aegean with ten Athenian ships and 3,000 troops, landing in Caria, where he was welcomed by his kinsman, the satrap Asander (A*Succ* 25.1). It was undoubtedly Antigonus' purpose to gain a foothold in Asia Minor and rally the disaffected satraps until Craterus and Antipater could cross the Hellespont. Menander immediately went over to Antigonus, angered by the high-handedness of Perdiccas, who had left him in charge of the satrapal forces but placed him under the authority of Cleopatra (A*Succ* 25.2). Furthermore, he gave damning evidence that Perdiccas intended to send Nicaea back to her father and marry Alexander's sister instead (A*Succ* 1.26). Reports of this hastened the invasion from the north by Craterus and Antipater, who persuaded White Cleitus to abandon the Perdiccan cause and allow their entry into Asia (A*Succ* 1.26).

Antigonus, in the meantime, had moved inland, intending to catch Eumenes in an ambush. But his troop movements were reported to Cleopatra at Sardis, and Eumenes managed to escape to Phrygia (A*Succ* 25.6–8). It was presumably soon afterwards that Antigonus joined Craterus and Antipater near the Hellespont where a council of war was held. Craterus, it was decided, would deal with Eumenes, while Antipater pushed on to Cilicia; Antigonus meanwhile was sent to Cyprus to engage the forces under the command of Aristonus (thus A*Succ* 1.30; cf. 24.6); Antigonus was perhaps accompanied by Dionysius of Heraclea Pontica (Memnon, *FGrH* 434 F2 §§3–6). Whether Antigonus won a clear victory there is debatable (*pace* Billows 68): nothing is recorded of the campaign except his participation in it. It appears that he came to terms with Aristonus' forces once news of Perdiccas' death became known. Of the enemy commanders there, at least one, Medius of Larissa, joined him. From Cyprus, Antigonus was summoned to northern Syria, where, at Triparadeisus, he was recognized as a virtual equal partner with Antipater, whom he had saved from the rampaging mob that had once been Perdiccas' Royal Army (A*Succ* 1.32–3;

Pol*Strat* 4.6.4). Antigonus was now confirmed as satrap of Phrygia (D 18.39.6; A*Succ* 1.37)[68] and appointed *hegemon* of the Royal Army (D 18.39.7; A*Succ* 1.38; cf. App*Syr* 53 [266]) and presumably recognized as *strategos* of Asia Minor (cf. D 18.50.1). In theory, he was second only to Antipater in the hierarchy of Alexander's orphaned empire. Perhaps Antipater sensed that his own end was near and regarded Antigonus as the most worthy to exercise the supreme authority. But the decision to leave the Kings with Antigonus and his chiliarch, Cassander, suggests that Antipater was content to rule Macedonia and Europe and to leave the problems of Asia and the misfit Kings to another. Antigonus and Cassander soon fell out, however, and Antipater, acting on his son's advice, took the Kings back to Europe. He had thus taken back the symbolic authority over the empire as a whole, but in fact left Asia to Antigonus, who lacked neither the ambition nor the resources to gain supremacy. Proclaimed "King" along with his son Demetrius in 306 after the naval victory over Ptolemy at Salamis (App*Syr* 54 [275]; P*Demetr* 17.2–6; D 20.53.2), Antigonus died on the battlefield of Ipsus in 301 (App*Syr* 55 [279–80]; P*Demetr* 29.7–8).

A towering man, larger than his own son Demetrius (P*Demetr* 2.2), who was himself reputedly tall (D 19.81.4; 20.92.3), Antigonus became exceedingly corpulent late in life – to the extent that this rather than old age hampered his performance on the battlefield (P*Demetr* 19.4; cf. P*M* 791e). Both jovial (P*Demetr* 28.8) and witty (P*Demetr* 14.3–4; P*M* 182d–e; cf. 633c), he could nevertheless be loud and boastful (P*Eum* 15.3; P*Demetr* 28.8). And, though affectionate at home (P*Demetr* 3) and clearly devoted to his wife Stratonice, he was driven by *philotimia* and *philarchia* to the extent that he alarmed Alexander (Ael*VH* 12.16; 14.47a) and alienated many others (D 18.50.1; 21.1.1; P*Demetr* 28.8). In some areas of his personal life he was less tolerant of criticism: he allegedly executed Theocritus for a tactless remark about his eyes (see s.v. **Theocritus**; cf. Teodorsson 1990: 380–2), though he had himself once joked that the characters of a letter were large enough for a blind man to read (P*M* 633c).

In his dealings with political and military foes, he could be ruthless: Alcetas' body was denied burial (D 18.47.3); and, of the officers taken captive at Cretopolis, only Docimus managed to save himself (and this was through treachery; D 18.45.3; 19.16; cf. Simpson 1957); White Cleitus and Arrhidaeus were driven from their satrapies (D 18.52.3–6); Peucestas was deposed (D 19.48.5), Peithon eliminated through treachery (D 19.46.1–4), and Antigenes burned alive in a pit (D 19.44.1). The claim that Eumenes was murdered by his guards without Antigonus' permission is feeble and transparent *apologia* (N*Eum* 12.4). In one case, his own son Demetrius was forced to betray his father's trust to secure the escape of his friend Mithridates (P*Demetr* 4).

Kaerst, *RE* s.v. "Antigonos (3)"; Berve ii.42–4 no. 87; Briant 1973; Anson 1988; Billows 1–80; Heckel 50–6. See Stemma VI.

Antigonus [2]. (Antigonos). Antigonus son of Callas, apparently from Amphipolis (cf. Bosworth i.59). A winner in athletic contests at Tyre in 332, his achievements are commemorated on an inscription now in the Amphipolis museum (Moretti no. 113). Nothing else is known about his career.

Antigonus [3]. (Antigonos). Apparently Macedonian. In late 331, Antigonus finished fifth in the contest of valor in Sittacene and thus became a *pentakosiarches* of the hypaspists (C 5.2.5).[69]

Heckel 305.

Antimenes. Rhodian. In 324 Antimenes succeeded Harpalus as the chief financial officer of the empire. He saw to it that royal storehouses were provisioned for troops on the march, instituted an insurance plan for slave-owners, which guaranteed the recovery of runaways or compensated owners for their loss, and revived an old Babylonian tithe that brought money into the imperial treasury ([Arist]*Oecon* 2.34 p.1352b; 2.38 p.1353a).[70] Otherwise, nothing is known about him.

Thalheim, *RE* s.v. "Antimenes (4)"; Berve ii.44–5 no. 89; Andréadès 1929: 5–10.

Antiochus [1]. (Antiochos). Possibly of Macedonian origin. Commander of the Macedonian archers (A 3.5.6), at Issus he was stationed on the right, next to the Paeonians (A 2.9.2; cf. C 3.9.9); the Cretan archers were on the left (A 2.9.3). He appears to have succeeded Cleander or possibly Clearchus in 334/3. In 332/1, Antiochus died of unknown causes – perhaps in Egypt, possibly in earlier campaigning. Alexander replaced him with the Cretan Ombrion (A 3.5.6).

Kirchner, *RE* s.v. "Antiochos (13)"; Berve ii.45 no. 91; Heckel 337.

Antiochus [2]. (Antiochos). Macedonian of unknown family background, Antiochus first appears in 327 BC as a chiliarch of the hypaspists. Alexander sent him, with his chiliarchy and two others, from Dyrta on a reconnaissance mission (A 4.30.5–6). Antiochus appears to have been subordinate to Nearchus, who took with him also the Agrianes and the light infantry (*psiloi*). Nothing else is known about him.

Badian 1975: 150–1; Berve ii.45 no. 90; Heckel 303.

Antipater [1]. (Antipatros). Son of Iolaus, from Paliura. Born in 399/8 BC (*Suda* 2704; cf. [L]*Macrob* 11; *MP* = *FGrH* 239 B12).[71] At least ten children are attested: four daughters and six sons, of whom the names of all but one *anonyma* (the wife of Alexander Lyncestes) are known. Phila, Nicaea, and Eurydice all played important roles in sealing political alliances in the years before and after Triparadeisus. Philip, Alexarchus,[72] Iolaus, Pleistarchus, and Nicanor are identified as either sons of Antipater or brothers of Cassander.

Antipater was already militarily active – and possibly influential at the court – during the reign of Perdiccas III (365–360/59). Antipater will have been almost 40 at the time of Philip's accession, and it is doubtful that he rose from obscurity at that age to become perhaps the most powerful of Philip's *hetairoi* (P*M* 179b; Ath 10.435d). He and Parmenion were involved in the peace negotiations in the spring of 346 (Dem 19.69; Aes 3.72; Din 1.28). About Antipater's diplomatic efforts in Athens little is known. It was at this time that he made the acquaintance of Isocrates; his friendship with Phocion may, however, belong to the period after Chaeronea.[73] Summer 342 saw Antipater representing Philip II as *theoros* at the Pythian games (Dem *Philippic* 3.32; cf. Lib 23.311) and as regent of Macedonia in the King's absence (Isoc*Ep* 4). In 340, when his services were needed in Thrace, Antipater turned over the affairs of the state to Alexander, now 16 (P*A* 9.1), and campaigned at Perinthus (D 16.76.3; Fr*Strat* 1.4.13)[74] and, later, against the Tetrachoritae (Theopompus, *FGrH* 115 F217). After Chaeronea (338), he was sent to Athens to negotiate a peace and awarded a proxeny.[75]

He played no small part in securing the throne for Alexander after Philip's assassination: it was undoubtedly at his urging that Alexander Lyncestes was the first to hail his namesake as "King" (A 1.25.2; C 7.1.6–7; cf. Ps-Call 1.26; J 11.2.2). Thereafter, Antipater appears to have acted as regent whenever the King was absent from Macedonia. Thus we find him sending an embassy – albeit ineffectual – to the Isthmus in an attempt to prevent the Arcadians from aiding Thebes in 335 (Din 1.18). Rumor at Thebes held that Antipater himself was coming to deal with their uprising (A 1.7.6), a story encouraged by false reports that Alexander had been defeated in the north (J 11.2.8). But Pol*Strat* 4.3.12 claims that Antipater played a significant role in the capture of Thebes.

This is contradicted by the Alexander historians and inherently improbable (the demand that the Macedonians surrender Antipater was not meant to be taken seriously: PA 11.8; cf. Hamilton 30). When he set out for Asia in 334, Alexander left Antipater firmly in charge of European affairs (A 1.11.3; C 4.1.39; J 11.7.1; D 18.12.1; cf. 17.118.1; *IA* 17) with 12,000 infantry and 1,500 horse, having ignored his advice to produce an heir to the throne before his departure (D 17.16.2).

By the time of Agis' war, Antipater's resources had been significantly depleted by the flow of reinforcements to Alexander in Asia. In response to the threat from Memnon, the rebellious *strategos* of Thrace, Antipater commissioned a fleet, commanded by Proteas, who defeated the Persian admiral, Datames, at Siphnos (A 2.2.4–5). In 331 Agis rallied the Peloponnesians and easily defeated Antipater's general, Corrhagus.[76] Agis then besieged Megalopolis (Aes 3.165) with a force of 20,000 infantry – to which we might add as many as 8,000 mercenaries who had escaped from Issus (C 6.1.39; D 17.48.1–2; but cf. Brunt i.481–2) – and 2,000 cavalry (D 17.62.7). Antipater received news of the uprising just as he was dealing with the rebellion in Thrace.[77] Concluding hostilities as best he could under the circumstances, he gathered a force of 40,000 (D 17.63.1) – greatly augmented by his Greek allies – and invaded the Peloponnese. At Megalopolis he was victorious, and Agis was killed in the engagement (P*Agis* 3; D 17.63.4; C 6.1.1–15; J 12.1.6–11). Order was restored to Greece in consultation with the League of Corinth (C 6.1.19–20).[78]

There was, however, a rift developing between Alexander and Antipater: Alexander had allegedly disparaged the victory at Megalopolis as a "battle of mice" (P*Ages* 15.6), and there were claims that Antipater had regal aspirations (C 10.10.14; cf. PM 180e), that he had entered into secret negotiations with the Aetolians (PA 49.14–15), and that he had quarrels with Alexander's mother, Olympias (PA 39.13; PM 180d; D 17.118.1; cf. 19.11.9). Hence Alexander's decision to replace him as regent of Macedon with Craterus (A 7.12.4; J 12.12.9) aroused the suspicions of both ancient and modern writers (C 10.10.15). And, not surprisingly, stories that Antipater and his sons conspired with several of the King's *hetairoi* to murder him soon began to circulate (see Heckel 1988, with testimonia).

The death of Alexander brought a measure of stability to Antipater's position in Macedonia: no one save the King himself could remove him from office, and the settlement at Babylon recognized that fact. The compromise proposal that Europe be shared by Craterus and Antipater (C 10.7.9; cf. A*Succ* 1.7) was soon abandoned and Antipater recognized as *strategos autokrator* of Macedonia and Greece.[79] Antipater nevertheless attempted to secure the cooperation of the leading marshals through marriage alliances: Nicaea was promised to Perdiccas, Phila to Craterus, and Eurydice to Ptolemy.[80]

In Greece, news of Alexander's death ignited the Hellenic War (cf. D 18.8). Leosthenes had gathered mercenaries, ostensibly for some private undertaking, in an attempt to deceive Antipater (D 18.9.2–3). But Athens soon declared its support for Leosthenes and, defraying his expenses with Harpalus' money, the Athenians allied themselves also with the Aetolians (D 18.9.4–5).[81] Antipater summoned Craterus and Leonnatus from Cilicia and Hellespontine Phrygia respectively (D 18.12.1 reads "Philotas"; D 18.16.4), promising Leonnatus the hand of one of his daughters in marriage. Leaving Sippas in charge of Macedonia, he moved into Thessaly with 13,000 Macedonians and 600 cavalry. Antipater also had a fleet of 110 ships, which had conveyed monies from Asia to Macedonia (D 18.12.2). But the desertion of the Thessalians to the Greek cause (D 18.12.3) proved to be a major setback, and Antipater soon found it necessary to take refuge in Lamia and await reinforcements from Asia (D 18.12.4; P*Dem* 27.1; P*Ph* 23.5).[82] Leosthenes invested the city (D 18.13.1–3), but at one point was struck by a stone or javelin (J 13.5.12) and killed (D 18.13.5; cf. P*Ph* 24.1; see also Hyp 6; cf. [P]*M* 849f); Antiphilus replaced him (D 18.13.6; P*Ph* 24.1).

Antipater now awaited Leonnatus, whom he had summoned through the agency of Hecataeus (D 18.14.4; cf. P*Eum* 3.6).[83] Upon his arrival, the Athenians abandoned the siege of Lamia and decided to meet him before he could join forces with Antipater (D 18.15.1).[84] In the ensuing battle, Leonnatus was killed (D 18.15.3); his infantry retreated to higher ground, where on the following day they were joined by Antipater (D 18.15.4–5). The engagement had freed Antipater from Lamia, rid him of a dangerous rival, and augmented his forces (J 13.5.15; A*Succ* 1.9). Nevertheless, Antipater chose to avoid giving battle on the plain, owing to his inferiority in cavalry; instead he withdrew over more rugged ground toward the Peneus (D 18.15.6–7; cf. 18.16.5; less accurately J 13.5.16).

In the meantime, Cleitus' naval victories had secured the crossing of the Hellespont for Craterus, who soon entered Thessaly with an additional 10,000 foot, 3,000 slingers and archers, and 1,500 cavalry, bringing to about 48,000 the entire Macedonian force (D 18.16.5), which confronted the Greeks near Crannon (D 18.17; P*Ph* 26; P*Dem* 28.1; P*Cam* 19; Paus 10.3.4; cf. A*Succ* 1.12) on August 5, 322 (7 Metageitnion: P*Cam* 19.8; P*Dem* 28.1); the Greeks, in comparison, had 25,000 infantry and 3,500 cavalry (D 18.17.2). Antipater, once the Macedonian cavalry had engaged its Greek counterpart, led the phalanx forward and drove the enemy infantry to the high ground. Seeing this, the Greek cavalry disengaged, and the victory went to the Macedonian forces, with more than 500 Greek dead and 130 Macedonians killed (D 18.17.4–5; Paus 7.10.5 says 200 of the Greek dead were Athenian). Menon and Antiphilus now sued for peace, but Antipater refused to deal with the Greeks collectively, demanding instead separate peace terms with each state. The Thessalian towns were taken by siege or storm and offered easy peace terms (D 18.17.7; cf. [P]*M* 846e, for the capture of Pharsalus), leaving the Athenians and Aetolians to face Macedon alone. In the Peloponnese, Antipater installed pro-Macedonian oligarchies, often headed by personal friends and supported by garrisons (D 18.18.8, 55.2, 57.1, 69.3).

In Athens there was great consternation, and a deputation led by Phocion and Demades was sent to Antipater, who had advanced into Boeotia; they met him at the Cadmea in Thebes (D 18.18; P*Ph* 26; Paus 7.10.4; N*Ph* 2). Mindful of Leosthenes' hard line at Lamia, Antipater demanded the unconditional surrender of the city, terms which Athens was forced to accept (D 18.18.1–3). Antipater, however, treated the Athenians with leniency, though he insisted on establishing a garrison on Munychia[85] and the punishment of leading anti-Macedonian politicians; the anti-Macedonian leaders were hunted down by Antipater's agent Archias and put to death.[86]

Having made peace with Athens, Antipater and Craterus turned their attention to the Aetolians (D 18.24–5), only to be forced by the situation in Asia to come to terms with them (D 18.25.5; cf. A*Succ* 1.24; J 13.6.9 wrongly speaks of peace with the Athenians). Antipater's decision was hastened by the arrival of Antigonus with news of Perdiccas' duplicity (D 18.23.4–24.1; 18.25.3; A*Succ* 1.21, 24; cf. J 13.6.5–6). Advancing to the Thracian Chersonese, Antipater sent envoys to secure the defection of White Cleitus and his own safe crossing of the Hellespont (A*Succ* 1.26). Friendship with Ptolemy in Egypt was renewed (D 18.14.2, 25.4).

On the Asian side, Antipater and Craterus were joined by Neoptolemus, who had recently abandoned Eumenes and offered promises of easy victory (A*Succ* 1.26; cf. D 18.29.4–5). Leaving Craterus to deal with Eumenes, Antipater pressed on in the direction of Cilicia (D 18.29.6; P*Eum* 6.4).

Craterus and Neoptolemus were defeated by Eumenes (D 18.30–2), but the remnants of their army escaped to Antipater (A*Succ* 1.28; D 18.33.1) who continued into Cilicia. There, it appears, he learned of Perdiccas' defeat at Kamelon Teichos and was given a favorable reception by Philoxenus.[87]

At Triparadeisus in Syria, Antipater met Peithon and Arrhidaeus who had brought the remnants of the Perdiccan army. These men were embroiled in a bitter dispute with the queen, Adea-Eurydice, who had usurped the prerogatives of her half-witted husband and was supported by the troops, who demanded their pay (A*Succ* 1.31–2; cf. D 18.39.1–2). Attalus son of Andromenes now heightened tensions further by journeying inland from Tyre in the hope of winning the army back to the Perdiccan cause (A*Succ* 1.33, 39). Hence Antipater was greeted, on his arrival, by an angry mob, which might have lynched him, had it not been for the efforts of Seleucus and Antigonus (A*Succ* 1.33; cf. Pol*Strat* 4.6.4; D 18.39.3–4).

Once order was restored, and the obstreperous Eurydice frightened into submission (D 18.39.4), Antipater, as *prostates*, assigned the satrapies of the empire anew (App*Syr* 52 [263]; D 18.39.5–7) and entrusted the war against the Perdiccans to Antigonus, with whom he left the "Kings," Philip III and Alexander IV (A*Succ* 1.34–8), and some 8,000 additional infantry (D 19.29.3). But Antipater took steps to limit Antigonus' power by designating his own son Cassander "chiliarch of the cavalry" (A*Succ* 1.38; D 18.39.7), so that Antigonus might not pursue an independent course without Antipater's knowledge.

Returning to the west, Antipater stopped at Sardis, where he and Cleopatra exchanged recriminations (A*Succ* 1.40). Asander was despatched to engage the forces of Attalus and Alcetas, only to be defeated (A*Succ* 1.41), and before he could leave Asia Antipater was met by Cassander, who had already fallen out with Antigonus. Persuaded that Antigonus harbored designs on a grander scale, he removed the Kings from the latter's custody and took them to Europe (A*Succ* 1.42–4). Removing the symbols of authority from Antigonus, Antipater had nevertheless tacitly recognized him as an equal partner in the empire, as the *strategos* of Asia, and he was content, for the time, to leave him preoccupied with the suppression of the outlawed party.

In the autumn of 319 he fell ill and soon died (D 18.48),[88] leaving the conduct of European affairs in the hands of Polyperchon and designating his son Cassander *chiliarchos* (see s.vv. **Cassander**, **Polyperchon**). Aristodemus brought news of his death to Antigonus the One-Eyed in the vicinity of Cretopolis (D 18.47.4), a signal to those in Asia to start working for their own ends (D 18.50.1).

Kaerst, *RE* s.v. "Antipatros (12)"; Berve ii.46–51 no. 94; Kanatsulis 1958/9: 14–64 and 1968: 121–84; Heckel 38–49. See Stemma V.

Antipater [2]. (Antipatros). Son of Asclepiodorus the satrap of Syria (A 4.13.4; cf. C 8.6.9).[89] Antipater was one of the *paides basilikoi* (Pages). Persuaded by Hermolaus and Sostratus to join their conspiracy in 327, he was later arrested, tortured, and executed for his involvement (C 8.8.20; A 4.13.7, 14.3; P*A* 55.6–7; J 12.7.2).

Kaerst, *RE* s.v. "Antipatros (15)"; Berve ii.45–6 no. 93; Hoffmann 179–80; Heckel 289.

Antipatrides. *Hetairos* of Alexander, apparently Macedonian – perhaps identical with the Antipatrides whom Pol*Strat* 5.35 describes as an "old friend" (*palaios philos*) of Nearchus.[90] He is known in the period 336–323 only from an anecdote illustrating Alexander's restraint in sexual matters. Antipatrides was said to have brought a beautiful harp-player (**F55**) to dinner. This girl aroused the King's interest, but, upon learning that Antipatrides was in love with her, he refrained from touching her (P*M* 180f, 760c–d).

Kirchner, *RE* s.v. "Antipatrides"; Berve ii.45 no. 92.

Antiphanes [1]. Apparently Macedonian. *Scriba equitum*, according to C 7.1.15, apparently the *grammateus* of the Companion Cavalry. In late 330, very shortly before the Philotas affair, Antiphanes had attempted to commandeer a number of horses from Amyntas son of Andromenes, who refused to surrender them and rebuffed Antiphanes with abusive language that included, allegedly, some discourteous remarks about Alexander himself (C 7.1.15–17). Antiphanes testified to this at the trial of Amyntas, who was suspected of complicity in the Philotas (Dimnus) affair, but Amyntas defended himself arguing that he had already surrendered eight of his ten horses and was reluctant to give up the remaining two, lest he should be compelled to fight on foot (C 7.1.32–4). Amyntas' apology to Antiphanes and Alexander gives some credence to Antiphanes' charge of insolence, but not of complicity in the Philotas "conspiracy" (C 7.1.35). But we cannot be entirely certain of the historicity either of the charge or of Antiphanes himself. He is not mentioned elsewhere.

Berve ii.51 no. 95.

Antiphanes [2]. Comic poet. Ath 13.555a says that Alexander did not particularly like one of his plays. If Antiphanes can be identified with the prodigious poet of Middle Comedy, who was said to have been born ca. 407 and to have lived seventy-four years, it may be that the *Philothebaios* was the play in question and that their meeting occurred in Greece, before Alexander's departure for Asia. A reference to "King Seleucus" in *Parekdidomene* appears to be a later interpolation.

Kaibel, *RE* s.v. "Antiphanes (15)."

Antiphilus (Antiphilos). Greek painter from Egypt (Pl*NH* 35.114, 138); student of Cleitodemus and contemporary of Apelles and Protogenes (Quint 12.10.6).[91] He is said to have painted Philip with the young Alexander as well as Philip, Alexander, and Athena (Pl*NH* 35.114; Berve ii.52 believes this may have been after the victory at Chaeronea); late in life, in Alexandria, Antiphilus painted a scene of Ptolemy I hunting (Pl*NH* 35.138). He was said to have been a rival of Apelles for Ptolemy's favor (Pollitt 163).

Rossbach, *RE* s.v. "Antiphilos (6)"; Berve ii.52 no. 96; Pollitt 174.

Apame [1]. (Apama). Daughter of Spitamenes (A 7.4.6; P*Demetr* 31.5; but Str 15.8.15 [578] confuses her with the daughter of Artabazus, below [2]),[92] she married Seleucus at Susa in 324; in all likelihood, Apame was born ca. 340. According to Malalas (8.198) she bore Seleucus two daughters, Laodice and Apame, one of whom may perhaps have been given in marriage to Sandrocottus (Str 15.2.9 [724]; App*Syr* 55 [282]). Her son was Antiochus (P*Demetr* 31.5), later known as Soter, who named the city of Apamea in Phrygia – to which he transferred the population of Celaenae – for her (Str 12.8.15 [578]; cf. Livy 38.13.5, using the title "Sister" of Seleucus), as he did Apamea near the Tigris (Pl*NH* 6.132); App*Syr* 57 [295] says that Seleucus Nicator named three cities after her (cf. Str 16.2.4 [750]; StByz s.v. "Apamea," who mistakenly calls her the "mother of Seleucus"). Apame may have died before Seleucus married Stratonice in 299 BC.

Wilcken, *RE* s.v. "Apama (1)"; Berve ii.52 no. 98; Tarn 1929; Macurdy 77–8; Grainger 1997: 38 no. 3.

Apame [2]. (Apama). Daughter of Artabazus. See s.v. **Artacama**.

Apelles. Son of Pytheas from Colophon (*Suda* A 3008) and, later, Ephesus (Str 14 [642]). Born ca. 370 (Pl*NH* 35.79, who says he was from Cos). Perhaps the greatest of the Greek painters, Apelles was a student of Ephorus of Ephesus and Pamphilus of Sicyon. Among his many paintings were depictions of Philip II (Pl*NH* 35.93) and

Alexander. Alexander was allegedly so impressed by his work that he allowed none other to paint him (Cic *Ad Familiares* 15.12.7; Horace, *Epistles* 2.1.239–40; Val Max 8.11 ext 2; Pl*NH* 7.125; cf. Stewart TT51–8). His painting of Alexander with thunderbolt, which was set up in the temple of Artemis in Ephesus, although it depicted his complexion as too swarthy, so impressed the King that he awarded the painter twenty talents (Cic *Verrine Orations* 6.60; Pl*NH* 35.92; cf. P*A* 4.3–4). The popular story that he fell in love with Alexander's favorite mistress (*paelix*), Pancaste, who posed nude for Apelles' Aphrodite Anadyomene, and received her as a gift from Alexander (Pl*NH* 35.86–7; Lucian, *Imagines* 7), is probably fictitious. In addition to Alexander, he painted several of his generals: Menander and Cleitus (Pl*NH* 35.93) and Neoptolemus on horseback, Antigonus walking beside his horse, and Archelaus with wife and daughter (Pl*NH* 35.96). Although he was on good terms with Antigonus the One-Eyed, managing to conceal his defect with his art, he fell out with Ptolemy during Alexander's lifetime and had the misfortune of being carried to Alexandria by a storm later when Ptolemy had become king (Pl*NH* 35.89–90). Apelles appears to have lived into the early third century BC.

Rossbach, *RE* s.v. "Apelles (13)"; Berve ii.53–5 no. 99; Pollitt 158–62; Stewart 33–5.

Aphobetus (Aphobetos). Macedonian. Conspired with Dimnus in 330 BC to murder Alexander; Philotas too was implicated in this plot. Aphobetus' name was given to Nicomachus (C 6.7.15) and, in turn, to Cebalinus, who brought the matter to Alexander's attention. He and the other conspirators were found guilty and stoned to death by the Macedonian army (C 6.11.38).

Berve ii.97 no. 190.

Aphrices (Aphrikes, Airikes, Erices, Ariplex). Perhaps a brother of Assacenus, the deceased dynast of the Assacenians, and of Amminais (*ME* 39); thus also a son of Cleophis, together with whom he is found at Massaga in spring 326 BC (*ME* 42). Aphrices attempted, after the capture of Aornus, to oppose the Macedonians in one of the passes of the Buner region (near Embolima) with a force of 20,000 Indians (C 8.12.1; D 17.86.2, giving him also fifteen elephants); he was killed by his own troops, who sent his head to Alexander in order to win his pardon (D 17.86.2; C 8.12.3 suggests that the troops may have acted out of hatred). Eggermont 183–4 sees Assacenus as ruler of the western Swat basin, Aphrices as chief of the eastern Swat (or Udyana[93]); Berve ii.26 identifies the unnamed brother of Assacenus (A 4.30.5) with Amminais (see above s.v.) and distinguishes him from Aphrices. But both are found in the city of Massaga (*ME* 39, 42, though only Amminais is described as *frater regis*; Ariplex belongs to the *amici*, that is, to the advisors, of Cleophis) and it seems odd (*pace* Berve ii.97–8) that we should find both opposing Alexander after the fall of Aornus. There are several possibilities: Arrian (4.30.5) may be wrong in calling the Indian leader Assacenus' brother; D 17.86.2 and C 8.12.1 wrongly name Aphrices (or Erices) in place of Amminais; or, what seems most likely, the vulgate simply failed to note that Aphrices was a member of the royal family.

Berve ii.97–8 no. 191; Eggermont 183–4.

Aphthonius (Aphtonius, Aphthonios). Named Elaptonius by C 8.6.9.[94] A member of the "conspiracy of the Pages," Aphthonius was arrested, tortured, and executed (C 8.8.20; cf. A 4.13.7, 14.2, who does not name either Elaptonius or Aphthonius; P*A* 55.6; J 12.7.2).

Berve ii.149 no. 296; Hoffmann 180; Heckel 289–90.

Apollodorus [1]. (Apollodoros). Macedonian from Amphipolis and one of Alexander's *hetairoi* (A 3.16.4; 7.18.1; D 17.64.5). In late 331, when Alexander made Mazaeus satrap of Babylon, he left Apollodorus behind as *strategos* of the troops left there (A 3.16.4; cf. 7.18.1; P*A* 73.3). C 5.1.43 gives him 2,000 troops and 1,000 talents with which to hire more mercenaries, but he says that Apollodorus and Menes were to govern Babylonia and Cilicia.[95] Apollodorus' *strategia* is almost certainly restricted to Babylonia, and the vulgate has conflated his office with the later appointment of Menes as *hyparchos* of Syria, Phoenicia, and Cilicia (A 3.16.9–10; for further discussion see s.v. **Menes**). He appears to have retained this office until the King's death (A 7.18.1). But Apollodorus feared Alexander, perhaps because of the purge the King had conducted after his return from India, and he was told by his brother, the seer Peithagoras, that Hephaestion and Alexander would soon be dead (A 7.18 = Aristobulus, *FGrH* 139 F54; P*A* 73.3; cf. App*BC* 2.152). The prophecies are clearly inventions *ex post facto* but Apollodorus' concerns will have been real.

Kaerst, *RE* s.v. "Apollodoros (43)"; Berve ii.55–6 no. 101; Papastavru no. 10; Abramenko 2000.

Apollodorus [2]. (Apollodoros). Son of Telestes, a cavalryman from Orchomenus. Served as a member of Alexander's allied cavalry until the expedition reached Ecbatana in 330. There he and his compatriots were discharged. On their return (ca. 329), they made a dedication to Zeus Soter in Orchomenus (*IG* vii.3206).

Berve ii.55 no. 100.

Apollonides [1]. Chian of the pro-Persian party (C 4.5.15; *SIG*[3] 283). His supporters were Athenagoras, Phesinus, and Megareus. All four were captured in 333/2 by Hegelochus and Amphoterus and taken to Alexander in Egypt (C 4.5.17; A 3.2.5). He sent them to Elephantine (A 3.2.7). Nothing further is known about Apollonides.

Wilcken, *RE* s.v. "Apollonides (20)"; Berve ii.56 no. 102; Hofstetter 20 no. 26.

Apollonides [2]. Greek or Macedonian, family background is unknown. Cavalry officer in the army of Eumenes, hence probably already an officer in Perdiccas' Royal Army and an officer of Alexander the Great (thus Berve ii.56). Before the battle of Orcynia in Cappadocia, Antigonus, whose army was inferior in numbers, suborned Apollonides (D 18.40.5) to desert in the midst of the battle, thus turning the tide against Eumenes, who lost 8,000 men in the defeat (D 18.40.8). Apollonides appears to have remained in Antigonus' service, although we hear nothing more about him.[96]

Kirchner, *RE* s.v. "Apollonides (10)"; Berve ii.56 no. 103; Engel 1971 (confusing Apollonides and Perdiccas).

Apollonius (Apollonios). Son of Charinus, apparently Greek. Appointed in 331 as governor of the region west of the Delta (A 3.5.4; C 4.8.5); whether, in financial matters, he was responsible to Cleomenes of Naucratis (thus C 4.8.5; cf. Atkinson i.367), who, in addition to governing the "Arabian" area east of the Delta, was the chief financial officer (A 3.5.4 speaks only of the nomarchs of Egypt as subject to Cleomenes; cf. Bosworth i.277), is uncertain. We do not know how long he remained in office or what became of him. Cf. also s.vv. **Doloaspis, Petisis, Cleomenes** [1].

Kaerst, *RE* s.v. "Apollonios (49)"; Atkinson i.367; Berve ii.56 no. 104; Bosworth i.275–7.

Apollophanes. Prominent Macedonian. In 325 Apollophanes was appointed satrap of the Oreitae (that is, of Gedrosia; cf. A*Ind* 23.5). He was left in Ora with Leonnatus and sufficient troops to deal with hostilities there and ensure safe passage of the coast for Nearchus (A 6.22.2–3), but in the military engagement that followed, although the Macedonians enjoyed an overwhelming victory, Apollophanes was killed (A*Ind* 23.5; cf. A 7.5.5 and C 9.10.19 for the battle). A 6.27.1 claims that Apollophanes was deposed when Alexander reached Pura, the capital of Gedrosia, for neglect of his duties. It appears that Arrian has confused Apollophanes with Astaspes of Carmania who was subsequently deposed for this very reason. Apollophanes' successor was Thoas.[97]

Kaerst, *RE* s.v. "Apollophanes (8)"; Berve ii.57 no. 105.

Arbupales (Arboupales). Son of that Darius who was son of Artaxerxes II; he was thus born no later than 362 (for Darius' death see Briant 681), and it may have been on account of his youth that he survived the purge that accompanied the accession of Artaxerxes III (Ochus) in 359/8 BC. Arbupales was among the dead commanders (*hegemones*) at the Granicus battle (A 1.16.3).

Cauer, *RE* s.v.; Justi 21; Berve ii.57 no. 106.

Arcesilaus (Arkesilaos). Macedonian, probably the father of Alcanor of Oropus (*IG* vii.4257, 10; Tataki 232 no. 84; cf. Hoffmann 202). Arcesilaus received the satrapy of Mesopotamia in the settlement of 323 BC (D 18.3.3; J 13.4.23; Dexippus = *FGrH* 100 F8 §6 calls him Archelaus). There is no mention of the satrapy during Alexander's lifetime (cf. Julien 27), but Leuze 460–2 may be right in assuming that it was detached from Babylonia when Mazaeus was placed in charge of the latter. Hence Arcesilaus may have administered Mesopotamia since 331/0 BC. Arcesilaus was perhaps deposed or forced to flee on account of his support of Perdiccas: in the Triparadeisus settlement (320 BC), the satrapy was awarded to Amphimachus (A*Succ* 1.35; D 18.39.6).[98]

Berve ii.75 no. 142; Tataki 265 nos. 278–9.

Archelaus [1]. (Archelaos). Son of Androcles. Macedonian and one of the *hetairoi*. Appointed *phrourarchos* of the Bactrian rock known as Aornus (A 3.29.1). What became of him we do not know. Berve ii.85 speculates that he may have been killed in the mercenary uprising in Bactria in 326/5.

Kaerst, *RE* s.v. "Archelaos (11)"; Berve ii.85 no. 157.

Archelaus [2]. (Archelaos). Macedonian. Son of Theodorus. Left behind in Susa in 334 as *strategos* (A 3.16.9; cf. C 5.2.16) with 3,000 troops with the satrap Abulites. Apelles is said to have painted him, together with his wife and daughter, probably soon after 331 (Pl*NH* 35.96). Identification with the *philos* of Demetrius Poliorcetes (D 19.100.7) is possible. It is much less likely that he is the *phrourarchos* of Tyre attested in 320 BC (D 18.37.4).

Kaerst, *RE* s.v. "Archelaos (10)"; Berve ii.85 no. 158.

Archelaus [3]. (Archelaos). Macedonian. *Phrourarchos* of Tyre. Perdiccas had left 800 talents with him in 321/0 for safe keeping, which he turned over to Attalus son of Andromenes after Perdiccas' death along with the affairs of the city (D 18.37.4). It does not necessarily follow that Archelaus was installed as *phrourarchos* by Perdiccas. He may have been appointed to that position during Alexander's reign.

Kirchner, *RE* s.v. "Archelaos (19)"; Berve ii.85 no. 159.

Archepolis. Macedonian of unknown origin. One of the fellow-conspirators of Dimnus in autumn 330 BC (C 6.7.15); his name was given by Dimnus to Nicomachus and came eventually to Alexander's attention. He was arrested and executed by stoning at Phrada for his part in the plot (C 6.11.38).

Berve ii.86 no. 161.

Archias [1]. Prominent Macedonian from Pella; son of Anaxidotus. Archias was one of the trierarchs of the Hydaspes fleet in 326 (A*Ind* 18.3) and also accompanied Nearchus on the voyage from the Indus delta to the Persian Gulf as a trusted officer and colleague. Archias acted as Nearchus' second-in-command in the capture of an unnamed coastal town (A*Ind* 27.8–28.9; perhaps in the Gwatar bay: thus Brunt ii.387 n. 5) and was one of a small group of Macedonians who marched inland to meet Alexander in Carmania; his meeting with Alexander hints at Archias' rank and intimacy with the King (A*Ind* 34–5). In 324/3 Alexander sent Archias to circumnavigate Arabia in a *triakontor*, but Archias went as far as the island of Tylus before turning back (A 7.20.7; cf. A*Ind* 43.8).[99] Nothing else is known about him.

Kirchner, *RE* s.v. "Archias (17)"; Berve ii.86 no. 162.

Archias [2]. Greek from Thurii (Paus 1.8.3; A*Succ* 1.14), in southern Italy. He was originally an actor ([P]*M* 849b; cf. P*Dem* 29.2–3, 6; Lenaean victor in 329: *IG* ii.977 u(z)), studied rhetoric with Anaximenes ([P]*M* 846f) and Lacritus, and was himself the teacher of Polus of Aegina (P*Dem* 28.3). In 322, he became Antipater's agent and hunted down the exiled Athenian politicians (especially Demosthenes and Hypereides), thus gaining the name "exile hunter." He captured Hypereides, Aristonicus, and Himeraeus (A*Succ* 1.13–14), and forced Demosthenes to commit suicide (P*Dem* 28–30; [P]*M* 846f, 849b; Str 8.6.14 [374]; Paus 1.8.3). He later died of hunger and in disgrace (A*Succ* 1.14).

Judeich, *RE* s.v. "Archias (10)"; O'Connor no. 87.

Archon. Macedonian from Pella. Son of Cleinias (A*Ind* 18.3) and Synesis, brother of Isocrates; honored at Delphi in 333/2 BC (Rhodes & Osborne no. 92).[100] In 326 he served as a trierarch of the Hydaspes fleet (A*Ind* 18.3). Archon appears to have succeeded Stamenes (Ditamenes) as satrap of Babylon in the last year of Alexander's life. He was confirmed as satrap in 323 (D 18.3.3; J 13.4.23). In 321, he may have colluded with Arrhidaeus and Ptolemy in the diversion of Alexander's funeral carriage to Egypt. Perdiccas did not trust him, and sent Docimus to assume control of Babylon and to kill Archon, who put up a gallant fight but later succumbed to his wounds (A*Succ* 24.3–5).

Kaerst, *RE* s.v. "Archon (5)"; Berve ii.86–7 no. 163; cf. Rhodes & Osborne 466–71 no. 92.

Aretes (Aretas). Named only in the accounts of Gaugamela, where he commanded the *sarissophoroi* (C 4.15.13), having replaced, at some point between 333 and 331, Protomachus. He was stationed on the right wing (A 3.12.3; cf. Bosworth i.303), next to the ilarch Ariston, commander of the Paeonians (cf. C 4.9.24). During the engagement, Aretes was sent to relieve the cavalry of Menidas, who were under heavy attack from the Scythian horse (A 3.13.3, 14.1, 3; C 4.15.13, 18). Nothing else is known about Aretes, who may, however, be identical with Aretis (below), Alexander's *anaboleus* at the Granicus (A 1.15.6).

Kaerst, *RE* s.v. "Aretes (1)"; Berve ii.58 no. 109; Bosworth i.303, 305; cf. i.122; Heckel 354.

Aretis. Termed *anaboleus* by A 1.15.6, he fought at the Granicus River but was unable to hand Alexander a lance since his, like that of the King, had been broken in the engagement. Possibly (*contra* Hoffmann 179) he is to be identified with the commander of the *hippeis prodromoi* at Gaugamela (A 3.12.3; C 4.15.13).[101] See s.v. **Aretes** (above).

Berve ii.58 no. 110; Hoffmann 179; Heckel 290.

Argaeus (Argaios). Berve ii.57 no. 107. See s.v. **Oropius**.

Argilias. Son of Laonicus. A cavalryman from Orchomenus, he served with Alexander's allied cavalry until the expedition reached Ecbatana in 330. There he and his compatriots were discharged. On their return (ca. 329), they made a dedication to Zeus Soter in Orchomenus (*IG* vii.3206).

Berve ii.57 no. 108.

Ariaces (Ariakes). Commander of the Cappadocian forces at Gaugamela (A 3.8.5). Ariaces is perhaps a corruption of the name Ariarathes (Meyer 1879: 28; Bosworth i.291). Berve (ii.58) rejects that identification, arguing that Ariaces was the successor of Mithrobuzanes, who fell at the Granicus, and that he fled to Darius. But Mithrobuzanes' troops, in all likelihood, dispersed to their homes after their leader's death; certainly, it is doubtful that they remained together as a unit beyond the battle of Issus (late 333). The Cappadocians at Gaugamela must be from Cappadocia-Pontus, and their leader Ariarathes. See below s.v. **Ariarathes.**

Berve ii.58 no. 111.

Ariamazes (Arimazes; Ariomazes; Arimases). Sogdianian dynast. Commanded the so-called "Rock of Sogdiana" (C 7.11.1–29; *ME* 15–18; Str 11.11.4 [517]). Trusting in the fortress, which he regarded as impregnable,[102] he refused to surrender to Alexander, arguing that the Macedonians would need men with wings in order to take his fortress. When Alexander sent climbers to occupy the heights above Ariamazes' position, the latter surrendered (Pol*Strat* 4.3.29). He was, however, scourged and crucified for his arrogance (C 7.11.28; but *ME* 18 says he was murdered by his own men). Arrian, who does not mention Ariamazes by name, says that it was here, at the Rock of Sogdiana, that Alexander captured and married Rhoxane (A 4.18.4, 19.5). This is, however, contradicted by all other sources, and Strabo clearly distinguishes between the Rock of Sogdiana and the place of Rhoxane's capture.[103]

Berve ii.59 no. 112; cf. Tomaschek, *RE* s.v. *Ἀριαμάζου πέρα*.

Ariarathes. Ariarathes I of Cappadocia. Born in 404/3 ([L]*Macrob* 13 = Hieronymus, *FGrH* 154 F4 says he lived to be 82), Ariarathes was the son of Ariaramnes (D 31.19.2 has Ariamnes) and brother of Orophernes, of whom he was exceedingly fond. The first to be called the "King of the Cappadocians," he annexed Cataonia, which had previously been a separate nation (Str 12.1.2 [534]). Ruled Cappadocia in Pontus already in the time of Artaxerxes III Ochus; for he sent his brother to serve with the Persian King against the Egyptian rebels (D 31.19.3). He avoided subjugation at the hands of Alexander, who was preoccupied with Darius III (D 18.16.1),[104] but, in 323, Eumenes was instructed to win the satrapy away from him (C 10.10.3; cf. P*Eum* 3.4). Perdiccas invaded Cappadocia in 322 or 321 and, after defeating Ariarathes in two battles (A*Succ* 1.11), captured and impaled him along with his prominent followers (D 18.16.1–3; cf. D 18.22.1; J 13.6.1; App*Mithr* 8 = *FGrH* 154 F3); but according to D 31 (frg. 19.3–5) Ariarathes fell in battle – his adopted son, Ariarathes, the biological son of Orophernes (D 31.19.4), escaped and later recovered the throne (D 31.19.5). The remainder of Ariarathes' subjects were granted immunity and placed under the rule of Eumenes of Cardia (P*Eum* 3.13; App*Mithr* 8).

Niese, *RE* s.v. "Ariarathes (1)"; Berve ii.59–60 no. 113; Meyer 1879: 28–9.

Arimmas. Berve ii.60 no. 114 and Bosworth i.285 reject Droysen's (i^2 326) emendation of A 3.6.8. I am inclined to see Arimmas as a corruption of Menon son of Cerdimmas. Hoffmann 193 suggests that Arimmas is an abbreviation of Arimachus, but the reading of the former in A 3.6.8 has been called into question and the latter is unattested in Macedonia. Comparison with Tyrimmas (Bosworth 1974: 52 n. 3) proves nothing. For a full discussion see s.v. **Menon** [1].

Ariobarzanes [1]. Son of Darius III by an earlier wife. He was probably a nephew of Pharnaces and brother-in-law of Mithridates, both of whom were killed at the Granicus (A 1.15.7, 16.3; D 17.21.3; cf. P*M* 326f). According to Aretades of Cnidus (*FGrH* 285 F1), Ariobarzanes plotted with

Alexander to betray his father but was exposed and executed. Berve ii.61 assumes that the cause of his grievance may have been the eclipse of his status by Darius' new family, especially Ochus, who may have had a stronger claim to the throne. The deaths of two prominent kinsmen must have contributed to Ariobarzanes' isolation.

Judeich, *RE* s.v. "Ariobarzanes (3)"; Berve ii.61 no. 116. See Stemma III.

Ariobarzanes [2]. Persian noble of unknown family – possibly he belonged to one of the aristocratic families that ruled Cappadocia-Pontus or Hellespontine Phrygia[105] – he was satrap of Persis since at least 331 (A 3.18.2). Identification with the son of Artabazus who later surrendered to Alexander (A 3.23.7) is ruled out by Curtius' claim (5.4.34, which we have no good reason to doubt) that the satrap of Persis died before Alexander's capture of Persepolis (cf. Bosworth i.325, against Berve ii.60). At Gaugamela, he commanded the Persians and, presumably, the neighboring Mardians (C 4.12.7; cf. A 3.8.5, "those bordering on the Persian Gulf"), though under the direction of Orxines. After the Persian defeat, he withdrew to his satrapy and, in late 331, he attempted to block Alexander's passage at the so-called Persian, or Susian, Gates with a force of 25,000 infantry (C 5.3.17; D 17.68.1, adding 300 cavalry; A 3.18.2: 40,000 and 700, exaggerated). Although he managed to stymie the initial (frontal) attack, Ariobarzanes soon found his position circumvented by Alexander and fled with but a few horsemen (A 3.18.9; cf. C 5.4.33; for the battle see A 3.18.2–9; C 5.3.17–4.34; D 17.68, badly confused; Pol*Strat* 4.3.27; cf. P*A* 37.1–2; Fuller 226–34). Returning to Persepolis, he found himself barred from the city and perished in a desperate battle with the Macedonians near the Araxes River (C 5.4.34).

Berve ii.60–1 no. 115; Bosworth i.324–5.

Ariobarzanes [3]. Son of Artabazus, born before 350 BC. According to D 16.52.4, Artabazus came to the court of Philip II (ca. 349/8; though the date is disputed) with eleven sons and ten daughters. Together with his father and his brothers, Arsames and Cophen, he surrendered to Alexander in Hyrcania (A 3.23.7; cf. C 6.5.4, who says that Artabazus surrendered along with nine sons). Nothing else is known about him. Identification with the satrap of Persis is impossible, since that man died in the defense of Persepolis (C 5.4.34; cf. Bosworth i.325).

Kaerst, *RE* s.v. "Ariobarzanes (4)"; Bosworth i.325, against Berve ii.60–1 no. 115; cf. also Hofstetter 34 no. 57 s.v. "Astyanax." See Stemma IV.

Aristander (Aristandros). Greek from Telmessus (Telmissus) (A 1.11.2, 25.8; 3.2.2; Lucian, *Philopseudes* 22), Aristander accompanied Alexander as a seer of great renown (D 17.17.6;[106] C 4.2.14, 6.12; cf. 5.4.2). Born perhaps ca. 380 (thus Berve ii.62), Aristander was already in Philip's entourage in 357/6, when he correctly interpreted a dream as revealing Olympias' pregnancy (P*A* 2.5). During Alexander's campaigns he interpreted various omens for the King: the sweating of the statue of Orpheus (A 1.11.2; P*A* 14.8–9; cf. Ps-Call 1.42; Jul Val 1.46); the toppling of the statue of Ariobarzanes (D 17.17.6); the actions of birds at Halicarnassus (A 1.25.6–8, relating to the plot of Alexander the Lyncestian) and at Gaza (A 2.26.4, 27.1; C 4.6.10–12) and at the founding of Alexandria in Egypt (A 3.2.1–2; cf. C 4.8.6); bleeding bread (C 4.2.14) or dreams about Heracles (A 2.18.1) at Tyre; and oil at the Oxus (A 4.15.8). Aristander's services were also sought before and at Gaugamela (A 3.7.6; C 4.13.15, 15.27; P*A* 31.9; cf. A 3.15.7), the Persian Gates (C 5.4.1–3), at the Iaxartes (A 4.4.3, 9; C 7.7.8, 22–9). It is also said that Aristander and Cleomenes were instructed by Alexander to sacrifice on behalf of Cleitus' safety (P*A* 50.3–5). Two other references to Aristander are almost certainly unhistorical: thirty days after Alexander's death Aristander was supposed to have predicted that the land that became home to his body would enjoy great prosperity, thus causing Ptolemy to bring it to Egypt (Ael*VH* 12.64); Aristander was also supposed to have predicted Lysimachus' kingship (App*Syr* 64 [338]). Fränkel and Robinson 1929 believed that Aristander was a feature of Callisthenes' history and they attribute his disappearance after 328/7 to the historian's demise. It is more likely, however, that Aristander simply died of illness or old age during the campaign.

Kaerst, *RE* s.v. "Aristandros (6)"; Berve ii.62–3 no. 117; Robinson 1929; Greenwalt 1982.

Aristarchus (Aristarchos). Apparently a leading Ambraciot, Aristarchus persuaded his fellow-citizens to expel the Macedonian garrison in the city immediately after Philip II's death (D 17.3.3). Since Alexander allowed the Ambraciots their freedom (D 17.4.3), it would appear that Aristarchus was unpunished for his role. Nothing else is known about him.

Kirchner, *RE* s.v. "Aristarchos (6)"; Schaefer iii^2 91; Berve ii.63 no. 118.

Aristeides (Aristides). Theban painter, son of Nicomachus (Pl*NH* 35.98); Aristeides the elder was apparently his grandfather (cf. Pl*NH* 35.75, 108). Aristeides was a contemporary of Apelles (Pl*NH* 35.98) and reportedly the first to depict human emotions. During the sack of Thebes, Alexander saw Aristeides' painting of a dying mother with child, which so impressed him that he had it taken to Pella (Pl*NH* 35.98; Sil 9.41ff.; *AP* 7.623). Another painting, depicting a battle with the Persians and containing 100 human figures, appears to have been inspired by one of Alexander's campaigns against Darius (Pl*NH* 35.99).[107]

Rossbach, *RE* s.v. "Aristeides (30)"; Berve ii.63 no. 119.

Aristion. Son of Aristobulus.[108] Young man of Plataean (Marsyas, *FGrH* 135/6 F2) or Samian (so Diyllus, *FGrH* 73 F2) origin, sent by Demosthenes to Hephaestion, asking him to intercede with Alexander on Demosthenes' behalf. Aristion's presence at Alexander's court is dated to 331 by an Athenian embassy which found him there (Aes 3.162).

Kirchner, *RE* s.v. "Aristion (12)"; Schaefer iii^2 195 n. 5; Berve ii.63 no. 120.

Aristobulus (Aristoboulos). Son of Aristobulus (A 6.28.2), from Cassandreia (P*Dem* 23.6; [L]*Macrob* 22). Since Cassandreia was not founded until 316, it may be that Aristobulus came from somewhere in Chalcidice, possibly Potidaea. But Aristobulus may have come from any part of the Greek world.[109] His birthdate is uncertain: he is said to have surpassed the age of 90 and did not begin writing his *History* until he was 84 ([L]*Macrob* 22).[110] Aristobulus seems to have accompanied Alexander from the beginning of the Asiatic campaign and remained with the King until his death (A *proem.* 2; cf. Str 15.1.17 [691], 15.1.45 [706]); his account of the Timocleia story does not prove that he was with the King at the sack of Thebes (*FGrH* 139 2a–b = P*M* 1093c, 259d–260d). He appears to have joined the expedition in what we would call the engineering corps. In fact, he was entrusted with the task of restoring Cyrus' tomb at Pasargadae after it had been plundered by thieves (Str 15.3.7 [730]; A 6.29.4–10). After Alexander's death he returned to Europe, perhaps in the company of Antipater in 320 (cf. Jacoby iiD, 508), and after the regent's death he may have become a supporter of Cassander and one of Cassandreia's first citizens. His *History* was used by Arrian, alongside that of Ptolemy son of Lagus, because of its favorable treatment of Alexander. He was noted for his flattering style (*FGrH.* 139 T5) and was not encumbered by the truth but was a blatant apologist for the King.[111] For the scope and nature of his *History*, of which some sixty-two genuine fragments survive, see Jacoby, *FGrH* 139 and Pearson 150–87.

Schwartz, *RE* s.v. "Aristobulos (14)"; Berve ii.64–6 no. 121.

Aristocrates (Aristokrates). A Theban harpist who performed at the Susan marriage festival (see also Heracleitus of Tarentum) in 324 BC (Chares, *FGrH* 125 F4 = Ath 12.538f). He is otherwise unknown.

Crusius, *RE* s.v. "Aristokrates (24)"; Berve ii.67 no. 124.

Aristocritus (Aristokritos). A tragic actor of unknown origin, Aristocritus served as messenger for the Carian prince Pixodarus, who sought a marriage alliance with Philip II in spring 336 (*PA* 10.1; for the date see Olmstead 490). He apparently returned with Philip's proposal that Pixodarus' daughter should marry Arrhidaeus. Alexander subsequently undermined these negotiations by sending another actor, Thessalus, to the Carian dynast. Aristocritus reappears (along with Thessalus and Athenodorus) in Susa, where he performed at the marriage festival in 324 (Chares, *FGrH* 125 F4 = Ath 12.538f). Thereafter he is not heard of again.

Kirchner, *RE* s.v. "Aristokritos (1)"; Berve ii.67 no. 125; O'Connor no. 65.

Aristogeiton [1]. Athenian. Son of Cydimachus (who had been condemned to death by the Athenians but went into exile in Eretria: [Dem] 25.54, 65, 77; Din 2.8). Berve ii.66 calls him "one of the most shameless demagogues and sycophants of his time," thus reflecting the judgment of his political opponents (cf. Dem 27, 28); *PPh* 10.3 portrays him as in the front ranks of those urging the *demos* to declare war but the first to shirk military service. Dinarchus alleged that he spent more time in prison than out of it (2.2), that he neglected his father when he was in exile (2.8), and that he had been fined the maximum amount for bringing false charges against the priestess of Artemis at Brauron and her family (2.12). In 324 he was charged with accepting bribes from Harpalus (Din 2.1 says he took twenty minae), a charge supported by the findings of the Areopagus. Dinarchus' speech, *Against Aristogeiton*, survives in an incomplete form and relies heavily on rhetorical topoi (see Worthington 287–312 for analysis and commentary). Despite his alleged history of abuses, Aristogeiton was acquitted (Dem*Ep* 3.37–8, 43; Goldstein 143, 231–2).

Thalheim, *RE* s.v. "Aristogeiton (2)"; Berve ii.66 no. 122; Kirchner no. 1775; Schaefer, *passim*; Sealy 1960; Worthington 287–312.

Aristogeiton [2]. An Athenian of unknown family background, Aristogeiton was sent as ambassador to Darius in 333/2 and was captured by Parmenion at Damascus (C 3.13.15, adding Iphicrates and Dropides). A 3.24.4, however, records the capture of Dropides in 330, in a context where Curtius (6.5.6–9) names Democrates, perhaps a mercenary captain (so, plausibly, Bosworth i.234). An Athenian embassy of three men was normal practice, and 333/2 BC makes eminently good sense.

Berve ii.66 no. 123; Hofstetter 27 no. 42; Atkinson i.464–5; Bosworth i.233–4; Develin 385, 392.

Aristomedes. A Thessalian from Pherae (A 2.13.2; cf. C 3.9.3), Aristomedes had joined the generals of the Great King in 341/0 in opposing Philip II, who mentioned him in a letter to the Athenians (Theopompus, *FGrH* 115 F222). He later served Darius at Issus (333 BC), where he commanded 20,000 barbarian infantry stationed on the left wing (C 3.9.3): whether these were Cardaces, as Berve ii.67 suggests, is not clear; from Arrian's description (2.8.6–7), it appears that the 60,000 Cardaces were positioned on either side of the Greek mercenaries but that an additional 20,000 troops (Aristomedes' force) were placed to the left of them. After the battle, Aristomedes managed to escape, along with Amyntas son of Antiochus and Bianor the Acarnanian, first to Tripolis in Phoenicia, where they had left the ships which brought them from Lesbos, and thence to Cyprus (A 2.13.2–3, with 8,000 troops; C 4.1.27 and D 17.48.2–3, only 4,000). D 17.48.4 says that the troops who continued on to Egypt perished to a man, but names no other officer except Amyntas. Bianor, Thymondas, and Aristomedes may have parted ways with Amyntas on Cyprus (Anaximenes, *FGrH* 72 F17 mentions only his flight to Cyprus), perhaps taking some of the mercenaries to Crete, which would account for the discrepancy in the numbers of mercenaries and failure of any source to mention deaths of the other three commanders (see Bosworth i.222–3).

Kirchner, *RE* s.v. "Aristomedes (2)"; Berve ii.67 no. 128; Hofstetter 27–8 no. 44.

Aristomenes [1]. Greek of unknown background. Aristomenes commanded a fleet of unknown size in the Hellespontine region. He was defeated by Hegelochus, perhaps early in 332 (C 4.1.36). That "Aristomenes" is an error for "Autophradates" seems unlikely (Atkinson i.289).

Berve ii.67 no. 126; Seibt 107; Hofstetter 28 no. 45.

Aristomenes [2]. Greek of unknown background. In 326/5 (i.e., the eleventh year of Alexander's reign) Aristomenes received land near Gambreion in Asia Minor from Crateuas (*SIG*[3] 302), who may have been the official in charge of royal land (*chora basilike*). Nothing else is known about him.

Berve ii.67 no. 127.

Ariston [1]. Nothing is known about the family and background of Ariston, who was undoubtedly a Macedonian of high standing. He is first attested at Gaugamela, where his squadron of Companions was stationed between those of Glaucias and Sopolis on the right wing (A 3.11.8); he may have been an ilarch since at least the beginning of Alexander's reign. Otherwise, nothing is known about the man. Berve and Billows identify him tentatively with the man who brought the remains of Craterus to his widow, Phila (D 19.59.3); he may, in fact, be identical with Ariston of Pharsalus (see below).

Kirchner, *RE* s.v. "Ariston (28)"; Berve ii.74 no. 137; Billows 375 no. 17.

Ariston [2]. Pharsalian (Ps-Call 3.31.8), apparently a Thessalian *hetairos* of Alexander and a friend of Medius of Larissa, whose dinner party he attended on 16 Daisios 323. Ariston is named by the author of the pamphlet on *The Last Days and Testament of Alexander the Great* as one of those who conspired to poison the King (Ps-Call 3.31.8); *LM* 97 mentions in this context "Polydorus," which may be a textual corruption or, what is remotely possible, the name of Ariston's father. The poisoning story, and hence Ariston's part in it, is almost certainly a fabrication of the Polyperchan party, but it does suggest close connections between Ariston and Medius, and perhaps also Antigonus the One-Eyed. It is tempting to see in Ariston the man who brought the remains of Craterus to his widow, Phila, at that time the wife of Demetrius Poliorcetes (D 19.59.3).

Berve ii.75 no. 139; Heckel 1988: 43–4.

Ariston [3]. Presumably a member of the Paeonian royal house, possibly even the brother of Patraus[112] and father of the later king Audoleon (for the apparent grandson, Ariston son of Audoleon, see Pol*Strat* 4.12.3; cf. Merker 1965: 6.45). His service with Alexander, like that of Sitalces and others, helped to ensure the loyalty of his nation to Macedon in the King's absence (Fr*Strat* 2.11.3; cf. J 11.5.3; see also s.v. **Sitalces**). From the beginning of the expedition, he commanded the single *ile* of Paeonians, who occupied a position on the right at the Granicus (A 1.14.1) and at Issus (A 2.9.2). In 331 the Paeonians fell in with some 1,000 cavalrymen left by Mazaeus in the vicinity of the Tigris (C 4.9.24–5) and routed them; Ariston for his part slew in single combat their leader Satropates (Atropates?) and brought his head to Alexander (C 4.9.25; *PA* 39.2; Merker 1965: 6.44–5 argues persuasively that the incident is commemorated on the coinage of Patraus).[113]

At Gaugamela, Ariston and his Paeonians were again stationed on the right wing, together with the *prodromoi*, immediately behind Menidas' mercenary horse (A 3.12.3; cf. Bosworth i.303; Marsden 1964: 48) and concealing from enemy view the Agrianes, archers, and *archaioi xenoi*. In the initial engagement, Ariston brought the Paeonians up to aid Menidas, who was hard pressed by the Scythian and Bactrian cavalry and, supported by the *prodromoi* and Cleander's mercenaries, succeeded in breaking the enemy formation (A 3.13.3–4). Nothing else is known about him.

Kirchner, *RE* s.v. "Ariston (32)"; Berve ii.74–5 no. 138; Atkinson i.384–5; Heckel 354–5; Marsden 1964: 31, 48, 50; Merker 1965: 35–46, esp. 44–6.

Ariston [4]. A comic actor, Ariston performed at the mass-marriage ceremony at Susa in 324 (Chares, *FGrH* 125 F4 = Ath 12.539a; see also s.vv. **Lycon**, **Phormion**). He is otherwise unknown.

v. Jan, *RE* s.v. "Ariston (40)"; Berve ii.75 no. 140; Ghiron-Bistagne 314; O'Connor no. 74.

Aristonicus [1]. (Aristonikos). A Greek of unknown family background, but presumably Methymnaean. In late 333 BC, as a consequence of Memnon's recapture of Lesbos (A 2.1.1), he was installed by the Persians as tyrant of Methymna (A 3.2.4; C 4.5.19, 8.11); whether he had any personal connections with his predecessor Aristonymus (cf. Pol*Strat* 5.44.3), who had been expelled in 334, we do not know; certainly there is no compelling reason for identifying the two. Aristonicus' tyranny appears to have been of short duration, for, coming to the aid of Pharnabazus in 332, he sailed into the harbor of Chios with five pirate ships (A 3.2.4; cf. C 4.5.19), unaware that it was in Macedonian hands. Captured by Alexander's admirals, Amphoterus and Hegelochus (C 4.5.19–21; A 3.2.4–5, naming Hegelochus only), Aristonicus was brought (along with Apollonides, Phesinus, and Magareus)[114] to the King in Egypt, who sent him back to Methymna to be punished by his own citizens (A 3.2.5, 7); they put him to death by torture in 331 (C 4.8.11).

Kaerst, *RE* s.v. "Aristonikos (13)"; Berve ii.68 no. 131, Berve 1967 i.337; Ormerod 1924: 120–1; Hofstetter 29 no. 48; Atkinson i.330.

Aristonicus [2]. (Aristonikos). Greek from Carystus, Aristonicus was a ballplayer (*sphairistes*) in Alexander's entourage. He was granted Athenian citizenship at an unspecified time and had a statue erected to him (Ath 1.19a). Nothing else is known about him.

Kaerst, *RE* s.v. "Aristonikos (5)"; Berve ii.68 no. 129.

Aristonicus [3]. (Aristonikos). Athenian politician from Marathon.[115] A follower of Demosthenes and Hypereides, Aristonicus was prosecuted in 324 in the Harpalus case (Dion Hal *Din* 10 [654] *PAnt* 2.62, on which see Worthington 54, 79–80; Din frag. 10A [Burtt]). He was exiled from Athens and fled to Aegina with Demosthenes, Hypereides, and Himeraeus, the brother of Demetrius of Phalerum (A*Succ* 1.13). Aristonicus was condemned to death *in absentia* on the proposal of Demades. This decree was executed by Antipater, who sent Archias of Thurii to capture him and send him to Cleonae, where he was executed (A*Succ* 1.13–14; P*Dem* 28.4; cf. Schaefer iii^2 392–3).

Kaerst, *RE* s.v. "Aristonikos (1)"; Berve ii.68 no. 130; Kirchner no. 2028.

Aristonicus [4]. (Aristonikos). Harpist (*kitharoidos*) from Olynthus (Pol*Strat* 5.44.1 connected with Memnon; Theopompus, *FGrH* 115 F236 says he was in Philip II's entourage after Chaeronea), Aristonicus may have accompanied Alexander since 334 BC. In 328, he was left behind at Zariaspa with the wounded and the non-military personnel. Forced to take up arms against the Massagetae, he fell in battle (A 4.16.6; not in Alexander's defense, as P*M* 334e says). Alexander ordered that a statue be erected at Delphi, depicting him with lyre in one hand and thrusting spear in the other (P*M* 334e–f).

Kaerst, *RE* s.v. "Aristonikos (6)"; Berve ii.68 no. 132; Gude no. 18.

Aristonus (Aristonous). The son of Peisaeus (A 6.28.4; A*Succ* 1.2), Aristonus is described as both Pellaean (A 6.28.4) and of Eordaean origin (A*Ind* 18.5), which must mean that he was from Eordaea but raised at the court in Pella (cf. s.v. **Leonnatus** [2]). Until his name appears in Arrian's list of the Somatophylakes (325 BC; A 6.28.4, from Aristobulus, *FGrH* 139 F50), he is unknown in the *Anabasis*. He may have been appointed to that office before 336, and we have a strong indication that Aristonus was Somatophylax already in 328. According to Plutarch, a certain Aristophanes, termed *somatophylax*, took away Alexander's sword when the King was quarreling with Cleitus (P*A* 51.5–6). Aristophanes was emended by Palmerius to read "Aristonus" (a known member of the Somatophylakes; cf. Hamilton 143), a simple and sensible correction. Berve's rejection of it (ii.69 n. 2) in favor of a historical hypaspist named Aristophanes (ii.74 no. 136) has been shown to be incorrect by Ziegler 1935, who pointed out that in the very sentence in which Aristophanes is described as *somatophylax* the term hypaspist occurs. The latter were summoned by Alexander, and it is doubtful that Plutarch used two different terms within the same sentence to apply to the same unit.

In 326, Aristonus assumed a trierarchy at the Hydaspes River (A*Ind* 18.5 = Nearchus, *FGrH* 133 F1), as did the other six Somatophylakes. Although he was wounded in the town of the Mallians (C 9.6.15ff.), this is not reported by Arrian (Ptolemy), perhaps because, after Alexander's death, Aristonus was a loyal supporter of Perdiccas (C 10.6.16; cf. Errington 1969: 235–6); the golden crown awarded him at Susa in 324 (A 7.5.6) supports Curtius' claim. In 323, Aristonus espoused the Perdiccan cause (C 10.6.16) and in 321/0 served as the commander-in-chief of the expedition against the Cypriot kings who had allied themselves with Ptolemy (A*Succ* 24.6). This undertaking was ill-fated, and Aristonus was apparently forced to surrender to Antigonus. Antipater, it appears, pardoned him and allowed him to return to Macedonia, perhaps on the understanding that he would retire to private life (cf. the case of Holcias, Pol*Strat* 4.6.6). In 319/8, in the turmoil that followed Antipater's death, Aristonus joined Polyperchon, who had allied himself with Eumenes and the remnants of the Perdiccan party. Nothing is known of his role in the early stages of the war between Polyperchon and Cassander, but in 316, when Olympias was forced to seek refuge in Pydna, Aristonus, on the queen mother's orders, took control of those troops who were still loyal to Alexander's house (D 19.35.4). Aristonus appears to have accomplished little: once Cassander had prevailed over Aeacides of Epirus and Polyperchon, both of whose armies were weakened by defections, Aristonus thought it prudent to fall back on Amphipolis. This town, however, he defended until early 315 (D 19.50.3) – indeed, he had actually defeated Cassander's general Crateuas at Bedyndia (19.50.7). He was induced by a letter of Olympias to surrender Amphipolis. Cassander, although he pledged Aristonus his safety (D 19.50.8), feared him on account of his popularity, which he derived from his high position in Alexander's lifetime, and had him killed through the agency of some of the relatives of Crateuas (D 19.51.1), though it is not clear if these represent the family of Aristonus' fellow-Somatophylax Peithon son of Crateuas.

Kaerst, *RE* s.v. "Aristonus (8)"; Berve ii.69 no. 133; Errington 1969: 235–6, 240–1; Heckel 275–6.

Aristonymus (Aristonymos). An Athenian harp-soloist who performed at the mass-marriage festival in Susa in 324 (Chares, *FGrH* 125 F4 = Ath 12.538e). Apart from Clearchus' (*ap.* Ath 10.452f) comment that Aristonymus was fond of riddles, nothing else is known about him.

Kirchner, *RE* s.v. "Aristonymos (4)"; Berve ii.75 no. 141; Kirchner no. 2186.

Aristophanes. P*A* 51.5–6. See s.v. **Aristonus**.

Aristotle (Aristoteles). (384–322 BC) Eminent Greek philosopher, born in Stageira in Chalcidice. Son of Nicomachus[116] and Phaestis. The father had been a physician of Amyntas III, father of Philip II, and it appears that Aristotle became familiar with the slightly younger prince during his stay in Pella. In 367, at the age of 17, Aristotle left Macedonia for Athens and became a student of Plato, but he did not succeed his teacher as head of the Academy, the position going to Plato's kinsman Speusippus. Aristotle and Xenocrates went to Asia Minor in 347 at the invitation of Hermias, tyrant of Assos and Atarneus.[117] Whether his departure from Athens was due to anti-Macedonian feeling there or bitterness over the appointment of Speusippus is unclear.[118] In the Troad, Aristotle married Pythias, the adopted daughter of Hermias (Str 13.1.57 [610], she was the daughter of Hermias' brother; cf. DL 5.4). In 343 he was invited to Pella by Philip II to become, for the next two years, the tutor of Alexander (P*M* 327e, 604d; P*A* 7–8; J 12.16; Pl*NH* 8.44; Ath 9.398e; Ael*VH* 4.19; Quint 1.1.23; Dio Chr 49.4). Although Str 13.1.57 [610] claims that Aristotle and Xenocrates escaped from the area when Memnon of Rhodes captured Hermias of Atarneus and sent him to the Great King to be executed, Hermias' death did not occur until 341. The relationship between the great philosopher (though at the time Aristotle had not yet earned that reputation) and the future world conqueror has captured the imagination of historians and philosophers since antiquity, but it appears that Alexander was not excessively influenced by his teacher's views and it is doubtful that Aristotle considered his pupil an intellectual prodigy. Aristotle later successfully petitioned Alexander to restore Stageira, which Philip had destroyed (D 16.52.9), and drew up a lawcode for the city (DL 5.4).[119] Aristotle inspired in Alexander a lifelong interest in literature and science (P*A* 8.1); and he is said to have produced an edition of the *Iliad* for him, later to become known as the "Casket Copy" (P*A* 8.2 = Onesicritus, *FGrH* 134 F38; Str 13.1.27 [594]; cf. P*A* 26.2). He presented his nephew Callisthenes to Alexander before his departure to Athens (Val Max 7.2 ext 11; cf. *Suda* K 240; see s.v. **Callisthenes** [1]). The execution of Callisthenes by Alexander in 327 gave rise to later rumors that Aristotle had been involved in a plot to poison the King (P*A* 77.3; A 7.27.1); P*A* 55.7 says that in a letter to Antipater, Alexander threatened to punish Aristotle for his connections with Callisthenes and for recommending him (DL 5.10).[120]

In 334 he returned to Athens, where he taught at the Lyceum, the walkway of which was the perfect place for teaching philosophy, whence he derived the name "Peripatetic" (DL 5.2). He taught Phanias and Theophrastus of Eresus (cf. Str 13.2.4 [618]) and Neleus, leaving his school and library to Theophrastus; Theophrastus in turn left the library to Neleus (Str 13.1.54 [608]); Neleus later sold the library to Ptolemy II Philadelphus (Ath 1.3a–b). In 322 he made his way to Chalcis on Euboea, where he ended his days (Str 10.1.11 [448]). Eurymedon the hierophant (or Demophilos, according to Favorinus) charged him with *asebeia* (DL 5.5). The impiety was that he wrote a hymn for Hermias and an inscription for his statue at Delphi. He died at Chalcis at the age of 70, drinking aconite (so Eumelus, in the fifth book of his history, cited by DL 5.6); but Diogenes corrects this and says that Aristotle died at age 63 and came to be Plato's student at 17 (DL 5.6). DL 5.1 gives a brief physical description of him: he spoke with a lisp, he had skinny legs and small eyes; he was conspicuous by his clothes and his rings, and his hair was cut short.

Gercke, *RE* s.v. "Aristoteles (18)"; Berve ii.70–4 no. 135. For a life of Aristotle see DL 5.1–35; the basic biographical information, from all ancient sources, is collected and discussed in Düring (see pp. 284–99 for Aristotle and Alexander). See also Guthrie for his life and philosophy. See also *OCD*[3] 165–9, with bibliography on 169.

Arrhabaeus (Arrhabaios; Arrabaeus). Lyncestian. Son of Aëropus and brother of Heromenes and Alexander (A 1.25). Apparently the father of Amyntas (A 1.12.7; rejected by Kaerst, *RE* s.v. "Arrabaios (3)") and Neoptolemus (A 1.20.10),[121] and thus born no later than ca. 380. Executed, along with Heromenes, for their complicity in the murder of Philip II (cf. D 17.2.1).[122] If there is any truth to the charge that they conspired against Philip, then it is most likely that they espoused the cause of Amyntas (IV), son of Perdiccas III (P*M* 327c).

Kaerst, *RE* s.v. "Arrabaios (2)"; Berve ii.80 no. 144; Bosworth 1971a. See Stemma XV.

Arrhidaeus [1]. (Arrhidaios; Arridaeus). Son of Philip II and Philine of Larissa (Satyrus, *ap.* Ath 13.557c; J 9.8.2; 13.2.11; App*Syr* 54 [275], mistakenly, a son of Olympias; J 14.6.13, incorrectly, the father of Thessalonice), in all probability a woman of the Aleuadae (cf. Ellis 61) and not a harlot, as the tradition records (J 13.2.11; Ptolemy son of Agesarchus of Megalopolis, *ap.* Ath 13.577f–578a = *FGrH* 161 F4; P*A* 77.1). Arrhidaeus was born in 358 or 357. That Amphimachus, the satrap of Mesopotamia in 320, was his half-brother is unlikely; A*Succ* 1.35 or his source confused Arrhidaeus the satrap with the King.[123] Arrhidaeus was of marriageable age in 337/6, when Philip considered an alliance with Pixodarus (P*A* 10.1), but afflicted since childhood with an incurable mental illness (P*A* 10.2; App*Syr* 52; J 13.2.11; 14.5.2; D 18.2.2; P*M* 337d; Porphyry of Tyre, *FGrH* 260 F2; *HE* 1 calls him "epileptic"), which Plutarch alleges was induced by mind-destroying drugs given to him by Olympias (P*A* 77.8). The marriage to Ada, daughter of Pixodarus, was preempted by the intervention of Alexander, who appears to have revealed to the Carian dynast what he did not know, that Arrhidaeus was mentally unstable (P*A* 10.2).

Nothing else is known about him during Alexander's lifetime. When the King died in 323, Arrhidaeus was already in Babylon (J 13.2.8; C 10.7.2ff.);[124] there is no indication as to how long he had been there. Paradoxically, he was declared King by the army under the name of Philip (C 10.7.1–7; D 18.2.2, 4; J 13.2.6–8, 3.1, 4.2; A*Succ* 1.1; Paus 1.6.2; App*Syr* 52 [261]; Porphyry of Tyre, *FGrH* 260 F2; cf. *LM* 115), and it was in his name that Perdiccas allotted the satrapies (A*Succ* 1.5; App*Syr* 52 [262]; cf. D 18.2.4), for Arrhidaeus was never anything more than a puppet (P*M* 791e). Although, by the terms of the compromise settlement in Babylon, Craterus had been designated Arrhidaeus' guardian (*prostates*), Arrhidaeus remained in Perdiccas' custody and accompanied him first into Cappadocia (D 18.22.1; cf. J 13.6.10)[125] and then to Egypt (Paus 1.6.3). At some point in between – perhaps in Pisidia – Arrhidaeus was married to Adea, the daughter of Cynnane (A*Succ* 1.23; cf. Pol*Strat* 8.60). After Perdiccas' murder in Egypt, Peithon and the other Arrhidaeus assumed the guardianship of the Kings (D 18.36.6–7; A*Succ* 1.30), but they soon found Adea-Eurydice impossible to deal with (A*Succ* 1.31–3) and surrendered this office to Antipater at Triparadeisus (D 18.39.1–2). Arrhidaeus was then left briefly with Antigonus (A*Succ* 1.38), before returning to Macedonia with Antipater (A*Succ* 1.45).[126] Upon Antipater's death in 319, the guardianship passed to Polyperchon (D 18.48.4), who in 318 issued a decree proclaiming the "Freedom of the Greeks" in the name of Philip III Arrhidaeus (D 18.56). Together with Polyperchon, and enthroned beneath a golden canopy, Philip Arrhidaeus received Phocion and his party in Phocis (N*Ph* 3.3; P*Ph* 33.8), and in an outburst of anger nearly impaled Hegemon with a spear (P*Ph* 33.11–12). Threatened by Polyperchon's summoning of Olympias to Macedonia, Adea-Eurydice transferred custody of Arrhidaeus to Cassander (J 14.5.1–4). An attempt was made to block the forces of Olympias and her kinsman Aeacides at Evia (J 14.5.9), but the troops deserted to Alexander's mother, who murdered Arrhidaeus soon afterwards (D 19.11.2–5;

Paus 1.11.3–4; 8.7.7; J 14.5.10); he was stabbed by his Thracian guards after a reign of six years and four months (D 19.11.5; cf. J 14.5.10, "six years"). Cassander later buried him and Adea-Eurydice, along with Cynnane, at Aegae (Diyllus, *FGrH* 73 F1 = Ath 4.155a; D 19.52.5).[127]

Kaerst, *RE* s.v. "Arridaios (4)"; Berve ii.385–6 no. 781. See Stemma I.

Arrhidaeus [2]. (Arrhidaios; Arridaeus). Prominent Macedonian, possibly son of Alexander (*IG* xii.9 212) and perhaps the brother of Amphimachus (A*Succ* 1.35). He was present in Babylon when Alexander died, but we have no indication of whether he accompanied the King from the beginning of the campaign or joined the expedition in progress. Arrhidaeus was given the responsibility of conveying the King's corpse to Egypt (D 18.3.5; J 13.4.6), a task which he completed with the aid of Ptolemy (D 18.28.2) despite Perdiccas' plan to bring the funeral carriage to Aegae (Paus 1.6.3; A*Succ* 1.25), resisting the forces of Polemon and Attalus, who had been set against him by Perdiccas (A*Succ* 1.25; 24.1). After the death of Perdiccas, Arrhidaeus and Peithon son of Crateuas were chosen *epimeletai* of the "Kings" by the army, primarily through the influence of Ptolemy (D 18.36.6–7). But, after taking the remnants of the Perdiccan army to Triparadeisus in Syria (D 18.39.1) and experiencing difficulties with Adea-Eurydice, they resigned their offices and Macedonians elected Antipater in their place (D 18.39.2). In the division of the satrapies at Triparadeisus, Arrhidaeus received Hellespontine Phrygia (D 18.39.6; A*Succ* 1.37), in place of Leonnatus. After the death of Antipater in 319, Arrhidaeus feared the expansionist designs of Antigonus and sought to strengthen his satrapy and garrison its cities (D 18.51.1). In the process he launched an attack on Cyzicus (*MP* B12 = *FGrH* 239; cf. Harding no. 1a, p. 2), which resisted and gave Antigonus an excuse for interfering;[128] when Arrhidaeus refused to withdraw from his satrapy, Antigonus sent forces against him (D 18.51–2). Arrhidaeus took refuge with Cleitus of Lydia, who assumed control of some of his forces (D 18.72.2–3), but after Cleitus' defeat and death in 317, Arrhidaeus may have come to terms with Antigonus. An Eretrian inscription honors an Arrhidaeus son of Alexander in 303/2, a man who had served Antigonus and Demetrius (*IG* xii.9 212; cf. Billows 1993). But the identification is tenuous at best. Nothing else is known about him.[129]

Kaerst, *RE* s.v. "Arridaios (5)"; Berve ii.80 no. 145; Hoffmann 264–6; Billows 375 no. 18.

Arsaces [1]. (Arsakes). Persian. In 330, Alexander appointed him satrap of Areia after the defection of Satibarzanes (A 3.25.7; cf. C 7.3.1); how he came to be in Alexander's entourage is unclear. At this time, it appears that Alexander placed Drangiana within the jurisdiction of the satrap of Areia (C 8.3.17; cf. A 4.18.3; Julien 38–9; Jacobs 75). Curtius calls him "Arsames," but there is nothing to warrant identification with the son of Artabazus (thus Berve ii.81). In fact, the failure of the sources to note the relationship, at a time when Artabazus was in Alexander's confidence, and the vague description of Arsaces as "a Persian,"[130] are telling. The confusion in Curtius is further emphasized by the fact that, immediately after discussing "Arsames" the satrap of the Drangae, he mistakenly calls Atropates "Arsaces." In the following year, Arsaces was deposed by Stasanor of Soli, who brought him in chains to Alexander at Bactra (A 4.7.1; cf. A 4.18.1).

Berve ii.80–1 no. 146.

Arsaces [2]. (Arsakes). Indian hyparch, ruler of Hazara (= Urasa, the territory east of the Indus and directly north of the kingdom of Taxiles). He appears to have been under the control of Abisares, king of the Kashmir (Abhisara), who lent support to the natives of Ora (Udegram) and took in the refugees from the Swat and Buner regions (A 4.27.7; 4.30.7; these fled directly across the river into Hazara). Nothing is known of Arsaces himself until he appears in Alexander's camp with Abisares' brother and other ambassadors from the Kashmir (A 5.29.4). His territory was included by Alexander in the administrative sphere of Abisares (A 5.29.5). Along with the kingdom of Kashmir, Urasa appears to have freed itself of Macedonian control soon after Alexander's return to the west. Arsaces himself does not reappear in our sources.

Berve ii.81 no. 147.

Arsames [1]. (Arsamenes; Pers. Arshama). Noble Persian, family background unknown. Satrap of Cilicia in 334/3 BC.[131] Arsames fought with his cavalry on the left wing at the Granicus, along with Memnon the Rhodian (D 17.19.4), and escaped from the battle to Cilicia, where he was unable to prevent the satrapy or the capital, Tarsus, from falling into Macedonian hands (C 3.4.3–5 suggests that Arsames' "scorched-earth" policy caused the native defenders of the Cilician gates to abandon their posts because Arsames was destroying the very territory they were defending). Arrian claims that Arsames had planned to put Tarsus to the torch but was prevented from doing so by the speedy arrival of the Macedonian troops (2.4.5–6; cf. C 3.4.14). Arsames fled to Darius (A 2.4.6), who was at this time in Syria. He died on the battlefield of Issus (A 2.11.8).

Berve ii.81–2 no. 149; Leuze 244ff.; Justi 29 "Arsames (7)."

Arsames [2]. (Pers. Arshama). One of at least eleven sons of Artabazus, Arsames accompanied his father, his brothers, and ten sisters into exile in 349/8 BC, finding refuge at the court of Philip II (D 16.52.4). Faithful to Darius III, Arsames and his family joined him in flight after the battle of Gaugamela (331) but surrendered to Alexander (along with his father, eight brothers, and Autophradates) after the Great King's death in 330 (A 3.23.7, naming Arsames, Cophen, and Ariobarzanes; C 6.5.4 speaks of nine sons without naming them). Although he was favorably received by Alexander, nothing further is known of Arsames' career.

Berve ii.81 no. 148; Justi 29. See Stemma IV.

Arsimas. A Persian of unknown origin (perhaps one of the King's *syngeneis*, cf. C 4.11.1); in early 332, while Alexander was at Marathos, Arsimas and a certain Meniscus (who most likely acted as translator) delivered a letter from Darius III to Alexander, asking for the return of his family (3.14.1–3; cf. C 4.1.8–10; D 17.39.1–2; P*A* 29.7). Arsimas and Meniscus were sent back to Darius along with Thersippus, Alexander's *epistoleus*, their mission unfulfilled (A 2.14.3–4; cf. C 4.1.14). Nothing else is known about him.

Berve ii.82, 150; Justi 31. For the letter of Darius to Alexander see Griffith 1968; Kaiser 1956; Bosworth i.227ff.

Arsites. Satrap of Hellespontine Phrygia (A 1.12.8; *hyparchos = satrapes*, see Bosworth i.112) since at least 340 (Paus 1.29.10, he sent an Athenian named Apollodorus with a mercenary force to defend Perinthus against Philip, perhaps on instructions from Artaxerxes III, thus Griffith, *HMac* ii.563 n. 2); father of Mithropastes (Nearchus, *FGrH* 133 F28 = Str 16.3.7 [767]). Arsites' territory included Paphlagonia, as is clear from his command of the Paphlagonian horse and from C 3.1.22–4. Arsites took part in the war-council at Zeleia (A 1.12.8) where he was foremost in opposing Memnon's scorched-earth policy (A 1.12.10). At the Granicus, he commanded the Paphlagonian cavalry, stationed on the left wing, just to the right of Arsames and Memnon (D 17.19.4). He fled from the battlefield at the Granicus but committed suicide soon afterwards because the blame for the disaster seemed to fall on his shoulders (A 1.16.3), presumably because he had opposed Memnon's strategy or because the defeat occurred in his territory.[132] His successor in the satrapy was Calas son of Harpalus.

Kaerst, *RE* s.v.; Berve ii.82 no. 151.

Artabazus (Artabazos). Son of Pharnabazus (the famous satrap of Hellespontine Phrygia) and the Achaemenid princess Apame (P*Art* 27.4; Xen*HG* 5.1.28, P*Ages* 3.3; cf. P*A* 21.9; *IG* ii^2 356 = Tod ii.199; cf. C 3.13.13; 5.9.1; and A 3.23.7 for his importance at the Persian court). Born ca. 387, or possibly as early as ca. 391 (thus Brunt 1975: 24 n. 3).[133] The history of the so-called "Great Revolt of the Satraps" is fraught with problems, which cannot be discussed here.[134] About Artabazus himself, we can say that he was initially a supporter of his grandfather Artaxerxes II, who sent him as *strategos* against the rebel Datames in Cappadocia (D 15.91, with Stylianou 1998: 541–3; the campaign is dated by Diodorus to 362/1 but probably belongs to 359) and installed him as satrap of Hellespontine Phrygia, in place of Ariobarzanes. Artabazus did, however, rebel against royal authority, receiving support first from Chares (356/5) and then from Pammenes the Theban (353/2); in 352 he fled to the court of Philip (D 16.52.3–4, under the year 349/8; cf. C 5.9.1; 6.5.2), where he remained an exile until perhaps the mid-340s. He had fathered eleven sons and ten daughters by the same woman (**F11**; D 16.52.4; cf. C 6.5.4, who mentions nine sons by the same mother who were with Artabazus in 330). The woman captured in Damascus (**F12**), along with her young son Ilioneus (C 3.13.13), was (*pace* Berve ii.83) probably not the Rhodian wife.

Artabazus was a staunch supporter of Darius (C 5.9.1) and in 330 attempted to defuse the tension between the King and Nabarzanes and Bessus (C 5.9.12–13, 17; 5.10.10–11). But although he remained vigilant in his defense of Darius (C 5.12.7–8), he could not prevent Bessus from arresting the King and chose instead to abandon the camp with his followers and seek refuge in the Elburz mountains (C 5.12.18; A 3.21.4). He surrendered to Alexander in Hyrcania (C 6.5.2–6; A 3.23.7), along with nine of his sons (C 6.5.3–4; A 3.23.7 names only three of them). He no doubt expected a favorable reception at Alexander's hands, since his daughter Barsine was at this point the King's mistress. Artabazus was soon sent with Erigyius, Caranus, and Andronicus against the rebel Satibarzanes in Aria (A 3.28.2; C 7.3.2). In 329 he was appointed satrap of Bactria (A 3.29.1)[135] but a year later asked to be excused from this office on account of old age (C 8.1.19; A 4.17.3). Alexander replaced him with Cleitus (C 8.1.19), and after Cleitus' death with Amyntas son of Nicolaus (A 4.17.3; see also **Amyntas** [9]). Artabazus is not heard of again.

Judeich, *RE* s.v. "Artabazos (3)"; Berve ii.82–4 no. 152; Weiskopf 1989; Krumbholz 71ff. See Stemma IV.

Artacama (Artakama). Daughter of Artabazus (A 7.4.6; P*Eum* 1.7 calls her Apama; Str 12.8.15 [578] confuses her with the daughter of Spitamenes).[136] Artacama was one of ten girls born to the sister of Mentor and Memnon the Rhodians (D 16.52.4; cf. Dem 23.154, 157). Since Artabazus and his family sought refuge at the court of Philip II at some time after 353/2 BC, and certainly before 344 (thus Griffith, *HMac* ii.484 n. 5), Apame's birth occurred, in all likelihood, between 355 and 345, since she will scarcely have been much older than 30 when she married in 324. Soon after 341, she returned to Asia with her family, and it may be that, in late 333, she was captured by Parmenion at Damascus, where the families of the noble Persians had been sent for safety (cf. C 3.13.12–14, naming her sister Barsine, her stepmother, and her half-brother, Ilioneus; cf. also A 2.11.9; D 17.32.3). If she and her sister Artonis were among the captives, they may have been taken by the Macedonians as far as Susa (cf. D 17.67.1), where, in 324, she married Ptolemy son of Lagus (P*Eum* 1.7; A 7.4.6). Nothing else is known about her, though it is likely that Ptolemy repudiated her soon after Alexander's death.

Judeich, *RE* s.v. "Artakama"; Berve ii.52 no. 97; Brosius 78, 185. See Stemma IV.

Artemius. (Artemios). A Greek of unknown family, from Colophon. In summer or autumn 328, he was present at the banquet at which Cleitus was murdered by the King (P*A* 51.4). Schubert may be right in suggesting that either Artemius or Xenodochus was the eye-witness source from which Chares (if he was not himself present) drew his information.[137]

Berve ii.84 no. 153; Schubert 1898: 99ff.; Hamilton 142.

Artiboles. Son of Mazaeus and, apparently, a Babylonian wife. Alexander enrolled him in the Companion Cavalry in 324 (A 7.6.4). The view that he is identical with the son who surrendered to Alexander in 330 (A 3.21.1; C 5.1.17) is remotely possible, but would force us to postulate a series of textual errors.

Berve ii.84 no. 154; Bosworth i.341.

Artonis (Artone). Daughter of Artabazus (A 7.4.6; P*Eum* 1.7). Artonis was one of ten girls born to the sister of Mentor and Memnon the Rhodians (D 16.52.4; cf. Dem 23.154, 157). Since Artabazus and his family sought refuge at the court of Philip II at some time after 353/2, and certainly before 344 (for the date see s.v. **Artacama**), her birth must have occurred between 355 and 345; for she will scarcely have been much older than 30 when she married in 324. Soon after 341, she returned to Asia with her family, and it may be that, in late 333, she was captured by Parmenion at Damascus, where the families of the noble Persians had been sent for safety (cf. C 3.13.12–14, naming her sister Barsine, her stepmother, and her half-brother, Ilioneus; cf. also A 2.11.9; D 17.32.3). If she and her sister Artacama (Apame) were among the captives, they may have been taken by the Macedonians as far as Susa (cf. D 17.67.1), where, in 324, she married Eumenes (P*Eum* 1.7; A 7.4.6). The remains of Eumenes' body were given to his wife and children, apparently Artonis and her children (P*Eum* 19.2), though, given the age of Eumenes, this could refer to the family Eumenes left behind when he went to Asia in 334.

Judeich, *RE* s.v.; Berve ii.84–5 no. 155; Brosius 78. See Stemma IV.

Arybbas [1]. Son of Alcetas and brother of Neoptolemus; married Troas (sister of Olympias and Alexander I of Epirus); father of Alcetas, whom he banished at some point before 342 (D 19.88.1; cf. Paus 1.11.5) and Aeacides, and thus grandfather of Pyrrhus (P*Pyr* 1.5; cf. J 7.6.11). Arybbas ruled Epirus until 342/1, when he was driven into exile by Philip II, who placed Alexander I on the throne (J 7.6.12; 8.6.7; D 16.72.1 confuses his exile with his death; *IG* ii^2 226 = Tod ii.173; Osborne i.59–60, D 14). A reference to an Illyrian campaign by Arybbas cannot be dated (Fr*Strat* 2.5.19). How long Arybbas lived after 342/1 is difficult to say. He may be the "Aryptaeus" mentioned by D 18.11.1, who joined the Hellenic cause in the Lamian War.

Kaerst, *RE* s.v. "Arybbas (1)"; Reuss 1881; Errington 1975; Heskel 1988. See Stemma II.

Arybbas [2]. Probably of Epirote origin and, to judge from his high standing at the Macedonian court, a member of the Molossian royal house (i.e., a relative of Olympias).[138] Arybbas was apparently one of the seven Somatophylakes inherited by Alexander from Philip II, who may have sought some type of regional representation. He died of illness in Egypt in the winter of 332/1 and was replaced as Somatophylax by Leonnatus (A 3.5.5).

Kaerst, *RE* s.v. "Arybbas (2)"; Berve ii.85 no. 156; Heckel 261; Hoffmann 176–7.

Asander [1]. (Asandros). Macedonian. Son of Philotas (A 1.17.7) but probably not Parmenion's brother (Heckel 1977c; cf. Bosworth i.130).[139] Asander was appointed satrap of Lydia (A 1.17.7) and, later, together with Ptolemaeus (identified as a brother of Antigonus the One-Eyed by Billows 425–6 no. 99, s.v. "Polemaios I"), defeated Orontobates (A 2.5.7, with Bosworth i.195–6). In 331, he was replaced as satrap by Menander (A 3.6.7) and rejoined Alexander in the Upper Satrapies (C 7.10.12). What became of him is unknown. Possibly identical with the [C]asander of D 17.17.4, if this man is not Asander son of Agathon.[140]

If Asander was, in fact, Parmenion's brother, the silence of the sources on both the relationship and its political ramifications is troubling. Alexander's act of recalling him from Sardis to the main camp (C 7.10.12) in order to have him executed cannot have been politically astute. This could only have revived unpleasant memories and accentuated the sufferings of the house of Parmenion. It is remarkable that his arrival created no recorded sensation in Alexander's camp, although there was a dissident faction in the army, which disapproved of Parmenion's murder (D 17.80.4; J 12.5.4–8; C 7.2.35–8). If we make Asander Parmenion's brother, we create a historical situation that the sources must have suppressed, i.e., the reaction of Alexander's camp to Asander's arrival. What became of Asander son of Philotas is unknown.

Kaerst, *RE* s.v. "Asandros (2)"; Berve ii.87 no. 165; Bosworth i.130; Heckel 385.

Asander [2]. (Asandros). Son of Agathon, from Beroea,[141] he had some family relationship with Antigonus the One-Eyed (A*Succ* 25.1). Satrap of Caria in 323 (A*Succ* 1.6; Dexippus, *FGrH* 100 F8 §2; C 10.10.2; D 18.3.1; *SIG*³ 311.2–3; cf. *LM* 117).[142] According to the propaganda pamphlet on *The Last Days and Testament of Alexander*, Asander attended the dinner-party of Medius but was ignorant of the plot against Alexander (*LM* 97–8); awarded Caria in the forged *Testamentum Alexandri* (*LM* 117). In 321/0 he received Antigonus on his return from Europe, thus defecting from Perdiccas (A*Succ* 25.1), but nothing further is known of his actions in the First Diadoch War. He was confirmed in his satrapy at Triparadeisus in 320 BC (D 18.39.6; A*Succ* 1.37), and fared poorly in an indecisive battle with Alcetas and Attalus in winter 320/19 (A*Succ* 1.41; cf. Wheatley 1995: 437). Intimidated by the growing power of Antigonus, he joined Ptolemy in 315 (D 19.62.2), who sent Myrmidon with mercenaries to give him aid against Antigonus' nephew Polemaeus (19.62.5). He crossed to Athens, where he was honored in a decree of Thrasycles son of Nausicrates (*SIG*³ 320.12–13). Aided by Cassander, who sent his general Prepelaus back to Asia Minor with him (D 19.68.5), Asander attempted to overcome the Antigonid forces by sending Eupolemus against Polemaeus (winter 313/12). But Eupolemus was captured by Polemaeus, who fell on his camp unexpectedly (D 19.68.5–7).[143] Asander was thus forced to come to terms with Antigonus: he surrendered his troops to Antigonus, relinquished his claims to the Greek cities of Caria, and gave his brother Agathon as a hostage to his new overlord (D 19.75.1–2). But he quickly regretted the decision, secured the escape of his brother, and turned to Ptolemy and Seleucus for help (D 19.75.2). Antigonus now took Asander's territory by force, and since Asander is not heard of again, we may assume that he fled with Agathon and played no further attested role in the history of the Successors.

Kaerst, *RE* s.v. "Asandros (3)"; Berve ii.87 no. 164; Tataki 76 no. 16.

Asclepiades (Asklepiades). Son of Hipparchus. Allegedly the first to bring the news of Alexander the Great's death to the Athenians (P*Ph* 22.5–6).

Kirchner no. 2590; Berve ii.87 no. 166.

Asclepiodorus [1]. (Asklepiodoros). Son of Eunicus. Prominent Macedonian, apparently from Pella. Father of the Page Antipater (A 4.13.4; C 8.6.9 mistakenly speaks of "Antipater and Asclepiodorus"). Asclepiodorus first joined Alexander in 331, when he brought 500 Thracian cavalry to the King at Memphis. He was soon appointed satrap of Syria, probably replacing Menon son of Cerdimmas (A 3.6.8 speaks of "Arimmas"). In 329 he relinquished this position to bring 4,000 infantry and 500 cavalry to the King in Zaraspa (A 4.7.2; C 7.10.12). In early 327, Asclepiodorus' son Antipater became involved in the conspiracy of the Pages (A 4.13.4; cf. C 8.6.9). The disgrace does not appear to have affected Asclepiodorus too badly: he reappears as a trierarch of the Hydaspes fleet in 326 (A*Ind* 18.3).[144] What became of him we do not know. Identification with Antigonus' satrap of Persis in 316 (D 19.48.5) is unlikely. Cassander's *strategos* in 315 is perhaps identical with Asclepiodorus the *grammateus* who supported Adea-Eurydice at Triparadeisus (D 19.60.2; A*Succ* 1.33).

Kaerst, *RE* s.v. "Asklepiodoros (5)"; Berve ii.88 no. 167.

Asclepiodorus [2]. (Asklepiodoros). Son of Timander, a Macedonian from Pella, trierarch of the Hydaspes fleet in 326 (A*Ind* 18.3). His father may have been the hypaspist commander who fought at Halicarnassus (A 1.22.7), but the hypaspist commanders were generally men of lower rank and it would be unusual to find the son of a man of this grade appointed trierarch.[145]

Kaerst, *RE* s.v. "Asklepiodoros (7)"; Berve ii.88 no. 168; Jacoby, *FGrH* IIB, 681; iiD, 450.

Asclepiodorus [3]. (Asklepiodoros). Son of Philon (A 3.16.4), place of origin unknown. Possibly Macedonian; perhaps Greek. Asclepiodorus was left behind in Babylon in late 331 and placed in charge of collecting tribute (A 3.16.4). Billows 376 tentatively identifies him with the man whom Antigonus established as satrap of Persis (316/5 BC), in the face of Persian opposition, in place of the popular Peucestas (D 19.48.5). Asclepiodorus is otherwise unattested. What became of him after Seleucus' recovery of Babylonia is unknown.

Kaerst, *RE* s.v. "Asklepiodoros (6)"; Berve ii.88 no. 169; Billows 376 no. 20.

Asclepiodorus [4]. (Asklepiodoros). Macedonian; *grammateus*, hence probably secretary of the "Royal Army" that withdrew to Triparadeisus after the death of Perdiccas. In the turmoil that followed the resignation of the *epimeletai*, Peithon and Arrhidaeus, Asclepiodorus supported Eurydice, who incited the army against the newly appointed guardian, Antipater. In this she was aided also by Attalus son of Andromenes (*ASucc* 1.33). Asclepiodorus' fate is uncertain: if he reached an accommodation with Antipater, he may be the later general of Cassander (D 19.60.2: 315 BC); otherwise, since the rioting initiated by Adea place Antipater's very life in peril (cf. Pol*Strat* 4.6.4), he may have been executed, if he did not escape from the camp. Identification with the son of Timander (**Asclepiodorus** [2]) is possible.

See Berve ii.88–9 no. 170.

Assacenus (Assakenos). Indian dynast; leader of the Assacenians, whose kingdom centered on the area between the Panjkora (Guraeus) and Swat rivers. The Assacenians were identified with the Aspasians (cf. Lassen ii^2 145 n. 2; *CHIndia* i.316 n. 1), and Berve ii.89 assumes that the *hyparchos* of the Aspasians (**M25**), who opposed the Macedonians at a certain river (there is a lacuna in the text of A 4.24.1, and we know the name of neither the river nor the city referred to), is Assacenus (C 8.10.22 says that he had died shortly before Alexander's arrival at Massaga; hence he cannot have been the *hegemon* of the troops at Massaga, A 4.27.2, **M24**). But Arrian makes a distinction between the Aspasians (4.24.1), the Guraeans (4.25.7), and the Assacenians (4.25.5; 4.26), and it seems far from certain that the leader of the Aspasians, who was killed in hand-to-hand combat with

Ptolemy son of Lagus, was Assacenus (A 4.24.3–5). When Alexander attacked Massaga, the capital of the Assacenians (so C 8.10.22; Str 15.1.27 [698] (Masoga); A 4.26.1 calls it the greatest city of that region[146]), Assacenus was already dead, and the kingdom was governed by his mother Cleophis (C 8.10.22; *ME* 39, she was aided by his brother Amminais). Cleophis and her granddaughter (*ME* 39, 45, grandson: **M19**) were captured along with the city (A 4.27.4; C 8.10.33–5 is somewhat different, and the child is Cleophis' *own son*; cf. *ME* 39, 45). See further s.vv. **Cleophis**, **Amminais**, **Aphrices**; cf. **F40**.

Berve ii.89 no. 172; Eggermont 178, 183–5; cf. Tomaschek, *RE* s.v. "Assakenoi."

Assagetes (Ashvajit). A local chieftain of the Assacenians; probably the hyparch of a small region south of Aornus (Pir-sar) and along the west banks of the Indus River, as A 4.28.6 suggests. Together with Cophaeus, Assagetes accompanied Alexander to Aornus, though we know of no role that he played in the campaign (A 4.28.6). He is most likely to have been the hyparch of the Assacenians, whose assassination by his people was reported by Sisicottus to Alexander sometime after the battle of the Hydaspes (A 5.20.7).[147]

Berve ii.89 no. 171.

Astaspes. Prominent Persian, satrap of Carmania. Astaspes was probably satrap under Darius III and was confirmed by Alexander in 330; for the King did not visit the area until his return from India. In early 324 he was suspected of plotting rebellion and executed (C 9.10.21, 29).

Berve ii.89 no. 173; Badian 2000a: 90–1.

Astis (Astes). The name appears thus in the MSS. of Arrian; Astes (Berve no. 691) is the emendation of B. Vulcanius (1575); Sanskrit "Hasti" (Smith[3] 50); but Rapson, *CHIndia* i.318, suggests that the name "is short for Ashtakaraja, king of the Ashtakas," which is more likely, if Astis, like Taxiles and Assacenus, is a dynastic name. Hyparch of Peucelaotis (Peukolaitis, Str 15.1.27 [698], that is, the territory of Gandhara, of which Pushkalavati was the capital), ruler of the Astacenians; he resisted the Macedonian advance-party under the command of Hephaestion and Perdiccas and held out in an unnamed city (probably his own capital, Pushkalavati, modern Charsadda[148]) in his territory, which fell to the Macedonians after a siege of thirty days. Astis himself perished in the defense and his territory was handed over to Sangaeus (apparently a local noble), who had rebelled from his authority (A 4.22.8). Peucelaotis, upon formal surrender to Alexander, was garrisoned by Macedonians under the command of Philip [13] (A 4.28.6). Anspach (i.13; cf. Berve ii.90) supposes that Astis was originally among the hyparchs who submitted to Alexander along with Taxiles (A 4.22.6), but it appears that Taxiles was accompanied by Sangaeus, a rival of Astis, who sought, with Taxiles' aid, to win Macedonian backing for his cause. Hence Astis' opposition to the forces of Hephaestion and Perdiccas (cf. Brunt i.415 n. 7).

Berve ii.89–90 no. 174; Anspach i.13–14; Lassen ii[2] 135; Eggermont 1970: 68–75; Badian 1987: 117–28.

Astycratidas (Astykratidas). Prominent Spartan. Lived at the time of Agis III's death at Megalopolis in 331 (whether he participated in the battle is not clear). One saying of his is preserved by *PM* 219, expressing the Spartans' determination to die rather than be enslaved by Macedon.

Berve ii.90 no. 175; Poralla no. 168.

Astylus (Astylos). Arcadian *strategos*. The Thebans, unable to persuade the Arcadians to abandon their alliance with Alexander, hoped to gain their help by bribing Astylus,[149] who demanded ten talents. This money the Thebans did not have, and Dinarchus (1.20) claims that Demosthenes, who had the money from Persia, would not part with it (Din 1.20; cf. Aes 3.240 who mentions nine talents). Nothing else is known about Astylus.

Berve ii.90 no. 176; Schaefer iii[2] 133.

Atalante (Atalanta). Daughter of Orontes, Macedonian from Orestis; sister of Perdiccas. She married Attalus son of Andromenes in 323 and appears to have borne him two daughters (D 19.35.5; **F38–39**). She accompanied her brother on his expedition against Ptolemy in 321/0, only to be murdered along with him (D 18.37.2).

Kaerst, *RE* s.v. "Atalante (5)"; Berve ii.90 no. 177; Heckel 381–4. See Stemma XII.

Atarrhias (Tarrhias). Son of Deinomenes (P*M* 339b). The only commander of "regular hypaspists" (excluding the *archihypaspistes* Nicanor) whose patronymic is attested. Fought with distinction at Halicarnassus in 334 (C 8.1.36; cf. A 1.21.5), and later won the military contest in Sittacene which determined the chiliarchs and pentakosiarchs of the regular hypaspists (C 5.2.5). As the foremost hypaspist officer, after Neoptolemus, Atarrhias appears in charge of the "police" force that arrested Philotas at Phrada (C 6.8.19–22), and he took an active role in demanding the execution of Alexander Lyncestes (C 7.1.5). Nothing further is recorded about Atarrhias, except that he was heavily in debt by the end of the campaign and attempted to defraud the King (P*M* 339b: "Tarrhias"; cf. Ael*VH* 14.47a: Alexander regarded him as undisciplined). Identification with the homonymous officer of Cassander, who appears in 317 BC (D 19.36.2), is possible but cannot be substantiated.

Berve ii.90–1 no. 178; Heckel 304; Hoffmann 203–4.

Athenagoras (Athanagoras). Family background unknown; Chian. Gained control of Chios, after the Persian counter-revolution in 334/3, along with Apollonides and other oligarchs supported by Memnon (C 4.5.15). Captured by Hegelochus (C 4.5.17); taken to Alexander in Egypt (cf. A 3.2.5–7, who mentions only Apollonides, Phesinus, and Megareus) and, presumably, sent to Elephantine. Cf. *SIG*[3] 283.

Berve ii.13–14 no. 26; Hofstetter 35 no. 60a.

Athenodorus [1]. (Athenodoros). Athenian, nicknamed "Imbrios," perhaps because he came from a cleruch family on Imbros (Berve ii.14). Mercenary leader (Aen Tact 24.10; Dem 23.12; *Suda* A 734 calls him *stratiotes*). He entered the service of Darius III and was captured at Sardis in 334, but released from prison through the efforts of Phocion (P*Ph* 18.6; Ael*VH* 1.25).[150]

Judeich, *RE* s.v. "Athenodoros (2)"; Berve ii.14 no. 27; Kirchner no. 280; Hofstetter 35–6 no. 61; Olmstead 421.

Athenodorus [2]. (Athenodoros). Native of Teos, harpist. According to Chares of Mytilene, in the tenth book of his *History of Alexander*, Athenodorus (along with Cratinus of Methymna and Aristonymus of Athens) entertained at the mass-wedding ceremony in Susa in 324 BC (Chares, *FGrH* 125 F4 = Ath 12.538e–f). Nothing else is known about him.

Kaerst, *RE* s.v. "Athenodoros (10)"; Berve ii.14 no. 28.

Athenodorus [3]. (Athenodoros). A Greek mercenary (perhaps an officer) of unknown origin, Athenodorus had been left with the garrison at Bactra in 327/6. In 325, when it was rumored that Alexander had died in India, he led his fellow-mercenaries in seizing the citadel of Bactra, putting to death those of his comrades who did not support him (C 9.7.1–2). Although he took the title of King, his chief aim was to lead the Greeks back to the coast (C 9.7.3), a plan which was preempted by the treachery of Biton and Boxus, who murdered him at a banquet, alleging that he had plotted against Biton's life (C 9.7.4–5).

Kaerst, *RE* s.v. "Athenodoros (11)"; Berve ii.14 no. 29.

Athenodorus [4]. (Athenodoros). A tragic actor of unknown origin, Athenodorus was a victor at the Dionysia in 342 (also a Lenaean victor in that year?) and 329 (O'Connor 73–4). He appears to have been among the prominent artists who joined Alexander in Egypt in 332/1 (A 3.1.4; cf. Bosworth i.262); he performed at Tyre (331), with Pasicrates of Soli acting as *choregos*, and was victorious over Thessalus, whom Nicocreon of Salamis supported and Alexander himself favored (P*A* 29.3–4; P*M* 334e). Soon afterwards he returned to the Greek mainland, as his Dionysiac victory of 329 BC shows. At some point, however, Athenodorus was fined by the Athenians for failing to appear at the festival, and he asked Alexander to intercede in writing on his behalf; the King instead paid his fine (P*A* 29.5). In 324 BC Athenodorus reappears at the Susan wedding festival, along with Aristocritus and Thessalus (Chares, *FGrH* 125 F4 = Ath 12.538f).

Kaerst, *RE* s.v. "Athenodoros (9)"; Berve ii.14–15 no. 30; Hamilton 76; O'Connor no. 13.

Athenophanes. Athenian of unknown family. Athenophanes attended Alexander when he bathed (P*A* 35.5). The only story told of him, that he smeared naphtha on the face of a homely youth named Stephanus and nearly killed him when it ignited (P*A* 35.5–9), smacks of sadism. Str 16.1.15 [743] attributes this act of cruelty to Alexander himself.

Berve ii.15 no. 31; Kirchner no. 285.

Atizyes (also Atixyes). Prominent Persian; satrap of Phrygia in 334 (A 1.25.3; it was to Atizyes that Sisines claimed to be going when he carried the letter from Darius to Alexander Lyncestes). Baumbach 56 n. 1 rejects the suggestion of Buchholz (58), that Atizyes became satrap of Phrygia only after the death of Spithridates, who administered Lydia, Ionia, and Phrygia. Although he is not named in the war-council at Zeleia or in actual description of the battle at the Granicus (D 17.21.3 wrongly says he died in that battle), A 2.11.8 is undoubtedly correct in naming him as one of the cavalry leaders (presumably of the Phrygian contingent) in that battle.[151] After the battle, he appears to have returned to Phrygia, whence he fled at Alexander's approach, leaving in Celaenae a garrison of 1,000 Carians and 100 Greek mercenaries (A 1.29.1; cf. C 3.1.6–8). He himself joined Darius to fight again at Issus, where he perished (A 2.11.8; C 3.11.10; D 17.34.5). His successor in Phrygia was Antigonus son of Philip (A 1.29.3).

Berve ii.91 no. 179; Krumbholz 71; Baumbach 56; Beloch iii^2 2.153; Bosworth i.111, 216; Atkinson i.231.

Atropates (Atropatos). Satrap of the Medes, whom he commanded at Gaugamela in 331 (A 3.8.4). He appears to have submitted to Alexander, perhaps after the death of Darius, by which time Alexander had already appointed Oxydates to his satrapy (A 3.20.3). Atropates must have remained with Alexander, for in winter 328/7 he was sent from Nautaca to remove Oxydates and administer Media (A 4.18.3; cf. C 8.3.17, wrongly calling him Arsaces). He rejoined Alexander in early 324 at Parsagadae, bringing Baryaxes and some other rebels (perhaps supporters of Oxydates) to Alexander for punishment (A 6.29.3). From Susa he was sent back to his satrapy (A 7.4.1), a clear indication that the King was satisfied with his performance. At Susa, Perdiccas son of Orontes married his (unnamed) daughter (A 7.4.5; cf. J 13.4.13, Atropatos). When Alexander arrived in Ecbatana in October 324, Atropates appears to have presented him with 100 women on horseback, dressed as Amazons (A 7.13.2, 6), something which may have contributed to the later fiction concerning Alexander's encounter with the Amazon queen (see s.v. **Thalestris**). He was confirmed as satrap of Lesser Media in 323 (J 13.4.13; D 18.3.3), which may mean that he was originally satrap of Media but restricted to Lesser Media in 323. But Atropates appears to have made himself independent of the

Macedonians and to have taken the title of king (Str 11.13.1 [523]), perhaps at some point soon after Gabiene and the removal of Peithon from Greater Media.[152] The area was known as Media Atropatene (StByz s.v. "Atropatia"; Str 11.13.1).

Kaerst, *RE* s.v.; Berve ii.91–2 no. 180. See Stemma XII.

Attalus [1]. (Attalos). Prominent Macedonian, patronymic unknown. Attalus was born ca. 390 BC. Uncle of Hippostratus (Satyrus *ap.* Ath 13.557d), and thus apparently the brother of Amyntas (Marsyas of Pella, *FGrH* 135/6 F17); both had died by the late summer or autumn of 337, when Philip II married Attalus' niece and ward, Cleopatra.[153] Nothing is known of his career until late summer 337, by which time he was an influential man at the court (D 16.93.7). Attalus' prayer at the wedding feast, that Cleopatra might produce legitimate heirs to the Macedonian throne,[154] was both tactless and fatal: Alexander never forgave him and considered him a threat to his life (C 8.8.7; cf. 6.9.17).

According to the popular account, Attalus was a friend of the younger Pausanias, who had confided to him the details of the insults uttered by Pausanias of Orestis and his own plans for a glorious death (D 16.93.5). The latter occurred in a battle with the Illyrians of King Pleurias, probably in early 336. Soon thereafter Attalus avenged his friend's death by plying Pausanias of Orestis with wine at a dinner-party and handing him over to his muleteers to be sexually abused.[155] By this time, Attalus had been designated general of the advance force that was to cross into Asia (D 16.93.8–9); for this reason, and because of their relationship (cf. 16.93.8), Philip was unwilling to reprimand Attalus for his crime against Pausanias, who in turn vented his rage on the King.

Attalus had crossed the Hellespont at the beginning of spring 336 (J 9.5.8; cf. D 16.91.2), sharing the command with Parmenion (D 17.2.4; cf. J 9.5.8–9), whose daughter he had married.[156] Their force of 10,000 advanced as far as Magnesia-on-the-Maeander, where they were defeated by Memnon the Rhodian, and thus forced to seek refuge in the city (Pol*Strat* 5.44.4). On the news of Philip's death, Attalus plotted rebellion,[157] trusting in his popularity with the troops and communicating with the anti-Macedonian party in Athens.[158] Whether he was in fact guilty is a moot point, since Alexander may have used these charges to justify his murder.[159] Judeich's suggestion (304–5), that the Macedonian retreat from Magnesia to the Hellespont can be explained by Attalus' rebellion against Alexander, is unlikely. Hecataeus was sent to secure his execution (D 17.2.5–6), which he could not have brought about without Parmenion's complicity (D 17.5.2; C 7.1.3; see also C 8.1.42; cf. 8.1.52; and 8.7.4; J 12.6.14). J's claim (11.5.1) that Alexander, before his departure for Asia, killed all Cleopatra's relatives is a rhetorical exaggeration: only Attalus is meant.

Kaerst, *RE* s.v. "Attalos (4)"; Berve ii.94 no. 182; Bosworth 1971a: 102ff.; Heckel 4–5; Judeich 302, 304–5; Schachermeyr 97. See Stemma XIV.

Attalus [2]. (Attalos). Macedonian, commander of the Agrianes at Issus (A 2.9.2) and, perhaps, since at least the beginning of the Asiatic campaign. At Gaugamela, as at Issus, he was positioned on the right wing, this time with half the Agrianes and adjacent to Cleitus' *ile basilike* (A 3.12.2; cf. C 4.13.31). When Alexander rushed ahead in pursuit of Bessus, who had by this time arrested Darius III, he ordered Attalus and the Agrianes, as well as the hypaspists under Nicanor, to follow as lightly equipped as possible; the rest of the infantry were to continue at their normal pace (A 3.21.8). This is our last reference to Attalus, although he may have retained his command until at least the end of the expedition. Certainly there is no record of his replacement by another officer.

Kaerst, *RE* s.v. "Attalos (6)"; Berve ii.94–5 no. 183; Heckel 332–3.

Attalus [3]. (Attalos). Macedonian from Tymphaea. Son of Andromenes. A Royal Hypaspist (*somatophylax*) of Philip II in 336 (D 16.94.4), Attalus had undoubtedly been one of that King's Pages and perhaps a *syntrophos* of Alexander. Hence a birthdate ca. 356 is consistent with the evidence for Attalus' career before and after Alexander's reign. Between 336 and 330 BC he was overshadowed by his brother Amyntas, but two years after the family's brief disgrace at Phrada, Attalus is found in command of Amyntas' *taxis* (A 4.16.1): in 328 in Bactria, he appears with Craterus, Gorgias, Polyperchon, and Meleager (A 4.16.1) and, in the following spring, he campaigned in Sogdiana with Craterus, Polyperchon, and Alcetas (A 4.22.1; cf. P*A* 55.6). During the Swat campaign, Attalus and his battalion served with Coenus, against the Aspasians (A 4.24.1), and Alcetas, in the siege of Ora (A 4.27.5). At the Hydaspes (Jhelum) River, he was stationed with the *taxeis* of Gorgias and Meleager halfway between the main camp and Alexander's crossing-point (A 5.12.1). In 325 BC he accompanied Craterus, Meleager, Antigenes, and (possibly) Polyperchon westward to Carmania via Arachosia and Drangiana (A 6.17.3).

In the eastern satrapies, Attalus had served with Alcetas (A 4.27.5), the brother of Perdiccas, on two attested missions, but more often he is associated with the more conservative leaders of the phalanx.[160] Hence it is not surprising to find him closely linked with Meleager in the days that followed Alexander's death. Coenus had died at the Hydaspes in 326; Craterus and Polyperchon were in Cilicia, bound for Macedonia. That left Attalus and Meleager as natural allies, and the spokesmen of the infantry (cf. J 13.3.2, 7–8). But their joint opposition to the *principes* in Babylon came to naught and Attalus was easily induced to abandon his colleague by the prospect of marriage to Perdiccas' sister Atalante (D 18.37.2; Heckel 381–4). This new alliance isolated Meleager, who, despite his appointment as Perdiccas' *hyparchos*, fell victim to the purge that followed the reconciliation of cavalry and infantry.

In winter 321/0, Attalus and Polemon failed in their attempt to recover Alexander's funeral carriage, which had been diverted at Damascus by Arrhidaeus and redirected to Egypt (A*Succ* 24.1; cf. 1.25, naming Polemon alone). Thereafter, he rejoined Perdiccas in Cilicia, who entrusted Attalus with a fleet, which skirted the coast of Phoenicia and secured the Pelousiac mouth of the Nile. There Attalus remained, guarding the entrance to the Delta against the naval forces of Antigonus and Antipater. It was here in May 320 that he learned of Perdiccas' assassination and the murder of Atalante by the raging army (D 18.37.3). From Pelusium, he took the fleet to Tyre, where the Macedonian garrison-commander Archelaus received him into the city and handed back 800 talents, which Perdiccas deposited there for safe-keeping. There too Attalus received those troops who had remained loyal to the Perdiccan cause and had fled from the army near Memphis (D 18.37.3–4). There were further defections at Triparadeisus, where Attalus appeared in person (A*Succ* 1.33, 39) to incite the army, which now rejected the leadership of Peithon and Arrhidaeus (cf. Errington 1970: 67 n. 131; Briant 1973: 278 n. 6; Billows 68). Attalus thus set sail for Caria with a force of 10,000 infantry and 800 cavalry, intending to attack Cnidus, Caunus, and Rhodes (A*Succ* 1.39).[161] Attalus soon rejoined that portion of the Perdiccan army under Alcetas, which had only recently separated from Eumenes in Phrygia (cf. P*Eum* 8.8). Reunited, Alcetas and Attalus successfully repulsed an attack from the Carian satrap Asander, who acted on Antipater's orders (A*Succ* 1.41). Nevertheless, they now withdrew into Pisidia, where in the following year they were defeated near Cretopolis by Antigonus (D 18.44–5; 18.50.1).[162] Attalus was captured, together with Polemon, Docimus, and two otherwise unattested commanders named Antipater and Philotas (D 18.45.3; 19.16.1). They were imprisoned in a secure fortress which, although unnamed, appears to have been in Greater Phrygia;[163] for Stratonice, Antigonus' wife, who resided in Celaenae, was said to have been nearby (D 19.16.4). In 317, the captives overpowered their guards and planned to escape, but Attalus' health was failing (D 19.16.3) and the Antigonid forces from neighboring garrisons arrived quickly to lay siege to the place. Docimus, who had planned the whole affair, escaped by a secret route and betrayed his former comrades. The fortress was recaptured after a siege of one year and four months (D 19.16.5). If Attalus did not die during the siege, he was almost certainly killed afterwards. The "daughters of Attalus" captured at Pydna with Olympias (**F38–39**) were apparently his and Atalante's.

Kaerst, *RE* s.v. "Attalos (5)"; Berve ii.92–3 no. 181; Schubert 1901: 467–8; Simpson 1957: 504–5; Schachermeyr 1970: 125; Heckel 180–3. See Stemma XII.

Attalus [4]. (Attalos). If not a literary fiction, Attalus was a Macedonian of unknown origin. Born probably in the mid-350s, he resembled Alexander and impersonated him at the Hydaspes River in order to divert Porus and his troops from the fact that the real Alexander had marched upriver to attempt another crossing (C 8.13.21; *ME* 58). Two points appear to rule out identification with the son of Andromenes (as suggested by Berve ii.93): the latter was stationed upstream from Alexander's camp during the manoeuvres against Porus (A 5.12.1) and the vulgate calls him *Attalus quidam* (*ME* 58), which suggests an otherwise unknown figure rather than a prominent *taxiarch*. The name Attalus is, furthermore, far too common to allow automatic identification with a well-known figure. Nothing else is known about him.

Heckel 1978d: 378 n. 8.

Attinas. Macedonian (Hoffmann 194) of unknown family background, Attinas had been appointed *phrourarchos* of an unnamed fort in Bactria (probably in 329/8 BC). This place was attacked by Spitamenes and a force of Massagetae, who lured Attinas and his 300 cavalrymen into an ambush and slaughtered them (C 8.1.3–5). The details of the incident as described by A 4.16.4–5 are somewhat different and the name of the *phrourarchos* is not given, but there can be little doubt that we are dealing with the same person. C 8.1.5 says Attinas was killed in the engagement; A 4.16.5 has him taken prisoner, in which case Attinas was probably executed afterwards.[164]

Berve ii.95 no. 185; Hoffmann 194; Bosworth ii.114–16.

Audata. Daughter of an Illyrian chieftain (Ath 13.557c), presumably Bardylis, whom Philip II defeated in 359/8 (D 16.4.3–7). First or possibly second wife of Philip II, Audata must have sealed the "glorious peace" that he had forged with the Illyrians (D 16.8.1). The fact that her name was changed to Eurydice (A*Succ* 1.22) may have some dynastic significance: for a brief period, she was Philip's "official" queen. Philip's mother, Eurydice, was herself partially Illyrian (see s.v. **Eurydice** [1]), and Carney suggests that Audata may have been related to her. The mother of Cynnane, Audata was the grandmother of Adea, who also took the name Eurydice (A*Succ* 1.22–3; Heckel 1983). The assignment of the name Eurydice to Cleopatra, the niece of Attalus, in 337/6 may suggest that Audata was no longer alive or at the court at that time, but Alexander will certainly have encountered her in Pella as a child.

Kaerst, *RE* s.v.; Heckel 1983; Carney 57–8; Ogden 22–4. See Stemma I.

Austanes (Haustanes; for the name see Justi 52). A local dynast in Paraetacene (Sogdiana) who supported the uprising of Spitamenes in 329; in 327 he and Catanes were arrested by Craterus who brought them to Alexander, who presumably executed them (C 8.5.2; A 4.22.1).

Berve ii.95 no. 186.

Autobares (Aigobares; Wata-para). Prominent Persian, brother of Mithrobaeus: their father is not named. Both were enrolled in the *agema* of the cavalry at Susa in 324 (A 7.6.5).

Berve ii.15 no. 32 ("Aigobares").

Autodicus (Autodikos; Autolycus; Autolykos). Brother of Lysimachus, and thus also of Philip and Alcimachus. Apparently the youngest of the sons of Agathocles, Autodicus was born in the early to mid-340s and appointed one of the four Somatophylakes of Philip III Arrhidaeus at Triparadeisus (A*Succ* 1.38). He appears later in an inscription as the husband of a certain Adeia (*SIG*^{3} 373).

Wilcken, *RE* s.v. "Autolykos (7)"; Berve ii.95 no. 187; Beloch iv^2 2.130; Heckel 282. See Stemma IX.

Autophradates [1]. (Wata-fradata). A Persian of unknown family background; possibly a relative of that Autophradates who participated in the Satraps' Revolt of the 360s (D 15.90.3; Pol*Strat* 7.27; cf. Weiskopf 1989: 38ff.). Commanded the Persian fleet in the Aegean in 333, under the supreme command of Memnon (cf. A 2.1.3); perhaps he was active in 337/6 against the pro-Macedonian party at Ephesus (Pol*Strat* 7.27.2). Together with Memnon's successor, Pharnabazus, Autophradates conducted the siege of Mytilene, which was later taken and occupied (A 2.1.3–5). While Pharnabazus turned his attention to Lycia, Autophradates campaigned in the islands, but the Persians soon despatched Datames to deal with the Cyclades, and Autophradates joined Pharnabazus in bringing Tenedos back under Persian domination (A 2.2.1–3), garrisoning Chios (cf. A 3.2.3–5) and attacking Siphnos (A 2.13.4). His dealings with Agis – ten triremes and thirty talents (A 2.13.4–6). But after Alexander's victory at Issus and his advance into Syria and Phoenicia, Autophradates' fleet began to disintegrate (A 2.20.1, 6: defection of Phoenicians). Berve ii.96 suggests that Autophradates may have gone with his remaining ships to Crete, to which island Alexander soon sent Amphoterus (A 3.6.3). The *hetaira* Antigone, who was captured by Autophradates (see s.v. **Antigone**) near Samothrace, was probably taken in the period immediately before Alexander's crossing into Asia (P*M* 339e); but see Berve ii.96 n. 3 for a plausible scenario in 334.

Kaerst, *RE* s.v. "Autophradates (1)"; Berve ii.96 no. 188; Baumbach 29ff., 50ff.; Weiskopf 1989.

Autophradates [2]. (Wata-fradata; C "Phradates"). Persian. Darius III's satrap of the Tapurians who dwelt near the Caspian Sea (A 3.23.7); he led the Caspian contingent at Gaugamela, positioned on the right wing (C 4.12.9). Berve ii.96 conjectures that Autophradates served under Phrataphernes; but Phradates could as easily be an error for Phrataphernes. Curtius' account is extremely confused. At 4.12.7 he speaks of the Persians, Mardians, and Sogdiani. The last are probably the Susiani (for the confusion of Sogdiana and Susiana cf. Dexippus, *FGrH* 100 F8). The Mardians ought to have been brigaded with the Tapurians, and the Caspians are perhaps the Hyrcanians subject to Phrataphernes: Arrian (3.8.4, 11.4) mentions Topeiri, Hyrcanians, and Parthians under his command. In 330, Autophradates surrendered voluntarily to Alexander in 330 (A 3.23.7); C 6.4.23–4 says he was brought to Alexander by Craterus and Erigyius (cf. A 3.23.2 for Craterus' and Erigyius' activities in the area). Alexander allowed him to keep his satrapy (A 3.23.7; C 6.4.25), which was soon enlarged to include the Mardians or Amardians (A 3.24.3; C 6.5.21). But in 329/8 he was arrested and replaced by Phrataphernes, whose satrapy was thus enlarged (A 4.18.2; C 8.3.17). On his return from India in 325/4, Alexander had Autophradates executed, allegedly for aspiring to the kingship (C 10.1.39).

Kaerst, *RE* s.v. "Autophradates (2)"; Berve ii.96–7 no. 189; Julien 36–7; Badian 2000a: 91–2.

Azemilcus (Azemilkos). For the name see Fleming 55 (Abdimilkutti in Assyrian inscriptions). Ruler of Tyre. Born before 370, since his son (**M39**) was in 333/2 old enough to rule in his absence while Azemilcus served with the Persian fleet of Autophradates (A 2.15.7). But Berve rightly suggests that the siege of Tyre will have summoned him back to Phoenicia before the general defection of Phoenician and Cypriot commanders (A 2.20.1–3). When the city was captured Azemilcus and many other prominent Tyrians fled to the temple of Melqart. Although he was pardoned (A 2.24.5), he appears to have been deposed (but see Grainger 1991: 36–8, 59).

Kaerst, *RE* s.v. "Azemilkos"; Rawlinson 1889: 513; Berve ii.13 no. 25.

B

Baeton (Baiton). Bematist (Ath 10.442b; Pl*NH* 6.61). Baeton's work appears to have been entitled *Asiatic Stages* (so Str 15.2.8 [723]) or *The Stages of Alexander's Journey* (Ath 10.442b). Eight fragments of his work survive, but nothing is known about his origins or his life beyond the fact that he accompanied Alexander and wrote the *Stages* (*Stathmoi*).

Schwartz, *RE* s.v. "Baiton"; Berve ii.99–100 no. 198; Jacoby, *FGrH* IIB, 119; on the bematists in general see Pearson 261.

Bagisthanes (Bagistanes). A Babylonian noble (A 3.21.1; but Ps-Call 2.19.7 calls him a eunuch), in 330, at the time of Alexander's pursuit of Darius, Bagisthanes fled from the Persian camp, which was not far from Alexander's (cf. A 3.21.3), together with Antibelus son of Mazaeus (Brochubelus, C 5.13.2: at Tabae, in the remotest part of Paraetacene) and reported Darius' arrest at the hands of Bessus and Nabarzanes (A 3.21.1; but C 5.13.3 claims that the king had not yet been harmed but was in danger of being murdered or put in chains). Nothing else is known about him.

Kaerst, *RE* s.v.; Berve ii.98 no. 193; Justi 59.

Bagoas [1]. (Bagoses, Jos*AJ* 11.300–1). Eunuch, apparently of Egyptian origin (Ael*VH* 6.8; *Suda* Λ 3), who rose to be the most powerful of Artaxerxes III's courtiers (D 16.47.3, 50.8). Despite his physical condition he was a man of great daring (D 16.47.4; 17.5.3) and acted as a military commander (cf. Jos*AJ* 11.300: *strategos*), at Sidon and in Egypt (350/49 BC) where he cooperated with Mentor the Rhodian (D 16.47.4, 49.4–6, 50.1–7). Having administered the Upper Satrapies (D 16.50.8; cf. Briant 746), he became chiliarch of Artaxerxes III (Ochus) and engineered that king's death, as well as that of his successor Arses (D 17.5.3–4; Str 15.3.24 [736]; for his role as king-maker see also P*M* 337e).[165] Bagoas was alleged to have hated Ochus because he killed the Apis calf; hence he had Artaxerxes' body dismembered and eaten, and made knife-handles out of his thigh-bones (Ael*VH* 6.8; cf. *Suda* Λ 3). Alexander was later to charge Darius with seizing the throne illegally from Arses through the agency of Bagoas (A 2.14.5; cf. C 6.3.12, 4.10; D 17.5.5; Grayson 1975: 24–37). Bagoas was, however, forced to drink his own poison when he plotted against Darius (D 17.5.6). The garden of Bagoas in Babylon and the house in Susa, which Alexander gave to Parmenion, may have been his (Pl*NH* 13.41; Theophr*HP* 2.6.7; P*A* 39.10). The name Bagoas became synonymous with eunuchs (Pl*NH* 13.41; *Judith* 12:11; Ovid, *Amores* 2.2.1), a type unworthy of respect or artistic representation (Quint 5.12.21).

Cauer, *RE* s.v. "Bagoas (1)"; Briant 769–80.

Bagoas [2a]. Prominent Persian, perhaps from Lycia (for Persians in Lycia see Goukowsky 220; Mosley 1971), son of Pharnuches. Bagoas is attested once, as a trierarch of the Hydaspes fleet in 326 BC (A*Ind* 18.8). Berve ii.98 rules out identification with the eunuch of the same name, but the possibility is not as remote as many would suggest.[166]

Berve ii.98 no. 194.

Bagoas [2b]. A good-looking eunuch of Darius III, with whom he had been sexually intimate, Bagoas surrendered to Alexander after the Great King's death in 330, along with Nabarzanes the regicide, whose life he saved through his persuasive charms (C 6.5.23). Bagoas soon became a favorite and a flatterer of Alexander (Ath 13.603b; P*M* 65d). Dicaearchus (*ap.* Ath 13.603a–b) claims that Alexander too became infatuated with the youth and, in Pura, the Gedrosian capital, he was overcome by Bagoas' performance and fondled and kissed him in the theater to the shouts and applause of the audience (P*A* 67.7–8; cf. C 10.1.26, for the charge that Alexander was intimate with Bagoas). C 10.1.22–38, 42 claims that Bagoas engineered the destruction of Orxines (Orsines), descended from the Seven, because he would not pay court to "one of Alexander's whores" (that is, to Bagoas), alleging that Orxines had plundered the tomb of Cyrus the Great at Parsagadae.[167]

Cauer, *RE* s.v. "Bagoas (2)"; Berve ii.98–9 no. 195; Justi 60 nos. 3–4; Badian 1958.

Bagodaras (Cobares, Gobares). For the name see Justi 60 (cf. Briant 740 for the rarity of Medes in the Alexander historians). A Mede – possibly a magus (C 7.4.8) – who remained with Bessus after he usurped the kingship (330/29). At a banquet, he advised Bessus to surrender to Alexander and seek his mercy, but Bessus became angry with Bagodaras, who escaped from the camp and joined Alexander. His favorable reception induced others to follow his example and contributed to the downfall of Bessus (C 7.4.8–19; D 17.83.7–8).

Kaerst, *RE* s.v.; Berve ii.99 no. 196.

Bagophanes. Commander of the Persian garrison and the treasures at Babylon in 330 BC; hence possibly a eunuch. Bagophanes surrendered to Alexander on his arrival (C 5.1.20), apparently induced by the actions of Mazaeus, who had taken refuge in the city (C 5.1.17–20), and welcomed the Macedonian King with pomp and circumstance (cf. 5.1.20–3). Despite Bagophanes' gesture of good faith, Alexander appointed Agathon (D 17.64.5; cf. A 3.16.4 for different arrangements and no mention of Agathon) commander of the Babylonian citadel and kept Bagophanes in his entourage (C 5.1.43–4). What became of him, we do not know.

Kaerst, *RE* s.v.; Berve ii.99 no. 197; Justi 60.

Balacrus [1]. (Balakros). Prominent Macedonian, son of Amyntas (A 1.29.3; 3.5.5). He appears to have accompanied Alexander's expedition from the beginning, and replaced Antigonus the One-Eyed at Celaenae (spring 333 BC) as commander (*strategos*) of the allied infantry (A 1.29.3), in which capacity he fought at Issus, Tyre, and Gaza. Early in 331, Balacrus was left, along with Peucestas son of Macartatus, as *strategos* of the army in Egypt (A 3.5.5); the command of the allied infantry was transferred to Coeranus (A 3.5.6, perhaps Caranus?). Nothing further is known about him.

Kaerst, *RE* s.v. "Balakros (2)"; Berve ii.100 no. 199; Heckel 335; Hoffmann 176 n. 82.

Balacrus [2]. (Balakros, Balagros).[168] Son of Nicanor (A 2.12.2; D 18.22.1), also father of another Nicanor (*Suda* N 376, Harp), possibly the later governor of Alexandria in Parapamisadae (A 4.22.5; Berve ii.275–6 no. 556; though Bosworth 1994 identifies him tentatively with Cassander's lieutenant in Piraeus), and possibly of Philip (Berve ii.383–4 no. 778; C 4.13.28; D 17.57.3). Born, in all likelihood, in the 380s, he appears to have been politically allied with Antipater, whose daughter he married (Antonius Diogenes *ap.* Phot*Bibl* 166,

p. 111a–b), perhaps just before the Asiatic campaign. Antipater son of Balagros (Balacrus) who appears in the Delian inscriptions, *IG* xi.2.287b, 57; and 161, 85, was probably their son (Heckel 1987a: 161–2; cf. Badian 1988). Balacrus had apparently been a Somatophylax of Philip II, unless he was appointed at the time of Alexander's accession, and served Alexander in that capacity until shortly after the battle of Issus, when he was named satrap of Cilicia (A 2.12.2; cf. D 18.22.1). He is almost certainly the Balacrus of C 4.5.13 (not Berve's no. 203), who in 332 joined with Antigonus (satrap of Phrygia) and Calas (Hellespontine Phrygia) in completing the conquest of Asia Minor (Schachermeyr 212; cf. also Briant 70; Bosworth i.219; Bosworth 1974: 58–9; and Billows 44–5; I see no reason to assume that Balacrus was killed in this campaign). As satrap he also controlled finances and minted coins bearing at first his own name, later merely the letter B (Aulock); perhaps, as Bosworth (1988a: 232) suggests, he was "primarily responsible for the payment of the army during the long siege of Tyre" (hence also the reference to Tyre in Antonius Diogenes *ap.* Phot*Bibl* p. 111a–b). Late in Alexander's reign – shortly before Harpalus' arrival at Tarsus – Balacrus was killed in an attempt to quell an insurrection by the Isaurians and Larandians (D 18.22.1; for this view, cf. Higgins 1980: 150; Bosworth i.219 argues for an earlier date, perhaps "associated with Antigonus' campaigns in Lycaonia during 332 (C 4.5.13)").

Kaerst, *RE* s.v. "Balakros (1)"; Aulock 1964; Badian 1988; Baumbach 45, 65, 69; Berve ii.100–1 no. 200, and ii.101–2 no. 203; Heckel 260–1. See Stemma V.

Balacrus [3]. (Balakros). A Macedonian of unknown family origin, Balacrus commanded the javelin-men, perhaps since the beginning of the expedition. At Gaugamela, these were stationed on the right, where they effectively negated the threat of the Persian scythe-chariots (A 3.12.3, 13.5; Marsden 1964: 66–7 estimates that Balacrus' men numbered about 1,000). This same Balacrus is undoubtedly the commander of *psiloi* who campaigned against the Scythians north of the Iaxartes (Syr-Darya) in 329 (A 4.4.6) and amongst the Aspasians in 327/6. On the latter occasion, his troops, along with Attalus' battalion of *pezhetairoi*, belonged to Leonnatus' third of the army (A 4.24.10). Balacrus led a detachment of men to reconnoiter Aornus and discovered that the Indians there had fled from the rock (C 8.11.22). Thereafter he is not heard of again. It is highly doubtful that he is identical with the Balacrus who defeated Hydarnes and recaptured Miletus (C 4.5.13); that man was probably the son of Nicanor, a former Somatophylax and satrap of Cilicia.

Kaerst, *RE* s.v. "Balakros (3)"; Berve ii.101 nos. 201 and 202; Bosworth 1973: 252–3; Heckel 332.

Barsaentes (Barzaentes). A noble Persian. Satrap of Arachosia (and Drangiana, A 3.21.1; cf. C 6.6.36) under Darius III, Barsaentes commanded his regional troops and the so-called "Mountain" Indians at Gaugamela (A 3.8.4; located on the left wing, 3.11.3). After this battle, he fled with Darius toward the Upper Satrapies and soon joined Bessus and Nabarzanes in arresting the King (A 3.21.1; cf. J 11.15.1) and later putting him to death (A 3.25.8; C 6.6.36; D 17.74.1). In 329, Barsaentes fled to his own satrapy. On the approach of the Macedonians and the appointment of Menon, with a force of 4,600, he took refuge with the dynast of the neighboring Indians, Samaxus (Sambus; see Eggermont 18–19; cf. Vogelsang 1985: 78), who harbored the regicide until 326 but then turned him over to Alexander (C 8.13.3–4; A 3.25.8, anticipating events some three years later; cf. also *ME* 3, where Ariobarzanes should be corrected to Barsaentes), presumably to win the King's favor. Alexander had Barsaentes executed (A 3.25.8).

Kaerst, *RE* s.v.; Berve ii.102 no. 205; Vogelsang 1985.

Barsine. Daughter of Artabazus (P*Eum* 1.7)[169] and a Rhodian woman, the sister of Mentor and Memnon (D 16.52.4; Dem 23.154, 157). Barsine was one of twenty-one children (eleven brothers, including Pharnabazus, Ariobarzanes, Arsames, Cophen, and, possibly, Ilioneus; nine sisters, of whom we know only the names of Artonis and Artacama or Apame). Barsine's birthdate depends on when she married Mentor, assuming that she married him at puberty or soon afterwards. She was still with her parents when they fled to Macedonia (between 352 and 344/3). On the other hand, she needed enough time to bear Mentor three children, if all three daughters mentioned by C 3.13.14 (**F14–16**) are in fact Barsine's. Mentor is last heard of in 342/1 and was certainly dead by 336. She was married to Memnon thereafter, and conceived a son no later than 334 (Memnon died in the spring of 333, and Barsine was captured along with her son at the end of 333). Barsine received a Greek education (P*A* 21.9), perhaps in connection with the family's stay in Macedonia (D 16.52.3–4), where she may have met Alexander for the first time. She was married first to her uncle Mentor, whom she may have borne three daughters (C 3.13.14); but only one of these daughters of Mentor, Nearchus' bride at Susa in 324 BC, can be identified with certainty as Barsine's child (A 7.4.6). After Mentor's death she married Memnon, by whom she had a son, born no later than 334 (C 3.13.14); these were sent to Darius as hostages before the battle of Issus (D 17.23.5–6), left at Damascus with the other women and children of noble Persians (A 2.11.9; D 17.32.3; cf. C 3.8.12), and captured in late 333 by Parmenion (C 3.13.14; J 11.10.2; cf. A 2.11.10). Thus she came to the attention of Alexander, who was captivated by her beauty (J 11.10.2–3); she was reputedly the only woman with whom Alexander had consorted before his marriage to Rhoxane (P*A* 21.7–9, who adds that Parmenion urged Alexander to marry her). In 327/6 (D 20.20.1; or 325/4, according to J 15.2.3), Barsine bore the King a son named Heracles (J 11.10.3; P*Eum* 1.7; cf. J 13.2.7; 15.2.3; Paus 9.7.2; C 10.6.11, 13; D 20.20.1; 20.28.1). Nearchus proposed, without success, that this son be recognized as King after Alexander's death (C 10.6.10–12; cf. also J 13.2.7). Barsine soon withdrew to Pergamum, where she was known to reside in mid-323 (J 13.2.7). In 309, Cassander persuaded Polyperchon to abandon Heracles and his mother; it appears that the mother was killed along with the son (J 15.2.3; Paus 9.7.2, who says Heracles was killed by poison, says nothing about the mother; cf. D 20.28.1; Brosius 78 locates the actual murder in Pergamum).

Kaerst, *RE* s.v.; Berve ii.102–4 no. 206; Brosius 78; Brunt 1975; Hofstetter 36–7 no. 63; Tarn 1921. See Stemma IV.

Barsine. (Aristobulus, *FGrH* 139 F52 = A 7.4.4; cf. Phot*Bibl* p.68b "Arsinoë"). See s.v. **Stateira** [2].

Baryaxes. A Mede who assumed the upright tiara and the title of king, probably after the replacement of Oxydates by Atropates (cf. A 4.18.3; cf. C 8.3.17). He and his followers were, however, defeated and arrested by Alexander's satrap of Media, Atropates, who brought them in early 324 to the King at Parsagadae, where they were executed (A 6.29.3).[170]

Kaerst, *RE* s.v.; Berve ii.104 no. 207; Justi 65; Badian 2000a: 93 no. 3; Briant 740.

Barzanes (or Brazanes). Persian supporter of Bessus, who in 330/29 left him in charge of Parthia. Alexander, however, reinstated Darius' satrap, Phrataphernes, who arrested Barzanes and brought him to the King in Zariaspa (Bactra) for punishment (A 4.7.1; cf. 4.18.1). He was presumably executed. Barzanes is otherwise unknown and the name looks sadly in need of a prefix. Perhaps we are dealing with [Na]barzanes (see s.v.).

Berve ii.102 no. 204.

Bas. Son of Boteiras. Bithynian dynast, born in 398/7. Ruled until 328/7. Alexander had apparently sent his satrap of Hellespontine Phrygia, Calas son of Harpalus, to subdue Bithynia, but the latter was defeated by Bas and forced to recognize his independence (Memnon, *FGrH* 434 F1 12.4).[171] His son and successor was Zipoetes.

Meyer, *RE* s.v.; Berve ii.104 no. 208.

Batis (Betis; "Babemesis" Jos*AJ* 11.320). Eunuch – according to Hegesias (*FGrH* 142 F5) he was corpulent and black – and *phrourarchos* of Gaza in the reign of Darius III (A 2.25.4; *IA* 45; cf. C 4.6.7), if not earlier. In September–October 332, he conducted a stubborn, two-month defense of Gaza (D 17.48.7; 10,000 Persians and Arabs were said to have died in the siege: C 4.6.30). When the city fell, he was taken by Leonnatus and Philotas son of Parmenion to Alexander (Hegesias, *FGrH* 142 F5; cf. C 4.6.26), who is said to have dragged him (alive) behind his chariot, thus imitating in a rather gruesome way Achilles' treatment of Hector (C 4.6.29). The imitation of Achilles may be part of the later tradition concerning Alexander, but we have no good reason for doubting the barbaric punishment meted out to Batis.

Kaerst, *RE* s.v.; Berve ii.104–5 no. 209; Tarn ii.265–70.

Belephantes. Leader of the Chaldaeans who spoke to Nearchus in 323 BC[172] and urged him to dissuade Alexander from entering Babylon, since this would bring about his death (D 17.112.3). The Chaldaeans also urged Alexander to avert the danger to himself by rebuilding the tomb of Belus, which the Persians had destroyed.

Baumstark, *RE* s.v.; Berve ii.105 no. 210.

Berenice (Berenike). Daughter of Antigone and Magas; granddaughter of Cassander, who was a brother of Antipater the regent (Theocritus, *Idyll* 17.61).[173] Born in the 340s, she married Philip (see n. 648), a man of obscure origins (ca. 325 BC) and produced two children: Antigone and Magas (Paus 1.7.1; P*Pyr* 4.7; Paus 1.11.5); a third child, Theoxene (who subsequently married Agathocles of Syracuse: J 23.2.6; cf. Geyer, *RE* s.v. "Theoxene"), may be the product of this marriage. What became of Philip, we do not know, but it appears that Berenice was already widowed in 320/19, when she accompanied her cousin, Eurydice, to Ptolemaic Egypt (Paus 1.5.8). She soon became Ptolemy's mistress and bore Arsinoë II and Ptolemy II (both later known as Philadelphus) as well as Philotera (Theocritus, *Idyll* 17.60; *MP* a.309/8; Callimachus, *Hymn to Delos* 160; cf. Str 16.4.5 [769]).

Wilcken, *RE* s.v. "Berenike (9)"; Berve ii.105 no. 211; Heckel 1989; Sandberger 55–61 no. 21; Beloch iv^2 2.180–1; Macurdy 104–9; Ogden 68–73. See Stemma X.

Bessus (Bessos). Prominent Persian, kinsman of Darius III (A 3.21.5). Satrap of Bactria (A 3.8.3; C 4.6.2; D 17.73.2). Darius summoned him from Central Asia after the battle of Issus and the failure of diplomatic negotiations (C 4.6.2, foreshadowing Bessus' betrayal of the King). At Gaugamela he commanded the Bactrian cavalry on the Persian left (A 3.8.3; C 4.12.6), with the aim of blunting Alexander's attack on that side (C 4.15.2; A 3.13.3–4). Nothing else is recorded of his participation in the battle. After the defeat he joined Darius in flight to Media with 3,300 cavalry (C 5.8.4; cf. A 3.16.1).[174] Bessus was joined by Nabarzanes, Barsaentes, and other prominent Persians in the plot to remove Darius. Nabarzanes bases Bessus' claim to the leadership on his position as satrap of Bactria, the region into which the Persian forces were fleeing (C 5.9.8; cf. A 3.21.4–5), but Bessus' authority must have been based largely on kinship; for Nabarzanes himself, as chiliarch, must have wielded considerable power. Together they arrested Darius (C 5.9–12; A 3.21.1, 4; D 17.73.2) and considered handing him over to Alexander in order to win his favor (A 3.21.5; C 5.9.2, 10.5).

Ultimately, they chose to kill the King (C 5.13.15–25; A 3.21.10; D 17.73.2) and fled toward Bactria (D 17.74.1) where Bessus assumed the military leadership and the title of King (D 17.74.2; C 6.6.13; A 3.25.3; *ME* 3). Satibarzanes, who had at first come to terms with Alexander, threw in his lot with Bessus and appealed for help (D 17.78.1–2; C 6.6.13, 20; A 3.25.5) but was defeated and killed before Bessus could be of aid. Bessus was, however, soon abandoned by his fellow-conspirators – some perhaps out of resentment, but others influenced by Alexander's lenient treatment of Nabarzanes and others who had surrendered.[175] But it also appears that the conspirators were convinced that Alexander would not pursue them into Bactria but turn instead to the warmer and richer lands of India. When their hopes were proved false, many dispersed and Bessus, with whatever followers remained, crossed the Oxus River into Sogdiana and proceeded toward the Iaxartes (C 7.4.20–1; A 3.28.8–10). Bessus was finally arrested by Spitamenes, Dataphernes, and Catanes and handed over to Alexander (A 3.29.6–30.5; C 7.5.19–26, 36–8; *ME* 5–6).[176] He was tortured briefly by some of those who had arrested him (C 7.5.40–2; A 3.30.5), and then sent on to Ecbatana to be punished by the Persians as a regicide (C 7.5.43; A 4.7.3).[177]

Kaerst, *RE* s.v.; Berve ii.105–8 no. 212.

Bianor. Acarnanian of unknown family, Bianor fought as a commander of Greek mercenaries in the Persian army at Issus in late 333 (A 2.13.2). After Darius' defeat there, Bianor joined Amyntas son of Antiochus, Thymondas, and Aristomedes in flight to Tripolis in Phoenicia. From there he appears to have accompanied Amyntas as far as Cyprus (D 17.48.3; A 2.13.2–3), but since we know only of Amyntas' death in Egypt, and no mention is made of the other officers, it may well be that they did not continue on with him to Egypt; perhaps Bianor went instead to Crete (cf. Bosworth i.222–3). Nothing else is known about him.[178]

Kaerst, *RE* s.v. "Bianor (5)"; Berve ii.109 no. 214; Hofstetter 38 no. 67.

Bion. Greek mercenary in the service of Darius III; he defected to the Macedonians on the eve of the battle of Gaugamela and revealed to Alexander the locations of traps set on the battlefield for the Macedonian cavalry by the Persians (C 4.13.36–7). This episode is mentioned only by Curtius and both the details and Bion himself may well be fictitious.

Berve ii.109–10 no. 217; Berve, *RE* Supplbd IV s.v. "Bion (3a)"; Hofstetter 38–9 no. 68; Marsden 1964: 41.

Bisthanes. Son of Artaxerxes III (Ochus), perhaps, as Bosworth i.335 suggests, by one of his concubines; D 17.5.4–5 says that Arses was the only son to survive Bagoas' initial purge of Ochus' family and that, after Arses' death, there was no successor to the throne. Bisthanes encountered Alexander when he was three days' march from Ecbatana in Media (A 3.19.4) and reported that Darius had fled from the city four days earlier with 7,000 talents from the treasury, 3,000 cavalrymen, and 6,000 infantry (A 3.19.5; cf. C 5.13.1, without naming Bisthanes). Whether he had accompanied Darius in flight from Gaugamela (thus Berve ii.109) or whether he had been in residence at Ecbatana is not clear. Nothing else is known about him, but we may assume that he remained in Alexander's entourage.

Kaerst, *RE* s.v.; Berve ii.109 no. 215; Bosworth i.335. See Stemma III.

Biton. A Greek mercenary leader of unknown origin, Biton was left behind with the garrison at Bactra in 327/6. When Athenodorus led an uprising of Greeks and seized the citadel of Bactra in 325 – for it was rumored that Alexander had died in India (D 17.99.5–6; cf. C 9.7.1; also D 18.7) – Biton induced a certain Bactrian named Boxus to invite Athenodorus to dinner and there to murder him (C 9.7.4). Biton then called a meeting of the Greek rebels and announced that Athenodorus had plotted against him and narrowly missed a lynching at the hands of Athenodorus' supporters. But those officers who had appealed to the mob to save Biton were also betrayed by him, and, although he was sentenced to be tortured, he escaped even this punishment and returned safely to Greece with some followers (C 9.7.5–11).

Berve ii.109 no. 216.

Bolon. A common Macedonian, a man of no refinement who had risen from the ranks to some lower military office (C 6.11.1), Bolon gave a speech at Phrada in 330 denouncing the arrogance of Philotas and thereby inciting hatred against him and contributing to his fall (C 6.11.2–8). He is, however, mentioned only by Curtius, who may have invented the individual and the sentiments expressed for dramatic effect.

Berve ii.110 no. 218; Hoffmann 222.

Boxus (Boxos). A Bactrian of unknown family;[179] supporter of the mercenary leader Biton, who induced him to murder Athenodorus at a dinner-party (C 9.7.4). Although Biton escaped punishment, Boxus was soon executed for his treachery (C 9.7.7–8).

Berve ii.110 no. 219.

Brison (A 3.12.2; Kaerst, *RE* s.v. "Brison (1)"; Berve ii.110–11 no. 223; Hoffmann 195). See s.v. **Ombrion**.

Brochubelus (Antibelus).[180] Son of Mazaeus and, perhaps, a Babylonian wife; both forms are legitimate Babylonian names (cf. Briant 724). Berve ii.40 identifies him with Antibelus, but Bosworth i.341 thinks that Arrian (or presumably his source) confused Antibelus and Artiboles, since "the two names . . . seem to be derived from the Babylonian Ardu-bel, and it is highly probable that they are alternative Hellenizations of the same original." Brochubelus deserted soon after the arrest of Darius by Bessus and Nabarzanes, surrendering to Alexander somewhere between Rhagae and Thara (C 5.13.11). A 3.21.1 places the surrender of Antibelus earlier (at Khar) and in conjunction with that of Bagisthanes (see Bosworth i.340–1). That we are dealing with two different sons of Mazaeus seems unlikely. What became of him we do not know.

Berve ii.40 no. 82 ("Antibelos"); Bosworth i.340–1; Hamilton 105.

Bubaces [1]. (Boubakes). The name may, however, be a corruption of Bubares/ Bupares, although identification with the Babylonian commander at Gaugamela is impossible. Prominent Persian of unknown family. Bubaces was killed in the battle of Issus in late 333 BC (A 2.11.8).[181]

Berve ii.110 no. 220; Justi 71.

Bubaces [2]. (Boubakes). A faithful eunuch who remained with Darius III to the end of the King's life. He appears to have acted as an interpreter (C 5.11.4), although we know that the King had an official interpreter in Melon (C 5.13.7). Whether Bubaces is historical or merely inserted into Curtius' account for dramatic effect cannot be determined. In a touching scene, Bubaces is praised by Darius for his loyalty and urged to save himself (C 5.12.10–11). Possibly he surrendered to Alexander soon afterwards.

Berve ii.110 no. 221.

Bupares (Boupares). Prominent Persian. Bupares is attested only once in the Alexander historians: A 3.8.5 says he led the Babylonian contingent at Gaugamela. He may have been satrap of Babylonia, but his subsequent disappearance must then be explained.[182] One possibility is that he was killed at Gaugamela and replaced after the battle by Mazaeus (thus Briant 849).

Berve ii.110 no. 222; Lehmann-Haupt 115, 142; Leuze 410–12; Bosworth i.291; Briant 849.

C

Cadmeia (Kadmeia). Daughter of Alexander I of Epirus and Cleopatra, daughter of Philip and Olympias. A birthdate for Cadmeia in the summer of 335 appears likely (Berve ii.186), since the parents were married in the summer of the preceding year and the girl's name appears to commemorate her uncle's victory at Thebes (cf. Heckel 1981a: 82, with n. 18). Cadmeia's father died when she was only 4, and she appears to have remained in Epirus in the charge of her grandmother, Olympias, when Cleopatra left to reside briefly in Macedonia, then in Sardis until her death in 308. Cadmeia herself was still alive in 296; for it was in her home that her brother Neoptolemus boasted that he would eliminate Pyrrhus – a remark overheard by a certain Phaenarete, who reported it to Pyrrhus' wife Antigone (P*Pyr* 5.11). What became of her, we do not know: she may have perished with her brother.

See Berve ii.186; Sandberger 115 no. 40. See Stemmata I, II.

Calanus (Kalanos; also Caranus, Callanus). Indian philosopher, originally named Sphines but better known by the nickname "Kalanos" for his habit of addressing Greeks and Macedonians with *kale* (instead of *chaire*), according to Onesicritus (*FGrH* 134 F17b = P*A* 65.5). This appears to be a false etymology and Calanus may in fact be a Graecism of the Indian Kalýana. Calanus was born in 397 BC (Str 15.1.68 [717]; D 17.107.2) and was among those philosophers summoned to Alexander at Taxila. A hostile tradition arose which contrasted the actions of Dandamis (Mandanis), who rejected Alexander's claims to divinity and was swayed neither by the promise of gifts nor by the threat of punishment, and Calanus who is depicted as lacking self-control and a slave to Alexander's dinner-table (i.e., a parasite). Calanus accompanied Alexander as far as Pasargadae, where he became ill for the first time in his life. On the borders of Susiana he mounted his own funeral pyre and was consumed by the flames. For the various accounts of his death see A 7.3.1–6; D 17.107.1–6; Val Max 1.8 ext 10; Str 15.1.68 [717–18], cf. 15.1.4 [686]. He was reported to have said to Alexander as he mounted his own funeral pyre, "I shall see you shortly," thus alluding to Alexander's imminent death (Val Max 1.8 ext 10).

Berve ii.187–8 no. 396.

Calanus (Kalanos). See s.v. **Caranus** [2].

Calas (Kalas; Kallas). Son of Harpalus (A 1.14.3; D 17.17.4), probably a kinsman (possibly a cousin) of Harpalus the Treasurer, hence a member of the Elimeiot royal house. Calas crossed into Asia Minor with Parmenion, Attalus, and (presumably) Amyntas son of Arrhabaeus in spring 336 (J 9.5.8–9; cf. D 16.91.2), unless, as Berve ii.188 conjectures, Calas was Attalus' successor and was not sent to Asia until later. Calas' conduct of the war in the Troad was far from successful: he nearly lost Cyzicus to Memnon (D 17.7.3–8; Pol*Strat* 5.44.5) and was driven back into Rhoetium (D 17.7.10; cf. McCoy 1989: 423–4; Judeich 305–6). When Alexander crossed in 334, Calas was appointed hipparch of the Thessalian cavalry (D 17.17.4), which he commanded at the Granicus (A 1.14.3), though he and the other officers on the left were subordinated to Parmenion (A 1.14.1). But he was soon assigned the satrapy of Hellespontine Phrygia and took up residence in Dascylium, which Parmenion occupied (A 1.17.1–2). Together with Lyncestian Alexander, who now commanded the Thessalian horse, Calas gained control of "Memnon's Land" (A 1.17.8; cf. Pol*Strat* 4.3.15). In 333, Paphlagonia was annexed to Hellespontine Phrygia (A 2.4.2; C 3.1.24), and Calas helped Antigonus the One-Eyed and Balacrus son of Nicanor suppress Persian resistance to Macedonian authority in Asia Minor (C 4.5.13; cf. Billows 43–5). Memnon of Heraclea (*FGrH* 434 F12 §4) records a defeat at the hands of a Bithynian dynast named Bas no later than 328/7 BC (cf. Bosworth i.127, with further literature). This need not have been the occasion of Calas' death, nor is it likely, as Billows suggests (45, with n. 85), that the campaign against Bas, and Calas' death, occurred in the late 330s. Alexander appointed Demarchus satrap of Hellespontine Phrygia, probably late in the campaign (A*Succ* 1.6). Badian's suggestion (1961: 18) that Calas was removed from office in the aftermath of Harpalus' misconduct is attractive but lacks proof.[183]

Berve ii.188 no. 397; Baumbach 29, 43, 56; Billows 38–40, 44–5; Heckel 355–7. See Stemma XIII.

Calis (possibly "Calas"; the name is attested only in Curtius). A Macedonian, apparently of high standing, Calis was exposed by Philotas, who was facing further torture at the hands of his accusers, and confessed that he and Demetrius the Bodyguard had planned the conspiracy against Alexander (C 6.11.36–7). He was, presumably, put to death together with the conspirators named by Dimnus and Nicomachus (C 6.11.38; cf. 6.7.15). He appears only in Curtius' heavily dramatized version of the Philotas affair, and this raises some doubts about the historicity of the individual and his involvement in the conspiracy.

Berve ii.189 no. 398.

Callias (Kallias). Son of Mnesarchus, from Chalcis (Aes 3.85), brother of Taurosthenes (Hyp 5.20). He was politically active in Euboea during the 340s, and was falsely accused of betraying the island to Philip. He gained Athenian citizenship through the efforts of Demosthenes (Din 1.44),[184] who in 332/1 appears to have sent him on a mission to Olympias – apparently at the same time as Aristion's mission to Hephaestion (Hyp 5.20; cf. Aes 3.162).

Swoboda, *RE* s.v. "Kallias (14)"; Berve ii.189 no. 399; Schaefer iii^2 195 n. 5.

Callicles (Kallikles). Athenian. Son of Arrheneides, of the deme Paeania (P*Dem* 25.7; *IG* ii^2 1632). Callicles was one of the politicians implicated in the Harpalus affair in 334 but, when the Athenians conducted a search of the houses of those suspected of taking Harpalus' money, they avoided his because he was newly married and his wife was in the house (Theopompus, *FGrH* 115 F330 = P*Dem* 25.7–8). He was trierarch in Athens in 322 (*IG* ii^2 1632).

Kroll, *RE* s.v. "Kallikles (2)"; Berve ii.189 no. 400; Kirchner no. 7934; Davies 68.

Callicrates (Kallikrates). Unknown background, perhaps Greek. Accompanied Alexander on the Asiatic expedition and was placed in charge of the treasures at Susa in late 331 (C 5.2.17). Identification with the *philos* of Ptolemy is possible but incapable of proof.

Berve ii.189 no. 401.

Callicratidas (Kallikratidas). Eminent Spartan, ambassador (along with Pausippus, Monimus, and Onomastoridas) to Darius III. According to C 3.13.15, he was captured by Parmenion at Damascus in late 333 BC, but A 3.24.4 places his capture after the death of Darius, in which case his embassy was probably linked with Agis III's efforts in Europe (thus Hofstetter 99).

Schoch, *RE* Supplbd IV s.v. "Kallikratidas (1a)"; Berve ii.189–90 no. 402; Poralla no. 409; Hofstetter 99 no. 171; Bosworth i.233–4.

Callicron (Kallikron). Son of Euryphaon. A cavalryman from Orchomenus, Callicron served as a member of Alexander's allied cavalry until the expedition reached Ecbatana in 330. There he and his compatriots were discharged. On their return (ca. 329), they made a dedication to Zeus Soter in Orchomenus (*IG* vii.3206).

Berve ii.190 no. 403.

Callimedon (Kallimedon). Athenian politician, surnamed *Karabos* (P*Dem* 27.2), "the Crab." Son of Callicrates, from Cottylus (*IG* ii^2 653, 7), and probably a kinsman of Callistratus of Aphidna (Davies 279). Pro-Macedonian and an adherent of Phocion – hence an opponent of Demosthenes (cf. Din 1.94, with Worthington 264–5). He was the butt of the jokes of the comic poets (Ath 3.100c–e, 104c–d; Lucian, *Encomium* 46, 48), perhaps already in the 340s, but he is best known for activities between 322 and 318. Soon after Alexander's death, he went first to Antipater in Macedonia and then accompanied Antipater's "friends and ambassadors" (*philoi kai presbeis*) as they traveled around Greece urging states not to join the Athenians in the Lamian War (P*Dem* 27.2). Callimedon was, however, not a mere sycophant and opposed, unsuccessfully, Antipater's plan to install a garrison in Munychia (P*Ph* 27.9). He is attested as a lessee of a mine at Thoricus (*IG* ii^2 1587, 12), probably around 320/19 (for the date see Crosby 1950: 280–1).[185] After the proclamation of Polyperchon's *diagramma* on the Freedom of the Greeks, when Hagnonides denounced Phocion and his party, Callimedon was among those who fled (P*Ph* 33.4), probably to the safety of Nicanor in Piraeus. He was condemned to death *in absentia* (P*Ph* 35.5)[186] but may have survived to return to Athens in the time of Demetrius of Phalerum (Ferguson 33).

Swoboda, *RE* s.v. "Kallimedon (1)"; Berve ii.190 no. 404; Kirchner no. 8032; Davies 279; Tritle 107, 124–5.

Callines (Kallines). Macedonian of unknown family. He appears only in Arrian's account of the Opis mutiny (324 BC), where he is described as an officer of the Companions, distinguished in age and rank. He acts as a spokesman for the Macedonians, indicating that they were hurt by the King's apparent preference for the Persians (namely, that he allowed the Persians to kiss him but did not extend the privilege to Macedonians: a strange reversal of the *proskynesis* episode). Callines then came forward and kissed Alexander, and others followed suit (A 7.11.6–7; cf. Roisman 2003: 300).

Berve ii.190 no. 405.

Callisthenes [1]. (Kallisthenes). Olynthian (A 4.10.1). Son of Demotimos (*SIG*^{3} 275; *Suda* K 240)[187] and Hero, who may have been a niece of Aristotle (P*A* 55.8; cf. 52.3). "Official" historian of Alexander's campaign (A 4.10.1; P*Sulla* 36). Callisthenes was a student of Aristotle (A 4.10.1; J 12.6.17; Cic *De oratore* 2.58; *Suda*), with whom he resided, and may have joined Alexander's expedition on Aristotle's recommendation (*Suda*; DL 5.4);[188] he had already written a Greek history (*Hellenica*). Aristotle is said to have recognized early the potential danger of Callisthenes' tendency to speak too freely in the presence of Alexander (DL 5.4–5). Callisthenes is wrongly depicted as one of Alexander's tutors (Str 13.1.27 [594]; Dio Chr 64.20; Solinus 9.18, p. 66). Although he accompanied Alexander from the beginning of the campaign, little is known of his personal relationship with Alexander until the last year of his life. It is certain, however, that although he wrote accounts that were favorable to the King (cf. Plb 12.12b, which must refer to his writings), in his personal speech he was brusque and critical, to the point of annoying and offending Alexander (DL 5.4–5; P*A* 52.7; Seneca, *Suasoriae* 1.5, confused; Cic *Tusculan Disputations* 3.21). He was, indeed, the victim of envious members of Alexander's entourage (P*A* 53.1–2); his manner and his lack of social graces – to say nothing of a perceived anti-Macedonian bias – contributed in no small way to his fall (P*A* 53–4; A 4.10.1; C 8.5.13, 6.1). On the morning after Alexander's murder of Cleitus, Callisthenes attempted to console the King with gentle words and circumlocutions, but he found himself trumped by his rival Anaxarchus, who resorted to flattery and insinuated himself with the King at Callisthenes' expense (P*A* 52.3–7; cf. A 4.9.7–9).[189] Furthermore, he incurred the hatred of Hephaestion and Hagnon (P*A* 55.1–2). He opposed the introduction of *proskynesis* in spring 327 (P*A* 54.4–6; A 4.12.3–5; J 12.7.2; C 8.5.13–20) and, because he was most likely the tutor of the Pages (*paides basilikoi*), was accused of participating in some way in the Hermolaus conspiracy and arrested (P*A* 55.3–5; A 4.12.7, 14.1; 8.6.24–5, 27), though not one of the Pages denounced Callisthenes. The place of his arrest was Cariatae in Bactria (Str 11.11.4 [517]); but A 4.22.2 says it occurred in Bactra (Zariaspa), where the Pages had earlier been left behind (A 4.16.6).[190] There is no agreement on the manner of Callisthenes' death (P*A* 55.9; A 4.14.3): Chares, *FGrH* 125 F15, says that he died of obesity and a disease of lice (cf. P*Sulla* 36.5; *Suda* K 240), which appears to be supported by Aristobulus, 139 F33 = A 4.14.3, who claims that he was imprisoned and thereafter died of illness.[191] This gives some credence to the view that Alexander intended to have Callisthenes tried by the League of Corinth for treason (P*A* 55.9). Ptolemy, 138 F17 = A 4.14.3, says that he was killed by hanging (cf. P*A* 55.9, crucifixion; C 8.8.21 says he died under torture – both accounts may go back to Ptolemy). A statue of Callisthenes by Amphistratus was located in Pliny's time in the Gardens of Servilius (Pl*NH* 36.36).

Berve ii.191–9 no. 408; Gude no. 74; Pearson 22–49; Jacoby, *FGrH* 124 TT1–36 (English translation in Robinson i.45–56); Golan 1988; Müller 135–68.

Callisthenes [2]. (Kallisthenes). Son of Menander. A cavalryman from Orchomenus, Callisthenes served with Alexander's allied cavalry until the expedition reached Ecbatana in 330. There he and his compatriots were discharged. On their return (ca. 329), they made a dedication to Zeus Soter in Orchomenus (*IG* vii.3206).

Berve ii.199 no. 409.

Callisthenes [3]. (Kallisthenes). Athenian politician with anti-Macedonian leanings. He is probably the mover of a decree urging the Athenians to accept an alliance with the Thracian Cetriporis, Lyppeus the Paeonian, and Grabus the Illyrian in 356/5 (SIG^3 196 = Rhodes & Osborne no. 53; cf. Kirchner no. 8090).[192] In 335 Alexander demanded his extradition along with other prominent enemies of Macedon (P*Dem* 23.4). That he was implicated in the Harpalus affair, we know only from a comic fragment of Timocles (Ath 8.341e–f).[193]

Berve ii.199 no. 410; Kirchner no. 8090.

Callixeina (Kallixeina). An exceptionally attractive Thessalian *hetaira*, who at the request of Philip and Olympias – they were worried about their son's indifference to women – slept with Alexander and was reputed to be the first woman to do so (Hieronymus, *Epistles*, frg. 10 [Hiller] = Ath 10.435a, quoting Theophrastus); though Alexander yielded to Olympias' wishes only after repeated entreaties. Ael*VH* 12.34, describing Pancaste, appears to have confused her with Callixeina. The historicity of

Hieronymus' story is suspect, coming as it does from a hostile Peripatetic tradition. In Athenaeus, Alexander's lack of interest in sex is connected with his love of drinking, which can not have been a serious factor in his youth. There is no good reason, however, to question the existence of Callixeina herself.

Berve ii.190–1 no. 406.

Caphisias (Kaphisias). Greek. Renowned flute-player and presumably a rival of Python (P*Pyr* 8.7; P*M* 184c, the anecdote demonstrates that Caphisias was still alive in the late fourth/early third century), Caphisias performed at the mass-marriage ceremony in Susa, along with Diophantus, Timotheus, Evius, and Phrynichus (Chares *ap*. Ath 12.538f = *FGrH* 125 F4; cf. Ath 14.629a–b and DL 7.19 for an anecdote relating to his interaction with one of his music students).

Berve ii.202–3 no. 416; Sandberger 116 no. 41.

Caphisodorus (Kaphisodoros). Son of Arxillus. A cavalryman from Orchomenus, Caphisodorus served as a member of Alexander's allied cavalry until the expedition reached Ecbatana in 330. There he and his compatriots were discharged. On their return (ca. 329), they made a dedication to Zeus Soter in Orchomenus (*IG* vii.3206).

Berve ii.203 no. 417.

Caranus [1]. (Karanos). Non-existent son of Philip II (J 11.2.3). Although many scholars have accepted Caranus as a son of Philip II and a half-brother and rival of Alexander, he is almost certainly fictitious (Tarn ii.260–2; Heckel 1979). Named only by Justin in his abbreviation of the *Philippic History* of Pompeius Trogus, Caranus is clearly nothing more than the son who, Alexander feared, might have fulfilled Attalus' wish that his niece Cleopatra would produce a legitimate heir to the Macedonian throne (Satyrus *ap*. Ath 13.557d; P*A* 9.7–8; J 9.7.3). Since Cleopatra's child turned out to be a daughter, Europa, and there was no time for a second child to be born before Cleopatra's murder in 336, Caranus must be dismissed as an invention. See s.vv. **Attalus** [1], **Cleopatra** [1].

Berve ii.199–200 no. 411; Heckel 1979.

Caranus [2]. (Karanos; Calanus, Kalanos; Coeranus, Koiranos). Macedonian, one of Alexander's *hetairoi* (A 3.28.2; 4.6.1). In 331, when Balacrus son of Amyntas was appointed *strategos* of Egypt, Caranus assumed command of the allied infantry (A 3.5.6 calls him "Calanus," which must be a scribal error).[194] It is not clear how long Caranus retained this command. A 3.12.4 names a certain "Coeranus" (again a possible scribal error for "Caranus"; cf. Brunt ii.262 n. 1; rejected by Bosworth i.303) in charge of allied *cavalry* on the Macedonian left; here he was stationed in close proximity to the mercenary cavalry of Andromachus [1], with whom he would again serve at the Polytimetus. In 330, Caranus was sent with Erigyius, Andronicus, and Artabazus against the rebellious satrap of Areia, Satibarzanes (A 3.28.2; C 7.3.2); his role in the campaign is overshadowed by Erigyius, who is said to have killed Satibarzanes in single combat (A 3.28.3; C 7.4.33–40). At the Polytimetus (Zeravshan) River (329 BC), Caranus led the 800 *misthophoroi hippeis* (A 4.3.7; at 4.5.7 he is called *hipparches*): possibly the allied horse continued to serve Alexander as mercenaries after their demobilization in 330. At the Polytimetus, Caranus and his colleagues – Andromachus appears to have commanded some sixty Companions, Menedemus the infantry – were ambushed and killed by Spitamenes (A 4.3.7, 5.7, 6.2), and it appears that some effort was made to cast the blame for the débâcle on Caranus himself (A 4.5.7).

Berve ii.186–7 no. 395 and ii.200–1 no. 412; Heckel 1981d: 64, 69–70.

Carthasis. The name appears only in its Latin form (C 7.7.1; *ME* 8). Carthasis was the brother of the king of the Scythians

(**M36**) who lived beyond the Iaxartes (Syr-Darya) River and was sent by him to destroy the newly founded Alexandria Eschate, which the Scythians regarded as menacing (C 7.7.1). His force was, however, attacked north of the Iaxartes (C 7.8–9, *ME* 10–12, and A 4.4.2–8 for the battle; cf. Fuller 238–41) and defeated with heavy casualties (C 7.9.16; cf. *ME* 12; A 4.4.8 speaks of 1,000 dead, including their commander, whom he calls Satraces, and 150 captured). Unless Carthasis is identical with Arrian's Satraces, we do not know what became of him.

Berve ii.201 no. 413.

Cassander (Kassandros, Kasandros, Casander). Son of Antipater (D 18.39.7, 48.5; 21.1.4; A*Succ* 1.14, 38; J 13.4.18; *LM* 96; Val Max 1.7 ext 2; App*Syr* 53 [270]) and hence brother of Nicanor, Iolaus, Philip, Pleistarchus (P*Demetr* 31.6, 32.4), Alexarchus,[195] Eurydice, Nicaea, and Phila. Married Thessalonice in 315 and produced three sons: Philip, Antipater, and Alexander (Paus 1.10.1; see s.v. **Thessalonice**). Cassander must have been born no later than 354 BC, if we accept the claim of Hegesander (*ap.* Ath 1.18a) that he continued to sit up at meals with his father at the age of 35 because he had not earned the right of reclining at dinner by killing a boar without a hunting net. He may have been a frail youth, and it appears that, at least later in life, he suffered from a lingering fatal illness, probably tuberculosis (Carney 1999: 209).[196] When Alexander crossed into Asia in 334, Cassander appears to have remained in Macedonia with his father. The text of D 17.17.4, assigning 900 Thracian and Paeonian *prodromoi* to Cassander, is probably corrupt: their commander was either Asander son of Philotas or Asander son of Agathon. In 324, he was sent by Antipater to Alexander in Babylon to answer charges against his father; rumors that he brought poison and formed a conspiracy to kill the King are the product of the propaganda wars of the successors (Val Max 1.7 ext 2; *LM* 89, 96, 100; see Heckel 1988). Although the charge of poisoning appears to be false, there is evidence of bad feeling between Alexander and Cassander (P*M* 180f; P*A* 74.2–6). After Alexander's death, he returned to Macedonia,[197] perhaps bearing news that Perdiccas was prepared to cooperate with the old regent. But Perdiccas' duplicity soon became apparent (see s.vv. **Cleopatra** [2], **Nicaea**, **Perdiccas** [1]). He accompanied his father as far as Triparadeisus in 320 and there was appointed *chiliarchos* of the cavalry and Antigonus' second-in-command, for Antipater was distrustful of Antigonus' ambition (D 18.39.7; A*Succ* 1.38; cf. *HE* 1.4). His suspicions were soon confirmed by Cassander, who quarreled with Antigonus and urged his father to remove the "Kings" from the latter's custody (A*Succ* 1.42). After his return from Asia, and during his father's illness, Cassander accused Demades of writing to Perdiccas and urging him to save the Greeks who were fastened by "an ancient and rotting thread," meaning Antipater; he killed Demades and his son, who had been taken to Macedonia (A*Succ* 1.14; P*Ph* 30.9–10). But Cassander was disappointed when his father, on his deathbed, entrusted the guardianship of the "Kings" to Polyperchon – which Cassander regarded as a birthright (D 18.49.1) – and appointed him, for a second time, *chiliarchos* (D 18.48.4–5). Going into the country, on the pretext of going on a hunting trip (D 18.49.3), Cassander met with his friends and plotted rebellion against Polyperchon (D 18.49.1–2; cf. 18.54.1–2; P*Eum* 12.1; P*Ph* 31.1, 32.1). He sent to Ptolemy asking to renew the alliance (D 18.49.3), which had been sealed by the marriage of Ptolemy to Cassander's sister Eurydice, and urged him to send ships from Phoenicia to the Hellespont. Later, he crossed to Asia and renewed the alliance with Antigonus (concluded during the war against Perdiccas): Antigonus promised (D 18.54.3) and delivered (D 18.68.1) both thirty-five ships and 4,000 infantry.

Polyperchon countered with a declaration of the "Freedom of the Greeks" in the name of King Philip III (D 18.56), thus attempting to destroy the base of Cassander's power, the garrisons and oligarchic governments in Greece, which were faithful to the house of Antipater (D 18.55.2–4). He hoped to secure the exile or execution of the pro-Antipatrid leader (D 18.57.1), and at first there was general support for Polyperchon in the Peloponnese, except in Megalopolis (D 18.69.3–4). Cassander had in effect been driven out of Macedonia (N*Ph* 3.2). But, through the services of Damis, Cassander managed to retain Megalopolis and gradually restore control over the Greek cities, which perceived Polyperchon as weak (D 18.74.1, 75.2; cf. Paus 1.4.1). Athens was secured for Cassander by Nicanor (see s.v. **Nicanor** [9]) and eventually entrusted to Demetrius of Phalerum (D 18.74.2–3; cf. Ath 12.542f); but Nicanor, who had won a naval victory over White Cleitus (D 18.72.3–8), incurred the suspicions of Cassander, who had him killed (D 18.75.1; Pol*Strat* 4.11.2).[198] Cassander's control of Athens lasted until its "liberation" by Demetrius Poliorcetes (P*Demetr* 8.1, 4; cf. 23.1–3 for Cassander's failed attempt to recover Attica in 304), who also removed Cassander's garrison from Megara (P*Demetr* 9.4–8).

In his struggle with Olympias, whose hostility toward Antipater extended also to his son (D 18.57.2; cf. Paus 1.11.3), he was aided by Adea-Eurydice, who had turned over the guardianship of Philip III to him (J 14.5.1–4); she soon summoned him back to Macedonia (D 19.11.1; J 14.5.8). But Olympias was victorious over Eurydice and Philip III and also killed a hundred of the most distinguished of Cassander's friends, as well as executing one brother, Nicanor, and overturning the grave of another, Iolaus (D 19.11.8). Cassander, learning of these events, made peace with the Tegeans and marched north (J 14.5.8), using barges to bypass Thermopylae and land in Thessaly (D 19.35.1–2). Keeping Polyperchon's forces in check, through the efforts of two generals, Callas and Deinias (D 19.35.3–4), Cassander proceeded to besiege Olympias and her entourage in Pydna (D 19.35.5–36.1; 19.49.1–50.5; J 14.6.2–5). Atarrhias was sent to prevent Aeacides of Epirus from bringing aid, and the action resulted in the deposing of the Epirote king (Paus 1.11.4; for his fate see s.v. **Aeacides**)[199] and the installation of Cassander's agent Lysiscus as *epimeletes* and *strategos* of Epirus (D 19.36.2–5); Callas meanwhile caused large numbers of Polyperchon's soldiers to defect (D 19.36.6). Having forced Olympias to surrender (Pol*Strat* 4.11.3), Cassander secured her murder (Paus 9.7.2; J 14.6.9–12; D 19.51.3–5), which he sanctioned by a vote of the Macedonian army (J 14.6.6–8; D 19.51.1–2),[200] and gained control of Rhoxane and her son, Alexander IV, whom he sent to Amphipolis (J 14.6.13; D 19.52.4). He also married Thessalonice (D 19.52.1; Paus 9.7.3; 8.7.7; J 14.6.13; cf. P*Demetr* 36.1; P*Pyr* 6.3),[201] who was captured at Pydna, and restored the city of Thebes (D 19.53.2; Paus 9.7.1, 4; 7.6.9; P*M* 814b), having first obtained the permission of the Boeotians to do so (D 19.54.1).[202] These were clear gestures that Cassander had chosen to link himself with the tradition of Philip II, abandoning all connections with Alexander the Great, whom he had personal reasons to hate (P*M* 180f; P*A* 74.2–6; P*Demetr* 37.3; cf. J 16.1.15, 16.2.5). The first child from his marriage with Thessalonice was named Philip (Paus 9.7.3),[203] and Cassander also gave royal burials to Adea-Eurydice and Philip III, as well as to Adea's mother, Cynnane (Ath 4.155a = Diyllus *FGrH* 73 F1; D 19.52.5).

Cassander was responsible for the murder of Alexander IV and his mother and, in the following year, persuaded Polyperchon to kill the illegitimate Heracles in return for a measure of power in the Peloponnese (Paus 9.7.2; J 15.2.3–5, confused; see below). The elimination of the last of Alexander's male relatives paved the way for Cassander's assumption of the kingship after the initial step had been taken by the Antigonids after their victory at Salamis (J 15.2.10–12),[204] and thus he was one of those considered responsible for the dismemberment of Alexander's empire (N*Eum* 13.3). During his reign he remained on good terms with Lysimachus (Paus 1.10.1), who was married to his sister Nicaea, and who joined him, as well as Ptolemy and Seleucus, in coalitions against Antigonus (App*Syr* 53; D 19.56.3; J 15.1.2, 15.2.15–17; cf. D 21.1.4[b]; Paus 1.6.4). The first coalition against the Antigonids came after the defeat of Eumenes and the expulsion of Seleucus from Babylon (D 19.56.3, 57.2); Antigonus' counter-arguments to Cassander were ineffective (D 19.56.4).[205] Instead the coalition demanded concessions, including that Cappadocia and Lycia be handed over to Cassander (D 19.57.1). For his part, Antigonus accused Cassander of murdering Olympias, mistreating Alexander IV and his mother, marrying Thessalonice by force, and rebuilding Thebes (D 19.61.1–2)[206] and urged that the Macedonians condemn him as an outlaw (D 19.61.3). The years after 315 saw Cassander struggling with Polyperchon and his son Alexander for control of the Greek cities (D 19.63–4), a problem which was partially overcome by Cassander's ability to detach Alexander from his father (D 19.64.4). This was followed by further campaigns in the northwestern regions of Greece, from Patrae in the south to Epirus in the north (D 19.66–7; 19.74.2–6; 19.88–9), as well as in Euboea (D 19.75.6–8, 77.5–6; cf. 19.78.2–3, 5), after an abortive attempt by Antigonus to make peace (D 19.75.6). In 310, Cassander took the bold step of ordering Glaucias to kill Alexander IV and his mother in Amphipolis (D 19.105.2), a move that was in fact welcomed by all the Successors who aspired to the kingship (D 19.105.3). But, when Polyperchon attempted to use Alexander's illegitimate son, Heracles, as a means of gaining power (D 20.20), Cassander induced him to murder the boy in exchange for a subordinate role as *strategos* of the Peloponnese (D 20.28.1–3; see s.v. **Heracles**). Although Cassander came to terms with Antigonus' nephew, Polemaeus, in 308 (D 20.37.1–2), he soon lost Athens to Demetrius (D 20.45.1–5). After the assumption of the kingship, Cassander renewed his alliance with Lysimachus, Ptolemy, and Seleucus (D 20.76.7); he responded to an appeal by the Rhodians (D 20.84.1) with a shipment of 10,000 medimnoi of barley (D 20.96.3), in return for which the Rhodians set up a statue of him (D 20.100.2). Demetrius Poliorcetes, however, countered by waging war on Cassander and Polyperchon in Greece (20.100.6; 20.102–3; 20.105.1–106.1), forcing Cassander to seek peace with Antigonus (D 20.106.2). But Antigonus' excessive demands merely resulted in a renewal of the alliance with Ptolemy, Lysimachus, and Seleucus (D 20.106.2–5), which led eventually to the battle of Ipsus. Cassander attempted to divert Demetrius' attention in Thessaly, but with no military success (D 20.110), and was forced to negotiate a truce that allowed Demetrius to cross to Asia in support of his father (D 20.111.1–2). But Cassander too had sent a substantial force under Prepelaus to serve with Lysimachus in Asia (D 20.107.1), and after recovering Thessaly in Demetrius' absence, he sent further forces with his brother Pleistarchus (D 20.112.1). Cassander benefited from the Antigonid defeat at Ipsus in 301, although he was not himself present (J 15.2.17; App*Syr* 55; Paus 1.6.7). We know also of an attack on Corcyra (in 299/8), in which Cassander's ships were burned by Agathocles of Syracuse, but the latter failed to follow up his victory and Cassander's forces escaped destruction (D 21.2.1–3). Cassander died in 297, perhaps of consumption, and he was succeeded by his son Philip IV (J 15.4.24, 16.1.1; P*Demetr* 36.1).

Stähelin, *RE* s.v. "Kassandros (2)"; Berve ii.201–2 no. 414; Sandberger 116–19 no. 42; Fortina; Adams 1984, 1993; Landucci Gattinoni. See Stemma V.

Catanes (Katanes). Perhaps Persian, though possibly a local dynast of Sogdianian

Paraetacene (A 4.22.1), Catanes was a trusted follower of Bessus (C 7.5.21). Together with Spitamenes and Dataphernes he conspired to arrest Bessus, who was then handed over to Alexander in chains (C 7.5.21–6; *ME* 5–6). Because of his skill in archery, he was assigned the task of keeping the birds off Bessus' crucified body (C 7.5.41–2). He persisted in his opposition to Alexander (C 7.6.14–15), however, until the spring of 327 when Craterus led a punitive expedition into Paraetacene against Catanes and his supporter Haustanes; the latter was captured but Catanes fell on the battlefield (C 8.5.2; cf. A 4.22.2, who estimates the barbarian casualties at 120 cavalry, 1,500 infantry); *ME* 23 curiously says that the Dahae arrested Catanes and Dataphernes and turned them over to Alexander in order to preempt an attack upon them.

Schoch, *RE* Supplbd IV s.v.; Berve ii.202 no. 415; cf. Heckel 1981d: 68.

Cebalinus (Kebalinos). Greek or Macedonian, apparently of low birth. Older brother of Nicomachus (P*A* 49.4; D 17.79.2; C 6.7.16), a male prostitute whose lover, Dimnus, was one of the *hetairoi* (D 17.79.1). Dimnus had tried to persuade Nicomachus to join a conspiracy against Alexander and divulged all its details to him (C 6.7.2–15, heavily dramatized). Nicomachus, however, informed Cebalinus, who attempted to bring the plot to the King's attention (D 17.79.2); in doing so he happened upon Philotas son of Parmenion (C 6.7.17–18; but P*A* 49.4 and D 17.79.3 imply that he sought him out). When Philotas failed to convey the news to Alexander (C 6.7.18–22; P*A* 49.5–6; D 17.79.3–4), Cebalinus used a Royal Page named Metron to take the information to the King (C 6.7.23; D 17.79.4), who told the full story. For Cebalinus there was considerable risk, since Alexander was slow to believe that he was telling the truth about Philotas' negligence (C 6.7.31–2). Ultimately, Cebalinus' testimony resulted in the arrest, conviction, and execution of Philotas (see further s.vv. **Nicomachus**, **Philotas** [4]).

Kroll, *RE* s.v.; Berve ii.203 no. 418; Adams 2003.

Cephisophon (Kephisophon). Athenian politician who, along with Demosthenes and Demades, had been investigated by the Areopagus for six months on the matter of having taken money from Harpalus (Din 1.45). The identity of Cephisophon is unclear. Berve ii.203 assumed that he was the son of Callibius (thus also Kirchner no. 8417). But he may have been dead by mid-century (Davies 149). Worthington 210 argues instead for Cephisophon son of Lysiphon Cholargeus (Kirchner no. 8419), but there can be no certainty.

Kroll, *RE* s.v. "Kephisophon (4)"; Berve ii.203 no. 419; Kirchner no. 8417; Davies 149; Worthington 210.

Chaereas (Chaireas). Greek. Sculptor. Produced statues of Philip II and Alexander (Pl*NH* 34.75 = Stewart T101). Nothing else is known about him or his work, unless he can be identified with Chares of Lindus (thus Stewart 106, following Schreiber 1903: 268–72).[207]

Robert, *RE* s.v. "Chaireas (9)"; Berve ii.403 no. 817.

Chaeron [1]. (Chairon). Greek from Megalopolis. Philip II sent him to Delphi in 356 to inquire about dreams he had had concerning Olympias. Chaeron returned with the response that Philip should revere the god Amun, and the prediction that he would lose the eye with which he watched the god in the form of a snake through a crack in Olympias' door (P*A* 3.1–2). The story is almost certainly a fiction, although Chaeron himself may be historical.[208]

Chaeron [2]. (Chairon). Tyrant of Pellene. Wrestler who was twice victorious at the Isthmian games and a four-time Olympic champion (Paus 7.27.7). Student of Plato and Xenocrates (Ath 11.509b). Alexander established him as tyrant of Pellene at some point before in 331 ([Dem] 17.10).

Chaeron remained loyal to Macedon during Agis' war (Aes 3.165) and this will account in no small way for the negative comments concerning his rule.[209] Nothing else is known about him.

Kroll, *RE* s.v. "Chairon (4)"; Berve ii.403 no. 818.

Chares [1]. Athenian of the deme Angele. Son of Theochares. Davies 568 comments: "Our ignorance of Chares' family remains complete." The father is otherwise unknown, and Chares' birthdate, on the assumption that he was at least 30 when he was first elected to the *strategia* in 367/6 (Xen*HG* 7.2.18–23, 4.1; D 15.75.3; cf. Develin 256), could not have been much later than 400 BC. Chares is attested as *strategos* on at least sixteen further occasions, the last time in 338 at Chaeronea ([P]*M* 843d; Pol*Strat* 4.2.8; D 16.85.2).[210] As an opponent of Macedon, he is listed amongst those whom Alexander demanded the Athenians to deliver after the sack of Thebes in 335 (A 1.10.4; *Suda* A 2704); Bosworth i.94 may be correct in assuming that Chares left Athens and retired to Sigeum soon after Chaeronea in order to escape prosecution (cf. the fate of Lysicles: D 16.88.1–2; [P]*M* 843d). Certainly, he is attested in Sigeum in 334 (A 1.12.1); for he greeted Alexander with a golden crown at Ilium at that time. Whatever concessions he received from the Macedonian ruler, Chares soon took up service with Persia. In 332, he occupied Mytilene, which had been recovered by the Persian fleet, with 2,000 mercenaries, but he soon handed the city over to Hegelochus on the understanding that he himself could leave unharmed (C 4.5.22; A 3.2.6).

Kirchner, *RE* s.v. "Chares (3)"; Kirchner no. 15292; Berve ii.403–4 no. 819.

Chares [2]. Chares of Mytilene (*FGrH* 125 T1, 3a). Accompanied Alexander from the beginning of the Asiatic expedition and held a high position at the court. Perhaps he was recommended to the King by the prominent Mytilenaeans, Laomedon and Erigyius. After the King's adoption of Persian court ceremonial, Chares became the Royal Usher (*eisangeleus*: P*A* 46.2); he was thus knowledgeable about everyday occurrences at the court and an eye-witness to events like the murder of Cleitus (P*A* 50–2, thought to be based primarily on Chares: Hamilton 139), the introduction of *proskynesis* (P*A* 54.4–6; cf. A 4.12.3–5) and the death of Callisthenes (P*A* 55.9), and the mass-marriages in Susa (Ath 12.538b–539a). Whether he had a personal dislike for Alexander's tutor, Lysimachus, is unclear (Berve ii.241; *contra* Pearson 56–7). Author of a *History of Alexander*, of which some nineteen fragments survive. The work is of greater interest to the social and cultural historian and presents little of value on politics or the military.[211]

Schwartz, *RE* s.v. "Chares (13)"; Berve ii.405–6 no. 820; Jacoby, *FGrH* 125; Pearson 50–61.

Charias. Origins unknown. Student of Polyeidus of Thessaly (Ath Mech 10; Vitr 10.13.3). Engineer in Alexander's entourage (Ath Mech 5, 10; cf. Whitehead & Blyth 71). He wrote a book on siege machinery (Vitr 7 *praef.* 14). See also s.v. **Diades**.

Hultsch, *RE* s.v. "Charias (11)"; Berve ii.406 no. 821; Marsden 1977; Whitehead & Blyth 71–2, 85–6.

Charicles [1]. (Charikles). Son of Menander (A 4.13.7), most likely the satrap of Lydia (see **Menander** [1]).[212] Perhaps one of the King's Pages in 327 BC. Though not party to the Hermolaus conspiracy, he was informed of it by his lover Epimenes and brought the matter to the attention of the latter's brother, Eurylochus (thus A 4.13.7; C 8.6.20 omits Charicles entirely), who revealed the plot to Alexander, through the agency of Ptolemy and Leonnatus. The conspirators themselves were arrested, tortured, and executed, but Charicles and Epimenes were spared (cf. C 8.6.26). Nothing further is known about him.

Berve ii.407 no. 824; Heckel 290; Hoffmann 180.

Charicles [2]. (Charikles). Athenian of unknown background. Charicles must have come from a prominent family, since he was deemed worthy to marry a daughter of Phocion (*PPh* 21.5), though Phocion may have had some reservations about the man's character (*PPh* 22.4). His connections with Harpalus and Pythionice may go back to the time of Harpalus' first flight (cf. A 3.6.4–7), but *PPh* 21.5, if taken literally, indicates that Harpalus befriended Charicles in 324 (see also Tritle 119). Charicles accepted thirty talents for the construction of a funeral monument to Pythionice, and this excessive amount may have included a substantial bribe (*PPh* 22.1–2); certainly he was brought up on bribery charges in connection with the Harpalus case (*PPh* 22.4). When Phocion and his associates were attacked by Hagnonides in 318, Charicles and Callimedon fled the city (*PPh* 33.4). Charicles was condemned to death *in absentia* (*PPh* 35.5). He was the guardian of the daughter of Harpalus and Pythionice (*PPh* 22.1, 3; **F58**).

Kirchner, *RE* s.v. "Charikles (2)"; Kirchner no. 15403; Berve ii.408 no. 825.

Charidemus (Charidemos). Son of Philoxenus, from Oreus on Euboea ([Arist]*Oecon* 2.1351b 19; Ael*VH* 2.41; Theopompus *ap.* Ath 10.436b–c; *IG* ii[2] 32, 36; cf. Davies 570). Born in the 390s, Charidemus first saw military action as a *psilos* when Chabrias attacked Oreus between 378 and 376 (cf. D 15.30.5). In the period 368/7–365, he fought with Iphicrates as a mercenary captain (*xenagos*) at Amphipolis (Dem 23.148–9). After the removal of Iphicrates from command, Charidemus delivered the Amphipolitan hostages back to their home rather than conveying them to Athens (Dem 23.149). Charidemus spent some time with Cotys of Thrace and was later captured en route to Amphipolis. He took up service with Timotheus (Dem 23.149–50). In 362 he went to Asia Minor to serve under Mentor and Memnon the Rhodians, waging war in Aeolia and taking control of Scepsis, Cebren, and Ilium (Dem 23.154ff.; Aen Tact 24.3; *PSer* 1.6; Pol*Strat* 3.14; for his further activities there see Dem 23.155–6, [Arist]*Oecon* 2.30.1351b 19ff.; *SIG*[3] 188). He returned to Thrace where he served Cotys and his son Cersobleptes and acted as an agent in Thracian dealings with Athens, whereupon he earned Athenian citizenship (Dem 23.141, 203; cf. Parke 1928: 170; Davies 571; Kelly 1990) and enrolled in the deme Acharnae (*SIG*[3] 962, 322). Charidemus reported the death of Philip II (Aes 3.77). After the sack of Thebes, he was exiled on Alexander's orders and took refuge with Darius III (A 1.10.4, 6; cf. *PPh* 17.2; *PDem* 23.4; *Suda* A 2704; Din 1.32–4). Shortly before the battle of Issus, he advised Darius to split his forces and entrust a portion of them to him (D 17.30.2–3), but he was suspected of planning to betray the Persians and put to death (D 17.30.4–5); C 3.2.10–19 gives an account strongly reminiscent of the Demaratus episode in Hdt 7.101–5.[213] Charidemus had three sons by a sister of Cersobleptes (Dem 23.129; cf. Davies 571): Eurymedon, Phylacus, and Troilus (*IG* ii[2] 1627. 207–16, 217–22); the sons paid a debt owed by their father for a trierarchy before 336 (cf. Dem 23.136, 138).

Kirchner, *RE* s.v. "Charidemos (5)"; Kirchner no. 15380; Schaefer iii[2] 143–4; Berve ii.406–7 no. 823; Blänsdorf 1971; Seibt 108–9; Atkinson i.462–3; Hofstetter 42–3 no. 74; Kelly 1990; Parke 1928: 170; cf. Parke 100, 125–32, 146–8, 183; Bengtson, *Staatsv* ii, no. 324; Judeich 213ff., 261, 279; Buckler 374–6, 431.

Charon. Greek from Chalcis in Alexander's entourage at an unspecified time. At a drinking-party in the quarters of Craterus, Alexander praised the young boy (**M78**) who was the *eromenos* of Charon. When the latter urged the boy to kiss Alexander, the King declined the offer on account of the pain it would cause Charon (Carystius *ap.* Ath 13.603b). Nothing else is known about him.

Berve ii.408 no. 827.

Charus (Charos). A member of Alexander's cohort (C 8.11.9–10) but apparently not a Page; hence a member of the "Royal Hypaspists." Charus commanded (together with Alexander) a troop of thirty hypaspists in an assault on Aornus, where he was killed in battle and fell upon the corpse of his friend Alexander (C 8.11.15–16). Curtius' description of their deaths recalls Virgil's account of Nisus and Euryalus (*Aeneid* 9.176ff.), but the historicity of the event (cf. P*A* 58.5) and of Charus and Alexander themselves need not be questioned.

Berve ii.408 no. 826; Heckel 296.

Cheirocrates (Berve ii.408 no. 828). See s.v. **Deinocrates.**

Choerilus (Choirilos). Execrable epic poet (Constantine "Porphyrogenitus" ad Hor. *Ars Poetica* 5.357 calls him *poeta pessimus*) from Iasus, Choerilus accompanied Alexander to Asia (C 8.5.8) and wrote a poem in which Alexander appeared as Achilles. Alexander is supposed to have remarked that he would rather be Thersites in Homer's *Iliad* than Choerilus' Achilles.

Crusius, *RE* s.v. "Choirilos"; Berve ii.408–9 no. 829.

Chorienes. See s.v. **Sisimithres.**

Chrysippus (Chrysippos). Greek dancer of unknown origin. Alexander mentions him in a letter to his financial officer Philoxenus (Ath 1.22d). Cf. also s.v. **Theodorus** [2].

Berve ii.409 no. 830.

Cissus (Kissos). A Greek who, together with Ephialtes, brought Alexander news of Harpalus' flight, only to be thrown into chains by the disbelieving King (P*A* 41.8). Presumably he was released once his report was verified. Berve ii.161, 203 has argued that Alexander's disbelief suggests that it is Harpalus' first flight (333 BC) that was reported by Cissus (cf. Hamilton 109). But we cannot be certain. Cissus is otherwise unknown, unless he is to be identified with the Athenian actor Cittus (*IG* ii^2 2418).

Berve ii.203 no. 420; Ghiron-Bistagne 72, 337.

Cleadas (the name appears only in its Latin form). A Theban who was captured when the city was sacked in 335 (J 11.4.1), Cleadas spoke in defense of the Theban uprising, alleging that Thebes had rebelled only on the false rumor of the King's death (J 11.4.1–6). His remarks fell on deaf ears. About the historicity of Cleadas and his appeal (cf. Hegesias, *FGrH* 142 FF6–20) we cannot be certain.

Berve ii.204 no. 421.

Cleander [1]. (Kleandros). Son of Polemocrates (A 1.24.2) and, in all probability, the brother of Coenus. He served Alexander since at least the beginning of the Asiatic campaign and, in late 334, was sent to recruit mercenaries from the Peloponnese (A 1.24.2; C 3.1.1: on the date see Heckel 1991). He rejoined Alexander at Sidon in early 332, bringing with him 4,000 mercenaries (A 2.20.5; cf. C 4.3.11). In 331 Cleander replaced Menander as commander of the *archaioi xenoi* (mercenaries); A 3.6.8 writes "Clearchus" in place of Cleander and the text should be emended (Bosworth i.285; Brunt i.240 n. 8; Heckel 1981d: 65). Cleander is securely attested as commander of the mercenaries at Gaugamela (A 3.12.2).

In the following year, Cleander remained with Parmenion in Ecbatana and, on the instructions brought by Polydamas, orchestrated the old general's murder (A 3.26.3; cf. C 7.2.19–32). In 324, he was summoned to Carmania, along with Heracon, Sitalces, and Agathon, and executed on charges of maladministration and crimes against the native population (A 6.27.4; C 10.1.1–7, who does not mention Cleander's own death but adds (10.1.8) that 600 common soldiers, who carried out the orders of Cleander and his fellow-officers, were executed *en masse*).[214]

Kroll, *RE* s.v. "Kleandros (6)"; Berve ii.204 no. 422; Badian 1961: 21–3; Heckel 340. See Stemma VII.

Cleander [2]. (Kleandros). Macedonian. Commander of archers (*strategos* of *toxotai* or *toxarches*). Cleander replaced Clearchus who was killed at Halicarnassus in 334 (A 1.22.7). Cleander was killed in the Pisidian campaign (334/3 BC: A 1.28.8). His successor was Antiochus.

Kroll, *RE* s.v. "Kleandros (5)"; Berve ii.205 no. 423.

Clearchus (Klearchos). Macedonian. Commander of archers, perhaps the successor of Eurybotas, who died at Thebes in 335 (A 1.8.4).[215] Clearchus was killed at Halicarnassus in 334 and replaced by Cleander (A 1.22.7).

Berve ii.205 no. 424.

Clearchus (Klearchos). Berve ii.205 no. 425. See **Cleander** [1].

Cleitarchus (Kleitarchos, Clitarchus). Greek from Alexandria in Egypt. Son of Deinon (Pl*NH* 10.136) the author of *Persica*. Author of what was perhaps the most popular *History of Alexander* in antiquity (see Jacoby, *FGrH* 137). Although there are only thirty-seven attested fragments of his work, he was almost certainly the chief source of Diodorus, Pompeius Trogus, and Q. Curtius Rufus. He appears not to have participated in the expedition. It is now generally believed that his work was published soon after 310 BC.

Berve ii.422–3, Abschn. II no. 40. For his work see Jacoby, *FGrH* 137; Brown 1950; Pearson 212–42; Prandi.

Cleitus [1]. (Kleitos, Clitus). Son of Bardylis (A 1.5.1); Illyrian, perhaps king of the southern Dardanians (Hammond 1966: 245). Together with Glaucias, king of the Taulantians, Cleitus rebelled against Alexander in 335 (A 1.5.1). Alexander attacked and hemmed him in at Pellion before Glaucias' arrival (A 1.5.8). After Glaucias was defeated and routed (A 1.6.10), Cleitus put Pellion to the torch and fled to the mountains to join the Taulantians (A 1.6.11). He appears to have been the grandfather of Bircenna, daughter of Bardylis, who later married Pyrrhus, king of Epirus (P*Pyr* 9.2–3).

Stähelin, *RE* s.v. "Kleitos (11)"; Berve ii.205–6 no. 426; Hammond 1966; Hammond 1974.

Cleitus [2]. (Kleitos, Clitus). Son of Dropidas (A 1.15.8; 3.11.8, 27.4; cf. 4.9.3), was surnamed Melas ("the Black": D 17.20.7, 57.1; P*A* 16.11) in order to distinguish him from his namesake, the taxiarch and later hipparch, White Cleitus (Ath 12.539c). Although we are reasonably well informed about his family, nothing is recorded about his place of birth or residence. Lanice, his sister, was Alexander's nurse (A 4.9.3; C 8.1.21 (Hellanice); cf. 8.2.8–9, and J 12.6.10): born ca. 375, she was apparently still alive in 328 and had at least three sons who served Alexander during the Asiatic expedition, two of whom died at Miletus in 334 BC (C 8.2.8; cf. A 4.9.4; **M41–42**), while a third son, Proteas – *syntrophos* and drinking-companion of Alexander (Ael*VH* 12.26; cf. Ath 4.129a and 10.434a) – was very likely the admiral who defeated Datames at Siphnos, hence the son of Andronicus (Berve ii.328–9 no. 664 = no. 665; thus Carney 1981: 152–3). If the identification is correct, Andronicus – almost certainly the son of Agerrus (so Carney 1981: 153) – would have been Lanice's husband and Cleitus' brother-in-law. Theodorus (Berve ii.176 no. 362), identified merely as a "brother of Proteas" but on intimate terms with Alexander (P*M* 760c), may also have been Lanice's son (cf. Carney 152, with n. 10).

Cleitus commanded the Royal Squadron (*ile basilike*) since at least the beginning of the expedition; in what capacity he had served under Philip II (C 8.1.20), we do not know. At the Granicus, he saved Alexander's life, killing either Rhoesaces or Spithridates, who was on the point of striking the King (A 1.15.8; P*A* 16.11; D 17.20.7; cf. C 8.1.20).[216] The episode may have been the inspiration for the Apelles' portrait of Cleitus on horseback (Pl*NH* 35.93).[217] At Gaugamela he continued to command the *ile basilike*, as he must have done at Issus, though he is not named in any account of the battle (A 3.11.8; D 17.57.1; C 4.13.26, the cavalry *agema*). When the King left Susa at the end of 331, Cleitus remained behind on account of illness. In the following spring, he proceeded to Ecbatana, taking from there those Macedonians who had been responsible for protecting the treasures that had been conveyed from Persepolis to Ecbatana and rejoining the King somewhere in Parthia (A 3.19.8).

After the fall of Philotas, Cleitus shared the command of the Companions with Hephaestion (A 3.27.4).[218] Shortly before he was killed in Maracanda (autumn 328), Cleitus had been designated satrap of Bactria and Sogdiana, which Artabazus had relinquished on account of age (C 8.1.19). Alexander had gradually replaced Philip's officers with men of his own generation, men who very often shared his vision of the empire or, even if they did not, were content to say that they did.[219] Cleitus' anger at the drinking-party in Maracanda has been attributed to offensive verses, mocking a Macedonian defeat (P*A* 50.8ff.), the excesses of Alexander's flatterers (A 4.8.2–3), the wrath of Dionysus (A 4.8.1–2, 9.5; or neglected sacrifices, P*A* 50.7), or Cleitus' own belligerence (A 4.8.6–9; C 8.1.49ff.; P*A* 51.8ff.). Certainly Cleitus objected publicly to Alexander's personal and political transformation. The King, though restrained by his Somatophylakes (C 8.1.45ff.; P*A* 51.6), grabbed a spear from a guard in the tent and killed Cleitus (A 4.8.8–9.1; C 8.1.49–52; P*A* 51.9–11; J 12.6.3) in a drunken rage. There is no reason to doubt that Alexander experienced genuine remorse (A 4.9.2ff.; C 8.2.1ff.; P*A* 52.1–2; J 12.6.7–11).

Kroll, *RE* s.v. "Kleitos (9)"; Berve ii.206–8 no. 427; Carney 1981; Heckel 34–7; Hoffmann 183; Müller 113–33. See Stemma VIII.

Cleitus [3]. (Kleitos, Clitus). Prominent Macedonian, family background unknown; nicknamed "the White" (Ath 12.539c) to distinguish him from "Black" Cleitus, the son of Dropidas. He first appears as a taxiarch in the Indian campaign (327): the *taxeis* of Cleitus, Gorgias, and Meleager, accompanied Perdiccas and Hephaestion to the Indus River (A 4.22.7). In the Hydaspes battle, Cleitus and Coenus made the river-crossing with the King (A 5.12.2), while the other five battalions remained on the western bank. Soon after the battle he was promoted to hipparch, in which capacity he fought in the Sangala campaign (A 5.22.6) and later against the Mallians (A 6.6.4). Who replaced Cleitus as taxiarch, we do not know. Cleitus himself was dismissed with the veterans at Opis and accompanied Craterus as far as Cilicia (J 12.12.8; cf. A 7.12.4). There Craterus appears to have entrusted him with the task of building a fleet which would secure the Hellespont crossing (cf. Beloch iv^2 1.72) for Craterus. Leonnatus' earlier crossing into Europe was clearly facilitated by the fleet of Antipater, some 110 ships sent in 324/3 by Alexander which defeated the Athenians near Abydos at the beginning of spring 322 (*IG* ii^2 398; ii^2 493, neither of which names Cleitus).[220] The death of Leonnatus and Antipater's deficiency in cavalry made it necessary for Craterus to leave Cilicia, probably in early June, and the Athenian admiral Euetion, having been unable to prevent reinforcements from reaching Antipater from Hellespontine Phrygia, now moved south to intercept Cleitus' fleet as it entered the Aegean. Near the island of Amorgos, Cleitus defeated the Athenian fleet in the last major naval engagement of the year of Cephisodorus (323/2 BC; *MP FGrH* 239 B9). At this point, Cleitus' fleet could not have numbered much more than 130 ships, a force which the Athenians, defeated at the Hellespont and forced to keep ships in reserve in the Malian Gulf, would have difficulty matching. After his victory near Amorgos, Cleitus added the Hellespontine fleet to his own and sailed to the Malian Gulf, where he caught the remainder of the Athenian fleet off the Lichades islands and inflicted heavy casualties (cf. Heckel 373–8; Bosworth 2003b: 16–19 believes that Cleitus' victories in 322 came at the Echinades off the coast of Acarnania).[221] Cleitus is said to have played the part of Poseidon and carried the trident (P*M* 338a); Phylarchus and Agatharchides go so far as to claim that he conducted business while walking on purple robes (Ath 12.539b–c = *FGrH* 81 F41, *FGrH* 86 F3). Although Cleitus commanded Perdiccas' fleet just before the latter's invasion of Egypt (J 13.6.16; cf. Keil 1913: 235 no. II*n*; commentary on 241, showing that he was still cooperating with Alcetas), he soon went over to Craterus and Antipater (A*Succ* 1.26). For this change of allegiance he received the satrapy of Lydia in the settlement at Triparadeisus (D 18.39.6; A*Succ* 1.37), replacing Antigonus' friend Menander, who had ruled there since 331 (A 3.6.7). Antipater's intention appears to have been to limit the ambitions of Antigonus the One-Eyed, by entrusting Hellespontine Phrygia to Arrhidaeus, Cilicia to Philoxenus, and Lydia to Cleitus; all these territories bordered on Antigonus' enlarged satrapy of Phrygia. Antigonus, however, moved against Arrhidaeus and Cleitus soon after Antipater's death. Cleitus fled to Macedonia and brought charges against Antigonus (D 18.52.5–8). He served Polyperchon briefly and took the Athenians arrested in Phocis, including Phocion, to Athens for execution (P*Ph* 34.2–4, 35.2). As admiral of Polyperchon's fleet he won an initial victory over Nicanor (son of Balacrus?) in the Propontis (D 18.72.2–4), but his ships were attacked while they were at anchor by lightly armed troops sent by Antigonus. The disorganized fleet then put out to sea and was destroyed by Nicanor (D 18.72.5–8; Pol*Strat* 4.6.8; cf. Engel 1973). Cleitus himself escaped to the Thracian shore only to be killed by Lysimachus' men (D 18.72.9).

Schoch, *RE* s.v. "Kleitos (10)"; Berve ii.209 no. 428; Hauben 43–51 no. 18; Heckel 185–7, 383–7.

Cleochares. Macedonian.[222] Sent by Alexander in 326 as an envoy to Porus, telling him that he must pay tribute and present himself to the King at the entrance to his realm (C 8.13.2). *ME* 55–6 claims that Porus had Cleochares whipped and sent an arrogant letter to Alexander. The letter is almost certainly a fabrication and a later addition. Hence the story of Cleochares' mistreatment may also be false.

Berve ii.214 no. 436.

Cleodice (Kleodike, also Cleonice, Kleonike). Sister of Holcias. Cleodice is known only from the propaganda pamphlet on the *Last Days and Testament of Alexander*, a product of the early age of the Successors. According to this document Cleodice was to marry Leonnatus (*LM* 119; Jul Val 3.58 [94]; Ps-Call 3.33.14). Although the testament of Alexander is a forgery, the individuals named therein are historical and we have no reason to doubt Cleodice's existence.

Berve ii.209–10 no. 429; Heckel 1988: 80.

Cleomantis. See s.v. **Cleomenes** [2].

Cleomenes [1]. (Kleomenes). Cleomenes of Naucratis. Ptolemy's hyparch in Egypt (J 13.4.11; A*Succ* 1.5; Dexippus, *FGrH* 100 F8 §2). Allegedly the man who built (*aedificaverat*) Alexandria (J 13.4.11). Cleomenes had been appointed by Alexander in 331 as governor of the Arabian portion of Egypt, around Heroönpolis (Pithom), east of the Delta (A 3.5.4), to which was added responsibility for Egyptian finances (A 3.5.4; cf. C 4.8.5; for the position of *arabarchos* see *OGIS* ii.570, pp. 256–8), which, in the opinion of Seibert 50, he handled with skill. A 7.23.6, 8, speaks of "wrong-doings," but this may reflect Egyptian complaints about over-zealous tax collection or tight-fisted financial management; D 18.14.1 says that Ptolemy found 8,000 talents in the Egyptian treasury. It is uncertain whether Cleomenes ever became satrap in Alexander's lifetime.[223] In all likelihood, Alexander (like Augustus and his successors) thought it wise not to entrust Egypt to a single official, a practice which may explain the decision of the marshals in Babylon to assign Cleomenes to Ptolemy as *hyparchos*; in effect, he continued in the functions originally assigned him by Alexander (cf. Julien 24: "Obersteuereinnehmer"). Killed by Ptolemy, who considered him friendly toward Perdiccas and therefore unfaithful to himself (Paus 1.6.3).

Stähelin, *RE* s.v. "Kleomenes (8)"; Berve ii.210–11 no. 431; Seibert 39–51.[224]

Cleomenes [2]. (Kleomenes). Greek. Possibly identical with "Cleomantis the Lacedaemonian" of P*A* 50.5, which appears to be a corruption of a text that originally read "the seers, Aristander and Cleomenes the Lacedaemonian"; Berve ii.212, for different reasons, concluded that Cleomenes must have been a seer or priest.[225] Cleomenes was thus a seer in Alexander's entourage who in 328 interpreted an unfavorable omen for the King at the time of the Cleitus affair (P*A* 50.4–5). Cleomenes was one of several men who slept in the temple of Serapis at the time of Alexander's fatal illness (A 7.26.2).[226] The entire episode has, however, been called into question, as has the existence of a temple of Serapis in Babylon at this time.[227]

Berve ii.211–12 no. 432; cf. Poralla no. 431.

Cleomenes [3]. (Kleomenes). Cleomenes II, Agiad king of Sparta. Son of Cleombrotus I and brother of Agesipolis II. He married the daughter of Gyrtias (Ath 4.142b–f; D 19.70.4; P*M* 53e) and was the father of Acrotatus and Cleonymus, and grandfather of Areus, who acceded to the throne in 309/8 (P*Agis* 3.6; Paus 1.13.4–5; 3.6.2). Although he succeeded Agesipolis in 370 and ruled until his death in 309 (D 20.29.1: he reigned for sixty years and ten months; D 15.60.4 wrongly thirty-four years), Cleomenes did not attract the attention of the Alexander historians. Berve includes Agesipolis II (ii.8 no. 13), arguing that Diodorus mistakenly reported his death, when he was merely deposed, and that Cleomenes surrendered his brother to Antipater as a hostage after Agis' was (P*M* 215b). But Agesipolis' death is reported also by Paus 1.13.4. Cartledge & Spawforth (1989: 16) call Cleomenes a "prodigious nonentity."

Poralla 77 no. 437.

Cleon (Kleon). Greek from Syracuse. Named by C 8.5.8 as one of the King's flatterers (*kolakes*) who advocated the public acknowledgment of Alexander's divinity (C 8.5.10). He may be identical with the author of a work *On Harbors* (also a Syracusan named Cleon from the fourth century) and thus one of Alexander's "technical" experts.[228] Nothing else is known about him.

Jacoby, *RE* s.v. "Kleon (8)"; Berve ii.215 no. 437; Müller, *FHG* iv.365.

Cleonice. See s.v. **Cleodice**.

Cleopatra [1]. (Kleopatra). Macedonian. A 3.6.5 calls her "Eurydice," which, if not an error, must be the name assumed at marriage (Heckel 1978a; Bosworth i.283; *contra* Badian 1982). Sister of Hippostratus and niece of Attalus (wrongly the sister of Attalus: D 17.2.3; J 9.5.9), Cleopatra was Philip's seventh and last wife (D 17.2.3; Satyrus *ap.* Ath 13.557d–e; cf. Ath 13.560c), and possibly the aunt of the ilarch and admiral Hegelochus (see s.v. **Hegelochus**). She had borne Philip a daughter named Europa (Satyrus *ap.* Ath 13.557e; cf. J 9.7.12) only a few days before the King's death (D 17.2.3). But this child was soon murdered along with her mother by Olympias (J 9.7.12; Paus 8.7.7). She may be the Eurydice, whose statue was housed, until its deliberate removal, in the Philippeum at Olympia (Paus 5.20.10; cf. 5.17.4 where, as Professor Palagia has pointed out, the text is corrupt).

Stähelin, *RE* s.v. "Kleopatra (12)"; Badian 1982; Berve ii.213 no. 434; Tarn ii.260–2; Heckel 1978a and 1979; Whitehorne 30–42. See Stemmata I, XIV.

Cleopatra [2]. (Kleopatra). Daughter of Philip II and Olympias (Satyrus *ap.* Ath 13.557c; D 16.91.4–6), sister of Alexander the Great (J 13.6.4; 14.1.7), Cleopatra was probably born sometime between 355 and 353.[229] In 336 she married her uncle, Alexander I of Epirus, in Aegae; it was during the celebrations associated with this wedding that Philip was assassinated (D 16.91.4–6; J 9.6.1–3, 7.7). In 335 Cleopatra gave birth to a daughter named Cadmeia and a son, Neoptolemus (P*Pyr* 5.11; cf. Sandberger 115 no. 40). After the departure of Alexander I from Epirus (see **Alexander** [1]; Aes 3.242 mentions an Athenian delegation that brought condolences; cf. Livy 8.24.14–17 for the return of his remains), Cleopatra appears to have exercised power as regent (cf. Carney 89).[230] After the death of Alexander I, Olympias returned to her native Epirus and sent Cleopatra back to Macedonia.[231] In the years after her brother's death Cleopatra became the political tool of others with regal aspirations, though she herself appears to have made an offer to marry Leonnatus (P*Eum* 3.9) along with the promise of supreme power. But Leonnatus died before the promise could be fulfilled (D 18.15.3–4; see s.v. **Leonnatus** [2]) and Cleopatra entered into negotiations with Perdiccas. These were, however, complicated by Perdiccas' previous commitment to marry Nicaea the daughter of Antipater (J 13.6.4, 7; D 18.23.1–3), an arrangement that Alcetas urged his brother to honor (A*Succ* 1.21); Eumenes at the same time acted as Perdiccas' go-between with Cleopatra, who had now taken up residence in Sardis (A*Succ* 1.26). Perdiccas' intrigues were reported by Antigonus to Antipater (D 18.25.3). After Perdiccas' death and the outlawing of his party, Eumenes came to Sardis in order to shore up his own authority as the defender of the royal cause through Cleopatra's support (J 14.1.7), but Cleopatra was afraid of compromising her position with Antipater and Eumenes departed (P*Eum* 8.6–7).[232] When Antipater himself reached Sardis, there was a heated exchange in which Cleopatra gave as good as she got (A*Succ* 1.40). Between 320 and 308, Cleopatra remained in Sardis until Ptolemy made an offer of marriage, in connection with his only serious bid for greater power (D 20.37.3; *HE* 4).[233] Antigonus, however, sensing the danger of such an alliance, had her killed (D 20.37.5–6).

Stähelin, *RE* s.v. "Kleopatra (13)"; Berve ii.212–13 no. 433; Macurdy 22–48; Whitehorne 57–69; Carney 75–6, 89–90, 123–8. See Stemmata I, II.

Cleophis. The name is found in Latin sources only and may have been invented in the Augustan age as a play on the name Cleopatra (cf. Gutschmid 1882: 553–4; Seel 1972: 181–2). Mother of Assacenus (C 8.10.22; *ME* 39; cf. A 4.27.4, who does not name her), the Indian dynast of the Assacenians of the Swat and Panjkora region. She conducted the defense of Massaga (a fortress in the Katgala Pass; cf. Caroe 51–3), the capital city of the Assacenians, since her son had died only shortly before the advent of Alexander (C 8.10.22); the actual operations appear to have been managed by Assacenus' brother (another son of Cleophis?), known in *ME* 39 as Amminais, and 9,000 mercenaries (C 8.10.23 says the city was garrisoned by 38,000 infantrymen, which may include the above-mentioned mercenaries, though Curtius, oddly, says nothing about their fate). After a valiant defense (C 8.10.27–33), in which the *hegemon* of the place (Amminais? or the commander of the mercenaries?) was killed (A 4.27.2), the

Assacenians sent a herald to Alexander to discuss terms of surrender. Arrian (4.27.3–4) differs from the vulgate in the details of this proposed capitulation, claiming that Alexander slaughtered the mercenaries because they planned to desert and took the city by force, capturing in the process the mother and *daughter* of Assacenus. Curtius writes that Cleophis and the noble women came in person to surrender to Alexander (cf. *ME* 45), that she placed *her own son* (Assacenus' son in *ME* 39, 45) on the King's knee and thereby won his pardon and retained her position as queen (C 8.10.34–5). Cleophis subsequently bore a son, named Alexander (C 8.10.36; J 12.7.10 claims that Alexander himself was the father, cf. Oros 3.19.1–2). Justin claims that she retained her kingdom through sexual favors and was thus called *scortum regium* (12.7.9–11). Berve ii.214 thinks that the romantic elements of this episode inspired the Candace story of the Alexander Romance (Ps-Call 3.18). See also s.vv. **Assacenus**, **Amminais**.

Berve ii.214 no. 435.

Codrus (Kodros). Ephesian, son of Echeanax. Together with his brothers Anaxagoras and Diodorus, he murdered Hegesias, tyrant of Ephesus. Philoxenus, acting on behalf of Alexander the Great, forced the Ephesians to surrender Codrus and his brothers and imprisoned them for some time in Sardis. From here Codrus and Anaxagoras escaped to Athens, but Diodorus was injured in the escape and recaptured. After Alexander's death, when Perdiccas sent Diodorus back to Ephesus to be tried, Codrus and Anaxagoras returned to save him (Pol*Strat* 6.49).

Berve ii.215 no. 438.

Coenus [1]. (Koinos). Son of Polemocrates (A 1.14.2; cf. *SIG*[3] 332, 7–8) and apparently the brother of Cleander (A 1.24.2). His father had been allotted estates in the Chalcidic peninsula, and Coenus too received additional land in Philip's reign, all of which Coenus' son Perdiccas inherited (*SIG*[3] 332). Born ca. 370: it is doubtful that he would have defended his right to speak out at the Hyphasis with reference to his age, had he not been at least 40 in 326 (A 5.27.3). His battalion is first attested in the surprise attack on Glaucias' Taulantians near Pellium in 335 (A 1.6.9), but Coenus may have held the command already in the final years of Philip's reign. He had married, perhaps in late 335, Parmenion's daughter (C 6.9.30), probably the widow of Attalus (**F33**, **34**). No later than the end of 333 BC she produced a son named Perdiccas.[234]

At the Granicus River, Coenus was stationed on the right, between the battalions of Perdiccas and Amyntas son of Andromenes (A 1.14.2). At Issus (A 2.8.3; C 3.9.7) and Gaugamela (A 3.11.9; D 17.57.2; C 4.13.28, wrongly claiming that Coenus' troops stood in reserve: cf. Atkinson i.422), his battalion held the position previously occupied by that of Perdiccas. During the winter 334/3 Coenus was sent on a recruiting mission from Caria to Macedonia (A 1.24.1–2); he rejoined Alexander at Gordium with 3,000 infantry and 300 cavalry from Macedonia, 200 Thessalian horse, and 150 Eleian cavalry (A 1.29.4; cf. C 3.1.24). Nothing is known of Coenus' role at Issus, but Griffith (*HMac* ii.712) regards his shift toward the center as a promotion based on the performance of the battalion. In the final assault on Tyre, Coenus' battalion (or rather a portion of it) boarded a ship suitable for landing troops, and once inside the city-walls distinguished itself in a particularly bloody engagement (A 2.23.2, 24.3). At Gaugamela he was wounded by an arrow in the heavy fighting (C 4.16.32; D 17.61.3; A 3.15.2; but cf. Bosworth i.311).

Coenus' battalion formed part of the contingent that attempted to encircle Ariobarzanes at the Persian Gates: the units of Coenus, Amyntas, Polyperchon, and Philotas son of Parmenion were detached from the encircling force in order to begin the bridging of the Araxes River (C 5.4.20,

30; A 3.18.6). After the sack of Persepolis, he accompanied Alexander as far as the Caspian Gates, where he was detached with a small party to forage for supplies needed in the pursuit of Darius (A 3.20.4).[235] But news of Darius' arrest caused Alexander to push ahead without awaiting Coenus' return (A 3.21.2); the latter rejoined Craterus, who followed the King at a more leisurely pace. In the campaigns against the Mardians (A 3.24.1) and Satibarzanes near Artacoana (A 3.25.6), Coenus was again directly under the King's command.

Allegations of Philotas' involvement in the conspiracy of Dimnus placed Coenus in jeopardy: Philotas was his brother-in-law (C 6.9.30), but Coenus belonged to the King's *consilium*, which was convened to discuss the matter (C 6.8.17). His actions are, in fact, quite understandable: the vehemence with which he assailed Philotas – denouncing him as a parricide and a traitor to his country (C 6.9.30) – reflects the danger in which he found himself. Few scholars today credit Curtius' statement that it was the law in Macedon to put to death the relatives of those who plotted against the King, yet Coenus, by inveighing against his wife's brother and calling for his torture, was attempting first and foremost to establish his own innocence (C 6.9.30–1; 6.11.10–11). Did his career suffer as a result of Philotas' disgrace? There is a brief hiatus in our knowledge of Coenus' activities between 330 and 328, but this may be due to the nature of the sources, which become confused and uneven at this point. To seek political causes for his brief disappearance from history is perhaps unwise; for we should then be hard pressed to explain the man's prominence in the years 328–326 BC. In 328, Alexander conducted a sweep-campaign in Sogdiana, dividing the mobile portion of the army into five units, one of them under Coenus' command.[236] He was instructed to take his troops and Artabazus (at that time the satrap of the region) in the direction of Scythia, where, it was reported, Spitamenes had taken refuge (A 4.16.3). This short campaign accomplished little, however, since Spitamenes had crossed the Oxus and attacked Bactra (Zariaspa), only to be driven out again by Craterus (A 4.16.4–17.2). In late summer or early autumn, Coenus rejoined Alexander at Maracanda where Artabazus relinquished his satrapy on account of old age (A 4.17.3; C 8.1.19). Hence Coenus was undoubtedly present at the drinking-party at which Artabazus' designated successor, Cleitus, was murdered by the King. As winter approached, Coenus remained in Sogdiana with the new satrap, Amyntas son of Nicolaus, two battalions of *pezhetairoi*, 400 Companion cavalry, and the *hippakontistai* with orders to guard the territory against Spitamenes and the Massagetae (A 4.17.3). Coenus retained his own battalion (perhaps already led by Peithon son of Agenor) and that of Meleager. The 400 Companions may represent what were to become Coenus' hipparchy (cf. A 5.16.3). On these he inflicted heavy casualties (A 4.17.5–6; 800 casualties), and after bringing the Massagetae to terms – they soon showed their good faith by sending Spitamenes' head to Alexander (A 4.17.7; a much different story in the vulgate: C 8.3.1–15; *ME* 20–3) – Coenus rejoined the King at Nautaca before the end of winter (A 4.18.1).

Coenus had proved himself in Sogdiana, and it is not surprising to find him in more independent roles during the Swat campaign (cf. Fuller 245ff.; Seibert 1985: 150–4). Against the Aspasian hyparch, he remained with Alexander (A 4.24.1) and also against the Guraeans and Assacenians as far as Massaga (A 4.25.6); from Massaga he was sent against Bazira (A 4.27.5, 7–8; C 8.10.22 (Beira); *IA* 107. Bazira = Bir-Kot: Stein 46–8; Eggermont 184), where he inflicted heavy losses on the natives while Alexander took the nearby town of Ora ("Ude-gram"; Stein 58–60; cf. Seibert 1985: 152, with n. 40, Maps 25–6). A 4.27.5 names Attalus, Alcetas, and Demetrius the hipparch as the commanders in charge of the siege; C 8.11.1 names Polyperchon and credits him with the capture of the town. A 4.27.7, 9 gives Alexander the honor of taking Ora. The natives of Bazeira fled to Aornus (Pir-Sar), to which the King advanced via Embolima, taking Coenus and some more nimble troops (A 4.28.8); in addition to Coenus' battalions, Alexander took the archers, the Agrianes, select troops from the phalanx, 200 Companion cavalry, and 100 mounted archers. On his return from Aornus, Alexander learned that Aphrices (or Airices?) was preparing to blockade his path, and he left Coenus to bring up the slower troops while he advanced to meet the enemy (D 17.86.2; C 8.12.1).

By the time the Macedonians reached the Hydaspes (Jhelum), Coenus had effectively become hipparch. His name continued to be applied to his former battalion, though the commander of that unit was in all probability Peithon son of Agenor (Tarn ii.190 implausibly assigns it to Antigenes). Before the battle with Porus, he was sent back to the Indus to dismantle the ships and transport them overland to the Hydaspes (A 5.8.4). In the actual engagement, Coenus' battalion and hipparchy crossed the river upstream along with the King and took part in the initial assault on Porus (A 5.12.2; C 8.14.15, 17; P*A* 60): he and Demetrius son of Althaemenes attacked the cavalry (about 2,000 in number) on the Indian right, pursuing them as they transferred their position to the left, where Porus' horsemen were outnumbered by Alexander's (A 5.16.3; 5.17.1; C 8.14.15 must be emended to make sense of Coenus' activities).

At the Acesines (Chenab) Coenus was left behind to oversee the crossing by the bulk of the army and to forage for supplies; a similar task was given also to Craterus (A 5.21.1, 4). He rejoined Alexander at or near the Hyphasis (Beas) after the bloody Sangala campaign. Here, when the troops were stubborn in their refusal to continue eastward, Coenus rose to put the soldiers' case to the King, reminding him of their sufferings and losses and their desire to see their homeland and loved ones (A 5.27.2–9; C 9.3.3–15). Curtius adds an appeal to the poor state of the soldiers' equipment, a point which may well be true, but which contributes to the general irony of the situation: Coenus, who spoke so passionately in favor of returning to Macedonia, died soon afterwards (C 9.3.20), and there arrived shortly after his death 25,000 splendid suits of armor (9.3.21). Whatever suspicions his death at the Hydaspes arouses (A 6.1.1, 2.1; cf. 5.29.5; C 9.3.20 puts it at the Acesines; for the confusion see Hammond 1983: 152–3), coming as it did so soon after his opposition to Alexander, there is no good reason to assume that it was not caused by illness.

Honigmann, *RE* s.v. "Koinos (1)"; Berve ii.215–18 no. 439; Heckel 58–64. See Stemma VII.

Coenus [2]. (Koinos). Macedonian of unknown background. Arrived in Persia in 324 with mercenaries and reports of the political situation in Europe (C 10.1.43). Ruled Susiana in 323 (J 13.4.14) after the brief rule of Oropius (Dexippus, *FGrH* 100 F8 §6; cf. *LM* 121), who had replaced Abulites. In 320, in the settlement of Triparadeisus, Susiana was awarded to Antigenes. What became of Coenus is unknown.

Honigmann, *RE* s.v. "Koinos (2)"; Berve ii.218 no. 440; Lehmann-Haupt 154.

Coeranus [1]. (Koiranos). Macedonian from Beroea (A 3.6.4). Coeranus appears to have been with Alexander since the beginning of the Asiatic expedition. Before the battle of Issus, when Harpalus fled to Greece (A 3.6.7), Alexander divided the control of the treasury between Coeranus and Philoxenus.[237] Upon Harpalus' return to favor, Coeranus was appointed the finance officer for Phoenicia, Cilicia, and Coele-Syria (A 3.6.4).[238] In 331, Alexander sent Menes son of Dionysius with 3,000 talents of silver to become *hyparchos* of this region (A 3.16.9–10). It does not follow (*pace* Berve ii.219) that he replaced

Coeranus as finance officer (see Brunt i.278 n. 11 and also s.v. **Philoxenus** [1]).

Berve ii.219 no. 441; Tataki no. 750.

Coeranus [2]. (Koiranos). A 3.12.4 calls the commander of the allied horse Coeranus. Possibly this is an error for Caranus (thus Roos emends the text; cf. Brunt i.262 n. 1; Heckel 1981d: 70) but Bosworth i.303 argues for retaining Coeranus. Coeranus is not heard of again; Caranus, on the other hand, is found commanding similar troops later in the campaign. See **Caranus** [2].

Schoch, *RE* Supplbd IV s.v. "Koiranos (9)"; Berve ii.219 no. 442 (Koiranos).

Combaphes (Kombaphes). Apparently an oriental (cf. Berve ii.219; for the name see Justi 165, "Kombaphis"). Slave of Alexander. According to the *Liber de Morte*, he and a fellow-slave, Hermogenes, were summoned to the King's deathbed, where one copied out his testament (which the King dictated) while the other held the lamp (*LM* 103). Alexander's testament itself is fictitious, but the *Liber de Morte* in other cases refers to historical individuals, and Combaphes and Hermogenes may, in fact, have been actual slaves of the King.

Berve ii.219 no. 443; Heckel 1988: 12.

Cophaeus (Kophaios). Indian dynast of the upper Cophen (Kabul) region (Lassen ii^2 147–8), Cophaeus surrendered to Alexander upon his arrival and retained the position of *hyparchos* of his country. Together with Assagetes, Cophaeus appears to have brought a contingent to Alexander at Peucelaotis and helped with the assault on Aornus (A 4.28.6). Nothing else is known of his career.

Wecker, *RE* s.v. "Kophen"; Berve ii.229 no. 458; Lassen ii^2 147–8.

Cophen (Kophen; Cophes). Son of Artabazus (A 2.11.9), and one of the nine sons of the same mother, the sister of Memnon and Mentor the Rhodians (Dem 23.154, 157), who spent some time in exile at the court of Philip II, ca. 349/8 (D 16.52.4); hence also the brother of Alexander's mistress, Barsine. Before the battle of Issus, Cophen was ordered to convey the royal treasures and the family members of the most prominent Persians to Damascus for safe-keeping (A 2.15.1; cf. 2.11.9; D 17.32.3; C 3.8.12). Damascus was, however, captured by Parmenion (A 2.15.1; C 3.13). Cophen himself appears either to have rejoined Darius at Issus, whence he escaped with the King, or to have escaped capture at Damascus (identification with Curtius' prefect of Damascus (3.13.2–3, 17) is impossible, since that man was murdered). In 330, after the arrest of Darius III by Bessus, Nabarzanes, and Barsaentes, Cophen (with his father and brothers) surrendered to Alexander (A 3.23.7), who later sent him to the Sogdianian rebel Ariamazes to negotiate his surrender (C 7.11.5, 22–3).[239] What became of him we do not know.[240]

Willrich 1899; Berve ii.230 no. 459. See Stemma IV.

Corrhagus [1]. (Korrhagos). Macedonian. Served as Antipater's *strategos* in the Peloponnese during Alexander's absence. In summer 331 his forces suffered a stunning defeat at the hands of Agis III and his allies (Aes 3.165). Whether he himself survived the battle is unknown. Identification with the father of Stratonice, the mother of Demetrius Poliorcetes (*PDemetr* 2.1), is possible but cannot be proved.

Schoch, *RE* Supplbd IV s.v. "Korragos (1)"; Berve ii.219–20 no. 444.

Corrhagus [2]. (Korrhagos). Prominent Macedonian and apparently one of Alexander's *hetairoi*. At a drinking-party in India (326/5 BC), he challenged the wrestler Dioxippus to single combat. Corrhagus, in full armor, was defeated by Dioxippus who fought without body armor and carried a club (C 9.7.16–26; D 17.100.1–101.6). Ael*VH* 10.22 wrongly adds that he was killed in the duel. Nothing further is known about him.

Schoch, *RE* Supplbd IV s.v. "Korragos (5)"; Berve ii.220 no. 445.

Corrhagus [3]. (Korrhagos). Macedonian. Son of Menoitas. One of the *hetairoi*. Participated in Alexander's Balkan campaign (see Clarysse & Schepens 1985; Hammond 1987; Whitby 2004). He could be identical with either [1] or [2].

Craterus (Krateros). Macedonian from Orestis. Son of Alexander (A*Ind* 18.5; A 1.25.9; cf. Perdrizet 1899: 274) and Aristopatra (Str 15.1.35 [702] = *FGrH* 153 F2);[241] Amphoterus was his brother (A 1.25.9; see s.v. **Amphoterus**). Born perhaps after 370, but this is no more than a guess. Wounds (P*A* 41.5; A 4.3.3) and illness (A 7.12.4; P*A* 41.6–7) appear to have taken their toll and hard campaigning may have aged him prematurely.

In 334 Craterus commanded a battalion of *pezhetairoi* on the left of the line at the Granicus (A 1.14.2, 3; cf. Bosworth 1976a: 126); he later commanded the entire infantry on the left at Issus (333 BC), though still subordinate to Parmenion (A 2.8.4; C 3.9.8). Early in 332, Craterus and Perdiccas directed the siege of Tyre in Alexander's absence (C 4.3.1) and Craterus' troops effectively countered a Tyrian sortie (Pol*Strat* 4.13). Alexander soon placed him in charge of the left wing, along with Pnytagoras of Salamis, in the naval assault on Tyre (A 2.20.6; C 4.3.11). At Gaugamela (331), as at Issus, he led the infantry-battalions on the left wing, again under Parmenion's general command (A 3.11.10; D 17.57.3; but C 4.13.29 is corrupt). His first independent command over a portion of the army other than his own battalion came in the Uxian campaign, where his troops occupied the heights, to which the enemy fled to escape Alexander's forces; large numbers were butchered by Craterus' men (A 3.17.4–5; cf., in general, D 17.67 and C 5.3.1–16).[242] Henceforth, Alexander regularly entrusted the larger, less mobile, forces to Craterus.[243] At the Persian Gates, only days later, Alexander led a select force to Ariobarzanes' rear, leaving the rest of his troops at the foot of the "Gates" under the direction of Craterus (A 3.18.4–8; C 5.4.14–34; Pol*Strat* 4.3.27 wrongly places Hephaestion and Philotas in charge of the main camp).

Soon after the fall of Persepolis, Alexander conducted a thirty-day campaign into the interior of Persia, while the bulk of the army remained behind with Parmenion and Craterus (C 5.6.11, probably to coordinate the removal of the treasures).[244] Later Craterus set out with Alexander from Ecbatana toward the Caspian Gates, and, when Alexander hurried after Darius and his captors, Craterus led the slower forces eastward from the Gates and awaited the return of Coenus and his foraging party (A 3.20.4; 3.21.2). In Hyrcania, Craterus and Erigyius each commanded one-third of the army, but Erigyius' task was merely to lead the baggage-train along the easiest route, while Craterus took his own battalion and that of Amyntas son of Andromenes, the archers, and some cavalry against the Tapurians (A 3.23.2; cf. C 6.4.2). C 6.4.2 claims that Craterus was left behind to guard Parthiene against invaders, but this is misleading. His mission was clearly to patrol, round up fugitive mercenaries (A 3.23.6), and restore order to Parthiene. Thus he and Erigyius reunited with Alexander at Zadracarta in Hyrcania; they were joined also by Autophradates, satrap of the Tapurians (A 3.23.6; C 6.4.23–4: "Phradates").

After the defection of Satibarzanes (330 BC), Craterus was left behind at the foot of a rocky outcrop, on the plateau of which – some thirty-two stades in circumference (C 6.6.23; about 3.5 miles) – 13,000 Areians had taken refuge. But Alexander, who had intended to pursue Satibarzanes, soon returned and conducted the siege in person; for he learned that Satibarzanes was too far off. Alexander's reconnaissance may have informed him that Satibarzanes had moved to Artacoana (usually identified as Herat and equated with Alexandria in Areia). Perhaps he sent Craterus ahead to Artacoana, which he besieged in the King's absence, but allowed him the honor of taking it (C 6.6.33). In Arrian's version, Alexander breaks off his march to Bactra, leaving him with the rest of the army, and rushes to Artacoana; no satisfactory account of the town's surrender is given. Some time later, when Alexander had already made administrative changes in the satrapy, Craterus and the remainder of the army joined him (A 3.25.6–8).

At Phrada (mod. Farah), Craterus took a leading role in the prosecution of Philotas, a political enemy and rival for command. Already in Egypt (331 BC), an informant had told Craterus of the "treasonous" remarks uttered by Philotas to his mistress, Antigone (P*A* 48.6; P*M* 339e–f). He wasted no time in bringing the matter, and Antigone, to the King's attention. And, while Alexander forgave Philotas, Craterus remained suspicious and kept him under surveillance (P*A* 48.7–49.1).[245] More than a year and a half later, when the opportunity presented itself in Phrada, Craterus was quick to act. Alexander at first made no firm decision on how he would deal with what amounted to a case of negligence, the only offense of which Philotas was clearly guilty (cf. C 6.7.34). For Philotas himself admitted that he had failed to pass on the news of a conspiracy involving some lesser-known Macedonians (see s.v. **Dimnus**). Philotas' fate was, in fact, decided at a council of the *hetairoi*. Craterus spoke first and most effectively, for he was dear to Alexander and exceedingly hostile to Philotas (A 7.12.3; P*A* 47.9–10; D 17.114.1–2; C 6.8.2). Whether or not Craterus was attempting to disguise his ill-will toward Philotas with a show of piety, as C 6.8.2, 4 claims, is debatable; for Craterus had already gained in power and importance as a result of Parmenion's relegation to Ecbatana. He was, most likely, sincere in both motives: he earnestly desired to protect Alexander from the insidious, and he sought to ruin Philotas for personal reasons. Craterus' speech was to the point and, in some respects, strongly reminiscent of the advice given concerning Alexander Lyncestes. Alexander could not go on excusing Philotas forever, nor would Philotas cease to plot against the King. Beware the enemy within, warned Craterus. And he had not forgotten the threat of Parmenion: the father would not endure the son's execution (C 6.8.7). Clearly, Craterus understood what was at stake, what could be gained from Philotas' removal. But his condemnation of Philotas served better the wishes of his accomplices in the conspiracy *against* Philotas. A clique of younger commanders, united against a common enemy, denounced Philotas, first in front of Alexander and then before the army, until even his relatives and friends saw fit to abandon him (see s.vv. **Coenus** [1], **Amyntas** [4]).

In Bactria-Sogdiana, as earlier in Hyrcania and Areia, Craterus had supreme authority over the army while Alexander led detachments on special missions. Thus, while Alexander subdued the rebellious outposts along the Iaxartes River (Syr-Darya), Craterus supervised the siege-work (A 4.2.2; C 7.6.16) at the largest of these, Cyropolis (Kurkath), which was then taken under the King's leadership (A 4.3.1–4; C 7.6.19–21) – though both Alexander and Craterus were wounded (A 4.3.3; P*M* 341b, incorrectly placing it in Hyrcania; C 7.6.22, saying the wound occurred at the town of the Memaceni, after the fall of Cyropolis). We know nothing of his role in the brief skirmish with the Scythians who lived beyond the Iaxartes. Curtius (7.7.9–10) says that he, along with Erigyius and Hephaestion, attended the council held in Alexander's tent before the battle, but no source records his participation in the actual fighting (A 4.4.1–9; C 7.8.6–9.17 is quite different; cf. Fuller 237–41 for analysis). It seems likely that he retained the bulk of the army on the south bank of the river when Alexander crossed with a select force to attack the Scythians.

On hearing of the disaster at the Polytimetus River (A 4.3.6–7, 4.5.2–6.2;

C 7.7.30–9; cf. 7.6.24; see s.v. **Spitamenes**) Alexander hurried south, leaving Craterus to follow with the main body at a more restrained pace (C 7.9.20).[246] In the spring of 328, Alexander moved out of winter quarters at Bactra (Balkh) and recrossed the Oxus River, leaving behind the battalions of Polyperchon, Attalus, Gorgias, and Meleager, all under the command of Craterus.[247] Their instructions were to prevent further defection in Bactria and to crush the insurrection (A 4.16.1). But, while Alexander and the mobile troops conducted a sweep-campaign in Sogdiana, the rebel Spitamenes, supported by horsemen of the Massagetae, attacked the smaller Macedonian garrisons in Bactria. Craterus drove the Massagetae to the edge of the desert, where he defeated them in a bitter struggle – killing 150 of 1,000 horsemen – only to be forced by the desert to abandon his pursuit.[248] But, by driving Spitamenes and his supporters out of Bactria, Craterus inadvertently took some of the luster off his own victory; for Coenus, who had been left in Sogdiana at the beginning of winter 328/7, won a more decisive battle, as a consequence of which the Massagetae delivered Spitamenes' head to Alexander (A 4.17.3–7; cf. C 8.3.1–15 and *ME* 20–3). Both Coenus and Craterus rejoined the main force at Nautaca for the remainder of that winter.[249]

Craterus was not present in Maracanda when Alexander murdered Cleitus in a drunken brawl, and we can only guess at what his reaction might have been. Like Cleitus, Craterus espoused the traditional values of Macedon (P*A* 47.9) and rejected the King's orientalism (P*Eum* 6.3), but his objections appear to have been tactful and restrained; for he retained the love and respect of Alexander. When the King moved south into Bactria, Craterus remained in Sogdiana with the battalions of Polyperchon, Attalus, and Alcetas, capturing the rebel Haustanes and killing Catanes (A 4.22.2; C 8.5.2). It was perhaps no coincidence that Alexander's attempt to introduce the Persian practice of *proskynesis* at his own court was made during Craterus' absence. But, even without him, the stubborn opposition of the Macedonian *hetairoi* forced Alexander to abandon the attempt. Details of the conspiracy of the Pages, which occurred soon afterwards, were reported to Craterus by letter (P*A* 55.6). Some time later, Craterus rejoined Alexander in Bactria, whence the army set out for India.

In early summer 327, they moved toward India (A 4.22.3–6). While Perdiccas and Hephaestion led the advance force to the Indus, Craterus at first remained with Alexander, following the course of the Choes. But the heavy infantry and siege-equipment crossed the river with great difficulty and made slow progress through the mountains (A 4.23.2), and Alexander left them behind to follow at their own speed, presumably under Craterus' command.[250] Probably they did not reunite with Alexander until they reached Andaca (A 4.23.5; C 8.10.5), where Craterus was left with instructions to subdue those neighboring cities that had not submitted voluntarily.[251] From Andaca, he advanced to Arigaeum, where Alexander again left him behind with instructions to fortify the main wall, to settle in the city those of the neighboring peoples who so wished, and to leave behind such Macedonians as were unfit for service (A 4.24.6–7). Next, Craterus led his troops and the siege-equipment into the land of the Assacenians, where he rejoined the King (A 4.25.5). From here he moved with the main army to Embolima, where he gathered provisions for the army's operations against Aornus (A 4.28.7). From Aornus, where Craterus is unattested, the main force advanced to the Indus, which had been bridged by Hephaestion and Perdiccas, and thence to the Hydaspes. Here Porus awaited the Macedonians with a sizeable force. In the ensuing battle – Alexander's last major engagement – Craterus' role was similar to that at the Persian Gates. He held the atten-tion of the enemy while Alexander conducted an encircling maneuver. When Porus turned to deal with Alexander, Craterus crossed the river in order to attack him from the rear (A 5.12.1, 18.1). But the battle appears to have been decided before Craterus' troops could play a significant part.

Craterus had perhaps advanced militarily as far as Alexander would allow. After the Hydaspes battle we hear of the fortification of Nicaea and Bucephala (A 5.20.2), of a foraging expedition conducted with Coenus near the Hydraotes River (A 5.21.4). In India he came into open conflict with Hephaestion (P*A* 47.11–12; P*M* 337a), forcing Alexander to intervene in person. For the remainder of the campaign, the Indus served to separate the foes and their armies, but the advantage shifted to Hephaestion, who, initially, commanded the larger force (A 6.2.2; A*Ind* 19.1) as they descended the river in stages (A 6.2.2, 4.1, 5.5, 5.7; A*Ind* 19.1, 3; D 17.96.1). After Alexander was critically wounded in the Mallian campaign, Craterus acted as the spokesman for the *hetairoi*, begging him not to risk his life unnecessarily (C 9.6.6–14). From the junction of the Indus and Acesines rivers, Craterus led the greater part of the army and the elephants along the left (east) bank of the Indus, arriving at Musicanus' capital (near Rohri and ancient Alor) after Alexander's fleet (end of spring 325). Craterus was ordered to garrison and fortify the town (see s.v. **Musicanus**). It was his last major operation – and one that he completed while Alexander himself was present (A 6.15.7) – before he was sent westward through Arachosia and Drangiana with instructions to rejoin Alexander in Carmania.[252]

Thus Craterus, with the battalions of Attalus, Meleager, Antigenes, and Polyperchon,[253] some of the archers, all the elephants and the *apomachoi*, moved westward, policing Arachosia and Drangiana and arresting the rebel leaders (A 6.27.3: Ordanes; C 9.10.19: Ozines and Zariaspes), whom he brought in chains to Alexander in Carmania (A 6.27.3; cf. Str 15.2.11 [725]).[254] At Susa (324 BC) Craterus married the daughter of Oxyathres, Amastris (A 7.4.5: see s.v. **Amastris**), whom he later repudiated and gave to Dionysius of Heraclea Pontica (Memnon, *FGrH* 434 F1 §4.4; Str 12.3.10). Soon afterwards he was ordered to lead some 10,000 veterans back to Macedonia, where he was to replace Antipater as regent and overseer of Greek affairs (A 7.12.4).[255] Craterus, however, made slow progress and had not advanced beyond Cilicia when Alexander died in June 323.[256] His progress was impeded initially by his own ill health (A 7.12.4) and, later, by the conditions in Cilicia itself: the satrap Balacrus had recently been killed in a campaign against the Pisidians (D 18.22.1) and Harpalus had passed through Tarsus before Craterus' arrival and created further disruptions (see s.v. **Harpalus**).

When Alexander died, the orders to replace Antipater were still in effect, at least until the army voted to cancel Alexander's "final plans,"[257] and soon the feuding marshals in Babylon designated him guardian (*prostates*) of Arrhidaeus (A*Succ* 1.3; Dexippus, *FGrH* 100 F8 §4; cf. J 13.4.5). But Antipater was urgently summoning reinforcements to help him in the Lamian War (D 18.12.1). In fact, Craterus remained cautious and did not leave Cilicia until it became clear that Leonnatus' help would prove insufficient.[258] At that point, patriotism won out over personal ambition and Craterus brought a force of about 12,500 to Macedonia (D 18.16.4).[259] Antipater's appeal included, in all probability, an offer of marriage to his eldest daughter Phila, widow of the satrap Balacrus. Craterus probably found her residing in Tarsus in 324 and now escorted her to Macedonia.[260] Craterus' arrival greatly augmented the Macedonian fighting force,[261] but he willingly yielded the supreme command to Antipater (D 18.16.5). Victory at Crannon proved decisive (A*Succ* 1.12; P*Dem* 28.2; P*Ph* 26.1; D 18.17), as the Thessalian cities were brought to terms one by one and the Hellenic alliance crumbled. When the Macedonian army reached Boeotia, Craterus favored an invasion of Attica (P*Ph* 26.6), but Antipater, for Phocion's sake, overruled him and the Athenians saved themselves through negotiation and accepted a garrison in Munychia on the twentieth day of Boëdromion (September 17, 322; cf. Beloch iv^2 1.76).[262]

Once back in Macedonia, Antipater celebrated the marriage of Craterus to Phila, heaping honors and gifts upon the groom and preparing for his "return to Asia" (D 18.18.7). But first it was necessary to deal with the Aetolians, the only Greeks who remained unsubdued (D 18.24–5). D 18.25 depicts Craterus as the chief prosecutor of this war; undoubtedly, he employed his experience gained in the east with Alexander to his advantage. It was now the height of winter, and Craterus built shelters for his troops, forcing the Aetolians, who had forsaken their cities for the highlands, to hold out against the elements and a shortage of food; for it appears that Craterus controlled the lines of communication (D 18.25.1). But events in Asia were to extricate the Aetolians from this grave situation and lead Craterus to his doom.

Perdiccas, in the meantime, wasted little time usurping the regency [of Philip Arrhidaeus] (cf. D 18.23.2), and in winter 321/0 Antigonus the One-Eyed arrived with news of Perdiccas' aspirations and duplicity. Craterus and Antipater now made peace with the Aetolians and prepared to confront Perdiccas in Asia.[263] Craterus departed from Macedonia for the last time in the spring of 320, leaving behind Phila and an infant son. Perdiccas, for his part, had left Eumenes to deal with Antipater and Craterus while he himself marched on Egypt. Nevertheless, things began auspiciously when Neoptolemus defected from Eumenes (D 18.29.1–30.3; P*Eum* 5; A*Succ* 1.26 says that he was lured away). Neoptolemus was aware of the impact Craterus' presence would have on the Macedonians who were stationed opposite him; but Eumenes had no intention of revealing to his forces with whom the issue was to be decided (N*Eum* 3.5–6; P*Eum* 6.7; A*Succ* 1.27). In the ensuing battle Craterus was thrown from his horse, felled by a nameless Thracian or Paphlagonian, or as some said, trampled by his own horse's hoofs (P*Eum* 7.5–6; A*Succ* 1.27; N*Eum* 4.3–4; D 18.30.5); P*Eum* 7.6 relates that a certain Gorgias (see s.v. **Gorgias** [2]), one of Eumenes' generals recognized the fallen Craterus. That Eumenes himself found him as he gasped out his life defies credulity, particularly if we are meant to believe that Eumenes had only shortly before overcome his arch-rival Neoptolemus in a bloody hand-to-hand encounter (N*Eum* 4.2; cf. J 13.8.8; P*Eum* 7.7–12; D 18.31). J 13.8.5, 7 writes Polyperchon where Craterus is clearly meant (cf. Tr*Prol* 13). Eumenes was almost certainly remorseful and treated Craterus' body with respect (P*Eum* 7.13; A*Succ* 26; N*Eum* 4.4; D 19.59.3 states that Eumenes kept the bones of Craterus and only when he himself was on the point of dying gave them to Ariston to convey to Phila in 315 BC).

Geyer, *RE* Supplbd IV s.v. "Krateros (1a)"; Berve ii.220–7 no. 446; Heckel 107–33. See Stemma VI.

Crates (Krates). Greek from Chalcis. Crates was a mining engineer (*metalleutes*) entrusted with draining Lake Copais in Boeotia, which was in flood and threatening neighboring towns. He wrote to Alexander concerning his activities and their disruption by civil strife in Boeotia (Str 9.2.18 [407]; cf. StByz s.v. "Athenai"). DL 4.23 mentions a miner named Crates who accompanied Alexander on his expedition and Ps-Call 1.31 speaks of a certain Carterus (or Craterus), an Olynthian, whom Alexander consulted on the construction of Alexandria in Egypt (cf. Jul Val 1.26). It appears that Crates may have been an Olynthian who settled in the Euboean mother-city, Chalcis, after the destruction of Olynthus in 348 by Philip II.

Fabricius, *RE* s.v. "Krates (21)"; Berve ii.227 no. 448.

Crateuas (Krateuas). Macedonian, possibly an official of Menander, satrap of Lydia.

In 326/5 (eleventh year of Alexander's reign) Crateuas made a gift of land (probably royal land *chora basilike*) near Gambreion to a certain Aristomenes (*SIG*[3] 302). I see no good reason for identifying this Crateuas with the father of the Somatophylax Peithon.

Berve ii.227 no. 447.

Cratinus (Kratinos). Methymnaean *psilokitharistes* of unknown family, Cratinus performed at the mass-marriage ceremony in Susa in 324 (Chares, *FGrH* 125 F4 = Ath 12.538e).

Berve ii.227 no. 449.

Cretheus (Kretheus). A Greek, patronymic unknown, from the Milesian colony of Callatis on the Black Sea coast of Thrace, he may have joined Alexander during the Danubian campaign of 335. During the Gedrosian march of 325, when the army came to a region of the satrapy where supplies were plentiful, he was instructed to gather provisions for Nearchus' fleet and convey them to a depot where they could avail the fleet (A 6.23.5). Nothing else is known about him.

Schoch, *RE* Supplbd IV s.v. "Kretheus"; Berve ii.228 no. 450.

Crison (Krison). A runner from Himera on Sicily, Crison once raced Alexander but lost deliberately, much to the King's annoyance (P*M* 471e, 58f). He is otherwise unattested.

Berve ii.228 no. 451.

Critobulus (Kritoboulos; Critobulus). A physician (C 9.5.25) from Cos, Critobulus was one of the trierarchs of the Hydaspes fleet (A*Ind* 18.7). Since the trierarchs were responsible for the expenses of fitting out the ships and not actually the commanders of the vessels themselves, there is no obstacle to identifying the trierarch and the physician. During the descent of the Indus river-system, Critobulus treated the near-fatal wound sustained by Alexander in the town of the Mallians (C 9.5.25). A 6.11.1 calls the physician Critodemus, but Curtius' version preserves the name of the man who is credited with extracting the arrow from Philip II's eye at Methone some twenty-eight years earlier (Pl*NH* 7.37).[264]

Kind, *RE* s.v.; Berve ii.228 nos. 452–3; cf. Heckel 1981e.

Critodemus (Kritodemos). See **Critobulus**.

Crobylus (Krobylos). Slave boy renowned in Corinth for his beauty. Hagnon of Teos was reported to have wished to buy him for Alexander, only to be rebuked for the offer (P*A* 22.3). He is otherwise unknown.

Berve ii.228 no. 454.

Ctesiphon (Ktesiphon). Athenian of the deme Anaphlystos; son of Leosthenes (Dem 18.54, 118). Introduced the motion to crown Demosthenes in 336, which was the basis of the charges brought by Aeschines in 330 (Aes 3 and Dem 18). Ctesiphon's personal link with Alexander came in 331/0, when he was sent as an ambassador to Alexander's sister, Cleopatra, offering Athenian condolences for the death of her husband, Alexander I of Epirus (Aes 3.242).

Hongimann, *RE* s.v. "Ktesiphon (2)"; Berve ii.228–9 no. 455; Kirchner no. 8894; Schaefer iii[2] 83, 86, 221, 292.

Cynnane (Kynane; Kyna; Kynnana; Cyna). Daughter of Philip II and Audata-Eurydice, the daughter of the Illyrian king Bardylis (Satyrus *ap.* Ath 13.557b–c; A*Succ* 1.22). Born ca. 358, Cynnane accompanied her father on an Illyrian campaign in the mid 340s in which she is said to have slain with her own hand an Illyrian queen (Pol*Strat* 8.60; **F43**). Soon thereafter she married Amyntas son of Perdiccas and bore him a daughter, Adea (A*Succ* 1.22). When Amyntas was executed by Alexander in 336/5, the widowed Cynnane was offered as a bride to Langarus, king of the

Agrianes (A 1.5.4); but he died of illness before he could come to Pella to receive his bride (A 1.5.5). She remained unmarried in Macedonia, raising her daughter, whom she trained in the Illyrian arts of war (Duris, *FGrH* 76 F52 = Ath 13.560f). After Alexander's death, she crossed the Strymon in spite of Antipater's attempt to prevent her journey and took her daughter to Asia, where she planned to arrange her marriage to Philip III Arrhidaeus. She was, however, met by Alcetas, the brother of Perdiccas, who sought to turn her back in the vicinity of Ephesus. Defiant, she was murdered by Alcetas (Pol*Strat* 8.60; A*Succ* 1.22, cf. 1.24 for the news of her death in Europe). Her murder helped to accomplish her goal;[265] for the army of Alcetas mutinied and demanded that Adea be taken to Philip III in order that Cynnane's death might not be in vain (Pol*Strat* 8.60; A*Succ* 1.23). She was later buried at Aegae, near the tomb of her daughter and son-in-law (Diyllus, *FGrH* 73 F1 = Ath 4.155a; D 19.52.5). According to Diyllus the funeral rites included four of Cassander's soldiers matched in single combat.

Berve ii.229 no. 456; Heckel 1983–4; Ogden 16–26; Carney 69–70, 129–31. See Stemma I.

Cyrsilus (Kyrsilos). Thessalian from Pharsalus, patronymic unknown. Accompanied Alexander on his expedition – perhaps as one of his Thessalian *hetairoi*, possibly as member of the Thessalian cavalry – and appears to have written, together with Medius of Larissa, an early history (*archaeologia*) of Armenia, claiming that the region was named for the Thessalian Armenus, who accompanied Jason on the *Argo* (Str 11.14.12).

Kroll, *RE* s.v.; Berve ii.229 no. 457; Müller, *FHG* 127; Jacoby, *FGrH* 130; Pearson 69.

D

Damis [1]. Spartan of unknown family. In 324, upon hearing that Alexander was requesting divine honors, Damis is supposed to have remarked, "Let's agree that Alexander be called a god, if he so wishes" (P*M* 219e–f; cf. Ael*VH* 2.19).[266] Nothing else is known about him.

Niese, *RE* s.v. "Damis (2)"; Berve ii.115 no. 239; Poralla no. 216.

Damis [2]. Megalopolitan. Damis served with Alexander in Asia, where he gained experience in the use of elephants in warfare (D 18.71.2). This knowledge he used to good effect in the successful defense of Megalopolis against Polyperchon in 318 (D 18.71). Whether or not Damis was a Megalopolitan himself is unclear. He appears to have been installed as the city's governor (*epimeletes*) by Antipater, perhaps after the Lamian War, and was confirmed in this position by Cassander in 315 (D 19.64.1). C 10.8.15 mentions a certain Amissus of Megalopolis as one of the agents who negotiated a settlement between the cavalry and infantry factions in Babylon after Alexander's death. This appears to be a corruption of the name Damis.

Kirchner, *RE* s.v. "Damis (1)"; Berve ii.115 no. 240.

Damon. Macedonian common soldier under the command of Parmenion (apparently in Syria, as the context of Plutarch's account suggests). Damon and Timotheus were charged with seducing the "wives" of certain Greek mercenaries (**F48–49**). Alexander instructed Parmenion to investigate and execute them if they were found guilty (P*A* 22.4). The outcome of the proceedings is unknown.

Berve ii.115 no. 241.

Damosthenes. Son of Pyrrhinus. Cavalryman from Orchomenus. Served as a member of Alexander's allied cavalry until the expedition reached Ecbatana in 330. There he and his compatriots were discharged. On their return (ca. 329), they made a dedication to Zeus Soter in Orchomenus (*IG* vii.3206).

Berve ii.116 no. 242.

Dandamis (Mandanis: Str 15.1.64 [715], 15.1.69 [718]). Indian philosopher. The oldest of the so-called Gymnosophists.[267] At Taxila he was summoned by Alexander through the agency of Onesicritus (Onesicritus, *FGrH* 134 F17a = Str 15.1.63–5; cf. F17b = P*A* 65.3), but Dandamis refused to present himself, denying the King's divine paternity and giving in to neither promises of gifts nor threats of punishment (A 7.2.2–4; cf. also P*A* 8.5, which shows that Alexander respected his independence). There appears to have developed a tradition that deliberately contrasted Dandamis and Calanus, depicting the former as a man of integrity and the latter as a parasite (Megasthenes, *FGrH* 715 F34a = Str 15.1.68 [718]).

Kaerst, *RE* s.v.; Berve ii.116 no. 243.

Darius (Dareios). (ca. 380–330; *regn.* 336–330). Son of Arsanes and grandson of Ostanes, who had been a brother of Artaxerxes II (D 17.5.5; for the family see s.v. **Sisygambis** and Stemma III). His mother was Sisygambis, apparently a sister of Arsanes. Darius clearly belonged to a cadet branch of the royal house, though certain hostile accounts depicted him a slave and courier (P*M* 326e; cf. *Suda* A3906; Ael*VH* 12.43; Str 15.3.24 [736]). Allegedly known as Codomannus before his accession (J 10.3.3). During the reign of Artaxerxes III Ochus, Darius volunteered to fight the champion of the Cadusians (**M38**) in single combat and, after defeating and killing him, was honored greatly by the King, who made him satrap of Armenia (J 10.3.3–4; D 17.6.1). Before Philip's death (D 17.7.1), Darius himself gained the throne through the machinations of the eunuch chiliarch Bagoas, who had poisoned Ochus, his son and successor Arses, and all the latter's brothers and children, thus eliminating the direct line of Ochus (D 17.5.3–6; P*M* 337e; cf. A 2.14.5). But Darius soon learned of Bagoas' plot against him and forced the eunuch to drink his own poison (D 17.5.6). Born ca. 380 – he was about 50 at the time of his death in 330 (A 3.22.2, 6) – Darius is described as the most handsome of men (P*A* 21.6), just as his second wife, his sister Stateira (P*A* 30.3; A 2.11.9; J 11.9.12; Gell 7.8.3; her name is given only by P*A* 30.5, 8), was the most beautiful woman in Asia (A 4.19.6; P*A* 21.6; P*M* 338e). By her Darius had at least three children: two daughters, Stateira and Drypetis, and a son named Ochus (see s.vv. **Stateira** [2], **Drypetis**, **Ochus**). He had also been married to a sister of Pharnaces (A 1.16.3; D 17.21.3), apparently a member of the Cappadocian-Pontic nobility (thus Berve ii.117), who bore him a son named Ariobarzanes (Aretades of Cnidus, *FGrH* 285 F1) and a daughter, who married Mithridates (A 1.15.7, 16.3; D 17.20.2, wrongly "Spithrodates").

Although Darius was not present in the west in 334/3, it is clear that he kept himself informed about Alexander's progress and took measures to deal with him. Darius had allegedly not taken Alexander seriously, on account of his youth (D 17.7.1), and entrusted the defense of the Aegean littoral to Memnon of Rhodes (D 17.7.2). In the first year of Alexander's expedition, it may be true that Darius despised his opponent, especially since the advance force under Parmenion had made little headway in 336–335. But Darius appears also to have been preoccupied with the revolt of Khababash and its aftermath (Nylander 1993: 148; Burstein 2000).[268] The first concerted action against the Macedonians was taken by a coalition of satraps, who distrusted Memnon and the Greek mercenaries. After the disaster at the Granicus, Darius gave greater authority to Memnon (A 1.20.3; cf. 2.1.1), who had sent him his wife, Barsine, and children as hostages (D 17.23.5–6; cf. C 3.13.14; J 11.10.2; P*A* 21.7–9). The Great King sent him funds with which to prosecute the war (D 17.29.1); but Memnon died soon afterwards of illness (D 17.29.4), and the command was handed to Pharnabazus. By the summer of 333,[269] Darius had assembled an army (D 17.31.1–2) and moved it to Sochi in northern Mesopotamia (A 2.6.1), having taken into his service the Athenian exile, Charidemus.[270] But he was advised by his courtiers that Charidemus was plotting treachery and had him arrested and executed (D 17.30.2–5; C 3.2.10–19). While there are good reasons for rejecting some of the Charidemus story as literary fiction, the reference to distrust of Greek advisors may be historical.[271] The alleged bribery of Philip of Acarnania (C 3.5.14–15, 3.6.4–13) appears to be a doublet for the negotiations conducted by Alexander the Lyncestian with the Persian King through the agency of Sisines (for details see s.vv. **Alexander** [3], **Sisines** [1]). From Sochi, Darius sent his money and a great number of the noncombatants in his army to Damascus (D 17.32.3; C 3.8.12; A 2.11.9–10) under the command of Cophen son of Artabazus (A 2.15.1).

Darius unwisely took his numerically superior army[272] away from the plains and moved into Cilicia via the Amanic Gates (A 2.7.1; C 3.8.13; Callisthenes *ap.* Plb 12.17.2; Jos*AJ* 11.314 wrongly says he crossed the Taurus), thinking that Alexander was deliberately avoiding battle (C 3.7.1, 8.10). It turned out to be a near-fatal miscalculation. The first major battle between Darius and Alexander thus took place at Issus (C 3.9–11; D 17.33–4; A 2.8–11) in November 333 (A 2.11.10 for the date); Alexander set out to attack him directly during the battle (D 17.33.5); but he was valiantly defended by his brother Oxyathres (D 17.34.2–4).[273] Darius' horses were wounded in battle (D 17.34.6), and after changing to another chariot he was seized with fear and led the flight from the battlefield (D 17.34.7–9; C 3.11.11). Darius mounted a horse that had followed the chariot precisely for this purpose[274] (A 2.11.4–7; P*A* 20.10), abandoning his family and possessions to the enemy (D 17.35.1–4; cf. 17.31.2, 36.2–4; A 2.11.9, 12.3–7; C 3.11.20–6, 12.4–16; P*A* 21.1–6; J 11.9.11–16; Jos*AJ* 11.316). At Darius' own tent, the Macedonian Pages welcomed their victorious King (D 17.36.5; P*A* 20.12–13; cf. C 3.12.1–3), who had broken off pursuit after some 200 stades (D 17.37.2), while Darius himself changed horses frequently and hurried to the heart of his empire (D 17.37.1). Amongst the captive Persians the rumor spread that Darius had been killed (D 17.37.3), but this was dispelled by Leonnatus, who had been sent by Alexander himself. Darius fled through the night with some 4,000 followers and crossed the Euphrates at Thapsacus (A 2.13.1); together with those who had accompanied him from Issus, he reached Babylon, where he wrote to Alexander about ransoming his family and concluding a peace-treaty which conceded Asia west of the Halys to Macedon (D 17.39.1; J 11.12.1), a proposal rejected by Alexander (D 17.39.2; J 11.12.2). Darius now prepared for an even greater engagement (D 17.39.3–4). Apart from the failed diplomatic negotiations (cf. Bernhardt 1988; Bloedow 1995), we learn little of Darius' activities between the time of his defeat at Issus and the preliminaries of Gaugamela. The defense of Tyre may have been an attempt by the Tyrians to prove their goodwill toward Darius (cf. the case of Straton of Sidon who was deposed for his stubborn adherence to Persia, D 17.47.1) and likewise give him an opportunity to regroup his forces (D 17.40.3), but the King appears to have done little on his part to aid the Tyrians, except perhaps by supplying ships, money, and mercenaries to Agis III (cf. D 17.48.1–2). Furthermore, he took no precautions to protect Egypt, whose satrap Sauaces had been killed at Issus, and instead allowed it to be disrupted by the mercenaries under Amyntas son of Antiochus (D 17.49.2–4). But, at least by the time Alexander returned to Syria in 331, Darius had assembled another and more powerful army (D 17.53.1), which he had equipped in a manner more suitable for fighting the Macedonians,[275] adding also some 200 scythe-bearing chariots. From Babylon he marched, with an army of some 800,000 infantry and 200,000 cavalry, in a northwesterly direction, keeping the Tigris on his right at first; but later he crossed the river and established a camp at Arbela (D 17.53.3–4). Despite his numerical advantage and the opportunity of choosing favorable terrain, Darius launched another peace initiative, this time offering all territory west of the Euphrates, 30,000 talents, and the hand of one of his daughters in marriage, an offer that was once again rejected (D 17.54.1–6; J 11.12.9–16). At about this time, his wife Stateira died (D 17.54.7).[276] Attempts to delay Alexander's progress were futile, and Darius finally met his opponent on the battlefield of Gaugamela (C 4.12–16; D 17.56–61; A 3.8–15; P*A* 31.6–33.11; cf. Pol*Strat* 4.3.5, 17; J 11.13.1–14.7; Oros 3.17.1–4),[277] where, despite his greater numbers, he was again soundly defeated and forced to flee (D 17.60.1–4; P*A* 33.8; J 11.14.3; C 4.15.30–3; A 3.14.3).[278] Immediately he escaped to

Arbela, which he reached in the middle of the night (C 4.16.8–9; 5.1.3),[279] and he now abandoned the centers of Babylon, Susa, and Persepolis and went instead directly to Ecbatana (D 17.64.1; A 3.16.1; C 5.1.9, 8.1; cf. Str 2.1.24 [79]). He gathered and rearmed stragglers (A 3.16.2; cf. C 5.8.3–5) as he went and hoped to rebuild his army (A 3.19.1–2).

But those generals and courtiers who remained with him were divided in their loyalties to the man and their strategies for saving the empire. To make matters worse, the base of his future military power was the region governed by his most dangerous enemy, Bessus, a man with some Achaemenid blood and, hence, at least marginal claims to the kingship. That Darius wrote to Abulites in Susa, telling him to turn the city and its riches over to Alexander in the hope of delaying his progress (D 17.65.5), makes a virtue of necessity. By contrast, the efforts of Madates, ruler of the Uxians and a kinsman of the King, to impede Alexander's progress (D 17.67.4) appear to have been a matter of policy, though they met with little success.

During Alexander's advance from Babylon to Persepolis, Darius had remained at Ecbatana, summoning troops from the Upper Satrapies. But these failed to materialize by the time Alexander set out for Media, and Darius began his flight toward Bactra (D 17.32.1; C 5.8.1) with a force of 30,000 Persians and mercenaries (D 17.73.2).[280] When Alexander was three days away from Ecbatana, he was met by Bisthanes, who reported that Darius had fled from there four days earlier (A 3.19.4–5). As Alexander gained ground in his pursuit (A 3.20–1), Darius was arrested (C 5.10–12, for a highly dramatized account; A 3.21.1, 4–5) and murdered by Bessus (D 17.73.2; J 11.15.1–14; C 5.13.15–25; A 3.21.10).[281] Alexander found him already dead and covered him with his cloak (P*M* 332f; P*A* 43.5); he also gave him an extravagant burial (D 17.73.3; A 3.22.1 says his body was sent to Persepolis to be entombed; cf. A 3.22.6; P*M* 343b; Pl*NH* 36.132; J 11.15.15; P*A* 43.7 says his body was sent to his mother). There was however a tradition that Alexander found the dying Darius, who begged him to avenge his death (D 17.73.4; Ps-Call 2.20).

Swoboda, *RE* s.v. "Dareios"; Berve ii.116–29 no. 244; Seibert 1987; Badian 2000b; Briant 2003. See Stemma III.

Datames. Persian noble, perhaps a relative of the famous Cappadocian satrap Datames. An officer in the Aegean fleet of Pharnabazus and Autophradates, he was given an independent command of ten Phoenician ships (cf. A 2.2.4) in 333 to subdue the Cyclades (A 2.2.2). He was, however, attacked at dawn, as he was anchored at Siphnos, by the Macedonian admiral Proteas, who captured eight of his ships. Datames himself escaped with the remaining two (A 2.2.4–5) and rejoined the main Persian fleet. Nothing else is known about him.

Berve ii.129 no. 245.

Dataphernes (Data-farnah). Prominent Persian. Dataphernes conspired with Catanes and Spitamenes in arresting the regicide Bessus (C 7.5.21; A 3.29.6; *ME* 5) and handing him over to Ptolemy, who had been sent out by Alexander (A 3.30.1, 5). Spitamenes and Dataphernes continued to resist Alexander and, after the former's death, Dataphernes was arrested by the Dahae and turned over to Alexander (C 8.3.16; *ME* 23).

Berve ii.129 no. 246; Kaerst, *RE* s.v.

Deinarchus [1]. (Deinarchos; Dinarchus). Son of Sostratus, from Corinth. Born ca. 360 and died not long after 292/1. [P]*M* 850c says he was still young when, during the time of Alexander's expedition, he came to Athens to study under Theophrastus; but it may be that Deinarchus arrived at the beginning of Alexander's reign (cf. Worthington 5). He wrote speeches for pay, but as a metic was not allowed to participate personally in the lawcourts. Some eighty-seven speeches were attributed to Deinarchus in antiquity, of which about sixty are authentic; his three surviving speeches – *Against Demosthenes, Against Aristogeiton, Against Philocles* – pertained to the Harpalus case in Athens ([P]*M* 850c–d). He was an imitator of Demosthenes and some speeches in the Demosthenic corpus have been, rightly or wrongly, attributed to him (Worthington 12; Cawkwell, *OCD*^{3} 469). A supporter of Antipater and Cassander, Deinarchus was particularly influential in Athens in the time of Demetrius of Phalerum (317–307 BC), but exiled when the city was "liberated" by Demetrius Poliorcetes. He returned as an old man, with failing eyesight, in 292 ([P]*M* 850d speaks of fifteen years of exile) and prosecuted Proxenus, thus making his only appearance in the Athenian courts ([P]*M* 850e). He had no personal contact with Alexander. Biographical information, late and somewhat unreliable, can be found in Ps-Plutarch's *Lives of the Ten Orators* (= [P]*M* 850c–e), cf. Photius; Dionysius of Halicarnassus, *On Dinarchus*; and *Suda* Δ 333, although there seems to be some confusion with Deinarchus [2] below.

Thalheim, *RE* iv.2386 no. 1; Berve ii.130 no. 247; Shoemaker 1968; Worthington 3–12.

Deinarchus [2]. (Deinarchos; Dinarchus). Corinthian of unknown family.[282] Pro-Macedonian politician during the reigns of Philip II and Alexander, and thus included by Demosthenes in a long list of Greeks who betrayed their fellow-citizens (Dem 18.295). The *Suda* (Δ 333) claims that Antipater made him *epimeletes* of the Peloponnese (cf. [Dem] *Ep* 6 for his pro-Antipatrid stance). He accompanied Phocion on his final embassy to Polyperchon (though Deinarchus fell ill on the way, P*Ph* 33.6), whom they encountered near Pharygae in Phocis. Deinarchus was, however, seized by Polyperchon's men, tortured, and executed (P*Ph* 33.8); for he was believed to be a supporter of Cassander.[283]

Berve ii.130 no. 248.

Deinocrates (Deinokrates; Dinocrates). Architect from Rhodes (Pl*NH* 5.62: "Deinochares"; Ps-Call 1.31–2; Jul Val 1.25), but Vitr 2 praef. 2 calls him *architectus Macedo*. It appears that the Alexander sources have confused the name of the architect, noted for his outrageous projects, and referred to him as Diocles, Cheirocrates, and Stasicrates. Diocles is said to have been from Rhegium and Stasicrates is listed as Bithynian, but the projects are the same. Stewart 28 opts for Stasicrates as the correct name, since the forms Deinocrates ("Marvel Master") and Cheirocrates ("Hand Master") are "overtly programmatic," but I see no way of deciding the matter. All are named as the proposers of a plan to convert Mount Athos into a giant statue of Alexander (Vitr 2 praef. 3; Str 14.1.23 [641]; P*M* 335c–f; P*A* 72.5–8)[284] and restorers of the temple of Artemis in Ephesus (Str 14.1.23 [641]; Solinus 40.5); only the layout of Alexandria in Egypt is attributed consistently to Deinocrates or the variant Deinochares (Val Max 1.4 ext 1; Ps-Call 1.31–32; Jul Val 1.25; Solinus 32.41; Pl*NH* 5.62).[285] P*A* 72.5 says that Alexander longed for Stasicrates when he needed someone to build Hephaestion's tomb (cf. D 17.115).

Berve ii.130 no. 249; Stewart 28–9, 41.

Delius (Delios). Ephesian of unknown family, companion (*hetairos*) of Plato. Sent by the Asiatic Greeks to Alexander (perhaps at Corinth in 336) to encourage him to campaign against Persia (P*M* 1126d).

Berve ii.131 no. 251.

Demades. Athenian orator, son of Demeas ([Demades] *On the Twelve Years* 7; Ael*VH* 12.43),[286] reputedly a sailor (*Suda* Δ 415). Like Demosthenes, from the deme Paeania. Born before 380 BC, perhaps as early as 390 (Davies 100): Antipater at some point in the 320s referred to him as an old man of whom little else remained except tongue and guts (P*Ph* 1.3; cf. P*M* 183f). He was amongst the captives at Chaeronea and rebuked Philip for, in his drunken state, "acting like Thersites when fortune had cast him in the role of Agamemnon" (D 16.87.1–2). Philip was won over by Demades' charm and released the Athenian prisoners (D 16.87.3). Not surprisingly, he advocated Athenian participation in the common peace, i.e., membership in the League of Corinth (P*Ph* 16.5). In 336, when the Greeks threatened to rebel against Macedonian authority, Demades worked to secure peace between Athens and Alexander. And, when in 335, after the sack of Thebes, Alexander demanded the extradition of certain politicians, including Demosthenes, Demades first proposed that ambassadors be sent to him, congratulating him on his safe return from Illyria and his suppression of the Theban revolt (A 1.10.3; [Demades] *On the Twelve Years* 17). Although the first mission accomplished little, a second embassy, led by Phocion (P*Ph* 17.6; A 1.10.6; P*Dem* 23) and including Demades (D 17.15.3) persuaded the King to relent.[287] The extent of Demades' contribution can be seen from the honors, including a statue, that were voted him by the Athenians (Din 1.101; P*M* 802f). He was pro-Macedonian in his politics (P*Ph* 1.1)[288] and opposed Athenian cooperation with Agis in 331/0 (P*M* 818e; P*Cleom* 27.1; cf. P*M* 191e). He proposed that Alexander be recognized as a god, only to be fined ten talents (Ath 6.251b; Ael*VH* 5.12, wrongly 100 talents; cf. Val Max 7.2 ext 13). Convicted of accepting bribes from Harpalus, he did not fight the charge and was fined (Din 1.104; 2.15) and deprived of his citizenship rights (P*Ph* 26.3; D 18.18.1–2); nevertheless he remained in Athens. After the Lamian War he was, however, reinstated and regarded as responsible for "betraying" Athens to Antipater (N*Ph* 2.2): it was his decree that called for the deaths of the anti-Macedonian leaders, including Demosthenes (N*Ph* 2.2; A*Succ* 1.13). He fell out with Phocion (cf. P*M* 811a), but he developed a reputation for dealing well with Macedon on Athens' behalf (D 18.48.1). In 319, as Antipater neared death and Demades came to Macedonia to request the removal of the garrison from Munychia (D 18.48.1), he was put to death by Cassander and Antipater, not only because of the accusations of Deinarchus of Corinth (A*Succ* 1.15; D 18.48.2), but also because letters found amongst the royal papers showed that he had written to Perdiccas to come and save Greece from an old and rotten thread which was binding it, meaning Antipater (A*Succ* 1.14). He was executed after first witnessing the slaughter of his son Demeas (A*Succ* 1.14; D 18.48.3–4; P*Ph* 30.8–9; P*Dem* 31.4–6).[289] In the end, the Athenians felt great hatred toward him and are said to have melted down his statues to make chamber-pots (P*M* 820f).[290]

Berve ii.131–2 no. 252; Kirchner no. 3263; Davies 99–101; Williams 1989; Worthington 271–2.

Demaratus [1]. (Demaratos, Demaretos). Corinthian. Born ca. 400 BC (P*A* 56.2 says he died of old age in 328/7). Demaratus, who campaigned with Timoleon in Sicily in 345 (P*Tim* 21, 24, 27), was prominent amongst the pro-Macedonians in his city (Dem 18.295). As a *xenos* of Philip II, he brought Bucephalas as a gift to the young Alexander (D 17.76.6; but P*A* 6.1 says that it was Philonicus of Thessaly who brought the horse), and in 337/6 he urged Philip to reconcile with his son, who had fled to Illyria (P*A* 9.12–14; P*M* 70b–c, 179c). He was almost certainly present in Aegae when Philip was assassinated in 336 (D 16.91.4–6), and in 334 he accompanied Alexander on the Asiatic expedition as one of his *hetairoi* (cf. A 1.15.6, at the Granicus). He is said to have wept with joy to see Alexander seated on Darius' throne at Susa (P*M* 329d; P*A* 37.7, 56.1; P*Ages* 15.4). Demaratus died shortly before the Indian campaign (P*A* 56.2); his remains were sent back to Corinth with appropriate honors.

Kirchner, *RE* s.v. "Demaratos (4)"; Berve ii.133 no. 253.

Demaratus [2]. (Demaratos). Rhodian, patronymic unknown, brother of Sparton. Demaratus and his brother were arrested at Sardis by Alexander but freed through the efforts of Phocion (*PPh* 18.6; Ael*VH* 1.25). The reason for his arrest is unknown; nor do we know anything about his personal or political connections with Phocion. Demaratus was undoubtedly a man of high standing amongst the Rhodians, for he reappears in 320 as their navarch, defeating the forces of Attalus son of Andromenes (A*Succ* 1.39).

Berve ii.133 no. 254; Hofstetter 46 no. 78.

Demarchus (Demarchos). Satrap of Hellespontine Phrygia from the death of Calas (at some point late in Alexander's lifetime) until 323, when he was succeeded by Leonnatus (A*Succ* 1.6; Dexippus = *FGrH* 100 F8 §2).

Berve ii.133–4 no. 255.

Demetrius [1]. (Demetrios). Son of Althaemenes (A 3.11.8), Demetrius is the only one of eight ilarchs named at Gaugamela who attained prominence in the latter half of the campaign. First attested in the battle-order at Gaugamela, where he was stationed between Heracleides and Meleager (A 3.11.8), Demetrius may have held the rank of ilarch since 334, if not earlier. He reappears during the Swat campaign of 327/6, now with the rank of hipparch, with Attalus son of Andromenes and Alcetas son of Orontes at the town of Ora (A 4.27.5), which was captured after Alexander's arrival (A 4.27.9). In the Hydaspes battle, Demetrius' hipparchy crossed the river with Alexander and was deployed on the right with that of Coenus (A 5.16.3). Demetrius' last recorded command was in the Mallian campaign (326/5): he and Peithon the taxiarch, along with some lightly armed troops, were sent to subdue those Mallians who had taken refuge in the woods near the river (A 6.8.2–3, presumably the Hydraotes; cf. A 6.7.1).

Demetrius vanishes from our records at this point. His prominence may be due to family connections. If Amyntor the father of Hephaestion can be identified with Amyntor son of Demetrius (*IG* ii^2 405 = Schwenk no. 24), then there may have been a relationship between Hephaestion and Demetrius: Althaemenes may have been the brother (or possibly brother-in-law) of Amyntor, making Hephaestion and Demetrius first cousins.

Kirchner, *RE* s.v. "Demetrios (25)"; Berve ii.134 no. 256; Hoffmann 183; Heckel 345–6.

Demetrius [2]. (Demetrios). Macedonian. Somatophylax of Alexander. Demetrius' family background is unknown, but the temptation to identify him with the brother of Antigonus Monophthalmus must be resisted.[291] Who Demetrius the Somatophylax was cannot be determined. Arrian (3.27.5) claims that Alexander deposed him from office in the land of the Ariaspians, "suspecting that he had a share in Philotas' conspiracy." Curtius includes his name in the list of conspirators given by Dimnus to his lover Nicomachus (6.7.15). Despite his vigorous defense (C 6.11.35), he was convicted by the testimony of a second witness (Calis: C 6.11.37) and executed along with the others (C 6.11.38). It is suspicious, however, that Demetrius (the only individual of note to be linked with Dimnus' plot) is given very little attention by Alexander or by the sources. It appears that Demetrius was removed from office, as Arrian says, on a mere suspicion, that his only crime was friendship with Philotas. Curtius' introduction of "Calis" (not named in 6.7.15) as Demetrius' accomplice suggests contamination from a second source. The original version (of Cleitarchus?) may not have named him at all. Ptolemy son of Lagus replaced him as Somatophylax.

Berve ii.135 no. 260; Kirchner, *RE* s.v. "Demetrios (24)"; Bosworth i.366–7; Heckel 261–2.

Demetrius [3]. (Demetrios). One of Alexander's *hetairoi* – hence probably Macedonian (Tataki 294 no. 34), but possibly Greek – son of Pythonax (A 4.12.5) and nicknamed *Pheidon* (P*A* 54.6). Although he is described as a flatterer (*kolax*) of Alexander (P*M* 65c), this does not rule out a military role in the campaign. In 327, when the King attempted to introduce *proskynesis*, Demetrius is alleged to have alerted Alexander to Callisthenes' failure to fulfill his promise to do obeisance (P*A* 54.6 = Chares, *FGrH* 125 F14; A 4.12.5). Demetrius may have remained with Alexander until the end of the King's life, but the evidence of Ps-Call 3.17 (cf. Jul Val 3.15–16), which appears to mention Pheidon, is all but worthless.

Berve ii.134–5 no. 258; Ribbeck, *RE* s.v. "Kolax (85)."

Demetrius [4]. (Demetrios). (ca. 336–282 BC). The famous successor of Alexander, distinguished by the epithet Poliorcetes ("the Besieger"). Son of Antigonus the One-Eyed and Stratonice, brother of Philip (P*Demetr* 2.1; Pl*NH* 7.56; P*Pyr* 4.3) was born ca. 336 in Macedonia. Demetrius came to Celaenae in Phrygia with his mother not much earlier than 330 BC (Wheatley 1999: 3) and spent his boyhood years there. He emerges from the shadows in 320, when he marries Phila, daughter of Antipater and widow of Craterus. Demetrius has no known personal connection with Alexander the Great.

Kaerst, *RE* s.v. "Demetrios (33)"; Berve ii.134 no. 257. Demetrius does not meet Berve's own criteria for inclusion in his prosopography. See, especially, Plutarch's *Life of Demetrius*; Diodorus, Books 19–20; Wehrli 1968; Sandberger 72–89 no. 30; Bengtson 1975: 64–90; Wheatley 1997a. The best discussion of Demetrius' youth is Wheatley 1999. See Stemma VI.

Democrates (Demokrates). Athenian. Democrates was sent as ambassador to Darius before Gaugamela and, after the King's defeat, attached himself to the Greek mercenaries in the Persian army. When these surrendered to Alexander, through the agency of Artabazus, in 330, Democrates despaired of obtaining mercy from Alexander because of his strong anti-Macedonian views and committed suicide (C 6.5.9).[292]

Kirchner, *RE* s.v. "Demokrates (6)"; Kirchner no. 3513; Berve ii.135 no. 261; Hofstetter 47–8 no. 81.

Demon. Athenian from the deme Paeania. Son of Demomeles, and a nephew or cousin[293] of Demosthenes (P*Dem* 27.6; [P]*M* 846d; cf. Dem 32.31). A member of the anti-Macedonian faction in Athens, he is named by Plutarch as one of those politicians whose extradition was demanded by Alexander after the sack of Thebes in 335 (P*Dem* 23.4).[294] In 324 he was charged with accepting money from Harpalus, but he appears not to have been convicted (cf. Timocles *ap.* Ath 8.341f). In the following year he secured the recall of Demosthenes, on the condition that Demosthenes use the thirty talents he owed to adorn the temple of Zeus the Savior in Piraeus ([P]*M* 846d; P*Dem* 27.6).

Kirchner, *RE* s.v. "Demon (3)"; Berve ii.142 no. 266; Davies 116–18.

Demonicus (Demonikos). A Macedonian from Pella, Demonicus son of Athenaeus was presumably one of Alexander's *hetairoi* and served in 326 as a trierarch of the Hydaspes fleet (A*Ind* 18.3). Nothing else is known about him.

Berve ii.136 no. 262.

Demophon [1]. Seer, apparently of Greek origin, in Alexander's entourage. The King ignored Demophon's prediction of danger before the attack on the Mallian town in India (D 17.98.3–4; C 9.4.27–9). Demophon was one of those who were said to have slept in the temple of Serapis in Babylon shortly before Alexander's death (A 7.26.2), and may have been, along with Cleomenes, the King's leading seer after the death of Aristander. Nothing else is known about him.

Berve ii.141 no. 264.

Demophon [2]. Perhaps Greek. One of Alexander's butlers (*trapezokomos* or *trapezopoios*), whose only claim to fame was that he felt cold in the sunshine but warm in the shade (DL 9.80; cf. Sextus Empiricus, *Outlines of Pyrrhonism* 1.82).

Berve ii.141–2 no. 265.

Demosthenes. Athenian. Son of Demosthenes (P*Dem* 4.1), from the deme Paeania (P*Dem* 20.3; see Kirchner no. 3597; Davies 113); Aeschines' assertions about the foreign and disreputable background of Demosthenes' mother, Cleobule the daughter of Gylon (3.171–2; cf. P*Dem* 4.2), are for the most part slanderous.[295] Born in 385/4 or 384/3 (Dem 21.154; cf. Davies 126 §XII), Demosthenes lost his father at the age of 7 and, although he inherited a considerable estate, much of this was squandered by his guardians.[296] Beginning his career as a speechwriter, Demosthenes soon took an active role in Athenian politics and is best known for his outspoken opposition to Philip II, and there is a story that he treated the news of Philip's death as a cause for celebration (P*Dem* 22.1–3; [P]*M* 847b; Aes 3.77, cf. 3.160). But his anti-Macedonian utterances, which continued into the reign of Alexander, were soon muted by Alexander's presence in Central Greece and his demand for Demosthenes' extradition. After Philip's death Demosthenes aroused the Athenians against Alexander, whom he derided as a child and a "Margites" (Aes 3.161; Marsyas, *FGrH* 135/6 F3; P*A* 11.6; P*Dem* 23.2; cf. Aes 1.166–8), and communicated with Attalus (D 17.3.2; P*Dem* 23.2), who later turned Demosthenes' letter over to Alexander in order to save himself (D 17.5.1). In 336, when Alexander made his first entry into Greece, Demosthenes was among the envoys sent to the King, but he went no further than Mount Cithaeron and returned to Athens (D 17.4.7; P*Dem* 23.3; Aes 3.161; cf. Din 1.82). Either he feared punishment for his anti-Macedonian policies or he had been in collusion with the Persian King, who had given him a large sum of money to oppose Macedon (D 17.4.7–8; Aes 3.238–40; Din 1.10, 18; cf. J 11.2.7),[297] evidence for which was supposed to have been found by Alexander in Sardis in 334 (P*Dem* 20.5). Demosthenes and Hypereides opposed Alexander's request for Athenian ships ([P]*M* 847c, 848e), probably for the Danubian campaign; for it would be hard to imagine such defiance in 334 when both orators had narrowly escaped Alexander's wrath. In 335, Demosthenes encouraged false rumors that Alexander had been killed fighting the Triballians (J 11.2.8) and incited the Thebans to rebel, going so far as to send them military equipment (D 17.8.5); and although he persuaded the Athenians to support the Thebans, no help ever materialized (D 17.8.6; Aes 3.156 holds Demosthenes responsible for Thebes' fate). After the destruction of the city, Alexander demanded the extradition of Athens' leading politicians and generals, including Demosthenes (A 1.10.4; P*Dem* 23.4; P*Ph* 17.2; *Suda* A 2704); it was also falsely stated that Demosthenes paid Demades five talents to intercede with Alexander (D 17.15.3). Although it was said that he hoped that Alexander would be defeated and killed by Darius (Aes 3.164), after Issus Demosthenes recognized the futility of such hopes and sent a certain Plataean named Aristion to Hephaestion in 332/1 for the sake of securing immunity and reconciliation (Aes 3.162; Marsyas, *FGrH* 135/6 F2). Significantly, he did nothing to help Agis III at the time of his uprising against Macedon (P*Dem* 24.1; Aes 3.165; Din 1.34–5). Aeschines' prosecution of Ctesiphon for illegally proposing a crown for Demosthenes occurred in 330, and although the speeches given by the two parties are rich in information about the careers and politics of the two orators, they belong primarily to the world of Athenian politics (see Aes 3, *Against Ctesiphon*, and Dem 18, *On the Crown*; cf. Pl*NH* 3.110). Demosthenes was also a political rival of both Demades (Ath 2.44e–f) and Phocion;[298] in 322, the former proposed the decree that condemned him to death and the latter did nothing to help him.

Of Demosthenes' activities vis-à-vis Macedon and Alexander in the years from 330 to 325, little is known. He was sent to Olympia in late summer 324 as *architheoros* and doubtless communicated with Nicanor of Stageira concerning the implementation of the Exiles' Decree (cf. D 17.109.1; C 10.2.4; J 13.5.3–4; see s.v. **Nicanor** [5]); his failure to oppose divine honors for Alexander (Din 1.94; Hyp 5, col. 31 [Burtt]) was doubtless an attempt to retain the goodwill of Alexander in the hope of mitigating the terms of the Exiles' Decree. At the games he publicly humiliated Lamachus, who delivered encomia on Philip and Alexander (P*Dem* 9.1; [P]*M* 845c). But on his return to Athens Demosthenes became embroiled in the Harpalus fiasco, the complexities of which are not discussed here.[299] Suffice it to say that after recommending that Harpalus be imprisoned and his money confiscated, Demosthenes was soon charged with having accepted bribes from Alexander's fleeing treasurer (D 17.108.8). An investigation by the Areopagus appears to have established his guilt, and although he claimed he would submit to the death-penalty if found guilty (Din 1.8, 40, 61, 108), this was pure bluster. He was exiled from Athens, and resided in the Megarid (J 13.5.9; D 18.13.6; A*Succ* 1.13); Demosthenes was forced to retire to Calauria, an island off Troezen (Paus 1.8.2). But he was recalled and banished again after the Lamian War (Paus 1.8.2; P*Ph* 26.2, 27.5); he went to Calauria on his second exile, and committed suicide by taking poison (P*Ph* 29.1); he was the only Greek fugitive whom Archias did not bring back to Antipater and the Macedonians (Paus 1.8.3). There was a statue of Demosthenes in Athens near the eponymoi and the sanctuary of Ares (Paus 1.8.2–4). Cineas the Thessalian, an advisor of Pyrrhus, was said to have been a student of Demosthenes (P*Pyr* 14.1). For ancient accounts of his life see P*Dem* and [P]*M* 844a–848d.

Berve ii.136–41 no. 263; Cawkwell, *OCD*[3] 456–8 no. 2; full discussion of Demosthenes and his family in Davies 113–39; see also Schaefer i–iii[2]; Sealey; Worthington (ed.) 2000. For the Harpalus affair, Jaschinski; Will 113–32; Blackwell.

Derdas. Apparently a relative of Alexander's treasurer Harpalus, possibly a son of the elder Derdas, who was the brother of Phila, Philip II's Elimeiot wife (Satyrus *ap.* Ath 13.557), or of the elder Harpalus and thus perhaps a brother of Calas. Derdas was sent as an ambassador to the (so-called "European") Scythians north of the Iaxartes River in 329 (C 7.6.9; cf. A 4.1.1–2).[300] He returned with a Scythian delegation in 328 (C 8.1.7; cf. A 4.15.1).

Berve ii.131 no. 250; Hoffmann 201–2. See Stemma XIII.

Diades. Thessalian engineer. Student of Polyeidus of Thessaly (Ath Mech 10.10–11; Vitr 10.13.3). Diades (along with Charias) was entrusted with the siege-work at Tyre (*LatAlex* col. 8, 12–15) and other cities, and was author of a work on siegecraft (Vitr 7 *praef.* 14; 10.13.3–8; Ath Mech 10.10–11, cf. 5.13). He claims to have invented movable towers, the borer, and the climbing machine, on which besiegers could be brought level with the top of the enemy's walls (Vitr 10.13.3).

Fabricius, *RE* s.v. "Diades (2)"; Berve ii.142 no. 267; Marsden 1977; Whitehead & Blyth 85–108, 176–87.

Didymeia. Sister of Seleucus Nicator, and thus daughter of Laodice and Antiochus. By an unnamed husband she bore two sons, Nicanor and Nicomedes (Malalas 8.198). The source of this otherwise uncorroborated information is late, and it may be that the name Didymeia is associated with Seleucid mythology, pertaining to Laodice's alleged sexual liaison with Apollo and to the allegation that the oracle of the Branchidae greeted Seleucus as "King" in 312 (D 19.90.4; cf. Hadley 1974: 53, 58–9; Grainger 3–4).

Willrich, *RE* s.v.; Berve ii.142; Beloch iv^2 2.198 is skeptical; not in Grainger 1997.

Dimnus (Dimnos; "Limnos" in Plutarch). Macedonian *hetairos* (D 17.79.1) from Chalaestra (*PA* 49.3). In autumn 330, he formed a conspiracy to murder Alexander (D 17.79.1; *PA* 49.3; but C 6.7.6 suggests he joined a conspiracy but was not the instigator). Dimnus enlisted his *eromenos* Nicomachus (D 17.79.2; C 6.7.2–14; *PA* 49.3) and revealed to him the names of the conspirators (C 6.7.15: Demetrius [2], Peucolaus [2], Nicanor [7], Aphobetus, Iolaus, Dioxenus, Archepolis, Amyntas [8]). But the plot was divulged by Cebalinus, who learned of the details from his brother, Nicomachus. Dimnus was thus arrested and later committed suicide (D 17.79.6; C 6.7.29–30; *PA* 49.7 says he was killed resisting arrest), indicating by his death the gravity of his crime (C 6.7.34). The resulting trial led to the execution of those whose names Dimnus had given to Nicomachus, as well as that of Philotas, who had failed to bring the matter to the King's attention, and the murder of his father, Parmenion. See also s.vv. **Cebalinus**, **Nicomachus**, **Philotas** [4].

Berve ii.142–3 no. 269. For the whole affair see Badian 1960a and 2000a; Rubinsohn 1977; Heckel 1977a and 2003; Adams 2003.

Diocles (Diokles). Greek from Rhegium in southern Italy. According to Eusthathius, commenting on *Iliad* 14.229 (for the commentary see Stewart T138), Diocles proposed to turn Mount Athos into a giant statue of Alexander, a plan that is otherwise ascribed to Stasicrates or Deinocrates or Cheiricrates.

Berve ii.144 no. 275; Fabricius, *RE* s.v. "Diokles (57)."

Diodorus [1]. (Diodoros). Brother of Anaxagoras and Codrus, all sons of Echeanax; they slew Hegesias, tyrant of Ephesus, shortly before 323. Philoxenus then satrap of Ionia demanded the extradition of the assassins, but the Ephesians refused. Philoxenus marched in and arrested the sons of Echeanax and imprisoned them for some time in Sardis (Pol*Strat* 6.49). The brothers made a daring escape attempt, in which Diodorus fell and became lame. He was recaptured and sent to Alexander (Berve ii.144 thinks Menander took him to the King in 323). But Alexander died before he could deal with Diodorus and Perdiccas sent him back to Ephesus to be tried. When word of this reached Anaxagoras and Codrus, who had escaped to Athens, they returned and saved their brother (Pol*Strat* 6.49).

He appears to have shifted his allegiance to Antigonus Monophthalmus and served as Demetrius Poliorcetes' mercenary captain, during the capture of Sicyon in 303 (Pol*Strat* 4.7.3; cf. Skalet 81). In 301, Demetrius, sailing off against Caria, left him as *phrourarchos* of Ephesus. Diodorus, however, made a pact to betray the city to Lysimachus for fifty talents; but Demetrius got wind of the plan and sailed back; he left his ships at anchor in one place and sailed into the harbor with only one boat [with Nicanor] and hid himself in the boat; Nicanor summoned Diodorus aboard his boat, pretending that he wished to discuss the handing over of soldiers [those in the garrison of Diodorus?]; when Diodorus felt safe and came near in a small boat, Demetrius jumped out of hiding and sank the boat. Some met their deaths by drowning, others were captured, but it is not stated which fate Diodorus suffered (Pol*Strat* 4.7.4).

Kirchner, *RE* s.v. "Diodoros (2)"; Berve ii.144 no. 273; Billows 380 no. 30.

Diodorus [2]. (Diodoros). Son of Telesarchus. Cavalryman from Orchomenus; served with Alexander's allied cavalry until the expedition reached Ecbatana in

330. There he and his compatriots were discharged. On their return (ca. 329), they made a dedication to Zeus Soter in Orchomenus (*IG* vii.3206).

Berve ii.144 no. 274.

Diodotus (Diodotos). Greek from Erythrae. Diodotus is identified as one of the authors of Alexander's *Ephemerides* (Ath 10.434b = *FGrH* 117 T1), working under the direction of Eumenes of Cardia (who is identified as *archigrammateus*). Nothing else is known about him.[301]

Berve ii.143–4 no. 272.

Diogenes [1]. Philosopher from Sinope, better known as "the Cynic." He spent a portion of his life in exile, in Athens and Corinth, and it is in the latter city that Alexander was said to have met him. In the famous, but almost certainly fictitious, tale of their meeting Alexander asked the philosopher if there was anything he could do for him. Diogenes replied that the King might move aside, since he was blocking Diogenes' enjoyment of the sun (P*A* 14.2–5; P*M* 331e–f, also 605d, 782a; Val Max 4.3 ext. 4a; A 7.2.1). That he died on the same day as Alexander is also false (DL 6.79), although it is true that he was an old man during the 113th Olympiad (324–321 BC). For his career see DL 6.20–81.

Berve ii.417–18 no. 22.

Diogenes [2]. Greek from Mytilene, Diogenes was a leader of the pro-Persian oligarchy. Although he was driven out when the Macedonians captured Lesbos in 334, he was installed as tyrant of Mytilene by Pharnabazus and Autophradates in the following year (A 2.1.5). In 332, Chares had come to the defense of Mytilene (A 3.2.6; C 4.5.19; see s.v. **Chares** [1]), but he surrendered the city in return for his safety. In 332/1, Hegelochus brought Diogenes to Egypt, where Alexander returned him to face the judgment of the Mytilenaeans, who in all likelihood had him executed (A 3.2.7).

Berve ii.143 no. 270; Berve 1967: i.336, ii.690; Olmstead 502; Hofstetter 51 no. 86.

Diognetus (Diognetos). Bematist (Pl*NH* 6.61), possibly from Erythrae. Nothing is known about his life beyond his participation in Alexander's expedition and his authorship of a work along the lines of Baeton's *Stages*, two fragments of which survive.

Berg, *RE* s.v. "Diognetos"; Berve ii.143 no. 271; Jacoby, *FGrH* 120.

Dionysius [1]. (Dionysios). Tyrant of Pontic Heraclea, 337/6–305 BC (*SIG*[3] 304.30ff.). Son of Clearchus (who ruled for twelve years, beginning in 364/3: D 15.81.5) and nephew of Satyrus (Memnon, *FGrH* 434); Clearchus gained the tyranny in 364/3 and ruled for twelve years (D 15.81.5; 16.36.3); he was succeeded by Dionysius' brother Timotheus, who in turn ruled for fifteen more (D 16.36.3, 88.5), until his death in 338/7 put Dionysius in power (D 16.88.5). Dionysius expanded his territory as a result of Persian weakness caused by Alexander's invasion in 334, but he was later threatened by those who had been exiled by the Heracleote tyranny, who asked Alexander to restore them. For this reason, Dionysius made contact with Cleopatra, the King's sister, who appears to have interceded with Alexander on Dionysius' behalf – although she may have done little more than delay the restoration of the exiles (Memnon, *FGrH* 434 F1 4.1; cf. Burstein 74). But upon Alexander's death, these exiles turned to Perdiccas, only to have their hopes dashed when Perdiccas was murdered in 320 (Memnon 4.3). He was a supporter of Antigonus. Married Amastris the daughter of Oxyathres (brother of Darius III) after she was repudiated by Craterus (Memnon 4.4). They had three children: Amastris, Clearchus, and Oxyathres (Memnon 4.8). The elder Amastris may be responsible for the development of closer ties between Dionysius and Antigonus; for Demetrius son of Antigonus had now married Craterus' widow, Phila, whom Amastris must have known since her arrival in Cilicia in late 324. The bond with Antigonus was strengthened when in 314 a daughter of Dionysius by an earlier wife married Polemaeus, Antigonus' nephew (Memnon 4.6; D 19.61.5). Late in his life, after Antigonus and Demetrius had been proclaimed "kings," Dionysius also took the title for himself (Memnon 4.7). By this time he had become extremely obese and ugly (Memnon 4.7; Ael*VH* 9.13; Ath 12.549a).[302] He died at the age of 53, having ruled for thirty-two years (Memnon 4.8; D 16.88.5).

Kaerst, *RE* s.v. "Dionysios (66)"; Berve ii.144–5 no. 276; Burstein 72–80. See Stemma III.

Dionysius [2]. (Dionysios). Heracleot flutist. Performed at the mass-marriage ceremony in Susa in 324 (Chares, *FGrH* 125 F4 = Ath 12.538f).

Berve ii.145 no. 277.

Dionysius [3]. (Dionysios). A native of Mesene (that is, of Characene in the Tigris region, rather than Messenia in Greece: see Abramenko 2000: 366). The name Dionysius is therefore suspect. During Alexander's final stay in Babylon, when the King had removed his robes to play ball, this man arrived unnoticed and, putting on the King's mantle and diadem, seated himself upon the throne. When this was discovered, he claimed that he had been imprisoned for some crime and brought to Babylon, but there had been freed by the god Serapis and told to do what he had done (P*A* 73.7–9; D 17.116.2–5, making no mention of Serapis). Diodorus goes on to say that the man was executed. What occurred was, in fact, no accident but the enactment of the Near Eastern "Substitute King" ritual, in which a substitute for the king is placed on the throne and later put to death to "fulfill" and deflect from the real king a portended death (see Bottéro 1992: 138–55).[303]

Berve ii.145 no. 278; Abramenko 2000: 366–9.

Dionysodorus (Dionysodoros). Theban, Olympic victor. Ambassador to the Persian King; captured at Damascus in late 333 (A 2.15.2). Alexander released him and his fellow-Theban Thessaliscus because of the former's Olympic victory and because he recognized that their attempts to win restoration of their city were understandable; presumably Alexander had cause to regret the severity of the punishment meted out to Thebes; P*M* 181b.

Kirchner, *RE* s.v. "Dionysodoros (12)"; Berve ii.145 no. 279; Hofstetter 52 no. 89.

Diophantus [1]. (Diophantos). Greek flutist. Performed at the mass-marriage ceremony in Susa in 324 (Chares, *FGrH* 125 F4 = Ath 12.538f).

Berve ii.146 no. 282.

Diophantus [2]. (Diophantos). Athenian. Diophantus was sent along with Achilleus on the Athenian state galley, *Paralos*, to Alexander to negotiate the release of their countrymen, who had been captured at the Granicus River in 334 and sentenced to hard labor in Macedonia (cf. A 1.29.5). They met Alexander at Tyre as he returned from Egypt in 331 and achieved their purpose, congratulating the King on his victories (A 3.6.2; C 4.8.12).

Schoch, *RE* Supplbd IV s.v. "Diophantes"; Berve ii.146 no. 283; Kirchner nos. 4419, 4435.

Diotimus (Diotimos). Athenian from the deme Euonymon, from a wealthy family that had mining interests at Laurium. Son of Diopeithes. Born ca. 375, he makes his first political appearance in 349/8 (Dem 21.208). Diotimus held various generalships (338/7, 337/6, 335/4, 334/3 BC) and trierarchies, dedicated shields after Chaeronea (Dem 18.114, 116; *IG* ii^2 1496,

22–5), and, in 335/4, conducted a naval expedition to suppress piracy (*IG* ii^2 1623, 276–85), for which he was honored in a decree moved by Lycurgus ([P]*M* 844a). He belonged to the anti-Macedonian party: as such he is associated with Demosthenes, Nausicles, Hypereides, and Polyeuctus ([P]*M* 845a), and was one of the orator-politicians whose extradition was demanded by Alexander in 335 (A 1.10.4; *Suda* A 2704; but P*Dem* 23.4 appears to have substituted Demon for Diotimus). Alexander relented in the case of Diotimus and some others, but Diotimus appears to have died at some point before 325/4 (cf. *IG* ii^2 1629). He has no other direct connections with Alexander.

Kirchner, *RE* s.v. "Diotimos (8)"; Kirchner no. 4384; Berve ii.146 no. 281; Lauffer 289ff.; Davies 163–5; Develin 343, 346, 373, 379.

Dioxippus (Dioxippos). Athenian pankratiast and Olympic champion[304] in the entourage of Alexander. At some point around 333 BC he attended the wedding of his sister, then a widow, to Charippus (Hyp 2.5–6). Hence we know he did not accompany Alexander from the beginning of the campaign. Certainly he was present in 326/5, when he was challenged to single combat by the Macedonian Corrhagus, whom Dioxippus defeated with relative ease (Ael*VH* 10.22 wrongly says that Dioxippus killed his opponent). But it is alleged that subsequently he was falsely accused of theft by agents of Alexander and driven to suicide (D 17.100–1; C 9.7.16–26). Dioxippus was regarded as one of Alexander's flatterers (*kolakes*) and was said to have likened the King's blood to the ichor of the immortal gods (Aristobulus, *FGrH* 139 F47 = Ath 6.251a).[305] His portrait was painted by Alcimachus (Pl*NH* 35.139).

Kirchner, *RE* s.v. "Dioxippos (2)"; Berve ii.146–7 no. 284.

Ditamenes. See s.v. **Stamenes**.

Docimus (Dokimos). Macedonian,[306] unattested in the Alexander historians, although it is probable that he served in the Asiatic campaign. Served Perdiccas, Antigonus, and Lysimachus in succession. As a supporter of Perdiccas, he captured Babylon and deposed Archon, who had colloborated with Arrhidaeus in diverting Alexander's corpse to Egypt (A*Succ* 24.3–5). After the failure of Perdiccas' expedition he joined Alcetas and Eumenes, but was reluctant to serve the latter (P*Eum* 8.8). Docimus served with Alcetas in Caria (cf. A*Succ* 1.41) and at Cretopolis, where he was captured (D 18.44–5; Pol*Strat* 4.6.7), along with Attalus and Polemon. Imprisoned in Phrygia (?), he planned to escape, eventually betraying his comrades to Antigonus' forces (D 19.16). Antigonus took him into his service, and in 313 Docimus and Medius captured Miletus (D 19.75.3–4). As general of the area around Synnada he founded, with Antigonus' approval, the town of Dokimeion (Robert 1934: 267–8). Shortly before the battle of Ipsus (301), Docimus went over to Lysimachus' general Prepelaus and secured for him Synnada and other strongholds (D 20.107.4); he also appears to have handed over to Lysimachus Pergamum, together with its wealth and the treasurer Philetaerus (Paus 1.8.1; cf. Str 13.4.1 [623]).[307]

Kaerst, *RE* s.v. "Dokimos (4)"; Berve ii.147 no. 285; Billows 382–3 no. 35; Schober 38–41; Simpson 1957; Hornblower 1981: 125–6; Launey 342.

Doloaspis. Egyptian. In 331, Alexander left Doloaspis and Petisis (another Egyptian) as nomarchs of Egypt; they must have been overseers of the lesser nomarchs of Upper and Lower Egypt, although we cannot say which of the two regions was assigned to Doloaspis. Petisis soon relinquished his position and the offices were combined under Doloaspis (A 3.5.2).

Berve ii.147 no. 286.

Dorceidas (Dorkeidas). Son of Melambichus. Cavalryman from Orchomenus, served with Alexander's allied cavalry until the expedition reached Ecbatana in 330. There he and his compatriots were discharged. On their return (ca. 329), they made a dedication to Zeus Soter in Orchomenus (*IG* vii.3206).

Berve ii.147 no. 288.

Doxares. Indian dynast (*nomarches*) of the upper Indus region; sent envoys to offer his submission to Alexander in 326 (A 5.8.3). He is otherwise unattested.

Berve ii.147 no. 287.

Dracon (Drakon). Coan doctor, son of Hippocrates. Personal physician of Rhoxane (*Suda* Δ 1497). His son, Hippocrates, succeeded him in this capacity and was killed along with Rhoxane and Alexander IV in 310.

Berve ii.147 no. 289; Sherwin-White 1978: no. 104.

Dropides. Athenian ambassador to Darius III. Dropides was captured, according to C 3.13.15, at Damascus by Parmenion in 333/2 BC. But A 2.15.2 mentions only Iphicrates and places the capture of Dropides in 330, after the death of Darius (A 3.24.4).

Kirchner no. 4575; Berve ii.148 no. 291; Hofstetter 55 no. 95; Atkinson i.261; Bosworth i.233–4.

Drypetis. Younger of the known daughters of Darius III and Stateira; sister of Stateira [2] and Ochus; granddaughter of Sisygambis (cf. C 3.11.25; 4.10.19, 21). Drypetis was born between 350 and 345. She accompanied her father to Issus in late 333, where she was captured along with her mother, siblings, and grandmother by the Macedonian troops (C 3.11.25; D 17.36.2; A 2.11.9; J 11.9.12; P*A* 21.1). She was treated with respect by Alexander (C 3.12.21; 4.11.3), who came in person to the captive family of Darius (C 3.12.13–26) and said he would surpass Darius in providing dowries for Drypetis and Stateira (D 17.38.1, 3; cf. 17.37.3–6; C 3.12.3–26 for events associated with her capture). She remained with Alexander's expedition until the end of 331 (C 4.10.19, 21 gives a dramatic story of her mother Stateira dying in her arms, and of Drypetis consoling Sisygambis), despite repeated attempts by Darius to ransom his family (cf. D 17.39.1, 54.2; C 4.11.5–6, 12–15; J 11.12.1–3; P*A* 29.7) and Parmenion's alleged advice that Alexander accept the offer (C 4.11.12–14). Drypetis was left behind at Susa with her sister and grandmother (C 5.2.17; D 17.67.1) and given instruction in the Greek language (D 17.67.1; C 5.2.18ff. has an implausible story about "wool-working"). Here she remained until 324, when she was given as a bride to Hephaestion (A 7.4.5; D 17.107.6),[308] from whom she was soon widowed (C 10.5.20; cf. A 7.14; P*A* 72). Soon after Alexander's death, she and her sister were murdered by Rhoxane and Perdiccas (P*A* 77.6).

Stähelin, *RE* Supplbd IV s.v.; Berve ii.148 no. 290; Justi 86; Brosius 77–8. See Stemma III.

E

Echecratidas (Echekratidas). Methymnaean, peripatetic philosopher, friend of Aristotle (StByz s.v. "Methymna"). Phocion interceded with Alexander to obtain the release of Echecratidas from prison in Sardis (P*Ph* 18.6; Ael*VH* 1.25). The exact date of his imprisonment or release is not known. Perhaps he was arrested in connection with the political upheavals in Lesbos (334/3 BC).

Berve ii.162 no. 333; Hofstetter 55 no. 96.

Echmon. Son of Echmon. Cavalryman from Orchomenus; served in Alexander's allied cavalry until the expedition reached Ecbatana in 330. There he and his compatriots were discharged. On their return (ca. 329), they made a dedication to Zeus Soter in Orchomenus (*IG* vii.3206).

Berve ii.175 no. 358.

Elaptonius. See s.v. **Aphthonius**.

Enylus (Enylos; Ainel[309]). Phoenician. Dynast of Byblos. In 333/2, upon learning of Alexander's capture of Byblos, Enylus defected (along with Gerostratus of Aradus) from the Persian fleet of Autophradates (A 2.20.1; cf. C 4.1.15). His ships joined Alexander at Sidon and played no small part in the siege and capture of Tyre in 332. Enylus appears to have retained his position in Byblos (A 2.20.3). Nothing further is known about him.

Berve ii.150 no. 299; cf. Hofstetter 56.

Ephialtes [1]. Athenian politician. Family background unknown. In 341/0 (Develin 335), Ephialtes was sent on an embassy to Artaxerxes III Ochus and received money with which he is said to have bribed both Demosthenes ([P]*M* 847f) and Hypereides ([P]*M* 848e). Politically, Ephialtes was an opponent of Macedon and in 335 his name was on the list of orators and generals whose surrender was demanded by Alexander (A 1.10.4; P*Dem* 23.4 = Idomeneus, *FGrH* 338 F11, and Duris, *FGrH* 76 F39; *Suda* A 2704). Although in the end Alexander insisted only on Charidemus, Ephialtes sailed away to Asia Minor (Din 1.33; D 17.25.6). He appears at Halicarnassus in 334 along with his fellow-Athenian exile, Thrasybulus, in the service of Memnon (D 17.25.6). Taking with him 2,000 picked mercenaries, Ephialtes made a sortie out of Halicarnassus against the Macedonian siege-engines, which he put to the torch, and got the better of the fighting against the Macedonians (cf. A 1.21.5); Ephialtes himself, being a man of some physical stature, slew in hand-to-hand combat many of the enemy who opposed him (D 17.26.1–7). But soon after Ephialtes' initial success (which was followed by the arrival of reinforcements under Memnon) the Macedonians turned the tide of the battle and drove the Persian forces back into the city; in this reversal, he was killed (D 17.27.1–4).

Berve ii.160–1 no. 329; Bosworth i.93ff., 147; Hofstetter 57 no. 99; Seibert 1979: 149, 393, 501.

Ephialtes [2]. A Greek who, together with Cissus, brought Alexander news of Harpalus' flight, only to be thrown into chains by the disbelieving King (*PA* 41.8). Presumably he was released once his report was verified. Berve ii.161, 203 has argued that Alexander's disbelief suggests that it is Harpalus' first flight (333 BC) that was reported by Ephialtes (cf. Hamilton 109; Heckel 219). But we cannot be certain. Nothing else is known about him. But, if Cissus is the Athenian actor Cittus (*IG* ii^2 2418; cf. Ghiron-Bistagne 72, 337), then Ephialtes might also have been an artist.

Berve ii.161 no. 330.

Ephippus [1]. (Ephippos). Son of Chalcideus. Nothing else is known about Ephippus' background. He accompanied Alexander on the Asiatic campaign and, in 332/1 BC, was left in Egypt as overseer (*episkopos*) of the mercenaries (A 3.5.3) along with Aeschylus. What became of him, we do not know.

Berve ii.161 no. 331.

Ephippus [2]. (Ephippos). Olynthian, family background unknown. Born before 348 (in which year the city was destroyed by Philip II). Identification with the *episkopos* of mercenaries in Egypt depends upon the doubtful emendation of A 3.5.3 to read "Ephippus the Chalcidian" (see Bosworth i.276; *contra* Berve ii.161, Pearson 61) and is rendered unlikely by the fact that certain fragments of the Olynthian's history (or, rather, political pamphlet) suggest an eye-witness knowledge of events that the *episkopos* could not have seen. Ephippus authored a work entitled *On the Deaths of Alexander and Hephaestion* (Jacoby, *FGrH* 126; cf. Ath 3.1210e, 4.146c, 10.434a, 12.537d). The hostile nature of the work may have its origins in Alexander's treatment of Ephippus' compatriot, Callisthenes. Berve's suggestion that it was published in Athens at the time of the Lamian War (ii.161) is pure speculation.

Berve ii.161 no. 331; Gude no. 55; Pearson 61–7.

Ephorus (Ephoros). (ca. 405–330 BC). Famous historian from Cyme (for the surviving fragments of his work see Jacoby, *FGrH* 70). A contemporary of Theopompus and, with him, a student of Isocrates, Ephorus composed a *History* in thirty books, which extended from the earliest times to 340 BC. Nothing is known about Ephorus' connections with Alexander except for the claim that he declined the King's request that he join his expedition, presumably as official historian (*PM* 1043). The truth of this claim cannot be determined.

Berve ii.162 no. 332; Barber 1935; Brown 1973: 107–15; cf. Fornara 1983: 42–6.

Epimenes. The son of Arsaeus (A 4.13.4, 7) and party to the "conspiracy of the Pages" (C 8.6.9), he appears to have undergone a change of heart (C 8.6.20) and revealed the plot either to his lover, Charicles (A 4.13.7), who in turn informed Epimenes' brother, Eurylochus, or to Eurylochus himself (C 8.6.22), who brought the matter to Alexander's attention (C 8.6.22; A 4.13.7). Epimenes was spared for his role in alerting Alexander to the danger (C 8.6.26). Nothing else is known about his career.

Berve ii.150 no. 300; Heckel 291; Hoffmann 180; cf. Carney 1980–1: 228–9.

Epocillus (Epokillos). Son of Polyeides. Epocillus appears only as an officer in charge of transporting troops to and from Alexander's camp. In 330 he escorted the discharged allied cavalry to the coast, leading his own squadron of cavalrymen, presumably mercenaries (A 3.19.6). He rejoined the King at Zariaspa (Bactra) at the end of winter 329/8, accompanied by Ptolemaeus and Menidas (A 4.7.2, reading "Melamnidas"; C 7.10.11, "Maenidas," emended by Hedicke to "Melanidas"; but cf. Hamilton 1955: 217). With the latter and the ilarch Sopolis, Epocillus left Bactria in the winter of 328/7 to fetch reinforcements from Macedonia (A 4.18.3). What became of him, we are not told.

Only Menidas is known to have rejoined Alexander (A 7.23.1; 7.26.2).

Berve ii.150–1 no. 301; Hamilton 1955: 217; Heckel 364–5; Hoffmann 195–6.

Erigyius (Erigyios). Son of Larichus and brother of Laomedon (A 3.6.5, 11.10). A Mytilenaean by birth (D 17.57.3), Erigyius was a naturalized Makedon, having been granted property in Amphipolis. An *hetairos* of Alexander, Erigyius is wrongly characterized as a "boyhood friend": C 7.4.34 describes him as "white haired" and *gravis aetate* in 330; it appears that he was born ca. 380 and had been appointed by Philip as an advisor of the young Alexander. He was banished in spring 336 for his role in the Pixodarus affair (A 3.6.5; P*A* 10.4) but returned soon after Philip's death (A 3.6.6). D 17.17.4 claims that Erigyius commanded 600 Greek allied cavalry since the beginning of the campaign; but it appears that Erigyius was not appointed hipparch until Alexander Lyncestes was deposed as commander of the Thessalians in the winter of 334/3 and replaced by Philip son of Menelaus (A 3.11.10; D 17.57.4; C 4.13.29); the Peloponnesian allies were then assigned to Erigyius (A 3.6.6). Thus he commanded the allied horse at Issus (A 2.8.9; C 3.9.8), and at Gaugamela (A 3.11.10; D 17.57.3).[310] Between these two battles, from winter 333/2 until spring 331, Erigyius appears to have remained with Menon son of Cerdimmas in Coele-Syria, protecting the area with the allied cavalry (A 2.13.7; cf. Berve ii.151).

In 330 Erigyius followed the King in his pursuit of Darius III, at least as far as the Caspian Gates (A 3.20.1). He is next attested leading the baggage-train through Parthiene (C 6.4.3) and rejoining the King at Arvae (C 6.4.23) or Zadracarta (A 3.23.6). At Phrada he participated in the King's council concerning the action to be taken against Philotas (C 6.8.17). Soon afterwards, he was sent against the rebel Satibarzanes (C 7.3.2; A 3.28.2), whom he slew in single combat (C 7.4.32–8; A 3.28.3). Thereafter he appears only as an advisor of the King at the Iaxartes, urging him not to campaign against the Scythians beyond the river (C 7.7.21ff.). In winter 328/7, Erigyius died in Sogdiana, apparently of illness, and was buried with suitable honors (C 8.2.40).

Berve ii.151–2 no. 302; Heckel 209–10; Lehmann-Haupt in Papastavru 85–6 no. 35.

Eteocles (Eteokles). Spartan. Ephor in 331/0. At the conclusion of the war of Agis III, Eteocles refused Antipater's demand for fifty Spartan boys to be given as hostages, offering instead a double number of old men or women (P*M* 235c). He is also credited with the remark that Sparta could not abide two Lysanders (Ael*VH* 11.7; cf. Ath 12.535d).

Berve ii.153 no. 306; Poralla no. 282.

Euctemon (Euktemon). One of the spokesmen of the mutilated Greeks (cf. s.v. **Theaetetus**) who encountered Alexander's army between the Araxes River and Persepolis. His name survives only in Curtius, but that is not to say that Curtius invented him: since D 17.69.5–8 preserves the same general arguments, it is likely that the story was told in greater detail by Cleitarchus (Pearson 239; cf. Hammond 1983: 56). Euctemon makes the case that they should not accept Alexander's offer of repatriation but instead remain together as a group in Asia. This group and its leaders are doubtless fictitious, the speeches of Euctemon and Theaetetus little more than rhetorical exercises.[311]

Berve ii.156 no. 316.

Eudamidas. Eudamidas I of Sparta. Eurypontid (*regn.* ca. 330–before 294). Son of Archidamus III and brother of Agis III. Husband of Archidamia, by whom he had Archidamus IV (Plb 4.35.13).[312] He became king of Sparta after the death of Agis III (P*Agis* 3.3; Paus 3.10.5).

Berve ii.154 no. 309; Poralla 161; Bradford 1977: 161 s.v. "Eudamidas (1)."

Eudamus [1]. (Eudamos). Brother of Peithon (D 19.14.1) the Somatophylax and thus presumably a son of Crateuas, from Alcomenae (cf. A*Ind* 18.6). He may have participated in Alexander's conquest of Asia but his role is unattested in the Alexander historians. In 317, he was installed as *strategos* of Parthia in place of Philip [10] (D 19.14.1, where "Philotas" is either an error in the MSS. or on Diodorus' part). Eudamus was soon driven out (and perhaps killed) by a coalition of eastern satraps (D 19.14.2).

Berve ii.154 no. 310.

Eudamus [2]. (Eudamos; Eudemus; Eudaemon). General of the Thracians, Eudamus had apparently been left in Taxiles' territory with the satrap Philip son of Machatas. When Philip was murdered, the satrapy was given by Alexander to Eudamus (C 10.1.21). In this capacity he appears to have been involved in the murder of Taxiles' old enemy, Porus, from whose kingdom he secured 120 elephants, which he brought, along with 500 cavalry and 300 infantry, to Eumenes in 317 (D 19.14.8); he commanded the left at the battle of Paraetacene (D 19.27.2, 30.3, 30.9–10). D 19.15.5 claims that Eumenes bribed Eudamus with 200 talents, but P*Eum* 16.3 depicts him as one of Eumenes' creditors. Eudamus was captured at Gabiene by Antigonus' troops and executed (D 19.44.1).[313]

Berve ii.154 no. 311; Heckel 333–4.

[Eu]dramenes. Thus Hammond 1987: 340. If Hammond's restoration is correct, Eudramenes may have been an Agrianian *phrourarchos*, whose troops were dismissed by Alexander during the Balkan campaign of 336/5 BC.[314] But the name is otherwise unattested and the emendation uncertain.

Eugnostus (Eugnostos). Son of Xenophantes. *Hetairos* of Alexander, hence apparently Macedonian (cf. Tataki 311 no. 35).[315] In 332/1 BC, Alexander appointed Eugnostus as secretary (*grammateus*) of the mercenaries in Egypt under Lycidas the Aetolian (A 3.5.3).[316] Nothing else is known about him.

Berve ii.154 no. 308.

Eumenes. Eumenes son of Hieronymus (A*Ind* 18.7) from Cardia (P*Eum* 1.1; N*Eum* 1.1) in the Thracian Chersonese. Born in 361/0 (he was 45 when he died in 316/5: N*Eum* 13.1), in 342, at the age of 19, he came to the court of Philip, who was impressed by the young man's intelligence (N*Eum* 1.6, 13.1; Anson 37 n. 14)[317] and soon made him one of his *hetairoi*. He appears also to have made a favorable impression on Olympias, and remained a lifelong supporter of the royal family (D 18.58.2–4). Claims that Hieronymus was a poor waggoner or funeral musician (P*Eum* 1.1; Ael*VH* 12.43) are inventions of the gossipmongers and virtually disproved by the threat posed to Eumenes by the ruling tyrant of Cardia, Hecataeus. This man's enmity may have had its origins in political upheavals as early as the 340s, in which Hieronymus played a significant role, and continued into the reign of Alexander and beyond (P*Eum* 3.7). Eumenes served Philip for seven years (N*Eum* 1.4–6, cf. 13.1; P*Eum* 1.1–3): probably he was secretary (*grammateus*) of Philip and Alexander successively (A 5.24.6–7; cf. P*Eum* 1.6);[318] he was said to have been the author of the *Ephemerides* (*FGrH* 117 T1, though others ascribed the work to Diodotus of Erythrae; cf. Anson 1996). In the Indian campaign (cf. P*Eum* 1.5), after the capture of Sangala in 326, Eumenes took 300 horsemen to two neighboring Cathaean towns in order to induce their surrender (A 5.24.6); but the Indians, learning of Sangala's fate, deserted their towns (cf. C 9.1.19). He was one of the trierarchs of the Hydaspes fleet (A*Ind* 18.7), and later in Susa he married Artonis, a daughter of Artabazus and sister of Alexander's mistress Barsine (A 7.4.6; P*Eum* 1.7).[319] In late 324, after the death of Hephaestion, Eumenes assumed the hipparchy of Perdiccas, who had been promoted to Hephaestion's position (P*Eum*

1.5; cf. N*Eum* 1.6). Little can be made of his alleged presence at the dinner-party of Medius, except that the author of the *Last Days and Testament* was clearly favorably inclined toward Eumenes and the party of Perdiccas (Ps-Call 3.31.9; *LM* 98).

About Eumenes' career under Alexander little else is known. Like several others, he found Hephaestion difficult to deal with (P*Eum* 2.1–3), but took the precaution of being amongst the first to praise Alexander's friend when he died at Ecbatana (P*Eum* 2.9–10), thereby not only deflecting the King's ill will but possibly procuring for himself a significant cavalry command. Stories of his avarice may be exaggerated (P*Eum* 2.4–6), but Eumenes appears to have had his share of "cash-flow" problems (P*Eum* 16.3). Despite his later prominence in the wars of the Diadochoi, Eumenes was hindered throughout his career by his Greek origins (N*Eum* 1.2; see Anson; Hornblower 1981: 156ff.; Westlake).

In the division of power at Babylon Eumenes was appointed satrap of Paphlagonia and the unconquered region of Cappadocia, which was still in the hands of Ariarathes (A*Succ* 1.5; D 18.3.1; C 10.10.3; J 13.4.16; P*Eum* 3.3–4; N*Eum* 2.2; Dexippus, *FGrH* 100 F8 §2; App*Syr* 53; App*Mithr* 8; D 31.19.4–5; cf. *LM* 116). A*Succ* 1.2 lists him as one of the officers of second rank in Babylon in 323, and he played no small part in reconciling the feuding factions in the days after the King's death (P*Eum* 3.2). Despite, or possibly because of, the great trust placed in him by Perdiccas, Eumenes received no help from Alcetas: instructions to both Antigonus and Alcetas to help Eumenes secure his satrapy were ignored by the two.[320] Leonnatus, too, who could have given assistance from Hellespontine Phrygia, intrigued with Olympias to marry Cleopatra and seize control of Macedonia, but he failed to persuade Eumenes to join him in this endeavor and allegedly plotted to kill Eumenes as a consequence; the latter escaped only by decamping during the night (P*Eum* 3.5–12; N*Eum* 2.4–5). Ultimately, it fell to Perdiccas to install Eumenes, and the two campaigned in Cappadocia, defeating Ariarathes and replacing him with Eumenes (D 18.16.1–3, 22.1; A*Succ* 1.11). When Perdiccas decided to deal first with Ptolemy in Egypt, he left Eumenes, whose forces had now been substantially augmented by a force of cavalry from his satrapy (D 18.29.3) to guard the Hellespontine region against Craterus and Antipater (D 18.25.6), ordering Alcetas and Neoptolemus to serve under Eumenes. He was, in effect, commander-in-chief of the region west of the Taurus (N*Eum* 3.2; J 13.6.14–15). But Alcetas refused to join forces with Eumenes, and Neoptolemus actively plotted against him: he deserted and joined Craterus and Antipater (A*Succ* 1.26; D 18.29.2, 4–6; J 13.8.3–5; cf. *PSI* xii.1284; Bosworth 1975), but Eumenes resisted their appeals and prevailed in the battle, which saw the deaths of both Craterus and Neoptolemus (A*Succ* 1.27). Whether Eumenes killed Neoptolemus in single combat is debatable, though modern scholars have accepted the story (D 18.31; J 13.8.8; N*Eum* 4.2; P*Eum* 7.7–13; Hornblower 1981: 194). After Perdiccas' defeat and murder in Egypt, Eumenes and the remnants of the Perdiccan party were outlawed (D 18.29ff.; 18.37.1–2; J 13.8.10; 14.1.1; App*Syr* 53; Bengtson i.171ff.). The task of dealing with them was assigned at Triparadeisus to Antigonus (D 18.39.7).[321]

Berve ii.156–8 no. 317. There are two ancient *Lives* of Eumenes, one by Nepos, the other (more detailed) by Plutarch. For a full discussion in English see Anson; Westlake; Bosworth 1992; cf. also Vezin, Engel, Schäfer 2002, Hornblower 1981: *passim*, and Billows, esp. 70–104.

Euphranor. Corinthian sculptor and painter (Quint 12.10.6). Born ca. 400 (his floruit was in the 360s, Pl*NH* 34.50; cf. 35.128). Euphranor produced statues of Alexander and Philip in four-horse chariots (Pl*NH* 34.78).[322] For his work see Palagia 1980.

Berve ii.160 no. 327.

Euphron. Son of Adeas and grandson of Euphron (on whom see Xen*HG* 7.1.43–4). Sicyonian (*IG* ii^2 448). Euphron drove out the Macedonian garrison in Sicyon after the death of Alexander and joined the Hellenic alliance that opposed Antipater in the Lamian War (cf. D 18.11.2; Paus 1.25.4; J 13.5.10). He was honored by the Athenians in 323/2, but his privileges were revoked by the oligarchic regime that dominated Athens after the war (cf. Habicht 1997: 45). In 318/7 the rights of Euphron and his descendants were reaffirmed on a motion by Hagnonides (see s.v. **Hagnonides**) and both the original decree and the new one were inscribed on a single stele (*IG* ii^2 448). After the defeat of the Greek forces in the Lamian War, Euphron died at the hands of his enemies (lines 53–5).

Berve ii.160 no. 328; Skalet 193–4 no. 136; Schwenk no. 83; Harding no. 123A; Griffin 76; Osborne i.80 (D 24); i.101–5 (D 38).

Europa (Europe). The daughter of Philip II and his seventh wife, Cleopatra-Eurydice (Satyrus *ap.* Ath 13.557e), Europa was born only a few days before Philip's death in midsummer 336 BC (D 17.2.3). The theory that Europa was born in 337, and that Caranus was her younger brother (Green 95–6, 141), must be rejected and Caranus with it (Heckel 1979). She was murdered in her mother's arms by Olympias (J 9.7.12; according to Paus 8.7.7 mother and daughter were dragged onto a brazen oven) during Alexander's absence and without his approval (P*A* 10.8; cf. Burstein 1982: 161).

Berve ii.160 no. 326; Beloch iii^2 2.71–2; Heckel 1979; Hoffmann 218. See Stemma I.

Eurybotadas. Son of Tallus, from Orchomenus; served as member of Alexander's allied cavalry until the expedition reached Ecbatana in 330. There he and his compatriots were discharged. On their return (ca. 329), they made a dedication to Zeus Soter in Orchomenus (*IG* vii.3206).

Berve ii.158 no. 319.

Eurybotas. Cretan of unknown family. Leader of the Cretan archers (*toxarches*), a position to which he may have been summoned already by Philip II, when he planned his Asiatic campaign. He was killed, along with seventy of his men, in the attack on Thebes in 335 (A 1.8.4). His successor appears to have been Ombrion.

Berve ii.158 no. 320; Bosworth i.82–3.

Eurydice [1]. (Eurydike). Granddaughter of Arrhabaeus of Lyncestis; daughter of Sirrhas (Str 7.7.8 [326]). Wife of Amyntas III, mother of Alexander II, Perdiccas III, Philip II, and Eurynoë (J 7.4.5). Stories of plots against her husband and her sons (J 7.4.7, 5.4–8) are fabricated and at odds with other historical evidence (N*Iph* 3.2). She was the paternal grandmother of Alexander the Great.

Carney 40–6; Mortensen 1991, 1992; cf. Kapetanopoulos 1994. See Stemmata I, XV.

Eurydice [2]. (Eurydike). Daughter (possibly the youngest) of Antipater, sister of Cassander (App*Syr* 62 [330]; Paus 1.6.8; see Stemma V). Nothing is known of her activities during the lifetime of Alexander the Great. Married to Ptolemy son of Lagus in 321/0 (Paus 1.6.8). She was the mother of numerous children including Ptolemy Ceraunus (App*Syr* 62 [330]) and Ptolemais (P*Demetr* 46.5), as well as Lysandra, who married Agathocles son of Lysimachus (Paus 1.9.6), but she did not produce the heir to the Ptolemaic throne. Ptolemy Soter's successor, Ptolemy II Philadelphus,[323] was the son of Eurydice's kinswoman Berenice. She is said to have freed the residents of Cassandreia, where she was apparently settled by her son Ptolemy Ceraunus ca. 280 BC, and to have been honored by a certain Apollodorus with a festival called the Eurydiceia (Pol*Strat* 6.7.2). Eurydice, the daughter of Lysimachus and Nicaea, was named for her aunt.

Macurdy 102–4. See Stemmata V, X.

Eurydice (Eurydike). See s.v. **Audata**.

Eurydice (Eurydike). See s.v. **Cleopatra** [1].

Eurydice (Eurydike). Wife of Philip III Arrhidaeus. See s.v. **Adea**.

Eurylochus [1]. (Eurylochos). Prominent Macedonian. Eurylochus served Philip II as an ambassador with Parmenion and Antipater in 346 (Theopompus, *FGrH* 115 F165; Hypothesis to Dem 19 §5) and as a mercenary commander on Euboea in 342 (Dem 9.58). Perhaps identical with the *hieromnemon* at Delphi in 342/1 (*SIG*^{3} 242 B6; but the text is uncertain). Eurylochus must have belonged to a political group or family that was hostile to Alexander: he was executed at the beginning of the new King's reign (J 12.6.14).

Berve ii.159 no. 323.

Eurylochus [2]. (Eurylochos). Brother of Epimenes (A 4.13.7; C 8.6.20) and presumably a son of Arsaeus (A 4.13.4). C 8.6.20 claims that Epimenes had wished to keep Eurylochus out of the conspiracy, suggesting that Eurylochus was also one of the Pages (if we assume that the plot was restricted to the Pages). Whether Eurylochus learned of the conspiracy directly from Epimenes or through Charicles, he brought the matter to Alexander's attention through the agency of Ptolemy (A 4.13.7) and Leonnatus (C 8.6.22). He was handsomely rewarded by the King, who gave him the rich estates of a certain Tiridates and spared Epimenes (C 8.6.26).

Berve ii.159 no. 322; Hoffmann 180; Heckel 291.

Eurylochus [3]. (Eurylochos). Macedonian from Aegae. Lover of the *hetaira* Telesippa, Eurylochus had himself fraudulently enrolled amongst those veterans destined for discharge in 324 in order to accompany her back to Greece. Alexander learned of the deception and the affair and, instead of punishing him, urged Eurylochus to persuade, with words or gifts, Telesippa to stay (P*A* 41.9–10; cf. P*M* 181a and 339c–d, where the same story is told of Antigenes of Pellene).[324]

Berve ii.159 no. 324.

Eurysilaus (Eurysilaos; Ersilaus). Greek from Eresus on the island of Lesbos (C 4.8.11 wrongly says he was from Methymna). Installed, along with Agonippus, as tyrant when Memnon recaptured most of Lesbos in 333 (A 2.1.1; D 17.29.2). The previous tyranny of Apollodorus and his brothers had been reinstated in 335/4 only to be driven out in 334 (see Rhodes & Osborne 417), probably through the efforts of Alcimachus son of Agathocles, whom Alexander had sent to establish democracies in the area (A 1.18.1–2). Eurysilaus and Agonippus exercised the tyranny in a most cruel fashion (*OGIS* i.8a, b = Tod ii.191). They were, however, overthrown by Hegelochus in 332 and taken to Alexander in Egypt (A 3.2.6; cf. C 4.8.11), who sent them back to Eresus to stand trial (A 3.2.7; cf. *OGIS* i.8a, lines 13–15). There they were convicted and executed (*OGIS* i.8b, lines 60–9). See also s.v. **Agonippus**.

Berve ii.159–60 no. 325; Baumbach 33ff., 79; Habicht^2 14ff.; Berve 1967: i.338; ii.691; Hofstetter 68 no. 115; Heisserer 39ff.; Harding no. 112 A and F; Lott 1996; Rhodes & Osborne no. 83.

Euthycles (Euthykles). Spartan, presumably a relative of the ambassador of the same name sent to the Persian court in 367 (Xen*HG* 7.1.33; Poralla no. 301; thus Berve ii.155; Badian 1967a: 174 n. 1; Hofstetter 69). Sent as ambassador to the Persian King, perhaps in connection with the early activities of Agis III (Beloch iii^2 1.646), and captured by Parmenion at Damascus after the battle of Issus in late 333 (A 2.15.2; for Curtius' confused list of Spartan captives see Bosworth i.233–4; Atkinson i.261–2). Euthycles may be the unnamed Spartan ambassador (held in honorary detention by Alexander) whose quip is preserved by P*A* 40.4 in the context of (apparently) the Sidonian lion-hunt (**M60**; cf. Willrich 1899: 231; Hamilton 107). Alexander was at first hostile to him (on account of the political posture of his homeland) but later released him (A 2.15.5), probably after the complete failure of Agis III and the Macedonian victory at Gaugamela.

Berve ii.155 no. 312; Poralla no. 302 (cf. no. 301); Badian 1967a: 174; Hofstetter 69 no. 118.

Evagoras (Euagoras). Son of Eucleon of Corinth. In 326 he was appointed *grammateus* of Alexander's Hydaspes fleet (A*Ind* 18.9). Nothing else is known about him. Whether he was the later satrap of Areia is uncertain (D 19.48.2). Identification with Evagoras the hunchback is less likely (Ath 6.244f).

Berve ii.153 no. 307.

Evius (Euios). Flute-player (*auletes*) from Euboian Chalcis. He performed at the mass-marriage ceremony in Susa in 324 (Chares, *FGrH* 125 F4 = Ath 12.538f). It was on this occasion that Evius was billeted by Hephaestion into a home previously assigned to Eumenes of Cardia, a move which further aggravated the unpleasant relationship between Hephaestion and the latter (P*Eum* 2.1–3).

Berve ii.155–6 no. 315.

G

Gerastratus (Gerastratos). Phoenician, king of Aradus and the neighboring regions (including Marathus, Sigon, and Mariamne); father of Straton, who surrendered himself and the above-mentioned territories to Alexander in 333/2 (A 2.13.7; C 4.1.5–6). Gerastratus himself, like the other kings of Cyprus and Phoenicia, was serving with the fleet of Autophradates (A 2.13.7). Perhaps encouraged by the treatment his son had received (or by the result of the battle of Issus, cf. Berve ii.111), Gerastratus deserted from Autophradates and, together with Enylus of Byblos, surrendered to Alexander at Sidon at the time of the siege of Tyre (A 2.20.1); presumably he took part in the final assault on the city. Alexander reinstated him as king of Aradus (A 2.20.3), though we do not know how long he continued to rule. The coin of Straton (Head, HN^2 788) is more convincingly dated by Bosworth i.226 to the period of Straton's regency than to the period after 323 BC.

Berve ii.111 no. 225; Hill 1910: xiv, xl; cf. Hofstetter 69.

Gergithius (Gergithios). Quintessential flatterer of Alexander. Gergithius inspired Clearchus of Soli to write a work on flattery called *Gergithios or Kolokeia* (Clearchus, frg. 25 = Ath 6.255).

Berve ii.111 no. 224.

Glaucias [1]. (Glaukias). King of the Taulantians, an Illyrian tribe of the western region near Epidamnus. In 335 he joined the Dardanian Cleitus in an uprising against Alexander (A 1.5.1), arriving when Alexander was blockading Cleitus in Pellion and occupying the high ground (A 1.5.9–11). Glaucias was defeated by the Macedonians and fled to the mountains (A 1.6.1–10); Cleitus, who then set fire to Pellion, took refuge with him. In 317 Glaucias took in the infant Pyrrhus (P*Pyr* 3.1–5) and refused to surrender him to Cassander even when offered 200 talents; for his wife Beroa belonged to the Molossian Aeacidae (J 17.3.19). In 314, when Cassander's general captured Apollonia, Glaucias met him near the Hebrus River only to be defeated and forced to make peace (D 19.67.5–7), but when Cassander turned his attention to the east, Glaucias besieged Apollonia, only to be compelled by the Spartan Acrotatus, who had been driven there with his forces by bad weather in the Adriatic, to come to terms with its inhabitants (D 19.70.7). In the following year the Corcyreans intervened and removed Cassander's garrison from Apollonia but allowed Glaucias to have possession of Epidamnus (D 19.78.1). Glaucias restored Pyrrhus to his kingdom in 307 (P*Pyr* 3.5). But Pyrrhus was again deprived of his kingdom (in 303/2) while he was absent, attending the wedding of Glaucias' son (P*Pyr* 4.1–2).

Berve ii.111–12 no. 227; Hammond 1966: 246; Hammond 1974: 66ff.; Sandberger 104–7 no. 34; Bosworth i.66.

Glaucias [2]. (Glaukias). Macedonian noble. Commander of an *ile* of the Companion Cavalry at Gaugamela, where his squadron was positioned between that of Cleitus (*ile basilike*) and Ariston (A 3.11.8). He is otherwise unattested in the Alexander historians but may be identical with the Glaucias who, on Cassander's orders, murdered Alexander IV and Rhoxane in 310 (D 19.52.4, 105.2–3).

Berve ii.111 no. 226; Heckel 348.

Glaucias [3]. (Glaukias; also Glaukos, Glaucus). Physician of unknown origin, presumably Greek. Glaucias attended Hephaestion during his final illness and was executed (by crucifixion) on Alexander's orders. Whether the charge of negligence was founded or unfounded is uncertain. Even if the latter, the fact of the physician's execution need not be discounted as fiction created by the tradition hostile to Alexander (A 7.14.4; P*A* 72.2). Arrian, as Berve ii.112 suggests, may preserve the official version which excused Alexander's behavior by charging Glaucias with giving Hephaestion "bad medicine."

Berve ii.112 no. 228.

Glaucippus (Glaukippos). Prominent Milesian. Sent in 334 by his fellow-citizens and the mercenary occupation force as an envoy to Alexander who was then besieging the city. He offered to open the city and its harbors to both Macedonians and Persians. Alexander rejected his proposal and sent him back (A 1.19.1–2). Nothing further is known about him.

Berve ii.112 no. 229.

Glaucus (Glaukos). Aetolian. Greek mercenary leader who remained with Darius III and some 2,000 men (A 3.16.2; C 5.12.4 says there were 4,000) after the disaster at Gaugamela (cf. C 5.9.15). In Curtius' highly dramatized account, Glaucus' fellow-commander, Patron, warns Darius of Bessus' treachery (5.11; cf. 5.12.7), but the Great King refuses to abandon his countrymen. Although Darius did not avail himself of the mercenaries' protection, some of them may have put up an unsuccessful fight or deserted. After the King's death, 1,500 (presumably including Glaucus) agreed through messengers to surrender unconditionally to Alexander's agent, Andronicus son of Agerrus (A 3.23.8–9).

Berve ii.112 no. 230; Seibt 117–18; Hofstetter 70 no. 121; Grainger 2000: 177 s.v. "Glaukos (1)".

Glycera (Glykera). Athenian courtesan. Daughter of Thalassis, if she is identical with the courtesan named by Hypereides in his speech *Against Mantitheus* (Ath 13.586b). She was summoned by Harpalus after the death of his favorite, Pythionice. According to Theopompus (*FGrH* 115 F254a–b = Ath 13.586c, 595d–e), whose comments are doubtless exaggerated, she resided in the palace of Tarsus, where she received *proskynesis* and was addressed as queen, receiving crowns whenever one was dedicated to Harpalus. A bronze statue of her was set up at Rhossus in Syria. This was corroborated by Cleitarchus (*FGrH* 137 F30), although all that survives in the extant Alexander historians is a brief reference in D 17.108.6. She was mentioned in a satyr-play attributed to Python of Catana, but the production date of the work is problematic (Ath 13.586d; 13.595e–596b).[325] She returned to Athens with Harpalus in 324, but nothing is known for certain of her life thereafter.[326]

Berve ii.112–13 no. 231.

Gobares (Gobryas). Darius' *phrourarchos* at Parsagadae; he surrendered to Alexander in 330 BC. The treasure taken there amounted to 6,000 talents (C 5.6.10). Nothing else is known about him.

Berve ii.115 no. 238; Justi 117.

Gobares (Cobares: C 7.4.8). See s.v. **Bagodaras**.

Gorgatas. A young Macedonian, Gorgatas was a favorite of the queen mother, Olympias, and taken against her wishes from the court to Asia by Amyntas son of Andromenes (C 7.1.38–9). He was probably one of the fifty Pages (*paides basilikoi*) brought to Alexander in 331 (cf. C 5.1.42; D 17.65.1).

Berve ii.113 no. 232; Hoffmann 205; Heckel 292.

Gorgias [1]. Macedonian. *Hetairos* of Alexander. He commanded a battalion of discharged veterans in 324, but this does not mean that he himself was born ca. 380, as Berve ii.113 maintains. Gorgias is first attested as a taxiarch in 328, commanding Craterus' former battalion in Bactria and in the company of Polyperchon and Attalus son of Andromenes (A 4.16.1, 17.1; Craterus appears to have had the supreme command on this mission). In India, Gorgias' battalion, along with that of Meleager and White Cleitus, accompanied Perdiccas and Hephaestion as an advance force to the Indus (A 4.22.7). At the Hydaspes he occupied a position upstream on the western bank of the river with Meleager and Attalus, and thus did not participate in the actual battle (A 5.12.1). Nothing further is known of his military career except that in 324 he was discharged along with Craterus and Polyperchon and led the veterans from Opis to Macedonia, via Cilicia (J 12.12.8).

Kirchner, *RE* s.v. "Gorgias (3)"; Berve ii.113 no. 233; Heckel 326–7.

Gorgias [2]. A young Macedonian, Gorgias was a favorite of the queen mother, Olympias, and taken against her wishes from the court to Asia by Amyntas son of Andromenes (C 7.1.38–9). He was probably one of the fifty Pages (*paides basilikoi*) brought to Alexander in 331 (cf. C 5.1.42; D 17.65.1). Identification with the officer of Eumenes who recognized the body of the fallen Craterus (P*Eum* 7.6) is remotely possible (thus Berve ii.114).

Berve ii.114 no. 234; Hoffmann 205; Heckel 292.

Gorgus [1]. (Gorgos). Greek from Iasus. Son of Theodotus and brother of Minnion (*SIG*^{3} 307). *Hoplophylax* of Alexander, Gorgus was apparently also a shameless flatterer; for in Ecbatana in 324 he offered the King, whom he addressed as "son of Amun," a golden crown worth some 3,000 staters and promised to supply armor and equipment for a siege of Athens (Ephippus, *FGrH* 126 F5 = Ath 12.537e–538b). He is honored by the Iasians for his help in getting Alexander to award a disputed waterway (perhaps formerly belonging to Mylasa; see Heisserer 177) called the "little sea" to the city. The date of this service is, however, uncertain. But a second inscription, this one from Samos (*SIG*^{3} 312), honors him and his brother Minnion for their help in restoring the Samian exiles living in Iasus, and this is clearly in connection with Alexander's Exiles' Decree.[327] Two fragmentary inscriptions from Epidaurus suggest that Gorgus had also helped the Epidaurians obtain what they sought from Alexander (cf. D 17.113.3–4), and confirm the title of *hoplophylax*.[328] What became of Gorgus, we do not know.

Berve ii.114 no. 236; Heisserer 169–203.

Gorgus [2]. (Gorgos). Apparently Greek. A mining expert (*metalleutes*) in Alexander's entourage, Gorgus reported that there were gold and silver mines in the territory of the Indian ruler, Sophytes (Str 15.1.30 [700]). The Indians were said to have had no expertise in mining, and there is no indication that the mines were exploited by the Macedonians. Nothing else is known about this Gorgus.

Berve ii.114–15 no. 237.

H

Habreas (Abreas). Macedonian soldier of unknown background; a *dimoirites* (A 6.9.3, 10.1, 11.7), a soldier with double-pay (for this rank cf. A 7.23.3), Habreas may have been one of the hypaspists, as Berve ii.5 suggests; or perhaps a soldier from Perdiccas' battalion (cf. A 6.9.2). Late in 326 BC, he accompanied Alexander into the town of the Mallians (A 6.9.3), along with Leonnatus, Peucestas, and a certain Limnaeus, and was killed when struck in the face by an arrow (A 6.10.1). Habreas' role in the battle was not recorded by the vulgate authors, and perhaps by only one of Arrian's chief sources (cf. A 6.11.7).

Berve ii.5–6 no. 6; Hoffmann 222.

Hagnon. Son of Caballas ("Andron son of Cabeleus": A*Ind* 18.8),[329] from Teos. Hagnon was one of Alexander's Greek *hetairoi*, but noted for his extravagance (Phylarchus, *FGrH* 81 F41 = Ath 12.539c; P*A* 40.1; Ael*VH* 9.3) and flattery (P*M* 65d), as well as his hostility toward Callisthenes (P*A* 55.2). He was, in short, "an influential courtier whose wealth and power excited envy" (thus Billows 387). P*A* 22.3 claims that Alexander was angry with Hagnon because he offered to buy a beautiful boy named Crobylus as a present for him (see s.v. **Crobylus**). Andron, the trierarch of the Hydaspes fleet (A*Ind* 18.8), is almost certainly the same man. In 321/0 Hagnon is attested as well disposed toward the Ephesians who supported Craterus (see Keil 1913: 242), and he appears soon to have joined Antigonus (perhaps through the influence of Nearchus?); for at some point between 317 and 315 he was defeated and captured off Cyprus by the Athenian Thymochares of Sphettus (*IG* ii^2 682 = *SIG*^{3} 409).[330] What became of Hagnon is unknown.

Berve ii.9–10 no. 17; Billows 386–8 no. 44; Hauben 40–1; Hauben 1974: 62–4; Habicht 1957: 162 n. 26.

Hagnonides (incorrectly Hagnon: N*Ph* 3.4). Athenian from Pergase (*IG* ii^2 1629a), son of Nikoxenos. Apart from appearing in an Athenian naval list of 325/4, Hagnonides is attested in the lifetime of Alexander only as one of those accused of accepting bribes from Harpalus.[331] A member of the anti-Macedonian party, he had apparently been exiled by Antipater, but Phocion succeeded in persuading the regent to permit him to live in the Peloponnese rather than in the remote areas beyond the Ceraunian mountains or Cape Taenarum (P*Ph* 29.4). Nevertheless, Hagnonides repaid the favor after Antipater's death by denouncing Phocion and his supporters for betraying Piraeus to Cassander (P*Ph* 33.4; cf. D 18.65.6) and by supporting a motion by Archestratus to send a delegation to Polyperchon (P*Ph* 33.6). Although Hagnonides ridiculed the proceedings, which had degenerated into farce (P*Ph* 33.9), he eventually attained his purpose and Phocion was returned to Athens for trial and execution in spring 318 (N*Ph* 3.4; P*Ph* 34.9, 35.2, Hagnonides' greatest hostility was directed toward Callimedon).[332] In 317, with the return of Demetrius of Phalerum, the Athenians, in typical fashion, soon regretted the decision to execute Phocion and they condemned Hagnonides to death (*PPh* 38.2). See also s.vv. **Callimedon, Phocion**.

Sundwall *RE* s.v. "Hagnonides"; Kirchner no. 176; Berve ii.10 no. 18.

Hamilcar (Hamilkas, Amilkas). Carthaginian, surnamed Rhodanus (Rhodinus, Fr*Strat* 1.2.3). He was allegedly a crafty and eloquent man and, for that reason, was sent by his government to Alexander in 331 to discern the intentions of the Macedonians, whose capture of Tyre and establishment of Alexandria in Egypt had given them cause for concern. Hamilcar gained access to Alexander through Parmenion and, claiming to be an exile, joined the Macedonian army as a common soldier (presumably a mercenary). He kept detailed records on wooden tablets covered with fresh wax, but on his return to Carthage was executed on the charge of planning to betray the city (J 21.6.1–7; Oros 4.6.21; Fr*Strat* 1.2.3). The story is plausible but appears not to come from a well-known primary historian of Alexander.[333]

Lenschau, *RE* s.v. "Hamilcar (3)"; Berve ii.25 no. 52.

Harpalus (Harpalos). Son of Machatas (A 3.6.4), in all probability the nephew of Philip's Elimeiot wife Phila (Satyrus *ap.* Ath 13.557c). Tauron and Philip (A 6.27.2; C 10.1.20; P*A* 60.16) were probably Harpalus' brothers; Calas son of Harpalus may have been a cousin (A 1.14.3; D 17.17.4), as was perhaps Derdas, whom Alexander sent as ambassador to the Scythians beyond the Iaxartes (C 7.6.12; 8.1.7). But we know little about the family, most of whose members vanish without a trace. Even Phila remains an enigma, though she was Philip's (second?) wife. The royal house of Elimeiotis, which enjoyed considerable prestige during Philip's reign and saw many of its members promoted by Alexander, lapses into obscurity after Harpalus' disgrace and Alexander's death.[334] Harpalus was physically unfit for military service (A 3.6.6), but the nature of his ailment is unknown. In 336, he was one of Alexander's advisors and banished for encouraging the prince to interfere in the negotiations with Pixodarus (P*A* 10.4; cf. A 3.6.5). No doubt he returned as soon as Alexander came to the throne. Harpalus accompanied the King to Asia and was appointed Imperial Treasurer, but he fled from the camp just before the battle of Issus, together with a scoundrel named Tauriscus who may have encouraged him to abscond with some of the King's money (A 3.6.4–7).[335] He remained for a time in the Megarid, having sent Tauriscus to Alexander of Epirus in Italy; Tauriscus died there.[336]

In 331 Harpalus rejoined Alexander in Phoenicia and was reinstated as treasurer (A 3.6.4). In the following year, he was left in Ecbatana, with 6,000 Macedonian troops, some cavalry and lightly armed infantry, Menidas, Sitalces, Cleander, and, for a time, Parmenion (A 3.19.7; cf. C 10.1.1ff.). He thus became Alexander's link with the west. Perhaps while he wintered in Bactria-Sogdiana, Alexander received from Harpalus a shipment of books (P*A* 8.3; cf. Hamilton 21). Earlier, it appears, he must have connived in the liquidation of Parmenion (thus Badian 1961: 22–3). At some point, he shifted the seat of his power to Babylon, almost certainly on Alexander's instructions, and was entrusted with the royal treasure and the collected revenues (D 17.108.4). Harpalus also enjoyed an extravagant lifestyle (D 17.108.4; P*M* 648c–d; P*A* 35.15).[337] In 326, 7,000 infantrymen reached India from Babylon, bearing 25,000 suits of exquisite armor (C 9.3.21) sent by Harpalus, but they brought also tales of debauchery: Harpalus had used the imperial treasures to buy and bring to Babylon the Athenian courtesan Pythionice, whom he pampered with gifts while she lived (D 17.108.5) and worshipped as Pythionice Aphrodite after her death (Theopompus, *FGrH* 115 F253 =

Ath 13.595c, *Letter to Alexander*; see s.v. **Pythionice**). From the resources of the empire, Harpalus erected two great monuments to harlotry: a temple in Babylon and, on the Sacred Way to Eleusis, a tomb, which Dicaearchus deemed "worthy of Pericles or Miltiades or Cimon" (Dicaearchus *ap.* Ath 13.594f). The tomb in Attica, impressive still in Pausanias' day (Paus 1.37.4), cost thirty talents, according to Plutarch; Theopompus claimed that both buildings were erected at an expense of 200 talents (cf. P*Ph* 22.1–2). And the cause of this extravagance, wrote Theopompus, a woman who was "thrice a slave and thrice a harlot" (*ap.* Ath 13.595a–c = *FGrH* 115 F253: *Letter to Alexander*). Still Harpalus' passion for courtesans continued unabated: he summoned Glycera from Athens (Theopompus, *FGrH* 115 F254; D 17.108.6), and ordered her to be revered as a queen in Tarsus; he even erected a statue to her in Syrian Rhossus.

The Alexander who emerged from Gedrosia was not the same man who had forgiven, or even laughed off, Harpalus' earlier indiscretions. Disappointed at the Hyphasis, he had suffered a serious wound in the town of the Mallians, where the lethargy of his troops had left him exposed to enemy fire. The incident fueled rumors of his death and, with them, defection in the northeastern satrapies. And, even when reports of his demise proved false, few gave much consideration to the possibility, much less the consequences, of his return. Harpalus' crimes, it turned out, could be viewed as part of larger, more sinister, activities, carried out in concert with Cleander, Sitalces, Agathon, and others. His dealings with native women transgressed both law and acceptable behavior (D 17.108.4; cf. C 10.1.1–5, for similar atrocities by the generals who had remained with him), and they brought shame upon the new Great King.

Nevertheless, we are told that, when Cissus and Ephialtes brought the news of Harpalus' flight, Alexander was so struck with disbelief that he ordered them placed in chains: for he believed that they were surely slandering and falsely accusing him (P*A* 41.8; see also s.vv. **Ephialtes** [2], **Cissus**). He did not yet understand the enormity of Harpalus' crime. But patterns of maladministration soon became evident, and nothing short of a purge would restore order and security to the heart of the empire. Harpalus himself had anticipated these measures and fled to Cilicia, whence he would make his way to Attica.

At this juncture, in 324, before Harpalus had made the decision to sail for Athens, the King retained a certain macabre sense of humor and allowed the production in the Macedonian camp of a satyr-play entitled *Agen*.[338] The author was Python, a Byzantine (or possibly Catanean), though it was alleged – quite implausibly – in antiquity that Alexander himself wrote the play. This work, which depicted Harpalus in the character of "Pallides," mocked his relationships with Pythionice and Glycera, and predicted that Agen (Alexander) would soon punish him for his crimes. For the troops, Harpalus' sex-life served as a useful diversion after the hard campaigning in Bactria and India, and the deprivations of the Gedrosian march. And the view, held by many scholars, that Alexander would not have allowed such political lampooning, fails to take into account the poem of Pranichus or Pierion, which purportedly raised the ire of Cleitus in Maracanda (P*A* 50.8).[339]

While the troops roared at Pallides, a more earnest Harpalus set out for Attica with thirty ships (C 10.2.1), bringing 6,000 mercenaries and 5,000 talents from the Babylonian treasury (D 17.108.6). A general uprising, led by Athens, seemed the only way to avoid punishment (A*Succ* 16). But the Athenians were uncertain about how to deal with Harpalus' arrival (Ashton 1983: 56–7), and at first rebuffed him. Taking the fleet and his mercenaries to Taenarum in the Peloponnese, he soon returned to Athens as a suppliant (P*Dem* 25.3), bringing with him 700 talents. Demosthenes, who had originally urged that he not be admitted to the city, now accepted a generous bribe (J 13.5.9; [P]*M* 846a [1,000 darics], 846c [thirty talents]; P*Dem* 25 [a golden drinking-cup and twenty talents]), for which he was later indicted by Hypereides, Pytheas, Menesaechmus, Himeraeus, and Stratocles ([P]*M* 846c, 848f; another opponent of Harpalus and those who accepted his money was Deinarchus: *M* 850c–d), convicted and forced to go into exile ([P]*M* 846c; Paus 2.33.3 claims that Demosthenes did not take any money; for his exile cf. D 18.13.6). Harpalus himself was imprisoned and his money confiscated, but he escaped ([P]*M* 846b) to Megara (J 13.5.9); eventually he went to Taenarum and Crete (P*M* 846b).[340] The Athenians, though enticed by Harpalus' bribes, were frightened by the appearance of Alexander's admiral, Philoxenus (P*M* 531a; Hyp *Against Demosthenes* col. 8; Paus 2.33.4). Olympias and Antipater had also demanded Harpalus' extradition (D 17.108.7).[341] Ultimately, his money helped finance the Lamian War (D 18.9.1); for the Athenians sent some of it to Leosthenes (D 18.9.4). But, by this time, it was too late for Harpalus. Disappointed by the Athenians, he sailed away, perhaps intending to go to Cyrene, where his forces went after his death. On Crete, he was killed by one of his friends (D 17.108.8; C 10.2.3), namely Thibron (D 18.19.2; A*Succ* 1.16; cf. Str 17.3.21 [837]) – though others say he was killed by a servant or by a certain Macedonian named Pausanias (Paus 2.33.4–5).

Berve ii.75–80 no. 143; Badian 1961; Heckel 213–21. See Stemma XIII.

Hecataeus [1]. (Hekataios). A young Macedonian and a favorite of the queen mother, Olympias (C 7.1.38–9), Hecataeus was taken to Asia against her wishes by Amyntas son of Andromenes when some fifty Pages (*paides basilikoi*) were brought to Alexander in 331 (C. 5.1.42; D 17.65.1). Nothing else is known about him.

Berve ii.149 no. 293; Hoffmann 205; Heckel 292.

Hecataeus [2]. (Hekataios). Agent (and *hetairos*) of Alexander, sent in 336 to Parmenion in Asia to arrange the arrest or death of Attalus (D 17.2.5–6), and soon thereafter murdered Attalus (D 17.5.2), undoubtedly with Parmenion's approval. He is presumably the Cardian, a mortal enemy of Eumenes. Greek from Cardia. Sent by Antipater in 323/2 to Leonnatus to request his aid in Europe (P*Eum* 3.6–8). And, although Leonnatus answered the call, Eumenes, who did not trust Hecataeus, slipped away (D 18.14.4).

Berve ii.148 no. 292 and ii.149 no. 294.

Hector (Hektor). Son of Parmenion (C 4.8.7; 6.9.27), brother of Philotas and Nicanor. Hector was apparently the youngest of Parmenion's attested sons (C 4.8.7) and probably held no military office. Berve's estimate (ii.149) that he was born ca. 360 is thus too high; ca. 350 is more likely. Hector was drowned in the Nile in 332/1 (C 4.8.7–8; cf. also C 6.9.27; P*A* 49.1)[342] and buried with great honors, befitting a son of Alexander's great marshal (C 4.8.9).

Berve ii.149 no. 295.

Hegelochus (Hegelochos). Macedonian. Son of Hippostratus (A 3.11.8) and, apparently, the nephew of Philip II's last wife Cleopatra (Satyrus *ap.* Ath 13.557d).[343] Hegelochus survived the disgrace of his relative, Attalus, who was murdered on Alexander's instructions in 336/5, but his military functions may have been somewhat curtailed. In the events leading up to the battle at the Granicus, he commanded a portion of the *hippeis prodromoi*, also called *sarissophoroi* (A 1.12.7), though clearly as a subordinate of Amyntas son of Arrhabaeus (A 1.31.1, with Bosworth i.114; cf. A 1.14.1). The treasonous activities of Amyntas' kinsman, Alexander Lyncestes, over the winter of 334/3 may have caused the King to keep an eye on Hegelochus. Hence he was appointed as a joint commander, this time in tandem with the trustworthy Amphoterus, of the Macedonian fleet, which had been reconstituted in 333 (C 3.1.19; cf. A 3.2.6).[344] In this capacity, Hegelochus effectively recaptured the Aegean states – Tenedos, Chios,[345] Mytilene and the rest of Lesbos, and Cos (through the efforts of Amphoterus) – that had defected from Alexander as a consequence of the activities of Memnon the Rhodian (A 3.2.3–7; C 4.5.14–22).

In Egypt 332/1 (A 3.2.3, 7), Hegelochus rejoined the land army and it was at this time that he is alleged to have urged Parmenion to conspire against Alexander (C 6.11.22–9). Many of the army's senior officers were offended by Alexander's apparent rejection of Philip II when he accepted Amun as his divine father, and Hegelochus may also have reacted negatively to the chastising of Philotas, whose derogatory comments about the King had been reported to Alexander. The "conspiracy" came to naught and was not brought to light until 330, long after Hegelochus' death. When the army moved out of Egypt, Hegelochus assumed command of an *ile* of the Companions. As such he fought and died at Gaugamela in 331 (C 6.11.22; A 3.11.8).

Berve ii.164–5 no. 341; Baumbach 49ff.; Heckel 1982a. See Stemma XIV.

Hegemon. Athenian politician. Family background unknown. Hegemon is attested as a leader of the pro-Macedonian party in Athens in the time of Philip II and Alexander (Dem 18.285; cf. Harpocration s.v. "Hegemon"). He is apparently identical with the supporter of Phocion, who in 318 met Polyperchon near Pharygae in Phocis and was nearly impaled on the spear of the enraged Philip III Arrhidaeus (P*Ph* 33.7, 10–12). He and his supporters were escorted by White Cleitus to Athens, where they were tried and executed (P*Ph* 34–5).

Berve ii.166 no. 342; Kirchner no. 6290.

Hegesias. Presumably a native of Ephesus. Hegesias established himself as tyrant of the city at some point during Alexander's Asiatic expedition with the support of the Macedonians.[346] Perhaps around 324,[347] he was murdered by the sons of Echeanax: Codrus, Anaxagoras, and Diodorus (Pol*Strat* 6.49).

Berve ii.166 no. 343; Baumbach 22.

Hegesimachus (Hegesimachos; Symmachos). Macedonian. Apparently a member of the "Royal Hypaspists." Hegesimachus (along with Nicanor) led a band of young men in an unsuccessful attack on an island in the Hydaspes River (C 8.13.13) and perished in the attempt (8.13.15–16).

Berve ii.166 no. 344; cf. Hoffmann 215 "Symmachus"; Heckel 296.

Hegesippus (Hegesippos). Son of Onymon. Together with Philon and Ptolemy son of Lagus (see s.vv. **Philon** [3], **Ptolemy** [6]), Hegesippus made a dedication to Apollo at Miletus, probably in 334, but certainly before 306 (Rehm, *IMiletos* no. 244). Nothing else is known about him, but he may have been an officer in Alexander's army.

Berve ii.166 no. 345.

Hegesistratus (Hegesistratos). Greek (perhaps Milesian), entrusted by Darius III with the garrison of Miletus. Hegesistratus had agreed by letter to surrender Miletus to Alexander in 334, but then, encouraged by the proximity of the Persian fleet, chose instead to defend the city against the Macedonian attack (A 1.18.4). Arrian tells us nothing further about his role in the defense of the city or his fate. He may have perished during the resistance, but neither his death nor his possible pardon (cf. A 1.19.6) is mentioned.

Berve ii.166–7 no. 346; Hofstetter 76 no. 135.

Helen (Helene). A Greek woman, the daughter of Timon, Helen lived in Egypt and painted the battle of Issus (Ptolemaeus Chennos *ap.* Phot p. 248 Hoesch = Stewart T84; cf. Pollitt 174–5), a painting which

Berve ii.149 thinks may have been the model for the Alexander mosaic of Pompey. The original was said by Ptolemaeus to have been housed in the *Templum Pacis* of Vespasian. Koerte, *Roem. Mitt.* 21 (1907) 1ff. rejects Ptolemaeus as unhistorical; Winter 1912: 8 regards Philoxenus of Eretria's painting (Pl*NH* 35.110; Pollitt 169) as the inspiration for the Alexander mosaic.

Berve ii.149–50 no. 297; Pollitt 174–5; Stewart T84.

Hellanicus (Hellanikos). Macedonian (Hoffmann 195) of unknown family background, Hellanicus, together with Philotas, saved some of the siege-equipment from destruction at Halicarnassus (334), when the defenders sallied forth from the city (A 1.21.5; D 17.27.1–2; cf. also C 8.1.36). What office he held at this time is uncertain, though clearly it was a minor one and, apparently, involving the hypaspists; for in 330, in the contests held in Sittacene, Hellanicus received the eighth prize and a pentakosiarchy of the hypaspists (C 5.2.5).

Berve ii.150 no. 298; Hoffmann 195; Bosworth i.146–7; Heckel 306.

Hephaestion (Hephaistion). Macedonian from Pella, son of Amyntor (A 6.28.4; A*Ind* 18.3). A childhood friend and *syntrophos* of Alexander (C 3.12.16; cf. Ps-Call 1.18.5; Jul Val 1.10). Born ca. 356, Hephaestion entered the ranks of the Pages ca. 343 and heard at Mieza the lectures of Aristotle (cf. DL 5.27). There is evidence of a lifelong friendship with Alexander (D 17.114.1, 3; *LDM* 12.4; *LPL* 8; *PA* 28.5, 39.8; *PM* 180d, 332f–333a);[348] but the story that he crowned the tomb of Patroclus at Troy, while Alexander honored that of Achilles, may be a literary fiction (A 1.12.1; cf. Ael*VH* 12.7; cf. Perrin 1895).[349] Nevertheless, the close bond between the two is clear: when the captive Persian queen mother, Sisygambis, mistook Hephaestion for the King and did obeisance to him, Alexander publicly acknowledged him as his *alter ego* (A 2.12.6–7; D 17.37.5–6, cf. 114.2; C 3.12.15ff.; Val Max 4.7 ext 2; *IA* 37; *Suda H* 660). In December 333 or January 332, Alexander permitted Hephaestion to choose a king for the Sidonians (C 4.1.15–26; *PM* 340c–d; D 17.46.6ff.).

In late summer 332, Hephaestion conveyed the fleet and the siege-equipment from Tyre to Gaza (C 4.5.10). In 331, he received a young Samian (or Plataean, so Diyllus, *FGrH* 73 F2) named Aristion (Marsyas, *FGrH* 135/6 F2 = Harpocration, s.v. "Aristion"), whom Demosthenes had sent in an effort to bring about a reconciliation with Alexander (cf. Aes 3.160, 162).[350] At Gaugamela Hephaestion was wounded (A 3.15.2; D 17.61.3; C 4.16.32) while "commanding the *somatophylakes*" (D 17.61.3), possibly a reference to his command of the *agema* of the hypaspists. He may have been promoted to this post in 332, when Admetus was killed at Tyre (A 2.23.5; D 17.45.6). At what point he became one of the Seven is unclear.[351] Pol*Strat* 4.3.27 claims that Hephaestion and Philotas commanded the forces directly opposed to Phrasaortes [*sic*], while Alexander led the encircling forces at the Persian Gates (late 331). But both A 3.18.4, 7–8 and C 5.4.14–15, 29 assign this role to Craterus, and correctly identify the Persian satrap as Ariobarzanes.

In autumn 330, Hephaestion was part of the King's *consilium*, which met to decide the fate of Philotas, who was implicated in the so-called Dimnus conspiracy (see s.vv. **Dimnus, Philotas** [4]). To what extent he influenced Alexander's thinking in private we cannot know, but we may suppose that Hephaestion was not loath to speak ill of Philotas.[352] His name heads the list of those who came to Alexander's tent during the second watch on the night of Philotas' arrest (C 6.8.17), and he appears as the foremost of Philotas' tormentors. The Macedonians demanded that Philotas be executed by stoning, but Hephaestion urged that he be tortured first (C 6.11.10; *PA* 49.12). He received, as his reward, command of one-half of the Companion Cavalry – a blatant case of nepotism involving a relatively inexperienced officer. Hence Alexander entrusted the other half to Black Cleitus (A 3.27.4). In 329, Hephaestion is named as one of the King's advisors before the battle with the Scythians at the Iaxartes River (C 7.7.9). In the spring of 328, when the army was divided into five parts, he commanded one contingent (A 4.16.2)[353] in a mission that appears to have done little more than win back several small fortresses to which the rebellious natives had fled.[354] When the columns reunited at Maracanda in the summer of 328, Hephaestion's role was adapted to suit his talents. Clearly, he had no extraordinary abilities as a general, as his undistinguished military record shows. But he did provide useful service as Alexander's "utility-man." His first mission in Sogdiana was to synoecize the local settlements (A 4.16.3), an assignment that was to guarantee the loyalty of the native population by means of the establishment of garrisons, while it provided Alexander with a network of communications in the region. Alexander used him regularly for non-military operations: the founding of cities, the building of bridges, and the securing of communications constitute Hephaestion's major contribution.[355] Ten days after the Cleitus affair, he was sent to collect provisions for the winter of 328/7 (C 8.2.13). There is no mention in the historical sources of Hephaestion's role at the wedding of Alexander and Rhoxane, though Aëtion's painting of the ceremony included him (Lucian, *Aëtion* 5; Pollitt 175–6).

In spring 327, Hephaestion and Perdiccas were sent ahead into India with a substantial force to act as an advance guard, subdue the area around Peucelaotis, and build a boat-bridge on the Indus (A 4.22.7–8; 4.23.1; 4.30.9; 5.3.5; C 8.10.2–3; 8.12.4; *ME* 48).[356] It appears that, nominally at least, Hephaestion had supreme command, for Curtius' account of the dealings with Omphis son of Taxiles makes no mention of Perdiccas, who must certainly have been present. Perdiccas' participation in the mission may be attributable both to the need for a competent military man to accompany the relatively inexperienced Hephaestion and to their apparent personal compatibility. In the late stages of the campaigns, both men developed strong personal ties with Alexander, and it is not surprising that Perdiccas replaced the dead Hephaestion as Alexander's most trusted general and friend. The two generals followed the Kabul River valley, subduing some natives who resisted and winning over others by negotiation and show of force. At Peucelaotis, however, they found that the local ruler, Astis, had rebelled (A 4.22.8). He had perhaps been among the Indian hyparchs who had submitted to Alexander along with Omphis (Taxiles) (A 4.22.6, so Anspach i.13), and his rebellion may have been caused not by anti-Macedonian sentiment but by fear of his rival Sangaeus, who had now allied himself with Omphis. Only after thirty days of siege did Hephaestion and Perdiccas take the city, handing it over to Sangaeus, who later made an official surrender to Alexander; Astis himself was killed in the defense of his city. By the time Alexander reached the Indus, Hephaestion had built the boat-bridge and acquired provisions, chiefly from Omphis, for the bulk of the army (A 5.3.5; C 8.10.2–3; 12.4.6, 15; *ME* 48; Fuller 126–7).

In the battle with Porus at the Hydaspes, Hephaestion commanded cavalry and was directly under Alexander's control on the left wing (A 5.12.2; C 8.14.15). In concert with the hipparch Demetrius son of Althaemenes, he led a smaller force into the kingdom of the so-called "cowardly" Porus, a cousin of the recently defeated king, who had fled eastward to the Gandaridae (D 17.91.1–2; cf. A 5.21.3–4). Alexander pursued him as far as the Hydraotes (Ravi) River, whence he sent Hephaestion into the defector's kingdom in order to hand it over to the friendly Porus (A 5.21.5; cf. D 17.91.2). Hephaestion's mission was primarily organizational – to oversee the transfer of the kingdom and establish a Macedonian outpost on the Acesines (cf. A

5.29.3) – and hardly a war of conquest.[357] He rejoined the King after the Sangala campaign – a particularly bloody undertaking (A 5.24.5) – and before the expedition reached the Hyphasis (D 17.93.1; C 9.1.35). His duties in India continued to be primarily non-military. With Perdiccas he had founded the city of Orobatis (A 4.28.5) *en route* to the Indus (which he bridged), and gathered provisions from Omphis. After transferring the territories of "bad" Porus to his namesake, he established a fortified site near the Acesines (A 5.29.3); later he founded settlements at Patala and in the land of the Oreitae (A 6.21.5). The latter, named Alexandria, may in fact have been the synoecism of Rhambacia, which Leonnatus completed (see Hamilton 1972).

Hephaestion is named as a trierarch of the Hydaspes fleet (Nearchus, *FGrH* 133 F1 = A*Ind* 18.3). In the actual descent of the Indus river system, Alexander divided the bulk of his land forces into two parts: Hephaestion took the larger portion, including 200 elephants, down the eastern bank, while Craterus with the smaller force descended on the west (A 6.2.2; A*Ind* 19.1–3; D 17.96.1). The separation of the two commanders had become a virtual necessity: friction between them had erupted during the Indian campaign into open hand-to-hand combat, with the troops ready to come to the aid of their respective leaders (P*A* 47.11–12; cf. D 17.114.1–2). The rivals were given instructions to proceed downstream, each on his side of the river, and to await the fleet, which would join them three days' sail from the point of departure (A*Ind* 19.3; A 6.4.1; cf. Milns 227). Two days after Alexander's arrival at the predestined location, Hephaestion continued south toward the junction of the Hydaspes and Acesines, toward the territory of the peoples allied to the Mallians (A 6.4.1). By the time he arrived, Alexander (who had sailed ahead) had subdued the tribes of that region and was preparing to march against the Mallians themselves.[358] In the ancient accounts of that campaign – which saw the destruction of the Mallian town (near modern Multan: Wood 1997: 199–200) and the near-fatal injury to Alexander – there is no mention of Hephaestion.

The army continued southward, with both Hephaestion and Craterus now occupying the eastern bank, since the terrain on the western side proved too difficult for Craterus' troops (A 6.15.4). But Craterus was soon despatched westward via the Bolan Pass to police the regions of Arachosia and Drangiana (A 6.17.3; on the error at 6.15.5 see Bosworth 1976a: 127–9; see also s.v. **Craterus**). Craterus' departure left Hephaestion as Alexander's second-in-command, but in fact the King continued to assign him organizational tasks. At Patala, in the delta, he built city-walls while Alexander sailed down the western arm of the Indus (A 6.18.1). On his return, the King found this task completed and instructed Hephaestion to fortify the harbor and build dockyards; he himself followed the river's eastern branch to the Ocean (A 6.20.1).[359]

On the journey westward, at the Arabius River, Alexander left Hephaestion behind with the main force, while he, Leonnatus, and Ptolemy ravaged the land of the Oreitae in three columns (A 6.21.3; C 9.10.6); the forces reunited at the borders of the Oreitae (A 6.21.5). In the land of the Oreitae, Hephaestion began the synoecism of Rhambacia, while Alexander attended to military matters on the frontiers of Gedrosia. Soon he was replaced by Leonnatus and rejoined Alexander, as he embarked on his march through the Gedrosian desert (A 6.21.5, 22.3). Of Hephaestion's part in the Gedrosian expedition we know nothing further. After the ordeal and a rest in Carmania, he led the slower troops and the baggage-train into Persia along the coastal route and rejoined Alexander – who took the lighter troops to Pasargadae and then through the Persian Gates (A 6.28.7–29.1) – on the road to Susa.

Various episodes in Hephaestion's career suggest that he was generally unliked and unlikable. We do not know the exact nature of his quarrel with Callisthenes, or why he maligned him. Perhaps he objected to the brusqueness and austerity of Callisthenes, who was himself not an endearing person (A 4.10; P*A* 53). Furthermore, Hephaestion showed an enthusiastic preference for Alexander's orientalisms and extravagances. P*A* 47.9 says that Alexander would employ Hephaestion in his dealings with the Persians. Perhaps this attitude toward the orientals earned him the disfavor of both Macedonians and Greeks, though his rise to power through Alexander's favoritism was a major cause of hostility.[360] Whether he organized the unpopular *proskynesis* affair is uncertain.[361] Hephaestion was to claim that Callisthenes had promised to do *proskynesis* and gone back on his word. He wasted no time in maligning Callisthenes, once the sycophant, Demetrius son of Pythonax (A 4.12.5), had drawn the man's misconduct to the attention of Alexander and his courtiers (P*A* 55.1). Plutarch mentions two separate occasions on which Hephaestion quarreled with Eumenes: the first time over the assignment of living-quarters (P*Eum* 2.2; see s.v. **Evius**), the second involving a gift or a prize (P*Eum* 2.8). Alexander, learning of these incidents, was angry with Hephaestion, but soon came to resent Eumenes. Fortunately for Eumenes, the animosity and Hephaestion were short-lived; nevertheless, Eumenes was careful to avert any suspicion that he rejoiced at Hephaestion's death by proposing that honors be granted to him posthumously (A 7.14.9; cf. D 17.115.1). Furthermore, the conflict between Hephaestion and Craterus in India is instructive. We are told (P*A* 47.11) that Alexander rode up and openly reproached Hephaestion, calling him a madman if he did not know that "without Alexander he would be nothing." This was not the case with Craterus, whom Alexander chided in private; for Craterus was not one to be dishonored before his own troops, and before the *hetairoi*. No two individuals are more aptly characterized than are Hephaestion and Craterus by the epithets *philalexandros* and *philobasileus* (P*A* 47.10; P*M* 181d; D 17.114.2). Craterus' departure for Europe in 324 (A 7.12.3–4) left him without a serious rival as Alexander's dearest friend and foremost general. Already he had become the army's most important officer, for he commanded the first hipparchy ("chiliarchy") of the Companions (A 7.14.10).

At Susa Hephaestion received a golden crown, as did the other Somatophylakes (A 7.5.6), and at the mass-marriage ceremony he married Drypetis, sister of Alexander's own bride Stateira, for, according to Arrian, Alexander wished their children to be first cousins (A 7.4.5; cf. D 17.107.6; cf. C 10.5.20). From Susa, Hephaestion led the bulk of the infantry to the Persian Gulf, while Alexander sailed down the Eulaeus River to the coast (A 7.7.1), and from here he followed the Tigris upstream where the army and fleet reunited (A 7.7.6). Together they proceeded to Opis, and from Opis to Ecbatana. It was now autumn 324 BC.

At Ecbatana Alexander offered sacrifice and celebrated athletic and literary contests. P*A* 72.1 says that some 3,000 artists had arrived from Greece; cf. A 7.14.1; D 17.110.7–8 (dramatic contests only). There were bouts of heavy drinking, and shortly thereafter Hephaestion fell ill with a fever. We do not know the precise nature of his ailment; even Plutarch, who gives the most detail, is vague (P*A* 72.2). Invariably, Hephaestion's death is linked with heavy drinking: Arrian implies that the drinking-bouts were the cause of his illness, Diodorus is more explicit, but Plutarch does not specify the cause of Hephaestion's fever, only that immoderate eating and drinking were the proximate cause of his death. For accounts of his death see A 7.14.1ff.; D 17.110.8; Pol*Strat* 4.3.31 (incorrectly, it happened at Babylon!); J 12.12.11; A 7.18.2–3; Epictetus 2.22.17; P*A* 72; P*Pel* 34.2; N*Eum* 2.2; App*BC* 2.152. Ephippus of Olynthus (*FGrH* 126), in his scandalous pamphlet *On the Deaths of Alexander and of Hephaestion*, will have attributed it solely to barbaric drinking habits. At any rate, it was on the seventh day of his illness that Hephaestion died (so A 7.14.1). The only other details are supplied by Plutarch, according to whom Hephaestion disregarded the strict diet imposed by his doctor Glaucus (*PA* 72.2; Glaucias in A 7.14.4), who had gone off to the theater. Eating a boiled fowl and drinking a great quantity of wine, Hephaestion heightened his fever and died (*PA* 72.2); news of his deteriorating condition reached Alexander at the stadium, where he was watching the boys' races, but he returned too late and found Hephaestion already dead (A 7.14.1). The King's grief was excessive.[362]

Magnificent, indeed ostentatious, were the funeral arrangements, some of which were later canceled at the instigation of Perdiccas, who conveyed Hephaestion's body to Babylon. The cost of his funeral pyre was estimated at 12,000 talents (J 12.12.12; D 17.115.5; cf. A 7.14.8, 10,000).[363] In his role as Great King, Alexander ordered that the sacred fire of Persia be extinguished (D 17.114.4; see also Schachermeyr 1970: 38–48, esp. 47) until such time as Hephaestion's last rites had been completed.[364] Not surprisingly, history was quick to discover prophecies of Hephaestion's death (A 7.18.2 = Aristobulus, *FGrH* 139 F54). The seer Peithagoras foretold the deaths of both Alexander and Hephaestion (cf. App*BC* 2.152). Alexander sent envoys of Siwah to inquire if Hephaestion should be worshipped as a god; the prudent oracle replied that he should be revered as a hero (A 7.14.7: envoys are sent to Amun; A 7.23.6: the response comes that he should be revered as a hero; cf. *PA* 72.3, but incorrectly that he should be deified D 17.115.6; J 12.12.12; L*Cal* 17).[365]

Hoffmann 170–1; Berve ii.169–75 no. 357. Cf. Schachermeyr 511–15 and *passim*; Schachermeyr 1970: 31–7; Heckel 65–90; Müller 217–37; Reames-Zimmerman 1998.

Heracleides [1]. (Heraclides; Herakleides). Macedonian. Son of Antiochus (A 3.11.8). Heracleides commanded the Bottiaean squadron of Companion Cavalry against the Triballians (A 1.2.5) and remained an ilarch until at least the Gaugamela campaign (A 3.11.8). After that he disappears from our sources.

Berve ii.167 no. 347; Heckel 348–9.

Heracleides [2]. (Heraclides; Herakleides). Son of Argaeus.[366] Early in 323 (that is, after the winter campaign against the Cossaeans), Alexander commissioned Heracleides to take some ship-builders to Hyrcania and construct a fleet of warships with which to explore the Caspian Sea and its connecting rivers (A 7.16.1–2). Since these formed part of Alexander's "final plans," Berve ii.167 rightly questions whether the task was ever undertaken or completed. Nothing else is known about him, unless he can be identified with Heracleides the Thracian, which is unlikely.

Berve ii.167 no. 348.

Heracleides [3]. (Heraclides; Herakleides). Family origin unknown; a Greek from Calchedon, he was found in 330 with Darius III as an ambassador of his state (A 3.24.5).

Berve ii.167 no. 349; Hofstetter 79 no. 141.

Heracleides [4]. (Heraclides; Herakleides). Thracian (Ps-Call 3.31.8; *LM* 97), presumably of high standing in Alexander's entourage. According to the *Liber de Morte*, Heracleides attended Medius' dinner-party, at which Alexander became fatally ill. The pamphlet alleges that Heracleides was one of those who conspired to poison the King (Ps-Call 3.31.8–9; *LM* 97–8). Identification with Heracleides son of Argaeus is not impossible but the father's name appears to rule out Thracian ancestry.[367]

Berve ii.167 no. 350; Heckel 1988: 44.

Heracleitus [1]. (Herakleitos, Heraclitus). A juggler (*thaumatopoios*) from Mytilene in Alexander's entourage (Ath 1.20a), Heracleitus performed at the mass-marriage ceremony at Susa in 324 (Chares, *FGrH* 125 F4 = Ath 12.538e). See also s.vv. **Philistides**, **Scymnus**.

Berve ii.167–8 no. 351.

Heracleitus [2]. (Herakleitos, Heraclitus). Harpist (cf. DL 9.17) from Tarentum; performed at the mass-marriage ceremony in Susa in 324 (Chares, *FGrH* 125 F4 = Ath 12.538f). He later became a jester (DL 9.17).

Berve ii.168 no. 352.

Heracles (Herakles, Hercules). Son of Alexander the Great and Barsine, daughter of Artabazus (D 20.20.1, 28.1; J 11.10.3; P*Eum* 1.7; cf. J 13.2.7; 15.2.3; Paus 9.7.2; C 10.6.11, 13). Born in 327/6 or 325/4 BC: according to D 20.20.1 and J 15.2.3 respectively, he was 17 or 15 years old in 310/9. Most of Heracles' life was spent at Pergamum, which had belonged to the former satrapal territory of Barsine's father's family (D 20.20.1; J 13.2.7). Both his youth and illegitimacy worked against him. Heracles was but a child when Alexander died in 323 (App*Syr* 52 [261]; Porphyry of Tyre *FHG* III, 4.1). His claim to his father's throne was advocated by Nearchus (C 10.6.10–12),[368] but rejected by the Macedonian officers (cf. C 10.6.13); but in 310/9, Polyperchon, recognizing the boy's potential, had him (and his mother) brought to Europe, with the intention of installing him as King of Macedon (D 20.20.1–2). This move was, however, pre-empted by Cassander, who bought off Polyperchon with promises of lands in Macedonia and the generalship of the Peloponnese, thereby inducing him to kill Heracles (D 20.28; cf. J 15.2.3; by poison, according to Paus 9.7.2). Heracles was the last male candidate for the Argead throne and not long after his death the Successors began to style themselves "Kings" (cf. App*Syr* 54 [275]).[369]

Tarn 1921; Berve ii.168 no. 353; Müller, *FHG*; Brunt 1975; Wheatley 1998: 12–23; Carney 149–50. See Stemmata I, IV.

Heracon (Herakon). Macedonian officer. In 330 BC, Heracon remained in Ecbatana with Parmenion, whom he (along with Cleander, Agathon, and Sitalces) later murdered on Alexander's orders (C 10.1.1; rejected by Berve ii.168 on the basis of A 3.26.3). Heracon may have commanded mercenaries, though nothing specific is recorded about his unit. Little else is known about his career except that he had apparently been shifted to an administrative post in Susa – perhaps when Harpalus moved from Ecbatana to Babylon.[370] Heracon and his colleagues were summoned to Carmania in 324 and there charged with maladministration and temple-robbery (C 10.1.1–4; A 6.27.3–4). Though Cleander and Sitalces were found guilty and executed, Heracon was acquitted, only to be indicted by the natives in Susa on similar charges and this time required to pay the penalty (A 6.27.5).

Berve ii.168–9 no. 354; Heckel 341.

Hermaeus (Hermaios). Son of Nicias, from Orchomenus, served as member of Alexander's allied cavalry until the expedition reached Ecbatana in 330. There he and his compatriots were discharged. On their return (ca. 329), they made a dedication to Zeus Soter in Orchomenus (*IG* vii.3206).

Berve ii.152 no. 303.

Hermogenes. Slave who was present when Alexander dictated his last will and testament (Ps-Call 3.32.9; *LM* 103). He may be fictitious.

Berve ii.152 no. 304.

Hermolaus (Hermolaos). Macedonian. Son of Sopolis (almost certainly the ilarch). *Pais basilikos* and student of Callisthenes (A 4.13.2; C 8.7.2–3), though the latter relationship was unduly emphasized in order to implicate Callisthenes, who was probably responsible for the education of all the Pages and was most likely innocent of involvement in the Pages' conspiracy (P*A* 55.6; C 8.7.10; 8.8.21; J 12.7.2). After he had been flogged for anticipating the King by striking a boar during the hunt (A 4.13.2; C 8.6.7), Hermolaus conspired with several other Pages to murder Alexander while he slept (A 4.13.3–4; C 8.6.8–10). In Curtius' version (8.6.8), it was Hermolaus' lover Sostratus who persuaded him to join a plot against the King. Whether there is any truth to the story of the boar hunt, we cannot say. But there were clearly political overtones (A 4.14.2; C 8.7.1ff.), and the "conspiracy of the Pages" was symptomatic of the friction between Alexander (and his faithful clique) and the more conservative elements in the Macedonian aristocracy. Betrayed by some of his accomplices and repudiated by his own father (C 8.7.2), Hermolaus was arrested, tried (C 8.7.1ff.; A 4.13.7–14.3), and condemned to death by stoning (A 4.14.3; P*A* 55.7; C 8.8.20 says that the Pages themselves put to death Hermolaus and his accomplices).

Hoffmann 179; Berve ii.152–3 no. 305; Heckel 292–3.

Herodas. Son of Terticon from Eresus. Grandson of the tyrant Heraeus, who, along with his brothers Hermus and Apollodorus, controlled the city before Alexander's invasion. He was banished when Eresus went over to the Macedonians. Herodas, together with Agesimenes, accompanied Hegelochus in 332/1 to Alexander in order to plead for a trial, leading to their restoration. But Alexander left the matter in the hands of the Eresian *demos*, which chose to uphold the banishment along with that of the unnamed sons of Apollodorus (*OGIS* i.8; Harding no. 112; Heisserer 36–45).

Berve ii.169 no. 356; see text in Heisserer 39, 45.

Heromenes. Lyncestian, son of Aëropus and brother of Arrhabaeus and Alexander (A 1.25.1). Heromenes and Arrhabaeus were accused of conspiring with Pausanias of Orestis to assassinate Philip II in October 336 and executed by Alexander the Great (A 1.25.1–2; cf. J 11.2.1). The charges were apparently false, unless the Lyncestians had hopes of placing Amyntas son of Perdiccas (III) on the throne.

Berve ii.169 no. 355.

Hieron. Greek from Soli on Cyprus. In 324/3 he was sent by Alexander in a *triakontor* to circumnavigate the Arabian peninsula. Although he traveled a considerable distance – farther than either Archias or Androsthenes – he was forced to turn back by the desolate nature of the coastline (A 7.20.7; cf. A*Ind* 43.8–9). Although he is not named in Arrian's *Indica*, it is likely that he participated in Nearchus' voyage from the Indus delta to the Persian Gulf. Nothing else is known about him.

Berve ii.183 no. 382.

Hieronymus (Hieronymos). Greek from Cardia (*Suda* I 201) and, perhaps, a kinsman of Eumenes (cf. D 18.50.4). Agatharchides (*FGrH* 86 F4 = [L]*Macrob* 22) says that he lived to the age of 104, and since Hieronymus recorded the death of Pyrrhus in 272 (*FGrH* 154 F15), it appears that Hieronymus' life ran from roughly mid-fourth to mid-third century. Hence it is conjectured (and it is nothing more than conjecture) that he lived from ca. 364 to 260 BC.[371] But, since Eumenes was 45 at the time of his death in 317/6 (N*Eum* 13.1; see also s.v. **Eumenes**) and there is a possibility that Eumenes was Hieronymus' uncle, a birthdate in the late 350s may be preferable (cf. Hornblower 1981: 6). Of his life we know little. In 320/19 he was sent to negotiate an agreement between Eumenes (who was besieged at Nora) and Antipater (D 18.42.1), and after Antipater's death he acted as a go-between for Antigonus and Eumenes (P*Eum* 12.2). He appears to have served with Eumenes in the war with Antigonus and become a prisoner-of-war after the defeat at Gabiene, but was held in a position of trust (316 BC: D 19.44.3). In 312, he was instructed to collect bitumen from the Dead Sea (D 19.100.1–2) but the project was thwarted by the Arabs. He was present at Antigonus' death at Ipsus (301: [L]*Macrob* 22). In 293, Demetrius left him as governor (*epimeletes kai harmostes*) of Thebes (P*Demetr* 39.3–7), and it appears that from this point on he developed closer links with Antigonus Gonatas, son of Demetrius Poliorcetes and Phila. Whether he was with Antigonus Gonatas in 272 when Pyrrhus died is unclear. Paus 1.9.8 says he was biased against all Successors except Antigonus. For his *History* see Jacoby, *FGrH* 154; Reuss; Brown 1947; Hornblower 1981.

Reuss; Berve ii.183 no. 383; Jacoby, *FGrH* 154; Brown 1947; Rosen 1967; Sandberger 113–14 no. 38; Hornblower 1981; Billows 390–2 no. 51; Olshausen nos. 1, 69.

Himeraeus (Himeraios). Son of Phanostratus, brother of Demetrius of Phalerum;[372] anti-Macedonian politician and supporter of Hypereides, he was nevertheless a prosecutor of Demosthenes in the Harpalus case ([P]*M* 846c; cf. Shoemaker 1968: 1274–6 and Worthington 52–4 for Himeraeus and Dinarchus' *Against Demosthenes*; see Tritle 120–1 for supposed political affiliations). Himeraeus fled Athens and went first to Aegina after the Lamian War; he was sentenced to death *in absentia* by the Athenians on Demades' proposal. Antipater had him hunted down and killed by Archias of Thurii (A*Succ* 1.13–14; cf. Carystius of Pergamum *ap*. Ath 12.542e).

Kirchner no. 7578; Berve ii.184 no. 385.

Hippias. Greek, presumably Spartan. An agent of the Spartan king Agis III, Hippias was sent in 333/2 to the king's brother, Agesilaus, conveying to Taenarum ten triremes and thirty talents of silver, which Agis had secured from Pharnabazus at Siphnos. He brought also Agis' instructions that Agesilaus should pay the crews and sail to Crete in order to prepare it as a safe retreat for the Persian fleet (A 2.13.6; cf. Bosworth i.224). What became of him is unknown.

Poralla 67 no. 388; Berve ii.184–5 no. 388; Hofstetter 89 no. 156.

Hippocrates (Hippokrates). Doctor from Cos. Son of Dracon, the personal physician of Rhoxane (see s.v. **Dracon**). Hippocrates appears to have succeeded his father in this position and was killed along with Rhoxane in 310 BC at Amphipolis. He was also the author of a work entitled *Iatrika* (*Suda* I 567).

Berve ii.185 no. 389; Sherwin-White 1978: 468.

Holcias (Holkias, Olkias, Olcias). Perhaps Illyrian, though Berve ii.283 identifies him as Macedonian (cf. Hoffmann 211–12). This enigmatic figure, who plays such an important role in the events described by the political pamphlet on *The Last Days and Testament of Alexander the Great*[373] and who may be the author of the tract, is attested only once outside the work: Holcias, a commander of infantry, led an uprising of some 3,000 troops against Antigonus in 319 BC. There was some concern that the rebels might make their way to the outlawed faction under Alcetas, and Antigonus captured Holcias' men through the agency and trickery of Leonidas. Their lives were spared on the condition that they would return to Macedonia and remain inactive (Pol*Strat* 4.6.6). In the pamphlet, Holcias is depicted as intimate with the King, and his sister Cleodice (or Cleonice) was considered a worthy bride for Leonnatus. His importance is almost certainly exaggerated, but it is possible that he belonged to a prominent Illyrian family – Holcias is awarded Illyria in the Testament: *LM* 122; Ps-Call 3.33.23 – who was educated at the court of Philip II and thus a *syntrophos* of Alexander (see further Heckel 1988). It appears that Holcias served with Alexander at some point in the Asiatic campaign (334–323), perhaps as a junior infantry officer; from 323 to 320, he belonged to the royal army of Perdiccas, and after his leader's death made his way to Triparadeisus. There he was assigned to Antigonus, to whom Antipater had assigned the extirpation of Eumenes and the Perdiccan party. Holcias' sympathies, however, lay with the latter, whom he attempted to join at the beginning of 319. After his capture by Leonidas he was paroled to Macedonia, but after Antipater's death Holcias became a supporter of Polyperchon, for whom he may have composed the *Last Days and Testament* as part of the propaganda war against Cassander.

Berve ii.283 no. 580; Billows 412–13 no. 83; Heckel 1988.

Hydarnes. Son of Mazaeus (A 7.6.4), Hydarnes had apparently served with the fleet of Pharnabazus, which recaptured Miletus in 333 (cf. C 4.1.37). Hydarnes was placed in command of the Persian forces there but was defeated in 333/2 by Balacrus (C 4.5.13). He may have rejoined his father Mazaeus in time to fight at Gaugamela. Whether he surrendered to Alexander along with his father at Babylon (C 5.1.17) is unknown. Two sons of Mazaeus were enrolled in the Companion Cavalry in 324 (A 7.6.4).

Berve ii.376 no. 759.

Hydraces (Hydrakes). Gedrosian. Hydraces acted as pilot for Nearchus, promising to take the fleet from the harbor of Mosarna to Carmania (A*Ind* 27.1). Nothing else is known about him.

Berve ii.376 no. 760.

Hyperbolus (Hyperbolos). Flute-player from Cyzicus, Hyperbolus performed at the mass-marriage ceremony in Susa in 324 (Ath 12.538f = Chares, *FGrH* 125 F4).

Berve ii.376 no. 761.

Hypereides (Hyperides). Athenian. Son of Glaucippus. Born 390 BC. He is said to have been a student of Plato and Isocrates (Ath 8.342c). Father of Glaucippus (P*Ph* 4.2). He began his career as a *logographos* (or speech-writer for others). His political stance was anti-Macedonian, and he was an opponent of Phocion (P*Ph* 23.3), as well as Demades (cf. his remark about the mother of Demeas: Ath 13.591f). Hypereides made a name for himself with his prosecution of Aristophon in 362 and of Philocrates in 343. He opposed the surrender of those generals and rhetors whose extradition was demanded by Alexander after the fall of Thebes in 335 ([P]*M* 848e), and his name appears (perhaps incorrectly) on three lists of those named by Alexander (A 1.10.4; *Suda* A 2704; P*Ph* 17.2; see P*Dem* 23.4 and Bosworth i.94). In 323 he went on a mission to the Peloponnese to encourage rebellion against Macedon (J 13.5.10) and, after the death of Leosthenes in the Lamian War, he was chosen to deliver the funeral oration for the Athenian dead, because he was foremost in both his eloquence and his hostility to Macedon (D 18.13.5). When Athens suffered defeat in the Lamian War, Hypereides fled the city (P*Ph* 26.2), and Antipater demanded that he and Demosthenes be delivered up (P*Ph* 27.5). He was hunted down by Archias of Thurii, who found Hypereides and Himeraeus, the brother of Demetrius of Phalerum, in Aegina and dragged them from the sanctuary of Aeacus. Archias sent them to Antipater at Cleonae, where Hypereides' tongue was cut out before he was killed (P*Dem* 28.4; A*Succ* 1.13; cf. P*Ph* 29.1). For a brief account of his life see [P]*M* 848d–850b.

Berve ii.376–8 no. 762.

Hypsides. Macedonian. Probably a lower-ranking officer, Hypsides was a friend of Menedemus. In the Polytimetus battle he remained by the side of his mortally wounded friend although Menedemus urged him to take his horse and save himself. Hypsides instead charged into the enemy and gained a glorious death (C 7.7.36–7). He is otherwise unknown.

His story may have been invented for dramatic effect.

Berve ii.378–9 no. 764.

Hystaspes. High-ranking Persian, Hystaspes was a kinsman of Darius III and the husband of an unnamed granddaughter of Artaxerxes III Ochus (**F10**),[374] captured in 330 after the death of Darius (C 6.2.7). Curtius adds that Hystaspes had been one of Darius' military commanders, and we may suppose that he was one of the many unnamed commanders of regional troops at Gaugamela. It seems highly likely that he is identical with Hystaspes "the Bactrian," who commanded the new oriental cavalry squadron (A 7.6.5); Berve's suggestion that he was a descendant of Hystaspes son of Xerxes (D 11.69.2) is rightly questioned by Briant 1033.

Berve ii.378 no. 763.

I

Ilioneus. Youngest son of Artabazus. The name is attested only in Curtius, but suits the family's interests in the Hellespontine region. Ilioneus was captured by Parmenion at Damascus in 333/2 (C 3.13.13). What became of him, we do not know.

Berve ii.183–4 no. 384. See Stemma IV.

Iolaus [1]. (Iolaos, Iollas). The youngest son of Antipater and, along with his brother Philip, probably a Page (*pais basilikos*) of Alexander during the latter portion of the Asiatic campaign (J 12.14.9). Iolaus is given the title *archioinochoos* or "wine-pourer" (P*A* 74.2; cf. A 7.27.2), but I see no difficulty in assuming that he held this position as one of the Pages (cf. Aretis the *anaboleus*, also identified as a Page). Except for rumors that he was the *eromenos* of Medius of Larissa (A 7.27.2) and responsible for poisoning the King (A 7.27.1–2; J 12.13.6ff., esp. 12.14.6–9; C 10.10.14–19; P*A* 77.2–3; D 17.118.1–2; [P]*M* 849f;[375] cf. Heckel 1988; *LM* 89, 96–100), nothing else is known of his career under Alexander. In 323/2, he acted as an intermediary for his father and Perdiccas, bringing to Asia in the following year his sister Nicaea, the latter's intended bride (A*Succ* 1.21). Thereafter, he appears to have returned to his father's court in Macedonia. By 317/6, he was already dead: Olympias, as an act of vengeance against her son's "murderers," overturned his grave (D 19.11.8; cf. 19.35.1).

Berve ii.184 no. 386; Heckel 293. See Stemma V.

Iolaus [2]. (Iolaos, Iollas). Prominent Macedonian; family background unknown. Iolaus was a member of the Dimnus conspiracy (330 BC), whose name was given by Dimnus to Nicomachus (C 6.7.15) and eventually reported to Alexander (cf. C 6.8.2). He and his accomplices were found guilty by the Macedonian army and stoned to death (C 6.11.38). He is mentioned only by Curtius, and we cannot be certain that he did not invent the conspirators' names for the sake of realism.

Berve ii.184 no. 387; Heckel 1977a: 21.

Iolaus [3]. (Iolaos, Iollas). Macedonian. Family background unknown. An inscription from Athens (*IG* ii^2 561) honors him, Philip, and, perhaps, a third individual as supporters of Demetrius and Antigonus and former *somatophylakes* of a certain King Alexander. Iolaus may have been appointed Somatophylax of Alexander IV at Triparadeisus. Apart from his continued support for the Antigonids and his *eunoia* toward the Athenians, nothing else is known about him.

Berve ii.420 no. 31; Billows 394–5 no. 57; cf. Habicht, *Akten VI. Kongr. Epig.* 373 n. 35; Heckel 1980d, 1981f; Burstein 1977.

Iphicrates (Iphikrates). Athenian from Rhamnus. Son of the famous general Iphicrates and a sister of the Thracian dynast Cotys, and thus born ca. 370 BC (Hofstetter 95 n. 2; Davies 249). Sent by the Athenians on an embassy to Darius,[376]

Iphicrates was captured, along with Euthycles the Spartiate and Thessaliscus and Dionysodorus the Thebans, in late 333 BC by Parmenion at Damascus (A 2.15.2; cf. C 3.13.15).[377] Iphicrates received kind treatment from Alexander, who respected both Athens and his father's fame, but died of illness soon after his capture; Alexander sent his remains to his relatives in Athens (A 2.15.4).

Berve ii.186 no. 393; Kirchner no. 7736; Davies 251; Hofstetter 95 no. 165; Hofstetter 1972: 99.

Isocrates (Isokrates). (436–338 BC). Athenian (Kirchner no. 7716). Son of Theodorus. Famous rhetor and teacher. He studied under, among others, the sophist Gorgias, and in 403 he spoke in favor of Theramenes, whom the Thirty sentenced to death. He was best known as a pamphleteer who promoted Panhellenism, urging the Greeks to unite under leader states or individuals (Athens, Sparta, Alexander of Pherae, Philip II) and wage war on Persia. In 342/1 he wrote a *Letter to Alexander* (*Ep* 5), which accompanied a letter to Philip. The letter is extremely short and comments on Alexander's education, praising him for not paying excessive attention to *eristic* (i.e., argument for its own sake) and for devoting himself to acquiring the kind of wisdom that will benefit a statesman. Although the authenticity of the *Letter* was once challenged, it is now generally regarded as genuine. We have no clear idea, however, to what extent Isocrates' ideas of Panhellenism and unity in the face of the common enemy (i.e., Persia) influenced Alexander's thinking (on which see Flower 2000). Isocrates died in 338 BC, the year of Chaeronea.

Berve ii.185–6 no. 391; Blass ii^2 327–8; Münscher, *RE* ix.2146ff.

Itanes. Son of Oxyartes; brother of Rhoxane. (Istanes = Wistana preferred by Marquart 162 n. 1). He was probably in Alexander's entourage since early 327, when the King married his sister.[378] In 324 he was enrolled in the *agema* of the Companions, along with other orientals (A 7.6.5). What became of him after the King's death, we do not know.

Berve ii.186 no. 392. See Stemma I.

L

Laches. Son of Melanopus, Athenian from the deme Aixone (Kirchner no. 9020). Imprisoned in Athens (at some undetermined point in Alexander's reign) for inability or failure to pay a fine but was freed as a result of a letter from Alexander (Dem*Ep* 3.24, 26).

Berve ii.232 no. 465; Kirchner no. 9020.

Lamachus (Lamachos). Sophist from Myrrhine on Lesbos,[379] Lamachus wrote a panegyric on Philip II and Alexander which was read out at Olympia and drew an angry response from Demosthenes. Lamachus was forced to leave the festival out of shame and fear for his safety (P*Dem* 9.1; [P]*M* 845c).

Berve ii.231 no. 461; Schaefer iii^2 317–18.

Langarus (Langaros). King of the Agrianes, a tribe of the Paeonians, who lived on the upper Strymon toward the Axius River. Their contingent later formed an important element in Alexander's expeditionary force. Langarus himself had developed close personal ties with Alexander already in Philip's lifetime, and had come to him personally on an embassy (A 1.5.2), perhaps while Alexander ruled in Philip's absence in 340 or 338/7. In 336/5, when Alexander was contemplating a campaign against the Autariatae, Langarus arrived with his best-equipped hypaspists, deriding the Autariatae as the least warlike of the tribes in that region, and offered to conduct the campaign against them in person. This he did successfully, leaving Alexander free to deal with the Illyrians and Taulantians under Cleitus and Glaucias (A 1.5.2–3). For his efforts he was handsomely rewarded by Alexander and summoned to Pella to marry the King's half-sister Cynnane (now the widow of Amyntas son of Perdiccas III). Langarus, however, died of illness on his return from the campaign against the Autariatae (A 1.5.4–5).

Berve ii.230 no. 460.

Lanice (Lanike; also Hellanice and Alacrinis). Daughter of Dropidas and sister of "Black" Cleitus (A 4.9.3; C 8.2.8). She was born, most likely, shortly after 380; for she is named as the mother of Proteas (Hippolochus *ap.* Ath 4.129a; Ael*VH* 12.26) and two other sons (**M41–42**) who died in battle at Miletus in 334 (C 8.2.8; cf. A 4.9.4). Lanice had been Alexander's nurse (C 8.1.21, 2.8–9; cf. A 4.9.3; Ael*VH* 26; Ath 4.129a; Ps-Call 1.13; Jul Val 1.17), a circumstance which only heightened the grief which Alexander felt for his murder of Cleitus. Her husband may have been Andronicus, though not the Olynthian (Berve ii.39, 231 is contradictory; see Carney 1981: 153, with n. 11).

Berve ii.231 no. 462; Staehelin, *RE* s.v. "Lanike." See also Samuel 1986: 430 n. 8. See Stemma VIII.

Laodice (Laodike). A woman of the Macedonian aristocracy, but of unknown family background, Laodice married

Antiochus (perhaps a member of the Orestian nobility, cf. Hoffmann 153). Mother of Seleucus Nicator. The story that she slept with Apollo and conceived Seleucus (J 15.4.3–6) is later invention, imitating Olympias' alleged liaison with Zeus-Amun (J 11.11.1–8; Grainger 2–3; Hadley 1969: 152, dating it to after Ipsus).[380] Seleucus is said to have founded five cities named in her honor (App*Syr* 57 [295]; Str 16.2.4 [749–50]; StByz s.v. "Laodikeia"; cf. Grainger 1990: 48–50).

Berve ii.231 no. 463; Volkmann, *Kl. Pauly* iii.479 no. 1; Bevan ii.275–6; Hoffmann 220. See Stemma XI.

Laomedon. Son of Larichus (A 3.6.5; A*Ind* 18.4) and younger brother of Erigyius. Mytilenaean by birth (A*Succ* 1.34; D 18.3.1, 39.6; J 13.4.12; App*Syr* 52 [263]; cf. D 17.57.3) but a naturalized Makedon settled in Amphipolis (A*Ind* 18.4). Possibly father of that Larichus honored at Priene (*OGIS* i.215, 13). An *hetairos* of Alexander, Laomedon was almost certainly not coeval with the King, but already mature when he settled in Amphipolis in the 350s or early 340s. His birthdate might belong to the late 370s. Laomedon was exiled by Philip in the spring of 336 (along with Erigyius, Harpalus, Nearchus, and Ptolemy) for his part in the so-called "Pixodarus affair" (A 3.6.5; cf. P*A* 10.5, naming Erigyius but omitting Laomedon), but recalled after Philip's death (A 3.6.6). He accompanied Alexander to Asia and was given charge of the Persian prisoners after Issus because he was bilingual (A 3.6.6).[381] At the Hydaspes he served as one of the trierarchs of Alexander's fleet (A*Ind* 18.4). Nothing else is known of his career under Alexander.

After the King's death in June 323, Laomedon received the satrapy of Coele-Syria (A*Succ* 1.5; Dexippus, *FGrH* 100 F8 §2; D 18.3.1; C 10.10.2; J 13.4.12; App*Syr* 52);[382] perhaps he aided his old friend Ptolemy in diverting Alexander's funeral carriage to Egypt (A*Succ* 1.25). At Triparadeisus in summer 320, his position as satrap was confirmed (A*Succ* 1.34; D 18.39.6; App*Syr* 52 [263]); Laomedon rejected Ptolemy's offer to "buy" the territory from him in 319 (App*Syr* 52 [264]). Not long after Antipater's return to Europe, Ptolemy sent his general Nicanor (otherwise unknown) to capture Laomedon and occupy the satrapy (D 18.43.2; cf. Paus 1.6.4; cf. App*Mithr* 9 [27], incorrectly saying that Antigonus expelled him). Laomedon bribed his guards and escaped to Alcetas in Caria (App*Syr* 52 [265]). What became of him, we do not know. He may have perished along with many of Alcetas' supporters at Cretopolis.[383]

Berve ii.231–2 no. 464; Heckel 211–12; Hoffmann 118 n. 2; Lehmann-Haupt in Papastavru 88–92 no. 50.

Leochares. Greek sculptor, apparently Athenian. Born ca. 390 – a letter attributed to Plato calls him a young man in 366 ([Plato]*Ep* 13.361a; cf. Pl*NH* 34.50) – and died ca. 310 BC. The statues of the royal family (Philip, Alexander, Amyntas III, Eurydice, and Olympias) in the *Philippeum* at Olympias, produced soon after Chaeronea, were the work of Leochares (Paus 5.20.10; Stewart T97–8). Leochares also worked with Lysippus on the lion hunt scene that included Alexander and Craterus at Delphi (P*A* 40.5; cf. Perdrizet 1899).[384]

Berve ii.237 no. 472.

Leon. Son of Leon, from Byzantium (*Suda Λ* 265). Author of several historical works including *Events concerning Philip and Byzantium* and *On the Sacred War*, as well as an Alexander history. He was perhaps a student of Aristotle (Jacoby, iiD, 444), but the *Suda* confuses him with the student of Plato (P*Ph* 14.7; Philostr*VS* 1.2; cf. Nicas of Nicaea *ap.* Ath 11.506c; DL 3.62) who led the Byzantine opposition to Philip II.[385]

Berve ii.235 no. 468; Jacoby, *FGrH* 132.

Leonidas [1]. (Leukonides; Leuconides: Ps-Call 1.13.4; Jul Val 1.7). Epirote, kinsman of Olympias and tutor of Alexander

(Diogenes of Babylon *ap*. Quint 1.1.9; Jerome, *Letters* 57; PI*NH* 12.62), noted for his austere nature (P*A* 5.7; 22; 25; cf. Ps-Call 1.13; Jul Val 1.7) and laconic discipline (illustrated in two anecdotes by P*A* 22.9–10). Leonidas was said to have shunned luxury and preached frugality to the extent of scolding Alexander for wasting incense: the King later sent Leonidas 100 talents of frankincense and cassia (PI*NH* 12.62; P*M* 179e–f; P*A* 25.6–8: 500 talents of frankincense and 100 of myrrh). Nothing else is known about him.

Berve ii.235–6 no. 469.

Leonidas [2]. Background unknown, presumably Macedonian. Commander of the *ataktoi*, or "Disciplinary Unit" (but see Welles 351 n. 3), formed by Alexander after the Philotas affair (330), Leonidas is said to have been a friend of Parmenion (C 7.2.35; rejected by Berve ii.236 n. 2 as "Erfindung"). Arrian does not mention the unit, but both the creation of the office (C 7.2.35–8; J 12.5.8; D 17.80.4) and the individual (named only by C) may be historical. Leonidas, the agent of Antigonus Monophthalmus who captured by trickery Holkias and his 3,000 rebellious troops in Cappadocia and escorted them back to Macedonia (Pol*Strat* 4.6.6), *may* have been the same man (Berve ii.236; Heckel 1988: 79; Billows no. 61). Identification with Ptolemy's *strategos*, sent against the Antigonid cities of Cilicia Tracheia in 310 BC (D 20.19.4; cf. *IG* xi.4, 161b, l. 77), is less likely: although many officers did change sides during the wars of the Successors, Leonidas, if he truly was a friend of Parmenion and one of the "old guard," may have been too old for such activity in 310.

Stähelin, *RE* s.v. "Leonidas (5–6)"; Berve ii.236 no. 470; Billows 397 no. 61; Heckel 1988: 79.

Leonnatus [1]. (Leonnatos). Son of Antipater, from Aegae (A*Ind* 18.6), Leonnatus' father is otherwise unknown. About Leonnatus himself we know only that he was one of the trierarchs of the Hydaspes fleet in autumn 326 (A*Ind* 18.6), hence a man of means. How long he had been in Alexander's entourage, and what became of him, we do not know. Berve ii.235 (followed tentatively by Bosworth ii.87) implausibly identifies him with the man who ridiculed *proskynesis* in 327 (A 4.12.2).

Geyer, *RE* s.v. "Leonnatos (2)"; Berve ii.235 no. 467.

Leonnatus [2]. (Leonnatos). Son of Anteas (a relative of Eurydice, mother of Philip II [A*Succ* 12 = *Suda Λ* 249; cf. C 10.7.8]), hence a member of the Lyncestian royal house (cf. Macurdy 17; Bosworth 1971a: 99–101); *syntrophos* of Alexander and presumably brought up at the court (A 6.28.4; A*Ind* 18.3).[386] First attested on the day of Philip II's assassination, along with Perdiccas and Attalus, Leonnatus was one of the *somatophylakes* (i.e., Royal Hypaspists) who pursued the assassin Pausanias (D 16.94.4).

It is alleged that Leonnatus was sent to the Persian queens captured at Issus to report that Darius had survived the battle and assure them of their own safety (A 2.12.4–5; C 3.12.4ff.; D 17.37.3; P*A* 21.1–2).[387] Hegesias (*FGrH* 142 F5) claims that Leonnatus and Philotas son of Parmenion brought Batis, the garrison commander of Gaza (A 2.25.4; cf. *IA* 45), in chains to Alexander. In 332/1 Leonnatus was appointed Somatophylax, replacing Arybbas, who died of illness in Egypt (A 3.5.5). He held no independent military command until 328/7 and functioned as a member of Alexander's "staff." He joined Perdiccas, Craterus, Hephaestion, Coenus, and Erigyius (and some others, unnamed) in Alexander's tent to discuss Philotas' arrest in 330 (C 6.8.17), acting as a member of the King's council (cf. A 1.25.4). Probably, he too condemned Philotas, but we have no explicit information about his involvement in Philotas' downfall. Certainly he was not an obvious beneficiary (Heckel

1977a; cf. Badian 1960a). Leonnatus is not heard of again until 328 when he attempted to disarm the King during the Cleitus affair (C 8.1.46). In 327, he incurred the King's wrath by ridiculing *proskynesis* (A 4.12.2).[388] Although Alexander's anger was short-lived, he might have dealt more severely with a lesser individual. His role in bringing the Hermolaus conspiracy to the King's attention may have helped to rehabilitate him. Leonnatus and Ptolemy son of Lagus learned of this from Eurylochus (thus C 8.6.22, but A 4.13.7 mentions only Ptolemy's role; cf. Seibert: 18–19; Strasburger 40). We know nothing further of his activities in this connection. Leonnatus' first military command came just before the conspiracy of the Pages: he conducted the nighttime operations of the siege of the Rock of Chorienes in rotation with his fellow-Somatophylakes Perdiccas and Ptolemy (A 4.21.4). When the army left Bactria for India and Hephaestion was sent ahead to the Indus with Perdiccas (A 4.22.7, 30.9; 5.3.5; C 8.10.2–3; *ME* 48), Leonnatus and Ptolemy emerged as prominent officers under Alexander's personal leadership. Both were wounded in the territory around the Choes (Kunar) River (A 4.23.3), though not seriously, for each commanded one-third of Alexander's forces in the campaign that drove the Aspasians into the hills; Leonnatus' forces included the *taxeis* of Attalus son of Andromenes and Balacrus (A 4.24.10). Leonnatus proved his military competence, driving the Aspasians from their positions in the hills and bringing about their defeat (A 4.25.3).

At the Hydaspes (Jhelum) River, Alexander faced Porus with his entire force and, since he had more experienced military men at his disposal, he used Leonnatus in a lesser capacity. He appears as an infantry commander, together with Antigenes and Tauron (C 8.14.15), crossing the Hydaspes some distance upstream from the main camp that faced Porus' army. These appear to have been lightly armed troops and hypaspists, and it is possible that Leonnatus is named by mistake in place of Seleucus (A 5.13.1, 4; Berve ii.233). Otherwise, there is no record of his involvement in the battle against Porus. We may assume that, as Somatophylax, Leonnatus remained close to Alexander when he crossed the Hydaspes and that he fought among the troops that were directly under Alexander's control (A 5.16; C 8.14.15).[389] Leonnatus next appears as one of about thirty trierarchs of the Hydaspes fleet some three or four months after the battle with Porus (A*Ind* 18.3–10 = Nearchus, *FGrH* 133 F1). Since he was among the forces that habitually accompanied the King, he very likely sailed downriver with him as far as the confluence of the Hydaspes and the Acesines (Chenab) and later accompanied him by land in the campaign against the Mallians, who lived between the Acesines and Hydraotes (Ravi) Rivers (A 6.4.3; C 9.3.24).

It was in this campaign against the Mallians that Leonnatus played one of his most noteworthy – though again disputed – roles. Alexander had taken the Mallians by surprise, crossing the desert that lay between the rivers, rather than marching north, as the Indians themselves anticipated, from the junction of the rivers (A 6.4, esp. 6.4.3; C 9.4.15). When the Mallians withdrew to their main city, Alexander sought to inspire his war-weary Macedonians by being the first to scale the city-walls. This nearly ended in disaster; for very few of the Macedonians managed to join Alexander at the top before the ladders gave way under the weight of the troops. Alexander, seeing that he was cut off, leapt from the walls inside the city, where he was wounded by an enemy missile (A 6.8.4–13.5; cf. C 9.4.26–5.30; D 17.98.1–100.1; P*A* 63).[390] From the city of the Mallians to the junction of the Acesines and Hydraotes, and thence to Patala, Leonnatus accompanied Alexander by ship both because he was wounded and because of his duties as Somatophylax (cf. C 9.8.3). At Patala, Leonnatus, now recovered from his wounds, led a force of 1,000 cavalry and 8,000 hoplites and lightly armed troops along the shore of the island (which formed the delta of the Indus) while Alexander took the fleet to the Ocean via the western arm of the river (A 6.18.3). With Alexander returning upstream, Leonnatus now retraced his steps to Patala. From there he accompanied the King, by land, along the eastern arm of the river as far as a great lake, where he remained in charge of his own troops and those ships with their crews that Alexander left behind as he took a smaller detachment to the Ocean (A 6.20.3). When Alexander returned, it seems, Leonnatus led the land forces back to Patala.

Having reached the Ocean, Alexander now gave thought to returning to the west. Presumably his native informants had told him that the region to the west lacked water, and so he sent Leonnatus ahead to dig wells along the route that the army was to follow (C 9.10.2). When he had completed this task (late summer 324: Beloch iii^2 2.320), he awaited Alexander on the borders of the land of the Oreitae. Reaching the Arabius River, Alexander left the bulk of the army under the command of Hephaestion and, dividing the rest of the army into three parts (as he had done against the Aspasians two years earlier), under the command of Ptolemy, Leonnatus, and himself, he moved south of the Arabius into the territory of the Oreitae, who had not submitted to him. By means of a vigorous sweep-programme, Alexander ravaged the land and subdued the Oreitae (C 9.10.6–7; D 17.104.5–6). The columns of Ptolemy and Leonnatus reunited first with Alexander and then with Hephaestion's troops. In one body they proceeded to Rhambacia, where Hephaestion was left to settle the city, while Alexander took a force to the Gedrosian border, where the Oreitae and the Gedrosians were preparing to resist (A 6.21.5–22.2). When these had been overcome without much difficulty, Alexander sent Leonnatus, together with Apollophanes, whom he had appointed satrap of the area, to Rhambacia. Leonnatus, with the Agrianes, some archers and cavalry, and a force of mercenary cavalry and infantry, was ordered to remain in the land of the Oreitae, with instructions "to await the fleet until it sailed past this region, to synoecize the city which had been established by Hephaestion (A 6.21.5) and to settle affairs among the Oreitae" (A 6.22.3; cf. Hamilton 1972: 605–6).[391]

Sometime between Alexander's departure and the arrival of Nearchus with the fleet, Leonnatus won an impressive victory over the Oreitae, who had risen against him, killing 6,000 of them, and all their leaders (A*Ind* 23.5 = Nearchus, *FGrH* 133 F1; cf. C 9.10.19). Of his own forces only fifteen cavalrymen and a handful of infantry were lost; though Apollophanes the satrap fell in the battle. When Nearchus arrived at the shore near Rhambacia (A 6.22.3; cf. A*Ind* 23), Leonnatus had prepared provisions for his Ocean voyage. He also exchanged troops with Nearchus, taking with him those men who, on account of their laziness, had caused or might cause disciplinary problems in the fleet (A*Ind* 23.8). After Nearchus' departure, Leonnatus put everything in order among the Oreitae (as he had been instructed) and set out for Gedrosia by land. The news of his exploits had already reached Alexander by letter (C 9.10.19), but it is uncertain where Leonnatus himself rejoined Alexander; perhaps it was in Carmania, though possibly only at Susa. At Susa (324), Leonnatus was awarded a golden crown in honor of his courage in India and his victory over the Oreitae (A 7.5.5–6; A*Ind* 23.6, 42.9). Presumably he took a Persian bride in the marriage ceremony, though we have no record of her or her fate.[392]

When Alexander died suddenly in Babylon, Leonnatus emerged as one of the leading men of the succession crisis: together with Perdiccas and Ptolemy, he belonged to the *megistoi*, as opposed to those lesser lights (A*Succ* 1.2). In the debate that followed, in which the supporters of Perdiccas proposed that Rhoxane's child (if male) should inherit the kingdom, it was suggested by Peithon, one of the

Bodyguard, that Leonnatus share with Perdiccas the guardianship of the child, on the grounds that both were of royal stock (C 10.7.8; cf. J 13.2.13–14). But when the common soldiery, incited by Meleager, declared for the feeble Arrhidaeus, whom they hailed as King under the title Philip III, Leonnatus led the cavalry, the backbone of Perdiccas' support, outside the city of Babylon, while Perdiccas himself remained within the city in the hope of winning over the infantry. Perdiccas' stay was brief, owing to the hostility of Meleager, who induced Arrhidaeus to order his assassination, and he soon rejoined Leonnatus and the cavalry (C 10.7.20, 8.4). That Leonnatus wholeheartedly supported Perdiccas' regency is doubtful, but the high-ranking officers will have been unanimous in their opposition to Meleager and Philip Arrhidaeus.

In the settlement at Babylon (323), Leonnatus was awarded the satrapy of Hellespontine Phrygia, which, despite its strategic location, must have disappointed him (A*Succ* 1.6; Dexippus, *FGrH* 100 F8 §2; C 10.10.2; D 18.3.1, cf. 18.12.1, wrongly "Philotas"; J 13.4.16). He began immediately to intrigue against Perdiccas and the marshals of the empire; for he had been contacted – perhaps at Olympias' instigation – by the sister of Alexander, the widow of Alexander of Epirus, Cleopatra, through whom he hoped to gain power, and such a marriage carried with it a serious – possibly "legitimate" – claim to the throne of Macedon (P*Eum* 3.9). When he received orders to aid Eumenes in Cappadocia (P*Eum* 3.4–5), he had already formulated his plan to overthrow Perdiccas. Renewed turmoil in Greece offered Leonnatus his pretext for crossing the Hellespont and seeking the throne; for Antipater, blockaded at Lamia in Thessaly by the allied Greek forces, sent Hecataeus of Cardia to summon him to Greece (P*Eum* 3.6; D 18.12.1, 14.4–5; J 13.5.14). Leonnatus attempted to persuade Eumenes to cross into Europe with him – ostensibly in aid of Antipater, but in reality to seize the Macedonian throne. He revealed to Eumenes the details of his correspondence with Cleopatra. But in this matter he misjudged Eumenes, who shunned the proposal, either from loyalty to Perdiccas or fear of his archrival Hecataeus. While Alexander lived, Eumenes had denounced Hecataeus, urging the King to depose him and restore freedom to the Cardians. Now he feared lest Antipater should kill him in order to please Hecataeus (P*Eum* 3.8–10). During the night, Eumenes and his forces slipped away from Leonnatus, bringing the news of his designs to Perdiccas (P*Eum* 3.10; N*Eum* 2.4–5 claims that he planned to kill Eumenes when he could not persuade him). Perhaps Eumenes' report induced Perdiccas to pursue the marriage with Cleopatra.

Leonnatus crossed into Europe with his satrapal army, which he augmented in Macedonia before pushing south toward Lamia with a force of more than 20,000 foot and 1,500 cavalry. The Athenian general Antiphilus moved to engage him before he could join forces with Antipater. The exact location of the battlefield is not given, but it could scarcely have been far north of Lamia itself; D 18.15.5 tells us that Antipater joined Leonnatus' army on the day after the battle. Although the infantry were evenly matched, Leonnatus, with less than half the enemy's number of cavalry, found himself cut off in a marshy region where he was overcome by wounds and carried from the battlefield by his men (D 18.15.3; J 13.5.14; cf. P*Ph* 25.5; Str 9.5.10 [434]). Antipater may indeed, as J 13.5.15 claims, have welcomed his death: not only had the engagement removed a dangerous rival (cf. A*Succ* 1.9), it had also lifted the siege of Lamia and added to Antipater's 13,600 forces an additional 20,000 foot and 1,500 horse.

In his arrogance, his fondness for Persian luxury (A*Succ* 12) – evinced by his dress and the decoration of his arms, even the gilded bridles of his Nesaean horses – and in the style of his hair, Leonnatus was clearly emulous of his kinsman Alexander and jealously eager to exercise at least some of his power. He was also passionately fond of wrestling and gymnastics (P*A* 40.1; Pl*NH* 35.168) or hunting (Ath 12.539d = Phylarchus, *FGrH* 81 F41 and/or Agatharchides of Cnidus, 86 F3; Ael*VH* 9.3).

Berve ii.232–5 no. 466; Heckel 91–106. See Stemmata I, XV.

Leosthenes. (For the name see *LGPN* ii.284 no. 6). Son of Leosthenes (who had been exiled by the Athenians after 362/1 and took up residence at the court of Philip II) of Cephale. Athenian *strategos* in 323/2 (Develin 408; he had held the generalship in 324/3 as well; for an earlier trierarchy see ii^2 1529.500, 606, 682, with discussion in Davies 342–3) and commander of the Greek forces in the Lamian War (A*Succ* 1.9); noted for his military skill (Paus 1.25.5; D 17.111.3), but thought by Phocion to lack caution (P*Ph* 23).[393] Before the news of Alexander's death was known, the Athenians authorized Leosthenes to recruit the mercenaries (D 17.111.3, he was given 50 talents; cf. D 18.9.1) at Taenarum – some 8,000 had recently been dismissed (Paus 8.52.5 gives the unrealistic figure of 50,000 mercenaries serving with Leosthenes)[394] – but to do so as if for his own private purpose, so that Antipater should not become suspicious of Athenian intentions (D 18.9.2–3). Certain news of the King's death precipitated the Lamian War and Leosthenes was given money that had been brought to Athens by Harpalus and ordered to win further allies (D 18.9.4–5);[395] he was elected commander-in-chief of the Greek forces (Paus 1.25.5). He marched north, defeated the Boeotians, and occupied Thermopylae (D 18.11.4–5),[396] thus anticipating Antipater who was moving down from the north. The defection of Thessaly was a serious setback for Antipater (cf. the role of Menon: P*Pyr* 1.6, see s.v. **Menon** [4]), and Leosthenes managed to defeat his troops and besiege Antipater in Lamia during the winter of 323/2 (hence the name of the war; D 18.12.3–13.3; P*Dem* 27.1). In the course of the siege, he must have offered Antipater harsh conditions for surrender, for the Macedonian regent threw these terms back at the Athenians when the war ended (P*Ph* 26.7). But while his troops were investing the city (Lamia), Antipater's soldiers made an attack on those who were digging a moat; Leosthenes coming to their aid was hit on the head by a stone (or some missile: J 13.5.12; D 18.13.5; Str 9.5.10 [434]; Paus 1.25.5); he swooned and was carried back to camp; on the third day he died. He was buried with the honors of a hero (D 18.13.5; cf. *Suda Λ* 276; P*Ph* 24.1) and in the absence of Demosthenes, who had been exiled on account of the Harpalus scandal, the funeral oration was given by Hypereides (D 18.13.5; Hyp 6; [P]*M* 849f). In Piraeus, in a precinct of Zeus and Athena (or at least in a long portico near a marketplace for those who live by the sea), there was a portrait of Leosthenes by Arcesilaus (Paus 1.1.3; cf. Paus 3.6.1, who puts him in the same class as Cleombrotus, who died at Leuctra, and Hippocrates, who fell at Delium; cf. Paus 1.29.13, 8.52.5).

Berve ii.236–7 no. 471; Geyer, *RE* s.v. "Leosthenes (2)"; Kirchner no. 9142 (= 9144); Davies 342ff.; Develin 408; cf. Lepore 1955.

Letodorus (Letodoros). Greek mercenary leader of unknown family and origin, possibly Aeaenian. Letodorus had been left behind in Bactria in 327 when Alexander marched into India. He took an active role in the uprising after the King's death, as is clear from the fact that he commanded 3,000 of the rebels, and may have had a role in the earlier disturbance of 326/5 (cf. C 9.7.1–11; see s.vv. **Boxus**, **Biton**). Letodorus was bribed by Peithon son of Crateuas, who had been sent by Perdiccas to put down the rebellion in 323, through the agency of a certain Aeaenian. During the battle Letodorus and his 3,000 men fled, thus giving Peithon complete victory (D 18.7.5–6). Doubtless he and his supporters were rewarded by Peithon, but what became of him is unknown.

Berve ii.237 no. 473.

Limnaeus (Limnaios; Curtius calls him Timaeus). The form Limnaeus (P*A* 63.7–8; P*M* 327b, 344d) is apparently correct.[397] One of the Royal Hypaspists (P*A* 63.5), Limnaeus accompanied Alexander into the town of the Mallians (near mod. Multan), where he was killed defending the King, who was himself seriously wounded (P*A* 63.8; P*M* 327b, 344d; C 9.5.15–16). A 6.9.3, 10.1–2 omits him; there was some disagreement about who defended Alexander on this occasion (A 6.11.7). Arrian names Habreas where the vulgate sources refer to Limnaeus (Berve ii.237 wrongly assumes a confusion of Limnaeus and Leonnatus).

Berve ii.237 no. 474; Heckel 296; Hoffmann 147.

Lycidas (Lykidas). Aetolian of unknown family. Lycidas' position before 332/1, when he was appointed commander of the *xenoi* at Memphis (A 3.5.3), is unclear. Berve ii.237 assumed that he had been a commander of Alexander's mercenaries since the beginning of the Asiatic campaign. But Tarn i.44 (cf. Schachermeyr 238 n. 263) regards the *xenoi* in Egypt as "military settlers" from the time of Persian occupation (i.e., precursors of the Hellenistic *katoikoi*), and Bosworth i.275 goes so far as to suggest that Lycidas "was an Egyptian resident who had served in the invasion of 343." Nothing else is known of Lycidas' career.

Berve ii.237–8 no. 475; Launey 1135; Grainger 2000: 217 s.v. "Lykidas (1)."

Lycomedes (Lykomedes). A Rhodian of unknown family background, Lycomedes had probably served as a mercenary captain with his compatriot Memnon. But the latter died in 333 (A 2.1.3), and Lycomedes remained with Pharnabazus and Autophradates, who installed him as garrison commander of Mytilene in support of the tyrant Diogenes, a Mytilenaean exile (A 2.1.5). Lycomedes himself is not mentioned again, but we are told that Chares, who came either to support or replace him, was expelled (or captured?) by Hegelochus (A 3.2.6; C 4.5.22).

Berve ii.238 no. 476; Olmstead 502; Hofstetter 117–18 no. 200; Bosworth i.183; Atkinson i.331–2.

Lycon (Lykon). A comic actor from Scarphe in Locris (P*A* 29.6), Lycon was twice victorious at the Lenaean festival ca. 350 (*IG* ii^2 670 [x]). He appears to have joined Alexander in 332/1 in Egypt (A 3.1.4), and, while performing in Phoenicia in early 331, inserted a line asking Alexander for a gift of ten talents, which the King good-naturedly provided (P*A* 29.6; cf. P*M* 334e). Lycon was among the notable comic actors who performed at the mass-marriage ceremony at Susa in 324 (Chares, *FGrH* 125 F4 *ap.* Ath 12.539a; see also s.vv. **Phormion**, **Ariston** [4]), and appears to have headed his own troupe of actors (P*M* 334e). We know nothing about his activities between 331 and 324, or afterwards. Antiphanes may have named his *Lycon* after him.

Berve ii.239 no. 478; O'Connor 114 no. 319.

Lycurgus (Lykourgos). Son of Lycophron, Athenian from the deme Boutadae. Born ca. 390 BC.[398] Married Callisto, the daughter of Habron, and by her had three sons: Lycurgus, Lycophron, and Habron ([P]*M* 842f–843a). Lycurgus gained particular prominence after Chaeronea as organizer and overseer of Athenian finances from 338 to 327 ([P]*M* 852b).[399] Strongly anti-Macedonian (*SIG*^{3} 326 = *IG* ii^2 457), and thus an opponent of Phocion and Demades (P*Ph* 9.10; see s.vv. **Demades**, **Phocion**). In 343 he is said to have accompanied Demosthenes and Polyeuctus to the Peloponnese and some other cities to garner support against Philip II ([P]*M* 841f). In 338/7, he prosecuted Lysicles for his generalship at Chaeronea (D 16.88.1; Hamel 1998: 156 no. 62) and secured the death sentence. He was one of a number of politicians whose extradition was sought by Alexander after the sack of Thebes in 335

(A 1.10.4; PPh 17.2; PDem 23.4; *Suda A* 2704; *IG* ii^2 457.17–18). But Alexander later relented (A 1.10.6). Lycurgus died in 325/4 and was thus untouched by the Harpalus scandal. Of his fifteen speeches ([P]*M* 843c), only the one *Against Leocrates* is extant. For his life see [P]*M* 841a–844a and 851f–852e.

Kirchner no. 9251; Berve ii.238–9 no. 477; Davies 350–1; *LGPN* ii.288 no. 4.

Lysanias. Macedonian. In spring 335, Lysanias (together with a certain Philotas) conveyed the booty taken from the "independent" Thracians to the coastal cities of Macedonia (A 1.2.1). Otherwise unattested during Alexander's reign, he may not have accompanied the King to Asia. Identification with the cavalry officer of the same name who served with Antigonus the One-Eyed in 316 (D 19.29.2) is remotely possible.

Berve ii.239 no. 479; cf. Billows 398 no. 64.

Lysimachus [1]. (Lysimachos). Acarnanian. Although somewhat uncultivated (P*A* 5.8), Lysimachus nevertheless served as tutor of Alexander and endeared himself to the young prince by referring to himself as Phoenix while calling his pupil Achilles and Philip II Peleus (P*A* 5.8; cf. 24.10). Although Plutarch mentions him after Olympias' kinsman, Leonidas, a stern disciplinarian, it is likely that Lysimachus educated Alexander at an earlier stage in life, as the playful references to Achilles suggest. As an educator he occupied a middle ground between the keen intellect of Aristotle and the laconic austerity of Leonidas. That Acarnanians found employment at Philip's court (cf. Philip of Acarnania, who was Alexander's physician; C 3.6.1) may be due to the influence of Olympias, who came from neighboring Epirus; certainly the allusions to the Aeacids will have found favor with her (cf. Heckel 1981a: 80–2). Lysimachus accompanied the King to Asia and, during an expedition against the Arabs of Antilebanon, failed, on account of his old age, to keep up with the Macedonian forces who had dismounted. Chares (*FGrH* 125 F7 = P*A* 24.10–14) faults him for his foolishness, which endangered the mission and the life of Alexander, who refused to abandon him. Nothing else is known about his career, except that a reference to his opposition to Callisthenes of Olynthus (P*A* 55.2) may indicate that he was still alive in 327 BC. What became of him, we do not know.

Berve ii.241 no. 481.

Lysimachus [2]. (Lysimachos). Son of Agathocles (A 6.28.4; A*Ind* 18.3; A*Succ* 1.2), a Thessalian from Crannon (Porphyry of Tyre *ap.* Euseb Arm = *FGrH* 260 F3 §8), whom Theopompus (*ap.* Ath 6.259f–260a = *FGrH* 115 F81; Geyer, *RE* xiv.1, *contra* Berve ii.239 and Hünerwadel 13) describes as a flatterer of Philip II. He was presumably not as humble as Theopompus claims (cf. Beloch iv^2 2.129). Agathocles and his sons were granted Macedonian citizenship (J 15.3.1; Paus 1.9.5; and P*Demetr* 44.6 who terms him *homophylos* with Demetrius Poliorcetes), and Lysimachus was educated at the court in Pella (A*Ind* 18.3). Brother of Philip (C 8.2.35; cf. Berve no. 774) and Autodicus, though a third brother, Alcimachus (A 1.18.1–2; cf. *IG* ii^2 239; Berve no. 47), is not positively identified as such. Born perhaps as early as 362/1 (Hieronymus *ap.* [L]*Macrob* 11), Lysimachus may have been appointed Somatophylax already during the reign of Philip II (Heckel 1978b: 224–8). Justin's claim that he was 74 when he died at Corupedium (J 17.1.10) must be treated with suspicion, since this appears to be a calculation that would make him coeval with Alexander. App*Syr* 64 puts his birth in 352/1, but this would make Lysimachus too young to have accompanied Alexander from the beginning of the expedition except as a *pais basilikos*.

C 8.1.13–17 first mentions Lysimachus as participating in a lion hunt in the forests of Bazeira in Sogdiana (328 BC); presumably in his capacity as Somatophylax (Paus 1.9.5, in a garbled version, calls him *doryphoros*), he tried to protect the King from a charging lion. Alexander, however, ordered him aside and killed the beast with his own spear, reminding Lysimachus of his misadventure during a lion hunt in Syria. There he had been seriously injured by a lion of great size (C 8.1.15). This story was soon embellished, and it was said that Lysimachus had been deliberately caged with a lion as punishment for giving poison to Callisthenes (J 15.3.3–9; cf. C 8.1.17; for further details see s.v. Callisthenes [1], and n. 191). P*Demetr* 27.3 gives the lion story a humorous context, and compares Lysimachus' scars, sustained while he was caged with a lion, with the bites on Demetrius' neck, inflicted by the flute-girl Lamia.[400] But the truth of the whole matter is probably very close to what Curtius tells us: Lysimachus once killed a lion of extraordinary size in Syria, but was severely mauled in the process; on a second occasion, in the Bazeiran woods, Alexander prevented him from making a similar mistake.

The Lysimachus of Plutarch's version of the Callisthenes affair (55.2) is not the son of Agathocles: Berve (ii.241 no. 481; cf. Hamilton 14, 153–4; Pearson 57) correctly recognized that this is Lysimachus, Alexander's Acarnanian tutor, the victim of Chares' hostility. It is puzzling, however, that Berve does not credit Lysimachus' participation in the Cleitus episode.[401] There is no good reason to disbelieve Curtius (8.1.46). For the political issues that lay behind Cleitus' confrontation with Alexander, Curtius' version demonstrates a sober approach to the affair. Nor does Plutarch's account, which claims that Aristophanes (read "Aristonus") disarmed the King, vitiate that of Curtius, for the former concerns the removal of Alexander's own sword (which was the first weapon that he might be expected to reach for, if he carried it on his person), while the latter involves a spear, which Alexander had taken from a bystander (C 8.1.45). P*A* 51.11 implies that all the Somatophylakes were present at the banquet, as we should expect. Presumably they did not stand idly by while Aristonus alone attempted to restrain the King. Very likely each one attempted, in his own way, to avert the disaster. Lysimachus, who appears in the company of Leonnatus, Perdiccas, and Ptolemy (all of whom were already Somatophylakes), undoubtedly held the same rank.

Not long after Cleitus' death, Lysimachus' younger brother, Philip, a Royal Hypaspist, accompanied the King some 500 stades on foot, refusing to mount the horse of Lysimachus, who rode nearby. Remaining ever by the King's side, both in the pursuit of the supporters of Sisimithres and in the skirmish that followed, Philip finally collapsed from exhaustion and expired in the King's arms. This story is told only by Curtius (8.2.35–9) and Justin (15.3.12). It is preceded in J 15.3.10–11 by a similar story, in which Lysimachus remains at the side of Alexander in India when all others have fallen behind. This story is surely a doublet (cf. Berve ii.240 n. 4), with further complications. App*Syr* 64 and J 15.3.13–14 relate that Lysimachus – here a hypaspist, which in the Indian campaign is entirely impossible – was wounded by Alexander's spear as Alexander leapt from his horse. He began to bleed profusely and the King, for want of proper bandages, placed his diadem on Lysimachus' head in an attempt to stop the bleeding (J 15.3.13). That Aristander (who vanished from the accounts of Alexander, probably with the end of Callisthenes' historical work) or any other seer prophesied that this act signified that Lysimachus would himself be King defies all credulity.[402] This tale of Lysimachus' wound is a later invention, as is Aristobulus' claim (*FGrH* 139 F54 = A 7.18.5) that the seer Peithagoras predicted Lysimachus' victory over Antigonus at Ipsus.

Near Sangala in India some 1,200 of Alexander's troops were wounded, among them Lysimachus the Somatophylax (A 5.24.5). He had earlier boarded a thirty-oared vessel at the Hydaspes (in the company of two other Somatophylakes), before the battle with Porus, though his role in the actual battle is not attested (A 5.13.1); presumably he fought in the immediate vicinity of Alexander himself. When Alexander decided to sail down the Indus river system to the Ocean, Lysimachus was one of those from Pella charged with a trierarchy in the Attic fashion (A*Ind* 18.3 = Nearchus, *FGrH* 133 F1). He is named by Arrian in the only complete list of the Somatophylakes (A 6.28.4). At Susa in spring 324, Lysimachus and the rest of the Somatophylakes were crowned by Alexander, though unlike Leonnatus, Lysimachus appears to have earned no special distinction (A 7.5.6). Very likely, he took a Persian bride: her name is not recorded, nor her fate. She may have been repudiated after Alexander's death, although it is worthy of note that in 302 Lysimachus married (albeit for only a brief time) Amastris, whom Craterus had married at Susa but put aside in favor of Antipater's daughter, Phila.

In 323 Lysimachus was assigned control of Thrace (C 10.10.4; D 18.3.2; A*Succ* 1.7; Dexippus, *FGrH* 100 F8 §3; J 13.4.16; cf. Paus 1.9.5; *LM* 111), and was probably *strategos* rather than satrap (Lund 54). The subordinate position of *strategos* may account for the failure of the sources to mention Lysimachus in the settlement of Triparadeisus; his brother Autodicus was, however, named as a Somatophylax of Philip III at that time (A*Succ* 1.38).[403] Before Antipater's death, he married Nicaea, who had been jilted by Perdiccas (see s.v. **Nicaea**) and, although he may have flirted with the idea of marrying Cleopatra for political advantage (D 20.37.4), he did not make another significant marriage until 302, when he took Amastris, the widow of Dionysius of Heraclea, whom he abandoned after the battle of Ipsus in favor of Arsinoë, the daughter of Ptolemy I and Berenice. In 306 or 305, he assumed the title of "King" (P*Demetr* 18.3; App*Syr* 1 [3], 54 [277], 55 [279]; cf. Ael*NA* 15.2), which he held until his death at Corupedium in 282/1 (App*Syr* 55 [270], 64; P*M* 970c; Ael*NA* 6.25; Duris *ap.* Pl*NH* 8.143; Hieronymus *ap.* [L]*Macrob* 11).

Hünerwadel; Hoffmann 171–2; Geyer, *RE* s.v. "Lysimachos (1)"; Berve ii.239–42 no. 480; Merker 1979; Heckel 1982b; Heckel 267–5; Lund; Landucci Gattinoni 1992. See Stemma IX.

Lysippus (Lysippos). Greek bronze sculptor, from Sicyon (Tzetz*Chil* 8.200, 417; Duris, *FGrH* 76 F32 = Pl*NH* 34.61, who adds that he was not the student of any artist, but originally a coppersmith). He had three sons, who were his pupils: Laippus, Boëdas, and Euthycrates (Pl*NH* 34.66). Lysippus knew Alexander before his accession to the throne, for he sculpted a youthful Alexander (Pl*NH* 34.63) as well as his friend Hephaestion (34.64), though we do not know the date of this work. It was Lysippus who gave Alexander the famous tilt of the head (Tzetz*Chil* 11.368, 97–108) and was the only sculptor permitted to make representations of him (P*A* 4.1–2; for the so-called "edict" concerning the depiction of Alexander see Stewart TT51–8). It was also Lysippus who made the bronze equestrian statues of the *hetairoi* who fell at the Granicus (A 1.16.4; P*A* 16.16; Vell Pat 1.11.3; J 11.6.13; Pl*NH* 34.64).[404]

Berve ii.241–3 no. 482; Groß, *Kl. Pauly* iii.843–4 no. 2.

M

Madates (Madetes, Medates). A relative of Darius III (D 17.67.4), Madates had married the daughter of Sisygambis' sister (C 5.3.12; see **F6, 7**) and was satrap of the Uxians who lived in the mountains east of the Pasitigris River (C 5.3.1–4; cf. D 17.67.1–4). He opposed, unsuccessfully, Alexander's entry into his territory and was soon defeated and besieged (C 5.3.5–11; cf. D 17.67.4–5; but the details are difficult to reconcile with A 3.17; see Bosworth i.321–4), so that in the end Sisygambis was forced to intercede on behalf of his people and for the sake of Madates' life (C 5.3.12–14).[405] Madates himself was pardoned (C 5.3.16), but his territory was assigned to Susiana and its satrap, Abulites. Nothing else is known of his career.

Berve ii.243 no. 483; Speck 2002: 22–37.

Maeander (Maiandros). Greek from Magnesia. Son of Mandrogenes. Maeander served as a trierarch of the Hydaspes fleet in 326 (A*Ind* 18.7). Otherwise unknown.

Berve ii.246–7 no. 488.

Marsyas. Son of Periander, raised in Pella as *syntrophos* of Alexander the Great (*Suda* M 227). Half-brother (by the same mother) of Antigonus Monophthalmus (P*M* 182c; *Suda*). Author of *Makedonika* (*FGrH* 135/136; cf. Heckel 1980b), which focused primarily on the reign of Philip II; the account of Alexander appears not to have been carried beyond the description of the campaign in Asia Minor. Born ca. 356, Marsyas appears to have accompanied Alexander to Asia but probably remained with his brother Antigonus in Phrygia in 333. In 307/6 he participated as a navarch in Demetrius' victory of Ptolemaic forces in the battle of Salamis (D 20.50.4). Nothing else is known about him except that he was involved in a legal dispute at an unspecified time, though certainly after 333, and possibly after Antigonus assumed the title of "King" in 306 (P*M* 182c).

Laqueur, *RE* s.v. "Marsyas (8)"; Berve ii.247–8 no. 489; Billows 399–400 no. 67; Hauben 59–60, 119; Heckel 1980b; Hornblower 1981: 130. See Stemma VI.

Mauaces. Commander of the Sacae (i.e., Scythian) mounted archers (*hippotoxotai*) at Gaugamela (A 3.8.3), located on the right wing and under the general command of Mazaeus (A 3.11.4). What became of Mauaces is unknown.

Berve ii.248 no. 490.

Mazaces (Mazakes). Ruler of Egypt in the absence of Sauaces (A 3.1.2), who took the Egyptian contingent to Issus and died there (C 3.11.10; 4.1.28). Mazaces defeated the invading forces of Amyntas son of Antiochus (C 4.1.32–3). In 332 he surrendered Memphis and its treasure to Alexander (C 4.7.4; A 3.1.2); he may have been retained in the King's entourage.

Berve ii.245–6 no. 485.

Mazaeus (Mazaios). Prominent Persian (C 5.1.18; D 17.55.1 calls him a *philos* of

Darius III; cf. *PA* 39.9). Born no later than 380 (he died of natural causes in 328: A 4.18.3; C 8.3.17); father of several sons, at least some by a Babylonian mother (Briant 783), though there seems to be some confusion in the names of Antibelus, Artiboles, and Brochubelus (see s.vv.). Satrap of Cilicia since no later than 350 (D 16.42.1; Head, HN^2 731ff.; Leuze 231), and – after the fall of Sidon and the demise (for reasons unknown) of Belesys – satrap of Syria (C 5.13.11, emending the text to read *praetoris*) and Mesopotamia (cf. A 3.8.6, 11.4). At some point around 351/0, Mazaeus, then satrap of Cilicia, and Belesys of Syria attempted to put down the Phoenician revolt led by Tennes of Sidon; they were, however, defeated by a force of 4,000 Greek mercenaries from Egypt led by Mentor the Rhodian (D 16.42.1–2). But in 346/5, Sidon surrendered through the treachery of Tennes and Mazaeus appears as satrap of both Cilicia and Abarnahara (Trans-Euphrates) in the reign of Artaxerxes III (Head, HN^2 732).[406]

In 331, he had been ordered by Darius to prevent Alexander's crossing of the Euphrates at Thapsacus, but he had insufficient numbers to do much more than prevent the completion of the bridges. Upon Alexander's arrival Mazaeus withdrew (A 3.7.1) and joined Darius, who was following the Tigris northward. D 17.55.1 claims that Mazaeus had been ordered to guard the Tigris crossing, a task which had perhaps been assigned to Satropates; C 4.9.7–25 conflates two sources (Ptolemy and Cleitarchus?) in a clumsy way that obscures the operations of both Mazaeus and Satropates. D 17.55.2 claims that Mazaeus neglected his duty here, because he considered the Tigris uncrossable, and turned to laying waste the countryside. At Gaugamela Mazaeus commanded the Persian cavalry on the right wing (D 17.59.5, 60.5) and led a charge of dense squadrons together with the scythe-chariots (D 17.58.2), where he inflicted heavy casualties and sent a Scythian squadron to capture the Macedonian camp (D 17.59.5–8). Soon he exerted pressure on Parmenion and the Thessalian cavalry on the Macedonian left (D 17.60.5–7) – Parmenion sent a force to summon Alexander to his aid, but they returned without having contacted him (D 17.60.7) – but was eventually overcome by the tenacity of the Thessalians and the flight of Darius (D 17.60.8). Mazaeus fled from the battlefield to Babylon (C 4.16.7; cf. 5.1.17), which he later surrendered to Alexander (C 5.1.17–19; cf. D 17.64.4; A 3.16.3), only to be installed as its satrap, the first Persian to be so honored by Alexander (A 3.16.4; C 5.1.44; cf. D 17.64.5–6).[407] He held this office until his death in late 328, whereupon he was replaced by Stamenes (A 4.18.3; cf. C 8.3.17 "Ditamenes"). Mazaeus was perhaps the intended occupant of the so-called Alexander sarcophagus in Sidon, if the details of sculptures relate to the life of the man who commissioned it (see Heckel 2006 for full discussion).

Berve ii.243–5 no. 484; Leuze (*passim*); Briant 848–9.

Mazarus (Mazaros). According to A 3.16.9, one of Alexander's *hetairoi* and *phrourarchos* of Susa (331 BC). The name sounds suspiciously Iranian and it is likely that the text is corrupt; possibly Arrian meant to record that Xenophilus replaced Mazarus as *phrourarchos* (see C 5.2.16; Bosworth i.319; Heckel 2002b) rather than that Mazarus was a Macedonian *phrourarchos* who was later replaced by Xenophilus (thus Brunt i.278 n. 10).

Berve ii.246 no. 486.

Mazenes. Persian *hyparchos*; governor of the island of Oaracta, which may have belonged to the satrapy of Carmania (thus Berve ii.246; cf. Tomaschek 47–8). Nearchus discovered him there in 325/4 along with Mithropastes, who had fled there (A*Ind* 37.2; cf. Str 16.3.7 [767]: Nearchus, *FGrH* 133 F28). He accompanied Nearchus as far as Susa where he appears to have submitted to the King in person.

Berve ii.246 no. 487.

Meda. Thracian princess. Daughter of Cothelas. Philip II married her at some point after his marriage to Olympias (Ath 13.557d), but the union probably dates to 342 (Ellis 166–7). She appears to have borne no children and her fate is unknown.

Ellis 166–7, 211–12; Carney 68.

Medius (Medeios, Medios, Medeius). Son of Oxythemis (A*Ind* 18.7; Str 11.14.12 [530]), from Larissa, where the grandfather, also named Medius, is attested as *dynastes* in 395 and an enemy of Lycophron of Pherae (D 14.82.5; cf. Westlake 1935: 59–66). A Thessalian *hetairos* of Alexander (cf. A 7.24.4; D 17.117.1), Medius appears to have accompanied the King from the beginning of the campaign (334),[408] but in no known military capacity; he is first attested as a trierarch of the Hydaspes fleet in 326 (A*Ind* 18.7).[409] Otherwise, he is described as a flatterer of Alexander (P*M* 65c) and the *erastes* of Iolaus son of Antipater (A 7.27.2). He gained notoriety as a result of the political pamphlet on *The Last Days and Testament of Alexander*, which alleged that it was at a drinking-party in the residence of Medius in Babylon (cf. A 7.25.1 = *FGrH* 117 F3a; P*A* 76 = *FGrH* 117 F3b) that the King was poisoned (*LM* 97–8; Ps-Call 3.31; cf. A 7.27.2; P*A* 75.4–6; Heckel 1988: 37–8). After the King's death, he was briefly a supporter of Perdiccas and served the admiral Sosigenes and the *strategos* Aristonus as commander of the mercenaries (*xenagos*) sent to Cyprus in 321/0 (A*Succ* 24.6). Medius entered Antigonus' service, either after the defeat of Sosigenes' expedition or upon the news of Perdiccas' death (whichever came first). Later he is found as an admiral of the Antigonid fleet (Hauben no. 23), defeating Cassander's ships as he sailed from Phoenicia to Caria in 313 (D 19.69.3) and, in the following year, continuing to serve in the Aegean and at the Hellespont (D 19.75.3–4, 75.7–8, 77.2–5). At Salamis (306) Medius commanded ships on the left wing of Demetrius' fleet (D 20.50.3). Afterwards, he participated in the unsuccessful move on Egypt (P*Demetr* 19.1–2). An Athenian inscription, dated 303/2, honors Medius for some unspecified service to the state in the period before 307/6 and mentions his role in attempting to liberate Greece (*SIG*[3] 342 = *IG* ii[2] 498), probably in 308/7.[410] Medius was the uncle of Oxythemis son of Hippostratus,[411] who was for a while a favorite at the Antigonid court but later executed by Antigonus Gonatas (Ath 13.578a–b; see also Billows 414 no. 86), and he himself appears to have remained a faithful supporter of Demetrius toward the end of his life (Habicht[2]). For his historical work see Jacoby, *FGrH* 129; Pearson 68–70.

Geyer, *RE* s.v. "Medios (2)"; Berve ii.261–2 no. 521; Billows 400–1 no. 68; Hauben 60–9, 110–17, 127; Hornblower 1981: 126–30.

Megabyxus (Megabyxos; but Greek literary texts have Megabyzos, Megabyzus). The form Megabyxus has both epigraphic and etymological support (Persian: *Bagabuksha*, which may mean "servant of the god" or "giving joy to the god"; thus Burkert 2004: 106). *SIG*[3] 282.1 calls him "Megabyxus son of Megabyxus, *neokoros* of Artemis of Ephesus," that is, the priest of Artemis (cf. Pl*NH* 35.93, 131–2), but the name appears rather to be a title[412] and the priests themselves were eunuchs (Str 14.1.23 [641]). The inscription shows the people of Priene honoring the Megabyxus with a crown and a bronze statue in 333 BC for his support of the rebuilding of the temple of Athena in their city; and they granted him *proxenia* and recognized him as a benefactor (lines 8–10). Apelles painted a *Procession of the Megabyxus* (Pl*NH* 35.93).[413] Alexander wrote to him, presumably in 324/3 (after the appointment of Antimenes of Rhodes as treasurer; see s.v. **Antimenes**), regarding a runaway slave (**M66**) who had taken refuge in the sanctuary of Artemis (P*A* 42.1), asking him to recapture the slave but not violate the sanctity of the temple.

Berve ii.248 no. 491; Burkert 2004: 105–7.

Megareus. A Chian of unknown family background, Megareus was a leader of the pro-Persian oligarchy at Chios (see also s.v. **Apollonides** [1] and **Phesinus**), which had been brought to power in the summer of 333 with the support of Pharnabazus' fleet. In 332 Megareus and his colleagues were captured by Hegelochus and brought to Alexander in Egypt (A 3.2.5); the latter sent them to Elephantine to be imprisoned (A 3.2.7), apparently countermanding thereby his own edict to Chios (Tod ii.192; see Bosworth i.268 for discussion).

Berve ii.248 no. 492; Berve 1967: i.339, ii.691; Hofstetter 124 no. 211.

Megasthenes. Greek of unknown origin, though apparently an Ionian Greek. He is said to have resided with Sibyrtius, the satrap of Arachosia (A 5.6.2), and it may be that he was a friend and compatriot of that man. From Arachosia he was sent as an envoy to Sandrocottus (Str 2.1.9 [70]; A 5.6.2) and Porus (A*Ind* 5.3), and if he visited both on the same mission, this must date to the period 322–317. Clement of Alexandria 1.72.5 says he lived in the time of Seleucus Nicator, which is technically correct, but it need not imply that his mission to Sandrocottus occurred late in the fourth century (but see Olshausen 174); nor need A 5.6.2 mean that he made several trips, though this cannot be ruled out.[414] He was the author of an *Indica* (see Jacoby, *FGrH* 715 for the fragments; cf. Brown 1955).

Stein, *RE* s.v. "Megasthenes (2)"; Grainger 103; Olshausen no. 127; Bosworth 1996b.

Melamnidas. See s.v. **Menidas**.

Meleager [1]. (Meleagros). Son of Neoptolemus (A 1.24.1, 29.4; Tataki 378 no. 8). His regional origins are unknown, but the father's name suggests the western highlands, the only attested examples in Alexander's reign coming from Epirus and Lyncestis (J 7.6.10; 17.3.14; P*Pyr* 5.2; P*Eum* 1.6; A 1.20.10; D 17.25.5; cf. Hoffmann 202 n. 119). Meleager's birthdate is unknown, but the fact that he was not dismissed with the veterans in 324 suggests that he may have been one of the younger marshals. Furthermore, he had only recently married in 334 (A 1.24.1), which implies (though it does not prove) a birthdate perhaps in the 360s (cf. Berve ii.249).

In 335 Meleager and a certain Philip[415] conveyed back to the Macedonian base the booty taken from the Getae beyond the Danube (A 1.4.5). From his association with Philip we may infer that he was already a taxiarch. He is not mentioned again in the accounts of Alexander's European campaigns, although three other taxiarchs are – Perdiccas, Coenus, Amyntas. Craterus too is conspicuously absent, and it may be that Alexander employed fewer, or different, battalions in Illyria and Greece. At the Granicus Meleager was stationed on the left, between the battalions of Philip and Craterus (A 1.14.3), and at Halicarnassus he joined Perdiccas and Amyntas, as Alexander led three battalions of infantry in an unsuccessful attack on Myndus (A 1.20.5). In winter 334/3 he was one of the leaders of the *neogamoi* (newly weds) – he too had recently married (A 1.24.1), though his wife's name and family are unknown – together with Coenus son of Polemocrates and Ptolemy son of Seleucus. These men spent the winter in Macedonia and secured new recruits for the expedition (A 1.24.1). Meleager rejoined the King at Gordium in the spring of 333, bringing 3,000 infantry and 300 cavalry from Macedonia, along with 200 Thessalian horse, and 150 Eleians under the command of Alcias (A 1.29.4). Of his participation in the battles at Issus and Gaugamela, nothing is known beyond his position in the battle-line.[416] At the Persian Gates, at the end of 331, Meleager and his battalion remained with Craterus, holding the attention of Ariobarzanes, while Alexander conducted the encircling maneuver (A 3.18.4; C 5.4.14).

In 329, in the campaign on the Iaxartes, Meleager and Perdiccas were entrusted with the besieging of the otherwise unknown Memaceni (C 7.6.17ff.), who were said to have killed some fifty Macedonian horsemen by treachery (C 7.6.17–18). As was often the case, the honor of taking the city was left to Alexander, who sustained a serious wound to the neck in the assault on the walls (C 7.6.22–3). A 4.3.3 claims that this injury occurred at Cyropolis. The discrepancy is hard to explain, but Curtius gives independent, circumstantial, evidence concerning Meleager's participation, and his account cannot be dismissed out of hand. In the spring of 328, when the main force returned to Sogdiana, Meleager was left with Polyperchon, Attalus, and Gorgias in Bactria (A 4.16.1). Berve ii.249 thinks that each taxiarch had his own command in a separate part of Bactria, but there is no good evidence for this. The cavalry units were active in Sogdiana, and it seems unlikely that individual battalions would have operated in Bactria without cavalry support. Meleager soon joined Coenus, with whom he spent the remainder of the campaigning season and the winter of 328/7 in Sogdiana (A 4.17.3).

In 327, his battalion, along with those of White Cleitus and Gorgias (that is, the non-*asthetairoi*), accompanied Perdiccas and Hephaestion to the Indus, subduing the local dynast Astis *en route* (A 4.22.7; cf. C 8.10.2). On this mission, Meleager will have met the son of the local dynast of Taxila, Omphis (Ambhi). Some time later, when Alexander gave Omphis 1,000 talents at a banquet, Meleager remarked to his King that "at least in India he had found a man worth one thousand talents" (C 8.12.17–18; cf. Str 15.1.28 [698]; P*A* 59.5). Whether this reflects Meleager's personal dislike of Omphis, or his opposition to Alexander's favorable treatment of orientals, or perhaps his own pettiness, we cannot say. Curtius claims that Alexander suppressed his anger, remembering Black Cleitus, but remarked that Meleager, in his envy, was tormenting only himself (C 8.12.18). Some modern scholars have seen in this episode, or perhaps in Meleager's personality in general, the reason for his failure to be promoted to hipparch (cf. Green 388). Certainly, he was the only surviving taxiarch of those who held the office in 334 who had not risen above that rank. Furthermore, he appears never to have exercised an independent command. Of his personality, little else is known, except that his conservative attitudes led him to reject the kingship of Alexander IV or of Heracles son of Barsine and to espouse the cause of the incompetent Arrhidaeus. His fondness for wrestling is attested by Pliny, who claims that he imported powdery dust from the Nile region for this very purpose (Pl*NH* 35.167–8). But he was clearly not a man of learning, nor politically astute (cf. Berve ii.250).

At the Hydaspes, Meleager, Attalus, and Gorgias occupied the camp at the halfway point between Craterus' position (opposite Porus) and Alexander's crossing-point (A 5.12.1). These three taxiarchs were placed in command of the mercenary cavalry and infantry, almost certainly in addition to their own battalions (Berve ii.249, following Anspach ii.7 n. 134; *contra* Bosworth 1973: 247 n. 2, who thinks they commanded *only* mercenaries). And, in accordance with their instructions, they crossed the Hydaspes, once Alexander's forces had successfully diverted Porus' attention, and helped to secure the Macedonian victory (A 5.18.1). In 325 Meleager returned from India via Arachosia and Drangiana along with Attalus and Antigenes, all under the leadership of Craterus (A 6.17.3).

In the events that followed Alexander's death, Meleager championed the cause of the conservative phalanx (D 18.2.2; A*Succ* 1.2 lists him as the only infantry officer amongst the *megistoi*) and opposed the kingship of Alexander's sons by barbarian women (J 13.2.6–8; C 10.6.20–1). He quickly became the spokesman for the common soldier and for those veteran commanders who had looked with disfavor on Alexander's orientalizing policies. In an unexpected move, which set the stage for the bitter struggles of the Diadochoi, Meleager espoused the hereditary claims of Arrhidaeus to the Macedonian kingship.[417] The aristocratic faction, stunned by the unexpected turn of events and cowed by the surging mob, withdrew from the phalanx, eventually leaving Babylon altogether (C 10.7.10–21). But Meleager's victory was temporary and hollow: agents sent to assassinate Perdiccas (C 10.8.1–3; but J 13.3.6–8 names Attalus as the instigator), who had remained briefly in the city in the hope of retaining some support with the infantry, were unwilling to do so, placing little confidence in the authority of Meleager or his puppet Arrhidaeus; Attalus son of Andromenes was easily detached by the prospect of alliance with Perdiccas, who offered his sister Atalante in marriage (D 18.37.2; cf. Heckel 381–4). The phalanx in general soon repented and called for Meleager's head and reconciliation with the cavalry (C 10.8.5ff.); Meleager appears to have bought time for himself by alleging that the order to murder Perdiccas had come from Philip Arrhidaeus himself. The cavalry, however, demanded that the leaders of the sedition be handed over, and the fact that the infantry made an exception of Meleager, whom they wanted as a third leader (along with Perdiccas and Craterus), shows that at this time there was still considerable support for him (C 10.8.14–22). The agreement, which ended the discord, recognized the kingship of Arrhidaeus, but it also saw Craterus replace Meleager as his guardian. This was, of course, much more to the liking of the common soldier, and Meleager, although recognized as *tertius dux* (C 10.8.22–3; A*Succ* 1.3 makes Meleager Perdiccas' *hyparch*os; J 13.4.5 treats them as equals), was now isolated and soon abandoned by the infantry, who saw his death as beneficial, indeed essential to the well-being of the empire (C 10.9.1). Disguising his intentions (J 13.4.7; cf. C 10.9.20), Perdiccas arranged with Meleager himself a lustration of the Macedonian army, officially on the instructions of the new King (C 10.9.7–11). But, at the head of the cavalry and the elephants, Perdiccas suddenly called for the surrender of the authors of the discord. Some 300 were handed over for punishment and trampled beneath the feet of the elephants (C 10.9.11–18). Meleager, their leader, sought refuge in a nearby temple, only to be murdered there (C 10.9.20–1; cf. A*Succ* 1.4; J 13.4.7–8 does not name Meleager, but it is clear that he was among those who were executed).[418]

Berve ii.249–50 no. 494; Hoffmann 146–7, 187; Heckel 165–70.

Meleager [2]. (Meleagros). Macedonian of aristocratic family. Meleager led a squadron of the Companion Cavalry at Gaugamela (A 3.11.8; C 4.13.27) and may have served as ilarch since at least 334. His connections with the Somatophylax, Peithon son of Crateuas, in whose service we find him in 317/6 (D 19.47.1), may go back into Alexander's reign and beyond. After the defeat of Eumenes of Cardia by the Antigonid forces, Meleager joined Peithon in an attempt to free Media from Monophthalmus' control. Although Peithon was deceived by Antigonus, who arrested and executed him (D 19.46), Meleager and Menoitas managed to collect a force of 800, some of whom had previously served with Eumenes (D 19.47.1). They attacked Antigonus' newly appointed satrap of Media, Orontobates, and his general Hippostratus (D 19.47.2), and, although they enjoyed some initial success, they were soon cut off and forced into an engagement in which Meleager was killed (D 19.47.3–4).

Berve ii.250 no. 495; Hoffmann 183; Heckel 1988: 40; Heckel 349.

Melon. A Greek of unknown family background, Melon served as interpreter for Darius III (C 5.13.7), though we do not know for how long.[419] Left behind, on account of illness, at the Parthian town of Thara (where Darius was arrested by Bessus and Nabarzanes) in 330, he fell into Alexander's hands (C 5.13.7). What became of him is unknown, though it is likely that, if he survived his illness, Alexander made use of his linguistic skills.

Berve ii.250 no. 496; Hofstetter 125 no. 214.

Memnon [1]. Rhodian (D 17.7.2). Brother of Mentor and brother-in-law of Artabazus (D 16.52.4; Dem 23.157), a relationship which accounts for his influence with Darius III (Seibt 106). Married Barsine, the widow of his brother Mentor and daughter of Artabazus (A 7.4.6; P*A* 21.8); the only known offspring of this marriage was captured, while still a child (**M2**), at Damascus in late 333 together with his mother (C 3.13.14). After the death of Philip II, Darius sent Memnon with a force of 5,000 mercenaries to traverse Mount Ida and gain possession of Cyzicus (D 17.7.2), a task which Memnon failed to accomplish (D 17.7.8); he did, however, prevent Parmenion and the Macedonian forces from capturing Pitane, compelling them to break off their siege (D 17.7.9). When Alexander crossed into Asia, he advocated a scorched-earth policy, advice which was rejected by the Persian commanders (D 17.18.2–3). At the Granicus River, Memnon and Arsames held the left wing (each with his own cavalry, says D 17.19.4; but earlier we heard only that Memnon had 5,000 Greek mercenaries, presumably infantry). Nothing else is recorded about his role in the battle; after the defeat, he and the Persian survivors took refuge in Miletus, only to be besieged by the Macedonians (D 17.22). After the fall of Miletus, Memnon and his supporters withdrew to Halicarnassus (D 17.23.4). Around this time, he also sent his wife and children to Darius, both for their safety and as a token of good faith; for he hoped to be given supreme command of the forces in Asia Minor (D 17.23.5). And this actually came about (D 17.23.6). At Halicarnassus, Memnon conducted a gallant defense (D 17.24.3–27.4), but in the end was forced to withdraw to Cos, leaving behind his best men to defend the acropolis of Halicarnassus (D 17.27.5). In spite of these setbacks, Darius appointed Memnon commander-in-chief of operations in Asia Minor and sent him money to hire mercenaries and man ships (D 17.29.1–2). Memnon captured Chios and the Lesbian towns of Antissa, Methymna, Pyrrha, and Eresus; finally also Mytilene, with heavy losses on his own side (D 17.29.2; A 2.1.1–2). But, just when Memnon was threatening to turn the war back on Greece (D 17.29.3; A 2.1.1; cf. D 17.30.1) – he had distributed bribes there – by sailing to Euboea, he died of illness (D 17.29.3–4; A 2.1.3; cf. C 3.1.21; 3.2.1). His successor was his kinsman Pharnabazus (C 3.3.1; A 2.1.3).

Berve ii.250–3 no. 497; Seibt 99–107; Hofstetter 125–7 no. 215 (with further bibliography). See Stemma IV.

Memnon [2]. Descendant of the great satrap Pharnabazus and his son Artabazus. Memnon was honored in Athens in 327/6 (*IG* ii^2 356 = Tod ii no. 199). There is no patronymic on the surviving portion of the inscription, but a reference to the euergetism of his ancestors (*progonoi*), Pharnabazus and Artabazus, follows eleven illegible lines of text which must have given the family details. A subsequent comment (lines 30–1) on "Mentor, the father of Thymondas," makes it virtually certain that Thymondas was his father and that either his mother or grandmother was a daughter of Artabazus.[420] If we are dealing with a relative of Barsine, the year is significant, since it was in 327 that Barsine was sent back to coastal Asia Minor, where she bore Alexander's son, Heracles. Athens was almost certainly attempting to curry favor with Alexander by means of the decree for Memnon (thus Hofstetter 127). Identification with the *strategos* of Thrace (thus Badian 1967a: 179–80) is rejected by Bosworth 1988a: 201 n. 15.

Berve ii.253–4 no. 498; Hofstetter 127–8 no. 216. See Stemma IV.

Memnon [3]. *Strategos* of Thrace in 331, rose in rebellion against Alexander and was defeated by Antipater (D 17.62.5–6). J relates in this chronological context the defeat of Memnon's successor Zopyrion at the hands of the Getae (12.1.4, 2.16–17; cf. C 10.1.44).

Berve ii.254 no. 499; Badian 1967a.

Menander [1]. (Menandros). Macedonian *hetairos* of Alexander (A 3.6.7) and father of the Page Charicles (A 4.13.7),[421] Menander commanded mercenary infantry from perhaps 334 until the spring of 331. At that point, he relinquished the command of the *xenoi* to Cleander (A 3.6.8; A 3.12.2) and became satrap of Lydia (A 3.6.7; cf. 7.23.1; *SIG*³ 302.4–5). As satrap, he appears to have been responsible for sending some 2,600 Lydian infantry and 300 cavalrymen to Alexander in Areia in 330 (C 6.6.35). In 323, Menander brought fresh troops to Alexander in Babylon (A 7.23.1); according to the forged *Last Days and Testament of Alexander*, he attended the dinner-party given by Medius, at which the King became fatally ill; he was allegedly one of those involved in the plot to poison the King (Ps-Call 3.31.8; *LM* 97–8). This appears to be hostile propaganda spread by the Polyperchon faction (Heckel 1988). Confirmed as satrap of Lydia in the settlement at Babylon (A *Succ.* 1.6; cf. 1.26; Dexippus, *FGrH* 100 F8 §2; C 10.10.2; D 18.3.1; J 13.4.15), he was soon humiliated by Perdiccas, who assigned control of the satrapy to Cleopatra, sister of Alexander the Great, and left Menander in charge of the army (A*Succ* 25.2). Menander defected to Antigonus, who had returned from Europe, having incited Antipater and Craterus to war with Perdiccas. But he received no reward for his betrayal of Perdiccas: at Triparadeisus his satrapy was assigned instead to White Cleitus. Menander, for his part, took refuge with Antigonus, perhaps in the vain hope of recovering Lydia. Although Menander served Antigonus faithfully, especially in the events following the battle of Orcynii (P*Eum* 9.8–12; cf. D 18.59.1–2), we hear of no further commands or administrative postings. Nor can we say what became of him.[422] Menander commissioned a painting of himself by Apelles, apparently during Alexander's lifetime (Pl*NH* 35.93, wrongly "*King* of the Carians," unless Pliny confuses him with Asander son of Agathon; cf. Pollitt 162).

Geyer, *RE* s.v. "Menandros (5)"; Berve ii.255 no. 501; Billows 402–3 no. 71; Heckel 1988: 39–40; Heckel 339–40.

Menander [2]. (Menandros). Prominent Macedonian, *hetairos* of Alexander. At some time ca. 329–327, he was left behind as the commander of a small fortress in Bactria-Sogdiana or perhaps in the territory bordering on India. He did not wish to remain there and rebelled against the King, who had him put to death (P*A* 57.3). Whether he had anything to do with the uprising of Orsodates (see s.v. **Orsodates**) is not clear.

Berve ii.255 no. 502.

Menedemus (Menedemos). Family and regional origins unknown; Hoffmann omits Menedemus, but the name is attested in Macedonia (*IG* ii² 1335, 35).[423] He is mentioned by the sources only in connection with the campaign in which he was killed, that at the Polytimetus (Zeravshan) against Spitamenes (329 BC). Here he commanded 1,500 mercenary infantry, as we may deduce from Arrian's description (4.3.7): Andromachus led sixty Companions, Caranus 800 mercenary cavalry; the Lycian Pharnuches was (allegedly) in charge of the entire expedition. Hence Menedemus must have been the commander of the mercenary infantry. But Curtius, who names only Menedemus in his account (7.6.24; 7.7.31–9; 7.9.21; cf. *ME* 13), gives him 3,000 foot in addition to 800 horse (7.6.24), a figure rejected by Berve (ii.256) without good reason. Whether Andronicus son of Agerrus served under Menedemus cannot be determined.

The mercenaries, largely through the incompetence of their Macedonian commanders, were lured into an ambush and defeated by Spitamenes (A 4.6.2, forty cavalry and 300 infantrymen escaped). Menedemus himself perished in the engagement and was duly buried by Alexander when he returned from the Iaxartes (C 7.9.21; *ME* 13).

Berve ii.256 no. 504; Heckel 343.

Menelaus (Menelaos). Prominent Macedonian. Son of Lagus and brother of Ptolemy (D 19.62.4), hence presumably from Eordaea. Menelaus is said to have been an avid hunter and, together with Leonnatus, carried with him curtains that measured 100 stades, with which to close off a hunting area (Phylarchus, *FGrH* 81 F41 = Ath 539d; cf. Ael*VH* 9.3). Nothing further is known about him until Ptolemy gained control of Cyprus in 315. He sent Menelaus to join forces with the exiled Seleucus and Nicocreon of Salamis (D 19.62.4). It was probably at this time that he was established as his *strategos* there (D 20.47.3; Paus 1.6.6 calls him satrap).[424] In 310 he supplied troops to Ptolemy's agents, Argaeus and Callicrates, who used them to surround the palace of Nicocles of Paphos and force his surrender and the noble deaths of his family (D 20.21.1–3; cf. Pol*Strat* 8.48 "Axiothea"; see also Gesche 1974). In 306, Demetrius Poliorcetes sailed to Cyprus and defeated Menelaus in a land battle (D 20.47.1–4). Menelaus, having lost many men, withdrew into the city of Salamis, sent to Ptolemy for aid (D 20.47.7–8), and took what action he could against Demetrius' siege-equipment (D 20.48.6). Ptolemy soon arrived with a larger fleet (P*Demetr* 15.2; Paus 1.6.6),[425] and summoned from Menelaus the sixty ships that lay at anchor in the harbor of Salamis. These, however, were blockaded by Demetrius' ships (D 20.49.3–6; cf. P*Demetr* 16.1–2, confused; cf. also Pol*Strat* 4.7.7). Nevertheless, in the ensuing battle, Menelaus assigned these ships to Menoetius, who, although they routed Demetrius' guard ships, could not join Ptolemy's fleet in time to make a difference (D 20.52.5).[426] Soon after the naval defeat of his brother Menelaus surrendered Salamis (P*Demetr* 16.7). After his capture, he was allowed by Demetrius to return, along with Ptolemy's son by Thaïs, Leontiscus, to Egypt (J 15.2.7; cf. P*Demetr* 17.1). The Menelaite Nome by the Canobic canal near Alexandria is named for Ptolemy's brother (Str 17.1.18 [801]). He is attested as eponymous priest of Alexander in 284/3 (year 40 of Ptolemy Soter: *PEleph* 2).

Berve ii.256 no. 505; Volkmann, *Kl. Pauly* iii.1210 no. 4; *Pros Ptol* 5196; Bagnall 40–2. See Stemma X.

Menes. Son of Dionysius, from Pella (D 17.64.5), Menes was appointed Somatophylax to replace Balacrus son of Nicanor, whom Alexander had designated satrap of Cilicia in late 333 BC (A 2.12.2). As Somatophylax he did nothing worthy of record, nor did he hold the office long: toward the end of 331, he was sent out from Susa as hyparch of Phoenicia, Syria, and Cilicia (A 3.16.9; cf. D 17.64.5; C 5.1.43). Alexander appears to have employed Menes temporarily as overseer of the area and of the existing satraps and financial officers.[427] Thus the vulgate refers to Menes and Apollodorus as "*strategoi* of Babylon and of the satrapies as far as Cilicia" (D 17.64.5; cf. C 5.1.43, as emended by Shackleton-Bailey 1981: 176). Considering the political situation in Europe and the need to press eastwards against Darius, Alexander entrusted the coastal region to a single individual. Hence he sent Menes to the coast with 3,000 talents (A 3.16.9; C 5.1.43 says 1,000), which were to be transported to Antipater for use in the war with Agis III. It was also his responsibility to see that the discharged Greek veterans (brought from Ecbatana by Epocillus son of Polyeides) found their way back to Europe (A 3.19.5–6). Coins minted in the region bearing the mark *M* will also belong to the time of Menes' coordination of affairs in this region (see Berve ii.257). Menes' disappearance from the sources, with no indication of his successor, suggests that his position was intended to be temporary.

Berve ii.257 no. 507; Julien 62 n. 2; Lehmann-Haupt 157–8; Brunt i.278–9 n. 11; Bosworth 1974: 59–60; Bosworth i.319; Shackleton-Bailey 1981: 176; Heckel 262–3.

Menesaechmus (Menesaichmos). Athenian orator and politician. Family background unknown. Lycurgus had once brought a charge against him ([P]*M* 843d; Dion Hal *de Din* 11; cf. [P]*M* 842e–f for their enmity). Menesaechmus was one of those who brought charges against Demosthenes for accepting money from Harpalus in 324 ([P]*M* 846c).

Kirchner no. 9983; Berve ii.255–6 no. 503; Develin 405.

Menestheus. Athenian from Rhamnus. Born ca. 381. Son of Iphicrates and Thressa, the daughter of the Thracian king Cotys (N*Iph* 3.4).[428] In 362 (Davies 251) he married a daughter of Timotheus (N*Timoth* 3.2; [Dem] 49.66). Appointed commander of a fleet of 100 triremes hastily organized by the Athenians in response to Hegelochus' seizure of the grain ships from the Hellespontine region ([Dem] 17.20). He died before 325/4: in that year a debt was paid on his behalf by his heirs (*IG* ii^2 1629.486–7; cf. [Dem]*Ep* 3.31).

Berve ii.256–7 no. 506; Kirchner 9988; Schaefer iii^2 175; Davies 250–1.

Menidas (Maenidas; Melamnidas). Macedonian. Menidas appears in all extant texts without patronymic.[429] At Gaugamela, Alexander positioned the mercenary horse on the right tip of his angled line, followed by the *prodromoi* and Paeonians, with the Agrianes, archers, and Cleander's mercenary infantry in reserve (A 3.12.2–3). Menidas had been instructed to attack the enemy cavalry, should they attempt to outflank the Macedonians (A 3.12.4). This is precisely what happened, but his force proved inadequate (A 3.13.3), on account of their small numbers, and had to be supported by the *prodromoi*, Paeonians, and the mercenary infantrymen, which managed to break the Persian formation (A 3.13.3–4).[430]

In 330, Menidas was left behind at Ecbatana with Parmenion's forces (A 3.26.3), and he must have played some part in the execution of the old general (A 3.26.4; cf. Berve ii.258). The command of the mercenary cavalry was turned over to Philip son of Menelaus, who brought them to Alexander in Areia (A 3.25.4; cf. C 6.6.35). Menidas rejoined Alexander at Zariaspa (Bactra) over the winter of 329/8, in the company of Ptolemy (the commander of the Thracians) and Epocillus (A 4.7.2: "Melamnidas" should be emended to read "Menidas," so Hamilton 1955: 217; C 7.10.11 says he and Ptolemy brought 5,000 mercenaries: 4,000 infantry and 1,000 cavalry). In the following year, Menidas was sent out from Nautaca, together with Epocillus and the ilarch Sopolis, to recruit new forces in Macedonia (A 4.18.3). It appears that these reinforcements did not reach Alexander until his return to Babylon (A 7.23.1: the cavalry which Menidas led were probably new recruits). Menidas is last attested sleeping in the temple of Sarapis in Babylon when the King had become fatally ill (A 7.26.2: but see the comments of Grainger 218–19).[431]

Berve ii.257–8 no. 508; Hamilton 1955: 217–18; Heckel 362–3.

Meniscus (Meniskos). Greek of unknown family in the service of Darius III. In 332, after the capture of Darius' family at Issus, Meniscus was sent along with Arsimas to deliver a letter from the Great King to Alexander. Thereafter he accompanied Thersippus, who bore Alexander's response, back to Darius (A 2.14.1, 3; C 4.1.7–14; P*A* 29.7–9).

Berve ii.258 no. 509; Hofstetter 128 no. 218; Schachermeyr 222–3.

Menoetas (Menoitas). Macedonian. Son of Hegesander. In 332/1 Menoetas brought 400 mercenary infantrymen to Alexander at Memphis in 332/1 (A 3.5.1), unless this man's name is a corruption of "Menidas" (thus Hamilton 1955: 217–18; *contra* Bosworth i.275). Menoetas may be identical with the cavalry officer who supported Peithon son of Crateuas in the events after the defeat of Eumenes of Cardia by Antigonus. He had perhaps been amongst those who served in the satrapal forces of Peithon since 323. In 316 he joined in Peithon's attempt to raise a rebellion in

Media. Although Peithon was tricked and captured by Monophthalmus, who executed him, Menoetas and Meleager collected a force of 800 men, some of whom had served with Eumenes. With these he attacked Antigonus' newly appointed satrap, Orontobates, and his general Hippostratus (D 19.46.5–47.2). After some initial success, the rebels, who were vastly outnumbered, especially with regard to infantry, were cut off and defeated. D 19.47.3–4 says that some were killed and others captured, and, since he names only Meleager and Ocranes as notable amongst the dead, we may assume that Menoetas either escaped or was captured. Perhaps he made his peace with the Antigonid officers and continued to serve in the east. Nothing else is known about him.

Berve ii.258–9 no. 510.

Menoetius (Menoitios). Apparently Macedonian (Hoffmann 211).[432] Menoetius was helmsman of Alexander's ship (cf. Bosworth i.103), with which he crossed the Hellespont. He presented the King with a golden crown at Troy (A 1.12.1). Menoetius is otherwise unknown unless it is possible to identify him with the *nauarchos* of Menelaus son of Lagus at Salamis in 306 (D 20.52.5).

Berve ii.259 no. 511; Bosworth i.102–3; Instinsky 71 n. 1.

Menon [1]. Macedonian. Son of Cerdimmas. Given charge of Coele-Syria in late 333 (A 2.13.7). C 4.8.11 says that, after the Samaritans murdered the Syrian satrap, Andromachus (apparently the ruler of Palestine), Alexander appointed "Memnon" in his place. This must be a reference to Menon son of Cerdimmas. A 3.6.8 says that Alexander, on his way to Thapsacus in 331, replaced "Arimmas" with Asclepiodorus. This creates a virtually insoluble set of problems concerning the administrative divisions of Syria and the various satraps.[433] Some have argued that Arimmas was Menon's successor in northern Syria when Menon replaced Andromachus. Others have suggested that Arrian's "Arimmas" is a scribal error for Cerdimmas, that Asclepiodorus replaced Menon son of Cerdimmas in 331. Is it mere coincidence that neither Menon nor Arimmas is heard of again? (See also s.vv. **Andromachus** [2], **Arimmas**).

Berve ii.259 no. 514.

Menon [2]. Macedonian. Patronymic unknown. Menon was appointed satrap of Arachosia in 330 and left with 4,000 infantry and 600 cavalry (C 7.3.5; A 3.28.1). He died of illness in 325 and was replaced by Sibyrtius (C 9.10.20).

Berve ii.259 no. 515; Julien 39; Lehmann-Haupt 146.

Menon [3]. Perhaps Macedonian. Menon was sent by Alexander to gold mines at Syspiritis (Hyspiritis) near Caballa in Armenia. He may have perished in the attempt at the hands of the natives (Str 11.14.9 [529]).[434] Berve ii.260 believes that Menon and his troops may have accompanied Mithrenes into Armenia in 331 (cf. A 3.16.5; D 17.64.6; C 5.1.44). The incident may also shed some light on Mithrenes' disappearance from our records.

Berve ii.260 no. 516.

Menon [4]. Thessalian from Pharsalus. Menon was apparently descended from the commander of the same name who served Cyrus the Younger at Cunaxa (see Xen*Anab* 2.6.21, for an unfavorable character sketch). That man was alleged to have been intimate with Tharyps the Molossian (Xen*Anab* 2.6.28), and it was the daughter of the younger Menon, Phthia, who married Aeacides, son of Arrybas and Troas, of the Molossian royal house (P*Pyr* 1.6; cf. Heckel 1981a: 81 n. 11). Menon commanded the Greek cavalry during the Lamian War: he fought with distinction alongside Leosthenes (P*Pyr* 1.6; cf. D 18.12.3, not naming Menon) and commanded the cavalry in the battle against Leonnatus, in which Antiphilus led the infantry (PPh 25.5; D 18.15.4). After the Lamian War, he led the Thessalians who numbered about 13,000 infantry and 1,100 horse (D 18.38.5).[435] He was defeated by Polyperchon and killed in battle (D 18.38.6; PPh 25.5). Most of his army was cut to pieces.

Berve ii.260 no. 517.

Mentor. Greek. Family background unknown. He was apparently a friend and supporter of Eumenes.[436] When on the return march from India Hephaestion had assigned quarters prepared for Eumenes to the flute-player Evius, Mentor accompanied Eumenes to lodge a complaint with Alexander (P*Eum* 2.2). Although Alexander reproached Hephaestion, the incident created ill will toward Eumenes (P*Eum* 2.3), and perhaps Mentor as well. Nothing else is known about him.

Berve ii.259 no. 512.

Menyllus (Menyllos). See n. 85.

Meroes. Indian of unknown background. He was a friend of Porus who had either defected to Alexander before the battle at the Hydaspes or surrendered during the course of it. The King sent him to Porus, who had suffered serious wounds, to urge him to surrender and to guarantee his safety (A 5.18.7). Nothing else is known about him.

Berve ii.260 no. 518.

Metron [1]. Son of Epicharmus. Macedonian from Pydna. Metron was a trierarch of the Hydaspes fleet in 326 BC (A*Ind* 18.5) and one of the King's *hetairoi*. He may be identical with Metron the Page.

Berve ii.260 no. 519.

Metron [2]. Macedonian, perhaps identical with the son of Epicharmus from Pydna (A*Ind* 18.5), unless this identification is rejected on the grounds of age.[437] When Cebalinus had no success in bringing the news of Dimnus' plot to the King's attention through Philotas, he informed Metron, one of the Pages.[438] Metron promptly reported Dimnus' conspiracy and Philotas' suspicious behavior (C 6.7.22–3; D 17.79.5; cf. P*A* 49.6; Hamilton 136). As a Page, he undoubtedly came from a good aristocratic family, and Alexander may have further enriched him for his part in bringing the Dimnus/Philotas affair to his attention. Hence a trierarchy in 326 is not entirely out of the question.

Berve ii.260–1 no. 520; Heckel 293–4.

Miccalus (Mikkalos). Greek from Clazomenae. In 323 he was sent with 500 talents to Phoenicia and Syria in order to recruit experienced sailors for Alexander's planned colonization of the coast of the Persian Gulf (A 7.19.5). The project was part of Alexander's so-called "final plans," which were canceled after his death. What became of Miccalus we do not know.

Berve ii.264 no. 530.

Micion (Mikion). Macedonian, perhaps *nauarchos*.[439] Micion led a force of Macedonians and mercenaries that landed at Rhamnus in Attica in 323/2. He was, however, met by the Athenians under Phocion, defeated and killed (P*Ph* 25.1–4, this occurred just before Leonnatus reinforced Antipater in Thessaly; cf. P*M* 188e). If this chronology is correct, Micion may have been the admiral who secured the Hellespont in preparation for Leonnatus' crossing and thus commander of Antipater's fleet, which was deployed before the arrival of White Cleitus in the Aegean.[440] About his earlier service under Antipater nothing is recorded.

Berve ii.264 no. 529; Hauben 71–2 no. 26.

Minnion (Minion, Minneon). Greek from Iasus. Son of Theodotus, brother of Gorgus the *hoplophylax*. Like his brother, Minnion appears to have served with Alexander, although we do not know in what capacity. He is honored, together with Gorgus, by both the Iasians and Samians for securing benefications from Alexander (*SIG*[3] 307, 312; cf. Heisserer 169–203). For details see s.v. **Gorgus** [1].

Berve ii.264 no. 531.

Mithraustes. Persian noble of unknown family background. Together with the satrap Orontes, Mithraustes led the Armenian troops at Gaugamela in 331 (A 3.8.5); Berve ii.262 (with n. 1) may be correct in assigning to him command of the infantry (cf. Bosworth i.291). What became of him is unknown. If he was not killed or captured in the battle, he may have returned to Armenia with Orontes.

Berve ii.262 no. 523; Bosworth i.291; Justi 217.

Mithrazenes (Mithracenes). For the name, see Justi 214; Mithracenes (C 5.13.9). A Persian of unknown origin. He and a certain Orsillus had apparently been with Darius III since, at least, the battle of Gaugamela. Both abandoned Bessus and the other conspirators who had taken the King prisoner, and, falling in with Alexander, reported that the conspirators were some 500 stades distant and offered to point out a shorter route (C 5.13.9). Mithrazenes is otherwise unknown.

Berve ii.262 no. 522; Justi 214.

Mithrenes (Mithrines, Mithrinnes). A Persian noble of unknown family background, Mithrenes was citadel-commander of Sardis under Darius III (A 1.17.3; cf. Dio Chr 73.2; cf. D 17.21.7).[441] In 334 he surrendered the city and its treasures to Alexander without resistance (D 17.21.7; cf. C 3.12.6; P*A* 17.1), meeting the King when he was still 70 stades from the city (A 1.17.3). He remained with Alexander (A 1.17.4), who later decided against sending him to the captive Persian queens with news about Darius III, lest the sight of a traitor should grieve them (C 3.12.6–7). This depiction of Mithrenes as a traitor to Darius (3.12.7; 5.8.12) is perhaps Curtius' own invention (cf. Atkinson i.247). In late 331, Alexander appointed him satrap of Armenia (A 3.16.5; D 17.64.6; C 5.1.44), an unconquered satrapy which he appears to have been unable to win (cf. Julien 28). Mithrenes is not heard of again, and he may have perished in an unsuccessful attempt to wrest the territory from Orontes (but see also s.v. **Menon** [1]); for the latter is found in command of the Armenians at Gaugamela (A 3.8.5) and again in 317 in charge of Armenia (D 19.23.3; Pol*Strat* 4.8.3). See further s.v. **Orontes**.

Badian 1965: 175 n. 1; Berve ii.262–3 no. 524; Bosworth i.315; Julien 27–8; Justi 217.

Mithridates. Noble Persian, son-in-law of Darius III (A 1.15.7, 16.3; **F8**). D 17.20.2 mentions "Spithrobates" as Darius' son-in-law (thus conflating Spithridates and Mithridates); the satrap of Ionia may also have married a daughter of Darius (**F9**), but it is more likely that Diodorus confused the two men, since there is no mention of Mithridates in either his account of the battle of Granicus or his casualty list. Berve ii.263 assumes that Mithridates was from the area of Pontus-Cappadocia, and that he was married to the daughter of Darius III and the sister of Pharnaces, a relative of Mithridates (as were also Ariobarzanes and Artabazus). But this is highly speculative. Alexander killed Mithridates in hand-to-hand combat at the Granicus River (334 BC), when he thrust his lance into his face (A 1.15.7; cf. 1.16.3; P*M* 326f).

Berve ii.263 no. 525.

Mithrobaeus (Mithrobaios). Prominent Persian, brother of Autobares (or Aegobares); their father is not named. Both were enrolled in the *agema* of the Companion Cavalry in 324 at Susa (A 7.6.5).

Berve ii.263 no. 526. Justi 208.

Mithrobuzanes (Mithrobouzanes). A Persian noble (possibly a son of Ariarathes; thus Marquart 1895: 495) and ruler of Cappadocia near the Taurus (A 1.16.3; for the division of Cappadocia, Str 12.1.4 [534]; Julien 18–19), Mithrobuzanes commanded the satrapal contingent at the Granicus (334 BC), where he lost his life (D 17.21.3; A 1.16.3). Alexander installed Sabictas in his place (A 2.4.2; C 3.4.1 incorrectly "Abistamenes").

Berve ii.263 no. 527; Justi 209; Julien 18–19.

Mithropastes. Son of Arsites (satrap of Hellespontine Phrygia). At some point, Mithropastes took refuge on the island of Oaracta in the Persian Gulf, where Nearchus encountered him in 325/4. He accompanied Nearchus on the remainder of his journey as a guide familiar with the voyage (Nearchus, *FGrH* 133 F28 = Str 16.3.7 [767]). There is no further record of him. Berve ii.263 speculates that Mithropastes' flight may in some way be connected with the Granicus fiasco or his father's subsequent suicide. It is more likely that he fought at Gaugamela and sought refuge on Oaracta in the hope of avoiding the Macedonians.

Berve ii.263–4 no. 528; Justi 216; Tomaschek 47–8.

Mnasicles (Mnasikles). Cretan mercenary captain (*hegemon*), Mnasicles accompanied Thibron from Cydonia on Crete to Cyrene (cf. A*Succ* 1.16), where he betrayed his leader after Thibron had captured the Cyrenaean harbor and extracted concessions from the city. In Thibron's absence, he recaptured the port of Cyrene and contributed indirectly to the destruction of Thibron's fleet (D 18.20.1–5). What became of Mnasicles is not recorded. If he survived the fighting in Libya, he may have been taken into the service of Ptolemy's *strategos*, Ophellas. Whether Mnasicles was recruited by Thibron on Crete or had been one of the mercenaries brought by Harpalus from Asia in 324 is uncertain (D 17.108.6; 18.19.2). If the latter, the Mnasicles may have served for a time with Alexander the Great.

Berve ii.264–5 no. 533.

Mnasidicus (Mnasidikos). Son of Athanodorus. Cavalryman from Orchomenus; served in Alexander's allied cavalry until the expedition reached Ecbatana in 330. There he and his compatriots were discharged. On their return (ca. 329), they made a dedication to Zeus Soter in Orchomenus (*IG* vii.3206).

Berve ii.264 no. 532.

Mnason. Tyrant of Elateia in Phocis during the reign of Alexander. Student of Aristotle (Timaeus, *FGrH* 566 F11a = Ath 6.264d; Ael*VH* 3.19; cf. Ath 6.264d, a companion of Aristotle). A man of considerable wealth (Ath 6.272b = *FGrH* 566 F116), Mnason is said to have purchased from Aristeides his painting of one of Alexander's battles with the Persians for the price of ten minae (Pl*NH* 35.99). Whether he had any personal contact with Alexander is unknown.

Berve ii.265 no. 534; Schaefer iii^2 39 n. 3.

Mnesitheus (Mnesitheos). Athenian dancer (*choreutes*). Demosthenes is said to have asked him to determine the amount of money Harpalus had brought with him to be deposited on the Acropolis. The answer was 700 talents (Hyp 5, col. 9 [Burtt]). He is perhaps identical with Mnesitheus of Myrrhinoussa (Aes 1.98), in which case he is the son of Tachybulus (Kirchner no. 10297).

Berve ii.265 no. 535.

Moeris.[442] The name comes up only in C 9.8.28. Indian dynast in the Patala region of the Indus delta. Marched north upon Alexander's approach and surrendered to the King (A 6.17.2). Alexander sent him back to his realm and ordered him to prepare everything for the Macedonian fleet (A 6.17.3). This Moeris appears to have failed to do, and he fled to the hills at the news of Alexander's approach (A 6.17.5; C 9.8.28). See D 17.104.1–2 for Patala's alleged dyarchy.

Berve ii.265 no. 536.

Moerocles (Moirokles). Athenian from Salamis; family background unknown (Harpocration; *Suda A* 1447). Convicted earlier in his career of extorting money from the lessees of the silver mines (Dem 19.293), Moerocles was one of the anti-Macedonian politicians whose extradition Alexander demanded after the sack of Thebes in 335 (A 1.10.4; P*Dem* 23.4; *Suda A* 2704 has "Patrocles"). In the end, Alexander relented and insisted only upon the surrender of Charidemus. Moerocles is named by the comic poet, Timocles, in a fragment of his *Delos* (Ath 8.341f) as accepting money from Harpalus.

Berve ii.266 no. 537; Kirchner no. 10400; cf. Schaefer iii[2] 137 n. 2, 321 n. 2, 349 n. 3; Sealey 204.

Monimus (Monimos). Spartan ambassador to Persia, probably sent out in connection with the activities of Agis III; captured by Alexander after the death of Darius in 330 (A 3.24.4).[443] But the name Monimus is not otherwise attested in Sparta.

Berve ii.266 no. 538; Hofstetter 135 no. 226; Poralla no. 540; Schachermeyr 308.

Moschion. Elean who served with Alexander in Asia; attested as the father of two distinguished boxers named Hippomachus and Theotimus (Paus 6.12.6, 17.5). Nothing specific is known about Moschion's participation in the campaign, though he may have been a member of the Elean cavalry contingent led by Alcias, which joined Alexander at Gordium (A 1.29.4). He was thus probably dismissed with the remainder of the allied troops at Ecbatana in 330.

Berve ii.266 no. 539.

Musicanus (Mousikanos). Indian dynast of southwestern Sogdia; ruler of the Mushika. Musicanus' kingdom lay to the east of the Indus, opposite that of Sambus, to the north of the realm of Oxicanus and south of the confluences of the various rivers of the Punjab.[444] The capital of this region was probably Alor, and Musicanus' rival, Sambus (A 6.16.3), presumably controlled the Kandahar to Alor trade route (Eggermont 5–9). Alexander arrived in Musicanus' kingdom before the news of the Macedonian advance and Musicanus quickly made his submission (A 6.15.6) and thus gained a pardon. He was allowed to retain his kingdom, although his capital was fortified and garrisoned by the Macedonians under Craterus' supervision (A 6.15.7; cf. C 9.8.10). But, when Alexander turned his attention toward Musicanus' neighbors, the ruler, influenced by the Brahmins, rebelled and was captured by Peithon (A 6.17.1). Peithon brought Musicanus captive to Alexander, who had him crucified (A 6.17.2; C 9.8.16).

Berve ii.266–7 no. 540; Jacobs 247 and 245 Abb. 4.

Mylleas. Son of Zoïlus. Macedonian from Beroea (see Tataki 231 no. 909). Possibly father of a certain Alexander (*IG* ii[2] 710). How long he served with Alexander in Asia is unknown, but in 326 he was appointed trierarch of the Hydaspes fleet (A*Ind* 18.6).

Berve ii.267 no. 541.

Myllenas (Mullinus). Apparently Macedonian. Described as *scriba regis* ("the King's Secretary"). Placed in charge of the lightly armed troops at Aornus (C 8.11.5). He may be identical with Myllenas son of Asander, who is honored by a decree of the Eretrians along with Tauron son of Harpalus (*IG* xii.9, 197; cf. Tataki 231–2 no. 910).

Berve ii.267–8 no. 542.

N

Nabarzanes.[445] Chiliarch of Darius III (A 3.21.1, 23.4; his seal was on the letter carried by Sisines, C 3.7.12–15). Commanded the cavalry and 20,000 slingers and archers on the Persian right at Issus (C 3.9.1). Together with Bessus, he plotted the arrest and murder of Darius (A 3.21.1; C 5.9.2–8; 5.9–12; cf. 6.4.8). Fled to Hyrcania (C 6.3.9) and eventually surrendered to Alexander along with Bagoas, who intervened on his behalf (C 6.5.22–3; A 3.23.4). He is probably identical with "Barzanes" (A 4.7.1; cf. 4.18.1; Heckel 1981d: 66–9). His career can be reconstructed as follows: after the death of Darius, Bessus assigned Hyrcania and Parthia to Nabarzanes (thus A 4.7.1, reading barzanes; the two satrapies were linked administratively: Str 11.9.1–2 [514]; cf. Julien 34–6). C 5.13.18 (cf. 6.3.9) says he went to Hyrcania, replacing Phrataphernes who had remained loyal to Darius and fled (cf. C 6.4.23). When Alexander approached, Nabarzanes surrendered, but only after cautious diplomatic exchanges (C 6.4.12–14, 5.22–3; the affair is compressed by A 3.23.4). Through the agency of Bagoas, Nabarzanes was pardoned (C 6.5.23), but he received no further honors from Alexander. He soon returned to Hyrcania but was arrested by Phrataphernes and delivered to Alexander (A 4.7.1, 18.1), who presumably had him executed.

Berve ii.268–9 no. 543.

Nearchus (Nearchos). Son of Androtimus (A 3.6.5; A*Ind* 18.4, 10; *SIG*[3] 266, 1–2). Cretan by birth (D 19.69.1; Pol*Strat* 5.35; A*Ind* 18.4), apparently from Lato,[446] but settled in Amphipolis during the reign of Philip II (A*Ind* 18.4, 10). His birthdate is unknown, though most scholars consider him coeval with the King and thus born ca. 360 (so Berve ii.269). But the crown prince's *hetairoi*, to which number Nearchus belonged in 336 (A 3.6.5; P*A* 10.4), should not be confused with Alexander's "boyhood friends": the latter were his *syntrophoi*. Alexander's *hetairoi* in 336 were, for the most part, older advisors of the prince (cf. D 19.69.1, for the case of Demetrius Poliorcetes; see Heckel 205–8). For his part in Alexander's dealings with Pixodarus, Nearchus was exiled along with his colleagues (A 3.6.5; P*A* 10.4) but promptly recalled after Philip's death. A grant of *proxenia* from the Delphians (*SIG*[3] 266) may date to this period (Tod ii.239 no. 182; Berve ii.269; but Wirth 1988: 258, with n. 85, argues for the late 290s).

In 334/3, Alexander installed him as satrap of Lycia and Pamphylia (A 3.6.6; cf. 1.24.4; cf. J 13.4.15), and it was perhaps in the period 334–330 that Nearchus developed ties with Antigonus the One-Eyed, with whom he is closely associated in the age of the Successors. Probably from Ecbatana, Alexander summoned Nearchus, who rejoined him at Bactra (Zariaspa) in the spring of 328, bringing mercenaries (A 4.7.2; cf. C 7.10.12: 4,000 infantry, 500 cavalry) in the company of Asander, the former satrap of Lydia.[447] Near Dyrta in the land of the Assacenians, Nearchus led a reconnaissance force of Agrianes and three chiliarchies of hypaspists under Antiochus

(A 4.30.5–6);[448] the results of the mission are not known.

In 326, Alexander ordered a fleet to be built at the Hydaspes (Jhelum), and Nearchus was designated its admiral (A 6.2.3; A*Ind* 18.10). This, at least, is Nearchus' own assertion. His trierarchy (A*Ind* 18.4) was, however, a financial responsibility, in the Attic fashion of public service (cf. P*Eum* 2.4–7 for Alexander's shortage of money). The voyage began in the autumn of that year (so Str 15.1.17 [691]), reaching the confluence of the Hydaspes and Acesines (Chenab) on the ninth or tenth day (thus A 6.4.1–4; but cf. Brunt ii.109). Here the fleet suffered considerable damage in the eddies and on the riverbanks where the ships ran aground (A 6.4.4–5.4; cf. C 9.4.9–14; D 17.97); Nearchus was entrusted with the repair of the vessels and ordered to sail to the borders of the Mallian territory and meet Alexander, who advanced by land.[449] Of Nearchus' activities from this point, until the fleet reached Patala, nothing is recorded. The descent of the river took, according to Aristobulus (*FGrH* 139 F35 = Str 15.1.17 [692]), ten months.[450]

From the Indus delta (perhaps from Xylinepolis, on the island of Cilluta: P*A* 66.1; Pl*NH* 6.96; cf. A 6.19.3), Nearchus and Onesicritus were ordered to sail to the Ocean and in the direction of the Euphrates (C 9.10.3; D 17.104.3; P*A* 66.3; A 6.19.5; A*Ind* 20ff.; Str 15.2.4 [721]). Despite Nearchus' attempts to make it seem otherwise (esp. A*Ind* 20), the actual naval responsibilities for the expedition were given to Onesicritus. Nearchus was commander-in-chief of the expedition (P*A* 66.3; Badian 1975: 153–60),[451] and his protestations about Onesicritus' mendacity appear to have been aimed at depriving the man of any credit for the undertaking.

The expedition is described in passionate detail by Nearchus (A*Ind* 20.1–42.10, contained in *FGrH* 133 F1) and Onesicritus (*ap.* Pl*NH* 6.96–100 = *FGrH* 134 F28) themselves. Attacks on the fleet by the natives, who were emboldened by Alexander's departure, forced Nearchus to set out on September 21 (20 Boedromion: A*Ind* 21.1; cf. Str 15.2.5 [721]) 325; but the fleet made slow progress, being forced by high winds to put in at a place which Nearchus named "Alexander's Harbor,"[452] where the island of Bibacta, two stades offshore, gave shelter for thirty-five days (A*Ind* 21.10–13). When the winds subsided (late October/early November), Nearchus led the expedition westward, establishing a camp at Cocala in Oreitan territory, where he received supplies for ten days from Leonnatus (A*Ind* 23.4–7).[453] Malnutrition and poor morale plagued the maritime expedition. Those who had posed disciplinary problems were left with Leonnatus; new sailors were recruited from the army (A*Ind* 23.8).

With fresh recruits Nearchus advanced to the Tomerus River (Hingol), about 300 stades east of what Nearchus called the last settlement of the Oreitae at Malana (A*Ind* 25.1; mod. Ras Malan). It was at the Tomerus River that he demonstrated his true talents, which reflect the nature of his training before he came to Macedonia from Crete. He had earlier been used by Alexander as a commander of light infantry (cf. A 4.30.5–6), and would be employed in a similar capacity by Antigonus in 317/6 (D 19.19.4–5). At this time, he led lightly armed troops, supported by archers on the ships anchored offshore, against the natives, who carried heavy wooden spears (with points hardened by fire), and easily routed them (A*Ind* 24). Nearchus' force must have included a sizeable contingent of Cretan archers (cf. A*Ind* 28.3, 5), and, although little is known about him, Archias son of Anaxidotus of Pella appears to have been placed on Nearchus' staff by Alexander for his military expertise.

The journey along the Makran coast and the villages of the Ichthyophagoi (or "Fish-Eaters") was marked by a scarcity of provisions, though date palms grew in places (A*Ind* 27.2; 29.1, 5), and plundering raids yielded little in the way of grain and a few animals (cf. A*Ind* 27.6–28.9, 29.5). At

Mosarna,[454] they took on board a Gedrosian guide, Hydraces, who led them as far as Carmania (*AInd* 26.10–27.1).[455] There, in December 325 (Beloch iii^2 2.321), Nearchus rejoined Alexander (C 10.1.10–15).[456] Alexander was allegedly reluctant to send him back to the coast and subject him to further risks (see Badian 1975: 160–5, rightly skeptical). In fact, it is hard to imagine that Alexander had any other plans for Nearchus than for him to sail on to the mouth of the Euphrates (C 10.1.16; D 17.107.1; cf. P*A* 68.6), whereafter he was to sail up the Pasitigris (Eulaeus) to Susa (A 6.28.6; *AInd* 36.4–9; Pl*NH* 6.99). The last leg of the voyage was considerably easier, and Nearchus' expedition proceeded to the mouth of the Euphrates and sailed as far as Diridotis, a village of Babylonia (Str 16.2.3 [766]). There it was learned that Alexander was not far from Susa (*AInd* 42.1), and Nearchus sailed back to the Pasitigris, eventually coming to a pontoon bridge, which Alexander's advance force had prepared for the King's crossing to Susa (*AInd* 42.7). The reuniting of the forces occurred in March 324.

Nearchus continued to Susa, witnessing on the way the self-immolation of Calanus (A 7.3.6 = *FGrH* 133 F4). At Susa, he was wedded to the daughter of Barsine and Mentor (A 7.4.6) – a fact which explains both Nearchus' support of Barsine's son, Heracles, as Alexander's successor (C 10.6.10–12) and his friendship with Eumenes (P*Eum* 18.6), who had married Artonis, a sister of Barsine (P*Eum* 1.7) – and crowned for his valorous achievements on the Ocean voyage (A 7.5.6; *AInd* 42.9 gives the impression that Nearchus and Leonnatus were crowned when the fleet and army were reunited; rejected by Badian 1975: 166). From Susa, Nearchus took Alexander by ship to the mouth of the Eulaeus (A 7.7.1), but thereafter the King sailed up the Tigris to rejoin Hephaestion at Opis (A 7.7.6), while Nearchus conducted the fleet up the Euphrates to Babylon (A 7.19.3). Here he was said to have brought the warnings of the Chaldaean astrologers to the King's attention (D 17.112.3–4; P*A* 73.1, with Hamilton 202–3). Alexander designated him admiral of his planned Arabian fleet (A 7.25.4; cf. P*A* 68.1, with Hamilton 187–9), a project cut short by the King's sudden death in Babylon. For it was after a banquet, which he had given in Nearchus' honor (P*A* 75.4), that Alexander went to the drinking-party in the home of Medius, at which he became fatally ill. Nearchus' part in the plot to poison Alexander is a fabrication of the Polyperchan camp (*LM* 97–8; Ps-Call 3.31.8–9; cf. Heckel 1988: 36).

J 13.4.15 says that Nearchus was assigned Lycia and Pamphylia in the division at Babylon, which appears to be an error, influenced by his earlier administration of the satrapy. But Nearchus clearly returned to Asia Minor and Antigonus' entourage, in whose service he captured Telmissus, where Antipatrides, an old friend of his (Pol*Strat* 5.35), had been installed, most likely by Attalus and Alcetas in 320/19 (cf. Billows 408). In 317/6 Antigonus sent him with a lightly armed force into Cossaean territory in order to seize passes of strategic importance to Eumenes (D 19.19.4–5). He accompanied Antigonus to Gabiene, and is said to have been one of the officers who begged him, unsuccessfully, to spare the life of the captive Eumenes (P*Eum* 18.6). Nearchus is last mentioned as one of four advisors (along with Andronicus, Peithon son of Agenor, and Philip) left by Antigonus with Demetrius Poliorcetes in Syria in 313/2 (D 19.69.1; chronology: Errington 1977: 498–500). Soon afterwards, he may have retired into private life, turning his attention to the publication of his historical account, an earlier version of which he had read to Alexander in the last days of his life (P*A* 76.3).[457]

Berve ii.269–72 no. 544; Tomaschek; Capelle, *RE* s.v. "Nearchos (3)"; Lehmann-Haupt in Papastavru 97–137 no. 61; Wirth 1972 and 1988; Badian 1975; Pédech 162–3; Sofman & Tsibukidis 1987; Billows 406–8 no. 77; Heckel 228–34. For his *History* see Jacoby, *FGrH* 133; Pearson 112–49.

Neiloxenus (Neiloxenos). Macedonian. Son of Satyrus. One of the *hetairoi*. In winter 330/29 he was installed as *episkopos* in Alexandria-in-the-Caucasus, along with the satrap Proexes (A 3.28.4). In 327, he was replaced by Nicanor, another *hetairos* (A 4.22.4–5).

Berve ii.272–3 no. 545.

Neon. Greek from Messenia. Son of Philiades. Leader of the pro-Macedonian party (Dem 18.295; cf. *Suda* N 231 = Theopompus, *FGrH* 115 F41; Plb 18.14.3). Neon and his brother Thrasylochus were exiled in 336/5, in the turmoil that followed Philip's death (Schaefer iii^2 115 n. 2), but reinstated as tyrants of Messenia soon afterwards on Alexander's orders ([Dem] 17.4, 7), probably in 333.

Berve ii.274 no. 550.

Neophon. See s.v. **Neophron**.

Neophron. (Perhaps Neophon). Sicyonian tragedian and friend of Callisthenes of Olynthus, Neophron accompanied Alexander on his campaign and, for allegedly plotting against the King, was tortured and killed along with Callisthenes (*Suda* N 218).[458]

Berve ii.273–4 no. 549.

Neoptolemus [1]. (Neoptolemos). Son of Arrhabaeus and brother of Amyntas (A 1.20.10). Arrian adds that he was one of those who deserted to the Persians, leaving little doubt that he was a grandson of Aëropus, and that he fled Macedonia after the arrest and execution of his father (cf. A 1.25.1). He perished in a skirmish at the gates of Halicarnassus (A 1.20.10; but D 17.25.5 places him on the Macedonian side, which is probably the result of carelessness).[459]

Berve ii.273 no. 547; Hofstetter 136 no. 230; Tataki 203 no. 12.

Neoptolemus [2]. (Neoptolemos). Neoptolemus' patronymic is unknown but he is described as one of the Aeacidae (A 2.27.6); hence he was a scion of the Molossian royal house (Beloch iv^2 2.145) and perhaps a relative of Arybbas the Somatophylax (cf. A 3.5.5). First attested at Gaza (late 332), where he was the first to scale the wall (A 2.27.6). This act of courage did not go unnoticed: he succeeded Nicanor son of Parmenion, who died of illness in 330, as *archihypaspistes* (P*Eum* 1.6), that is, as commander of the regular hypaspists (cf. Berve ii.273).[460] Neoptolemus may have been awarded the satrapy of Armenia in the settlement of 323, but the doctored text of Dexippus (*FGrH* 100 F8 §6) is suspect.[461] Briant 152 n. 8 is probably correct to regard him as *strategos* rather than satrap (cf. P*Eum* 4.1; 5.2). D 19.14.1, however, calls Philotas (sc. Philip; cf. Billows 90 n. 17) *strategos*, although he was clearly satrap of Parthia (D 18.39.6; A*Succ* 1.35). The satrapy was assigned by Alexander to Mithrenes in 331 (C 5.1.44); but Orontes, who commanded the Armenians at Gaugamela (A 3.8.5), is found ruling it in 317. He may have regained his ancestral territory at Triparadeisus, perhaps through the influence of his friend Peucestas. That Neoptolemus managed only to create havoc in Armenia (P*Eum* 4.1) suggests that he was not cooperating with any existing satrap.

When it became clear that war with Craterus and Antipater was imminent, Perdiccas assigned Cappadocia and Armenia to Eumenes and instructed both his brother Alcetas and Neoptolemus to obey the Greek commander (P*Eum* 5.2; D 18.29.2; J 13.6.15). Alcetas refused to serve, arguing that his Macedonians would be ashamed to fight against Craterus (P*Eum* 5.3). Neoptolemus remained with Eumenes but soon intrigued with Antipater (A*Succ* 1.26) and plotted betrayal (P*Eum* 5.4), presumably intending to defect with his forces to the enemy once the engagement had begun. Schubert 163 imagines a more important role for Neoptolemus: that he would keep Eumenes in check in Asia Minor while

Craterus and Antipater proceeded to Egypt. Eumenes, discovering the plot, brought him to battle and defeated him (P*Eum* 5.5; D 18.29.4–5; A*Succ* 1.27; cf. *PSI* xii.1284, with Bosworth 1978); Neoptolemus, however, escaped with some 300 horsemen (D 18.29.6; cf. P*Eum* 5.6; A*Succ* 1.27; J 13.8.5). Taking refuge with Craterus, he persuaded him that the Macedonians in Eumenes' service would receive him favorably (P*Eum* 6.1–2); for the mere sight of Craterus would be sufficient to turn the tide of battle. But, when Eumenes learned that Neoptolemus was stationed on the left (D 18.30.3, 31.1), he placed his Macedonian troops opposite him and deployed his barbarians on his own left, facing Craterus (P*Eum* 6.7; 7.3). The stratagem worked, and Craterus, uttering curses against Neoptolemus (P*Eum* 7.4), found the enemy stubborn in its resistance. As fate would have it, he perished in the engagement.[462] Felled by his adversary, and prevented by a wound to the knee from rising from the ground, Neoptolemus directed a feeble blow to Eumenes' groin as the Greek was already stripping the armor from his body, a heroic scene which does for Eumenes what Callisthenes had intended for Alexander in his description of the Granicus battle. One final thrust to the neck ended Neoptolemus' life (D 18.31.5; J 13.8.8). Since Craterus had already fallen, and with the right wing in disarray, Neoptolemus' death signaled total defeat (D 18.32.1; cf. 18.37.1). Eumenes' attitude to his defeated adversaries was mixed: he regarded Craterus with honor, Neoptolemus with contempt (P*Eum* 7.13). But to have overcome both opponents greatly enhanced his reputation (D 18.53.3). Neoptolemus was a man of great pride and warlike spirit (A*Succ* 1.27). At some point after 330 he, or perhaps his family, commissioned Apelles to depict him on horseback, fighting the Persians (Pl*NH* 35.96; Pollitt 162).

Anson 1990; Beloch iv^2 2.145–6; Berve ii.273 no. 548; Bosworth 1978; Heckel 300–2; Wirth 1965.

Neoptolemus [3]. (Neoptolemos). Neoptolemus II of Epirus (*regn.* 317–312, 302–297 BC). Son of Alexander I and Cleopatra, brother of Cadmeia; ruled Epirus after Pyrrhus was driven out. His rule was harsh and many Epirotes welcomed the return of Pyrrhus who shared power with him but soon put Neoptolemus to death (P*Pyr* 5). Cross 106–8 identifies him as grandson of Alcetas II (who also had a son Alexander), but this seems unlikely (cf. Hammond 1967: 558–68).

Berve ii.273 no. 546; Sandberger 164–70 no. 58.

Nicaea (Nikaia). Daughter of Antipater (Str 12.4.7 [565]; D 18.23.3; A*Succ* 1.21; StByz s.v. "Nikaia") and sister of Phila and Eurydice. In 322 she was brought by her brother Iolaus and a certain Archias to marry Perdiccas (A*Succ* 1.21); when Perdiccas was faced with the choice, Eumenes recommended that he marry Cleopatra, while Alcetas, his brother, favored Nicaea, and the latter won out, at least, temporarily (A*Succ* 1.21). Perdiccas had actually sought Nicaea's hand (D 18.23.1) to seal a pact with Antipater, but when Cleopatra became available he wanted to marry her and disguised his plot by marrying Nicaea first (D 18.23.2–3; J 13.6.5–6). Antipater learned of the deception (J 13.6.7) and made war on Perdiccas. Nicaea was subsequently given as a bride to Lysimachus.[463] By him she had at least three children:[464] Agathocles, Eurydice, and Arsinoë (I), who married Ptolemy II Philadelphus and bore Ptolemy III Euergetes. Whether Nicaea was still alive in 302, when Lysimachus married Amastris, is unknown.

Berve ii.274 no. 552; Seibert 1967: 16, 93; Ogden 57–8. See Stemmata V, IX.

Nicagoras (Nikagoras). Tyrant of Zeleia (Ath 7.289c). Aristus of Salamis (*FGrH* 143 F4)[465] claims that he lived in the time of Alexander and both dressed and had himself addressed as Hermes (cf. Baton of Sinope, *FGrH* 268 F2).[466] Supporter of

Darius III (that is, his regime was supported by the Persians). After the battle of the Granicus, Alexander pardoned the Zeleians since they had opposed him under pressure from Nicagoras (A 1.17.2), but in the city a democracy was instituted in 334/3 (*SIG*[3] 279) and Nicagoras was probably banished.

Berve ii.274 no. 551; Berve 1967: i.314, ii.679; Hofstetter 136 no. 231.

Nicanor [1]. (Nikanor). The second (?) of Parmenion's sons (A 1.14.2; 2.8.3; 3.11.9; D 17.57.2; C 3.9.7; 4.13.27; *Suda* N 376), Nicanor was the brother of Philotas and Hector. Philotas was apparently coeval with Amyntas son of Perdiccas and born ca. 365; Nicanor can scarcely have been born much later. The prominence of these brothers already in 335/4 must be seen as a reward for Parmenion's help in eliminating Alexander's rival Attalus (D 17.2.4–6, 5.2; C 7.1.3), his own son-in-law (C 6.9.17). Hence Nicanor, presumably as commander of the hypaspists, was given charge of the phalanx in the Getic campaign of 335 (A 1.4.2; cf. Berve ii.275). At the Granicus River (334), Nicanor is first positively identified as the hypaspist commander, holding a position just to the right of center on the Macedonian line, between the Companions and the battalions of the *pezhetairoi* (A 1.14.2). At Issus, Nicanor's hypaspists occupied the far right wing, with the *pezhetairoi* to their immediate left (A 2.8.3; C 3.9.7). But in the battle of Gaugamela they were again stationed in the center between the Companions and *pezhetairoi* (A 3.11.9; cf. C 4.13.27). Of Nicanor's actual participation in these battles nothing is known.

Alexander took with him in his pursuit of Darius, in the final days of that King's life, the most mobile of the infantry, the hypaspists and the Agrianes. But, when it became necessary to proceed only on horseback, he substituted some 500 mounted infantrymen for cavalry and pushed ahead with these *dimachae*, as they were called (C 5.13.8 says they were 300 strong).[467] Nicanor and Attalus (the commander of the Agrianes) were ordered to follow with the remaining troops (cf. C 5.13.19). Although the *archihypaspistes* would seem to be the superior officer, Arrian (3.21.8) treats Nicanor and Attalus as equals – perhaps Attalus was considerably senior, perhaps the special position of the Agrianes in Alexander's army was a factor. Not long afterwards, Nicanor died of illness in Areia (A 3.25.4; C 6.6.18), where Philotas remained to perform the funeral rites, retaining 2,600 men while Alexander himself continued in pursuit of the rebel Bessus (C 6.6.19). Nicanor's successor appears to have been Neoptolemus.

Berve ii.275 no. 554; Heckel 299–300; Tataki 383 no. 44. See Stemma VII.

Nicanor [2]. (Nikanor). Macedonian of unknown family. Born perhaps ca. 360. Commander of the "Hellenic fleet" in 334, which anchored at Lade and then moved into the harbor of Miletus to complete the blockade of the city (A 1.18.4–5, 19.3ff.). But Alexander soon disbanded this fleet (A 1.20.1) and Nicanor found himself without a command. The reconstituted Aegean fleet was entrusted to Hegelochus and Amphoterus. What became of Nicanor we do not know, although he could be identical with the son of Balacrus (*Suda* N 376, Harp). But if this is the case, his mother cannot have been Antipater's daughter, Phila (who can scarcely have been born earlier than 360), and it is less likely that his father was Alexander's Somatophylax (see s.v. **Balacrus** [2]). Given his naval experience it is tempting to identify him as Cassander's lieutenant in Munychia (see s.v. **Nicanor** [9]), the man who defeated Cleitus in the Propontis (but see the arguments of Bosworth 1994). See now Heckel 2007b.

Berve ii.275 no. 555; Bosworth i.137; Hauben 1972: 55–6; Tataki 380 no. 23.

Nicanor [3]. (Nikanor). Son of Antipater, brother of Cassander (D 19.11.8), and thus apparently from Paliura (Tataki 146). Berve ii.274 assumes that he was born ca. 350 and spent Alexander's reign at the court of his father, cf. Beloch iii[2] 2.84. In 317, after the deaths of Philip III Arrhidaeus and Adea-Eurydice, Olympias put Nicanor to death, claiming that she was avenging Alexander's death (D 19.11.8). Identification with Nicanor [10], the satrap of Cappadocia (D 18.39.6; A*Succ* 1.37; cf. App*Mithr* 8), and possibly the Nicanor of *LM* 117, makes it difficult to account for his presence in Macedonia in 317.

Berve ii.274 no. 553; Tataki 382 no. 40.

Nicanor [4]. (Nikanor). Macedonian. Son of Balacrus (*Suda N* 376, Harp), possibly the son of Alexander's Somatophylax, the later satrap of Cilicia (see s.v. **Balacrus** [2]), and an earlier wife (hence born ca. 360 and a brother of Philip [3]) or possibly a son of Antipater's daughter, Phila. Nothing is known for certain about his career. Bosworth speculates that he may have been born ca. 340 and Cassander's lieutenant in Athens. This Nicanor is usually identified as the Stageirite (e.g., Ferguson 28 n. 4; Berve ii.277), though the evidence is far from compelling (see s.v. **Nicanor** [9]). On the other hand, the view that Cassander's lieutenant and admiral was also his nephew makes it difficult to explain the elimination of Nicanor, a stepson of Demetrius Poliorcetes, at a time when Cassander was attempting to strengthen his alliances with his sister's husbands (see s.v. **Cassander**). It is equally, if not more, likely that Nicanor son of Balacrus is identical with Nicanor [12].

Bosworth 1994.

Nicanor [5]. (Nikanor). From Stageira (*Suda N* 376, Harp; Tataki 175 no. 5). Berve ii.276 suggests that the Nicanor described by StByz s.v. "Mieza" as *Miezaios* ("from Mieza") may be the same man and that he was educated with Alexander at Mieza and was thus a contemporary of the King. In 324 he was sent by Alexander to proclaim the "Exiles' Decree" at Olympia (D 18.8.3–4; DL 5.12; Hyp 1.14; Din 1.169; 1.175; D 17.109.1; C 10.2; J 13.5.3–4; Hyp 1.18.9–10). Whether he is identical with Cassander's commander of Munychia, as has generally been assumed, has now been called into question (see s.v. **Nicanor** [9]).

Berve ii.276–7 no. 557.

Nicanor [6]. (Nikanor). Macedonian. *Hetairos* of Alexander. In 327, Nicanor was left to set in order the affairs of Alexandria-in-the-Caucasus in tandem with the new satrap of Parapamisadae, Tyriespis (A 4.22.5). Nicanor replaced Neiloxenus, who had been appointed in 330/29 (A 3.28.4) and was apparently the *hyparchos* of the city deposed in 327 (A 4.22.4; *contra* Bosworth ii.145). He should not, however, be identified as *phrourarchos*. Nicanor may be the same man who was made satrap of the region to the west of the Indus (A 4.28.6), hence apparently also the *hyparchos* who was killed by the Assacenians in 326 (A 5.20.7).

Berve ii.275–6 no. 556.

Nicanor [7]. (Nikanor). Macedonian of unknown family. He was implicated in the Dimnus conspiracy of 330 (C 6.7.15), denounced and executed by stoning (C 6.11.38).

Berve ii.277 no. 558.

Nicanor [8]. (Nikanor). A prominent young Macedonian (*nobilis iuvenis*), probably a member of the "Royal Hypaspists," Nicanor (along with Hegesimachus) led a band of young men in an unsuccessful attack on an island in the Hydaspes River and perished in the attempt (C 8.13.13–16).

Berve ii.277 no. 560; Heckel 297.

Nicanor [9]. (Nikanor). Macedonian *phrourarchos* of Munychia, installed in 319/8 (P*Ph* 31.1–2). He was encouraged by Phocion to act as *agonothetes* and put on games in Athens (*PPh* 31.3). When he heard that Polyperchon was on his way to Attica – while Cassander had gone to Antigonus – he tried to persuade the Athenians to remain loyal to Cassander, stalling for time and secretly introducing more troops until he had sufficient troops to withstand a siege (D 18.64.1–2); furthermore, he captured Piraeus as well (D 18.64.3–4; N*Ph* 2.4–5; cf. 3.4; *PPh* 32). The Athenians sent Phocion, Conon son of Timotheus, and Clearchus son of Nausicles to negotiate autonomy for Athens, but Nicanor said he could do nothing without Cassander's approval (D 18.64.5–6). Olympias also wrote to Nicanor demanding that he restore Munychia and Piraeus, but Nicanor put off doing so. In Athens, Nicanor had the support of Phocion and the pro-Antipater politicians, and he also entered into negotiations with Alexander son of Polyperchon (D 18.65.3–5; *PPh* 33.1, 3), thus making it clear that neither party was interested in the good of the Athenians.[468] When Cassander arrived from Asia, Nicanor had firm control of Munychia and Piraeus (18.68.1–2). In 317, Nicanor was sent by Cassander with the entire fleet to oppose Cleitus in the Hellespont and Propontis (18.72.3–8; Pol*Strat* 4.6.8). After an initial setback, he defeated Cleitus in the Propontis and sailed into Piraeus with his fleet ornamented with the beaks of Cleitus' ships (D 18.75.1). His success went to his head and he incurred the suspicions of Cassander, who had him assassinated (D 18.75.1; Pol*Strat* 4.11.2). The long-accepted view that he is identical with the Stageirite, a nephew of Aristotle (Ferguson 28 with n. 4; see s.v. Nicanor [5]) is based on no good evidence. The most likely candidate is Nicanor [2].

Berve ii.276–7 no. 557; Bosworth 1994; Habicht 1997: 47–5.

Nicanor [10]. (Nikanor). Macedonian. Installed as satrap of Cappadocia (in place of Eumenes of Cardia) at Triparadeisus (D 18.39.6; A*Succ* 1.37; cf. App*Mithr* 8). Billows assumes that Nicanor did not take up his position in Cappadocia but remained with Antigonus; but D 18.59.1–2 does not require the replacement of Nicanor by Menander. Nicanor, the lieutenant of Antigonus Monophthalmus, who negotiated the surrender of Eumenes (*PEum* 17.5), is probably a different indiviual. See s.vv. **Menander** [1] and **Nicanor** [3], with notes.

Billows 409–10 no. 79; Takaki 380 no. 26.

Nicanor [11]. (Nikanor). Macedonian, *philos* of Ptolemy I Soter. At some point in 320/19 he took an adequate force into Coele-Syria, capturing the territory and its satrap Laomedon; Nicanor placed garrisons in Phoenicia and returned to Egypt after a "short and effective campaign" (D 18.43.2). Nothing else is known about him, but Berve ii.277 reasonably assumes that he held some higher office already under Alexander.

Berve ii.277 no. 559.

Nicanor [12]. (Nikanor). Macedonian. Officer and presumably *philos* of Antigonus the One-Eyed. He negotiated the surrender of Eumenes after the battle of Gabiene (*PEum* 17.5). He appears to have been the same man whom Antigonus installed as satrap of Media in 315, assigning him the *strategia* of the Upper Satrapies (D 19.92.1–5, 100.3; App*Syr* 55 [278], 57 [292–3]; cf. Schober 97–103; Bengtson i.183–5). He may, however, be identical with Nicanor son of Balacrus, assuming that this man was a son of Balacrus by a wife other than Phila.

Nicarchides [1]. (Nikarchides). Apparently Macedonian; family background unknown. In 331/0 he was appointed *phrourarchos* of Persepolis and placed in charge of a garrison of 3,000 men (C 5.6.11). Identification with the trierarch of the Hydaspes fleet (below), though unlikely, is not impossible.

Berve ii.278 no. 563; Tataki 384 no. 49.

Nicarchides [2]. (Nikarchides). Macedonian from Pydna. Son of Simus. In 326 he was appointed a trierarch of the Hydaspes fleet (A*Ind* 18.5). Nothing else is known about him.

Berve ii.278 no. 562; Tataki 171 no. 12.

Nicesias (Nikesias). Flatterer in Alexander's entourage. Apparently a Greek, though his family background is unknown. He was one of the flatterers (*kolakes*) who encouraged Alexander's belief in his own divinity (Phylarchus *ap.* Ath 6.251c = *FGrH* 81 F11; Hegesander *ap.* Ath 6.249d–e).

Berve ii.278 no. 564.

Nicesipolis (Nikasipolis, Nikesipolis). Thessalian (Paus 8.7.7; Ath 13.557d). Niece of Jason of Pherae (StByz s.v. "Thessalonike"), a relationship which seems to rule out the suggestion (Green 1982: 143–4) that she was a mere concubine. Married Philip II in 352 or 346, as the name of her daughter suggests (Paus 9.7.3). Since Thessalonice did not marry until 315, the latter date is far more likely.[469] Her beauty won the admiration of even her rival Olympias (P*M* 141b–c). Mother of Thessalonice (Satyrus *ap.* Ath 13.557d). She died on the twentieth day after giving birth to her daughter (StByz s.v. "Thessalonike").

Carney 60–1; Ogden 18–19. See Stemma I.

Nicias (Nikias). Family background unknown and place of origin unknown; apparently a Greek in Alexander's entourage.[470] Nicias was placed in charge of the assessment and collection of tribute in Lydia in 334. He was probably subordinate to the newly appointed satrap, Asander son of Philotas (A 1.17.7). Nothing else is known about him.

Berve ii.278 no. 565.

Nicocles [1]. (Nikokles). Son of Pasicrates of Soli (A*Ind* 18.8), possibly brother of Eunostus. He accompanied Alexander since 331, if not already in 332, and is named as one of the trierarchs of the Hydaspes fleet; hence Nicocles may be counted among Alexander's non-Macedonian *hetairoi*. Identification with the envoy sent to Abisares in 326 is a strong possibility.

Berve ii.278–9 no. 566; Berve, *RE* s.v. "Nikokles (4)."

Nicocles [2]. (Nikokles). Apparently the son of Timarchus. Dynast of Paphos[471] on Cyprus and husband of Axiothea (D 20.21.2; Pol*Strat* 8.48). He was a rival of Straton of Sidon (Ael*VH* 7.2). In 321/0 he sided with Ptolemy against Perdiccas (A*Succ* 24.6). In 310, however, it was discovered that he had secretly formed an alliance with Antigonus the One-Eyed, and Menelaus, the brother of Ptolemy, sent Argaeus and Callicrates against him. These ordered him to commit suicide, which he did; his wife Axiothea slew their daughters and committed suicide as well (D 20.21.1–3; cf. Pol*Strat* 8.48). For the confusion of Nicocles and Nicocreon see Gesche 1974.

Stähelin, *RE* s.v. "Nikokles (3)"; Berve ii.279 no. 567; Bagnall 40–2.

Nicocles [3]. (Nikokles). Greek. Sent by Alexander in 326 to negotiate the submission of the Indian dynast Abisares (*ME* 55; cf. D 17.90.4 and C 9.1.7–8, neither of whom names Nicocles). Nicocles appears to have rejoined Alexander on the way to the Hyphasis (thus *ME* 65) or at the Acesines, when Alexander had returned from the Hyphasis (A 5.29.4–5). Berve identifies him with the son of Pasicrates.

Berve ii.278–9 no. 566.

Nicocreon (Nikokreon). Son and successor of Pnytagoras as king of Cypriot Salamis. Pnytagoras had defected to Alexander after Issus and served with his ships at Tyre (A 2.22.2). In 332/1, when Alexander returned from Egypt to Phoenicia, Nicocreon is already attested as king of Salamis, and he and Pasicrates of Soli served as *choregoi* for dramatic competitions: Nicocreon supported Thessalus (Alexander's favorite, who was defeated in the contest) and Pasicrates, Athenodorus (P*A* 29.2–4). He was also insulted by Anaxarchus, whom he later captured and put to death (see s.v. **Anaxarchus**; DL 9.58; cf. *PA* 28.4; DL 9.59; Val Max 3.3 ext 4; P*M* 449e).[472] He supported Ptolemy against Perdiccas in 321/0 (A*Succ* 24.6), and remained a supporter of Ptolemy (D 19.59.1, 62.5), who made him *strategos* of Cyprus (D 19.79.5),[473] until his death in 311/0 (*MP*, *FGrH* 239 F17). He is wrongly identified by Machon *ap*. Ath 8.349e as the husband of Axiothea (but see Gesche 1974).

Berve ii.279 no. 568; *Pros Ptol* 15059; Gesche 1974; Bagnall 39–40.

Nicomachus (Nikomachos). Low-born Macedonian – Curtius calls him *exoletus* (6.7.2, 8) and *scortum* (6.7.33), that is, a male prostitute – who despite his station in life retained a modicum of decency (C 6.7.13). Brother of Cebalinus and lover of Dimnus (D 17.79.1–2; C 6.7.2, 16; *PA* 49.3–4) of Chalaestra, whose "conspiracy" set the stage for the so-called "Philotas affair." Dimnus attempted to involve him in the plot and revealed the identities of the conspirators, and Nicomachus reported all the details to his brother (C 6.7.2–16; *PA* 49.4). Nicomachus remained in his tent while Cebalinus attempted to bring the matter to the King's attention (C 6.7.16), but two days later he was summoned by the King and corroborated Cebalinus' information (C 6.8.1–2). Nicomachus later gave testimony before the Macedonian assembly (C 6.9.7; cf. D 17.79.6), to which Philotas later responded, questioning Nicomachus' reliability (C 6.10.5–7, 16; see s.v. **Philotas** [4] for his part). But ultimately, Philotas, and those named by Nicomachus – as well as Calis, who had not been named but confessed – were executed (C 6.11.37–8). See also s.vv. **Dimnus**, **Cebalinus**. It appears that Nicomachus himself escaped punishment.

Berve ii.279–80 no. 569.

Nicon (Nikon). Runaway slave of Craterus, Nicon was recaptured, presumably in Persia, by Peucestas, who received written praise from Alexander (*PA* 42.1). The episode seems to have occurred in 324, after Peucestas' appointment as satrap and before Craterus left Opis with the discharged veterans.

Berve ii.280 no. 571.

Niphates. Prominent Persian. Niphates was one of the commanders at the Granicus battle (A 1.12.8); he was killed in the engagement (A 1.16.3).

Berve ii.280 no. 573.

Nithaphon. Cypriot. Son of King Pnytagoras of Salamis. In 332 or 331 he appears to have joined Alexander's entourage, along with his younger brother Nicocreon, perhaps as hostages. He is attested in India as a trierarch of the Hydaspes fleet (A*Ind* 18.8). Nothing else is known of his career.

Berve ii.280 no. 572.

O

Ochus (Ochos). Son of Darius III and Stateira, his name occurs only in Curtius (4.11.6, 14.22) and the *Fragmentum Sabbaiticum* (*FGrH* 151 F1 §5). Born in 338 (he was in his sixth year at the end of 333: C 3.11.24; D 17.38.2). Ochus accompanied his father to Issus, where he was captured, along with his mother, sisters, and grandmother (D 17.36.2, 37.3–38.3; C 3.11.24–12.26; cf. 4.14.22; A 2.11.9). Alexander and Hephaestion admired his courage, which they deemed greater than that of his father (D 17.38.2; cf. C 3.12.26). J neither mentions his capture nor includes him in the terms of the diplomatic negotiations that occurred between the winter of 333/2 and summer 331 (cf. C 4.11.6, where Darius proposes that Alexander retain Ochus as a hostage in exchange for a peace settlement); but the omission of Ochus can be attributed to imprecise abbreviation of Trogus. Ochus was left behind in Susa in 330, with his grandmother and sisters (D 17.67.1; C 5.2.17). What became of him we do not know. If he did not die of natural causes before 324/3, he may have been murdered shortly before, or soon after, Alexander's death: certainly, the political motives behind the murder of Stateira and her sister by Rhoxane and Perdiccas (P*A* 77.6) must have pertained to Ochus as well.

Berve ii.409–10 no. 833. See Stemma III.

Olympias. Epirot princess. Daughter of Neoptolemus and sister of Troas (J 7.6.10–11) and Alexander I of Epirus (J 8.6.4–5; cf. 17.3.14–16; D 19.51.6, 72.1); niece and sister-in-law of Arybbas (J 7.6.10–11). Descended from Pyrrhus son of Achilles and, on her mother's side, from the Trojan prince Helenus (Theopompus, *FGrH* 115 F355); hence one of the Aeacidae.[474] Leonidas, Alexander the Great's tutor, was also a kinsman (P*A* 5.7). As a child she was called Polyxena and then, at marriage, Myrtale; later in life she was also known as Olympias and Stratonice (P*M* 401a–b; J 9.7.13; cf. Heckel 1981a). In 357 BC she married Philip II, whom she had met as a child on Samothrace (P*A* 2.2; cf. C 8.1.26; Himerius *ap.* Phot p.367a [ed. Bekker]; J 7.6.10–11; Satyrus *ap.* Ath 13.557c), to whom she bore first Alexander on July 20, 356 BC[475] and later Cleopatra (D 16.91.4; Ath 13.557c; see s.v. **Cleopatra** [2]); App*Syr* 54 [275] wrongly calls Arrhidaeus Olympias' son. Since the news of Alexander's birth coincided with that of Philip's Olympic victory, it may be at this point and for this reason that Myrtale's name was changed to Olympias (P*A* 3.8; cf. J 12.16.6; Macurdy 24). Her pedigree is celebrated in an anonymous epigram (P*M* 747f–748a; cf. D 19.51.6). Stories that she slept with Zeus (= Amun), who disguised himself as a snake, were doubtless fabricated after Alexander's visit to Siwah (P*A* 3.3–4; cf. Gell 13.4.13; A 4.10.2; cf. Cic *De divinatione* 2.135); that she was a devotee of exotic cults and maenadism (P*A* 2.8–9; Ath 14.659f–660a; cf. Duris, *FGrH* 76 F52 = Ath 13.560f) is probably true. As far as her personality is concerned, she is described as high-minded (P*M* 243d), jealous, and brooding (PA 9.5). As a mother she was domineering and interfering, yet she retained her son's love until the end (cf. PA 39.13; C 5.2.22; 9.6.26; 10.5.30) and corresponded with him during his absence (Ath 14.659f–660a; A 6.1.4–5; *ME* 87; PA 39.7–8; cf. her complaints about Antipater, below). Her concern about her son's apparent lack of interest in women caused her (in consultation with Philip) to encourage him to have sexual relationships with the courtesan Callixeina (Hieronymus of Rhodes, citing Theophrastus *ap.* Ath 10.435a). Philip's letters to Olympias were intercepted but unopened by the Athenians (PM 799e; P*Demetr* 22.2); and the fact that in 341 Anaxinus of Oreus was making purchases for Olympias in Athens (Dem 18.137; cf. Aes 3.223) shows that her relationship with Philip endured well beyond the births of their two children.

Although jealous of Philip's other wives, she appears to have been complimentary about the charms of Nicesipolis (PM 141b–c). Her rivalry with Cleopatra, the niece of Attalus, will have had to do with her concerns about Alexander's rights of inheritance (A 3.6.5; Ath 13.557d–e; PA 9.6–10), but the story that she was "divorced" on the grounds of adultery (*stuprum*) is a fabrication (J 9.5.9), as is the claim that she corrupted the mind of young Arrhidaeus (Philip's son by Philine) by giving him drugs (PA 77.8). Nevertheless, A 3.6.5, speaking of the dishonoring of Olympias, may well refer to Cleopatra's recognition as Philip's "queen" (Heckel 1978a). After the quarrel of Alexander and Attalus on the occasion of Philip's wedding to Cleopatra (Ath 13.557d; PA 9.6–10; J 9.7.3–4), Olympias took refuge with her brother Alexander I of Epirus, whom she tried unsuccessfully to incite to war against her husband (J 9.7.5, 7; PA 9.11). But Philip's decision to marry his (and Olympias') daughter, Cleopatra, to Alexander I was intended not, as some scholars have claimed,[476] to drive a wedge between brother and sister but rather to effect a reconciliation with his Epirote family. Although she returned to Pella,[477] Olympias was not fully reconciled with her husband and encouraged Alexander to believe that his father meant to cut him out of the succession; for thus she appears to have depicted Philip's plans to marry Arrhidaeus to the daughter of Pixodarus (PA 10.1; see s.vv. **Ada** [2], **Pixodarus**). She was also believed to have incited the assassin Pausanias, who had been humiliated by Attalus (J 9.7.2). That she favored and perhaps encouraged Philip's assassination is credible but there can be no proof (J 9.7.1–2, 8; PA 10.5), but accounts that she openly acknowledged her role are doubtless false (J 9.7.10–14). On the other hand, it is quite plausible that she brought about the murder of Cleopatra and her young child (PA 10.7; J 9.7.12; Paus 8.7.7). Alexander was distressed by this action, if not for personal, then certainly for political reasons (PA 10.8; cf. Burstein 1982).

Of her activities in Macedonia during her son's absence we know little: she is said to have written to warn him against Alexander Lyncestes (D 17.32.1; cf. C 7.1.6); she made a dedication to Hygeia in Athens in 333 (Hyp *In Defense of Euxenippus* 19); and, in 332/1, she objected to the recruitment by Amyntas son of Andromenes of some youths from her court (C 7.1.37–8).[478] Whether she was still in Macedonia when she made the dedication of spoils at Delphi in 331/0 (*SIG*[3] 252) is unclear. Certainly it was not much later that she quarreled with Antipater (perhaps after his return from the Peloponnese) and withdrew to Epirus, sending Cleopatra back to Macedonia at some point after 330 (*LM* 87–8; 96–7; D 18.49.4; Paus 1.11.3; PA 68.4–5; cf. 77.21; A 7.12.6–7; D 18.49.4; J 12.14.3; Hyp *In Defense of Euxenippus* 25).[479]

After her son's death (for her grief see Ael*VH* 13.30), she could not refrain from meddling in the affairs of the Successors: after inducing Cleopatra to offer herself in marriage to Leonnatus (who promptly met his death in the Lamian War), she sent her to Perdiccas (A*Succ* 1.21; J 13.6.4–5,

11–13). Although this scheme also came to naught, she soon received an appeal from Polyperchon that she return to Macedonia and assume the *epimeleia* and *prostasia* of Alexander IV (D 18.49.4, 57.2; hence also her favorable treatment in the *Last Days and Testament*: *LM* 115–16, 122; cf. Heckel 1988: 52; cf. Baynham 1998b); if Polyperchon imagined that Olympias would be content to act as a mere figurehead, he was mistaken. Olympias wrote first to Eumenes for his advice (D 18.58.2–3) and received a reply that urged caution and suggested that she remain in Epirus for the time being (D 18.58.4). Olympias did, however, play a role in the struggle between Polyperchon and Cassander, writing a letter to Nicanor, the commander of Munychia, ordering him to restore the fort and Piraeus to the Athenians (D 18.65.1–2), but her orders were disregarded (D 18.74.1). With the help of her nephew Aeacides, she prepared to return to Macedonia, and met her opponent Adea-Eurydice at Euia (Paus 1.11.3–4; Duris *ap.* Ath 13.560f = *FGrH* 76 F52; J 14.5.1–10; D 19.11.1–8; Ael*VH* 13.36; P*A* 77.2); her very presence induced the Macedonians to desert, but she followed up the victory by putting to death Philip III Arrhidaeus (J 14.5.10; D 19.11.4–5) and Adea-Eurydice (J 14.5.10; D 19.11.6–7; Ael*VH* 13.36),[480] and taking vengeance on her political enemies (D 19.11.8–9, 35.1; cf. Paus 1.11.4). But the tide soon turned against Polyperchon and his supporters,[481] and Olympias and her entourage, which included Thessalonice, Rhoxane, Alexander IV, and his betrothed, Deidameia (D 19.35.5; J 14.6.2–3), were besieged at Pydna (D 19.36.1–2; J 14.6.4), waiting in vain for help from Aeacides and Polyperchon (D 19.36.2, 5–6). An escape attempt apparently miscarried (Pol*Strat* 4.11.3; D 19.50.4) and, on the point of starvation (D 19.49.1–50.2), Olympias surrendered to Cassander on the promise of her own personal safety (D 19.50.5; J 14.6.5). This was, however, disregarded and Cassander, after first gaining approval for the act from the assembled Macedonians, had her put to death by relatives of her victims (D 19.51; J 14.6.6–12).

Berve ii.283–8 no. 581; Strasburger, *RE* s.v. "Olympias (5)"; Macurdy 22–44; Carney 1987a and 1993; O'Neil 1999; Carney 62–7, 85–8, 119–23. See Stemmata I, II.

Omares. Persian. Commander of 20,000 mercenaries at the Granicus River (A 1.14.4; cf. 1.16.3);[482] Omares died in the battle (A 1.16.3).

Berve ii.409 no. 832.

Ombrion. Cretan. Ombrion was appointed *toxarches* by Alexander in Egypt in 331 (A 3.5.6) to replace the Macedonian Antiochus. At Gaugamela we find the Macedonian archers commanded by a certain Brison (A 3.12.2). Neither *toxarches* is heard of again and it is likely that Brison is an error for Ombrion.[483]

Berve ii.288 no. 582.

Onesicritus (Onesikritos). Greek from Aegina or Astypylaea (A*Ind* 18.9; Ael*NA* 16.39; DL 6.84). Son of Philiscus (A*Ind* 18.9), father of the younger Philiscus and Androsthenes. The elder Philiscus was said to have been a teacher (*grammatodidaskalos*) of Alexander (*Suda* Φ 359; see s.v. **Philiscus**), but this may be an invention based on the fact that Onesicritus wrote a work on the education of Alexander. Onesicritus is said to have sent first one, then the other, of his sons to Diogenes of Sinope, and that both fell under the philosopher's spell. Finally, Onesicritus too became a student of Diogenes (DL 6.75–6;[484] cf. P*A* 65.2; P*M* 331e; Str 15.1.65 [716]). The story, if it is true, means that Onesicritus must have been around 40 in the mid-330s and in his early fifties when he participated in Alexander's naval expedition down the Indus and on to Mesopotamia. What Onesicritus did in the years before the Indian campaign is unknown, although it seems he was with the expedition from the start (DL 6.84). At Taxila, he was sent to Calanus and

Dandamis (Onesicritus, *FGrH* 134 F17a = Str 15.1.63–5; cf. F17b = P*A* 65.3). When the Hydaspes fleet was formed, he was appointed helmsman of Alexander's ship (A 7.5.6; A 7.20.9; A*Ind* 18.9; and, perhaps, by virtue of this position, *archikybernetes* or "chief helmsman"; Str 15.1.28, 2.4; P*A* 66.3; A 6.2.3 criticizes Onesicritus for falsely claiming to be *nauarchos*). It appears that Onesicritus had the naval (technical) expertise that Nearchus lacked, and once the ocean voyage began Nearchus was in charge of the direction of the expedition and the command of the forces, whereas Onesicritus was responsible for the safety of the ships (the disagreement at Maceta is one of policy: A*Ind* 32.9–13).[485] In 324, Onesicritus and Nearchus both received a golden crown for their achievements (A 7.5.6; A*Ind* 42.9, which derives from Nearchus, makes no mention of Onesicritus). Very soon after Alexander's death, he wrote that the King had been poisoned – perhaps his aim was to discredit his political enemies – though he did not name the perpetrators of the crime for fear of reprisals; but he no doubt thought that most contemporaries were familiar with the names of those who attended Medeius' dinner-party, at which the King became ill (*LM* 97). How long Onesicritus lived is uncertain: P*A* 46.4 speaks of Onesicritus reading his *History* to Lysimachus, "who was already king," which implies that he was still alive in 306.[486]

As a historian (see Jacoby, *FGrH* 134; Brown; Pearson 83–111), Onesicritus modeled himself on Xenophon, writing an *Education of Alexander* to rival Xenophon's *Cyropaedia*,[487] though his style was said to have been inferior (DL 6.84); he was noted for his flattery (Lucian, *How to Write History* 40) but not for his veracity (P*A* 46.4; Str 15.1.28; cf. Str 11.1.9; Gell 9.4.1–3; A*Ind* 3.6, 6.8).

Berve ii.288–90 no. 583; Brown.

Onomastoridas (Onomas). Spartan ambassador to Darius III, sent out in all likelihood in connection with the activities of Agis III in Greece. He was captured, along with Callicratidas, Monimus, and Pausippus, soon after the death of Darius in 330 (A 3.24.4). C 3.13.15 mistakenly places his capture at Damascus in 333.

Berve ii.290–1 no. 584; Poralla no. 580; Hofstetter 140 no. 240.

Ophellas [1]. Olynthian of unknown family. Ophellas is attested only once, in [Arist]*Oecon* 2.35 p. 1353a, who reports that he was guilty of extortion in Athribis in the southern Nile Delta, perhaps in the period shortly before Alexander's death when Cleomenes was supposed to have been guilty of financial mismanagement. Identification with Ophellas son of Seilenus is impossible. Nothing else is known about him.

Berve ii.297 no. 599; Wilcken 1901: 195–6.

Ophellas [2]. (Ophelas). For the name see Hoffmann 199. Son of Seilenus; Macedonian from Pella (A*Ind* 18.3, A*Succ* 1.17). Of his career under Alexander, we know virtually nothing, except for his role as trierarch in 326 (cf. D 20.40.1 for his service under Alexander). He appears to have gone to Egypt with Ptolemy in 323. When Thibron made his bid to control Cyrene (see s.v. **Thibron**), some of the well-to-do exiles appealed to Ptolemy, who sent Ophellas as *strategos* to the aid of the city with a large force of infantry and ships (D 18.21.7; A*Succ* 1.17); he defeated the Cyrenaeans and captured Thibron, whom he handed over to the people of Teucheira to torture (D 18.21.8–9; A*Succ* 1.18). Cyrene became part of the Ptolemaic kingdom, and Ophellas appears to have remained as its governor. But we hear nothing about him until 309/8, when Agathocles of Syracuse sent Orthon to Cyrene to urge Ophellas to join in the subjugation of the Carthaginians. The alliance appealed to Thibron, who aspired to greater power, especially since Agathocles relinquished any claims to Libya (D 20.40.1–4;

J 22.7.5, saying that Ophellas initiated the alliance). Ophellas, furthermore, recruited mercenaries from the Athenians – he had married Euthydice, daughter of Miltiades, a descendant of the famous Athenian general (D 20.40.5; P*Demetr* 14.1; see Davies 309), by whom he had a son named Miltiades (*IG* ii^2 6630)[488] – and other Greek states (D 20.40.6–7). With a large army he marched westward (D 20.41.1–2), suffering great hardships along the way and finally linking up with Agathocles' forces (D 20.42.1–2). Soon after their arrival, however, Agathocles betrayed Ophellas and, claiming that he was plotting against him, attacked the Cyrenaean force, killed Ophellas and took over his army (D 20.42.3–5; cf. 20.43.3–4; cf. J 22.7.5–6; *Suda* O 994; cf. *Suda* Δ 431). There is a story that Ophellas was infatuated with Agathocles' son, Heracleides, whom Agathocles had sent to him as hostage and a distraction, knowing that he was fond of boys (Pol*Strat* 5.3.4; J 22.7.6 says he adopted the boy). Thus caught off guard, Ophellas was attacked by Agathocles. His death occurred in 308.

Berve ii.296 no. 598; Gude no. 102 (confused); *Pros Ptol* 15062; Osborne T86.

Ordanes. Justi 351, "Wardan (1)"; C calls him Ozines. Persian leader who had incited rebellion in Drangiana or Arachosia. He was captured and brought to Alexander by Craterus, who had returned from India via the Bolan Pass. The King learned of the arrest of Ordanes (and Zariaspes) while he was in Gedrosia; Craterus and his captives rejoined Alexander in Carmania (A 6.27.3; C 9.10.19; 10.1.9), where Ordanes and Zariaspes were executed.

Berve ii.293–4 no. 590.

Orontes. A Persian noble, descended from Hydarnes, one of the Seven, as we learn from Str 11.14.15 [531], referring to the last member of this family, which ruled Armenia from at least the reign of Artaxerxes II (Xen*Anab* 3.4.17; cf. 4.3.4; Lehmann-Haupt 127) until the time of Antiochus III. Hence Orontes is probably to be identified as the satrap of Armenia under Darius III (he may, in fact, have succeeded Darius in this position; J 10.3.4; cf. Osborne 1973: 520), commanding the satrapal contingent at Gaugamela (A 3.8.5; Mithraustes, who is named with him, appears to have led the infantry; cf. Berve ii.295). It appears that, after the battle, he escaped to his satrapy, which Alexander assigned to Mithrenes, the former citadel-commander of Sardis (A 3.16.5; D 17.64.6; C 5.1.44). But the latter is not heard of again, and may have perished in an unsuccessful attempt to wrest the territory from Orontes, who is found again in charge of Armenia in 317 (D 19.23.3; Pol*Strat* 4.8.3). Bosworth i.315–16 thinks that he may have surrendered to Alexander soon after Gaugamela, and that the friendship between Peucestas and Orontes (Pol*Strat* 4.8.3) developed in the years 331–324, when Orontes was at the court of Alexander. But it seems not unlikely that Peucestas, satrap of Persis, came to know the most important members of the Persian aristocracy. In all likelihood, Armenia, which was bypassed by the Macedonian army, was never part of Alexander's empire.

The possible awarding of the satrapy to Neoptolemus in 323 (Dexippus, *FGrH* 100 F8 §6; cf. P*Eum* 4.1; 5.2; Briant 1973: 152 n. 8 thinks he was *strategos* rather than *satrapes*) may have been contingent upon his ability to conquer the territory (cf. P*Eum* 4.1; 5.2). Neoptolemus created havoc in the satrapy (P*Eum* 4.1), but Orontes appears to have regained his position after the former's death in 320 BC. Nothing further is known about him. Berve wrongly asserts that he married the daughter of Artaxerxes II, Rhodogune (P*Art* 27.4; cf. Xen*Anab* 2.4.8), who may, however, have been his mother (cf. Beloch iii^2 2.141, dating Orontes' birth ca. 386)[489] or grandmother (Judeich 225).

Berve ii.295 no. 593; Justi 235 no. 7; Osborne 1973; Bosworth i.315–16.

Orontopates (Orontobates).[490] Prominent Persian, as is clear from his later position at Gaugamela (331 BC) and son-in-law of Pixodarus, who had usurped the satrapy of Caria (A 1.23.8); he was thus the husband of the younger Ada, who had at one point been offered to Arrhidaeus. Orontopates was given charge of the satrapy by Darius III after the death of Pixodarus in 334, and he defended it, and its chief city, Halicarnassus, with the help of Memnon, even after Alexander had returned Caria to Ada (A 1.23.8; cf. D 17.24.2). After a spirited but unsuccessful defense of Halicarnassus, Orontopates escaped to join Darius and is attested as one of the commanders at Gaugamela, but nothing is known of his role in the battle or his subsequent fate (A 3.8.5; C 4.12.7).[491]

Berve ii.295–6 no. 594. See Stemma XVI.

Oropius (Oropios). The name is uncertain and looks more like an ethnic, but it could be a corruption of an Iranian name. Dexippus makes the curious comment that Oropius ruled Susiana not by "ancestral right" but as an appointee of Alexander (Dexippus, *FGrH* 100 F8 §6). Such a remark would not have been made about a Graeco-Macedonian official. Berve ii.57 no. 107 wishes to identify him with Argaeus of Oropus (cf. *LM* 121). But there is no indication that Argaeus came from Oropus and a greater likelihood that Argaeus is a corruption of, or error for, Oropius. Oropius was undoubtedly appointed to replace Abulites, who was executed in 324 for failure to supply Alexander during the Gedrosian campaign. Charged with inciting rebellion, Oropius was deposed, fled, and perished. His successor was Coenus (Dexippus, *FGrH* 100 F8 §6; cf. *LM* 121; J 13.4.14).

Berve ii.57 no. 107 ("Argaios").

Orsilus (Orsilos; Orsillus).[492] Prominent Persian. Orsilus surrendered to Alexander, together with Mithrazenes, in 330 after Darius' arrest by Bessus and the conspirators (C 5.13.9). Nothing else is known about him.

Berve ii.296 no. 595; Justi 236.

Orsodates. A barbarian rebel, Orsodates was reportedly killed by Alexander himself (*PA* 57.3). The context of the incident is unknown.[493]

Berve ii.296 no. 596.

Orthagoras. Str 16.3.5 [766]; Ael*NA* 17.6. Author of a work called *Indikoi Logoi*, mentioned by both Nearchus and Onesicritus. Berve believes he was a contemporary and companion of the two. But there is nothing to link him directly with Alexander.[494]

Berve ii.294 no. 591.

Orxines (Orsines). Descended from one of the Seven and also from Cyrus the Great (C 4.12.8; 10.1.23); commanded the Persians, Mardians, and Sogdiani at Gaugamela (C 4.12.8; less accurately, A 3.8.5) and later governed Persia (without Alexander's approval) since the death of Phrasaortes, which occurred while Alexander was in India (A 6.29.2, 30.1). Alexander executed him in 324 on charges of plundering temples and royal tombs and putting innocent Persians to death; he was hanged (impaled) by those to whom the task was assigned (A 6.30.2); Peucestas was his successor. Curtius ascribes Orxines' death to the machinations of the eunuch Bagoas (C 10.1.22–38).

Berve ii.294 no. 592.

Ostanes. A magus who, on Alexander's order, accompanied the King from Persis onward (Pl*NH* 30.3, 11; Apul*Apol* 1.326; Euseb 1.43; Syncellus 198; Tatian *ad Gr* 75 Schw.). Nothing else is known about him.

Berve ii.296 no. 597.

Oxathres (Oxanthes; Oxoathres). Perhaps more correctly "Oxyathres" (cf. below s.v.); *PA* 68.7 has "Oxyartes." Son of Abulites, satrap of Susiana, Oxathres commanded at Gaugamela the Uxians and Susians (A

3.8.5), who were positioned on the left side toward the center (A 3.11.3); he was thus acting as military leader on behalf of his father, who may have been unfit for such service. The fact that Oxathres appears to have acted as the agent in Abulites' surrender to Alexander may support this view (A 3.16.6). Alexander appointed Oxathres satrap of Paraetacene (A 3.19.2; C 5.2.8–9), which he appears to have governed until 325, when he was executed along with his father for maladministration (A 7.4.1; cf. *PA* 68.7, who says that Abulites had failed to send supplies in accordance with Alexander's instructions, apparently during the Gedrosian campaign, and that Alexander felled Oxathres with his lance).

Berve ii.291 no. 585; Justi 232 no. 4.

Oxicanus (Oxykanos). The form Oxycanus (given by Berve no. 587) is unattested in the MSS. Indian dynast, *nomarches* of a region of Sind, perhaps based at the city of Azeika (Pt*Geog* 7.1.57; Eggermont 12). He did not submit to Alexander, who was sailing down the Indus from Alor (Musicanus' realm; summer 325) and took two of his cities by assault, capturing Oxicanus in the second (A 6.16.1–2). His fate is not recorded, but it is likely that Alexander had him executed. Berve ii.293 identifies him with Porticanus (Str 15.1.33 [701]; C 9.8.11–12; D 17.102.5; cf. Jacobs 247, 251), but the names and the details concerning them are sufficiently different that we may suspect conflation of two successive incidents, with Arrian preserving the name Oxicanus, the vulgate Porticanus. See further s.v. **Porticanus**.

Anspach iii.33 n. 374; Berve ii.293 no. 589; Eggermont 9–15.

Oxyartes. Bactrian or Sogdianian noble (C 8.4.21–4, but the text is corrupt); father of Rhoxane, father-in-law of Alexander (D 18.3.3, 39.6; *PM* 332e; Paus 1.6.3; A 6.15.3; cf. C 10.3.11; *LM* 118, 121; C 8.4.21–7; for the details of the marriage see s.v. **Rhoxane**); for his other children see **F31–32** and s.v. **Itanes**. Oxyartes was one of those nobles of Bactria-Sogdiana who continued to resist Alexander after the execution of Bessus (see s.v.), but it appears that he submitted to Alexander at the time of the Macedonian siege of the Rock of Sisimithres, where he had left his family for safekeeping, and acted as a go-between for Alexander and Sisimithres (C 8.2.25–31; cf. A 4.21.6; *PA* 58.3–4; Str 11.11.4 [517]; see also s.v. **Sisimithres**). He is also known to have had a son named Itanes, but the three sons ascribed to him by C 8.4.21 appear to belong to Chorienes (Sisimithres). A 4.18–19 claims that Oxyartes' wife and daughter were captured at the so-called "Rock of Sogdiana," and he dates this to spring 327. But this "Rock" is clearly the fortress of Ariamazes, whom Alexander crucified along with many of his followers, selling the remainder into slavery.[495] Rhoxane may have influenced her husband's decision to give Oxyartes the satrapy of the Parapamisadae (or Paropanisadae) in 325 in place of Tyriespis (A 6.15.3); C 9.8.9 calls the governor of Parapamisus Terioltes and says that he was tried for greed and tyrannical acts and executed; he adds that Oxyartes, *praetor Bactrianorum*, was acquitted and given a more extensive territory (9.8.10), but there appears be considerable confusion here. C appears to have forgotten at this point that Oxyartes was Rhoxane's father; he mistakenly reports that he was put on trial; and he has wrongly called him the governor of Bactriana. That Oxyartes shared the satrapy with Peithon son of Agenor is highly unlikely and editors are right to emend the text of A 6.15.4: Oxyartes' satrapy is described by A 6.15.3 as Parapamisadae; perhaps this was extended in a southeasterly direction to the confluence of the Indus and Acesines (Chenab) and was thus adjacent to Peithon's. He retained Paropanisadae in the settlement of 323 (Dexippus, *FGrH* 100 F8 §5; D 18.3.3; J 13.4.21; cf. *LM* 121), and again at Triparadeisus (D 18.39.6). Although he gave aid to Eumenes in 317, he did not come in person but rather sent troops under the command of Androbazus (D 19.14.6, 27.5). After the battle of Gabiene, Antigonus allowed Oxyartes to retain his satrapy, considering it too difficult to dislodge him from there (D 19.48.2). What became of him, we do not know.

Berve ii.292–3 no. 587. See Stemma I.

Oxyathres (Oxathres, Oxyatres, Exathres). Son of Arsanes and Sisygambis. Brother of Darius III (D 17.34.2; C 3.11.8; 6.2.9; A 7.4.5; Str 12.3.10 [544]; Ps-Call 2.7.5) and of Stateira, who had given him Timosa, a beautiful captive sent by the king of Egypt, as a concubine (Ath 13.609a–b).[496] He was younger – we do not know by how much – than Darius, who was born in ca. 380 (A 3.22.6). Fought with distinction in defense of his brother at Issus (D 17.34.2–3; C 3.11.8; for his merits see also C 6.2.9). After his brother's death he was amongst some 1,000 noble Persian captives (C 6.2.9) and later enrolled in Alexander's *hetairoi* (P*A* 43.7; C 6.2.11) and as one of his bodyguard (D 17.77.4; C 7.5.40; *ME* 2).[497] The captive regicide Bessus was handed over to Oxyathres for punishment (C 7.5.40–1; J 12.5.11). He was the father of Amastris, who married Craterus in 324 at Susa (A 7.4.5; Str 12.3.10 [544]; Memnon, *FGrH* 434 F4.4; D 20.109.7; see s.v. **Amastris**), and perhaps a second daughter, captured at Damascus in 333 (C 3.13.13: **F1**). He was apparently still alive in 323 (assuming that the remark in C 10.5.23, that only one of Sisygambis' seven children remained alive, refers to Oxyathres). What became of him is unknown, although it may be speculated that all of the immediate relatives of Darius III were quietly eliminated after Alexander's death.[498]

Berve ii.291–2 no. 586. See Stemma III.

Oxydates. For the name, see Justi 233; cf. Marquart 26, *Waxsu-data*. A prominent Persian (his family background is unknown) who had been arrested by Darius III and imprisoned at Susa (we do not know the charge against him or the historical context, but C 6.2.11 says that he had been condemned to death). Oxydates was found there and released by Alexander, whom he accompanied as far as Rhagae (Rey), where, in 330 BC, he was appointed satrap of Media; for, as a victim of Darius, he was considered trustworthy (A 3.20.3; cf. C 6.2.11, who dates his appointment to after Darius' death). In late 328, however, Oxydates was considered guilty of misconduct and replaced by Atropates (A 4.18.3; C 8.3.17, wrongly names Arsaces).[499] It is hard to imagine that Atropates was not instructed to arrest (if not execute) him. If he fled at Atropates' approach, there is no record of him afterwards. Nor is it clear if he had anything to do with the rebels who were later taken to Alexander at Pasargadae (A 6.29.3; see s.v. **Baryaxes**).[500]

Berve ii.293 no. 588; Bosworth 1981: 21.

Ozines. See s.v. **Ordanes**.

P

Pancaste (Pankaste, Pancaspe, or Pakate). Pl*NH* 35.86 (Pancaspe); Lucian 43.7 (Pakate); Ael*VH* 12.34 says she was from Larissa and that she was the first woman with whom Alexander was intimate (which suggests that Aelian confused her with Callixeina the Thessalian courtesan; Ath 10.435a). The favorite mistress of Alexander (Ael*VH* 12.34 calls her exceedingly good looking); Alexander commissioned a nude painting of her by Apelles, and, when the latter fell in love with his subject, Alexander presented her to him as a gift (Pl*NH* 35.86); she was rumored to be the model for his Aphrodite Anadyomene (Pl*NH* 35.87).

Berve ii.297 no. 600; Pollitt 160.

Pancles (Pankles). Son of Dorotheus, a cavalryman from Orchomenus. Served as a member of Alexander's allied cavalry until the expedition reached Ecbatana in 330. There he and his compatriots were discharged. On their return (ca. 329), they made a dedication to Zeus Soter in Orchomenus (*IG* vii.3206).

Berve ii.297 no. 601.

Panegorus (Panegoros). Macedonian. Son of Lycagoras (or Lycagorus) and *hetairos* of Alexander. Left behind with an undisclosed force to occupy the city of Priapus (A 1.12.7), which surrendered to Alexander as he advanced to the Granicus in 334 BC. Nothing else is known about Panegorus.

Berve ii.297 no. 602.

Pantaleon. Macedonian *hetairos* from Pydna. Pantaleon was appointed *phrourarchos* of Memphis in Egypt in 332/1 BC (A 3.5.3). He is otherwise unknown.

Berve ii.297 no. 603.

Pantauchus (Pantauchos). Macedonian. Son of Nicolaus. Trierarch of the Hydaspes fleet in 326 (A*Ind* 18.6). Identification with the officer of Demetrius Poliorcetes (= Sandberger 175–7 no. 64) who was left behind in Aetolia in 289 (P*Pyr* 7.4–1; cf. P*Demetr* 41.2–3) is highly unlikely, though not entirely impossible.

Berve ii.298 no. 604.

Pantordanus (Pantordanos). Son of Cleander (A 2.9.3), of otherwise unknown family. That he was the son of Cleander son of Polemocrates, or possibly a relative of Cleander the *toxarches*, is impossible to determine given the frequent occurrence of the name in Macedonia. Pantordanus commanded the so-called "Leugaean" squadron[501] in the battle of Issus, occupying at first the left wing but then being transferred (along with the squadron of Peroedas) to the right, just as the battle began (A 2.9.3). He is not heard of again, and the battle-order at Gaugamela (A 3.11.8) shows that he had been replaced. A 2.10.7 says that some 120 Macedonians of note died at Issus, but names only Ptolemaeus son of Seleucus. It is not impossible that Pantordanus was killed at Issus, but, since Arrian drew attention to his maneuver at the beginning of the battle, it would be unusual for him to omit his death, had it occurred.

Berve ii.298 no. 605; Heckel 349–50; Hoffmann 183–4.

Parmenion (Parmenio). Macedonian. Son of Philotas (A 3.11.10).[502] Macedon's foremost general in the years leading up to Alexander's accession (C 4.13.4; J 12.5.3; cf. P*A* 49.13; P*M* 177c) and no less influential at the court (P*M* 179b). Together with Antipater and Eurylochus, Parmenion negotiated the Peace of 346 (Dem 19.69; Aes 3.72; Din 1.28; cf. Theopompus, *FGrH* 115 F165). Born ca. 400 BC (C 6.11.32; cf. 7.2.33), he was already a dominant force in Pella in the first years of Philip II, on whose orders he arrested and killed at Oreus Euphraeus, an adherent of Perdiccas III (Carystius *ap.* Ath 11.508e). In 356 he campaigned successfully against Grabus the Illyrian (P*A* 3.8), and the value of his generalship is summed up in Philip's remark that whereas the Athenians elected ten generals every year, he himself had found only one general in many years – Parmenion (P*M* 177c).

Parmenion had three attested sons: Philotas, Nicanor, and Hector; an unnamed daughter is known to have married Attalus, the uncle of Cleopatra (C 6.9.18). The family may have had estates in the highlands: Philotas commanded in the Triballian campaign the cavalry from Upper Macedonia (A 1.2.5) and his friends included the sons of Andromenes from Tymphaea (C 7.1.11); Parmenion himself normally commanded the infantry, on the left, where at least four of six taxiarchs were from Upper Macedonia; he was also associated with Polyperchon of Tymphaea (C 4.13.7ff.) and the sons of Polemocrates (Elimea), one of whom, Coenus, appears to have married Parmenion's daughter after Attalus' death (C 6.9.30; cf. A 1.24.1, 29.4).

Sent ahead with Attalus and Amyntas to prepare for Philip's invasion (D 16.91.2; 17.2.4; J 9.5.8; cf. Tr*Prol* 9), Parmenion enjoyed mixed success in Asia Minor: Pol*Strat* 5.44.4 provides a vague account of a defeat at Magnesia-on-the-Maeander inflicted by Memnon the Rhodian.[503] In 336/5, on Alexander's orders, he eliminated Attalus (D 17.2.4–6, 5.2).[504] Some time later, he captured Grynium and sold its inhabitants into slavery; Memnon, however, forced him to abandon the siege of Pitane (D 17.7.9) and drove his accomplice, Calas son of Harpalus, back to Rhoetium (D 17.7.10). The campaign had not been an overwhelming success, but Parmenion had only limited resources with which to secure a beachhead in Asia. In winter of 335/4, he rejoined Alexander in Europe and, in the spring, transported most of the infantry and cavalry from Sestos to Abydos; in Asia Minor, he commanded the infantry – 12,000 Macedonians, 7,000 allies, and 5,000 mercenaries (A 1.11.6; D 17.17.3).

At the Granicus, Parmenion counseled Alexander not to attack late in the day, advice rejected by the King (A 1.13.2ff.; P*A* 16.3).[505] In the actual battle he commanded the left, including the Thessalian cavalry (A 1.14.1), who acquitted themselves well in the engagement (D 17.19.6). After the battle, Parmenion captured and garrisoned Dascylium (A 1.17.2), the residence of the satrap of Hellespontine Phrygia. Hence, he ensured that Calas son of Harpalus, Alexander's newly appointed satrap of the region, was securely established there.[506] Upon his return, Parmenion secured Magnesia and Tralles (which had surrendered) with 2,500 infantry, an equal number of Macedonians, and 200 of the Companions (A 1.18.1). He rejoined the King at Miletus, where he advised against disbanding the fleet,[507] and continued with him into Caria. With winter approaching, Parmenion moved to Sardis, taking a hipparchy of Companions, the Thessalian horse, the allies, and the wagons; from there to march into Phrygia and await the King (A 1.24.3; cf. 1.29.3). There he apprehended Darius' agent, Sisines, who had been sent to induce Alexander Lyncestes to murder the Macedonian King. Sisines was sent in chains to Alexander (now at Phaselis) and interrogated. On the basis of his testimony, Alexander sent Amphoterus back to Parmenion with orders to arrest the Lyncestian.[508] In spring 333, Parmenion rejoined the remainder of the army at Gordium (A 1.29.3–4).

When the expedition moved out of Cappadocia to Cilicia, Parmenion remained at the so-called "Camp of Cyrus" with the heavy infantry while Alexander took the hypaspists, archers, and Agrianes in order to occupy the Cilician Gates (A 2.4.3). These had been abandoned by Arsames' guards, who were frightened by the King's approach and alarmed by Arsames' "scorched-earth" policy; and Alexander, fearing lest the satrap should destroy Tarsus, sent Parmenion ahead to capture the city. This, at least, is Curtius' version; Arrian says nothing about his contribution (C 3.4.14–15; A 2.4.5–6).[509] It was near Tarsus that Alexander fell ill, and Justin's claim that Parmenion wrote to Alexander from Cappadocia, warning the King to beware of Philip, the Acarnanian physician, may reflect his (or rather Trogus') belief that Parmenion had remained in Cappadocia while Alexander rushed ahead to Tarsus.[510] Now it is precisely in this context that the vulgate discusses the arrest of Alexander Lyncestes, who, like the doctor Philip, had allegedly been bribed by the Persian King. On this occasion, as on others, Parmenion's advice was disregarded and proved to be wrong.

From Tarsus, Parmenion advanced to the "other" or Syrian Gates (A 2.5.1; D 17.32.2), which he secured before rejoining the King at Castabalum (C 3.7.5; cf. A 2.6.1–2, with Bosworth i.199); thereafter he took Issus and advised Alexander to fight Darius in the narrows where the numerical supremacy of the Persians could be negated. The advice was accepted (C 3.7.6–10)![511] At Issus, Parmenion acted as commander-in-chief of the forces on the left, and was told to extend his line to the sea (C 3.9.8–10; A 2.8.4, 9–10). To his contingent Alexander added the Thessalian cavalry (A 2.8.9; C 3.11.3), who again fought with distinction. After the battle, Parmenion captured without difficulty the treasures at Damascus.[512] Alexander instructed him to send on only the captive Greek envoys and to take the remaining spoils back to Damascus (A 2.15.1–2). The captives included Barsine, the widow of both Mentor and Memnon the Rhodians and allegedly the first woman with whom Alexander was intimate. Parmenion, it is said, urged him to take up this relationship;[513] she may have been brought to the King at Marathus. Parmenion himself became military overseer of Coele-Syria,[514] a temporary command: the satrapy was soon assigned to Andromachus, whom the Samaritans later put to death (C 4.5.9; cf. 4.8.9–11).[515] From Gaza, Parmenion accompanied the King to Egypt. There he used his influence to pacify Hegelochus (C 6.11.27–9), and his mere presence in the camp sufficed to save Philotas from charges of treason (A 3.26.1). Still his sojourn in Egypt was not free of tragedy: his youngest son Hector drowned in the Nile (C 4.8.7ff.; 6.9.27; cf. *PA* 49.13).

Alexander undoubtedly sought to free himself from Parmenion's influence and the belief that his military victories were owed to the old general (cf. C 7.2.33). But it is difficult to determine what role Alexander played in blackening Parmenion's memory or if this was even done in the King's lifetime. Certainly, we have a collection of stories that put him in a bad light: he urges acceptance of Darius' peace offer (*PA* 29.7–9: 10,000 talents; cf. A 2.25.1, in a different chronological context; D 17.54; C 4.11.1–14 and J 11.12.1–10: 30,000 talents), which Alexander arrogantly rejects; the old general's advice that they attack the Persians by night at Gaugamela is dismissed as a plan to "steal victory" (C 4.13.4, 8–9; A 3.10.1–2; *PA* 31.11–12); Parmenion's anxiety before the battle is contrasted with Alexander's confidence in the face of danger (D 17.56.2; C 4.13.17ff., *PA* 32.1–4); and, in the actual battle, he is depicted as incompetent and tarnishing the King's victory over Darius (*PA* 33.10).[516]

Parmenion commanded the Macedonian left at Gaugamela (A 3.11.10; cf. 3.15) and soon found himself hard pressed by the Persian cavalry under Mazaeus (D 17.60.5–7); Scythian horsemen had, furthermore, broken through Macedonian lines and begun to plunder the camp (C 4.15.2ff.). A detachment sent to recall Alexander failed to make contact with the King and returned with its mission unfulfilled (D 17.60.7).[517] Parmenion, with the Thessalian cavalry, managed to hold Mazaeus until Darius' flight signaled the collapse of the Persian effort (D 17.60.8). He had thus fulfilled his role in the battle by holding the enemy in check on the left while Alexander turned the tide of battle on the right. Despite later claims that his performance was lackluster (*PA* 33.10 = Callisthenes, *FGrH* 124 F37), his contribution should not be diminished. Once the Persians were routed, and Alexander had established his camp beyond the Lycus River, Parmenion occupied the Persian camp, capturing the baggage, the camels, and the elephants (A 3.15.4).

From Susa to Persepolis, Parmenion led the slower troops and the baggage-train along the wagon road into Persis (A 3.18.1), while Alexander took an unencumbered force through the Persian Gates. At Persepolis he advised Alexander not to destroy the palace; for it was unwise to destroy one's own property (A 3.18.11). Alexander may have wished to accept Parmenion's advice for once, but he had little choice: constrained by his own claims to be the "avenger of Greece," he was forced to make at least a symbolic gesture at Persepolis. From Persepolis the King sent him to Ecbatana with the accumulated treasure (J 12.1.3; A 3.19.7), details of which are again provided in a letter from Parmenion to Alexander (Ath 11.781f–782a).

When Alexander continued his pursuit of Darius in 330, he left Parmenion in Ecbatana, presumably as *strategos* of Media and possibly as a temporary measure.[518] The matter is academic, since Alexander's decision to execute Philotas sealed the old man's fate. Polydamas was sent in disguise to deliver the order that Parmenion be executed (A 3.26.3; C 7.2.11ff.). In Media, Cleander, Agathon, Sitalces, and Menidas carried out the sentence (A 3.26.3; cf. C 7.2.19ff.; C 10.1.1 adds Heracon), as the old man learned of this conviction and of the charges (cf. C 6.9.13–24, 11.21ff.) against him (A 3.26.3–4; *PA* 49.13; D 17.80.3; J 12.5.3; C 7.2.11–32, with a eulogy at 7.2.33–4).

Beloch iv² 2.290–306, Abschn. XV: "Alexander und Parmenion"; Berve ii.298–306 no. 606; Heckel 13–23; Carney 2000: 264–73; Müller 55–79. See Stemma VII.

Parysatis. The youngest daughter of Artaxerxes III Ochus (A 7.4.4), Parysatis and her two older sisters (**F3–4**) were captured at Damascus by Parmenion in 333 (C 3.13.12). From that point, she remained in Alexander's camp until late 331 and, presumably, was left behind at Susa in 331 with Darius III's womenfolk, when Alexander the Great continued on to Persepolis (cf. C 5.2.17; D 17.67.1). There, in 324, she married Alexander (A 7.4.4). What became of her or whether she was treated with suspicion by Rhoxane after Alexander's death and eliminated (cf. Stateira and Drypetis; *PA* 77.6), we do not know.

Berve ii.306 no. 607; Brosius 77. See Stemma III.

Pasas. Thessalian. Family background unknown. Pasas appears, along with Damis (Amissus) and Perillus, as an intermediary in the dispute between the cavalry and infantry factions after the death of Alexander in Babylon (C 10.8.15). It is impossible to determine the precise nature of his service under Alexander or how long he had participated in the campaign. Unlike Damis and, possibly, Perillus, he does not resurface in the accounts of the Successors.

Berve ii.306–7 no. 608.

Pasicrates [1]. (Pasikrates). Ruler of Curium; son of Aristocrates and brother of Themistagoras. Pasicrates, like the other kings of Cyprus, joined the Aegean fleet of Pharnabazus and Autophradates in 334, only to defect after the battle of Issus and submit to Alexander at Sidon in 332 (A 2.20.3). The Cyprian fleet played an important role in the final assault on Tyre, though Pasicrates' own quinquereme (along with those of Pnytagoras of Salamis and Androcles of Amathos) was destroyed by a Tyrian counterattack as it lay at anchor in the harbor (A 2.22.2). Nothing else is known of his career.

Berve ii.307 no. 609.

Pasicrates [2]. (Pasikrates). Ruler of Cypriot Soli (P*A* 29.3). Father of Nicocles (A*Ind* 18.8) and, probably, Eunostus (Ath 13.576c). He appears to have defected to Alexander along with the other Cypriot kings soon after Issus. In early 331, when Alexander conducted dramatic contests in Phoenicia and enlisted the Cypriot kings as *choregoi*, there was particularly keen competition between Pasicrates and Nicocreon of Salamis (P*A* 29.3). But Pasicrates' actor Athenodorus defeated Thessalus, a favorite of Alexander's who had been assigned to Nicocreon (P*A* 29.1–4). In the first war of the Diadochoi, Pasicrates and other rulers of Cyprus made an alliance with Ptolemy (A*Succ* 24.6); Perdiccan forces sent against him were unsuccessful. He remained an ally of Ptolemy and resisted Antigonus' overtures in 315 (D 19.59.1; cf. Olshausen 87 no. 62). His successor was Eunostus (Ath 13.576c).[519]

Berve ii.307 no. 610.

Patron. Phocian. Mercenary in the service of Darius III; Patron commanded those Greek mercenaries who remained with the King after the disaster at Gaugamela (C 5.9.15).[520] In Curtius' highly dramatized account, he makes an effort to warn Darius of Bessus' treachery (5.11; cf. 5.12.7), speaking Greek to the King in the very presence of the unilingual conspirator. Although Darius did not avail himself of the mercenaries' protection, some of them may have put up an unsuccessful fight or deserted. After the King's death, 1,500 (presumably including Patron) agreed through messengers to surrender unconditionally to Alexander's agent, Andronicus son of Agerrus (A 3.23.8–9). See also s.v. **Glaucus**.

Berve ii.307–8 no. 612; Seibt 117–18; Hofstetter 142–3 no. 245.

Pausanias [1]. Macedonian, apparently of high standing (he was one of the King's *hetairoi*); in 334 Pausanias was appointed commandant (*epimeletes*, in effect, as *phrourarchos*) of the citadel of Sardis (A 1.17.7). As such he was presumably responsible to the newly appointed satrap of Lydia, Asander son of Philotas. Nothing else is known about him.[521]

Berve ii.308 no. 613.

Pausanias [2]. A young Macedonian of unknown family, identified merely as a lover of Philip II and friend of Attalus (D 16.93.4–5), Pausanias was apparently close in age to his namesake from Orestis, whose rival he had become for Philip's favor. Their homosexual relations with the King had presumably begun during their terms as Pages at the court. The Orestian is described as *somatophylax* (D 16.93.3), and the fact that Pausanias died fighting on foot at the side of Philip II suggests that he too was a Royal Hypaspist, that is, a member of the *agema*. His death occurred in a battle with the Illyrians (D 16.93.6), presumably in early 336 (Heckel 1981c: 56).

Fears 1975; cf. also Ogden 1996: 120–1.

Pausanias [3]. Son of Cerastus (Jos*AJ* 11.8.1 [304]), Macedonian from Orestis (D 16.93.3). Pausanias was born in the mid-350s: as a Page (*pais basilikos*) he appears to have become an *eromenos* of Philip II, but as he approached manhood he found himself replaced by another young man, also named Pausanias, as Philip's favorite (D 16.93.3–4). The rival was abused by Pausanias as effeminate and sought to prove his manliness by dying on the battlefield (presumably in an Illyrian campaign in 337/6) in defense of Philip II (D 16.93.5–6). Attalus, who was a friend of the dead Pausanias, invited Pausanias of Orestis to a drinking-party where he was allegedly gang-raped by muleteers at Attalus' instigation (J 9.6.5–6; D 16.93.7–8; Arist*Pol* 5.10 1311^{b}; *PA* 10.6 includes Attalus' niece Cleopatra as an instigator). Pausanias sought redress from Philip, who failed to take action because the culprit was a kinsman and would soon be sent to Asia Minor with the advance force (D 16.93.9). Hence Pausanias directed his hostility against the King and murdered him as he entered the theater in Aegae (D 16.94.3; J 9.6.4; *PA* 10.6–7; Jos*AJ* 11.8.1 [304]; 19.1.13 [95]; Arist*Pol* 5.10 1311^{b}; cf. Ael*VH* 3.45; Val Max 1.8 ext. 9; Cic *De fato* 3.5).[522] It was alleged that he was incited by Olympias, or even Alexander, to kill Philip (J 9.7.1ff.; *PA* 10.6); D 16.94.1–2 claims he was inspired by the sophist Hermocrates. Pausanias was killed by other Royal Hypaspists as he tried to escape (D 16.94.4; cf. J 9.7.9, where the reference to "getaway horses" suggests that J is compressing a similar story), and his body crucified (J 9.7.10; 11.2.1; cf. *POxy* 1798).

Berve ii.308–9 no. 614; Bosworth 1971a; Fears 1975; Heckel 297–8; Hoffmann 212.

Pausanias [4]. Macedonian. Pausanias accompanied Harpalus to Athens in 324 and then Crete, where he murdered him (Paus 2.33.4), perhaps on the orders of Thibron (D 17.108.8; Str 17.3.21 [837]; A*Succ* 1.16). Nothing else is known about him.

Berve ii.309 no. 615.

Pausanias [5]. Apparently Macedonian. Physician who treated Craterus at some point (perhaps in 324) and received a letter from Alexander concerning the use of hellebore (*PA* 41.7). Nothing else is known about him.

Berve ii.309 no. 616.

Pausippus (Pausippos; Pasippus). Spartan. Sent as ambassador to Darius III, perhaps in the period leading up to Agis' war, along with Callicratidas, Monimus, and Onomastoridas. All were captured by Alexander after Darius' death in 330 (A 3.24.4). C 3.13.15 mistakenly places their capture at Damascus (333/2 BC), in which context A 2.15.2 names Euthycles (partially corroborated by *PA* 40.4).[523]

Berve ii.310 no. 617; Poralla no. 598; Hofstetter 145 no. 247.

Peithagoras (Pythagoras). Seer. Macedonian from Amphipolis, brother of Apollodorus (*PA* 73.3–4). He appears to have set out on the Asiatic expedition with his brother – though we do not know when they left Macedonia – and remained in Babylon with Apollodorus in 331/0 (A 3.16.4). Peithagoras is said to have predicted the deaths of Hephaestion and Alexander as well as those of Perdiccas and Antigonus (A 7.18.1–5 = Aristobulus, *FGrH* 139 F54; App*BC* 2.152). Hence, he must have lived until at least 301 BC.

Berve ii.310 no. 618.

Peithon [1]. (Pitho, Pithon). Son of Antigenes. According to Nearchus (*ap.* A*Ind* 15.10), Peithon captured a snake of considerable length in India. That he was a man of some importance is suggested by the use of both the name and patronymic, as Berve observed, but that need not require us to identify him with the only attested Peithon without a patronymic, namely the taxiarch, who is probably to be equated with the son of Agenor. Whether this Peithon's father is identifiable with the commander of the Argyraspids (or Antigenes of Pallene, if this was a separate or historical individual) is impossible to determine.

Berve ii.311 no. 620.

Peithon [2]. (Pitho, Pithon). Macedonian. Son of Sosicles. Peithon was placed in charge of the Royal Pages, who had been left in Zariaspa-Bactra in 328, in which place there were also some mercenary cavalry and several of the *hetairoi* who were suffering from illness. When the town was attacked by the Massagetae, a force of eighty mercenaries, a few Companions, Pages, and Peithon, along with the harpist Aristonicus, rode out and defeated them. On their return, however, they were ambushed by Spitamenes and a force of Scythians: some sixty mercenaries, seven Companions, and Aristonicus were all killed. Peithon was captured alive and doubtless killed later (A 4.16.6–7). Arrian says that he was responsible for the Pages (i.e., the *therapeia basilike*); cf. *IA* 98. And we need not assume that he was more than the equivalent of a "cadet instructor"; this is surely the point of Arrian's comment that the force was without a leader (4.16.7).

Berve ii.311–12 no. 622.

Peithon [3]. (Pitho, Pithon). Son of Crateuas (A*Succ* 1.2), from Alcomenae in Deuriopus (Str 7 [326]); perhaps a relative of Cassander's general Crateuas (D 19.50–1).[524] Although he first appears as a trierarch of the Hydaspes fleet in 326 (A*Ind* 18.6), Peithon had been a Somatophylax for an unspecified time (A 6.28.4), perhaps since at least 336. He received a golden crown at Susa in 324 (A 7.5.6), but we are not told of any distinguished contribution; nor do we know the name of his Persian bride at the Susan mass-marriage. At the time of Alexander's fatal illness in Babylon, Peithon, along with Seleucus and others, slept in the temple of Sarapis (A 7.26.2).[525] Peithon opposed the kingship of Arrhidaeus and supported Perdiccas: his proposed joint guardianship of Rhoxane's child by Perdiccas and Leonnatus, leaving the direction of European affairs to Antipater and Craterus (C 10.7.8–9), was intended to prevent the complete erosion of Perdiccas' authority (C 10.7.4–5).[526] In return for his support, Peithon received the satrapy of Media Maior (J 13.4.13; C 10.10.4; D 18.3.1; A*Succ* 1.5; Dexippus, *FGrH* 100 F8 §2; cf. *LM* 117, with Heckel 1988: 66–7), and also the task of suppressing the Greek rebellion in the Upper Satrapies (D 18.4.8; 18.7.3–9). For this purpose, he received special powers, perhaps as "*strategos* of the Upper Satrapies" (cf. D 19.14.1), to levy troops from the neighboring satraps and to act as commander-in-chief of the expedition. Peithon took 3,000 infantry and 800 horse from Babylon, as well as written orders to the satraps to supply a further 10,000 infantry and 8,000 cavalry for the expedition. This command fueled Peithon's ambitions, and he planned to come to terms with the insurgents and translate his *strategia* into greater powers in the Upper Satrapies (D 18.7.4). But Perdiccas, suspecting his designs, gave instructions that the rebels be slaughtered upon their surrender. Despite Peithon's intrigues and the cooperation of Letodorus the Aenianian, the troops were moved more by the expectation of plunder than by compassion and carried out Perdiccas' orders (D 18.7.3–9). Rejoining Perdiccas, probably in time to participate in the expedition against Ariarathes of Cappadocia, Peithon later accompanied him to Egypt, where he was foremost of the mutineers who killed him near Memphis (D 18.36.5).[527] With Ptolemy's approval, he and Arrhidaeus become *epimeletai* of the Kings (D 18.36.6–7), but Ptolemy left them with the dregs of the Royal Army and problems of back-pay. At Triparadeisus in Syria, Peithon and his colleague found themselves upstaged by Adea-Eurydice, who courted the troops. Peithon and Arrhidaeus thus resigned the *epimeleia* and the office was given to Antipater (D 18.39.1–2); it was enough, for the time, to be reaffirmed as satrap of Media (D 18.39.6; A*Succ* 1.35).

In the turmoil that followed Antipater's death in 319 Peithon revived for himself the title of *strategos* of the Upper Satrapies and he expelled the Parthian satrap Philip,[528] installing in his place his own brother

Eudamus. But the neighboring satraps joined Peucestas in driving Peithon (and Eudamus) out of Parthia (D 19.14.2). When Eumenes asked him to support the Kings, he was already intriguing with Seleucus, now satrap of Babylonia (D 19.14.3). The two joined forces against Eumenes (D 19.12.1–2, 5; cf. D 19.17.2), but Seleucus chose to recognize the authority of Antigonus. Peithon joined Antigonus as well (D 19.19.4), giving him useful advice, which Antigonus rejected at his own peril (D 19.19.8). Before the battle of Paraetacene, Peithon was sent by Antigonus to bring reinforcements and pack animals from Media (D 19.20.2), which he supplied in large numbers (D 19.20.3; cf. 19.27.1). That Antigonus had complete trust in him is doubtful, though he valued his generalship and assigned to him the less mobile forces while he pursued the enemy with his cavalry (D 19.26.7). In Paraetacene Peithon commanded the cavalry on the left (D 19.29.2–3), but his force was routed (D 19.30.1–4).[529] While the army was in Peithon's satrapy (D 19.32.4), it was important for Antigonus to keep his goodwill, and we find Peithon closely associated with his commander until the final defeat of Eumenes at Gabiene (D 19.38.4, 40.1, 43.4). Soon, however, Peithon was suspected of plotting rebellion. Antigonus pretended that he was about to hand over troops to him and to leave him as *strategos* of the Upper Satrapies. Catching him off guard, he arrested and executed him (D 19.46.1, 3; Pol*Strat* 4.6.14).[530]

Berve ii.311 no. 621; Bengtson i.178ff.; Schober 15–26, 88, 91–6, 158–60; Heckel 1988: 38–9, 66–7, 74–5; Heckel 276–9; Billows 415–16 no. 88.

Peithon [4]. (Pitho, Pithon). Macedonian. Son of Agenor (A 6.17.1; J 13.4.21; A*Succ* 1.36). Peithon assumed command of Coenus' battalion of *asthetairoi*, perhaps as early as the Hydaspes battle (326). He accompanied Alexander against the Mallians (A 6.6.1), capturing and enslaving those who had fled to a neighboring fortress (A 6.7.2–3). Together with Demetrius the hipparch, he led further reprisals against the Mallians (A 6.8.2–3).[531] It appears that, as a reward for his efforts and because of his experience in this region, Alexander appointed the son of Agenor satrap of India from the confluence of the Indus and Acesines rivers to the Indian Ocean (A 6.15.4) – that is, the west bank of the Indus, down to the sea and including Patala.[532] As satrap, he brought the rebellious Musicanus captive to Alexander, who crucified him (C 9.8.16; A 6.17.1–2). Although J 13.4.21 implies that Peithon retained this satrapy after Alexander's death (cf. C 10.10.4), it appears that, probably after the death of Philip son of Machatas, he was transferred to the Cophen satrapy (Gandhara), between Parapamisus and the Indus (so D 18.3.3; Dexippus, *FGrH* 100 F8; cf. Bosworth 1983: esp. 39ff.). At Triparadeisus (320 BC) his position was confirmed (D 18.39.6; A*Succ* 1.36; J 13.4.21).

Nothing further is heard of Peithon until 315, when Antigonus appointed him satrap of Babylonia in place of Seleucus, who had fled to Egypt (D 19.56.4). It is not possible to determine whether he took part in the battle of Gabiene or if he had, perhaps, been recalled from India when Antigonus reformed the administration of the east (D 19.48.1–2).[533] Since he was not in a position to remove Peithon from India – for he could not even exert his authority over Tlepolemus, Stasanor, and Oxyartes (D 19.48.1–2) – it seems likely that Peithon left his satrapy soon after Gabiene, because of the instability there (Tarn 1951: 168; cf. Billows 415); perhaps he arrived at the same time as, if not together with, Sibyrtius, whom Antigonus reinstated as governor of Arachosia (D 19.48.3). Peithon himself was appointed satrap of Babylon by Antigonus (D 19.56.4), replacing Seleucus who had taken refuge with Ptolemy in Egypt. From Babylon he was summoned to Syria in 314/3 – though not necessarily relieved of his satrapy, since no successor is named in the sources.[534] Possibly on account of his experience in India with elephants, he became an advisor of Demetrius Poliorcetes

(D 19.69.1) and joint commander of his forces (cf. D 19.82.1). In 313, Demetrius left him with the elephants and heavily armed troops to hold Coele-Syria while he tried in vain to deal with the enemy in Cilicia (D 19.80.1). When Demetrius returned and engaged Ptolemy at Gaza, Peithon fought on Demetrius' left wing, sharing the command (D 19.82.1); in this engagement, he fell and his body was recovered under truce (D 19.85.2).

Berve ii.310 no. 619; Billows 415–16 no. 88; Bosworth 1983: 39ff.; Heckel 323–6.

Pelagon. Ephesian; son of Syrphax, a leader of the pro-Persian oligarchy in Ephesus. After the restoration of the democracy, Pelagon and Syrphax had taken refuge in the temple (of Artemis), from which they were dragged out and stoned to death (A 1.17.12). Their fate was shared also by Syrphax's nephews.

Berve ii.312 no. 624; Berve 1967: i.335–6, ii.690; Hofstetter 146 no. 249.

Pelignas. A cook purchased by Olympias and sent to Alexander at some point during the campaign in Asia Minor (Ath 14.659f, 660a). He is otherwise unknown.

Berve ii.312 no. 625.

Perdiccas [1]. (Perdikkas). Son of Orontes (A 3.11.9; 6.28.4; A*Ind* 18.5) from Orestis (A 6.28.4; D 17.57.2), a member of that canton's royal house and possibly even of Argead descent (C 10.7.8). Born ca. 360 BC (cf. Berve ii.313). Brother of Alcetas (A*Succ* 1.21) and Atalante (D 18.37.2), who later married Attalus son of Andromenes. A steadfast supporter of Alexander, Perdiccas declined Alexander's gifts in 334, preferring to share the King's fortune (P*A* 15.4–5; cf. P*M* 342d–e). A member of the Royal Hypaspists at the time of Philip II's assassination in October 336, Perdiccas pursued and killed the regicide Pausanias (D 16.94.4). In 335, he commanded the *taxis* of Orestians and Lyncestians (D 17.57.2) in the campaign against Cleitus and Glaucias (A 1.6.9).

A 1.8.1–3 claims that Perdiccas' troops acted without orders from Alexander when they attacked Thebes (but this is refuted by D 17.12.3) and that he was wounded in the engagement. At the Granicus River he was stationed between the hypaspists of Nicanor and Coenus' battalion (A 1.14.2), roughly the same position that he occupied at Issus and Gaugamela (A 2.8.3; C 3.9.7 [Issus]; A 3.11.9; C 4.13.28). In an abortive attempt on Myndus Alexander took with him the *taxeis* of Perdiccas, Amyntas, and Meleager (A 1.20.5; cf. Fuller 202); a second reference to Perdiccas at Halicarnassus is less creditable: two of his men, motivated by drunkenness and *philotimia*, led an unauthorized assault on the city-walls that ended in failure (thus A 1.21.1–3; the poor discipline of Perdiccas' troops is corroborated by D 17.25.5; Fuller 200–6; cf. Welles 189 n. 2). In 332, Perdiccas and Craterus shared the command over the besieging forces at Tyre, while Alexander raided the neighboring Arabs (C 4.3.1; Craterus' role is corroborated by Pol*Strat* 4.13, but Arrian says nothing of joint command; cf. Errington 1969: 237; Fuller 206–16).

Not one to lead from the rear, Perdiccas was wounded at Gaugamela (C 4.16.32; D 17.61.3).[535] At the Persian Gates, he joined Alexander's force which encircled Ariobarzanes (A 3.18.5). What part he played in the Philotas affair can be determined only from Curtius: Perdiccas came to Alexander's tent on the night of Philotas' arrest, accompanied by Hephaestion, Craterus, Coenus, Erigyius, and Leonnatus, to discuss the crisis (C 6.8.17). Probably, he belonged to the *consilium amicorum*, which had met with Alexander earlier that day and urged that Philotas be punished: in short, he was party to the conspiracy *against* Philotas (C 6.8.1ff.). What Perdiccas gained from Philotas' fall is less clear; for he was already well advanced in the Macedonian chain of command. He appears to have replaced Menes as Somatophylax[536] but served as both taxiarch and Somatophylax from late 331 to early 329. In Sogdiana, Meleager and Perdiccas, functioning as taxiarchs, besieged one of the seven fortresses along the Iaxartes (Syr-Darya) (C 7.6.19, 21; cf. Holt 54–5). In 328 Perdiccas was promoted to hipparch and led one of five divisions that swept Sogdiana (A 4.16.2); the *pezhetairoi* of Orestis and Lyncestis were now entrusted to his younger brother, Alcetas (cf. A 4.22.1). As Somatophylax, on the other hand, he occupied a seat near the King at the fateful banquet in Maracanda (late summer 328), and joined Ptolemy in trying to restrain the King, who was incensed by Cleitus' outspokenness (C 8.1.45, 48). Three Somatophylakes – Ptolemy, Leonnatus, Perdiccas – conducted the night operations against the Rock of Chorienes (Koh-i-nor) early in the following spring (A 4.21.4).

With Hephaestion, Perdiccas led the advance force to the Indus, which they were to bridge (A 4.22.7; cf. C 8.10.2), subduing on the way Peucelaotis, whose ruler Astis offered stubborn resistance (A 4.22.8; see s.v. **Astis**). By the time Alexander reached the Indus, Perdiccas and Hephaestion had brought the natives under Alexander's sway, gathered provisions from Taxiles (C 8.12.6, 15; *ME* 48), and bridged the river by means of what clearly was a boat-bridge (C 8.10.2; cf. A 5.7.1–2). On their way they had also fortified a city called Orobatis, in which they left an armed guard (A 4.28.5).

At the Hydaspes (Jhelum), Perdiccas crossed the river in the same triakontor as Alexander, Lysimachus, Ptolemy, and Seleucus (A 5.13.1) and, in the actual battle, commanded one of the hipparchies directly under Alexander's control, the main striking force against Porus (A 5.12.2; cf. 5.13.1; C 8.14.15; Fuller 180–99, esp. 186–7). In the Sangala campaign, Perdiccas led his own hipparchy and the infantry battalions on the left (A 5.22.6); but Arrian describes in detail only the action on the right. After the battle Perdiccas was sent to ravage the region around Sangala with a lightly armed force (C 9.1.19). During the descent of the Indus river system in 326, Perdiccas took a special force against one of the Mallian towns, which he captured, killing those inhabitants who did not manage to escape into the marshes (A 6.6.4, 6). Reunited with Alexander for the assault on the main Mallian stronghold, he commanded a portion of the army, which Arrian (Ptolemy) implies was, through its sluggishness, responsible for Alexander's critical wounding there (A 6.9.1–2).[537] According to at least one (unnamed) source, it was Perdiccas who cut the arrow from Alexander's body (A 6.11.1).[538] While Alexander convalesced, Perdiccas completed the subjugation of the region before rejoining the main force (A 6.15.1; he subdued the Abastani).

At Susa in 324 he married the daughter of Atropates (A 7.4.5; cf. J 13.4.13) and was crowned, along with the other Somatophylakes (A 7.5.6). Later in 324 he conveyed Hephaestion's corpse from Ecbatana to Babylon for burial (D 17.110.8) and received Hephaestion's (the first) hipparchy or chiliarchy of the Companion Cavalry – though the unit, out of respect for the dead Hephaestion, retained the name of its original commander (A 7.14.10); in effect, he was Alexander's second-in-command.[539] Perdiccas was thus the most influential of the marshals in Babylon at the time of Alexander's death (N*Eum* 2.2), indeed, it was reported that the King, on his deathbed and in the presence of the other generals, handed Perdiccas his signet ring (C 10.5.4, 6.4–5; J 12.15.12; D 17.117.3; 18.2.4; N*Eum* 2.1; *LM* 112). Alexander may also have entrusted to him his wife, Rhoxane, with instructions that he should marry her (*LM* 112, 118), a reasonable move in view of the fact that she was carrying Alexander's child (C 10.6.9; J 13.2.5; cf. 12.15.9; A*Succ* 1.1; Dexippus, *FGrH* 100 F8 §1). Despite early support from Aristonus (C 10.6.16–18) and Peithon (C 10.7.4–8), his position was soon undermined by the unexpected proclamation of Arrhidaeus, who was renamed Philip (see s.v. **Arrhidaeus** [1]). A compromise[540] saw Craterus appointed *prostates* of the mentally deficient King, while Perdiccas retained his rank of *chiliarchos*, which was further restricted by the appointment of Meleager as *hyparchos* (A*Succ* 1.3).[541] Perdiccas, however, worked to eliminate his rival and encouraged rumors that Meleager was plotting against him (D 18.4.7; cf. C 10.9.7ff.) and then conducted a lustration of the army, using the opportunity to round up and execute the ringleaders of the uprising (C 10.9.11ff.; J 13.4.7; cf. D 18.4.7) and Meleager himself (C 10.9.20–1; A*Succ* 1.4–5; J 13.4.7–8; cf. D 18.4.7).

In the name of the King, Perdiccas assigned some satrapies to the leading men in Babylon while retaining some of the existing satraps (D 18.3.1–3; J 13.4.10–23; C 10.10.1–4; A*Succ* 1.5–7; Dexippus, *FGrH* 100 F8 §§2–7). He also arranged the murder of Stateira and her sister Drypetis (P*A* 77.6); what Plutarch depicts as an act of jealousy on Rhoxane's part was meant to secure the interests of her unborn child and eliminate the Achaemenid princesses as political tools for the ambitions of others. Perdiccas also held an assembly of the Macedonian troops and canceled Alexander's plans, as they were set out in the *Hypomnemata*, thereby protecting himself against any possible future charge of having failed to carry out the King's instructions and canceling Craterus' orders to replace Antipater as regent of Macedonia (D 18.4.1–6; Badian 1967b: 201–4). In this scheme he may have had the support of Eumenes who, as Royal Secretary, had prepared the *Hypomnemata*. Perdiccas' motive must have been to secure the goodwill and support of the old regent, and at this time he must have entered into negotiations for the hand of his daughter, Nicaea. Perdiccas entered into negotiations with Antipater when his own position was not yet secure, before he had taken control of the "royal armies and the guardianship (*prostasia*) of the Kings" (thus D 18.23.2). Now the reference to the "royal armies" cannot be accurate, for it is certain that Perdiccas commanded them from the start by virtue of his *chiliarchia* (C 10.10.4; J 13.4.5; D 18.3.1). As chief commander he conducted the lustration of the army (J 13.4.7ff.; A*Succ* 1.4; C 10.9.11ff.). But the *prostasia* may well – and very likely does – refer to the time of the birth of Alexander IV, Rhoxane's son; for Diodorus speaks of the *prostasia* of the Kings, not just of Arrhidaeus, with whom alone the enigmatic *prostasia* of Craterus is linked. At that point in time Perdiccas was formidable: he was *epimeletes* for Philip Arrhidaeus, *prostates* (or guardian) for Alexander IV, and *strategos* of the imperial forces in Asia. But Craterus' position had become weak indeed. Before the birth of Alexander's son, however, Perdiccas had isolated Craterus in Cilicia and was himself in a precarious state, having incurred the suspicion of the Macedonians in Babylon through his treacherous elimination of Meleager (A*Succ* 1.5). But Antipater too was prepared to deal: there was the matter of the Lamian War, and he wanted Craterus in Europe. Thus he recognized Perdiccas' claim to a share of the supremacy in Asia and bound him to a political alliance by promising his daughter Nicaea. In return Perdiccas acknowledged Antipater's sole authority in Europe. The negotiations must belong to the period of instability at Babylon. One of those who brought Nicaea to Perdiccas in the following year was Iolaus (A*Succ* 1.21), the girl's brother, who had been present at Alexander's death (see s.vv. **Iolaus** [1], **Nicaea**). Perdiccas' assumption of the regency may thus be seen not so much as an act of usurpation as a realistic political solution, similar to the case of Baldwin V, appointed co-ruler along with Baldwin the leper king in Jerusalem in 1183, who at the age of 5 (or possibly a year or two later) was assigned a different regent from the one who was exercising power in the name of the invalid Baldwin IV (see Hamilton 2000: 194–5).

In the Upper Satrapies, where Alexander had settled the Greek mercenaries, there was rebellion, a direct consequence of Alexander's death (D 18.4.8, 7.1). Accordingly, Perdiccas sent out Peithon (D

18.7.3), formerly one of the Somatophylakes, who had been allotted Media and now showed the first signs of seditious intent. His army, augmented by contributions from the other satraps (in accordance with Perdiccas' instructions), overcame the Greek force partly by deceit (D 18.7.5–7). Whether the ensuing slaughter of the Greeks who had surrendered was indeed ordered by Perdiccas at the outset of the campaign is difficult to determine (D 18.7.5, 8–9). In view of Perdiccas' growing dependence on Eumenes, the annihilation of the Greek force was scarcely good politics. It is possible, however, that Peithon's troops got out of control and that the blame for the slaughter devolved upon Perdiccas.

In the west, Antigonus and Leonnatus had been instructed to aid Eumenes in conquering his satrapy of Cappadocia, which had been bypassed by Alexander (P*Eum* 3.4). Antigonus defected from the Perdiccan cause and refused aid to Eumenes; but Leonnatus joined him in the spring (P*Eum* 3.5). At that point, however, Hecataeus, tyrant of Cardia, arrived with an urgent appeal from Antipater, asking Leonnatus to come with all haste to Europe (D 18.14.4–5; P*Eum* 3.6); for he was besieged in Lamia by the Hellenic forces under Leosthenes. For Leonnatus it was the perfect opportunity for seeking the throne. He had already had communications with Olympias, the unyielding foe of Antipater, and had received from her daughter Cleopatra, Alexander's sister, a promise of marriage (P*Eum* 3.9; cf. Macurdy 37–8; Seibert 1967: 20; see s.v. **Cleopatra** [2]). So much he confided to Eumenes, with whose support he hoped to gain the throne. But Eumenes, whether wary of Leonnatus' impetuosity or sincerely devoted to the Perdiccan cause, rejected the appeal on the grounds that he feared that Antipater would betray him to his arch-enemy Hecataeus (P*Eum* 3.8). Therefore, he slipped away from Leonnatus' camp during the night, leaving Leonnatus to take his chances in Europe (P*Eum* 3.10; cf. N*Eum* 2.4–5, who claims that Leonnatus planned to kill Eumenes when he failed to win his support).

Perdiccas came to regard Cleopatra as a means of gaining supreme power. Eumenes, deserted by Antigonus and Leonnatus, appealed to Perdiccas for help and divulged the details of Leonnatus' intrigues. Perdiccas moved to join Eumenes for an invasion of Cappadocia; it was late spring or early summer 322 (cf. Anson 1986: 214). In the Cappadocian campaign, Perdiccas continued the conquest of Alexander's empire and punished Ariarathes for his refusal to submit; he defeated him in two decisive engagements (A*Succ* 1.11; cf. D 18.16.1–3, 22.1; App*Mithr* 8 = Hieronymus, *FGrH* 154 F3; J 13.6.1–3; [L]*Macrob* 13 = *FGrH* 154 F4; Hornblower 1981: 239–43). In a single campaigning season, he had extended the boundaries of Alexander's empire and taken a barbarian king captive. But the victory was tarnished by his cruel treatment of Ariarathes, who was impaled (A*Succ* 1.11) along with his relatives (D 18.16.3; P*Eum* 3.13 says only that he was captured; D 31, frg. 19.3–5, from a different source, says Ariarathes fell in battle). Thereafter, he instructed Eumenes to settle affairs in Armenia, which had been thrown into confusion by Neoptolemus (P*Eum* 4.1), while he himself directed his attention to Pisidia (D 18.22.1). Here the Isaurians and Larandians had risen against and killed Alexander's satrap Balacrus son of Nicanor (D 18.22.1). These cities Perdiccas took without great difficulty, and they proved a source of plunder for his men. Victorious in the field and offering lucrative rewards to his soldiers, Perdiccas now enjoyed his greatest success (D 18.22.2–8; J 13.6.1–3; but J and Diodorus disagree on the question of booty).

It was at this time that Antipater's daughter Nicaea was brought to Asia by Iolaus and Archias (D 18.23.1; A*Succ* 1.21; J 13.6.4–6). But Perdiccas, who had found a marriage alliance with Antipater's family desirable in 323, now had second thoughts. To make matters worse, Cleopatra, Alexander's sister, had arrived in Sardis, having been sent out (no doubt) at the instigation of Olympias (A*Succ* 1.21; cf. J 13.6.4). Eumenes may have had a hand in the affair: Leonnatus had opened his eyes to Cleopatra's potential, and Eumenes, who urged Perdiccas to marry her in place of Nicaea, may have corresponded with the scheming Olympias, encouraging her to send out her daughter. For his part, Perdiccas had begun to formulate a new policy, one that he hoped would win for him the throne. With the Kings securely in his possession and the army favorably disposed toward him on account of his recent successes in Cappadocia and Pisidia, Perdiccas was prepared to take two final steps to the kingship: union with Cleopatra and the ceremonious return of Alexander's body to Macedonia. What army would oppose the man returning to Macedonia with the son of Philip II, the wife, son, and sister – indeed, the very body – of Alexander himself?

The almost contemporaneous arrivals of Nicaea and Cleopatra were most inopportune. In fact, Nicaea's very presence was an indication of changing events: the Macedonians had been victorious in the Lamian War, Antipater's power restored. And he meant to achieve stability by wedding Phila to Craterus, Nicaea to Perdiccas. By rejecting Nicaea now, Perdiccas would certainly invite civil war (D 18.23.3; the sentiment at least is expressed by J 13.6.5; see also Macurdy 37–8; Vezin 39; cf. Beloch iv^2 1.83). But there was also the matter of the rebellious Antigonus, satrap of Phrygia and friend of Antipater. What Perdiccas needed was time enough to settle affairs in Asia to his satisfaction. To this time belongs the restoration of the Samian exiles, a matter referred by Antipater to the Kings and carried out by Perdiccas in the name of Philip Arrhidaeus (D 18.18.6, 9).[542] Perhaps Perdiccas received news of this from Iolaus and Archias, when they brought out Nicaea.

Perdiccas now called Antigonus to account, planning to remove him under the guise of legality (D 18.23.3–4). But Antigonus, who understood Perdiccas' intention – and, indeed, would use similar methods in the future – made no attempt to clear himself of the charges brought against him: guilty of insubordination, he now fled from his satrapy (D 18.23.4, 25.3; J 13.6.7–9; A*Succ* 1.24) and joined Craterus and Antipater, revealing Perdiccas' ambitions and duplicity in his dealings with Nicaea; he also reported Alcetas' murder of Cynnane (A*Succ* 1.24; see s.vv. **Alcetas**, **Cynnane**), which must have been committed without Perdiccas' approval.[543] At any rate, the army mutinied and demanded that Cynnane's purpose be fulfilled, that Adea be taken to Arrhidaeus (Pol*Strat* 8.60; A*Succ* 1.22–4). Antigonus thus sought refuge with Antipater and Craterus, warning them of Perdiccas' intention to march on Macedonia (D 18.23.4, 25.3–4; J 13.6.7–9; A*Succ* 1.24; cf. Vezin 37; Kaerst ii^2 21). Ptolemy, who had long feared Perdiccan intervention in Egypt (D 18.14.2, 25.4), made an alliance with the *strategoi* in Europe, who now abandoned their Aetolian war in mid-winter 321/0 and prepared to cross into Asia (D 18.25.5; J 13.6.9). Polyperchon held Europe (J 13.6.9).

Perdiccas abandoned Nicaea and openly courted Cleopatra, sending Eumenes with gifts to Sardis, where she had taken up residence (A*Succ* 1.26). Antigonus' defection had been followed by that of Asander, the Carian satrap, and now Menander of Lydia also took flight (A*Succ* 1.26; 25.2; cf. Engel 1972b: 215–19). Perdiccas knew that a confrontation with Antipater and his allies was inevitable, and he meant to bolster his position by marrying Cleopatra before he took to the field and marched on Macedonia. But at this point the bottom fell out of Perdiccas' carefully conceived scheme: Arrhidaeus had completed the funeral car in Babylon and had begun to transport the King's body to Egypt. This had clearly been the King's intention, but Arrhidaeus (see s.v. **Arrhidaeus** [2]), who spent almost two years overseeing the funeral arrangements, was surely instructed by Perdiccas that there would be a change in plans: Alexander's body would be taken to Macedonia, not Egypt (D 18.3.5; J 12.15.7; 13.4.6; C 10.5.4). Paus 1.6.3 does say that the body was destined for Aegae, but this was in accordance with Perdiccas' change of policy; there is no mention of Alexander's wishes here.[544] We can only assume, as Perdiccas himself did, that there had been collusion between Ptolemy and the satrap of Babylonia, Archon; it was symptomatic of widespread disaffection among the officials of the empire (A*Succ* 24.3). Word came to Perdiccas that Arrhidaeus had turned southward and was making for Egypt. A contingent headed by the sons of Andromenes (A*Succ* 1.25; 24.1), sent out to retrieve Alexander's body, proved inadequate; for Ptolemy had marched out in full force to meet Arrhidaeus' procession and escort it to Egypt (D 18.28.2ff.; A*Succ* 1.25; Paus 1.6.4; cf. C 10.10.20). News of the "body-snatching" emphasized the need to secure Asia first (D 18.25.6; J 13.6.10–13; A*Succ* 24.1; Seibert 110–17). Perdiccas had other grievances against Ptolemy: his execution of the hyparch Cleomenes and his expansionist war against Cyrene. Making what arrangements he felt necessary for the security of Asia Minor,[545] Perdiccas began his assault on Egypt,[546] where Ptolemy had spent the two years after the settlement at Babylon fortifying his satrapy and winning the loyalty of his followers (D 18.33.3–4). Perdiccas, if indeed he did try to win support among his generals through gifts and promises (so D 18.33.5), was less successful; for he seems not to have been well liked by the army or its officers (J 13.8.2; A*Succ* 1.28; *Suda Π* 1040; cf. Beloch iv^2 1.88). Failing to take Kamelon Teichos by storm, Perdiccas broke camp on the following night and marched upstream to an island that lay opposite Memphis. But in the attempt to reach the island, he lost many men in the river, which was unexpectedly swift and deep. Once across, Perdiccas recognized that he had too few men for an assault on Memphis and was forced to recross the treacherous river. In all, according to D 18.36.1, some 2,000 men were lost, including some prominent officers, though none of these is named. It was as much as the army was willing to endure from Perdiccas, whom they held responsible for their present miseries. He had failed for the last time. The foremost of his generals, including Peithon and Seleucus, conspired against him during the night and murdered him in his tent. For Perdiccas' campaign against Ptolemy see D 18.33–7 (the only extensive account); also A*Succ* 1.28; P*Eum* 8.2–3; J 13.8.1–2; see Seibert 118–28 for an analysis of the accounts. For his death: A 7.18.5 (it was prophesied by the seer Peithagoras); N*Eum* 5.1; J 13.8.10; 14.1.1, 4.11; 15.1.1; D 18.36.5; Paus 1.6.3; *Suda Π* 1040; *HE* 1.

Hoffmann 153, 168; Berve ii.313–16 no. 627; Geyer, *RE* s.v. "Perdikkas (4)"; Wirth 1967; Heckel 134–63. See Stemma XII.

Perdiccas [2]. (Perdikkas). A Macedonian officer in the army of Eumenes, Perdiccas defected with 3,000 infantry and 500 horse in Cappadocia in spring 320, shortly before the battle of Orcynia. Phoenix of Tenedos, who had been sent after the mutineers with 4,000 foot and 1,000 horse, surprised Perdiccas' forces as they slept and captured them with their leader. The leaders, including Perdiccas (though this is not stated explicitly), were executed, though Eumenes spared the common soldiers (D 18.40.2–4).[547] Nothing is known of Perdiccas' earlier career, but his association with Eumenes, who was outlawed at Triparadeisus with the other leaders of the Perdiccan party and who had received no reinforcements from Europe between 323 and 320, suggests that he was already serving in Asia during Alexander's lifetime.

Berve ii.317 no. 628.

Perilaus [1]. (Perilaos; Perillos; Perillus). *Hetairos* of Alexander, perhaps of Greek origin. Perilaus asked Alexander for a dowry for his daughters and received fifty talents (P*M* 179f). The story itself is one of many illustrating the generosity of kings, and we may place no faith in the figures given. If this anecdote did, in fact, have its roots in some historical event, then we must suppose that it dates to after 331/0 BC – after Alexander's capture of the Persian treasures – and that Perilaus, who had daughters of marriageable age at that time, was born not later than the mid-360s. He may well be identical with that Perilaus who, along with Pasas the Thessalian and Damis [MSS. Amissus] of Megalopolis, acted as negotiators for the Macedonian cavalry and infantry in Babylon immediately after Alexander's death (C 10.8.15). Given the fact that the three other mediators at Babylon were Greeks (including Eumenes, P*Eum* 3.1) and the frequency of the name outside Macedonia (cf. Pape & Benseler s.v.), it appears that Perilaus was one of Alexander's Greek *hetairoi*. He is perhaps identical with the Perilaus who led the land forces, in concert with the fleet of Antigonus' *nauarchos* Theodotus, to Patara in Lycia, in 315 BC. He was captured by Ptolemy's admiral Polycleitus but soon ransomed by Antigonus (D 19.64.5–8). Identification with Antipater's son (below) is highly unlikely, since Cassander and Antigonus were at war at this time and Diodorus (Hieronymus) would no doubt have commented on the relationship, if Perilaus had defected to Antigonus.

Berve ii.317 no. 630; Billows 416 no. 89.

Perilaus [2]. (Perilaos; Perillus). Son of Antipater and younger brother of Cassander (P*M* 486a); he seems to have remained in Pella with his father during the period 334–323.

Berve ii.317 no. 629.

Peroedas (Peroidas). Son of Menestheus. Commander of the *ile* of Companions from Anthemus,[548] Peroedas appears to have accompanied Alexander from the beginning of the campaign. At Issus, his squadron was transferred, along with that of Pantordanus, from the left to the right wing before the battle began (A 2.9.3). Nothing further is known of his role in that engagement. Like Pantordanus, he was no longer an ilarch at Gaugamela, and it seems unlikely that both died at Issus. Who his replacement was is unclear: Ariston, Demetrius, Glaucias, Hegelochus, and Meleager all appear for the first time at Gaugamela, though two of them may well have been ilarchs at Issus.

Berve ii.317 no. 631; Heckel 350; Hoffmann 184–5.

Petenes. A high-ranking Persian commander at the Granicus battle (A 1.12.8), who was killed during the cavalry engagement (A 1.16.3; D 17.21.3 appears to have confused Petenes with Atizyes, whose death he records a second time at Issus: 17.34.5).

Berve ii.317 no. 632 ("Petines").

Petisis. Egyptian. In 331, Alexander left Petisis and Doloaspis (another Egyptian) as nomarchs of Egypt; they must have been overseers of the lesser nomarchs of Upper and Lower Egypt, although we cannot say which of the two regions was assigned to Petisis. At any rate, Petisis relinquished the position for unspecified reasons very soon afterwards and the offices were combined under Doloaspis (A 3.5.2).

Berve ii.317–18 no. 633.

Peucestas [1]. (Peukestas; Peukestes; Peucestes). Son of Macartatus; *strategos* in Egypt together with Theramenes (A 3.5.5; C 4.8.4, naming only Peucestas and numbering his force at 4,000). Lehmann-Haupt 152 suggests that Upper and Lower Egypt were divided between Peucestas and Theramenes, though we do not know who received which.[549]

Berve ii.319 no. 635.

Peucestas [2]. (Peukestas; Peukestes; Peucestes). Macedonian. Son of Alexander, from Mieza, where Alexander and the Pages were educated by Aristotle (A*Ind* 18.6; cf. A*Succ* 1.38), born most likely in the early 350s; Amyntas, a Somatophylax of Philip III Arrhidaeus in 320, was his brother (see s.v. **Amyntas** [11]). Peucestas is first mentioned as a trierarch of the Hydaspes fleet (A*Ind* 18.6), an indication of his high standing and financial status. Not much later, in the Mallian campaign, he was seriously wounded in an attempt to save the King's life (C 9.5.14–18; A 6.9.3, 10.1–2, 11.7–8; 6.28.4; A*Ind* 19.8; D 17.99.4; PA 63.5; cf. Ps-Call 3.4.14–15; *IA* 115). About this most memorable event in Peucestas' career (cf. D 19.14.5) there is no dispute in the ancient sources, but there is some disagreement amongst modern scholars concerning the unit to which he belonged.[550]

As a reward for his bravery, Alexander made him an exceptional eighth Bodyguard (A 6.28.4; cf. 7.5.4: he was also awarded a golden crown at Susa in 324) and very soon thereafter assigned him the satrapy of Persis (A 6.30.2), which Peucestas administered with such zeal that he adopted Persian dress and became the first Macedonian of record to learn the Persian language (A 6.30.3). This conduct, though pleasing to Alexander himself, earned the disapproval of his countrymen (A 7.6.3; cf. 7.23.3). D 19.14.5, however, says that, on account of his heroism, Peucestas alone received Alexander's *permission* to adopt Persian dress.

Peucestas was in Babylon at the time of Alexander's death in June 323, having brought recruits from the Cossaeans and Tapurians (A 7.23.1; cf. D 17.110.2: 20,000 Persian archers and slingers). He is said to have attended the drinking-party hosted by Medius of Larissa, at which the King became fatally ill; indeed, it is alleged that he was involved in a conspiracy to poison the King (Ps-Call 3.31.8; cf. Heckel 1988: 38–9; 74–5). Along with Attalus, Peithon, Seleucus, and others, Peucestas spent the night in the temple of Sarapis, inquiring about the health of Alexander (A 7.26.2). Little is known about Peucestas in the years between Alexander's death and the settlement of Triparadeisus, where his brother, Amyntas, was appointed Somatophylax of Philip III in 320 (A*Succ* 1.38). He himself was confirmed as satrap of Persis (at Babylon: D 18.3.3; J 13.4.23; Dexippus, *FGrH* 100 F8 §6; cf. *LM* 121; at Triparadeisus: D 18.39.6; A*Succ* 1.35).

Peucestas' immense popularity in the east and the importance of his satrapy made him a natural leader of the resistance to Peithon, who in 317 tried to revive for himself the position of "*strategos* of the Upper Satrapies," which he had held temporarily under Perdiccas in 323/2 (D 19.14.1–4). And he had gathered, in addition to his own forces (10,000 Persian archers and slingers; 3,000 Macedonian-style infantrymen; and 400 Persian horsemen: D 19.14.5), contingents led by the satraps Tlepolemus, Stasander, and Sibyrtius; Oxyartes had sent troops under the care of Androbazus, and Eudamus had come from India (D 19.14.6–8). It was this army, assembled to oppose Peithon, that Eumenes sought to bring under his own control in Susiana (D 19.15.1; P*Eum* 13.9). But the question of leadership went beyond the rivalry of the respective commanders (N*Eum* 7.1); the division of sentiment appears to have followed racial lines (D 19.15.1; cf. P*Eum* 14.8ff.). Peucestas, it appears, did not formally acknowledge Eumenes' leadership, but accepted for the time a joint command in the name of Alexander the Great, a face-saving proposal. Fear of Antigonus, who threatened to remove him from his satrapy and perhaps end his life, induced Peucestas to throw in his lot with Eumenes (D 19.17.5). Reluctantly, Peucestas summoned 10,000 archers from Persia (D 19.17.4–6). But, upon reaching his home province, Peucestas attempted to gain the supreme command through an extravagant show of pomp (D 19.21.2–23.1; cf. P*Eum* 14.5), which might have succeeded, had not Eumenes resorted to deception in order to win back the troops. Producing forged letters, purportedly from the Armenian satrap Orontas, Eumenes announced that Olympias had expelled Cassander from Macedonia and placed Alexander IV on the throne;

Polyperchon, the letter alleged, was approaching Cappadocia in order to attack Antigonus from the west (D 19.23.2–3; Pol*Strat* 4.8.3).

Rivalry between Eumenes and Peucestas was intense (N*Eum* 7.1), despite their friendship in Alexander's lifetime (P*Eum* 13.9): Eumenes further undermined Peucestas' authority by bringing charges against the latter's friend Sibyrtius (D 19.23.4), and, when he fled, Eumenes led Peucestas on with idle promises (D 19.24.1). In the end, however, it was the will of the Macedonian element, almost certainly the Argyraspids, that prevailed and Eumenes, despite an illness contracted in Persia (D 19.24.6; P*Eum* 14.6), was hailed as the commander-in-chief. In Paraetacene, Peucestas' subordinate position may be seen in the fact that Eumenes had an *agema* of horsemen (300 strong), whereas a corresponding *agema* was shared by Peucestas and Antigenes (D 19.28.3).

Perhaps disillusionment affected his performance. Peucestas appears now to have been seeking a pretext for breaking with Eumenes and his ally Antigenes. The dispersal of the troops in winter quarters in Media might have facilitated a withdrawal. But the army of Antigonus had sought to catch the enemy disunited, only to be forced by the weather to make its size and presence known. Natives on dromedaries, sent out on a spying mission (D 19.37.6), brought news of Antigonus' army which prompted Peucestas to consider flight (P*Eum* 15.7–8). But the accounts, deriving from Hieronymus (Hornblower 1981: 151), are hostile to Peucestas and depict him as overcome by fear (P*Eum* 15.8; cf. D 19.38.1), and the defeat at Gabiene is attributed to his poor showing in the cavalry engagement (P*Eum* 16.9; D 19.42.4, 43.2–3 and esp. 19.43.5). After the battle, when it was learned that Antigonus had captured the baggage camp and was offering to restore their property to those who defected, Peucestas and his Persian force abandoned Eumenes, though only after the desertion of the Argyraspids had sealed his fate (Pol*Strat* 4.6.13). That Peucestas betrayed his allies during the battle is almost certainly not the case, for the hostile sources would not have failed to bring this charge against him both through vindictiveness and to exculpate Eumenes. Perhaps the intervention of Sibyrtius helped him escape the fate of the other prominent officers who had surrendered (D 19.44.1). Antigonus removed him from his satrapy but kept him in his entourage until he returned to Asia Minor, where Peucestas resurfaces on an inscription from Carian Theangela (*Staatsv.* iii.249; Momigliano 1931: 245–6; Buraselis 21 n. 70; Billows 1989: 180). Phylarchus (*ap.* Ath 14. 614f = *FGrH* 81 F12) suggests that Peucestas was still active at the court of Demetrius Poliorcetes at some time after the battle of Ipsus.

Berve ii. 318–19 no. 634; Billows 417–18 no. 90; Billows 1989: 180, 185; Buraselis 21 n. 70; Momigliano 1931; Hornblower 1981: *passim*; Milns 1982; Heckel 263–7.

Peucolaus [1]. (Peukolaos). Macedonian. Peucolaus was left with 3,000 men in Sogdiana, when Alexander returned to Zariaspa-Bactra for the winter of 329/8 (C 7.10.10). The small number of men and the relative obscurity of Peucolaus suggest that he was left as *phrourarchos* of a fortified place. Nothing further is known about him or the fate of his garrison.

Berve ii.319 no. 636.

Peucolaus [2]. (Peukolaos). Macedonian of unknown origin. One of the fellow-conspirators of Dimnus in 330 BC (C 6.7.15, 9.5); his name was given by Dimnus to Nicomachus and came eventually to Alexander's attention. He was arrested and executed at Phrada for his part in the plot (C 6.11.38).

Berve ii.319–20 no. 637.

Peucolaus [3]. (Peukolaos). A Macedonian of humble origins, Peucolaus is alleged to have made a tearful speech to Alexander as he lay on his deathbed and to have elicited a grateful response from the dying

King (*LM* 105–6; Ps-Call 3.32.14–15). Whether he is a historical figure or a fiction is impossible to determine.

Berve ii.320 no. 638.

Pharasmenes. Ruler of the Chorasmians, who lived on the lower Oxus in the region beyond Bokhara (A 4.15.4; C 8.1.8 wrongly calls him Phrataphernes). Bessus had hoped in vain for his support (C 7.4.6), as did Spitamenes (Str 11.8.8 [513]), but Pharasmenes had wisely refrained from joining the resistance to Alexander. In 328 he came to Zariaspa (Bactra) to make submission and to offer his services in a campaign against the Amazons and Colchians (A 4.15.4; cf. C 8.1.8). Pharasmenes' activities were apparently monitored by Artabazus, satrap of Bactria (A 4.15.5), and, although Alexander declined his offer at that time, he suggests that he might avail himself of it on a later occasion (A 4.15.6). Pharasmenes is not heard of again.

Berve ii.379 no. 765.

Pharismenes (Pharasmenes?). Son of Phrataphernes the satrap of Hyrcania and Parthia. Sent to Carmania by his father with supplies for Alexander, who had finished the Gedrosian march (A 6.27.3, 6).[551] He may be that son of Phrataphernes who is elsewhere referred to as Phradasmenes (A 7.6.4; cf. Berve ii.400 no. 812; Bosworth ii.105), but the identification is far from certain.

Pharnabazus (Pharnabazos). Persian. Son of Artabazus and a Rhodian woman; hence also nephew of Memnon and Mentor. When Memnon died in 333 he entrusted the affairs of the Aegean littoral to Pharnabazus, along with the fleet-commander Autophradates, pending the approval of Darius III (A 2.1.3). Pharnabazus and Autophradates secured Mytilene, which they forced to renounce its alliance with Alexander, and exacted monies from the citizens (A 2.1.4–5);[552] the city was garrisoned, with Lycomedes the Rhodian as *phrourarchos*, and entrusted to the tyrant Diogenes (A 2.1.5).[553] From Lesbos Pharnabazus sailed to Lycia, where he was met by Thymondas son of Mentor, who brought news that Pharnabazus' position as Memnon's successor had been confirmed by Darius but took from him the mercenary troops to lead back to the King (A 2.2.1; C 3.3.1). Pharnabazus now sailed to join Autophradates' in whose company he took Tenedos (A 2.2.2–3) and Chios (A 2.13.4); some ships were sent to Cos and Halicarnassus. At Siphnos Pharnabazus met Agis III of Sparta and received from the east news of the disaster at Issus. Leaving Autophradates to deal with Agis, he sailed to Chios to prevent its defection (A 2.13.5). But Pharnabazus soon lost Chios and, although he was captured in the process by Hegelochus (A 3.2.3–4; C 4.5.15–18), he managed to escape at Cos (A 3.2.7). He reappears in 321/0, after a long absence. His support of Eumenes will be due in part to the fact that Eumenes had married his sister, Artonis. When Eumenes fought Craterus in Hellespontine Phrygia, he did not set Macedonians opposite him – for he was afraid of Craterus' popularity with the Macedonian troops – but instead two commanders of mercenary cavalry: Pharnabazus son of Artabazus and Phoenix of Tenedos. They were ordered to attack quickly and not let Craterus send a herald to induce the troops to defect (P*Eum* 7.1). What became of Pharnabazus is unknown.

Berve ii.379–80 no. 766. See Stemma IV.

Pharnaces (Pharnakes). The brother of an earlier wife of Darius III (**F5**), his name and that of (apparently) his nephew, Ariobarzanes, suggest that Pharnaces belonged to the Cappadocian-Pontic aristocracy (thus Berve ii.380) or that he was related to the family of Artabazus (cf. Bosworth i.125). Certainly, his presence as one of the Persian leaders in the Granicus battle, where he perished (A 1.16.3; D

17.21.3), supports the assumption that he came from Asia Minor.

Berve ii.380 no. 767.

Pharnuches. Lycian by birth but an expert in the languages of Bactria and Sogdiana. He had probably entered Alexander's entourage after the death of Darius, unless he was found in one of the Persian capitals.[554] He was sent in 329 with Menedemus, Caranus, and Andromachus against the rebel Spitamenes (A 4.3.7). The force was, however, ambushed at the Polytimetus River and annihilated (A 4.5.3–9 = Ptolemy, *FGrH* 138 F34). In Aristobulus' version, Pharnuches attempted to resign his command but found no one willing to accept it (A 4.6.1–2 = *FGrH* 139 F27). Pharnuches was almost certainly the father of Bagoas the trierarch (A*Ind* 18). But the identity of this Bagoas is less certain.

Berve ii.380–1 no. 768.

Phasimelus (Phasimelos). A harpist of unknown origin, Phasimelus performed at the mass-marriage ceremony in Susa in 324 (Chares, *FGrH* 125 F4 = Ath 12.539a). He is otherwise unknown.

Berve ii.381 no. 769.

Phegeus. Indian ruler, who lived east of the kingdom of Sophytes and near the Hyphasis. His name appears to be formed from the region he ruled, that is, the Begas River area (Anspach ii.38 n. 245). Phegeus submitted to Alexander (who made him subordinate to Porus), bearing gifts and reporting the existence, extent, and power of the Nanda kingdom to the east (D 17.93.1–2; C 9.1.36–2.4).

Berve ii.381 no. 770.

Pheidon. See s.v. **Demetrius** [3].

Phesinus (Phesinos). Chian rebel and member of the oligarchic pro-Persian party. Captured when Hegelochus took the city and brought by him to Alexander in Egypt (332/1 BC). Phesinus, Apollonides, Megareus, and a few others (C 4.5.17 adds Athenagoras) were imprisoned in Elephantine (A 3.2.5, 7).

Berve ii.381–2 no. 771; Baumbach 35ff.; Berve 1967: i.339, ii.691; Hofstetter 149 no. 254.

Phila [1]. Sister of Derdas and Machatas (Ath 13.557c), a woman of the Elimeiot royal house[555] and thus probably a relative of Alexander's treasurer, Harpalus. Born soon after 375, in all likelihood. She was apparently the first or second wife of Philip II, but Satyrus' list as preserved in Athenaeus is not necessarily in chronological order. She appears to have remained childless, and the view that she was the mother of Caranus (Berve ii.200; Milns 18) is unsupported by the evidence.

Carney 59–60.

Phila [2]. Theban girl, enslaved as a result of Alexander's sack of the city in 335, ransomed for twenty minas by Hypereides, who kept her at his estate in Eleusis ([P]*M* 849d; cf. Idomeneus, *FGrH* 338 F14 = Ath 13.590d).

Berve ii.382 no. 773.

Phila [3]. Eldest of at least four daughters of Antipater son of Iolaus (D 18.18.7; P*Demetr* 14.2); her sisters were Nicaea, Eurydice (P*Demetr* 46.5), and an *anonyma* who married Alexander Lyncestes (J 12.14.1; C 7.1.7). Born shortly before 350 BC, she married Balacrus son of Nicanor in the mid-330s and bore him a son, Antipater (*IG* xi.2 161b, line 85; xi.2 287b, line 57). She appears to have remained with her father in Macedonia until at least 331 or 330. Antonius Diogenes *ap.* Phot*Bibl* 111a–b mentions a letter written by Balacrus to Phila at some time after the fall of Tyre in August 332; the details of the letter need not be believed. She may have been escorted to Cilicia, where her husband was now satrap, by Amyntas son of Andromenes (but this is merely speculation). Her son, Antipater, if he was not born in the mid-330s, will have been born at some time between 330/29 and 324; for in 324 Balacrus was killed in a skirmish with the Pisidians (D 18.22.1). She appears to have returned to Macedonia with Craterus, whom she married in 322/1 (Memnon, *FGrH* 434 F1 §4.4; D 18.18.7; P*Demetr* 14.2). To him she bore a son of the same name (cf. Perdrizet 1899), but she was soon widowed a second time; for Craterus died in the battle with Eumenes (his remains were entrusted by Eumenes to Ariston, who returned them to Phila for burial in 316 or 315: D 19.59.3). Soon after the settlement at Triparadeisus in 320, Phila married Demetrius Poliorcetes although she was considerably older than he (P*Demetr* 14.2–4, 27.8), to whom she bore Antigonus Gonatas (cf. P*Demetr* 37.4) and a daughter, Stratonice (P*Demetr* 31.5, 53.8). (Perhaps an indication of the kind of abuse Demetrius subjected her to: Demetrius had a daughter by Lamia the prostitute, whom she called Phila, Ath 13.577c).[556] After Demetrius was driven out of Macedonia in 288, she could no longer bear her husband's misfortunes and committed suicide by poison (P*Demetr* 45.1). Her exceptional personal qualities are spelled out by D 19.59.3–5, and her dedication to her husband[557] and her brother recalls the behavior of Octavia.

Berve ii.382 no. 772; Macurdy 58–69; Wehrli 1964; Heckel 1987a; Carney 165–9. See Stemmata V, VI.

Philine (Philinna). From Larissa. Wife of Philip II and mother of Arrhidaeus (Satyrus *ap.* Ath 13.557c; A*Succ* 1.1). Philip appears to have married her in 358 and her son was born before Alexander but soon showed signs of mental impairment (see s.v. **Arrhidaeus** [1]). Stories that she was a dancing-girl (*saltatrix*) and a harlot are, as Carney 61 notes, later inventions meant to discredit Philip III and his guardians (Ath 13.577f–578a = Ptolemy of Megalopolis, *FGrH* 161 F4; J 9.8.2; 13.2.11). Since the marriage was meant to strengthen the bond between Philip and his Larissan allies, it is likely that Philine belonged to the aristocracy, probably to the Aleuadae.[558] That she was the mother of Amphimachus by another marriage is highly unlikely (see A*Succ* 1.35 with Jacoby, iiD, 563; Beloch iv^2 2.316): the suggestion is based on a misunderstanding on the part of Arrian's source, possibly Duris of Samos.[559]

Carney 61–2; Ogden 17–27. See Stemma I.

Philip [1]. (Philippus; Philippos). Philip II of Macedon (*regn.* 360/59–336). Born in 383/2, Philip was the third son of Amyntas III (*regn.* 393–369) and Eurydice (D 16.1.3; see s.v. **Eurydice** [1]), and brother of Alexander II, Perdiccas III, and Eurynoë (J 7.4.5). Hostage in Thebes, probably during the reign of Alexander II, and briefly during the regency of Ptolemy of Alorus, his brother-in-law (J 7.5.2–3; D 15.67.4; PM 178c); he may earlier have been a hostage of the Illyrians (D 16.2.2; J 7.5.1). On the death of Perdiccas III in battle against the Illyrians, Philip ruled either as regent (J 7.5.9–10; Satyrus *ap.* Ath 13.557b) for his nephew (see s.v. **Amyntas** [1]), or as king in his place (D 16.1.3, 2.1; cf. Griffith, *HMac* ii.208–9, 702–4). If he served as regent, he assumed the kingship very soon afterwards. Philip took the reins of power at a critical time: over 4,000 Macedonians had been killed in the Illyrian disaster and the confidence of those who survived was badly shaken (D 16.2.5); and, in addition to numerous external enemies, Philip had to overcome challenges from his three half-brothers, the sons of Gygaea (J 7.4.5; 8.3.10), at least one of whom, Archelaus, was probably executed in 359 (J 7.6.3; cf. Ellis 1973; Griffith, *HMac* ii.699–701). Immediately, Philip placed the Macedonian army on a stronger footing by improving discipline, training, and equipment (D 16.3.1–2). His introduction of the *sarissa*, an 18-foot pike, revolutionized Greek warfare and proved to be the basis of Macedonian power. In the first year of his rule, he was challenged by Argaeus, who claimed the Macedonian throne with Athenian support but was defeated by Philip's general, Mantias; the Paeonians and Thracians were for the time being bought off. With his reformed army, he defeated the Illyrian king, Bardylis, in 358 (J 7.6.7; D 16.4.3–7, 8.1), and cemented the peace by marrying his daughter Audata, who later bore him a daughter (Ath 13.557c; see s.v. **Cynnane**). In 358, he intervened in northern Thessaly (J 7.6.8–9; D 16.14.1–2) and took another political wife, Philine of Larissa, who, in 357, gave birth to Arrhidaeus [1] (Ath 13.557c; J 9.8.2 calls her a dancer and a prostitute, 13.2.11; but see s.v. **Philine**). His alliance with Epirus was accompanied by a marriage to Olympias, who was to be the mother of Alexander the Great and Cleopatra [2] (Ath 13.557d), and he later removed the Epirote heir, Alexander [1], to Macedonia (J 7.6.10–12; 8.6.4–8). When Alexander reached maturity in 342, Philip installed him as king of Epirus, driving out his former ally, Arybbas (D 16.72.1; cf. *IG* ii^2 226 = Rhodes & Osborne no. 70, with commentary on 352–5; see s.vv. **Arybbas**, **Alexander** [1]).

Philip exploited the Athenians' troubles in the Social War (357–355) to gain control of Amphipolis and Pydna (357) and Potidaea (356). On the day Potidaea fell, he learned of the birth of Alexander the Great, Parmenion's victory over the Illyrians, and the success of his chariot team at Olympia (P*A* 3.8). In 354 he captured Methone but lost his right eye to a defender's arrow (J 7.6.14–15; P*A* 3.2). Philip soon became involved in the Sacred War against the Phocians who had violated the sanctuary of Delphi; he posed as champion of the Greeks and, in the process, secured control of the remainder of Thessaly. After two military setbacks in 353, in at least one of which the Phocians used artillery to great advantage (Pol*Strat* 2.38.2; D 16.35.2), Philip defeated the enemy in the battle of the Crocus Field in 352 (J 8.2.1–4; D 16.35.4–5, 38.1). A final reckoning with the Phocians was thwarted when they occupied Thermopylae against him. Pherae now fell into his hands and with it control of the Thessalian League, which elected him as its *archon*. Again he strengthened his position by political marriage, this time to Nicesipolis of Pherae, who bore him another daughter; Ellis 212, with n. 10, puts the marriage in 352 but the date is not certain and might belong to 346/5 (Ath 13.557c; see s.v. **Thessalonice** for details). The steady growth of Philip's power created great anxiety in Athens, which was only increased when Philip attacked and destroyed Olynthus, which was harboring his political rivals (J 8.3.10–11); despite Demosthenes' impassioned *Olynthiac* orations, the Athenians were slow to respond to the threat. In 346, an agreement with the Greeks left Philip free to fortify Thermopylae, dismantle Phocian power (D 16.59–6; J 8.4–5), and pursue his interests in the northeast.

It may be that he had already conceived a plan to attack the Persian Empire (thus D 16.60.5); and it is at this time that Isocrates wrote his *Philippus*, urging Philip to do just that. Artabazus, the rebellious satrap of Hellepontine Phrygia, had been received as a suppliant in Pella along with his large family around 353/2 (thus Ellis 92), and D 16.52.3 speaks of them as still resident there in 349. Furthermore, Philip may have had an "agent" in Asia Minor in Aristotle, son of the former court physician Nicomachus (see Guthrie 35–6; cf. Ellis 97–8), who would soon be invited to Macedonia as tutor of the young Alexander (P*A* 7.2–4; see s.v. **Aristotle** for further details). That Philip seriously considered an expedition against Persia before bringing the Greek states under his control is doubtful. But it does not follow that, because he initiated the Persian war only after the creation of the League of Corinth, he could not have launched such an expedition without the subjugation of the Greeks. Access to Greece via Thermopylae was, however, important, and Philip also held out hope of Athenian cooperation. But this was not forthcoming. His activities in the north in the years that followed 346 may indeed have been in preparation for a large undertaking, but it appears as if many of his moves were intended to pressure the Athenians, who had agreed to the Peace of Philocrates reluctantly. The anti-Macedonian faction, led by Demosthenes and Hegesippus ([Dem] 7, *On Halonnesus*, is apparently his speech) incited the Athenians against Philip. Although the Macedonian King made sincere attempts to reach an agreement, the terms were clearly intended to work in his favor. For the Athenians, opposition to Macedon was an attempt to salvage lost pride, a futile and dangerous undertaking. Philip's subsequent activities in Thrace and Illyria were essential to Macedonian security. But Perinthus and Byzantium, against which he moved in 340 (D 16.74.2–76.4; J 9.1.1–7), lay on Athens' economic lifeline, as did the Thracian Chersonese, and the aim was clearly to force a showdown with the Athenians.

In 338, Philip defeated a coalition of Thebans and Athenians at Chaeronea (D 16.85.2–86.4; Pol*Strat* 4.2.2, 7; J 9.3.4–11), in a battle that saw the 18-year-old Alexander commanding the Macedonian left, where the vaunted Sacred Band of the Thebans were annihilated (P*A* 9.2). The victory brought Boeotia into Philip's power and cowed the Athenians into submission. Philip took no punitive action against the Athenians (J 9.4.1–3; P*M* 177e–f) – indeed, he had taken to heart the rebuke of Demades who, when Philip celebrated his victory in a drunken stupor, charged him with "playing the part of Thersites, when history had cast him in the rôle of Agamemnon" (D 16.87.1–2). They in turn accepted Macedonian hegemony (albeit reluctantly) and joined the League of Corinth, which the King convened in the spring of 337 (J 9.5.1; D 16.89.1–3; *IG* ii^2 236 = Harding no. 99 = Rhodes & Osborne no. 76). The winter of 338/7 appears to have been spent imposing a Macedonian settlement on the Peloponnese (see Roebuck 1948). The Spartans, however, remained aloof, militarily impotent but politically obstinate.

Domestic (i.e., matrimonial) problems would prove to be Philip's undoing. He had married six times before becoming master of Greece, beginning perhaps with a member of the Upper Macedonian aristocracy, Phila, the sister of Derdas and Machatas (Ath 13.557c; for the family see s.v. **Harpalus**; cf. Stemma XIII), and ending with a Thracian princess (Ath 13.557d; see s.v. **Meda**); he considered adoption by the Scythian king, Atheas, no doubt for want of a suitable bride (J 9.2.1–3; *contra* Hammond 1994: 182). But his decision to marry Cleopatra, a daughter of the Macedonian nobleman Attalus (see s.vv. **Cleopatra** [1], **Hegelochus**), threw the household and the state into confusion (Ath 13.560c; P*A* 9.5). It was not the marriage itself that caused a rift between Philip and Alexander, for Alexander was present at the wedding-feast, and his mother, Olympias, was still in Pella. Instead, a tactless prayer by the bride's guardian, that the marriage might produce *legitimate* heirs, was interpreted by Alexander as a challenge and an insult (P*A* 9.7–10; Satyrus *ap.* Ath 13.557d; cf. J 9.7.3–4). The resulting feud between father and son was ended through the intervention of Demaratus of Corinth (P*M* 179c) and the arranged marriage of Alexander's sister, Cleopatra, to her uncle, Alexander I of Epirus (J 9.7.7; D 16.91.4). The reconciliation was genuine but the young prince came to question the motives of Philip's every action, and his insecurity was exploited by the jealous Queen Mother, who felt herself dishonored by the new bride and her family (Heckel 1978a, 1981c). Hence, Philip's plans to marry Arrhidaeus to Ada [2], the daughter of Pixodarus, were misinterpreted by Alexander and his advisors (P*A* 10.1–5; A 3.6.5). Furthermore, Alexander's flight to Illyria in late 337 (P*A* 9.11; J 9.7.5) necessitated a punitive campaign on the western marches of the kingdom (D 16.93.6; often confused with the campaign of 334/3: D 16.69.7). In October 336, after celebrating the nuptials of Cleopatra and Alexander I, Philip was assassinated as he entered the theater in Aegae (modern Vergina) by a member of the royal hypaspists (D 16.91.2–94.4; J 9.7; see s.v. **Pausanias**).

J 9.8.1 says that Philip was 47 years old at the time of his death, having ruled twenty-five years, but these numbers should perhaps be taken as ordinals: he died in his 47th year of life and the 25th year of his reign (D 16.1.3, 95.1; 17.1.1 says he ruled for twenty-four years; Hammond 1992: 361–4 explains the discrepancy in terms of calculation by Athenian and Macedonian years). Despite his injuries (Marsyas, *FGrH* 135/6 F17) – broken collarbone (P*M* 177f; cf. 178a); an eye lost at Methone (J 7.6.14; Duris, *FGrH* 76 F36; Theopompus, *FGrH* 115 F52); and a wound to the thigh in campaign against the Triballians (J 9.3.2, the weapon passed through his leg and killed the horse) – Philip remained for the most part a vigorous and charming man. His fondness for drinking was legendary (*FGrH* 115 F282), but Theopompus saw heavy drinking as a Macedonian trait (FF 163, 236) and depicted the *pezhetairoi* as male-sodomizers (F225b). Philip himself was both a womanizer and an admirer of boys (J 8.6.5–8; D 16.93.3–4); excesses in both cases played no small part in his death. His relationship with Alexander, despite the unfortunate break in 337, was close and cordial. Indeed, after the victory at Chaeronea, Philip is supposed to have been fond of hearing the troops remark that "Philip was their general and Alexander their King" (P*A* 9.4). Although J 9.8 contrasts the characters and actions of the two men, their methods and manners were in many respects the same, and Alexander could truly be seen as Philip's son – except perhaps for Alexander's apparent rejection of pederasty (P*A* 22.1). Not merely for the splendid Macedonian army and the forcible unification of the Greek states was Alexander indebted to his father; he appears to have learned a great deal about the power of propaganda and to have developed a firm grasp of political expediency. Alexander's use of political marriage and his elevation of the conquered nobility to positions amongst his *hetairoi* and administrators, as well as the use of foreign, specialist troops, were all learned in his youth from his brilliant and dynamic father.

Philip so dominated his times that he was the central subject of Theopompus of Chios' historical work, *Philippica*, in fifty-eight books (on which see Jacoby, *FGrH* 115; Shrimpton 1991: 58–126; Flower 1994: 98–135); the major portion of the *Macedonica* of Marsyas of Pella (see s.v. **Marsyas**) also recounted the affairs of Philip II (*FGrH* 135/6; Heckel 1980b); many of the political speeches of Demosthenes deal with Philip, especially the *Philippics*, *Olynthiacs*, *On the Peace*, and *On the Crown*, as do the three extant speeches of Aeschines and Isocrates' *Philippus*. For a collection of readings with commentary see Ellis & Milns 1970 and Phillips 2004: 67–186. For a brief discussion of Tomb II at Vergina (ancient Aegae), often identified as that of Philip II, see Borza 1999: 68–74; for discussions of the physical remains, a reconstruction of the skull from Tomb II, and two possible representations of Philip, see Prag, Musgrave, & Neave 1984; Xirotiris & Langenscheidt 1981; Riginos 1994).

Ellis; Cawkwell 1978; Wirth 1985; Griffith, *HMac* ii.203–726; Errington 1990: 35–102; Borza 1990: 198–230 and 1999: 51–74; Hammond 1994.

Philip [2]. (Philippus; Philippos). A 1.14.2 mentions a Philip son of Amyntas in the Macedonian line at the Granicus. There are, however, some textual difficulties and Philip's patronymic may have been corrupted by the proximity of the name Amyntas (i.e. the son of Andromenes) in the preceding line. He may thus have been the son of Balacrus (below).[560]

Philip [3]. (Philippus; Philippos). Son of Balacrus (D 17.57.3; C 4.13.28) and possibly a brother of Nicanor. Taxiarch; together with Meleager he was responsible for conveying the booty taken from the Getae in 335 back to the Macedonian base (A 1.4.5, naming Philip without patronymic). Philip's association with the taxiarch Meleager son of Neoptolemus suggests that he is identical with the taxiarch Philip attested at the Granicus (A 1.14.2–3).[561] At

Gaugamela he commanded the battalion of Amyntas son of Andromenes during the latter's absence (D 17.57.3; C 4.13.28; but A 3.11.9 assigns this battalion to Amyntas' younger brother Simmias). Nothing else is known about him unless he can be identified with the friend of Demetrius, honored together with a certain Iolaus in Athens in 307 (*IG* ii^2 561).[562]

Berve ii.383–4 no. 778; Billows 796–9 no. 93; Wheatley 1997b.

Philip [4]. (Philippus; Philippos). Philip son of Menelaus was clearly a Macedonian, though his precise origin is unknown. He is first attested as hipparch of the allied cavalry (from the Peloponnese) at the Granicus (A 1.14.3), a unit which he appears to have led from the very beginning of the Asiatic expedition. Philip's name does not reappear until the accounts of Gaugamela, where he leads the Thessalian cavalry (A 3.11.10; D 17.57.4; C 4.13.29); his former hipparchy is now commanded by Erigyius son of Larichus (see s.v. **Erigyius**). It appears that Philip was promoted to hipparch of the Thessalians in the winter of 334/3, after the arrest of Alexander Lyncestes (A 1.25), or at the latest in the spring of 333 at Gordium; at that time Erigyius was assigned the allied cavalry, though neither is mentioned by name until the campaign of Gaugamela.[563]

After the battle of Issus, Philip and the Thessalians were taken by Parmenion to Damascus, where they captured the Persian treasures and many relatives of Persian notables (P*A* 24.1–3). Probably, like Erigyius, Philip remained with Menon son of Cerdimmas in Coele-Syria between early 332 and spring 331 (A 2.13.7). At Ecbatana, however, Alexander dismissed the Thessalian cavalry, and Philip was reassigned to the command of the mercenary horse (A 3.25.4; cf. Berve ii.384), replacing Menidas, who remained in Media with Parmenion. Philip remained for some time in Ecbatana and rejoined the King in Areia ("on the way to Bactra," A 3.25.4), bringing the mercenary cavalry, the *xenoi* of Andromachus, and those of the Thessalians who had volunteered to continue serving Alexander (A 3.25.4; C 6.6.35 says the Thessalians numbered 130). The son of Menelaus is not heard of again. He may, however, have been identical with the later satrap of Bactria and Sogdiana, whom Alexander appointed after the death of Amyntas son of Nicolaus, or possibly the friend of Antigonus the One-Eyed and advisor and general of Demetrius Poliorcetes.

Berve ii.384 no. 779; Heckel 358–9; Wheatley 1997b.

Philip [5]. (Philippus; Philippos). Macedonian. Son of Machatas (A 5.8.3) and probably brother of Harpalus and Tauron. Although Philip is attested with patronymic only once in the Alexander historians, his career can be reconstructed with a measure of certainty. He first appears in the Aspasian campaign of 327/6 BC, leading a battalion of light infantry under the command of Ptolemy son of Lagus (A 4.24.10). At Taxila, Philip was ordered to govern the newly formed satrapy east of the Indus (A 5.8.3), and on the death of Nicanor (A 5.20.7) his province was extended to include Gandhara (A 6.2.3), where he restored order with the help of Tyriespis, satrap of the Parapamisadae. The Philip who was installed as *phrourarchos* of Peucelaotis (= Charsada), under the general supervision of Nicanor, who ruled the Cophen (Gandhara) satrapy (A 4.28.6), is unlikely to have been the son of Machatas. As the Macedonian conquests continued, he received additional territory between the Acesines and Indus rivers as far south as their confluence (A 6.14.3, 15.2; cf. P*A* 60.16), regions which he had himself helped to subdue (A 6.2.3, 4.1; cf. A*Ind* 19.4).

When Alexander moved south toward Sogdia and the kingdom of Musicanus (with its capital at Alor; cf. Eggermont 5–9), Philip remained in the enlarged satrapy, supported by all the Thracians (presumably under Eudamus' command) and a force of mercenaries, with instructions to found a city at the junction of the rivers and build dockyards (A 6.15.2).[564] In 325 Philip was assassinated by mercenaries, some of whom were killed in the act by the satrap's Bodyguard, others were arrested and executed. Alexander, who learned of Philip's death as he marched from Gedrosia to Carmania, appointed Eudamus as his replacement (A 6.27.2; C 10.1.20).

Berve ii.384–5 no. 780, and ii.386–7 no. 784; Bosworth 1973: 252–3.

Philip [6] (Philippus, Philippos). Macedonian. *Patronymikon* unknown (for the difficulties associated with the restoration of the *patronymikon* see Heckel 1981f; Billows 422; Wheatley 1997b: 66). Philip was honored in Athens at some point between 307 and 301, on a motion by Stratocles, a strong supporter of Demetrius Poliorcetes (*IG* ii^2 561). He and a certain Iolaus (see s.v. **Iolaus** [3]) are described as former *somatophylakes* of King Alexander, which presumably means that they were two of the three Somatophylakes assigned to Alexander IV at Triparadeisus in 320 (A*Succ* 1.38 names four for Philip III, and it follows that the infant Alexander received three to bring the total to the traditional seven). At some point, perhaps after the capture of Alexander IV at Pydna, Philip entered the service of Antigonus and Demetrius. What became of him after Ipsus, we do not know.

Berve ii.420 includes Philip's colleague Iolaus amongst individuals who are wrongly associated with Alexander (Abschnitt 2 no. 31) but does not list Philip; Burstein 1977; Heckel 1980d, 1981f; Billows 421–3 no. 93; Wheatley 1997b.

Philip [7]. (Philippus; Philippos). Brother of Lysimachus (C 8.2.35; J 15.3.12), hence also a son of Agathocles (A 6.28.4; A*Ind* 18.3; A*Succ* 1.2), and brother of Autodicus and, perhaps, Alcimachus. On a campaign in Sogdiana, Philip accompanied on foot the King (who rode), declining to take Lysimachus' horse (C 8.2.35–6). Later, after fighting by Alexander's side, he fainted and died in his arms (C 8.2.37–40; cf. J 15.3.12). The wording of C 8.2.35 implies that Philip was a member of the Royal Hypaspists at the time of his death.

Berve ii.382–3 no. 774; Lund 3; Heckel 298. See Stemma IX.

Philip [8]. (Philippus; Philippos). Son of Antipater (J 12.14.6), brother of Iolaus and Cassander. He and Iolaus were apparently Pages (*paides basilikoi*) of Alexander at the time of his death in Babylon and implicated in the alleged plot to poison the King (J 12.14.6–9; cf. Heckel 1988). It appears that, after the death of Alexander and the settlement of affairs in Babylon, Philip returned to Macedonia with his brother Iolaus. He later served his brother Cassander as *strategos* in the campaign against the Aetolians, and won a victory over King Aeacides of Epirus at Oeniadae in 313 BC, in which Aeacides himself died (D 19.74.3–5; Paus 1.11.4; cf. Sandberger 19 no. 5). His successes in Acarnania frightened the Aetolians, who took refuge in the mountains (D 19.74.6), but nothing else is recorded about Philip's generalship or his life. His son Antipater ruled Macedonia for forty-five days in 280 BC (Porphyry, *FGrH* 260 F3 §10), following the death of Ptolemaeus Ceraunus and the brief reign of the latter's brother, Meleager (cf. Walbank, *HMac* iii.253).[565]

Berve ii.383 no. 777; Sandberger 19. See Stemma V.

Philip [9]. (Philippus; Philippos). Physician from Acarnania (D 17.31.5; C 3.6.1; A 2.4.8; P*A* 19.4), he had been Alexander's most trusted physician since the King's boyhood (C 3.6.1). When Alexander became ill in Cilicia, he used an untried potion to treat him and thereby saved his life (D 17.31.5–6) – although, for a time, it looked as if the treatment might fail. Alexander subsequently treated him as one of his most loyal friends (D 17.31.6).[566] There is, however, a tradition that Parmenion sent Alexander a letter warning him that

Philip had been bribed by the Great King to administer poison (A 2.4.9–10; *PA* 19.5–10; Val Max 3.8 ext 6; C 3.6.4–17; Sen*de Ira* 2.23.2; J 11.8.5–8; cf. Ps-Call 2.8.5; Jul Val 2.24), a story which appears to have been confused in some way with the alleged conspiracy of Alexander the Lyncestian (see s.v. **Alexander** [4]). Later, at Gaza (332 BC), Philip treated an arrow wound to Alexander's shoulder (C 4.6.17). But from that point onwards nothing else is recorded about him, unless he is to be identified with Philip the physician, named in the *Last Days and Testament* (Ps-Call 3.31.8). His name may have been added to the list of conspirators because of the earlier charge of attempted poisoning.

Berve ii.388–9 no. 788.

Philip [10]. (Philippus, Philippos). Macedonian. Patronymic unknown. Philip appears to have replaced Amyntas son of Nicolaus as satrap of Bactria and Sogdiana. He retained his satrapy in the settlement of 323 (D 18.3.3; Dexippus, *FGrH* 100 F8 §6; *LM* 121; Ps-Call 3.33.22; cf. J 13.4.23, confused) but was shuffled to Parthia in the reorganization at Triparadeisus in 320 (D 18.39.6; A*Succ* 1.35). Some three years later, Peithon son of Crateuas deposed and killed a *strategos* of Parthia named Philotas and installed his own brother Eudamus as satrap of the region (D 19.14.1). It is generally assumed that Diodorus wrongly named the satrap Philotas instead of Philip (Wheatley 1997b: 62; Billows 90 n. 17). But Schäfer 2002: 159 (without comment) identifies the Philip who served Eumenes at Gabiene as the former satrap of Parthia, and it may be that Peithon had deposed and killed, in Philip's absence, his subordinate, the *strategos* Philotas.[567] It is more likely, however, that Diodorus' text is corrupt, especially since the virtually certain restoration of Philip in *PSI* xii.1284, line 14 increases the likelihood that the Philip who served Eumenes at Gabiene was already with him in 320 BC (cf. Hornblower 1981: 123–4). See below, s.v. **Philip** [11].

Berve ii.387 no. 785.

Philip [11]. (Philippus; Philippos). Macedonian. A senior officer who had campaigned with Alexander (D 19.69.1). He was probably the officer of Eumenes, who is named in *PSI* xii.1284, line 14, and thus already with Eumenes in 321/0. He is later found in Eumenes' service, as commander of elephants and cavalry, at Gabiene (D 19.40.4, 42.7). Presumably, he survived the battle and surrendered to Antigonus, who in 314 appointed him, together with Nearchus, Peithon son of Agenor, and Andronicus of Olynthus, as an advisor of young Demetrius Poliorcetes in 314 (D 19.69.1; cf. Wheatley 1997b). He is not actually named in the account of the battle of Gaza, though Peithon and Andronicus play prominent roles. Whether he is identical with the friend of Antigonus who occupied the acropolis of Sardis in 302 is unclear (D 20.107.5). To identify him with any of the known officers of Alexander is nothing more than guesswork: he may be the son of Menelaus, the son of Balacrus, Philip *mechanikos*. Possibly, he is the man honored with Iolaus in Athens in 307–301 (*IG* ii^2 561).[568]

Berve ii.387 no. 786; Billows 421–3 no. 93; Wheatley 1997b.

Philip [12]. (Philippus; Philippos). Macedonian. One of Alexander's *hetairoi*. Philip had been sent to the oracle of Amun at Siwah to inquire about the honors due to the dead Hephaestion. He returned with the news that he should be revered as a hero (D 17.115.6). He is probably identical with one of the other attested individuals named Philip, but it is impossible to establish which one. Berve identifies him with the Philip of *LM* 92–4.

Berve ii.386 no. 782.

Philip [13]. (Philippus; Philippos). Macedonian of unknown family background. In 326, Alexander appointed Philip as *phrourarchos* of Peucelaotis (A 4.28.6). Bosworth ii.185 tentatively identifies him with the son of Machatas, but the office of *phrourarchos* was generally reserved for men of lower rank. Arrian identifies him neither by patronymic nor as one of the *hetairoi*.[569]

Berve ii.386 no. 783.

Philip [14]. (Philippus; Philippos). Ethnic and *patronymikon* unknown; an engineer (*mechanikos*). He was one of the guests at Medius' dinner-party, and allegedly one of the poisoners of Alexander (Ps-Call 3.31; *LM* 97). Identification with any other known Philip is at best tenuous.

Berve ii.389 no. 789; Heckel 1988: 42–3.

Philip [15]. (Philippus; Philippos). Son of Antigonus the One-Eyed and Stratonice (P*M* 182b; P*Demetr* 2.1–2, 3.4, 23.6). Born perhaps ca. 334 in Macedonia (thus Billows 420); Berve ii.383 believes he may have been born in Celaenae. Philip was named for his paternal grandfather, although he was the second son, Demetrius took the name of his uncle, who had probably died shortly before Demetrius' birth (P*Demetr* 2.1–2). For stories of his early years see P*M* 182b, 506c; Cic *De officiis* 2.48; Fr*Strat* 4.1.10. Like his brother, he was voted a crown by the Scepsians, when they honored Antigonus in 311 (*OGIS* i.6 = Bagnall & Derow no. 6). Philip's first attested command was in 310 (D 20.19.5). He died in 306 in his mid-twenties (D 20.73.1, wrongly calling him Phoenix). He had no personal contact with Alexander.

Berve ii.383 no. 776; Billows 419–21 no. 92. See Stemma VI.

Philip, first husband of Berenice. See n. 648.

Philiscus (Philiskos). Greek from Aegina and apparently father of Onesicritus.[570] *Suda* Φ 359 claims that he was a teacher of the young Alexander (*grammatodidaskalos*), and Ael*VH* 14.11 preserves some advice given by Philiscus to Alexander on statecraft. Onesicritus may have been introduced to the King by his father and inspired to write a work on Alexander's "education" along the lines of Xenophon's *Cyropaedia* (see s.v. **Onesicritus**). Nothing else is known about Philiscus and there is, of course, the risk that the few "biographical" observations that survive were invented.

Berve ii.389 no. 790.

Philistides. A juggler from Syracuse in Alexander's entourage (Ath 1.20a), Philistides performed at the mass-marriage ceremony at Susa in 324 (Chares, *FGrH* 125 F4 = Ath 12.538e). See also s.vv. **Heracleitus** [1] and **Scymnus**.

Berve ii.389 no. 791.

Philocles (Philokles). Athenian. Possibly the son of Phormion of Eroeadae.[571] *Strategos* in 325/4 (Develin 402). He was in charge of Munychia and ordered to refuse Harpalus admission into Piraeus (Din 3.1). This he did on the first occasion when he first appeared (cf. P*Dem* 25.3, 7; [P]*M* 846a), but he later admitted Harpalus and was accused of having accepted a bribe from him (Din 3 repeats the charge but is short on details). He was convicted and apparently fined (Dem*Ep* 3.32), although Din 3.2 claims that he proposed a decree "against himself" that he should be put to death if found guilty.

Berve ii.389 no. 792; Kirchner no. 14521; Davies 539–41; Worthington 315–16.

Philon [1]. Son of Antipater (though not the famous regent). Sculptor (Pl*NH* 34.91). Philon produced a statue of Hephaestion (Tatian *ad Gr* 55 p. 121 Worth), either early in Alexander's reign or perhaps in Alexandria, after Hephaestion's death, when the latter's hero-cult had been established there.[572]

Berve ii.391–2 no. 797.

Philon [2]. Aenianian. Philon was chosen *strategos* by the rebellious mercenaries in the Upper Satrapies; their forces numbered 20,000 foot, 3,000 horse (D 18.7.2). He had served as a mercenary (probably as an officer) in Alexander's lifetime and, like many others, been relegated to garrison duty in a remote part of the empire. Philon thus played an unattested role in the upheavals of 325, which followed the false report of Alexander's death in India (C 9.7.1–11; see s.vv. **Athenodorus** [3], **Biton**, **Boxus**). In 323, Philon and his troops were defeated by Peithon son of Crateuas, who had suborned one of Philon's officers, Letodorus, through the agency of another Aenianian (D 18.7.5). Whether Philon died in the battle or in the treacherous slaughter of the prisoners that followed, we do not know.

Berve ii.392 no. 798.

Philon [3]. Apparently Macedonian. Family background unknown. Philon, together with Hegesippus son of Onymon and Ptolemy son of Lagus, made a dedication to Apollo at Miletus, presumably in 334 (Rheim, *IMilet* no. 244). Nothing else is known about him.

Berve ii.392 no. 799.

Philonides. Son of Zoitus. Greek from Chersonessus on Crete (*SIG*^{3} 303 = Harding no. 110; Paus 6.16.5). Philonides was a *hemerodromos* (*cursor*) of Alexander and a bematist of the Asia expedition. He is said to have covered the distance from Sicyon to Elis, 1,200 stades, in nine hours, though the return trip took him longer (Pl*NH* 2.181; 7.84). For his work, which must have resembled that of Diognetus, see Pl*NH* 1.4, 5.129; Jacoby, *FGrH* 121. Nothing else is known about him.

Berve ii.392 no. 800.

Philotas [1]. A high-ranking Macedonian of unknown family, Philotas was in 335 *phrourarchos* of the Cadmea (D 17.8.7), a position which he may have held since 338. Besieged by the Thebans (D 17.8.3–7), he held out until the arrival of the King, who demanded the surrender of the Thebans Phoenix and Prothytes; in an absurd counterdemand, the Thebans asked for Philotas and Antipater (*PA* 11.8).[573] What became of Philotas after the destruction of Thebes is unknown. Identification with the commandant of Tyre (332) is remotely possible (C 4.5.9).[574]

Berve ii.399 no. 808; Hamilton 30.

Philotas [2]. Macedonian of unknown family. In spring 335, along with Lysanias, he conveyed the booty acquired from the "independent" Thracians to the coastal cities of Macedonia to be sold (A 1.2.1). Identification with Philotas [6] the taxiarch is possible but cannot be proved.

Berve ii.398 no. 805.

Philotas [3]. Philotas Augaeus (C 5.2.5); possibly from Augaea in Chalcidice (thus Berve ii.398).[575] In the contest of valor, held in Sittacene in late 331, Philotas took third place and thus became a chiliarch of the hypaspists (C 5.2.5). He may be the same Philotas who, along with Hellanicus, distinguished himself during the siege of Halicarnassus (A 1.21.5). Note that Atarrhias (like Philotas and Hellanicus, a victor in Sittacene) was also conspicuous at Halicarnassus (C 8.1.36). Nothing else is known about about him. If he survived Alexander and participated in the wars of the Successors, it was most likely as one of the Argyraspids.

Berve ii.398–9 no. 807; Heckel 304–5.

Philotas [4]. Son of Parmenion; brother of Nicanor the *archihypaspistes*, Hector, and at least one unnamed sister, who in 336 had married Attalus, the guardian of Cleopatra-Eurydice (C 6.9.17). Born probably in the late 360s, Philotas appears to have been a *syntrophos* of Amyntas son of Perdiccas (see s.v. **Amyntas** [1]); the sons of Andromenes (C 7.1.10–11; cf. A 1.27.1) and, perhaps, also Amyntas son of Antiochus were personal friends. An early friendship with Alexander may be implied by *PA* 10.3, who records that in 336, Philip had brought Philotas with him "as a witness" (so Hamilton 26) when he reproached his son for his dealings with Pixodarus. Whether this means that Philotas had informed against the prince or, what seems more likely, Philip was using Philotas as a paradigm of good behavior, the incident cannot have endeared him to Alexander. Philotas is first attested as a commander of cavalry (from Upper Macedonia) in the Triballian campaign (A 1.2.5; cf. also Hammond 1987: 340, lines 32–3). In the following year, during the attack on Pellium, Alexander sent Philotas with sufficient horsemen to protect a foraging party. These, however, were surrounded by Glaucias and the Taulantians, who had come to Cleitus' aid, and had to be rescued by the King (A 1.5.9–11). By the beginning of the Asiatic expedition, he commanded the entire Companion Cavalry (D 17.17.4; cf. C 6.9.21), perhaps as a reward for his father's elimination of Attalus (see s.v. **Parmenion**).

At the Granicus, Philotas' cavalry were drawn up on the right, alongside the archers and the Agrianes (A 1.14.1; there is no evidence, *pace* Berve ii.393, that these other units were under Philotas' command). Nothing else is known of his role in the battle. When the army moved to Miletus, Philotas was sent with the cavalry and three battalions of infantry to Mycale to prevent the Persian fleet from disembarking and obtaining water and supplies (A 1.19.7–8). In the Halicarnassus campaign, he participated in the abortive attempt on Myndus (A 1.20.5–7). It appears that he spent the winter of 334/3 with Alexander in Pamphylia and Lycia.[576] When the reunited army moved from Gordium to Tarsus, the Companion Cavalry accompanied Alexander and were probably instrumental in capturing Tarsus before it could be put to the torch by the satrap Arsames.[577] After Alexander's recovery from his illness at the Cydnus, Philotas accompanied him to Soli and via Anchiale to the Aleian plain. Here Alexander turned south to the coastal town of Magarsus, sending Philotas across the plain to Mallus, where the army was later reunited (A 2.5.5–9). Of his role in the battle of Issus, nothing is recorded except his position in the battleline: on the right wing with the King (A 2.8.3). Hegesias (*FGrH* 142 F5) claims that during the capture of Gaza Philotas and Leonnatus brought the eunuch (A 2.25.4; *IA* 45) Batis, whom Darius had entrusted with the defense of the city, to Alexander as a captive.[578] Whatever the truth concerning the nature of Batis' death, there is no good reason for doubting Philotas' involvement in his arrest. Nor does Alexander's treatment of Batis, if it is indeed historical, reflect badly on Philotas. Alexander's adoption by Amun-Re (winter 332/1) marked a turning-point in the relationship between Philotas and the King. The "friendship," of which some writers (ancient and modern) speak, may never have been warm. In Egypt, Philotas made his true feelings about the King known to his mistress, Antigone, who had been with him since her capture at Damascus in late 333 (see s.v. **Antigone**): he told her that Alexander's achievements were due to the efforts of his father, Parmenion, and complained about the King's pretensions to be the son of Amun. But these comments were carelessly passed on to others, who reported the matter to Craterus, and through him they came to Alexander's attention. These disloyal rumblings constituted Philotas' so-called "Egyptian conspiracy" (A 3.26.1; cf. P*A* 48.4–49.2), and Alexander rightly took no action against him. Nor was he aware of Philotas' conversations with Hegelochus, whose treasonous remarks did not come to light until 330 (C 6.11.22–9; see s.v. **Hegelochus**).

At Gaugamela, Philotas commanded the Companions (A 3.11.8; C 4.13.26; D 17.57.1), probably in the immediate vicinity of the King, and followed him in his pursuit of the fleeing Persians, which, rumor held, was cut short by Parmenion's request for help. At Susa, he is said to have witnessed Alexander sitting on the throne of the Great King and to have treated with disdain the laments of those Persians who saw Alexander resting his feet on the table from which Darius used to eat (C 5.2.13–15; D 17.66.3–7). At the Persian Gates, Philotas was sent with the infantry battalions of Coenus, Amyntas, and Polyperchon (C 5.4.20, 30; A 3.18.6) to circumvent the forces of Ariobarzanes and perhaps begin the bridging of the Araxes River (Thus A 3.18.6); but C 5.4.30 has Philotas and the taxiarchs participating in the attack on Ariobarzanes, with the bridging of the Araxes taking place later under Alexander's direction (5.5.3–4); Pol*Strat* 4.3.27 wrongly assigns command of the main camp to Philotas and Hephaestion (cf. Heckel 1980c: 169–71). Nothing else is recorded about Philotas until the death of his brother Nicanor in the autumn of 330. He remained behind in Areia for several days to see to his brother's funeral.

Philotas rejoined the army in Phrada (modern Farah?), the capital of Drangiana (D 17.78.4), soon to be renamed Prophthasia ("Anticipation"; cf. StByz s.v. "Phrada") for the events which would unfold. There Philotas was implicated in a plot to kill the King, though it is clear that he could not have been a member of the conspiracy.[579] About this plot virtually nothing is known: motive and mode of execution are completely absent; the conspirators, with the exception of Demetrius the Somatophylax, notable for their obscurity.[580] Dimnus either planned the deed (P*A* 49.3) or was a member of a conspiracy,[581] but was betrayed by his lover Nicomachus, who revealed everything to his own brother Cebalinus. Cebalinus reported the matter to Philotas, who failed to act on the information. Cebalinus then approached the Royal Page, Metron, who reported the matter to the King. Dimnus could not be taken alive and the old maxim that "dead men tell no tales" lends credence to the view that Alexander did not want him to testify.[582] And Philotas, who was certainly not a participant in Dimnus' plot,[583] was eventually arrested and brought to trial. Nothing could be asserted with confidence, however, either by the prosecution or the King's historians, except that Philotas had been negligent. But this negligence may well indicate Philotas' hopes that the plot should succeed. With Alexander dead, the army would almost certainly turn back, and Parmenion in Ecbatana would be the logical man to assume control of affairs until a new king could be selected. Parmenion's position should not be underestimated: the old general controlled Alexander's lifeline to Macedonia.

Philotas owed much to his father's influence. But he was arrogant and outspoken (P*A* 48.1–3; cf. Them*Or* 19.229c–d), and his prestigious command was coveted by the younger commanders, who through their connections with Alexander hoped for greater power. He had foolishly disregarded Parmenion's advice to "make less of himself" (P*A* 48.3), and his arrogance and general unpopularity made his fall all but inevitable. What amounted to little more than an error in judgment – albeit a serious one – afforded the perfect opportunity for securing his elimination (C 6.8.4). What we know from the detailed but highly dramatized account of Curtius is that several of the younger *hetairoi* of Alexander – Craterus, Hephaestion, Coenus, Leonnatus, Perdiccas (C 6.8.17, adding Erigyius) – took leading roles in securing his condemnation. Craterus renewed his prosecution of an old enemy. Alexander was told to guard himself against the enemy within (C 6.8.4), a warning that masked their personal enmity and ambitions. If Alexander himself desired Philotas' removal from office, there were several who supported such a move, if they did not in fact initiate it. Certainly they took an active part in torturing the prisoner (C 6.8.15) and Philotas was right to remark that the bitterness of his enemies had overcome Alexander's goodwill (C 6.8.22). They had all hated Philotas for a long time (P*A* 49.8), particularly Hephaestion and Craterus. The latter had already monitored his activities in Egypt, and the former was feared by many for his influence with the King. Coenus, Philotas' brother-in-law, was his most outspoken prosecutor (C 6.9.30), but this may have been an act of self-preservation. Similarly, Amyntas son of Andromenes averted danger by repudiating his friendship with Philotas (C 7.1.18ff.). For a full but dramatic account see C 6.7–11; cf. D 17.79; P*A* 49.3–12; A 3.26.1–2; J 12.5.1–3. Convicted by the Macedonian assembly he was killed by stoning (C 6.11.10; cf. D 17.80.2) or with javelins (A 3.26.3). For his death see also P*A* 49.13; J 12.5.3; C 7.1.1.[584]

Berve ii.393–7 no. 802; Heckel 23–33. See Stemma VII.

Philotas [5]. Son of Carsis (A 4.13.4), a Thracian who may have married the daughter of a Macedonian aristocrat named Philotas (thus Hoffmann 180). Philotas was born between 345 and 340, since he is named as one of the Pages involved in Hermolaus' conpiracy of 327 (C 8.6.9; A 4.13.4). He is not mentioned again by name, but it is virtually certain that he was executed by stoning (A 4.14.3) for his part in the conspiracy, after first being tortured (A 4.13.7; P*A* 55.6; cf. C 8.6.20).

Hoffmann 180; Berve ii.392 no. 801; Heckel 295.

Philotas [6]. Macedonian. Family background unknown. A taxiarch and later satrap of Cilicia, Philotas' early career is entirely obscure. It is tempting to identify him with the officer who, in the company of Lysanias, conveyed the Thracian booty to Amphipolis in 335 (A 1.2.1), an identification made more attractive by the possibility that Lysanias is the cavalry commander of Antigonus the One-Eyed (D 19.29.2; cf. Billows 398 no. 64). Hence, both would have found their way eventually into Antigonus' service. Otherwise, Philotas is attested as the commander of an infantry battalion sent with Ptolemy son of Lagus to arrest the regicide Bessus (A 3.29.7) and again in the Aspasian campaign of 327/6 (A 4.24.10).[585]

In 323 Philotas resurfaces as satrap of Cilicia (D 18.3.1; J 13.4.12; A*Succ* 1.5; Dexippus, *FGrH* 100 F8 §2; cf. J 13.6.16; D 18.12.1 confuses him with Leonnatus), an appointment which was perhaps made by Alexander himself; for the previous satrap, Balacrus son of Nicanor, had been killed by the Pisidians while Alexander was still alive (D 18.22.1). He appears to be the Philotas named as one of the King's poisoners (Ps-Call 3.31.8–9); the charge was almost certainly fabricated but suggests nevertheless that he was still in Babylon in May/June 323.[586] Perdiccas removed him from his satrapy in 321/0, perceiving that he was loyal to Craterus (A*Succ* 24.2; J 13.6.16; cf. Boerma 185). Philotas may now have joined the forces of Antipater, if he did not go directly to Antigonus. If Philotas had been a *philos* of Antigonus before the settlement at Triparadeisus, Antipater may have failed to reinstate him as satrap of Cilicia in 320 for this very reason, allowing Philoxenus to remain in office (A*Succ* 1.34; D 18.39.6; Philoxenus was Perdiccas' appointee, and we must assume that he remained in office because he had defected to Antipater after Craterus' defeat at the Hellespont in 320).[587] In 318, Philotas was sent with thirty other Macedonians to seduce the Argyraspids away from their allegiance to Eumenes. For this purpose, he bore a letter from Antigonus himself (D 18.62.4). Philotas suborned Teutamus to approach Antigenes in an effort to bring about his defection, but instead the latter succeeded in bringing Teutamus back into Eumenes' camp (D 18.62.5–7). Although he read out to the Argyraspids Antigonus' letter, urging them to arrest Eumenes, whom the Macedonians had outlawed at Triparadeisus, he met with no success and returned to Antigonus (D 18.63.1–5). Nothing else is known about him.[588]

Berve ii.397–8 nos. 803–4; Billows 423–4 no. 95; Heckel 328–30.

Philotas [7]. One of Alcetas' commanders, captured at Cretopolis along with Attalus, Polemon, Docimus, and Antipater (D 19.16.1). There is a strong likelihood that he had seen service with Alexander, but there is no compelling evidence for identification with any known Philotas from that period.

Philotas [8]. Commandant (*phrourarchos*) of Tyre in 332 (C 4.5.9). Nothing else is known about him, unless he is identical with the man captured at Cretopolis (above).

Berve ii.398 no. 806.

Philotas. D 19.14.1. *Strategos* of Parthia in 317; killed by Peithon son of Crateuas. Probably an error for Philip. See s.v. **Philip** [10].

Philoxenus [1]. (Philoxenos). Macedonian. Family background unknown. In late 333, after the flight of Harpalus, he was appointed financial officer in charge of tax collection in Asia west of the Taurus mountains (A 3.6.4). P*A* 22.1 calls him *strategos* of the forces on the coast, and he seems to have exercised, in addition to his functions as a financial officer, the role of satrap or *hyparchos* (cf. Pol*Strat* 6.49, speaking of the *hyparchos* of Ionia; cf. P*M* 333a: *hyparchos* of the coastal region);[589] his residence was probably Sardis, where he imprisoned the murderers of Hegesias of Ephesus (Pol*Strat* 6.49). In fact, Philoxenus appears to have had an overarching authority, reminiscent of the younger Cyrus' powers as *karanos* in the late fifth century (Xen*HG* 1.4.3; cf. Briant 600).[590] According to P*A* 22.1–2 (cf. P*M* 333a; Ath 1.22d) he wanted to send Alexander some good-looking slave boys (**M67–68**), but Alexander indignantly declined the offer. The date of this offer is not given, and it could belong to the 330s. The official who demanded the extradition of Harpalus, arrested the steward of Harpalus' money (**M64**), and reported to the Athenians the names of those who had received bribes (Paus 2.33.4–5; cf. Hyp 1.8) could just as easily have been the satrap of Caria. Even the *hyparchos* can be identified with the satrap of Caria (see below) – as Bosworth i.280–2 suggests – but not the later satrap of Cilicia; Philoxenus plays no role in the history of the Successors, and he may have died or returned to Macedonia, perhaps with Craterus in 322. His special command appears to have ended with the death of Alexander.[591]

Berve ii.389–90 no. 793.

Philoxenus [2]. (Philoxenos). Macedonian of obscure origins and undistinguished military service (A*Succ* 24.2),[592] Philoxenus was installed as satrap of Cilicia by Perdiccas in place of Philotas, who was known to be a friend of Craterus (A*Succ* 24.2; J 13.6.16). Philoxenus, despite his appointment by Perdiccas, must have cooperated with Antipater and was consequently confirmed as satrap of Cilicia at Triparadeisus (D 18.39.6; A*Succ* 1.34). It appears that he is identical with the Philoxenus who was, after the death of Ada, satrap of Caria ([Arist]*Oecon* 2.31, 1351; but see Bosworth i.280–2).[593] In 323, he brought troops from the coast to Alexander in Babylon (A 7.23.1, 24.1), but he was overlooked in the settlement of 323. His sojourn in Babylon may, however, explain how he came to be in Perdiccas' camp in 321/0. What became of him is unknown.

Berve ii.390–1 no. 794.

Philoxenus (Philoxenos). Berve ii.391 no. 795. A 3.16.6. See s.v. **Xenophilus**.

Phocion (Phokion). Athenian. Son of Phocus (Kirchner no. 15076).[594] Born 402/1 (P*Ph* 24.5; N*Ph* 2.1). Student of Plato and friend of Xenocrates (P*Ph* 4.2; 14.7; P*M* 1126c). In his early years he served with Chabrias (P*Ph* 6–7; P*M* 791a), but he died in 357.[595] Phocion held the *strategia* forty-five times, more than any other Athenian, and is first attested in a military capacity in 349/8 on Euboea (Aes 3.86–8; Dem 21.162ff.; P*Ph* 12.1–14.2), unless his command of mercenaries on Cyprus is correctly dated by D 16.42.7ff. to 351/0. It is more likely, however, that this campaign in the service of Idrieus of Caria and in conjunction with Evagoras II belongs to 344/3. In 343/2 he supported Aeschines in the *Parapresbeia* trial and in 341/0 he defeated Cleitarchus of Eretria, whom Philip II had installed as tyrant there (D 16.74.1; cf. Gehrke 45 n. 29; Dem 18.71, 295). His intervention in Byzantium in 340/39, made possible by the trust its citizens placed in him and on account of his friendship with Leon (P*Ph* 14.7; the Byzantines had refused to accept help from Chares, whom they distrusted, 14.3–4), kept the city out of Philip's hands. Hence, although he can be called a conservative, with leanings toward the policies of Eubulus, he was prepared to act in the interests of the state and thus appears on these occasions to be following a Demosthenic policy. But Phocion's actions were dictated by principle rather than by party politics, and the charge that Demosthenes had often defended Phocion only to be betrayed by him (N*Ph* 2.2–3)[596] fails to take account of the complexities of Athenian politics and Phocion's adherence to his own beliefs. He did not join Demosthenes in ridiculing the youth of Alexander (P*Ph* 17.1) or opposing his request for ships (P*Ph* 21.1; P*M* 188c). Certainly, Phocion regarded Alexander's demand for the extradition of the most bellicose orators and generals after the sack of Thebes perfectly reasonable (P*Ph* 9.10, although it is not clear whether Phocion's advice that the men be surrendered was made in earnest). Although he argued that Athens should surrender the mischief-makers rather than go to war with Alexander, he later used his influence to persuade the King to relent (P*Ph* 17.3–6). During Alexander's lifetime Phocion steered a course between the ardent opponents of Macedon[597] and the dangers of the King's friendship. In fact, his lifestyle was simple and frugal (Ael*VH* 2.43, 7.9; N*Ph* 1.1) – though stories of his low origins must be rejected (Ael*VH* 12.43; Idomeneus, *FGrH* 338 F15 = P*Ph* 4.2) – and he is said to have rejected gifts of money from various Macedonian leaders (N*Ph* 1.3–4; Ael*VH* 1.25, 11.9; P*Ph* 18.1–4, 7–8; 30.1–4; P*M* 188c, 188f).[598] Instead of accepting bribes from Alexander – for it is thus that his gifts would be perceived – Phocion secured the release of political prisoners from Sardis (P*Ph* 18.6), and it said that Alexander used the polite form of address (*chairein*) only in his letters to Antipater and Phocion (P*Ph* 17.9–10 = Duris, *FGrH* 76 F51 and Chares, *FGrH* 125 F10). In 324 he also resisted attempts by Harpalus to buy his favor (P*Ph* 21.3–4), only to find that his son-in-law, Charicles, had become a confidant of the deserter, to his own detriment (P*Ph* 21.5–22.4). In fact, when Charicles was charged by the Athenians for his dealings with Harpalus, Phocion would not speak in his defense (P*Ph* 22.4). Nor did Phocion support Leosthenes and those who favored war after Alexander's death; for he felt that Athenian chances in the long run were not very good (P*M* 803a–b; P*Ph* 23). There may be some truth to the belief that he was deliberately passed over for supreme command when Leosthenes was killed (P*Ph* 24.1–2). Nevertheless, he did serve his country in the Lamian War, when he led out forces to Rhamnus to defeat and kill Micion, who had invaded Attica (P*Ph* 25.1–4).

But Phocion's policy of avoiding war with Macedon, and his friendship with Macedonian leaders, brought him to grief when he supported Demades in turning over the city to Antipater (P*Ph* 30.8)[599] and later allowed Nicanor to control both Munychia and Piraeus (N*Ph* 2.4–5; P*Ph* 31.2–3, 32.4–10; D 18.64.5); together with Demetrius of Phalerum he was the outspoken voice of the aristocratic party that sided with Cassander (N*Ph* 3.1). But when Polyperchon gained temporary supremacy in Macedon, the democratic party expelled Phocion and his supporters (N*Ph* 3.2; D 18.65.6); indeed, Polyperchon had sparse hopes of achieving his purpose as long as Phocion remained influential in Athens (P*Ph* 32.2). When he went to Polyperchon, now at Pharygae in Phocia, to plead his case – ostensibly before Philip III Arrhidaeus – he was shouted down by the regent and charged with betraying Piraeus (N*Ph* 3.3; P*Ph* 33.4–12; cf. Ael*VH* 3.47; 12.49; D 18.66.3). Phocion was sent to Athens for trial (N*Ph* 3.4; D 18.66.4), but had to be taken to court by carriage since he was too old to walk. Nevertheless, although the crowd pitied him, the Athenians' anger over his betrayal of Piraeus was so great (cf. P*M* 189a) that they would not even allow him to speak in his own defense (D 18.66.5–67.2). Hence, he was condemned – some even wanted to subject him to torture (P*Ph* 35.1) – and handed over to the Eleven for execution (N*Ph* 4.1–2; cf. P*M* 189a–b; D 18.67.5–6; P*Ph* 35–6).[600] Even then, as a final insult, his enemies decreed that he should not have a proper burial within the limits of Attica (P*Ph* 37.3). His funeral rites were conducted in private by a servant and his wife (N*Ph* 4.3–4; P*Ph* 37.3–5), though later the Athenians regretted their actions and gave him a public funeral and statue (P*Ph* 38.1). At his death, he was 83 or 84 years old (cf. P*M* 791e–f; Pol*Strat* 3.12). The Athenians condemned Hagnonides to death, and Phocion's son, Phocus, tracked down and punished Demophilus and Epicurus (P*Ph* 38.2).

Kirchner no. 15076; Berve ii.402–3 no. 816; Lenschau, *RE* s.v. "Phokion (2)"; Davies 559–60; Tritle; Gehrke.

Phoenix [1]. (Phoinix). Theban. A leader of the anti-Macedonian faction. In 335, Alexander demanded that the Thebans surrender him and Prothytes in return for amnesty; but the Thebans arrogantly demanded the surrender of Philotas and Antipater (P*A* 11.7–8). This can easily be reconciled with the admittedly apologetic version of A 1.7.10–11, which shows that there was in Thebes a party willing to negotiate, but that their efforts were undermined by the anti-Macedonian faction (cf. D 17.9.4).

Berve ii.399 no. 809.

Phoenix [2]. (Phoinix). Greek from Tenedos. Whether Phoenix had served with Alexander or had been recruited by Eumenes in northwestern Asia Minor is unclear. In the battle with Craterus, Phoenix and Pharnabazus commanded the mercenary cavalry, with orders to attack quickly before a herald from Craterus' army could come to persuade them to defect (P*Eum* 7.1). After Triparadeisus he remained faithful to Eumenes and, when 3,000 infantry and 500 cavalry led by a certain Perdiccas deserted Eumenes in Cappadocia, Phoenix was sent against them with 4,000 infantry and 1,000 cavalry; he caught the deserters in their camp during the second watch and brought them back to Eumenes for punishment (D 18.40.2–4). After the defeat of Eumenes, Phoenix appears to have entered Antigonus' service, becoming a close friend of Antigonus' nephew Polemaeus. When he rebelled against his uncle (310 BC), Polemaeus left Phoenix in charge of Hellespontine Phrygia, where he was subsequently attacked by Philip son of Antigonus (D 20.19.2, 5). We are not told the outcome of events in the Hellespont but, since Polemaeus was murdered by Ptolemy on Cos in 309 (D 20.27.3), it may be that Phoenix came to terms with Antigonus and was pardoned for his indiscretion.[601] In 302, we find Phoenix again in Antigonus' service but now betraying Sardis to Lysimachus (D 20.107.5). Nothing else is known about him.

Berve ii.399 no. 810; Billows 424 no. 96; Hornblower 1981: 130 n. 105.

Phormion (Phormio). Greek. Phormion was among the notable comic actors who performed at the mass-marriage ceremony at Susa in 324 (Chares, *FGrH* 125 F4 = Ath 12.539a; possibly a Lenaean victor ca. 350 (*IG* ii^2 670 [x], but the name is restored and far from secure; see also s.vv. **Lycon**, **Ariston** [4]).

Berve ii.399 no. 811; O'Connor 138 no. 498.

Phradasmenes. Son of Phrataphernes. Phradasmenes was enrolled, along with his brother Sisines [2], in the *agema* of the cavalry (A 7.6.4). Nothing further is known about him, unless he is identical with Pharismenes son of Phrataphernes.

Berve ii.400 no. 812.

Phrasaortes. Persian. Son of Rheomithres. Appointed by Alexander as satrap of Persis (A 3.18.11) after the death of Ariobarzanes.[602] Phrasaortes died of illness while Alexander was in India. His position was taken, without the King's permission, by Orxines (A 6.29.2, 30.1).

Berve ii.400 no. 813.

Phrataphernes. Persian. Father of Sisines, Pharismenes, and Phradasmenes.[603] In the reign of Darius III Phrataphernes was satrap of Parthia and Hyrcania and commanded the regional troops at Gaugamela (A 3.8.4; cf. C 4.12.9, 11). He remained faithful to Darius until the King's death and when he surrendered to Alexander, he may have been restored to the satrapy of Parthia (A 3.23.4, 28.2). In 330 he was ordered to accompany Erigyius and Caranus, who were sent to subdue Areia. Later he met Alexander in Zariaspa (A 4.7.1) or Nautaca (A 4.18.1), bringing Arsaces captive. Alexander made him satrap of Hyrcania, adding control of the Mardians and Tapurians, and ordering him to arrest Autophradates, who was guilty of misrule (C 8.3.17).[604] In India he returned to Alexander the Thracians who had been assigned to him for this purpose (A 5.20.7). Alexander appealed to him for supplies during his Gedrosian march (C 9.10.17) and these were brought to him in Carmania by Phrataphernes' son Pharismenes (A 6.27.3, 6). Two of Phrataphernes' sons – Phradasmenes and Sisines – were enrolled in the *agema* of the cavalry in 324 (A 7.6.4). In the settlement that followed Alexander's death in Babylon Phrataphernes retained his satrapy (D 18.3.3; cf. *LM* 121; J 13.4.23 gives only Hyrcania, assigning the Parthians to Philip, but this looks ahead to 320). He is not named in the satrapal reorganization at Triparadeisus.[605]

Berve ii.400–1 no. 814.

Phrynichus (Phrynichos). Flutist, apparently of Greek origin. Phrynichus performed at the mass-marriage ceremony in Susa in 324 (Chares, *FGrH* 125 F4 = Ath 12.538f).

Berve ii.401 no. 815.

Pierion (Pierio). Greek poet in Alexander's entourage, whose verses at the dinner-party in Maracanda in 328 ridiculed a recent Macedonian defeat and prompted Cleitus to the outburst that resulted in his death at Alexander's hands (*PA* 50.8). Plutarch tells us that some sources reported the poet's name as Pranichus. Whether this means that only the form of the name is disputed or that both Pranichus and Pierion were known to have been in Alexander's camp is uncertain (Berve ii.320 presumes that the latter is the case).

Berve ii.320 no. 639.

Pixodarus (Pixodaros; Pixodoros; also Pizodaros). Son of Hecatomnus, younger brother of Idrieus (D 16.74.2); brother of Ada, from whom he seized the rule of Caria in 339 (A 1.23.7; cf. D 16.69.2). In the spring of 336, he had sent Aristocritus to Pella in order to seek a marriage alliance; Philip II responded by proposing the marriage of Pixodarus' daughter, the younger Ada, to Arrhidaeus (*PA* 10.1), but these plans were disrupted by Alexander, who sent Thessalus to Caria and offered himself in Arrhidaeus' place (*PA* 10.1–2). The alliance came to naught, and Pixodarus gave his daughter to a Persian named Orontopates. When Alexander reached Halicarnassus, Pixodarus had already died and Darius had entrusted the rule of Caria to Orontopates (A 1.23.8; cf. D 16.74.2).

Berve ii.320–1 no. 640; Judeich 251ff. See Stemma XVI.

Pleistarchus (Pleistarchos). Younger brother of Cassander (Paus 1.15.1); son of Antipater. He may have been a child when Alexander left for Asia and appears to have remained at his father's court until Antipater's death in 319. Certainly, he plays no personal role in the history of Alexander and is not attested until 313 BC (D 19.77.6).

Berve ii.321 no. 641; Beloch iii[1] 2.84. See Stemma V.

Pnytagoras. King of Salamis on Cyprus from ca. 351 to 332/1, Pnytagoras was a relative of Evagoras I, although the relationship is not clearly spelled out.[606] In 351, he drove out Evagoras II (who had succeeded Nicocles) and joined the other kings of Cyprus in their revolt from Artaxerxes III (Olmstead 434–5); Evagoras II had the temporary support of Artaxerxes and Phocion, but lost this advantage through the slanders of Pnytagoras, who appears to have won the Great King's recognition in return for his promise of loyalty to Persia after the submission of the Phoenicians in 345/4 (D 16.46.2; cf. Beloch iii[2] 2.287 for the date). Pnytagoras and the other kings of Cyprus joined the Aegean fleet of Pharnabazus and Autophradates in 334, but, after Darius' defeat at Issus, they defected to Alexander at Sidon in 332 (A 2.20.3). Pnytagoras played no small part in the final assault on Tyre (July/August 332): together with Craterus, he commanded the ships on the left wing of the assault force (A 2.20.6; C 4.3.11), and, when the Tyrians would not engage in a sea battle, since they were outnumbered, he and the other Cyprians blockaded the harbor that looked toward Sidon (A 2.20.10). Pnytagoras' own quinquereme (along with those of Androcles of Amathus and Pasicrates of Curium) was sunk in a Tyrian counterattack as it lay at anchor (A 2.22.2).

For his services, he was richly rewarded: Tamasus in the territory of Citium, which had formerly belonged to Pymiathon's realm (Duris, *FGrH* 76 F4 = Ath 4.167c; *CIS* i.10–11; Hill 1949: 150). Pnytagoras appears not to have lived long to enjoy his reward, for in spring 331 we find his son Nicocreon ruling in Salamis (P*A* 29.3; cf. DL 9.58).[607] A second son, Nithaphon, is named as one of the trierarchs of Alexander's Hydaspes fleet (A*Ind* 18.8).

Berve ii.321 no. 642.

Polemaeus (Polemaios; also Ptolemaeus, Ptolemaios: P*Eum* 10.5). A nephew of Antigonus the One-Eyed (D 20.27.3) and the son of Ptolemy (Polemaios) son of Philip (see s.v. **Ptolemy** [2]). His activities belong entirely to the age of the Successors. Billows' identification of him with the Somatophylax of Philip III (A*Succ* 1.38) is attractive but speculative nonetheless.

Berve ii.321–2 no. 643; Billows 426–30 no. 100. See Stemma VI.

Polemon [1]. (Polemo). Macedonian *hetairos*. Son of Megacles, from Pella. In 332/1 he was appointed *phrourarchos* of Pelusium in Egypt (A 3.5.3). Nothing else is known about him.

Berve ii.322 no. 645.

Polemon [2]. (Polemo). Macedonian. Son of Theramenes. Left in Egypt as admiral of the fleet in 331 BC (A 3.5.5); he was given thirty triremes with which to protect the mouths of the Nile (C 4.8.4). Nothing else is known about him.

Berve ii.322 no. 646.

Polemon [3]. (Polemo). Youngest of the attested sons of Andromenes, brother of Amyntas, Simmias, and Attalus. Born not long after 350 BC, Polemon appears to have been in his late teens – and thus a member of either the *paides basilikoi* or the *hypaspistai basilikoi* – when Amyntas was implicated in the Philotas affair (C 7.2.4). His flight from the camp at that time heightened suspicions that Amyntas and his brothers had been in some way involved in the Philotas affair (A 3.27.1–2; C 7.1.1). But Polemon was persuaded by Amyntas to return and, in the subsequent trial, acquitted (A 3.27.3; cf. C 7.2.1–10 for a different version).[608] He is not heard of again during Alexander's lifetime. The marriage of Attalus to Perdiccas' sister Atalante brought the sons of Andromenes into the Perdiccan camp. In 321/0 Polemon (*ASucc* 1.25) and Attalus (*ASucc* 24.1) were sent to stop the funeral carriage of Alexander from continuing south to Egypt. Their force was, however, repulsed and they returned to Perdiccas empty-handed. Whether Polemon served with the land army that approached Memphis or remained with his brother and the fleet, we cannot say. He is found with Attalus and Alcetas (cf. P*Eum* 8.8) after Perdiccas' death: at Cretopolis (319 BC) Polemon, Attalus, Docimus, Antipater, and Philotas were captured by Antigonus (D 18.45.3; 19.16.1). Imprisoned in a fortress not far from Celaenae, he and his fellow-captives made a desperate bid for freedom, only to be hemmed in and besieged for one year and four months (D 19.16). He was probably executed upon his surrender.[609]

Berve ii.322 no. 644; Hoffmann 157; Heckel 183–4. See Stemma XII.

Poluxenus (Polouxenos). Son of Xenotimus. Cavalryman from Orchomenus who served in Alexander's allied cavalry (*IG* vii.3206) until the expedition reached Ecbatana in 330. There he and his compatriots were discharged. On their return (ca. 329), they made a dedication to Zeus Soter in Orchomenus (*IG* vii.3206).

Berve ii.322 no. 647.

Polycleitus (Polykleitos). Thessalian from Larissa. Polycleitus wrote what appears to have been an eye-witness account of Alexander's expedition in at least eight books (Ath 12.539a, the reference to Alexander's extended drinking-bouts probably refers to the last years of his life). Fragments of his work deal with geography, Persian antiquities, and gossip; for example, Polycleitus is cited by P*A* 46.1 as one of those who credited the story of the visit of the Amazon queen. Nevertheless, for a work of its size, Polycleitus' book does not seem to have attracted much attention, and it appears to have been more a collection of stories than a serious history. Furthermore, Polycleitus has been confused with Polycritus of Mende, a "paradoxographer." On the identity of the man and his career, little can be said with certainty. He may have belonged to a prominent Thessalian family and it is likely that he was a friend or acquaintance of his compatriot Medius. Two other prominent men named Polycleitus come to mind: a Polycleitus of Larissa had a daughter named Olympias, who married Demetrius the Fair and bore Antigonus Doson; another Polycleitus is attested as admiral of Ptolemy I Soter (D 19.62.4).[610] There is, however, no compelling reason to identify the historian with either of these men.

Berve ii.324 no. 651; Jacoby, *FGrH* 128.

Polycles [1]. (Polykles). Macedonian. Served as a *strategos* of Antipater, who had crossed into Asia (321/0) to confront the Perdiccans; hence, a subordinate of Polyperchon. Polycles confronted the Aetolians who had invaded Locris and was killed in battle (D 18.38.2). If he, like Polyperchon, had returned to Europe with Craterus, he may have served with Alexander in Asia.

Berve ii.324–5 no. 652; Ziegler, *RE* s.v. "Polykles (4)"; Tataki 411–12 no. 93.

Polycles [2]. (Polykles). Macedonian. Advisor of Adea-Eurydice. He fled with her, after the battle of Evia (317), but was captured on the way to Amphipolis and presumably executed (D 19.11.3). If, like Asclepiodorus [4], the *grammateus*, he was a supporter of the young queen from the time of Triparadeisus, Polycles may have been a member of the "Royal Army" and perhaps an officer of Alexander the Great.

Polydamas. *Hetairos* (A 3.26.3), possibly Macedonian[611] but, more likely, one of the

Thessalian *hetairoi* (cf. Ariston of Pharsalus and Medius of Larissa).[612] A 3.11.10 describes Parmenion leading the left, accompanied by the Pharsalian horse, and Polydamas may have been included in Parmenion's guard. During the battle he was sent by Parmenion to seek help from Alexander, when Parmenion's troops were hard pressed on the left (C 4.15.6–7). Ironically, he was later sent (in Arab dress) by Alexander to Cleander with the orders that Parmenion be put to death (A 3.26.3; C 7.2.11–33; Str 15.2.10 [724]; D 17.80.3)[613] and was nearly lynched by Parmenion's troops after the order was carried out (C 7.2.29). Nothing else is known of his career, except that he was dismissed with the veterans at Opis and returned to Macedonia with Craterus (J 12.12.8). Nothing else is known about him.[614]

Berve ii.322–3 no. 648; Heckel 359–61.

Polydorus (Polydoros). Apparently Macedonian. Polydorus is named as one of the guests at the house of Medius who allegedly conspired to poison Alexander. He is known only from the pamphlet on *The Last Days and Testament of Alexander* (*LM* 97). Unless we are dealing with a corruption in the manuscript – possibly Polydorus was the name of the father of Ariston of Pharsalus – there is no reason to assume that he is fictitious (thus Berve ii.429). He may be the physician from Teos, who once dined with Antipater (Cephisodorus of Thebes *ap.* Ath 12.548e, *FGrH* 112 F2), and the fact that he was named among the prominent individuals who attended Medius' drinking-party (and the very fact that his name was included in the political pamphlet) suggests that he was a man of high standing, perhaps a friend of Antigonus or Antipater.[615]

Berve ii.429 no. 68; Heckel 1988: 44–5.

Polyeuctus (Polyeuktos). Athenian orator[616] and politician from Sphettus (*PPh* 5.5; *PDem* 10.3). One of the anti-Macedonian politicians (*PPh* 9.9), in 343/2 he had gone with Demosthenes, Hegesippus, and others to stir up hostilities against Philip (Dem 9.72; cf. [P]*M* 841e). His surrender was demanded by Alexander in 335, after the fall of Thebes (A 1.10.4; *PDem* 23.4; *Suda* A 2704). Phocion criticized him for being fat and out of breath, a man who would advocate war with Philip but be unfit to fight one (*PPh* 9.9). A supporter of Demosthenes,[617] Polyeuctus may have been charged with accepting bribes from Harpalus in 324 and acquitted, though the evidence is flimsy (Din 1.100; cf. Worthington 55–6; 270–1). Before the outbreak of the Peloponnesian War, Polyeuctus was sent to the Arcadians but failed to persuade them to break with Antipater until he had the aid of the exiled Demosthenes ([P]*M* 846c–d).

Berve ii.323–4 no. 650; Kirchner no. 11950.

Polyperchon (Polypercon; Polysperchon).[618] Macedonian. Son of Simmias (A 2.12.2; 3.11.9) from Tymphaea (Tzetz, *ad Lycophron* 802; cf. D 17.57.2; 20.28.10), hence perhaps a kinsman of Andromenes. Born between 390 and 380 BC, Polyperchon was among the prominent veterans sent home in 324 from Opis (J 12.12.8); his son, Alexander, was born probably in the late 340s (see s.v. **Alexander** [6]). Polyperchon replaced Ptolemaeus son of Seleucus, who died at Issus (A 2.12.2), as taxiarch of the Tymphaean battalion of *pezhetairoi*; thus at Gaugamela, Polyperchon and his *taxis* of "so-called Stymphaeans" (D 17.57.2) are found between Meleager and Amyntas (A 3.11.9; cf. D 17.57.2–3 and C 4.13.28).[619] At the Persian Gates (winter 331/0), Polyperchon, Amyntas, and Coenus, along with some cavalry under Philotas' command, were sent ahead to bridge the Araxes River, while Alexander dealt with Ariobarzanes (C 5.4.20, 30; but A 3.18.6 omits him). Polyperchon is next attested in 328, when he is left at Bactra with Meleager, Attalus, and Gorgias, with instructions to protect the area against the incursions of rebels like Spitamenes (A 4.16.1). Hence, C 8.5.22–6.1

must be wrong when he claims that Polyperchon mocked *proskynesis* in 327; this is refuted by A 4.12.2, who names Leonnatus instead, and by the fact that Polyperchon was absent when the alleged episode took place (Heckel 1978c).[620] At the beginning of the Indian campaign (327), Polyperchon accompanied Craterus, whom Alexander left in the vicinity of Andaca to subdue the neighboring towns (A 4.23.5)[621] and rejoined Alexander briefly at Arigaeum, only to be left there again with Craterus to restore and fortify the city (A 4.24.6–7). He reunited with Alexander a second time to attack the Assacenians (A 4.25.6) and fight at Massaga (A 4.26.1–27.4).[622] For the remainder of the Indian campaign, Polyperchon is regularly found with Craterus. At the Hydaspes, his battalion, and that of Alcetas, remained with Craterus in the main camp, opposite Porus, and thus played only a secondary role in the defeat of Alexander's most formidable Indian adversary (A 5.11.3; cf. 5.15.3ff.). In the descent of the Indus river system, he served briefly under Hephaestion, but was soon transferred to the west bank, thus rejoining Craterus (A 6.5.5).[623] In 324, when Craterus was sent from Opis, with some 10,000 discharged veterans, to replace Antipater as regent of Macedonia, Polyperchon was designated his second-in-command (A 7.12.4; cf. J 12.12.8).

But, when Alexander died (June 323), Polyperchon, Craterus, and the veterans had not advanced beyond Cilicia, where they now remained for a second winter. In 322, they answered Antipater's call and returned to Macedonia and Thessaly. Augmenting the Macedonian forces, they contributed in no small way to the defeat of Antiphilus at Crannon (D 18.16.4ff.). And, when Craterus and Antipater made a truce with the Aetolians in the winter of 321/0, in order to give themselves a free hand to deal with Perdiccas (D 18.25.4–5), Polyperchon was entrusted with the defense of Macedonia in their absence (J 13.6.9).[624] The Aetolians, however, had made a secret pact with Perdiccas to invade Thessaly in order to distract Antipater. Quickly they attacked Amphissa, defeating and killing the Macedonian general, Polycles [1],[625] who had been left behind in Locris, and moved into Thessaly where they incited rebellion and threatened Macedon with a force of 25,000 infantry and 1,500 horse; Alexander the Aetolian had brought 12,000 infantry and 400 cavalry, which are surely included in this number (D 18.38.1, 3). But the danger was lessened by the sudden departure of the Aetolians themselves – in response to an attack by the Acarnanians – and Polyperchon won a decisive victory over the Thessalians and Menon of Pharsalus (D 18.38.5–6).

Antipater, on his deathbed (319), named Polyperchon *epimeletes* of the Kings, with Cassander as his chiliarch (D 18.49.1–3; cf. P*Ph* 31.1; *HE* 1.4 = *FGrH* 155 F1). Thus he inherited the political and military leadership of Macedonia (D 18.47.4, 48.4; cf. P*Ph* 31.1).[626] But Cassander, who had served as Antigonus' chiliarch in 320 (A*Succ* 1.38; D 18.39.7), did not welcome the subordinate role, and Polyperchon sought to strengthen his own position by offering the guardianship of Alexander IV to Olympias and by proclaiming the "Freedom of the Greeks" (D 18.55.2–57.1; P*Ph* 32.1). At first Polyperchon found strong support in Macedonia (D 18.54.2), and he was joined by White Cleitus, whom Antigonus had driven from Asia (D 18.52.6); Olympias took a more cautious approach.[627] Threatened by Cassander, Polyperchon extended an amnesty to Eumenes and the outlaws, if they supported the cause of the Kings, promising also to come in person to Asia with an army to oppose Antigonus (D 18.57.3–4). Indeed, he wrote to the Argyraspids, now in Cyinda (D 18.58.1), instructing them to cooperate with Eumenes. Athens in February 318 made public its enthusiasm for Polyperchon (*SIG*^{3} 315 = *IG* ii^2 387; cf. N*Ph* 3.1). But the March deadline for the implementation of Philip III's decree passed, with Nicanor still firmly entrenched in Munychia (D 18.56.5; Ferguson 30–2; but see Williams 1984). A force led by Polyperchon's son Alexander advanced to Attica (D 18.65.3ff.), bringing with it many of the exiles and putting pressure on Nicanor, who had seized and fortified Piraeus and was ignoring orders from Olympias to withdraw his garrison (D 18.65.1). But Polyperchon's duplicity soon became evident: Alexander entered into frequent and secret negotiations with Nicanor, perhaps even through the agency of Phocion, who thought to ingratiate himself with the Polyperchan party and to protect himself at home if he could persuade Nicanor to turn over Munychia and Piraeus to Alexander (D 18.65.3–5; but P*Ph* 33 omits Phocion's role; cf. Gehrke 115 n. 39).

Polyperchon, meanwhile, held the bulk of the Macedonian army in reserve in Phocis, that is, inside Thermopylae, where he was met by delegations of the Athenians (D 18.68.2; P*Ph* 33.4–12; cf. N*Ph* 3.3). One of these was headed by Phocion, whose crimes included collaborating with Nicanor in his seizure of Piraeus and whose favorable stance toward the house of Iolaus now placed him in jeopardy; nevertheless, his recent negotiations with Alexander must have caused him to hope for a better reception from Polyperchon (cf. Gehrke 115 n. 39). The latter made a great show of ceremony – with Philip III enthroned beneath a golden canopy – but the process quickly degenerated into a shouting match, and Polyperchon was forced to restrain the enraged King, who nearly transfixed Phocion's comrade, Hegemon, with his spear (P*Ph* 33.7–12). In the end, White Cleitus was instructed to take the opponents of the new regime under guard to Athens, where they were denounced and executed (P*Ph* 34–5).

Unable to win Athens for himself (though he did manage to send relief to Salamis, which was being besieged by Cassander's forces: D 18.69.2), Polyperchon left behind a small force under Alexander, and proceeded against Megalopolis, which had mustered some 15,000 men and prepared to withstand a siege (D 18.70.1–3). Elsewhere in the Peloponnese, his envoys called upon the cities to overthrow the oligarchies of Antipater and even to put the latter's supporters to death, and in this Polyperchon was generally successful (D 18.69.3–4). The Megalopolitans, however, held out under the leadership of Damis, a veteran of Alexander's campaigns (D 18.70–1; cf. Pol*Strat* 4.14), and Polyperchon soon withdrew to tackle more pressing matters (D 18.72.1). It appears that he returned to Macedonia to guard against an invasion by Cassander. But, having taken precautions there, he moved south to Epirus – in order to prepare for Olympias' return to Macedonia, which he entrusted to his ally, and Olympias' own nephew, Aeacides (D 19.11.1–2) – and, from there, perhaps to the Aetolians, whose friendship he cultivated (cf. Mendels 1984: 158ff.). In his absence, Adea-Eurydice transferred the guardianship of her husband, Philip III, to Cassander (cf. J 14.5.1–3).

This move, perhaps instigated by Cassander himself during his first return to Macedonia (probably in spring 317; so Hammond, *HMac* iii.137; D 18.75.2; cf. 19.35.7 and Poly*Strat* 4.11.2), severely damaged Polyperchon's prestige. It is, most likely, in this historical context that a pamphlet on *The Last Days and Testament of Alexander the Great* was published. The emphasis placed on the legitimate kingship of Alexander IV and the favorable treatment of Olympias and Rhoxane, in sharp contrast to the accusations of regicide leveled against the family of Cassander and the supporters of Antigonus, leave little doubt that the original version of this pamphlet – which was soon embellished, contaminated, and otherwise distorted in the interests of other parties – originated in the Polyperchan camp (Heckel 1988; but see Bosworth 2000).

The failure at Megalopolis had had devastating effects in the south: contemptuous of Polyperchon (Pol*Strat* 4.11.2), some Greek cities went over to Cassander (D 18.74.1 exaggerates Cassander's popularity; cf. Beloch iv^2 2.440–1), who had pursued his goals with great energy and through the formidable alliances secured by his father in the first years that followed Alexander's death. To counter the most dangerous of these alliances – that with Antigonus, who had supplied Cassander with thirty-five ships to secure Nicanor's position in Piraeus – Polyperchon sent out Cleitus with the Macedonian fleet. This man had a score to settle with Antigonus, who had driven him from Lydia soon after Antipater's death. But his initial success near Byzantium, in which he destroyed or captured about half Nicanor's fleet, was followed by an overwhelming disaster; for Antigonus, with a large contingent of lightly armed troops, fell upon Cleitus' sailors after they had disembarked for the night. Those who managed to board ship and make for open water fell in with the remnants of Nicanor's fleet and were annihilated. Cleitus himself fled to shore and attempted to reach Macedonia by land, only to fall in with Lysimachus' troops, who put him to death (D 18.72.2–9; Pol*Strat* 4.6.8; cf. Engel 1973: 141–5; Beloch iv^2 1.103–4; Billows 86–8).[628]

In contrast to the lethargy and ineffectiveness of Polyperchon's party, Cassander had shown himself a force to be reckoned with. Now the return of Nicanor's fleet, sailing into Piraeus with the beaks of Cleitus' warships, spelled the end of Polyperchon's hopes in Athens (D 18.75.1). The Athenians, having flirted briefly with democratic revolution, came to terms with Antipater's son and Greece in general reverted to a pro-Antipatrid stance. Polyperchon could do little but concentrate his efforts on driving Cassander and his supporters from Macedonia, while hoping that his son Alexander could keep in check the dissension in the Peloponnese.

In the northwest, Olympias and Aeacides brought their forces to Euia, on the Macedonian–Epeirot border (Hammond, *HMac* iii.140, with n. 2), where they confronted Philip III and Eurydice. Duris' description of the battle as one fought between women, with Olympias in Bacchic attire and Eurydice in Macedonian armor, is surely a later embellishment (Duris *ap.* Ath 13.560f = *FGrH* 76 F52; cf. Heckel 1981a: 83–4; Carney 1987b: 496ff., esp. 500). At first, the benefits of alliance with Olympias became clear: overawed by the prestige of the queen mother, the troops of Philip and Eurydice deserted, leaving their "King" to fall into enemy hands and his bride to make a desperate bid at escape (D 19.11.1–7). She was captured as she made her way to Amphipolis with her advisor, Polycles (D 19.11.3), perhaps a relative of the general who had been killed by the Aetolians in 321/0 (D 18.38.2). But Polyperchon would have been wise to curtail Olympias' power: her reprisals against personal enemies, and those of her family, soon turned the reverence of the Macedonians into disgust, and this feeling for the woman was extended also to the man who had summoned her (D 19.11.4–9).

Cassander was, at the time, besieging Tegea, and Polyperchon occupied Perrhaebia, while his son Alexander threatened the Peloponnese; the Aetolians, meanwhile, blocked Cassander's advance at Thermopylae (D 19.35.1–2). But Cassander ferried his men around the pass, landing them in southern Thessaly, and sent one of his officers, Callas, to hold Polyperchon in check. A second general, Deinias, secured the entrances to Macedonia before Olympias' forces could seize them (D 19.35.3), and the queen mother took refuge in Pydna (D 19.35.5–7; J 14.6.1–4), entrusting the campaign against Cassander to Aristonus (D 19.35.4). Besieged at Azorus (or Azorius, D 19.52.6), Polyperchon watched his troops desert to Callas (D 19.36.6), and was forced to sit idle as Cassander starved Olympias and the remnants of the royal family into submission (D 19.35.5; cf. J 14.6.2–3).[629] Indeed, it was only with difficulty that he escaped to Aetolia (D 19.52.6). Little remained of his former power, except perhaps those cities of the Peloponnese that retained their allegiance thanks to the presence of

Alexander (D 19.35.1, 53.1) – and even he was hard pressed by Cassander.[630]

A rift between Cassander and Antigonus offered Polyperchon some hope of recouping his losses. In 315, Antigonus sent his agent Aristodemus to secure a pact with Polyperchon and his son, whereby Polyperchon was recognized as *strategos* in the Peloponnese. Oaths were exchanged by Aristodemus and Polyperchon; Alexander sailed to Asia to complete negotiations with Antigonus (D 19.57.5, 60.1, 61.1; cf. 62.5). But Polyperchon had clearly accepted a subordinate role in return for Antigonid support in Greece (D 19.61.3; cf. Billows 114, with n. 41); for Aristodemus brought to his new allies some 8,000 mercenaries recruited in the Peloponnese (D 19.60.1). Cassander meanwhile secured Orchomenus in Arcadia but failed to make further gains in Messenia and prepared to return to the north, stopping first to celebrate the Nemean games (D 19.64.1). It was presumably during this brief respite that he tried, in vain, to persuade Polyperchon to abandon Monophthalmus (D 19.63.3). On his return to Macedonia, Cassander sent Prepelaus to Alexander (D 19.64.3–5), offering him the title of "general of the Peloponnese" – the very office which the father exercised for Antigonus – and inducing him to defect. Thus Cassander did even greater harm to Polyperchon's credibility. Antigonus meanwhile sent his nephew Telesphorus to liberate the cities in which Alexander (and Cassander) had placed garrisons. Soon only Sicyon and Corinth held out against Antigonus (D 19.74.2). It appears also that the willingness of the Aetolians to join Aristodemus – they had formerly been allies of Polyperchon – was prompted by an alliance between Polyperchon and Cassander, and Beloch iv^2 2.443 suggests, plausibly, that Alexander served as Cassander's *strategos* because Polyperchon could not bring himself to serve the younger man. Now 70 years old, Polyperchon may have relinquished control of affairs to his son, allowing him to make his best deal, which, in this case, involved abandoning Antigonus in favor of his father's bitter enemy. Polyperchon's "retirement" thus paved the way for *rapprochement*. But Alexander was quickly swept aside by Aristodemus, and his alliance with Cassander was perhaps the cause of his assassination and the uprising in Sicyon in 314 (D 19.66–7). These events drew Polyperchon out of retirement to pursue an independent policy. Hence, in the Peace of 311, Polyperchon plays no part, and Antigonus' letter to Scepsis (*OGIS* i.5 = Welles, *RC* 1) shows that Antigonus at least was anxious to deprive him of allies.

Polyperchon made one last bid for power, bringing Heracles, son of Alexander and Barsine, from Pergamum to Greece. The claims of this child to the throne had been rejected in 323 (C 10 6.11–12; cf. J 13.2.7), but at that time the marshals were already divided on the question of Rhoxane's unborn child. In 310, Cassander laid that problem to rest by ordering the murder of Alexander IV and his mother in Amphipolis (D 19.105.1–2; Paus 9.7.2; J 15.2.5). Heracles, now 17 or 18, could be exploited for political gain (D 20.20). Polyperchon brought him to his native Tymphaea in Upper Macedonia, at the head of an army of 20,000 infantry and 1,000 horse, and seriously threatened Cassander. But Cassander understood Polyperchon's nature and the limits of his ambitions, and persuaded the old man to murder the boy in exchange for a share of power, which amounted, in fact, to little more than the theoretical *strategia* of the Peloponnese (D 20.28.2).[631] The murder of Alexander's son cost Polyperchon what little remained of his credibility. Satisfied that he had obtained as much as he could from the exercise, he attempted to return to the south, only to be forced by a coaliton of Peloponnesians and Boeotians to winter in Locris (D 20.28.4; Tr*Prol* 15). Cassander had given him 4,000 Macedonian infantry and 500 Thessalian horse (D 20.28.3). Cratesipolis, holding Corinth and Sicyon in his absence, was forced to turn the cities over to Ptolemy Soter (D 20.37.1), who in 308 made his only serious bid for power in Europe and revived the old slogan of "Greek Liberty."

Polyperchon nevertheless continued to wreak havoc in the Peloponnese in the years between Ptolemy's defeat at Salamis and the battle of Ipsus in 301. In 304, Demetrius was still intent on liberating the Greek cities from Cassander and Polyperchon, and indeed he captured and crucified the latter's garrison commander in Arcadian Orchomenus (D 20.100.6, 103.5–7). What became of Polyperchon himself is unknown. Demetrius' campaign against Messene in 295 (P*Demetr* 13.3–4) may have been directed against him, though he was by now nearly 90 years old!

Berve ii.325–6 no. 654; Hoffmann 156; Beloch iv^2 1.97ff.; Lenschau, *RE* s.v. "Polyperchon (1)"; Sandberger 179 no. 67; Heckel 1988: 48–54; Heckel 188–204. See Stemma XII.

Polystratus (Polystratos). A Macedonian soldier who was reported by the source of the vulgate to have found Darius when he had been left by his assassins to die (P*A* 43.3–4; C 5.13.24). Although the story that he found the Persian King still alive and received his dying words (cf. J 11.15.5–14, referring only to "one of Alexander's men") is undoubtedly a fiction, Polystratus may, nevertheless, have been a genuine historical figure.

Berve ii.326 no. 655.

Porticanus (Portikanos). Indian dynast (Str 15.1.33 [701]), ruler of the Praesti (C 9.8.11; cf. Lassen ii^2 186). Eggermont 11–12 would make him ruler of Pardabathra (Pt*Geog* 7.1.58); hence we should distinguish between Oxicanus (A 6.16.1–2), who ruled Azeika (Axika; Pt*Geog* 7.1.57). Indeed the details are sufficiently different to argue against identification of the two (*pace* Berve ii.293 no. 587). Porticanus was captured in the citadel (of Pardabathra?) on the third day, after Alexander had destroyed two of the city's towers and before Porticanus could send envoys to negotiate his surrender (C 9.8.11–12; summer 325). D 17.102.5, however, adds that Alexander had taken two of Porticanus' cities, and that the Indian died fighting in the third. The two cities that were taken earlier may well have been those of Oxicanus, who was captured in the second (A 6.16.2).

Berve ii.293 no. 589 ("Oxykanos"); Eggermont 9–15; Jacobs 247, 251 "Porti-/Oxycanus."

Porus [1]. (Poros). Indian dynast, ruler of the Paurava. Porus was thus his official, rather than personal, name; the latter is unrecorded. He was physically imposing (J 12.8.1; A 5.19.1; C 8.13.7, 14.13; cf. *IA* 111; *ME* 54; *Suda Π* 2180), with a height of at least five cubits (A 5.19.1; D 17.88.4; P*A* 60.12),[632] which contrasted with the shortness of Alexander (cf. Ps-Call 3.4.3; Jul Val 3.7). An enemy of Taxiles, Porus had an ally in Abisares, with whom he had previously campaigned against the Sudracae (A 5.22.2), and even on his own was perhaps the most powerful of the rulers of the Punjab (cf. C 8.12.13); certainly his kingdom lay beyond the limits of the Persian empire. Not surprisingly, he rejected the demand for tribute brought by Alexander's envoy, Cleochares (C 8.13.2; *ME* 56–7 says that Porus had Cleochares whipped and sent Alexander an arrogant letter; cf. Ps-Call 3.2).

Instead Porus moved to prevent Alexander's crossing of the Hydaspes (Jhelum) in April 326 (A 5.9.1; P*A* 60), occupying a position that proved unassailable, and forcing Alexander to resort to various feints (A 5.10; C 8.13.18–19; P*A* 60; Pol*Strat* 4.3.9) in an attempt to confuse him. Eventually, Alexander under the cover of heavy rain and thunder effected a crossing of the river some 28 km upstream after leaving Craterus to watch the main river-crossing (A 5.11.3–4). Once Porus' position had been turned (cf. **M15**), a major engagement followed, in which his troops were routed. Wounded and defeated, Porus nevertheless refused to treat with Taxiles, whom Alexander had sent to urge his surrender; instead he attempted to kill him with a javelin, which Taxiles evaded

(A 5.18.6–7; C 8.14.35–6 says that it was Taxiles' brother who was sent to Porus, and that Porus killed him). His surrender was negotiated by another Indian, Meroes (A 5.18.7). Porus' haughty demeanor is perhaps somewhat exaggerated by the sources, but Alexander respected him as a worthy opponent and a valuable ally (P*A* 60.14–15; P*M* 181e, 332e, 458b; A 5.19.2–3; Them*Or* 7.89d; C 8.14.41–5). Alexander arranged an alliance between Taxiles and Porus (C 9.3.22). News sent by Porus and Taxiles in 324 that Abisares had died (C 10.1.20) suggests that the alliance was still in existence. After Alexander's death, Perdiccas did not disturb the organization of the eastern satrapies and allowed Porus to retain his kingdom (D 18.3.2; Dexippus, *FGrH* 100 F8 §5a; cf. *LM* 121). This right was reaffirmed at Triparadeisus in 320 (D 18.39.6; A*Succ* 1.36). But in 318/7 he was treacherously killed by Eudamus, who subsequently joined Eumenes with 120 taken from the region (D 19.14.8). Porus' kingdom was soon absorbed into the empire of Sandrocottus (Chandragupta Maurya).

Berve ii.340–5 no. 683.

Porus [2]. (Poros). Distinguished from his cousin (D 17.91.1; Str 15.1.30 [699]) and namesake by the epithet *kakos* ("bad" or "cowardly"). His official name, like that of most Indian dynasts, derives from the people he ruled, in this case those of the Paurava who lived east of the Acesines River (cf. A 5.21.4–5).[633] He sent envoys to Alexander offering to surrender (A 5.20.6), apparently in the hope of gaining power and territory at the expense of his kinsman who was actively opposing the Macedonians. But when Alexander treated that man favorably, Porus (*kakos*) fled to the Gandaridae (D 17.91.1)[634] with a number of warlike tribesmen (A 5.21.2–3). His initial contact with Alexander was doubtless regarded as submission to Macedonian authority, and Alexander, who now regarded him as a defector, sent Hephaestion and Demetrius son of Althaemenes (along with two battalions of *pezhetairoi*) into his territory; they were to hand his territory over to the good Porus (A 5.21.5; D 17.91.2), a mission which was successfully carried out (D 17.93.1). That he was later an agitator at the court of Chandragupta (see s.v. **Sandrocottus**), as Bosworth ii.325 suggests, is plausible but little more than speculation. What became of the second Porus is unknown.

Berve ii.345 no. 684; Anspach ii.25–6, with nn. 197, 199; Bosworth ii.320, 325.

Poseidonius (Poseidonios). Macedonian engineer in Alexander's army. The bematist, Baeton, records that he built a particularly effective siege-engine, but the historical context is not known (cf. Kern 1999: 210). One suspects that this was done in the context of the sieges of either Tyre or Gaza.

Berve ii.327 no. 656.

Pranichus (Pranichos). Poet in Alexander's entourage (apparently Greek), who in 328 sang verses ridiculing a recent Macedonian defeat and thus angered Cleitus sufficiently to begin quarreling with Alexander (P*A* 50.8). Plutarch tells us that some sources reported the poet's name as Pierion. Whether this means that only the form of the name is disputed or that both Pranichus and Pierion were known to have been in Alexander's camp is uncertain.

Berve ii.327 no. 657.

Procles (Prokles). Athenian. One of the accusers of Demosthenes in the Harpalus proceedings in 324/3 ([P]*M* 846c, wrongly emended to Patrocles; Phot*Bibl* 494a, 38). Possibly identical with the Procles named by Demosthenes himself in 348 (Dem 37.48).

Berve ii.327 no. 659; Schaefer iii^2 329 n. 1; Kirchner no. 12208.

Proexes. Prominent Persian (see Justi 225). In 330/29 he was appointed satrap of Parapamisadae, apparently residing in the new settlement of Alexandria-in-the-

Caucasus (A 3.28.4); his activities were curtailed by an *episkopos*, Neiloxenus son of Satyrus, with an unspecified number of troops. In 327, Proexes was replaced as satrap by Tyriespes (A 4.22.5).

Berve ii.327 no. 658.

Promachus (Promachos). Macedonian. Perhaps a common soldier in Alexander's army. In 324 at Susa, when a drinking contest was held in connection with the funeral of the Indian Calanus, Promachus drank the equivalent of 13 litres of unmixed wine and won the first prize of a talent (or possibly a golden crown worth a talent). He died three days later from the after-effects of the drinking (Chares, *FGrH* 124 F19a = Ath 10.437b; F19b = P*A* 70.1–2; cf. Ael*VH* 2.41). Forty-one other contestants allegedly died of alcohol poisoning.

Berve ii.327 no. 660.

Proppei. Son of Thiogiton. Cavalryman from Orchomenus; served in Alexander's allied cavalry until the expedition reached Ecbatana in 330. There he and his compatriots were discharged. On their return (ca. 329), they made a dedication to Zeus Soter in Orchomenus (*IG* vii.3206).

Berve ii.328 no. 663.

Proteas. Macedonian. Son of Andronicus and, in all likelihood, of Lanice, Alexander's nurse (Ath 4.129a; cf. A 4.9.3; see Carney 1981: 152); hence also the nephew of Black Cleitus and brother of two men killed near Miletus in 334 (C 8.2.8; **M41–42**). A *syntrophos* of Alexander, Proteas was born in the mid-350s BC (Ael*VH* 12.26). He had been sent with fifteen ships by Antipater to protect the islands and the Greek mainland against Persian attack. Putting in at Chalcis on Euboea he advanced to Cythnus and then caught the Persian admiral Datames at Siphnos at dawn, capturing eight of his ten ships (A 2.2.4–5); there is no mention of Macedonian losses. Proteas came with a fifty-oared ship from Macedon to join Alexander at Sidon (A 2.20.2). Whether he came on official state business – hence the reference to the single *pentekontoros* – or if he participated in the naval action around Tyre is unclear.[635] Like Hegelochus, who served with the fleet, Proteas soon joined Alexander's expedition and accompanied him by land from at least Egypt (cf. Berve ii.328). Of his military actions nothing further is known. He was a notorious drinking companion of Alexander (Hippolochus *ap*. Ath 4.129a; Ael*VH* 12.26), and the King on one occasion gave him five talents to prove that he was no longer angry with him (P*A* 39.6). How he reacted to the death of his uncle in 328 is unknown, but Ephippus may have implied some form of poetic justice when he claimed that Alexander became ill and died as a result of a drinking contest with Proteas (*FGrH* 126 F3 = Ath 10.434a–b).

Berve ii.328 no. 664; ii.328–9 no. 665; Carney 1981: 152; cf. Wirth 1989: 1–4. See Stemma VIII.

Prothytes. Theban. A leader of the anti-Macedonian faction. In 335 Alexander demanded that the Thebans surrender him and Phoenix in return for amnesty; but the Thebans arrogantly demanded the surrender of Philotas and Antipater (P*A* 11.7–8). This can easily be reconciled with the admittedly apologetic version of A 1.7.10–11, which shows that there was in Thebes a party willing to negotiate, but that their efforts were undermined by the anti-Macedonian faction (cf. D 17.9.4).[636]

Berve ii.328 no. 661.

Protogenes. Greek from Caunus (Pl*NH* 35.101; P*Demetr* 22.4; Paus 1.3.5). Born perhaps in the 370s: Pliny claims that he was a ship painter until he was 50. Famous painter and sculptor; friend of Apelles (Pl*NH* 35.81–3, 87–8). Protogenes appears to have spent some time in Athens, where he painted numerous famous individuals, including writers, athletes, the mother of Aristotle, Antigonus the One-Eyed, and Alexander himself (Pl*NH* 35.106). He also painted the state triremes Paralus and Ammonias, but his masterpiece appears to have been the Ialysus, which had been commissioned by the Rhodians and which the artist was in the process of completing in the suburbs of Rhodes when the city was besieged by Demetrius Poliorcetes. Demetrius spared the painter and his work, thus winning great renown (P*Demetr* 22.4–7; Pl*NH* 35.104–5; PM 183a–b). Protogenes was noted for the laborious care and accuracy he put into his work (Quint 12.10.6) – his Ialysus was already seven years in the making when Demetrius attacked Rhodes (P*Demetr* 22.5) – and was counted amongst the greatest of painters (Cic *Brutus* 70).

Berve ii.329 no. 666; Pollitt 171–3.

Protomachus (Protomachos). A Macedonian of unknown family background, Protomachus is once attested: at Issus, he commanded the *prodromoi* (A 2.9.2). He replaced Amyntas son of Arrhabaeus in this office, perhaps, as Berve ii.329 suggests,[637] at Gordium in spring 333. But by the time of the Gaugamela campaign (summer 331) he had himself been replaced by Aretes. What became of him is unknown.

Berve ii.329 no. 667; Heckel 353.

Proxenus (Proxenos). Macedonian or Greek of unknown background. Proxenus is found in Alexander's entourage as the man in charge of the household equipment (*stromatophylax*). As he was pitching the King's tent at the Oxus River in 329, he discovered petroleum. The discovery was reported by Alexander in a letter to Antipater (P*A* 57.5–8; cf. Ath 2.42f).

Berve ii.328 no. 662.

Psammon. Egyptian philosopher of unknown family, though Hamilton 73 suggests plausibly that Psammon is merely a variation of Ammon (cf. P*M* 180d). While in Egypt, Alexander listened with approval to his lectures on the nature of the divine (P*A* 27.10–11). Nothing else is known about him.

Berve ii.409 no. 831; Hamilton 73.

Ptolemy [1]. (Ptolemaeus, Ptolemaios). *Somatophylax basilikos*, who commanded two *taxeis* of hypaspists (those of Adaeus and Timander) in the skirmish with those defenders who had made a sortie from the Tripylon at Halicarnassus (A 1.22.4). Ptolemy himself was killed in that engagement (A 1.22.7). He may have been commander of the *agema* of the hypaspists and, thus, the predecessor of Admetus.[638]

Berve ii.337 no. 672.

Ptolemy [2]. (Ptolemaeus, Ptolemaios; possibly Polemaios, Polemaeus). Son of Philip (A 1.14.6), Ptolemy led, in a special but unspecified capacity, a battalion of infantry and a squadron of Companions – that of Socrates – at the Granicus River in 334 and conducted the initial assault on the Persian position (A 1.14.6; cf. 1.15.1, 16.1). This infantry battalion appears to have comprised hypaspists (cf. Berve ii.336) which are described in the battle-order as next to Socrates' *ile* (A 1.14.6). In the settlement at Triparadeisus, Philip III was assigned four Somatophylakes, including a certain Ptolemaeus son of Ptolemaeus (A*Succ* 1.38), whom Billows 425–30 identifies with the nephew of Antigonus (but see s.v. **Ptolemy** [7] below). Billows 425 makes the attractive suggestion that the correct form of the name of both father and son is Polemaios and that Polemaeus the elder was a brother of Antigonus the One-Eyed. The best we can say is that Ptolemy son of Philip *may* have been Antigonus' brother. The names Ptolemy and Philip are far too common to permit certainty.

Berve ii.336 no. 671; Billows 425 no. 99, s.v. "Polemaios I"; Heckel 259. See Stemma VI (possibly).

Ptolemy [3]. (Ptolemaeus, Ptolemaios). Son of Seleucus, probably from Tymphaea (so Berve ii.335) or from Orestis and a relative of Seleucus son of Antiochus (Hoffmann 174). A 1.24.1 calls him "one of the royal bodyguard," which must mean that he was one of the Royal Hypaspists. In late 334 Ptolemy led the newly-weds back to Macedonia for the winter (A 1.24.1), returning to Gordium in the spring of 333 with these men and 3,000 infantry and 300 horse from Macedonia, 200 Thessalian cavalry, and 150 Eleians under Alcias (A 1.29.4; cf. C 3.1.24). Later that year, he appears as taxiarch of the Tymphaean battalion, perhaps that commanded at the Granicus by Philip son of Amyntas (or Balacrus?). Ptolemy died on the battlefield of Issus and his battalion was assigned to the Tymphaean Polyperchon (A 2.12.2).

Berve ii.335–6 no. 670; Hoffmann 174; Beloch iii^2 2.327; Heckel 286. See Stemma XI (possibly).

Ptolemy [4]. (Ptolemaeus, Ptolemaios). Commander of the Thracians (A 4.7.2), Ptolemy was apparently the Macedonian officer in charge of all Thracian infantry, except the Agrianes, during the first half of the expedition. Of the native commanders, only Sitalces is known to us. In 329/8, Ptolemy returned from the coast of Phoenicia and Cilicia to Alexander in Zariaspa (A 4.7.2; cf. C 7.10.11: he returned with 5,000 mercenaries),[639] having been sent there in the winter of 331/0 to accompany Menes the hyparch and the discharged Thessalian cavalrymen (cf. A 3.16.9). On his departure for the coast, he was replaced by Eudamus. What became of Ptolemy after his return to Bactria is unknown.

Berve ii.337 no. 673; Heckel 333.

Ptolemy [5]. (Ptolemaeus, Ptolemaios). Macedonian. In 334, Alexander left Ptolemy behind as *strategos* of Caria,[640] in support of the reinstated queen Ada, with 3,000 mercenary infantry and 200 horse (A 1.23.6). Ptolemy, together with Asander, the satrap of Lydia, eventually defeated those who were holding the citadel of Halicarnassus, driving out Orontopates and killing some 700 infantry and fifty cavalry, while taking 1,000 prisoners. Hence he gained control also of Myndus, Caunus, Thera, Callipolis, Cos, and Triopium (A 2.5.7; cf. C 3.7.4). The remainder of Ptolemy's career is unknown, unless he can be identified with the son of Philip (a brother of Antigonus the One-Eyed).

Berve ii.337 no. 674.

Ptolemy [6]. (Ptolemaeus, Ptolemaios). Son of Lagus (A 2.11.8; 3.6.5 etc.; on Lagus see also P*M* 458a–b) and Arsinoë (Porphyry *ap.* Euseb Arm p. 74, 19ff. = *FGrH* 260 F2 §2), purportedly a member of a lesser branch of the Macedonian royal house (Satyrus, frg. 21 = *FHG* 3.165; Theocritus 17.26, with Gow ii.331; C 9.8.22; *OGIS* i.54, line 6). Ptolemy came from Eordaea (A 6.28.4; A*Ind* 18.5)[641] and may have been brought up at the court in Pella. Rumors that he was an illegitimate son of Philip II (Paus 1.6.2; C 9.8.22; Ael frg. 285; *Suda* *Λ* 25) are just that and originated in the early years of the Diadochic age, when blood relationship with the house of Philip had tremendous propaganda value (cf. Errington 1976: 155–6). The only source for Ptolemy's birthdate is of dubious worth: [L]*Macrob* 12 places it in 367/6 BC, a date generally rejected because it conflicts with the popularly accepted view that Ptolemy was coeval with Alexander (see Heckel 205, 207).

Banished by Philip II in spring 336 for his role in the Pixodarus affair – Ptolemy, along with Erigyius, Laomedon, Nearchus, and Harpalus, had induced the crown prince to conduct private negotiations with the Carian dynast – he appears not to have returned to Macedonia until after Philip's death (P*A* 10.4; A 3.6.5). Although he crossed into Asia with Alexander in 334,[642] nothing is known about his participation in the campaign in the early years. He appears to have joined in the pursuit of the Persians who fled from the battlefield of Issus, though he embellished his account with images of the Persians crossing a ravine on the bodies of their own dead (A 2.11.8; cf. Bosworth i.216–17, with earlier literature). There is no mention of an independent command until late 331, at the Persian Gates. Here Arrian (3.18.9) – probably drawing on Ptolemy's own *History* – assigns to him the command of 3,000 troops guarding one of Ariobarzanes' possible escape routes. But the vulgate authors say nothing about Ptolemy's role, and we may be justified in questioning the veracity of Arrian's account.[643] Certainly, Ptolemy's lack of achievement up to this point, combined with the conspicuous silence of the vulgate, raises suspicions about the man's sudden prominence in an account based, most likely, on his own record of events.[644]

In autumn 330, after Demetrius had been deposed (and presumably executed) on allegations of involvement in Dimnus' conspiracy, Alexander appointed Ptolemy Somatophylax (A 3.27.5; cf. 6.28.4 = Aristobulus, *FGrH* 139 F50). A 3.6.6, in a passage that anticipates the appointment, regards it as a reward for Ptolemy's loyalty to the King in the past, especially in 337/6. When J 13.4.10 writes that he had been "promoted from the ranks (*ex gregario milite*) on account of his *virtus*," he is merely indicating that Ptolemy, up to this point, had had no unit under his command. It was at about this time that Alexander began to make greater use of his Somatophylakes on an ad hoc basis. This is almost certainly because the composition of the unit had changed significantly and its members were all younger men whom the King felt he could trust. Thus, in 329, we find Ptolemy assigned the task of bringing in the regicide Bessus, whom Spitamenes and Dataphernes had arrested and were prepared to extradite, presumably in exchange for immunity (A 3.29.6–30.5; cf Seibert 10–16). Here again, Arrian, when he follows Ptolemy (*FGrH* 138 F14), shows signs of embellishment; for other accounts of Bessus' arrest see A 3.30.5 = Aristobulus, *FGrH* 139 F24; D 17.83.7–9; C 7.5.19–26, 38–43; J 12.5.10–11; *IA* 34. But, from his account, we do gain a sense of how delicate the extradition process was and how great the fear of betrayal. Spitamenes and Dataphernes had asked that only a small force be sent to them; Ptolemy's contingent probably exceeded 5,000 men: three hipparchies of Companions; the battalion of Philotas; one chiliarchy of hypaspists, all the Agrianes, and half the archers. Seibert 11 n. 33, following Berve, puts the figure at ca. 5,000. But the calculation of 300 men per hipparchy (*ile*) is probably incorrect, since the hipparchies had by this time been reformed (cf. Bosworth i.375–6), and the strength of a battalion of *psiloi* (i.e., Philotas' battalion) was not necessarily equal to that of its counterpart in the *pezhetairoi*. Alexander had clearly not forgotten Satibarzanes' treachery and the death of Anaxippus (A 3.25.2, 5).

In 328, Ptolemy commanded one of five columns that swept through Sogdiana (A 4.16.2–3; cf. Holt 60–6; C 8.1.1, 10, however, mentions only three contingents). His claim to have reported the discovery of oil at the Oxus (A 4.15.7–8) is contradicted by *PA* 57.5ff. and C 7.10.14 (cf. Seibert 16–17). In late summer or autumn of that year, he attended the banquet in Maracanda where Alexander killed Cleitus. Although it is generally agreed that he made some attempt to restrain Cleitus (A 4.8.9 = Aristobulus, *FGrH* 139 F29) or Alexander himself (C 8.1.45, 48), it could be argued that he had failed to prevent the murder, and it is difficult to determine what, if anything, Ptolemy said about the episode in his *History*. Over the winter, when the Macedonian forces besieged the fortress of Sisimithres (the Rock of Chorienes), Ptolemy and his fellow-Somatophylakes, Perdiccas and Leonnatus, conducted the night operations in shifts (A 4.21.4).

In the spring of 327, after Alexander's marriage to Rhoxane and before the departure for India, Ptolemy played a major role in bringing the conspiracy of Hermolaus and the Pages to Alexander's attention. The details of the plot had been divulged to him by Eurylochus, and, in Arrian's version (4.13.7), Ptolemy alone informed

Alexander. Curtius (8.6.22) says that Ptolemy *and Leonnatus* were approached by Eurylochus, and it appears that, in his own *History*, Ptolemy took full credit by suppressing Leonnatus' contribution (Errington 1969: 234; cf. A 4.25.3). During the Swat campaign, Ptolemy was wounded in a skirmish with the Aspasians near the Choes River (A 4.23.3). The wound could not have been serious, for Ptolemy soon afterwards pursued the Indian hyparch up a hill and killed him in single combat, the account of which almost certainly comes from Ptolemy's own pen (A 4.24.3–4; Jacoby rightly includes Ptolemy's *aristeia* in F18; cf. Brunt i.421 n. 3; and Seibert 19, with n. 54). Once the Macedonians had advanced beyond Arigaeum, Ptolemy was again sent ahead to reconnoiter, and he reported large numbers of enemy campfires (A 4.24.8). In the attack on this concentration of Indian forces, Alexander divided his troops into three contingents, assigning the command of one-third to Ptolemy, to whom he assigned the lightly armed battalions of Philotas and Philip, as well as one-third of the hypaspists (A 4.24.10). While Alexander dealt with the Indians who had rushed down onto the plain, Ptolemy successfully dislodged those who occupied the hills (A 4.25.2–3). And Ptolemy himself reported that in the engagement more than 40,000 Indians and 230,000 oxen were captured by the Macedonians (A 4.25.4 = *FGrH* 138 F18). But, despite Ptolemy's tendency to focus in his *History* on his own achievements, there is little to support Curtius' remark that "Ptolemy took the most cities, but Alexander captured the greatest ones" (8.10.21). Not surprisingly, Ptolemy also played a key role in the assault on Aornus in Arrian's version (4.29.1–6). The vulgate knows nothing of it, and Curtius in particular (8.11.5) ascribes a similar command to Myllinas (probably the son of Asander, a Beroean; cf. Tataki no. 910).

The vulgate preserves a story that Ptolemy was one of many Macedonians wounded at Harmatelia, a town of Brahmins – located by Diodorus and Curtius in the kingdom of Sambus, but placed by Str (15.2.7 [723], followed by Eggermont 125ff.) in the land of the Oreitae. These Indians smeared the tips of their weapons with poison extracted from snakes, thus causing the wounded to die in excruciating pain (D 17.103.3–6; C 9.8.20; Str 15.2.7 [723]). Apart from the implausible tale that Alexander saw in a dream a serpent carrying in its mouth the plant which was the antidote to the poison, it is clear that the whole story is a fiction invented to glorify Ptolemy. Like the false report that Ptolemy saved Alexander's life in the town of the Mallians (C 9.5.21; Paus 1.6.2; cf. P*M* 327b), which is disproved by Ptolemy's own *History* (A 6.11.8), this story contains late elements which render it even more suspect. Diodorus (17.103.6–7; cf. C 9.8.23–4) emphasizes the character and popularity of the later ruler of Egypt; Curtius (9.8.22; cf. Paus 1.6.2) adds that Ptolemy was thought to be an illegitimate son of Philip II. The snake itself is thought by some to be connected with the cult of Sarapis (see Eggermont 112–14, with earlier literature; cf. also Bosworth 1988b: 167–70; Fraser 1967: 23–45), instituted in Egypt by Ptolemy.

He was responsible for building the funeral pyre on which the famed Indian philosopher Calanus committed suicide amidst the flames shortly before the army reached Susa (A 7.3.2). At Susa in 324, Ptolemy married Artacama, a daughter of Artabazus (A 7.4.6; cf. P*Eum* 1.7, who calls her Apame) – hence a sister of Alexander's mistress Barsine – and, along with his fellow-Somatophylakes, was awarded a golden crown (A 7.5.6). There is no evidence that Ptolemy had been previously married. The Athenian courtesan Thaïs, who had accompanied the expedition, became Ptolemy's mistress (P*A* 38.2; Hamilton 100) – possibly she joined the expedition in that capacity – and bore him two sons (Lagus and Leontiscus) and a daughter, Eirene, who later married Eunostus, king of Cypriot Soli (Ath 13.576e).

Ptolemy's last commission under Alexander came against the Cossaeans, whose territory the King invaded in the winter of 324/3. Here he seems to have been Alexander's second-in-command, but Arrian's narrative (undoubtedly based on Ptolemy's own account: Strasburger 47), though vague and abbreviated (A 7.15.1–3), suffices to depict Ptolemy as a full partner in the undertaking and, consequently, equally responsible for its success (Seibert 25–6).[645] The forty-day campaign, which served to divert Alexander's attention away from the recent loss of Hephaestion (cf. P*A* 72.4), was not as successful as D 17.111.5–6 claims, as Antigonus discovered in 317 (D 19.19.3–8; Billows 92–3; cf. Bosworth 1988a: 165).

When Alexander died in 323, Ptolemy was one of the first to reject the legitimacy of the inept candidates for the throne – the half-witted Arrhidaeus, the illegitimate Heracles, and the half-barbarian and as-yet-unborn Alexander IV – proposing instead a ruling junta of officers (C 10.6.13–16). When an agreement was reached in Babylon, he was given Egypt as his satrapy (C 10.10.1; D 18.3.1; J 13.4.10), but assigned Cleomenes as his *hyparchos*, doubtless because Perdiccas distrusted him (A*Succ* 1.5; Dexippus, *FGrH* 100 F8 §2; J 13.4.11). Ptolemy, however, soon eliminated Cleomenes (Paus 1.6.3), whose mismanagement of affairs already in Alexander's lifetime provided a convenient pretext (A 7.23.6, 8), and began to forge closer ties with Antipater (D 18.14.2, 25.4). Sending a force to Syria in 321/0, he made sure that Alexander's funeral carriage would come to Egypt (A*Succ* 1.25; 24.1; D 18.28.2–3), as the King had originally intended, though Perdiccas had instead hoped to bring it back to Europe.[646] This move drew Perdiccas' forces to Egypt (D 18.25.6, 29.1), but Ptolemy had prepared for this eventuality (J 13.6.18–19, 8.1) and after a disastrous campaign at Kamelon Teichos Perdiccas was killed by his own men (A*Succ* 1.28; D 18.33–6; J 13.8.10). Ptolemy treated the remnants of the Perdiccan army and its mutinous commanders with respect (D 18.36.1–2, 6) and, after selecting the best troops for his own service, he sent the remainder under the leadership of Peithon and Arrhidaeus to northern Syria (D 18.36.6, 39.1; A*Succ* 1.30). There the empire was divided up anew, and Ptolemy retained Egypt (D 18.39.5; A*Succ* 1.34), to which he could add Libyan Cyrene, whither he had sent his general Ophellas to suppress the army of Thibron (D 18.19–21; A*Succ* 1.16–19; J 13.6.20; see s.vv. **Ophellas** [2], **Thibron**). Later he would send his stepson, Magas, to administer the area.[647] He had sealed his alliance with Antipater by marrying Eurydice, whose cousin, Berenice, accompanied her and later became his mistress.[648] The kingship which he established in Egypt, officially in 306 or 305, devolved in 285 upon his son by Berenice, Ptolemy II Philadelphus (Stemma X). It appears that in the period of co-rule with Philadelphus (285–283), Ptolemy composed his *History of Alexander*, which was used extensively by Arrian, and to a lesser extent by Curtius; Errington, however, proposes a much earlier date for the composition of the work.

Berve ii.329–35 no. 668; Volkmann, *RE* s.v. "Ptolemaios (18)"; Seibert; Heckel 222–7; Bengtson 1975: 10–35; Pédech 215–22; Ellis 1994; Collins 1997. For his historical work see Jacoby, *FGrH* 138; Errington 1969; Roisman 1984. See Stemma X.

Ptolemy [7]. (Ptolemaeus, Ptolemaios). Son of Ptolemy (perhaps the *somatophylax basilikos* who was killed at Halicarnassus or even the son of Ptolemy son of Seleucus;[649] but see also s.vv. **Polemaeus** and **Ptolemy** [2]). Appointed Somatophylax of Philip III Arrhidaeus at Triparadeisus (A*Succ* 1.38). He may be the same Ptolemy son of Ptolemy whose sale of land was ratified by Cassander, king of the Macedonians (*SIG*[3] 332).

Berve ii.335 no. 669.

Pulamachus (Poulamachos; Polymachos; Pulamachos, thus Hoffmann 212–13; Berve ii.339). A prominent Macedonian from Pella, Pulamachus was left behind in Persis in 330 BC. At an unspecified time, he plundered the tomb of Cyrus the Great and, on Alexander's return in 324, was convicted and executed (P*A* 69.3–4).

Berve ii.339 no. 679; Hoffmann 212–13; Tataki 159 no. 75.

Pymiathon. King of Citium; apparently the son and successor of Meleciaton (for the form Pymiathon, see Head, *HN*^{2} 788; cf. D 19.79.4, incorrectly "Pygmalion"[650]). Born at least by the late 380s, he acceded to the throne ca. 362/1. Among his possessions was Tamassus, an area rich in copper, which he had purchased for fifty talents from its bankrupt king, Pasicyprus (otherwise unknown), who subsequently retired into private life in Amathus (Duris *ap.* Ath 4.167c = *FGrH* 76 F4). That the territory in question was Tamassus seems to be confirmed by *CIS* i.10–11 (cf. Hill 1949: 150 n. 2; *CIS* i.10 dates to the twenty-first year of Pymiathon's reign [342/1] and mentions Tamassus as one of his possessions; *CIS* i.11, from the thirty-seventh year [326/5], no longer includes Tamassus). Pymiathon appears not to have given Alexander his wholehearted support (perhaps he did not report to Alexander at Sidon as the other Cypriot kings had done; cf. A 2.20.3), but sought instead to buy the King's favor by sending him a splendid sword (P*A* 32.10). Alexander allowed him to retain his throne, although Pymiathon did not mint coins independently until after Alexander's death (Head, *HN*^{2} 788; cf. Bagnall 187–8), but gave Tamassus as a gift to Pnytagoras (Duris, *FGrH* 76 F4).

Pymiathon remained in power in Citium until 312. In 315 he entered into negotiations with Antigonus the One-Eyed through the agency of Agesilaus (D 19.57.4; cf. Olshausen 87 no. 62) and agreed to an alliance (D 19.59.1). When Ptolemy counterattacked in 312, the Cypriot rulers who had gone over to Antigonus came to terms, but Pymiathon, who held out, was put to death (D 19.79.4; cf. also Hill 1949: 159 n. 5).

Berve ii.339–40 no. 680; Hill 1949: 151–2, 158–9.

Pyrgoteles. Greek engraver. His depictions of Alexander were regarded as so authentic that he was allegedly the only artist whom the King allowed to portray him in this medium (Pl*NH* 7.125, 37.8; Apul*Flor* 7). He may have been responsible for the Alexander with "horns of Amun" images on the Lysimachus coinage and the Ashmolean quartz ringstone of the same type (Pollitt 1986: 26), but this is speculation at best.

Berve ii.340 no. 681 (inaccurate); Pollitt 217–18.

Pyrrhon. Son of Pleistarchus. Philosopher from Elis (Str 9.1.8 [393]). His career is summarized by DL 9.61–108, followed by *Suda Π* 3238. Pyrrhon was originally a painter but then studied philosophy under Bryson. He went on Alexander's expedition in the company of Anaxarchus of Abdera. As a result of his travels he was influenced by the Gymnosophists and the Magi. Alexander gave him 10,000 pieces of gold the first time he met him (P*M* 331e).

Berve ii.340 no. 682.

Pytheas. Athenian orator and demagogue; hence not surprisingly depicted as of low origin (*Suda Π* 3125) and of unscrupulous character (Ael*VH* 14.28; P*Ph* 21.2; Dem*Ep* 3.30). Born perhaps ca. 360,[651] he was a supporter of Antipater, with whom he had on at least two occasions taken refuge (*Suda*; P*Dem* 27.2), and, perhaps for that reason, opposed to the granting of divine honors to Alexander (P*M* 804b); he was thus also an opponent of Demosthenes and Demades (Ath 2.44e–f). In 324, he was one of those who brought charges against Demosthenes in the Harpalus bribery scandal ([P]*M* 846c; Dem*Ep* 3.29).[652] In 323 he was entrusted by the city with the traditional sacrifices at Delphi (Dem*Ep* 3.30). After Alexander's death he belonged to those *philoi kai presbeis* who went round the Peloponnese urging states to remain loyal to Macedon and not join a Greek uprising (P*Dem* 27.2), and in Arcadia he openly debated with Demosthenes, without success, it appears

(PDem 27.4–5; cf. Phylarchus, *FGrH* 81 F75).

Berve ii.337–8 no. 675; Kirchner no. 12342.

Pythionice (Pythionike; Pythonike). Pythionice's family background is unknown. She was, according to Theopompus (*FGrH* 115 F253 = Ath 13.595a), a slave of the *hetaira* Bacchis and became a courtesan first in Corinth and then in Athens (Paus 1.37.5), becoming the most glamorous *hetaira* of her time (D 17.108.5).[653] She may have met Harpalus in 333/2, during his first flight from Alexander's camp (cf. A 3.6.7), when Harpalus spent some time in the Megarid. At some point after 330, when Harpalus was securely in charge of the imperial treasures, she joined him in Babylon, where Alexander's treasurer lavished gifts upon her and treated her like a queen; after her death he erected a magnificent tomb for her of the Attic type (D 17.108.5) and a similar monument near Eleusis (Paus 1.37.5; Ath 13.595b; cf. Dicaearchus *ap.* Ath 13.594f);[654] according to Theopompus (*FGrH* 115 F 253 = Ath 13.595c), he also set up a shrine where she was worshipped as Pythionice Aphrodite. She bore him a daughter (P*Ph* 22.1; **F58**), who after Harpalus' death was raised in the home of Charicles, a kinsman of Phocion (P*Ph* 22.3). Pythionice and Harpalus were the subjects of a satyr-play performed in front of the army in Asia (see below **Python** [1]).

Berve ii.338 no. 676. See Stemma XIII.

Python [1]. Greek poet from Catane or Byzantium (Ath 2.50f, 13.595e), allegedly the author of the satyr-play *Agen*, which satirized the activities of Harpalus in Babylon (Cleitarchus, *FGrH* 137 F30 = Ath 13.586c–d; cf. Theopompus, *FGrH* 115 F254) and, according to Athenaeus, was produced at the Hydaspes River. It seems virtually impossible that the performance could have taken place in India (although this is accepted by Snell 1964: 113–17), since the play speaks of Harpalus' affair with Pythionice, who was by this time dead, of Harpalus' treatment of Glycera in Tarsus and Rhossus (see s.v. **Glycera**), and his dealings with the Athenians. This makes it likely that the play was written after Harpalus' flight: indeed, it would perhaps not have been safe to criticize Alexander's *hetairos* before that time. Droysen i^3 406 n. 101 suggested the Choaspes River, and Goukowsky ii.77 and Bosworth 1988a: 149 believe it was produced in Carmania in 324. But Beloch iv^2 2.434–6 thinks of the Medus Hydaspes (Virgil, *Georgics* 4.211), possibly the Karkheh is meant. Identification of the poet with Python of Byzantium, the highly regarded orator in the service of Philip II (Aes 2.125; cf. *Suda Π* 3139), is unlikely.

Berve ii.338–9 no. 677; Snell 1964: 99–138, for the *Agen*.

Python [2]. Greek. As a young man, Python was the *eromenos* of the flute-player Evius. Cassander is said to have kissed him against his wishes and thus incurred Alexander's displeasure (P*M* 180f). The story appears to have been set in the last year of Alexander's life,[655] probably in Babylon, and belongs to a set of anecdotes that illustrate the King's hostility toward Cassander. Berve ii.339 believes that Python may have become the famous flute-player of Pyrrhus' time (P*M* 184c; P*Pyr* 8.7).

Berve ii.339 no. 678.

R

Rhebulas (Rheobulas). Son of Seuthes III, younger brother of Cotys (*IG* ii^2 349; Schwenk no. 45). Rhebulas and Cotys had both been honored earlier with citizenship (Dem 23.118). Rhebulas was sent to Athens in 330, in the archonship of Aristophanes, by his father, perhaps in the context of the unrest in Thrace (cf. Memnon), although it is difficult to see a clear connection with the later Odrysian uprising (C 10.1.45).

Berve ii.346 no. 686; Beloch iii^2 2.89–91.

Rheomithres. For the name ("to whom Mithra is friendly") see Justi 260. Noble Persian, father of Phrasaortes – who was appointed satrap of Persis in 330 (A 3.18.11) – and other children, who along with their mother were left as hostages with the Egyptian ruler Tachos, whom Rheomithres betrayed in 362 during the Satraps' Revolt (Xen*Cyr* 8.8.4; D 15.92.1). This identification was rejected by Leuze (403 n. 1; cf. Atkinson i.231), without compelling chronological reasons; a birthdate for Rheomithres in the mid-380s is perfectly compatible with all the other evidence (Justi 260; cf. Bosworth i.111). He commanded 2,000 cavalry on the right wing (between 1,000 Medes and 2,000 Bactrians) at the Granicus River (D 17.19.4; cf. A 1.12.8); after that battle he joined Darius III and fought at Issus, where he lost his life (A 2.11.8; C 3.11.10; D 17.34.5).

Judeich 205–6; Berve ii.346 no. 685; Briant 663–4, 674.

Rhoesaces (Rhoisakes; Rhosakes; Rhosaces). Persian nobleman and brother of Spithridates (D 17.20.6) the satrap of Lydia and Ionia under Darius III (A 1.12.8; cf. D 17.20.2), Rhoesaces was descended from the "Seven" Persians (D 16.47.2).[656] In the battle at the Granicus, Rhoesaces struck Alexander on the helmet but was himself killed by the King (A 1.16.7, by a lance; P*A* 16.8, 11, by Alexander's sword, with Spithridates striking the King's helmet); Cleitus cut off the arm of his brother as he intended to deal Alexander a fatal blow (A 1.16.8; P*A* 16.8–11).[657]

Berve ii.346 no. 687; Justi 262.

Rhoxane (Roxane). "Roshanak" ("Little Star," so Rawlinson 1912: 46 n. 2). The daughter of Oxyartes, a Bactrian noble (D 18.3.3; 19.48.2; Paus 1.6.3; C 10.3.11; Str 11.11.4; *LM* 118, 121); wrongly identified as daughter of Darius III in the *Alexander Romance* (Ps-Call 2.20.11; 2.22.3; cf. also Malalas 8.194). Rhoxane was born not long before 342 BC; for she was of marriageable age in late 328, when she took refuge, together with her mother and sisters (**F30, 31–32**), at Koh-i-nor with Sisimithres (Str 11.11.4 [517]), whose surrender was, in fact, negotiated by Oxyartes himself (C 8.2.25–31 "Oxartes"). After his campaign against the Sacae, Alexander was entertained by Sisimithres (Chorienes, *ME* 28; C 8.4.21 MSS. *cohortandus*) and on that occasion met Rhoxane, who was among thirty maidens introduced at the banquet

(C 8.4.23; cf. *ME* 28–9; A 4.18.4, 19.4–5 wrongly places her capture on the Rock of Ariamazes, which was taken by Alexander in the spring of 328). Arrian calls it the "Rock of Sogdiana" and dates its capture to the spring of 327; C 7.11 puts it in its proper context, sometime before the summer in which Cleitus was murdered. In Cleitus' criticisms of Alexander there is no mention of the marriage to Rhoxane – which suggests that the marriage had not yet occurred in mid-328. Different is the interpretation of Bosworth 1981: 31 n. 98, who thinks that Rhoxane was captured on the Rock of Ariamazes and married on that of Chorienes. But Bosworth rejects the identification of Chorienes and Sisimithres. According to the romantic tradition Alexander was so impressed by her beauty – she was reputed to be the most beautiful woman in Asia after the wife of Darius (A 4.19.5; cf. C 8.4.25) – that he married her (P*A* 47.7–8; *ME* 29–31; cf. P*M* 332e, 338d; C 8.2.26–9).[658] But the chief motive will have been political: the marriage helped to end the opposition to him in the northeast (cf. Hamilton 129–30; cf. C 10.3.11); Curtius compares her with Briseis for literary effect (8.4.26). Rhoxane bore a son (**M40**), who appears to have been stillborn or to have died within days of his birth at the Acesines River in autumn 326 (*ME* 70); the silence of the other extant sources carries little weight. Otherwise we know nothing of Rhoxane during the campaign until the last days of Alexander's life. She may have influenced her husband's decision to give Oxyartes the satrapy of the Parapamisadae (or Paropanisadae) in 325 (A 6.15.3; cf. C 9.8.9–10, confused).

Rhoxane's political influence was undoubtedly diminished when Alexander married at Susa first Stateira, daughter of Darius III, and then Parysatis, daughter of Ochus (A 7.4.4 = Aristobulus, *FGrH* 139 F52, calling Stateira "Barsine"); but in October (J 13.2.5) or December (C 10.6.9) 324 she became pregnant with Alexander's child, whose birthright she sought to protect by murdering Stateira and her sister, Drypetis, soon after Alexander's death in early June 323 (P*A* 77.6). The tender scenes of Rhoxane and Alexander during his final days are romanticized by the author of the *Liber de Morte* and perhaps exaggerated in the interests of the claims of Alexander IV (*LM* 101–2, 110, 112; Ps-Call 3.32.4–7; cf. A 7.27.3), but there is no good reason to deny that the two felt genuine love for each other; and, if Curtius' date for Rhoxane's conception is correct (10.6.9), then Alexander may have turned to her for consolation, as Green 467 notes, when Hephaestion died in October of 324.

The status of Rhoxane's child became a matter of great contention, both because of the uncertainty about the child's sex and on account of Rhoxane's "Persian" origin (J 13.2.5–6, 9; C 10.6.9, 13–14); in the end a compromise was reached, whereby Rhoxane's child, if male, should become *symbasileus* with Philip III Arrhidaeus (A*Succ* 1.1, 8; somewhat different is App*Syr* 52; *HE* 1), a fact supported by the epigraphic evidence (*OGIS* i.4) but denied by the author of the *Liber de Morte* (*LM* 115; Ps-Call 3.33.13). Rhoxane, along with her son, accompanied Perdiccas to Egypt, in the campaign against Ptolemy (Paus 1.6.3), and after Perdiccas' death was taken to Macedonia by Antipater (A*Succ* 1.44; D 18.39.7; *HE* 2), although she was briefly in the camp of Antigonus the One-Eyed (A*Succ* 1.38, 42–3). Rhoxane and her son took refuge with Olympias at Pydna over the winter 317/6,[659] where they were subsequently captured (D 19.35.5; J 14.6.2, confusing her son with Heracles, son of Barsine; J 15.1.3). She and Alexander IV were soon imprisoned at Amphipolis by Cassander (D 19.52.4; cf. 19.61.1, 3; J 14.6.13) and later murdered by Glaucias, a henchman of Cassander (D 19.105.1–2; J 15.2.2–5; Paus 9.7.2; cf. Tr*Prol* 15; *HE* 1–2).[660]

Berve ii.346–7 no. 688; Justi 262; Schachermeyr 1920; Macurdy 1932; Renard and Servais 1955; Schoder 1982; Holt 2005; 86–91. See Stemma I.

S

Sabeil. *Pap. Berolin.* 13044 = *FGrH* 153 F9. See **Sambus** [1].

Sabictas (Sabiktas). Possibly a high-ranking Persian – or perhaps a native Cappadocian – Sabictas was appointed satrap of Cappadocia near Taurus (cf. Baumbach 59; Julien 18–19) by Alexander in the summer of 333 (A 2.4.2; cf. C 3.4.1, "Abistamenes"). Berve suggests that Abistamenes was Sabictas' successor (ii.348), but it is more likely that we are dealing here with a corruption of the name Sabictas.[661] How long he remained in office – or if he was involved in any way with the Persians who fled into Cappadocia after Issus (C 4.1.34–5) – we do not know.

Berve ii.348 no. 690; Justi 269; Baumbach 59 n. 2; Julien 18–19.

Samaxus. Ruler (*regulus*) of an Indian region adjacent to Arachosia. He had apparently served with Barsaentes at Gaugamela (see A 3.8.4, with Eggermont 18) and had given refuge to the regicide Barsaentes. After the deaths of Satibarzanes and Bessus, Samaxus joined in a rebellion with Barsaentes, but both men were captured and brought in chains to Alexander at the Hydaspes (C 8.13.3–4). Barsaentes was executed by Alexander (A 3.25.8); but we cannot be certain what became of Samaxus. Eggermont 16–21 plausibly suggests that Samaxus is identical with Sambus, since both appear to have ruled the territory controlling the Khojak and Bolan passes. "Samaxus" may be little more than a corruption of the name Sambus, perhaps brought on by the confusion of another Indian *hyparchos*, Doraxes, who met Alexander near the Hydaspes in the presence of ambassadors from Abisares (A 5.8.3; cf. C 8.13.1 for Abisares' ambassadors). It appears that the original source may have mentioned both Sambus and Doraxes, which Curtius conflated into a single individual named "Samaxus."[662] If this is the case, the remainder of his career can be found s.v. **Sambus** [1] below. If Samaxus is indeed a separate individual, he may have been executed along with Barsaentes.

Berve ii.348 no. 692; Eggermont 16–21.

Sambus [1]. (Sambos; also Sabbas, Sabos; perhaps Samaxus).[663] Ruler of the Indian region centered on Sindimana (traditionally identified with Sehwan, but Eggermont 22 suggests that it lay somewhere west of Alor on the road to Kandahar). Alexander had himself appointed Sambus satrap of the area (A 6.16.3), which suggests an earlier meeting (perhaps at the Hydaspes: see s.v. **Samaxus** above; C 9.8.17 speaks of Sambus' recent surrender).[664] He is said to have fled when Alexander reinstated his enemy Musicanus in the adjacent region; his relatives opened the gates of Sindimana and explained that Sambus' flight was due to fear of Musicanus (A 6.16.3–4).[665] The real instigators of the rebellion against Alexander were those of the Brahmin class (*Pap. Berolin.* 13044 = *FGrH* 153 F9; *PA* 64.1; cf. C 9.8.15 and D 17.102.7, both from

Cleitarchus, for the death of 80,000 Brahmins), but the details of the conflict are hopelessly confused. What happened to Sambus is unknown.

Berve ii.348–9 no. 693; Eggermont, *passim*; Jacobs 246–7.

Sambus [2]. (Sambos). Indian commander, who during the defense of the Mallian town was transfixed by a 3-ft catapult dart (*ME* 75). The author of the *Metz Epitome* may have confused the name of this commander with that of the more famous king, whom he otherwise appears not to know; but the name may have been common in the region. We are clearly dealing with two separate individuals.

Berve ii.349 no. 694.

Sanballat (Sanaballetes). A Horonite. Darius III's satrap in Samaria (Jos*AJ* 11.302), Sanballat was already an old man at the time of Alexander's invasion (Jos*AJ* 11.311). He was the father of Nicaso and father-in-law of Manasses, the brother of the high priest of Jerusalem, Iaddus (Jos*AJ* 11.302–3; but Nehemiah 13:28 says that Sanballat's son-in-law was son of the high priest Eliashib and grandson of Jehoiada).[666] The mixed marriage was frowned upon and Sanballat planned to make Manasses high priest of a new temple he was to found on Mount Gerizim (Jos*AJ* 11.310). But the war between Alexander and Darius intervened, and after the battle of Issus Sanballat abandoned Darius and brought 8,000 men to Alexander at Tyre (Jos*AJ* 11.321), thus retaining his position and gaining permission for the construction of the temple on Mount Gerizim. At this point the classical sources speak of the appointment of Andromachus in Coele-Syria, presumably as *strategos* (C 4.5.9). Sanballat died before Alexander had completed the siege of Gaza (Jos*AJ* 11.322–5). The remainder of Josephus' story, which has Alexander coming to Jerusalem and revering the Hebrew god, is dismissed by many scholars as fiction (Bickerman 1988: 5).[667] The value of the details of Sanballat's administration of Samaria and submission to Alexander is also uncertain (cf. Briant 1048).

Berve ii.349 no. 695.

Sandrocottus (Sandrokottos; Sandrakottos, also Andrakottos). Chandragupta Maurya, king of Magadha and founder of the Mauryan dynasty. There is no firm evidence of any personal connection between Sandrocottus and Alexander. *PA* 62.9 says that when he was still a youth he saw Alexander, presumably when his army reached the limits of the Punjab. But this appears to be a later embellishment. But Sandrocottus clearly exploited the weakness of the Nanda dynasty that is reported by King Phegeus (and verified by Porus) to Alexander at the Hyphasis (C 9.2.5–7; D 17.93.2–3). J 15.4.13–19 gives us a "rags to riches" story of the allegedly low-born Sandrocottus, who fled into exile, fearing the wrath of "Nandrus" (apparently Mahapadma Nanda; see s.v. **Xandrames**). Smith[3] 117 assumes that this occurred before Alexander's advance and that it was during this exile that Sandrocottus saw Alexander. According to Buddhist tradition, he overthrew the Nanda king in 322 and established himself at Pataliputra[668] (mod. Patna) on the Ganges. The Greek sources say nothing about the pivotal role played by Kautilya in Sandrocottus' rise to power. Soon after gaining the throne of Magadha, Sandrocottus expelled Macedonian garrisons from the Punjab (J 15.4.12, 19). The historian Megasthenes appears to have been sent on an embassy to Sandrocottus by Sibyrtius, satrap of Arachosia (A 5.6.2; cf. Str 2.1.9 [70], 15.1.36 [702]), at some point between Sandrocottus' accession and the death of Porus (cf. Bosworth 1996b: 121). After the death of Porus (318/7), Sandrocottus extended his empire into the Indus region, and he came into conflict with Seleucus ca. 304 BC. Impressed by Sandrocottus' army of 400,000 (Megasthenes, *FGrH* 715 F32 = Str 15.1.53 [709]; Pl*NH* 6.68 has 600,000 infantry and 9,000 elephants), Seleucus made peace with him, ceding the territories adjacent to the Indus (Parapamisadae, Arachosia, Gedrosia) in return for a large number of elephants (cf. P*A* 62.4) and a marriage alliance (J 15.4.21; App*Syr* 55 [282]; Str 15.2.9 [724]).[669] Appian's story of Seleucus' waging war against Sandrocottus east of the Indus is face-saving propaganda. Sandrocottus ruled for twenty-four years, dying ca. 298.

Berve ii.349–50 no. 696; Smith[3] 113–20; Hamilton 172ff.; Bosworth 1996b.

Sangaeus (Sangaios). "Sangaja" ("Victory," so Lassen ii[2] 135 n. 3; Anspach i.13 n. 35). An Indian leader and, apparently, a subordinate of Astis – if not a neighboring chieftain whose territory was threatened by Astis – who fled to the army of Perdiccas and Hephaestion, which was at that time advancing to the Indus. After the defeat of Astis, Sangaeus was made ruler of Peucelaotis in the territory of Gandhara (A 4.22.8; cf. Bosworth *ad loc.*). By the terms of Alexander's settlement of the area, he was responsible to the Macedonian satrap (Philip son of Machatas and, later, Peithon son of Agenor). Nothing else is known about him.

Berve ii.348 no. 691; Lassen ii[2] 135 n. 3; Anspach i.13 n. 35.

Satibarzanes. Noble Persian. Satrap of Areia and commander of the satrapal levies at Gaugamela (A 3.8.4). He is otherwise unattested in the battle. A 3.21.10 calls Satibarzanes a regicide, which may be due to confusion with Nabarzanes. On the other hand, he may very well have participated in the plot against Darius (cf. *ME* 3, where *Ariobarzanes* should read *Satibarzanes*). Satibarzanes surrendered to Alexander at Susia (Tus) in Areia, and was confirmed in his satrapy (A 3.25.1; C 6.6.20; he brought news that Bessus had assumed the tiara and title of "Artaxerxes" and was mobilizing the Scythians, C 6.6.13). But Satibarzanes murdered Anaxippus and the forty javelin-men whom Alexander had sent with him (A 3.25.2), butchering them once Alexander had set out for Bactria and then gathering the rebellious Areians at Artacoana, the satrapal capital (A 3.25.5; C 6.6.20–34).[670] Within two days of receiving the news of Satibarzanes' treachery, Alexander arrived at Artacoana, from which the satrap fled to Bactria with 2,000 horsemen (C 6.6.22; cf. A 3.25.6–7). In his place Alexander appointed Arsaces, a Persian (A 3.25.7), but Satibarzanes soon returned to his satrapy to incite rebellion (C 7.3.2; A 3.28.2; D 17.81.3), whereupon he was killed in single combat by Erigyius (A 3.28.3; C 7.4.33–7; D 17.83.4–6), who returned to Alexander with the barbarian's head (C 7.4.40).

Berve ii.350–1 no. 697; Justi 291.

Satraces (Satrakes). Leader of the Sacae. Satraces opposed Alexander on the north bank of the Iaxartes (Syr-Darya) River in 329 and died in battle against him (A 4.4.8). Curtius and *ME* speak, in this context, of a certain Carthasis, brother of the Scythian king. See s.v. **Carthasis**.

Berve ii.351 no. 698.

Satropates (Perhaps "Atropates"). A Persian cavalry officer, Satropates was sent by Darius with 1,000 picked horsemen to prevent Alexander's crossing of the Tigris shortly before the eclipse of September 20, 331 (C 4.9.7). Curtius' account is, however, unclear: Satropates is given 1,000 men and sent ahead by Darius to patrol the east side of the Tigris, while Mazaeus with 6,000 is ordered to prevent Alexander's crossing *the river* – clearly the Euphrates; C 4.9.12 (Atkinson i.379). Yet at C 4.9.7 we find only 1,000 horsemen sent by Mazaeus against Alexander at the *Tigris*, and in the ensuing battle Satropates is killed by the Paeonian Ariston, who brings his head to Alexander (C 4.9.25; cf. P*A* 39.2). A 3.7.7–8.2 appears to be referring to the same battle, which he dates to four days after the eclipse. Either Mazaeus had nothing to do with the battle near the Tigris (and Curtius has conflated the missions of Satropates and Mazaeus), or Mazaeus, after withdrawing from Thapsacus, joined forces with Satropates (cf. also Berve ii.244–5). Satropates' death may be depicted on the coinage of the Paeonian king, Patraus, who appears to have been Ariston's brother (Merker 1965: 44–5; Atkinson i.384–5).

Berve ii.351 no. 699; Marsden 1964: 31.

Sauaces (Sabakes; Sauakes; also Sataces, Tasiakes or Stasiakes). Satrap of Egypt under Darius III, in late 333 BC Sauaces led the Egyptian contingent to Issus where he fell on the battlefield (A 2.11.8; D 17.34.5; C 3.11.10; 4.1.28). His administrative duties appear to have been assumed by Mazaces.

Berve ii.348 no. 689; Justi 268.

Scymnus (Skymnos). A juggler from Tarentum in Alexander's entourage (Ath 1.20a), Skymnos performed at the mass-marriage ceremony at Susa in 324 (Chares, *FGrH* 125 F4 = Ath 12.538e). See also s.vv. **Heracleitus** [1] and **Philistides**.

Berve ii.357 no. 713.

Seleucus (Seleukos). Son of Antiochus (*OGIS* i.413; J 13.4.17; 15.4.3; A*Succ* 1.2; also Str 16.2.4 [749]; App*Syr* 57; Oros 3.23.10; Lib 11.93), a prominent officer of Philip II (J 15.4.3), and Laodice (J 15.4.3; Str 16.2.4 [750]; App*Syr* 57; StByz s.v. "Laodikeia"); from Europus (StByz s.v. "Oropos," cf. App*Syr* 57 [298]) in Macedonia. Ptolemaeus son of Seleucus may have been Tymphaean, as was his successor Polyperchon son of Simmias. The existence of a sister, named Didymeia, is uncertain (see s.v. **Didymeia** and Stemma XI). Stories of Laodice's liaisons with Apollo are creations of the Diadochic era and influenced in part by Olympias' alleged affair with Amun, who visited her in the form of a snake (J 15.4.1–6; for stories of Olympias and Amun see P*A* 2.6; 3.1–2; J 11.11.3; 12.16.2; Gell 13.4.1–3; cf. also Mehl 5–6; Grainger 2–3; Hadley 1969: 144, 152). Born in the early 350s,[671] probably in Europus near the Axius River, Seleucus came to Pella in the mid-to-late 340s as a Page of Philip II and slightly older *syntrophos* of the crown prince.[672] A member of Alexander's *hetairoi*, his aristocratic standing is virtually proved by his promotion – probably in 330 – to the command of the Royal Hypaspists. Hephaestion held this office at Gaugamela and must surely have relinquished it when he was appointed hipparch in 330, upon the death of Philotas (A 3.27.4). When Seleucus appears as commander of the Royal Hypaspists at the Hydaspes (A 5.13.1, 4), he must have held the office for almost four years. Certainly the fact that Seleucus coordinated the infantry (i.e., hypaspists, archers) against Porus (A 5.16.3; C 8.14.15 incorrectly substitutes Leonnatus for Seleucus in his account of the Hydaspes battle) suggests that by this time he had acquired considerable experience in command – primarily in the campaigns of Bactria and Sogdiana.

For the remainder of Seleucus' career during Alexander's lifetime there is no evidence of military activity, though he must certainly have played a prominent role in the Indus campaign and will most likely have accompanied the King to Gedrosia and the west. At Susa in 324 he received as his bride Apame, the daughter of Spitamenes (A 7.4.6; cf. P*Demetr* 31.5; App*Syr* 57 [295–6]; Str 12.8.15 [578] calls her daughter of Artabazus; cf. 16.2.4 [750]; Pl*NH* 6.132); she was to become the mother of Antiochus I Soter, and Seleucus later named at least three cities for her. (App*Syr* 57 [295]; Livy 38.13.5 calls Apame "sister" of Seleucus; StByz s.v. "Apamea"; cf. Str 16.2.4 [750]). Whether there is any significance in the fact that Apame was the only bride from the northeast, besides Alexander's wife Rhoxane (as Mehl 18 points out), it cannot be determined. At any rate, we do not know the names of all the brides of prominent *hetairoi*; there may have been others from Bactria and Sogdiana. Seleucus is mentioned in connection with perhaps three episodes in Babylonia – a sailing trip on the marshes near Babylon (A 7.22.5; App*Syr* 56 [288–9]); the dinner-party of Medius the Thessalian (Ps-Call 3.31.8?);

and the visit to the temple of Sarapis (A 7.26.2; P*A* 76.9) – all associated with the King's death.

In the first of these episodes, Seleucus recovered Alexander's diadem, which had been blown off his head and had settled on some reeds near the tombs of Assyrian kings. In order to keep it dry, he placed the diadem on his head while he swam back to the King's ship. The actions were regarded as ominous: the diadem, landing near the tombs, foretold the King's death; placed on Seleucus' head, it presaged the kingship of the bearer (App*Syr* 56 [287–91]). But, according to Aristobulus (*FGrH* 139 F55 = A 7.22.5), it was a Phoenician sailor (**M72**) and not Seleucus who recovered the diadem, and J 15.3.13–14 tells a similar story about Lysimachus' future kingship. Such stories circulated in the Diadochic age, almost certainly after 307/6, to support the regal pretensions of one Successor or another. We may place very little faith in their historicity.[673]

That Seleucus attended the dinner-party of Medius, at which Alexander became fatally ill, may be true. That he was involved in a plot to poison the King is, however, unlikely. The story that Seleucus (accompanied by Peithon, Attalus, Menidas, Demophon, Peucestas, and Cleomenes) slept in the temple of Sarapis in Babylon in the hope that Alexander's health might improve (A 7.26.2; P*A* 76.9) has also been challenged by scholars, since the cult of Sarapis is generally thought to have been instituted by Ptolemy I in Egypt (discussion in Hamilton 212–13). Grainger 218–19 may be right in assigning this story to the propaganda wars of the Diadochoi as well. In the factional strife that broke out after Alexander's death in June 323, Seleucus is scarcely mentioned. He is referred to once as a marshal of the second rank: the most powerful leaders in Babylon were Perdiccas, Leonnatus, and Ptolemy; with them, but clearly of lesser importance, were Lysimachus, Aristonus, Peithon, Seleucus, and Eumenes (A*Succ* 1.2). Seleucus was, however, a man whom Perdiccas trusted – perhaps wrongly, as events would show. When Perdiccas had eliminated his rival Meleager and distributed the satrapies, he took steps to secure for himself the "guardianship" of (first) Philip III Arrhidaeus and (later) Alexander IV. Hence he named Seleucus his second-in-command (at least in the military sphere: *summus castrorum tribunatus*, J 13.4.17), assigning to him "the hipparchy of the Companions, which was the most distinguished" (D 18.3.4), namely the "first hipparchy" or "Hephaestion's chiliarchy" (A 7.14.10), which Perdiccas himself had once commanded. As such, he was, in theory, second only to Perdiccas who exercised power "in the name of the Kings." But this power depended on Perdiccas' ability to preserve the integrity of Alexander's empire and to impose the "Royal Will" on the satraps and the *strategos* of Europe. In this endeavor Perdiccas failed miserably, only to be confronted by a mutiny of his officers – among them Antigenes, Peithon, and Seleucus – who murdered him in his tent as the Royal Army was encamped near Memphis (N*Eum* 5.1; cf. A*Succ* 1.28, 35; D 18.33.2ff.; Paus 1.6.3; Str 17.1.8 [794]; *Diadochoi Chronicle*, BM 34660, col. 4). At Triparadeisus, he was rewarded for his betrayal of Perdiccas with the satrapy of Babylonia (D 18.39.6; A*Succ* 1.35; *HE* 1.4 = *FGrH* 155 F1 §1.4). He continued to support the decision of the assembly at Triparadeisus, which had outlawed the Perdiccan party, and he attempted to impede Eumenes' progress eastward (D 18.73.3–4; cf. 19.12.1–2). After a fruitless struggle to keep Eumenes from crossing the Tigris, he negotiated a truce (19.13.5) under which Eumenes would leave the satrapy (D 18.12–13). But Seleucus also urged Antigonus to come with his army to deal with Eumenes (D 19.13.5). Meanwhile, Peithon son of Crateuas was also making a bid for power in the Upper Satrapies and trying to enlist Seleucus in his cause, but the satrap of Babylon remained non-committal (D 19.14.3). Antigonus assigned Susiana, and the task of bringing

Xenophilus to heel, to Seleucus (D 19.18.1) and, although we hear of reinforcements from Seleucus and Peithon at Paraetacene (D 19.27.1), it appears that only Peithon fought in Antigonus' forces at Paraetacene (D 19.29.3) and Gabiene (D 19.38.4). Seleucus meanwhile came to terms with Xenophilus, who greeted the returning Antigonus at the Pasitigris River (D 19.48.6), and prepared to entertain Antigonus in Babylon (D 19.55.2). But Antigonus sought to relieve Seleucus of his satrapy by demanding an audit of his accounts – a similar trick had been used by Perdiccas against Antigonus himself, and he was quick to learn the lesson – and charging him with taking actions against a subordinate without his authority (D 19.55.3–4; App*Syr* 53 [268]). Seleucus, alert to the danger and mindful of Peithon's fate (see s.v. **Peithon** [3]), fled to Ptolemy (19.55.5–6).[674] Revealing to Ptolemy the details of Antigonus' actions and ambitions, he persuaded him to form a coalition with Lysimachus and Cassander (D 19.56.1–4; App*Syr* 53 [270]). Consequently, envoys sent to Antigonus demanded, *inter alia*, that Seleucus be reinstated as satrap of Babylonia (D 19.57.1; cf. App*Syr* 53 [271] for the ultimatum).

Berve ii.351–2 no. 700; Stähelin, *RE* s.v. "Seleucus (2)"; Bevan i.28–73; Hadley 1969; Mehl 1–28; Grainger 1–23; cf. Heckel 253–7. See Stemma XI.

Serapion. Youth in Alexander's entourage with whom the King used to play ball (P*A* 39.5), to whom the King, allegedly, did not give gifts because he did not ask for them. The boy's name (and thus his existence) has been called into question because it implies that the cult of Serapis existed before the time of Ptolemy I (see Hamilton 103 and 212–13, with bibliography).[675]

Berve ii.352–3 no. 701; Hamilton 103.

Seuthes. Cf. Besevliev 2–3; Tomaschek, *SB Wien* 131, 42. King of the Odrysian Thracians (Str 7, frg. 47), Seuthes III (*regn.* ca. 300–ca. 300/295) is attested as father of Rhebulas and Cotys (*IG* ii^2 349 = Tod ii.193). The Odrysians were reluctant allies of Macedon (cf. A 3.12.4 for Odrysian cavalry in Alexander's service), and Seuthes' position doubtless was one of vassalage. In June 330 he sent his son Rhebulas to Athens to forge an alliance, probably in the aftermath of the rebellion by the Macedonian *strategos* of Thrace, Memnon. The Athenians appear to have done little more than renew old ties with Thrace and honor Rhebulas with citizenship (*IG* ii^2 349 = Tod ii.193); after the defeat of Memnon and the failure of Agis' war, they could scarcely do more. The disastrous campaign of Zopyrion led Seuthes into open rebellion (C 10.1.45). Founder of Seuthopolis (on which see Danoff, *RE* Supplbd ix.1370–8; id., *Kl. Pauly* v.152; Dimitrov & Cicikova 1978).

In 323/2, when Thrace was awarded to Lysimachus, the latter invaded Seuthes' territory (from "the middle and upper reaches of the Tonsus, extending west perhaps as far as the Stryama River and east to the Sasliyka," Lund 24) with a force of 4,000 foot and 2,000 horse, against which the Thracian king mustered 20,000 infantry and 8,000 cavalry (D 18.14.2). In the stubborn ensuing battle, Lysimachus claimed a doubtful victory, and killed large numbers of Seuthes' men. But the outcome was clearly indecisive (D 18.14.3–4; A*Succ* 1.10 incorrectly says that Lysimachus was killed in the engagement). On the other hand, Seuthes' lack of further action suggests that he entered into some kind of alliance with Lysimachus until 313 (D 19.73.8; Pol*Strat* 7.25). For his coinage see Mørkholm 83 (**192**), who notes that many of Seuthes III's coins "are overstruck on Macedonian ones, especially on bronze issues of Cassander."

Berve ii.353 no. 702; Swoboda, *RE* s.v. "Seuthes (4)"; Badian 1967a. Cf. Lund 19ff.

Sibyrtius (Sibyrtios). Macedonian. We do not know how long he had been in

Alexander's entourage before his appointment as satrap of Carmania in 325 and almost immediate transfer to Gedrosia (A 6.27.1).[676] Upon the death of Menon, Arachosia was added to Sibyrtius' satrapy, and he retained both regions in the subsequent distribution of satrapies at Babylon in 323 (D 18.3.3; J 13.4.22; Dexippus, *FGrH* 100 F8 §6; cf. *LM* 121) and at Triparadeisus in 320 (A*Succ* 1.36; cf. A 5.6.2). In 317 he appears to have joined the coalition of "Upper Satraps" against Peithon son of Crateuas; we find him in command of 1,000 infantry and 610 cavalry in 316, directly under the authority of Peucestas (D 19.14.6), who was a personal friend. Sibyrtius fled the camp after being called to account by Eumenes (D 19.23.4); his troops were assigned to Cephalon (D 19.27.4, on whom see further Heckel 1980a). He appears to have joined Antigonus, though there is no record of military command in 316/5, who restored him to his satrapy and assigned some 1,000 Argyraspids to him with orders that he should wear them out with service (Pol*Strat* 4.6.15; P*Eum* 19.3; D 19.48.3). Nothing else is known about his career except that he retained his position under Seleucus I Nicator, whose agent to India, Megasthenes, visited him on his way to Sandrocottus (A 5.6.2).

Berve ii.353 no. 703; Billows 432–3 no. 106.

Simmias [1]. Born ca. 360, Simmias appears to have been the second oldest of Andromenes' sons (perhaps named for the maternal grandfather, possibly the father of Polyperchon; cf. Heckel 189 for stemma) and the logical choice to command Amyntas' battalion in his absence. Since Amyntas did not rejoin the expedition until after Gaugamela, his battalion was commanded on that occasion by Simmias (A 3.11.9; D 17.57.3 names Philip son of Balacrus in this context; cf. C 4.13.28).[677] It may be that, because of Simmias' inexperience and the importance of the battle, Amyntas' battalion was commanded by Philip son of Balacrus, with Simmias in a subordinate role.

Upon his return in late 331, Amyntas resumed command of his battalion. The absence of Simmias from our records and the appointment of Attalus as Amyntas' successor as taxiarch suggest that Simmias was deliberately passed over in favor of his younger brother, perhaps because of his earlier associations with Philotas and Amyntas son of Perdiccas. The charge that Simmias was, indirectly, responsible for the attack on the Macedonian camp may have been used to justify Alexander's decision to give Amyntas' command to Attalus, one of his own *syntrophoi*. On the other hand, Simmias may have left the army in 331/0 or died of illness (but see s.v. **Sippas** below).

Berve ii.353–4 no. 704; Bosworth i.300–1; Bosworth 1976a: 125 and 1976b: 9–14; Heckel 179. See Stemma XII.

Simmias [2]. Son of Phaiyllus; cavalryman from Orchomenus. Simmias served in Alexander's allied cavalry until the expedition reached Ecbatana in 330. There he and his compatriots were discharged. On their return (ca. 329), they made a dedication to Zeus Soter in Orchomenus (*IG* vii.3206).

Berve ii.354 no. 705.

Sippas. The name is otherwise unattested. Sippas was left as *strategos* in Macedonia, when Antipater moved south into Thessaly in 323 (D 18.12.2). Perhaps the correct form of the name is Simmias (but Sirrhas is also possible, if not more likely, cf. Hoffmann 214). Identification with the son of Andromenes is made less likely by that man's limited military experience.

Berve ii.354 no. 706; Hoffmann 214.

Sisicottus (Sisikottos). Sanskrit "Sasigupta," Prakrit "Sasigutta" (Eggermont 185). Native dynast, and originally a supporter of Bessus, whom Alexander appointed ruler of the Assacenians (Udyana) after the capture of Aornus (A 4.30.4; C 8.11.25), though clearly under the watchful eye of the satrap Nicanor, whose death in 326 he later reported to the King (A 5.20.7).

Anspach i.28, 81; ii.27, 200; Berve ii.354 no. 707; Eggermont 185, 188; Bosworth ii.192–3, 321–2.

Sisimithres. A local chieftain of eastern Sogdiana (Paraetacene), apparently also known as Chorienes (A 4.21.6–10; cf. *ME* 28), which may be an official name taken from the territory he ruled. According to native custom, he had married his own mother (C 8.2.19, 28; **F26**), on whom he fathered at least two sons, who had reached military age in 328/7 (C 8.2.19; 8.4.21 gives Chorienes three sons), and three daughters (*ME* 19). Thus he could not have been born much later than 370 BC (cf. Berve ii.354: "vor 365").

In late autumn 328, Sisimithres took refuge, along with the other hyparchs of the region, on the so-called "Rock of Chorienes" (Koh-i-nor, Kaerst i.440 n. 3, following Schwarz 83ff.), which was said to be twenty stades high and sixty stades in circumference (A 4.21.2; cf. Str 11.11.4, [517], who says it was fifteen stades in height with a circuit of eighty) and was surrounded by a deep ravine. This ravine Alexander filled with rocks and trees in order to facilitate the approach of the army (C 8.2.23–4; A 4.21.3–4; the work was supervised in shifts during the night by Perdiccas, Ptolemy, and Leonnatus, whereas Alexander himself conducted the assault by day). Alexander sent to Sisimithres Oxyartes (C 8.2.25ff. has "Oxartes"; A 4.21.6 says that Chorienes asked that Oxyartes be sent to him), who induced him to surrender (A 4.21.6–8; C 8.2.27–31). This voluntary surrender probably saved Sisimithres' life (cf. the punishment of Ariamazes), and he was allowed to retain his territory, which was perhaps around Gazaba (C 8.4.1; cf. *ME* 28, Gazabes), although his two sons were retained as hostages in Alexander's army (C 8.2.33). Not much can be inferred from Plutarch's claim (*PA* 58.4) that Oxyartes told Alexander that Sisimithres was the greatest coward in the world, although this opinion is echoed by C 8.2.28, where Sisimithres' mother shows more courage than her son. *PM* 181c probably refers to Sisimithres but wrongly makes him the commander of Aornus.

Alexander found that Sisimithres had surrendered after consuming only one-tenth of his provisions, which supported the view that he had capitulated out of good-will rather than necessity (A 4.21.10). Sisimithres was later (early 327) able to supply Alexander's army (A 4.21.10, supplies for two months; C 8.4.19, "a large number of pack animals, 2,000 camels, and flocks of sheep and herds of cattle"), which had suffered from adverse weather in the region (A 4.21.10 says that they experienced heavy snowfall *during the siege*; C 8.4.2–18 and *ME* 24–7 claim the privations occurred after the capture of the Rock).

Not to be outdone in generosity, Alexander plundered the territory of the Sacae and returned to Sisimithres with a gift of 30,000 head of cattle (C 8.4.20). This was almost certainly the occasion of the banquet given by Chorienes (*cohortandus* in C 8.4.21, with textual difficulties),[678] at which Rhoxane was introduced to Alexander, along with the host's own unmarried daughters, and Alexander took his first oriental bride (C 8.4.22–30; *ME* 28–31; Str 11.11.4 [517]; but A 4.19.4–5 places the marriage after the capture of the Rock of Sogdiana; see further s.v. **Rhoxane**). Otherwise, Sisimithres is not heard of again.

Berve ii.354–5 no. 708; Bosworth 1981; Heckel 1986a.

Sisines [1]. (Also Sisenes). Prominent Persian, but of unknown family background. According to Curtius (3.7.11) he had been sent to Philip's court by the ruler of Egypt. There is considerable confusion about Sisines' role, though it is clear that he acted as an agent of some sort. Arrian reports that he was sent to corrupt Alexander Lyncestes but was arrested by

Parmenion and sent to Alexander for interrogation. See C 3.7.11–15 and A 1.25.3–4 with the commentaries of Atkinson and Bosworth.

Berve ii.356 no. 710.

Sisines [2]. Son of Phrataphernes (A 7.6.4; A*Succ* 3), satrap of Hyrcania and Parthia, and brother of Phradasmenes. Both Sisines and his brother were enrolled in the cavalry *agema* in 324 at Susa (A 7.6.4). Whether they had been in Alexander's entourage since Phrataphernes' surrender to the King in 330 (as Berve ii.355 assumes) is unclear. A*Succ* 3 shows that he played some part in the early history of the Successors, but says only that his name was mentioned in the first two books of Arrian's *Events after Alexander*. See further s.v. **Phrataphernes**.

Berve ii.355 no. 709.

Sisygambis (also Sisyngambris). Mother of Darius III, Oxyathres, and (possibly) Stateira and four other children (C 10.5.23). If she was both sister and wife of Arsanes, then her father was Ostanes, a son of Darius II and brother of Artaxerxes II.[679] Sisygambis, her daughter, and three grandchildren accompanied Darius to Issus (C 3.3.22; D 17.31.2), where they were captured (A 2.11.9; C 3.11.24; D 17.36.2), and received a false report that Darius had been killed (P*A* 21.1; D 17.37.3; C 13.12.3–5). The truth was reported to them by Leonnatus (D 17.37.3; C 3.12.6–12; P*A* 21.2), and his visit was followed by another by Alexander himself; there followed the famous episode in which Sisygambis mistook Hephaestion for Alexander.[680] At Gaugamela, she and the other captives were kept in the baggage-camp (C 4.13.35), where she allegedly refused to celebrate a Persian victory prematurely when the Scythians broke through (D 17.59.7; C 4.15.10–11). Left behind at Susa, with tutors to teach her Greek (D 17.67.1; C 5.2.18–22 has a different story), she appears to have intervened on behalf of the Uxians and their satrap Madates (her niece's husband: C 5.3.12) by writing a letter to Alexander (C 5.3.12–15; confirmed to some extent by Ptolemy, *FGrH* 138 F12 = A 3.17.6; but see Bosworth i.321–4). In 330, Alexander sent her Darius' corpse for burial (P*A* 43.7).[681] When she learned of Alexander's death in June 323, Sisygambis refused food and died five days later (C 10.5.19–25; D 17.118.3; J 13.1.5); in the vulgate sources she is depicted as a second mother to Alexander (C 3.12.17; 5.2.22; J 13.1.5; cf. Brosius 21).

Berve ii.356–7 no. 711; Neuhaus 1902; Brosius 21, 67–8; Briant 772–3. See Stemma III.

Sitalces (Sitalkes). Apparently a prince of the Odrysian royal house (Hoffmann 182; Bosworth i.171), possibly even the son of Cersobleptes, Sitalces commanded the Thracian javelin-men (*akontistai*) since at least the beginning of the Asiatic campaign, and in this capacity served also as a hostage for the good conduct of his father; according to Fr*Strat* 2.11.3 (cf. J 11.5.3), Alexander took the sons of Thracian kings with him in order to ensure the loyalty of their fathers at home (cf. s.v. **Ariston** [3]). Sitalces first appears in the Pisidian campaign, in the attack on Sagalassus (334/3). Here the natives had occupied a hill-fort near the city and could only be dislodged by an attack of the lightly armed troops – the archers and Agrianes on the right, Sitalces' javelin-men on the left (A 1.28.4). Doubtless, the latter played an important role in defeating the enemy, though Arrian's account concentrates on the activities of the right wing, where Alexander himself was present (1.28.5–8).

In late 333, Sitalces accompanied Parmenion, when he occupied the "other" Gates that led from Cilicia to Syria (A 2.5.1; for their location see Bosworth i.192–3). At Issus (A 2.9.3), as at Gaugamela (A 3.12.4), he was stationed on the left wing. In 330, he remained with Parmenion at Ecbatana and later received, through the agency of Polydamas, orders to kill the old general (A 3.26.3–4). But, when Alexander returned from India, Sitalces, like his colleagues

Cleander, Heracon, and Agathon, who had participated in the murder of Parmenion, was found guilty of maladministration and executed (A 6.27.4; cf. C 10.1.1).

Berve ii.357 no. 712; Hoffmann 182; Heckel 334.

Socrates (Sokrates). Son of Sathon (A 1.12.7), commanded the squadron from Apollonia since at least the beginning of the Asiatic expedition. In 334, he joined Amyntas son of Arrhabaeus and the four squadrons of *prodromoi* in a scouting mission from Hermotus in the direction of the Granicus River (A 1.12.7). At the river, he was again stationed next to Amyntas on the right wing (A 1.14.1), and their units, along with an infantry battalion led by Ptolemy son of Philip, initiated the fighting by being the first to cross to the opposite bank (A 1.14.6–15.1). Arrian does not name Socrates again. No full list is provided for the battle of Issus (late 333), but Socrates is no longer amongst the ilarchs at Gaugamela (A 3.11.8). If Curtius (4.5.9) is not mistaken, Socrates took over, temporarily, the governorship of Cilicia; for Balacrus, whom Alexander had appointed after the battle of Issus (A 2.12.2), is soon found campaigning at, and capturing, Miletus (C 4.5.13). Berve assumes that the Platon who brought reinforcements from Cilicia to Alexander in 331/0 (C 5.7.12) is actually Socrates – with the vulgate or Curtius himself confused by the names of two prominent philosophers (ii.367; cf. ii.429, Abschn. II no. 67; rejected by Bosworth 1974: 59 n. 1). Curtius, however, calls Platon "an Athenian" and, if Berve's theory is correct, we have a confusion of both the man's name and his nationality. What became of Socrates the ilarch we do not know.

Berve ii.367 no. 732; Bosworth i.120; Heckel 350–1; Hoffmann 186.

Sopater (Sopatros). Greek of unknown origin, though it is remotely possible that he is identical with the poet from Paphos who lived from the time of Alexander the Great to that of Ptolemy II Philadelphus (Ath 2.71a).[682] Sopater was said to have given the hoof of a Scythian donkey to Alexander; this was subsequently dedicated by the King to Delphi (Ael*NA* 10.40).[683] The truth of the story and the historicity of Sopater cannot be known. Whether the story has any bearing on that of Alexander's alleged poisoning, where the poisonous waters of the Arcadian Styx were transported to Babylon in an ass's hoof (P*A* 77; cf. C 10.10.16; A 7.27.1; Ps-Call 3.31; Paus 8.18.6; J 12.14.7), cannot be determined.

Berve ii.367 no. 733.

Sopeithes. See s.v. **Sophytes**.

Sophytes (Sopeithes, Sophites).[684] Indian king, whose realm was situated between the Hydraotes and Hyphasis, and between that of the Adrestae and Cathaeans (D 17.91.2–4) and of Phegeus (C 9.1.35–6). Sophytes surrendered voluntarily to Alexander (C 9.1.28–30), together with his sons (**M17–18**), and was allowed to retain his kingdom (D 17.91.7) – though probably as a vassal of Porus – which was reputed for its good institutions and the beauty of its inhabitants (D 17.91.4–7; C 9.1.24–6; *ME* 66–8), and the Alexander historians comment on the good looks of the king himself. It was in Sophytes' kingdom that Alexander was treated to a demonstration of the courage and tenacity of Indian dogs (D 17.92; C 9.1.31–3; *ME* 66–7; Str 15.1.31). Arrian, who does not mention Sophytes or Phegeus, says that when the fleet began its descent of the Hydaspes, Hephaestion, whose forces marched along the eastern bank of the river, was to hurry to the capital city of King Sopeithes (A 6.2.2). Sophytes' kingdom cannot have extended in that direction, and we must assume that either there were two men named Sophytes/Sopeithes (certainly there were two rulers named Porus, but their territories were at least adjacent and they ruled different groups of the Pauravas) or Arrian's source is mistaken about the location of Sophytes' kingdom.

The latter seems likely; for Str 15.1.30 [699] mentions just such a discrepancy in the sources and then tells the story of the king's hunting dogs (Str 15.1.31 [700]).[685]

Berve ii.367–8 nos. 734–5.

Sopolis. Son of Hermodorus (A 3.11.8), commanded the Amphipolitan squadron of Companion Cavalry since at least the Triballian campaign of 335 (A 1.2.5), in which he appears together with Heracleides son of Antiochus, who led the Bottiaeans. At Gaugamela, Sopolis' squadron was stationed between those of Ariston and Heracleides (A 3.11.8). That he belonged to the Macedonian aristocracy is indicated not only by his important cavalry command but also by the fact that his son, Hermolaus, served as one of Alexander's Pages in 327. In the winter of 328/7 Sopolis was sent from Nautaca, in the company of Menidas and Epocillus, to bring new recruits from Macedonia (A 4.18.3). There is no record of his return to Alexander's camp, and we may assume that, after the disgrace of his son in 327, he did not think it wise to do so. Alexander may have sent orders that he be arrested and, perhaps, executed. But this is far from certain.[686] It appears that Asclepiodorus, father of Hermolaus' fellow-conspirator, Antipater, was a trierarch of the Hydaspes fleet (A*Ind* 18.3, with Jacoby's emendation); cf. Heckel 1986b: 300.

Berve ii.368–9 no. 736; Hoffmann 186; Heckel 351.

Sosigenes. Rhodian. Served as *nauarchos* of the fleet of about 200 ships sent by Perdiccas against the pro-Ptolemaic forces in Cyprus in 321/0 (A*Succ* 24.6). Although the expedition achieved little – in part because of the efforts of Antigonus the One-Eyed, but also because of Perdiccas' defeat and death in Egypt – Sosigenes and his fleet appear to have remained with Eumenes. Sosigenes' fleet defected with its treasure to Antigonus in 318, while the helpless admiral looked on from the Cilician shore (Pol*Strat* 4.6.9). He may have come to terms with Antigonus, for P*Demetr* 49.7 mentions a man of that name who is described as a *hetairos* of Demetrius Poliorcetes. It is not certain whether Sosigenes held any command under Alexander the Great.

Berve ii.369 no. 737.

Sostratus (Sostratos). Son of Amyntas, lover of Hermolaus (A 4.13.3; C 8.6.8). Sostratus joined (A) or instigated (C) the "conspiracy of the Pages" on account of the outrage done to Hermolaus. For his part he was arrested, tortured, and executed (A 4.13.7–14.2; C 8.8.20; P*A* 55.6; J 12.7.2). C 8.6.9 lists a conspirator named Nicostratus (Berve ii.280 no. 570; Hoffmann 180); this is probably a corruption of the name Sostratus.

Berve ii.369 no. 738; Hoffmann 179; Heckel 295.

Sparton. Rhodian, patronymic unknown, brother of Demaratus. He and his brother were arrested at Sardis by Alexander but freed through the efforts of Phocion (P*Ph* 18.6; Ael*VH* 1.25). The reason for his arrest is unknown; nor do we know anything about his personal or political connections with Phocion. It is possible that he and his brother belonged to the anti-Macedonian faction in Rhodes, which reasserted itself in 323. Sparton himself is not heard of again, but Demaratus reappears in 320 as a Rhodian navarch, defeating the forces of Attalus son of Andromenes (A*Succ* 1.39).

Berve ii.358 no. 714; Hofstetter 167 no. 295.

Spitaces (Spitakes, also Pittakos, Pittacus). A 5.18.2 speaks of an Indian nomarch named Spitaces who was killed in the battle at the Hydaspes. He does not, however, identify him as a relative of Porus, but instead mentions also two sons of Porus who were killed in the same battle. Hence, it is unlikely that Arrian regarded Spitaces as one of Porus' relatives. Pol*Strat* 4.3.21 corrupts the name Spitaces into Pittacus and calls him a nephew of the Indian ruler (cf. C 8.14.2 who speaks of a brother of Porus).[687] Polyaenus' story clearly refers to an incident before the Hydaspes battle, an attempt to ambush Alexander *en route* to the Hydaspes (cf. Stein 1937: 11, with n. 7).[688] Thus it seems that after the unsuccessful ambush, Spitaces withdrew to Porus' main force and then was sent with 100 chariots and 4,000 cavalry to oppose Alexander's crossing to the north of Porus' main camp (C 8.14.2). Spitaces was apparently killed in the skirmish that followed (C 8.14.2–8; A 5.18.2). It appears that the primary sources were confused about the identity of Spitaces and his role in the battle. It is clear that the command attributed by some to a son of Porus was ascribed by others to Spitaces.[689]

Berve ii.358 no. 716.

Spitamenes. Prominent leader in Bactria or Sogdiana, perhaps of Iranian ancestry. Born in all likelihood before 370: he had three grown-up children in 328 (C 8.3.3; **M30–32**). Although he is depicted as a supporter and close friend of Bessus (C 7.5.19; *ME* 6), Spitamenes may not have been with Darius at Gaugamela, and perhaps joined Bessus only in Bactria. He accompanied him across the Oxus River into Sogdiana when Alexander invaded Bactria (A 3.28.10) but soon plotted to arrest Bessus and hand him over to the Macedonians (A 3.29.6, 30.1; C 7.5.19–26; *ME* 5–6). Whether he surrendered Bessus in person (C 7.5.36–8; A 3.30.5 = Aristobulus, *FGrH* 139 F24) or left him in chains to be picked up by Ptolemy son of Lagus (A 3.30.2–4) is unclear. Certainly, Spitamenes did not trust Alexander, for in 329 he refused to attend a conference at Bactra (A 4.1.5, Zariaspa = Bactra) and continued to resist the Macedonians (C 7.6.14–15). Spitamenes besieged the Macedonian garrison at Maracanda when Alexander advanced to the Iaxartes (A 4.3.6, 5.2–3). When the King sent Andromachus, Menedemus, Caranus, and Pharnuches against him (A 4.3.7), Spitamenes with the aid of some 600 Scythian horsemen ambushed the Macedonian force at the Polytimetus River (A 4.5.4–9; a slightly different version in Aristobulus: A 4.6.1–2 = *FGrH* 139 F27; C 7.7.31–9; *ME* 9) and then withdrew at the news of Alexander's return (C 7.9.20 says he fled to Bactra, which may be an error for Bactria, i.e., he went south of the Oxus; A 4.6.3–4 does not say where he went, but it is certain that he spent the winter with his allies the Massagetae, perhaps in the vicinity of Bokhara as Brunt i.505 suggests; cf. *ME* 13, 20). In spring 328 Spitamenes recrossed the Oxus with a force of 800 Scythian cavalry and attacked an unnamed fort (C 8.1.3; A 4.16.4 gives him 600 horsemen), capturing its commandant, Attinas (C 8.1.4–5; A 4.16.5, for details see s.v. **Attinas** and n. 164). Then he fell upon Bactra, which was lightly defended, killing several, including Aristonicus [4] the harpist, and taking Peithon [2] son of Sosicles prisoner (A 4.16.4–7; *IA* 98). His incursions were checked by Craterus and Coenus (A 4.17), and soon Spitamenes was betrayed by the Massagetae, who sent his head to Alexander (A 4.17.7; *IA* 98; Str 11.11.6 [518]). C 8.3.1–16 and *ME* 20–1 have a different version of Spitamenes' death, reporting that he was murdered by his own wife (**F25**), who brought his head into the Macedonian camp.[690] His daughter Apame married Seleucus at the mass-marriage in Susa in 324 (A 7.4.6; P*Demetr* 31.5; see also s.v. **Apame** [1] and Grainger 67).

Berve ii.359–61 no. 717; Holt 1994. See Stemma XI.

Spithridates ("Spithrobates": D 17.20.2; "Spinther": Ps-Call 1.39, 2.10; Jul Val 1.41, 2.18). A Persian noble descended from the "Seven" (cf. D 16.47.2) – perhaps a relative of that Spithridates who was active in the Hellespontine region and Paphlagonia at the beginning of the fourth century (Xen*HG* 3.4.10; 4.1.3, 20, 26–7) and apparently the son of Rhoesaces, the satrap of Ionia ca. 344/3 (D 16.47.1–2; further discussion s.v. **Rhoesaces**) – Spithridates was a son-in-law of Darius III (unless Diodorus confuses him with Mithridates, A 1.16.3; cf. Berve ii.358 n. 2; **F8, 9**) and satrap of Ionia in 334 (D 17.20.2; A 1.12.8, "Lydia and Ionia"); the younger Rhoesaces was his brother (D 17.20.6, "Rhosaces"). Spithridates led some forty of the Persian "Kinsmen" against the Macedonian line at the Granicus River (D 17.20.2), and, according to D 17.20.3–5 (cf. C 8.1.20), he engaged in single combat with Alexander only to be killed by him. A 1.15.7–8 and P*A* 16.8–11 reverse the roles of the brothers, but Spithridates' death in the battle is certain (A 1.16.3; P*M* 326f).

Berve ii.358 no. 715; Krumbholz 70.

Stamenes (Ditamenes, C 8.3.17). Apparently an Iranian, but both forms of the name may be corrupt. In the winter of 328/7, at Nautaca, Alexander appointed Stamenes satrap of Babylonia, to replace Mazaeus, who had recently died (A 4.28.3; cf. C 8.3.17).[691] How long Stamenes remained in office is unclear. In the settlement that followed Alexander's death, Archon of Pella was appointed satrap of Babylonia, but it is not clear whether this was a new appointment or the confirmation of one made by Alexander himself after the death or removal from office of Stamenes. The latter seems more likely (see s.v. **Archon**). Nothing else is known about Stamenes.

Stasander (Stasandros). Cypriot Greek, possibly a relative or friend of Stasanor of Soli. When Stasanor was appointed satrap of Bactria-Sogdiana, Stasander replaced him in Aria-Drangiana (D 18.39.6). Stasander supported Eumenes of Cardia in 318–317, bringing also a contingent of Bactrians (D 19.14.7; 19.27.3), and vanished after Gabiene. Whether he was executed along with the other prominent supporters of Eumenes we cannot say.[692] What we do know is that his satrapy was assigned by Antigonus to a certain Evitus, who soon died and was in turn replaced by Evagoras (D 19.48.2; Klinkott 75).

Stasanor. Cypriot Greek from Soli, probably a member of the ruling house, Stasanor accompanied Alexander since 332/1 as one of his *hetairoi* (Str 14.6.3 [683]; A 3.29.5).[693] In 330/29 he was assigned the task of arresting and replacing the rebellious satrap of Aria, Arsaces (A 3.29.5). In winter 328/7 he brought Arsaces in chains to Alexander at Nautaca (A 4.18.1) and had his satrapy enlarged to include Drangiana (A 4.18.3).[694] When Alexander reached Carmania, Stasanor joined him with Phrataphernes' son Pharismenes (A 6.27.3), bringing a large number of pack animals and camels (A 6.27.6). Alexander again sent him back to his satrapy (A 6.29.1) but he appears to have rejoined the King in Susa, bringing barbarian troops to serve in his army (A 7.6.1, 3). According to the pamphlet on the *Last Days and Testament of Alexander*, Stasanor was present at the dinner-party given by Medeius of Larissa, at which the King was poisoned; Stasanor is named as one of the conspirators (*LM* 97–8; Ps-Call 3.31.8–9). In the settlement at Babylon, he was confirmed as satrap of Aria and Drangiana (D 18.3.3; J 13.4.22–3, with textual problems; cf. *LM* 121). In 320, at Triparadeisus, he was reassigned to Bactria-Sogdiana (D 18.39.6; A*Succ* 1.36). He appears to have sent troops to aid Eumenes but did not come in person (D 19.14.7; these were led by Stasander). Antigonus did not attempt to dislodge him from his satrapy after Gabiene because of the remoteness of the area and the difficulty involved (D 19.48.1). Nothing else is known about him.

Berve ii.361–2 no. 719; Julien 38; Lehmann-Haupt 158; Badian 1961: 18.

Stasicrates (Stasikrates; Berve ii.362 no. 720). See s.v. **Deinocrates**.

Stateira [1]. (Statira). Her name is given only by P*A* 30.5, 8. The wife and sister of Darius III (P*A* 30.3; A 2.11.9; J 11.9.12; Gell 7.8.3), Stateira need not, however, have been the daughter of Sisygambis. The sources describe the latter as "mother of Darius" and "grandmother of Darius' children" but never as Stateira's mother. She may thus have been the daughter of Arsanes (D 17.5.5), by another wife or concubine (cf. the brother–sister relationship of Darius II and Parysatis, who were children of Artaxerxes I by different Babylonian concubines, if Ctesias, *FGrH* 688 F15 §47, is to be believed). Born perhaps between 370 and 365, Stateira married Darius not much later than 350; for their daughters, Stateira (below) and Drypetis, are described as *adultae virgines* in late 333 BC (C 3.12.25). A son, Ochus, was born in 339/8 (D 17.38.2; C 3.11.24). According to the romantic tradition, she was the most beautiful woman in Asia (A 4.19.5–6; P*A* 21.6; C 3.11.24, 12.22; 4.10.24), a claim which serves to emphasize Alexander's restraint. In 333 Stateira, together with her mother and childen, accompanied Darius to Issus, where, after his flight from the battlefield, they were captured by Alexander (C 3.11.24ff.; P*A* 21; D 17.36.2–4; A 2.11.9). Alexander's moderation and respectful treatment of the Persian queens, and his famous visit to their tent, became well-worn themes of the Alexander vulgate (P*A* 21; C 3.12.15–26; D 17.37.5–38.3; J 11.9.12–16; A 2.12.3–8; cf. Val Max 4.7 ext 2). But Alexander must have given serious consideration to the value of the King's wife and daughters as hostages (cf. their importance in the diplomatic exchanges: A 2.25.1; C 4.1.8; cf. 4.5.1ff.; D 17.54.1–5) or for their political impact (cf. Bosworth i.221). Ptolemy and Aristobulus (*FGrH* 138 F6, 139 F10 = A 2.12.3–6) imply that Alexander never saw Stateira (cf. P*M* 338e, 522a; Gell 7.8.3: he would not even hear about her beauty). Yet, the date and circumstances of her death cloud the issue considerably: the vulgate is consistent in dating Stateira's death to shortly before the battle of Gaugamela (J 11.12.6; C 4.10.18ff.; D 17.54.7; P*A* 30.1) and J agrees with Plutarch that she died in childbirth (miscarriage). Berve (ii.363; cf. Hamilton 78) places her death in 332, which cannot be inferred from A 4.20.1–2 (conflating the eunuch who escaped after Issus with Teireus; note that Darius learns that his wife and children are alive). Either pregnancy played no part in Stateira's death or she was not carrying Darius' child (cf. Welles 275 n. 3; Bosworth i.221). On the other hand, it was certainly not the aim of the vulgate to suggest (even in the most subtle way) that Stateira was pregnant with Alexander's child, since the same tradition reiterates that Alexander had seen her only once (C 4.10.24), in late 333. Furthermore, the eunuch Teireus brings the news of her death, and of Alexander's grief and honorable conduct, to Darius (P*A* 30.2ff.; C 4.10.25–34, with dramatic embellishment, calling the eunuch Tyriotes). Why her death would have been recorded in the wrong historical context (Atkinson i.392) is difficult to understand; but the diplomatic negotiations of 331 BC, admittedly, make no further reference to Darius' wife (C 4.5.1ff.; D 17.54.1–5). Alexander ordered a sumptuous funeral, in keeping with the woman's former station (C 4.10.23; D 17.54.7; P*A* 30.1; P*M* 338e).

Berve ii.362–3 no. 721. See Stemma III.

Stateira [2]. (Statira). The name occurs in the vulgate (C 4.5.1; D 17.107.6; J 12.10.9; P*A* 70.3; 77.6; P*M* 338d; cf. *Fragmentum Sabbaiticum* = *FGrH* 151 F1 §5); Aristobulus calls her Barsine.[695] Stateira was apparently the elder of the known daughters of Darius III and Stateira, an assumption based on the fact that Alexander married her instead of Drypetis but otherwise unsubstantiated. Granddaughter of Sisygambis (cf. C 3.11.25; 4.10.19, 21); sister of Drypetis and Ochus; cousin of Amastris (Memnon, *FGrH* 434 F1 §4.4). She and her mother, grandmother, and siblings accompanied Darius III to Issus, where, after Darius' flight, they were captured by Alexander (C 3.11.25; D 17.36.2; A 2.11.9; J 11.9.12; P*A* 21.1) and visited by both Leonnatus (P*A* 21.2–5; C 3.12.7–12) and the King himself (C 3.12.15–26). Alexander treated her with respect (C 3.12.21; 4.11.3, respecting her royal status) and said he would see to their dowries better than even Darius would have (D 17.38.1). Although Darius wrote Alexander, shortly before the battle at Gaugamela (A 2.25.1 places it in the preceding year, during the siege of Tyre; cf. C 4.5.1; see also Bosworth i.256–7; Atkinson i.320–1), offering to pay a ransom – of 10,000 talents each – for the members of his family (C 4.11.6, 12; P*A* 29.7; D 17.54.2; J 11.12.10) and to give one of his daughters (C 4.5.1 names Stateira in an earlier context) to Alexander as his wife (C 4.11.5–6, the return of *duas virgines filias* demanded by Darius in §6 does not rule out that Stateira was the intended bride in §5; D 17.54.2; J 11.12.3), the offers – favored by Parmenion (C 4.11.12) – were rejected (C 4.11.15; J 11.12.2). Left behind at Susa[696] at the very end of 331 (C 5.2.17) – she was given instruction in the Greek language (D 17.67.1; Curtius' story about "wool-working" sounds implausible, 5.2.18–22) – where she remained until Alexander's return in 324, when she became (along with Parysatis, daughter of Ochus) one of his royal brides (D 17.107.6; J 12.10.9; P*A* 70.3; P*M* 338d; Aristobulus, *FGrH* 139 F52 = A 7.4.4; cf. C 10.3.12; Memnon, *FGrH* 434 F1 §4.4; A 3.22.6); her sister Drypetis married Hephaestion (A 7.4.5; D 17.107.6). Soon after the marriage, however, Alexander died, leaving his first wife, Rhoxane, pregnant; the latter, concerned for the birthright of her child, summoned Stateira and her sister to her, murdered them both, and threw them into a well (P*A* 77.6); the fact that she was aided in this by Perdiccas underscores the political background to Stateira's murder.

Berve ii.363 no. 722. See Stemma III.

Stephanus (Stephanos). Greek youth in Alexander's entourage and, because of his ugliness, the object of ridicule. He was nearly killed as a result of a cruel joke played by an Athenian named Athenophanes, who smeared naphtha on the boy's face and set it on fire (P*A* 35.5–9). Str 16.1.15 [743] attributes this act of cruelty to Alexander himself, an unlikely story. Nevertheless, the King appears to have condoned the mockery, at least in its early stages.[697]

Berve ii.15 no. 31; Kirchner no. 285.

Straton [1]. (Strato). A Graecism of the Phoenician Abdastart ("servant of Astarte"). The son of Gerostratus, Straton ruled Arados (also Marathos, Sigon, and Mariamme) in the absence of his father (cf. C 4.1.6), who served with the Persian fleet under Autophradates. On Alexander's entry into Phoenicia, Straton met him (near Marathos), surrendered himself and his territories, and presented the King with a golden crown (A 2.13.7–8; C 4.1.5–6). It appears, however, that Gerostratus was reinstated as ruler of Arados upon his own surrender (cf. A 2.20.1); the coin issued in Straton's name (Head, *HN*² 788) probably belongs to the period of Straton's regency in 333/2 (cf. Bosworth i.226). Aside from this coin, of disputed date, we have no further record of him.

Berve ii.363 no. 727.

Straton [2]. (Strato). (Abdastart). Phoenician, king of Sidon; son of Tennes, or Tabnit II (Head, *HN*² 796), who had rebelled against Artaxerxes III in 351 and later sought to save himself by betraying the city to the Great King in 345 (D 16.43); but Tabnit's treachery did not save him, and he was executed on Ochus' instructions once Sidon had fallen into Persian hands (D 16.45.4). Straton succeeded his father in 345/4 (cf. Rawlinson 1889: 505); but, as the son of the traitor Tabnit and a Persian appointee (presumably he remained under the watchful eye of Mazaeus, to whose satrapy of Cilicia Syria had been added; cf. Olmstead 437), he was not generally popular. Even after the Persian defeat at Issus, Straton remained loyal, and he was consequently deposed by Alexander upon his arrival in Sidon (C 4.1.16; D 17.47.1). His pro-Persian stance was not popular with the Sidonians themselves, who appear to have forced Straton into submitting to the

King (A 2.15.6; cf. C 4.1.16). On the basis of C 4.1.17–23, Berve ii.3 sees the opponents of Abdalonymus as the supporters of Straton and the wealthy nobility ("Geldadel"). If Sidon was, in fact, destroyed on the scale depicted by D 16.45 (questioned by Beloch iii^2 1.535 n. 2), then Straton must have taken important measures to revive the city, ones which doubtless benefited the business class. Straton was perhaps executed, or turned over to the Sidonians for punishment: Ath 12.531d–e (based on Anaximenes) speaks of a violent death. His successor was Abdalonymus.

Rawlinson 1889: 501–10; Keller 1904: 19–20; Hill 1910: LX–LXV; Bosworth i.235; P. Naster, *Proceedings of the International Numismatic Convention* (Jerusalem 1967): 19–21; Cawkwell 1963: 136–8; Beloch iii^2 1.535; Olmstead 437; Babelon 1891: 311–13.

Stratonice (Stratonike). Macedonian. According to *PDemetr* 2.1, the daughter of Corrhagus, wife of Antigonus the One-Eyed, and mother of Demetrius Poliorcetes (D 21.1.4b) and Philip; though Plutarch reports a rumor that she was previously married to Antigonus' brother Demetrius. She followed her husband to Asia Minor and resided in or near Celaenae – at least, not far from where Docimus and Attalus son of Andromenes were imprisoned. She appears to have intrigued with the former to secure his escape, and his subsequent loyalty to the Antigonids (D 19.16.4). At the time of the battle of Ipsus (301) she remained in Cilicia with all her possessions, and after the battle and Antigonus' death, she was taken by Demetrius to Salamis on Cyprus, an Antigonid possession (D 21.1.4b). In 297, however, Salamis was taken by Ptolemy, and Stratonice and Demetrius' young children were captured but soon released (*PDemetr* 35.5; 38.1).

Macurdy 62, 64–6. See Stemma VI.

Strattis. Olynthian of unknown family. Born before the destruction of the city by Philip in 348, Strattis may have accompanied Alexander on the expedition, possibly as a member of the chancellery (thus Berve ii.365). Of his actual activities nothing is known, but he is named as an author of a work *On Rivers, Springs, and Lakes*, as well as what appears to have been a commentary in five books of the *Ephemerides* (*Suda* Σ 1179). Nothing that is recorded about him or his works can be taken as certain.

Berve ii.365 no. 726; Bosworth 1988b: 180–2; Gude no. 112; Jacoby, *FGrH* 118; omitted by Pearson.

Stroebus (Stroibos). Greek slave who used to read aloud to Callisthenes. Stroebus had apparently accompanied his master from the beginning of the campaign. He gave a written account to Aristotle of Callisthenes' quarrel with Alexander, which Plutarch used via Hermippus (*PA* 54.1). Nothing else is known about him.

Berve ii.366 no. 799; Hamilton 149.

Syrmus (Syrmos; also Syrmios). Triballian ruler who, upon hearing of Alexander's approach in spring 335, sent the women and children to the island of Peuce on the Danube, where he too took refuge, joining the Thracians who had also fled there (A 1.2.2–3; Str 7.3.8 [301]). A large number of Triballian fighting men doubled back to the Lyginus River and were defeated there, with 3,000 dead, by Alexander (A 1.2.4–7; cf. *PA* 11.5 says Alexander "defeated Syrmus in a great battle" but this need not mean that Syrmus was at the Lyginus in person). An attempt to take the island by means of ships that sailed up the Danube from the Black Sea failed because the defenders controlled the banks of the island and because of the small number of ships (A 1.3.3–4; cf. Str 7.3.8). After Alexander's success against the Getae, Syrmus sent ambassadors to make peace (A 1.4.6; Str 7.3.8). Whether the peace terms included a requirement to contribute troops is unclear: D 17.17.4 mentions 7,000

Odrysians, Illyrians, and Triballians at the beginning of the Asiatic campaign.

Berve ii.366 no. 730; Fuller 221–3; Bosworth i.57ff.

Syrphax. Ephesian, *patronymikon* unknown. A leader of the pro-Persian oligarchy in Ephesus, after the restoration of the democracy, Syrphax, together with his son, had taken refuge in the temple (of Artemis), from which they were dragged out and stoned to death (A 1.17.12) by their political opponents, who slew Syrphax's nephews as well.

Baumbach 12, 22; Berve ii.366 no. 731; Berve 1967: i.335–6, ii.690; Hofstetter 169–70 no. 302; Judeich 303 n. 1.

T

Tauriscus (Tauriskos). Man of unknown family, apparently a Greek (cf. Pape & Benseler 1495).[698] He was perhaps a member of Alexander's army or entourage and befriended Harpalus, whom he persuaded to flee from Alexander shortly before the battle of Issus. Little is known about the man or the circumstances of his flight with Harpalus. Arrian, our only source for the episode, calls him an "evil man," and it appears that he had some mischief in mind when he befriended Alexander's treasurer. That their crime was theft or embezzlement seems likely, given Harpalus' position, but it cannot be proved. Tauriscus accompanied Harpalus to Greece and thence to Alexander of Epirus in Italy, where he met his end (A 3.6.7).

Berve ii.371 no. 740; Heckel 1977b; Carney 1982; Worthington 1984.

Tauron. Son of Machatas (*IG* ix.9, 197), apparently brother of Philip and Harpalus and a member of the royal house of Elimeia. Tauron first appears in late 331: Alexander, intending to attack a town of the Uxians, sent him with a force of 1,500 mercenary archers and 1,000 Agrianes to occupy the heights above that town (C 5.3.6; cf. D 17.67.4–5). A 3.17.4 assigns to Craterus the command of this force, which in his version was intended to cut down the Uxians who fled to the heights. Now it may be that Tauron commanded only the archers, with the supreme command belonging to Craterus. But Bosworth i.321–2 argues persuasively for two different engagements fought on the journey from Susa to the Persian Gates. Tauron's maneuver was carried out successfully and the appearance of the archers and Agrianes disheartened the Uxians, who were now under attack by Alexander (C 5.3.10). Tauron is not mentioned again until 326, this time with the title *toxarches,* in the battle with Porus (A 5.14.1). Along with Seleucus and Antigenes, he commanded infantrymen who were clearly not *pezhetairoi* (A 5.16.3; cf. C 8.14.15, wrongly substituting Leonnatus for Seleucus). According to Diodorus (17.88.5) the archers were used to make a direct attack on Porus himself.

Tauron's career appears to have suffered as a result of Harpalus' disgrace. Perhaps he is identical with a certain Taur[i]on honored in a late fourth-century inscription from Eretria together with Myllenas son of Asander (*IG* xii.9, 197), a *grammateus* of Alexander. Since most of the honorific decrees of Eretria in this period concern men in the service of Antigonus and his son, it would appear that Tauron too became an Antigonid supporter (Billows 450, "Taurion").[699] Nothing further is known about him.

Berve ii.371–2 no. 741; cf. Billows 450 no. 139; Heckel 338; Hoffmann 201. See Stemma XIII.

Taxiles. Indian dynast, ruler of Taxila, which can be located in the vicinity of Rawalpindi.[700] His personal name was Omphis (C 8.12.5; Sanskrit Ambhi) or

Mophis (D 17.86.4; *ME* 49–52), but in the fashion of that region he later took the official name Taxiles (C 8.12.14). While Alexander was still in Sogdiana (D 17.86.4), Omphis induced his father, Taxiles, to offer submission. But the elder Taxiles died very soon thereafter and Omphis awaited Alexander's approval before assuming the kingship (C 8.12.5–6). He communicated with the advance forces of Hephaestion and Perdiccas, sending them supplies for the army, but would not make formal submission to anyone but Alexander himself (C 8.12.6).[701] His motive was clearly to win Macedonian support against his neighbors, Abisares and Porus. But when Omphis came out to meet Alexander at the head of his army, the gesture was mistakenly interpreted as a hostile move and military action narrowly averted (C 8.12.7–11; D 17.86.5–6; cf. A 5.3.5–6, 8.2, without the drama). Omphis was now given lavish gifts by Alexander, to the extent that the Macedonians resented Alexander's generosity (C 8.12.15–17; cf. Str 15.1.28 [698]; see s.v. **Meleager** [1]). He took the name of his father and his kingdom (C 8.12.14; D 17.86.7) and Alexander turned over to him the thirty elephants captured with Barsaentes (C 8.13.3–5). Taxiles accompanied Alexander to the Hydaspes with 5,000 troops (A 5.8.5). As it became clear that Porus was defeated, Alexander sent Taxiles to urge his enemy to surrender and accept terms. Porus, however, attempted to kill him with a javelin but Taxiles evaded him (A 5.18.6–7; this story is transformed by Curtius, who says that Taxiles' brother (**M20**) was sent to urge Porus to surrender, only to be killed by him: C 8.14.35–6). Alexander arranged an alliance between Taxiles and Porus (C 9.3.22). Nothing else is known about Taxiles in Alexander's lifetime except that in 324 he reported the death of Abisares (C 10.1.20).[702] After the King's death, he retained control of his kingdom (D 18.3.2; Dexippus, *FGrH* 100 F8 §5; J 13.4.20; cf. *LM* 121); this was confirmed at Triparadeisus in 320 (D 18.39.6; A*Succ* 1.36), for neither he nor Porus could be removed without a royal army and an outstanding general.

Berve ii.369–71 no. 739.

Teireus (Teireos; Curtius: Tyriotes). Eunuch of the Persian queen, Stateira, he had been captured at Issus (333 BC) along with the family of Darius. In 331 he escaped from Alexander's camp to Darius, bringing the news that his mistress had died (perhaps in childbirth, P*A* 30.1; J 11.12.6; but see s.v. **Stateira** [1] for the date and circumstances) and that Alexander had ordered a sumptuous burial for her (cf. D 17.54.7; P*M* 338e). Alexander's grief over Stateira's death led Darius to suspect that the conqueror had been intimate with her (C 4.10.31), but Teireus testified that Alexander's treatment of the queen had always been honorable (C 4.10.25–34; P*A* 30.2–6).[703] The story, and Teireus himself, may very well have been invented, though the fact that Teireus does not appear elsewhere is not, in itself, proof that he is fictitious.

Berve ii.372 no. 742.

Telephus (Telephos). One of Alexander's *hetairoi*, hence apparently a prominent Macedonian. During the Gedrosian campaign, Telephus was ordered to convey a small quantity of ground corn to an unnamed location, where it could be used by Nearchus' fleet (A 6.23.6). Nothing else is known about him.

Berve ii.372 no. 745; Tataki 440 no. 11.

Telesippa. Greek *hetaira*. Telesippa had among her lovers a certain Eurylochus of Aegae, who, upon hearing of her planned return to Greece in 324, tried to have himself declared unfit for battle in order to return with her. The matter was brought to the attention of Alexander, who ordered Eurylochus to attempt to persuade Telesippa to remain, but not to force her (P*A* 41.9–10; P*M* 181a). The same story is told, implausibly, of Antigenes, who was in fact discharged in 324 (P*M* 339c–d).

Berve ii.372 no. 743.

Teutamus (Teutamos). Unattested in the Alexander historians, but possibly a member of the hypaspists (Argyraspids) during the King's lifetime; he may, however, have been appointed by Antipater at Triparadeisus to keep a watchful eye on his colleague, Antigenes. The two are regularly spoken of as commanders of the Silver Shields, but Teutamus was clearly the junior colleague. D 18.62.6–7 says that both men were satraps, and if this is correct Teutamus' satrapy must have been a minor one, perhaps Paraetacene (thus Bosworth 1992: 66–7).[704]

In 318, Polyperchon, writing in the name of the Kings, instructed Teutamus and Antigenes to support Eumenes, who had been appointed General of Asia (D 18.58.1); they joined forces with Eumenes (P*Eum* 13.2–4), whom they congratulated on his escape from Nora (D 18.59.3) but served with some reluctance on account of his ethnic origins. Teutamus was willing to accept the theoretical leadership of Alexander (P*Eum* 13.7–8; Pol*Strat* 4.8.2). He appears to have resisted the appeals of Ptolemy, who had landed at Zephyrium in Cilicia and urged the Argyraspid commanders to abandon Eumenes (D 18.62.1); but a second embassy, by Antigonus' agent Philotas, would have persuaded Teutamus, had not Antigenes intervened to keep him loyal (D 18.62.4–6). He commanded the Argyraspids at Paraetacene (D 19.28.1); but soon he plotted with some of the other commanders to make use of Eumenes in the coming battle in Media and then to eliminate him (P*Eum* 16.2). The conspiracy was, however, reported to Eumenes by Eudamus and Phaedimus. When the Macedonian baggage was captured at Gabiene, Teutamus took the lead in negotiating with Antigonus, who promised to return the property of the Silver Shields in exchange for Eumenes (P*Eum* 17.1–2). J 14.3.11 says the Silver Shields sent a deputation *ignaris ducibus*, which must mean that they did so without the knowledge of Antigenes and other officers in the army, but Teutamus was clearly not ignorant of the proceedings.

What became of Teutamus, we are not told. It appears that he avoided Antigenes' fate by initiating the arrest and betrayal of Eumenes (P*Eum* 17.1).[705] There is no indication that he served under Antigonus – perhaps he was dismissed on account of his age. It is possible that he commanded the remnants of the Silver Shields, whom Antigonus entrusted to Sibyrtius and thus consigned to difficult service and obscurity. Pol*Strat* 4.6.15; P*Eum* 19.3; D 19.48.3–4 says that the Argyraspids who went with Sibyrtius to Arachosia included "those who had betrayed Eumenes." It would be in character for Antigonus to "double-cross" Teutamus; cf. his treatment of Seleucus (D 19.55.2ff.).

Berve ii.372 no. 744; Billows 85 n. 8; Heckel 316–19.

Thaïs. Athenian courtesan. Thaïs may have accompanied Alexander from the beginning of the campaign – or perhaps since Alexander's sojourn in Egypt. She was present when Persepolis was destroyed (Ath 13.576d–e), perhaps already as the mistress of Ptolemy son of Lagus (Cleitarchus *ap.* P*A* 38.2). The vulgate depicts her as the person who induced Alexander to burn the royal palaces in a drunken revel (D 17.72; C 5.7.3–7).[706] She bore Ptolemy three children (Lagus, Leontiscus, Eirene) – perhaps all before she accompanied him to Egypt in 323 BC[707] – and at some point actually married him (Ath 13.576e). What became of her we do not know.

Berve ii.175 no. 359; Tarn ii.324 n. 7; Ogden 68–9, 241. See Stemma X.

Thalestris (also Thallestris; Minythyia). Fictitious Amazon queen encountered by Alexander in 330 (full accounts in C 6.5.24–32; J 12.3.5–7; D 17.77.1–3); P*A*

46.1–2 dismisses the story as fictitious but records the names of writers who either accepted or rejected the tale.[708] According to J 2.4.33 and 12.3.5 (cf. Oros 3.18.5) she was also known as Minythyia. Thalestris allegedly came to Alexander in Hyrcania from her home on the plains of Themiscyra near Thermodon (C 6.5.24), traveling for thirty-five days (J 12.3.5; Str 11.5.4 [505] claims that the distance was 6,000 stades), and arrived at Alexander's camp with 300 women, having left the remainder of her army at the borders of Hyrcania (C 6.5.26; D 17.77.1). Her purpose was to have a child by Alexander, believing that two superior beings would produce a remarkable child (D 17.77.3). After thirteen days of sexual relations with the King, in which she showed herself to be the more enthusiastic partner, she departed convinced that she had conceived (J 12.3.7; cf. C 6.5.32; D 17.77.3).

Berve ii.419, Abschn. II no. 26; Baynham 2001.

Theaetetus (Theaitetos). Athenian (C 5.5.17). One of the spokesmen of the mutilated Greeks who encountered Alexander's army between the Araxes River and Persepolis. His name survives only in Curtius, but that is not to say that C invented him: since D 17.69.5–8 preserves the same general arguments, it is likely that the story was told in greater detail by Cleitarchus (Pearson 239; cf. Hammond 1983: 56). Theaetetus makes the case that they should accept Alexander's offer of repatriation (C 5.5.17–20). This group and its leaders are doubtless fictitious, the speeches of Theaetetus and Euctemon little more than rhetorical exercises (see s.v. **Euctemon**).

Berve ii.175–6 no. 360.

Theocritus (Theokritos). Greek from Chios. Theocritus was an orator and poet (the author of *Chreai*, as well as a *History of Libya*) who had studied with Metrodorus, a student of Isocrates (*Suda Θ* 166); he was an enemy of Theopompus the historian, also a Chian (Str 14.1.35 [645]), as well as of Anaximnes (Ath 1.21c). A man of low origins, he was later prone to extravagance (Ath 6.230f). Nevertheless, he is supposed to have criticized Aristotle for developing a taste for life at the Macedonian court (P*M* 603c; cf. DL 5.11). He made light of Alexander's request for purple dye from the Chians, with which to adorn the garments of his *hetairoi* (Ath 12.540a; P*M* 11a–b). He was put to death at some point after 306, as is clear from the reference to King Antigonus, for making a tasteless joke about Monophthalmus (P*M* 11b–c, 633c).[709]

Laquer, *RE* s.v. "Theokritos (2)"; Berve ii.176–7 no. 364; Billows 436–7 no. 114; Teodorsson 1990.

Theodorus [1]. (Theodoros). Macedonian. Brother of Proteas and thus probably son of Lanice (the sister of Black Cleitus and Alexander's former nurse). He is known only from P*M* 760c, who records correspondence between the King and Theodorus concerning a *hetaira*/musician (**F54**).[710]

Berve ii.176 no. 362. See Stemma VIII.

Theodorus [2]. (Theodoros). Dancer from Tarentum. At an unspecified time in the campaign, Theodorus was with Philoxenus in Asia Minor and in possession of two slave boys (**M67–68**) whom he was trying to sell. Philoxenus offered to buy these for Alexander, whose letter in response to the offer was a stinging rebuke of Philoxenus and a general condemnation of Theodorus (P*A* 22.1–2; cf. Ath 1.22d).

Berve ii.176 no. 363.

Theodotus (Theodotos). Macedonian. Theodotus was awarded seventh place in the contest of valor in Sittacene (331 BC); hence he became a pentakosiarch of the hypaspists (C 5.2.5). He is otherwise unknown. That he was Lysimachus' *thesaurophylax* of the late 280s (Pol*Strat* 4.9.4) is only a very remote possibility; nor can a good case be made for identification with the navarch of Antigonus the One-Eyed of 314 (D 19.64.5–7).

Berve ii.176 no. 361; Billows 436 no. 113; Hauben 100 no. 35; Heckel 305.

Theophilus (Theophilos). Greek or possibly Macedonian craftsman who made the polished iron helmet that Alexander wore at Gaugamela (*PA* 32.9).[711] Nothing else is known about him.

Berve ii.178 no. 366.

Theopompus (Theopompos). Son of Damasistratus, from Chios (Str 14.1.35 [645]; Paus 2.9.5, 6.18.5; *Suda Θ* 172). Born in 377/6 (we are told that when he returned to Chios in 332 from exile he was 45 years old).[712] Rhetor and historian, Theopompus was a student of Isocrates and fellow-student of Ephorus (Cic *De Oratore* 2.13, 22–3; 3.9 = Quint 2.8.11). He had left Chios as a child in the company of his exiled "Spartanizing" father, and Memnon's capture of Chios in 333 (A 2.1.1; D 17.29.2) will have prevented any plans to return. He was, however, recalled as a result of Alexander's decree in 332 (*SIG*[3] 283), but Heisserer 83–95 makes a good case for the issuing of this decree in 334. At any rate, Theopompus is unlikely to have returned until 332. As an opponent of the oligarchic party, he was an enemy of Theocritus (see s.v.) and a supporter of Alexander (Str 14.1.35 [645]; Ath 6.230f).[713] The author of an *Epitome of Herodotus' Histories*, *Hellenica*, and *Philippica*, Theopompus wrote only *Letters* to Alexander (of which we have five fragments: *FGrH* 115 FF250–4), primarily itemizing the misdeeds of Harpalus, and an *Encomium* (F257),[714] but there are references to Alexander's expedition in the *Philippica*. For his historical work see Jacoby, *FGrH* 115; cf. Shrimpton 1991: 196–274 for *testimonia* and fragments). At some point after Alexander's death, Theopompus was again exiled from Chios. He sailed to Egypt but did not receive a good reception from Ptolemy, possibly for his negative comments about Harpalus (Photius, *Life of Theopompus*).

Berve ii.177–8 no. 365; Shrimpton 1991; Flower 1994.

Theoxenus (possibly Dioxenus; the name appears only in C, in its Latin form). Macedonian of unknown family, Theoxenus conspired with Dimnus against Alexander at Phrada in 330 (C 6.7.15). On the evidence of Nicomachus (or his brother Cebalinus) he was arrested and executed (C 6.11.38).

Berve ii.146 no. 280 (s.v. "Dioxenos").

Thersippus (Thersippos). Apparently Greek. Envoy of Alexander. In the diplomatic negotiations of 332, which followed Alexander's victory at Issus and the capture of Darius' family, Thersippus was sent from Marathus to Darius with the Persian envoys (see s.vv. **Arsimas, Meniscus**) and a letter that rejected the Great King's offers and charged him with crimes against Macedon (A 2.14.4; C 4.1.14; for the contents of Alexander's letter see A 2.14.4–9; C 4.1.7–14). He is honored by the Nesiotic League for his services to the state during the reigns of Philip III and Alexander IV and during the regencies of Antipater and Polyperchon (*OGIS* i.4), an inscription that attests to his high standing with the Macedonian kings and generals.

Berve ii.179 no. 368; Hofstetter 1972: 179 no. 312; Poddighe 2001.

Thessaliscus (Thessaliskos). Theban. Son of Ismenias (Arist*Rhet* 2.1398b.3ff.). He had been sent on an embassy to Darius at some point before the destruction of his city in 335. He was captured at Damascus, together with Dionysodorus, by Parmenion after the battle of Issus (A 2.15.2). Alexander released both prisoners, in part because he regretted the severity of the action (cf. *PA* 13.5; *PM* 181b) he had taken against Thebes, and in Thessaliscus' case out of respect for his lineage (A 2.15.4).

Swoboda, *RE* s.v. "Ismenias (2)"; Berve ii.179 no. 369; Hofstetter 99, 179 no. 313.

Thessalonice (Thettalonike; Thessalonike). Daughter of Nicesipolis of Pherae and Philip II (Satyrus *ap.* Ath 13.557c; Paus 9.7.3; cf. 8.7.7; J 14.6.13 wrongly calls her daughter of Philip Arrhidaeus(!); *HE* 2; D 19.35.5, 52.1); a niece of Jason of Pherae (StByz s.v. "Thessalonike"). Thessalonice's birth dates in all likelihood to ca. 345/4, for Philip will have married Nicesipolis soon after he gained possession of Pherae in 346 (but Ellis 212, with n. 10, prefers 352 for the marriage). Nothing is known of her life before 316/5, when she was found with Olympias – who appears to have acted as her guardian, since Nicesipolis died twenty days after the girl's birth (StByz[715]) – during the siege of Pydna (J 14.6.13; D 19.35.5). In 315 she was compelled to marry Cassander (D 19.52.1, 61.2; cf. Paus 8.7.7; J 14.6.13; Porphyry of Tyre, *FGrH* 260 F3 §4), to whom she bore three sons: Philip, Alexander, and Antipater (P*Demetr* 36.1–2; Porphyry of Tyre §5; cf. P*Pyr* 6.3; P*Demetr* 36.1). He founded the city of Thessalonice in her honor (Str 7. frgs. 21, 24; *HE* 2, ascribing the foundation to Thessalonice herself). She was killed, perhaps in 296, by her own son, Antipater (P*Demetr* 36.1; P*Pyr* 6.3; D 21.7.1; Porphyry of Tyre §5), because she favored his younger brother, Alexander (J 16.1.1–4; Paus 9.7.3). According to the forged Testament of Alexander, she is designated as the bride of Lysimachus (Ps-Call 3.33.13).

Beloch iii^2 2.69; iv^2 2.127–8; Berve ii.179–80 no. 370; Macurdy 52–5; Carney 1988; Carney 155–8. See Stemmata I, V.

Thessalus (Thessalos; Thettalos). Tragic actor; victor in the Dionysiac festival in 347 and 341 (*IG* ii^2 2318, 2320) as well as the Lenaean (for the second time ca. 356, *IG* ii^2 2325). He acted as the envoy of Alexander to Pixodarus of Caria in 336 (P*A* 10.2), bringing about the failure of the proposed marriage of Arrhidaeus to Ada [2], and therefore Philip II ordered him to be arrested and imprisoned (P*A* 10.4). Thessalus appears to have come to no harm, perhaps because Philip II died before the orders to arrest him could be carried out. In 332/1 he was defeated by the actor Athenodorus, much to Alexander's dismay (P*A* 29.4; P*M* 334e; A 3.1.4). Thessalus later performed, again in the company of Athenodorus, at the mass-marriage ceremony in Susa in 324 BC (Chares, *FGrH* 125 F4 = Ath 12.538f).

Berve ii.180 no. 371; O'Connor 103 no. 239 (with numerous factual errors).

Thibron. Spartan, family background unknown (A*Succ* 1.16). Thibron was amongst the friends of Harpalus who joined him in his flight to Athens in 324 (D 18.19.2).[716] Later he sailed with Harpalus to Cydonia on Crete, where he murdered him (D 17.108.8; 18.19.2) or, possibly, instructed an agent to do so (Paus 2.33.4; cf. Str 17.3.21 [837]) and took control of the 6,000 or 7,000 mercenaries who had come with the disgraced treasurer from Asia.[717] After Alexander's death, Thibron was induced by Cyrenaean and Barcaean exiles to attack Cyrene, which at that point was independent of Macedonian rule, with an army of 6,000 (A*Succ* 1.16; D 18.19.2; Str 17.3.21). After some initial successes on the battlefield, Thibron besieged the harbor and extracted from the Cyrenaeans 500 talents of silver and a contribution of half their chariots to his army; furthermore, he plundered the merchant ships in the port in order to pay his troops (D 18.19.3–5). But a quarrel soon arose with one of his commanders, the Cretan Mnasicles, over the division of spoils, and Mnasicles defected to the Cyrenaeans and encouraged them to stop paying the indemnity, of which they had turned over only sixty talents at that point. Thibron countered by seizing eighty Cyrenaeans in the port and marching on the city, but he accomplished little. Later he went to the aid of his allies, the Barcaeans and Hesperitae, which were under attack from Cyrene, but in Thibron's absence Mnasicles recaptured the harbor (D 18.20.1–5). For Thibron's fleet and its sailors, this created serious supply problems: many were killed or captured by the

Libyans as they foraged, and the fleet was subsequently destroyed by bad weather (D 18.20.6–7). Thibron nevertheless took Taucheira[718] by siege (D 18.20.6) and continued his campaign after summoning 2,500 mercenaries from Taenarum (D 18.21.1–3). Although he won a decisive victory against a larger force of Cyrenaeans, Thibron's fate was sealed when exiles from Cyrene summoned aid from Ptolemy in Egypt, who sent a force under Ophellas to deal with him (D 18.21.4–7). Captured by the Libyans, Thibron was taken in chains to Epicydes of Olynthus, whom Ophellas had placed in charge of Taucheira. He allowed the Taucheirans to torture Thibron before sending him to Cyrene where he was crucified in the harbor (A*Succ* 1.17–18; cf. D 18.21.7–9).

Poralla 65–6 no. 376; Berve ii.180 no. 372.

Thiodexilas. Son of Mnasicles. Cavalryman from Orchomenus; served in Alexander's allied cavalry until the expedition reached Ecbatana in 330. There he and his compatriots were discharged. On their return (ca. 329), they made a dedication to Zeus Soter in Orchomenus (*IG* vii.3206).

Berve ii.180 no. 373.

Thiodotus (Thiodotos). Patronymic lost. Cavalryman from Orchomenus; served in Alexander's allied cavalry until the expedition reached Ecbatana in 330. There he and his compatriots were discharged. On their return (ca. 329), they made a dedication to Zeus Soter in Orchomenus (*IG* vii.3206).

Berve ii.180–1 no. 374.

Thiopompus (Thiopompos). Son of Olympiochus. Cavalryman from Orchomenus; served in Alexander's allied cavalry until the expedition reached Ecbatana in 330. There he and his compatriots were discharged. On their return (ca. 329), they made a dedication to Zeus Soter in Orchomenus (*IG* vii.3206).

Berve ii.181 no. 375.

Thoas. Son of Mandrodorus from Magnesia-on-the-Maeander (A 6.23.2; A*Ind* 18.7 calls him son of Menodorus). He is first encountered as a trierarch of the Hydaspes fleet in 326 (A*Ind* 18.7). During the Gedrosian march he operated by land and secured landing places and water supplies for the fleet (A 6.23.2). He replaced Apollophanes, who had been killed in battle with the Oreitae, but soon died of illness and was in turn replaced by Sibyrtius (A 6.27.1, incorrectly claiming that Apollophanes was deposed; see s.v. **Apollophanes**).

Berve ii.181 no. 376.

Thoenon (Thoinon). Son of Timogiton. Cavalryman from Orchomenus; served in Alexander's allied cavalry until the expedition reached Ecbatana in 330. There he and his compatriots were discharged. On their return (ca. 329), they made a dedication to Zeus Soter in Orchomenus (*IG* vii.3206).

Berve ii.181 no. 377.

Thrasybulus (Thrasyboulos; Thrasyboulus). Athenian. Son of Thrason. Born no later than 375; he appears in a naval list of 353/2 (*IG* ii^2 1613.270); he served with Chares at the Hellespont. He is named as one of the Athenian generals and politicians whose extradition was demanded by Alexander after the sack of Thebes in 335 (*Suda* A 2704), but the list given by the *Suda* may not be reliable. Certainly, Thrasybulus fled from Athens, probably in the company of Ephialtes, soon after the sack of Thebes, and served with Memnon of Rhodes at Halicarnassus (D 17.25.6). Ephialtes was killed during the siege (D 17.27.3) but Thrasybulus escaped from the city with Memnon (cf. D 17.27.5). In 326/5 he reappears in Athens as *strategos* (*IG* ii^2 1628.40–1; cf. Develin 400) and makes a dedication at Eleusis (*IG* ii^2 2969).

Berve ii.181–2 no. 378; Kirchner no. 7304; Davies 239; Seibt 105 n. 3; Hofstetter 181 no. 317.

Thrasylochus (Thrasylochos). Greek from Messenia. Son of Philiades. Leader of the pro-Macedonian party (Dem 18.295). Thrasylochus and his brother Neon were exiled in 336/5, in the turmoil that followed Philip's death, but reinstated as tyrants of Messenia soon afterwards on Alexander's orders ([Dem] 17.4, 7).

Berve ii.182 no. 379.

Thymondas (Thimodes). Son of Mentor the Rhodian (C 3.3.1; A 2.13.2), Thymondas was born ca. 355, as we may gather from his father's age (Dem 23.157) and Curtius' description of him as *impiger iuvenis* in 334/3 (C 3.3.1). He had perhaps spent the time before the death of his uncle Memnon at the court of the Great King; then he was sent out to confirm Pharnabazus as Memnon's successor (A 2.2.1; C 3.3.1). Thymondas joined Darius at Sochi and in the battle of Issus commanded 30,000 infantry on the right wing (C 3.9.2; cf. A 2.13.2). After the Persian defeat, he and other mercenary captains (Amyntas son of Antiochus, Bianor, and Aristomedes) fled to Tripolis in Syria and from there took ships to Cyprus. Although Amyntas went on to Egypt with 4,000 mercenaries, all of whom perished there, there is no evidence that Thymondas accompanied him. What happened to him, we do not know. He appears to have been the father of Memnon, honored by the Athenians in 327/6 (*IG* ii^2 356; see s.v. **Memnon** [2] for the implications of such a relationship).

Berve ii.182 no. 380; Seibt 110–13; Hofstetter 182 no. 319. See Stemma IV.

Timander (Timandros). Commander of a battalion (*taxis*) of hypaspists. He is attested at Halicarnassus, together with Adaeus, under the command of the Somatophylax Ptolemy (A 1.22.4). Identification with Timander, father of Asclepiodorus, is doubtful. The name Timander may be the result of a textual error in A*Ind* 18.3 (Jacoby, *FGrH* iiB, p. 450). If the text is correct, it is unlikely that an officer of relatively low standing would have been the father of one of the Hydaspes trierarchs. What became of Timander is unknown.

Berve ii.373 no. 746; Heckel 303.

Timanthes. Son of Pantiades, a Macedonian from Pella, one of the trierarchs of the Hydaspes fleet in 326 (A*Ind* 18.3 = Nearchus, *FGrH* 133 F1). Nothing else is known about him or his father.

Berve ii.373 no. 747.

Timarchus (Timarchos). Son of Nicocles (Pl*NH* 11.167) and grandson of Evagoras I ([P]*M* 838a). Very little is known about him, most of that trivial: Pliny comments on his teeth, that he had two rows of maxillaries (*NH* 11.167). He was the father of that Nicocles who ruled Paphos from at least 321. The exact relationship of Timarchus to [Cha]ridamus (Berve no. 822) is uncertain, though it appears that Timarchus replaced [Cha]ridamus at some point in Alexander's reign.

Berve ii.373 no. 748.

Timocleia (Timoclea; Timokleia). Theban woman; sister of Theagenes who died on the Greek side at Chaeronea (P*M* 259d; cf. Din 1.74). Raped by Thracians during the sack of Thebes (335 BC), she killed their leader (see s.v. **Alexander** [7]) by tricking him into thinking that she had hidden her gold and silver in a well. When he climbed down to see, she (aided by her maidservants) threw rocks down upon him and killed him. She was brought to Alexander, who acquitted her (Pol*Strat* 8.40; P*A* 12).[719]

Berve ii.374 no. 751; Hamilton 31–2; Stadter 1965: 112–15.

Timocles (Timokles). Comic poet of the late fourth century BC (*Suda* T 623). Timocles' comedies touched on contemporary events like the Harpalus scandal (Ath 8.341e).[720] There is, however, no known personal connection between Timocles and Alexander.

Berve ii.374 no. 753.

Timolaus (Timolaos). Theban, leader of the pro-Macedonian party, described by Theopompus (*FGrH* 115 F210 = Ath 10.436b) as one of the most dissolute public figures. Demosthenes, in the *de Corona*, depicts him as a traitor to his country (18.48, 295; cf. Plb 18.14.4, citing Demosthenes). He was among those supporters of Macedon (Din 1.74 says he took bribes from Philip II) who resided on the Cadmea and in 335 he and Amyntas (i.e., Anemoetas) were caught off guard and murdered by Theban exiles who had slipped into the city (A 1.7.1). Timolaus' death was followed by rebellion, which ultimately led to the city's destruction.

Berve ii.374 no. 752.

Timotheus [1]. (Timotheos). Macedonian common soldier under the command of Parmenion (apparently in Syria, as the context of Plutarch's account suggests). He and Damon were charged with seducing the "wives" of certain Greek mercenaries (**F48–49**). Alexander instructed Parmenion to investigate and execute Timotheus and Damon if they were guilty (P*A* 22.4). The outcome of the proceedings is unknown.

Berve ii.373–4 no. 750.

Timotheus [2]. (Timotheos). Son of Oeniades (Didymus col. 12.61–2; Gibson 2002: 97). Flutist (*auletes*), noted for his long beard (Ath 13.565a), who performed at the court of Philip II and gave martial inspiration to young Alexander (Dio Chr 1.1).[721] Later he joined Alexander in Memphis, where he took part in the musical competitions (*Suda*; A 3.1.4); he also performed at the mass-marriage ceremony in Susa in 324 (Chares, *FGrH* 125 F4 = Ath 12.538f; see also s.vv. **Phrynichus**, **Caphisias**, **Diophantus**, and **Evius**).

Berve ii.373 no. 749.

Tiridates [1]. Persian, possibly a eunuch.[722] Royal treasurer (*gazophylax*) at Persepolis (C 5.5.2; D 17.69.1 describes him vaguely as "the man in charge of the city"), Tiridates offered to betray the city to Alexander (D 17.69.1; C 5.5.2) and was probably instrumental in shutting the city's gates to the defeated satrap Ariobarzanes (C 5.4.34; cf. Bosworth i.329; Briant 467). Alexander thus secured a treasure of 120,000 talents of silver (D 17.71.1; C 5.6.9) before it could be plundered by the Persian garrison (A 3.18.10). Tiridates was retained as treasurer, but with a Macedonian garrison and Nicarchides as *phrourarchos* (C 5.6.11) and Phrasaortes as satrap of Persis (A 3.18.11). His tenure appears to have been brief, for the treasures were transferred from Persepolis to Ecbatana and placed in the charge of Alexander's Imperial Treasurer, Harpalus (A 3.19.7). What became of him we do not know.[723]

Berve ii.374–5 no. 754.

Tiridates [2]. Persian or possibly a native of the region around Lake Sistan. According to D 17.81.2, Alexander appointed Tiridates to the *strategia* of the Gedrosians and Ariaspians. C 7.3.4, however, says that Amedines, the former secretary of Darius III (*scriba regis*), was made satrap of the Ariaspians (Euergetae).[724] It is remotely possible (*pace* Berve) that Tiridates is the same man who surrendered Persepolis; cf. the case of Mithrenes, who surrendered Sardis and then became satrap of Armenia.

Berve ii.375 no. 755.

Tiridates [3]. Prominent Persian. His estates in an unspecified area (perhaps Bactria) were given to Eurylochus as a reward for bringing the Hermolaus conspiracy to Alexander's attention (C 8.6.26). One may conclude that Tiridates had been an enemy of the King and that his property had thus been confiscated.[725]

Berve ii.375 no. 756.

Tlepolemus (Tlepolemos; Tleptolemus). Macedonian. Son of Pythophanes (A 3.22.1; 6.27.1); *hetairos* of Alexander (A 3.22.1). Tlepolemus first appears in 330 BC as the *episkopos* in Parthia-Hyrcania (cf. Anaxippus and Neiloxenus), that is, the military watchdog of the Amminapes, the native satrap (A 3.22.1; cf. Bosworth i.346). He continued in that capacity when Amminapes was replaced by Phrataphernes, sometime between 330 and 326. In 325 Tlepolemus was appointed satrap of Carmania – succeeding Sibyrtius, who moved to Gedrosia and Arachosia (A 6.27.1; cf. C 9.10.20, without reference to Tlepolemus) – but he had not succeeded in establishing order there when Nearchus arrived (A*Ind* 36.8; some confusion here; A appears to be referring to Gedrosia-Arachosia, where Apollophanes had been deposed and Thoas had died of illness). Tlepolemus was recognized as satrap of Carmania in 323 (J 13.4.23; D 18.3.3),[726] and his position was confirmed at Triparadeisus (D 18.39.6; A*Succ* 1.35). In the war between Eumenes and Antigonus, Tlepolemus supported the former (D 19.28.3); Antigonus' failure to depose him after Gabiene may reflect the fact that he fled to his satrapy after the battle (cf. Heckel 1980a: 44, with n. 6) as much as his popularity with the Carmanians, whom he had governed well (D 19.48.1).

Berve ii.375–6 no. 757; Lehmann-Haupt 145–6 §118.

Troas. Epirote. Daughter and eldest surviving child of Neoptolemus the Molossian; sister of Olympias and Alexander I (J 7.6.10–11; cf. 8.6.4), and thus an aunt of Alexander the Great. Troas was born perhaps ca. 375 BC. After the death of her father, she married her uncle, Arybbas son of Alcetas, and became the mother of Aeacides (P*Pyr* 1.5). Nothing else is known about her life. Troas, the daughter of Aeacides and Phthia (and thus sister of Pyrrhus), was named for the maternal grandmother (P*Pyr* 1.7).

See Stemma II.

Tyriespis (Terioltes). Iranian. Installed as satrap of Parapamisadae in 327, with Nicanor entrusted with the administration of Alexandria-in-the-Caucasus (A 4.22.5). When Nicanor was moved to the satrapy to the west of the Indus and killed by an uprising of the Assacenians, Tyriespis and Philip son of Machatas were sent to put down the revolt (A 5.20.7). Tyriespis' administration of Parapamisadae was marked by cases of improper behavior and he was removed in 325 and replaced by Oxyartes (A 6.15.3). Tyriespis was put on trial and executed (C 9.8.9).

Berve ii.376 no. 758. Terioltes (C 9.8.9).

Wanaxion. Son of Saondas. Cavalryman from Orchomenus; served in Alexander's allied cavalry until the expedition reached Ecbatana in 330. There he and his compatriots were discharged. On their return (ca. 329), they made a dedication to Zeus Soter in Orchomenus (*IG* vii.3206).

Berve ii.162 no. 334.

X

Xandrames (Aggrammes; Sanskrit Chandramas = "Moon god," so McCrindle 409; Nandrus: J 15.4.16). Ruler of the Prasii and Gandaridae, Xandrames commanded an army of 200,000 infantry, 20,000 cavalry, and 2,000 chariots (D 17.93.2; C 9.2.3; *ME* 68).[727] He is Mahapadma Nanda, last king of the Nanda dynasty, which ruled the Magadha kingdom on the Ganges in the mid-fourth century. Alexander learned about him from Phegeus at the Hyphasis (Beas) River in 326 BC. According to the report, Xandrames was the son of the king's barber (**M23**), who killed his master (**M22**) and married the queen (**F41**; C 9.2.6–7; D 17.93.2–3 claims that it was the queen herself who killed her husband). P*A* 62.9 says that Chandragupta (Sandrocottus) sneered at the base origins of Xandrames. Chandragupta himself deposed and killed Xandrames and established the Mauryan dynasty not long after Alexander's departure from India (ca. 322 according to Buddhist tradition).

Berve ii.281 no. 574.

Xennias. Macedonian.[728] Xennias served in some capacity, and perhaps not solely as a herald, in the army of Eumenes of Cardia. Since he is found with Eumenes in the campaign against Neoptolemus (thus Bosworth 1978) in early 320, it is virtually certain that he had served in Asia during Alexander's lifetime. Eumenes sent him, because he was a Macedonian speaker (*PSI* xii.1284, 6), to address the Macedonian nucleus of Neoptolemus' force and gain a truce by threatening to cut off Neoptolemus' forces from their supplies. Nothing else is known about Xennias.

Bosworth 1978; Tataki 389 no. 2.

Xenocles (Xenokles). *Gazophylax* (Str 2.1.6 [69]). See s.v. **Xenophilus**.

Xenocrates (Xenokrates). Son of Agathenor. Born ca. 395 BC (DL 4.14). Greek philosopher from Calchedon (Str 12.4.9 [566]), Xenocrates was a student and successor of Speusippus (*Suda* s.v.), heading the Academy from 339 to his death in 314 BC.[729] He was associated with both Plato and Aristotle, accompanying the former to Sicily and spending time with the latter at Assos, where he went at the invitation of Hermias of Atarneus; when Memnon of Rhodes arrested Hermias and sent him to the Great King to be executed, Xenocrates and Aristotle escaped from the area (Str 13.1.57 [610]). Xenocrates' connections with Alexander are slight: when the King sent Xenocrates a gift of fifty talents, he returned it saying that money was for kings, not philosophers (P*M* 181e, 331e, 333b; Val Max 4.3 ext. 3b; *Suda* s.v.; for his integrity in general see Val Max 2.10 ext. 2).[730] He dedicated a work *On Kingship* in four books to Alexander (cf. P*M* 1126d), as well as works for Arybbas[731] and Hephaestion (DL 4.14). In 322, after their defeat in the Lamian War, the Athenians sent him as one of their ambassadors to Antipater, but Xenocrates' tone was defiant and Antipater's treatment of him cool (P*Ph* 27.1–3, 6; but DL 4.9 paints a different picture); his relationship with Polyperchon appears to have been better (P*M* 533c). Soon afterwards he was offered, but declined, citizenship by the pro-Macedonian Athenian regime (P*Ph* 29.6). An account of his career is given by DL 4.6–16.

Berve ii.281–2 no. 576.

Xenodochus (Xenodochos). Greek from Cardia. Xenodochus and Artemius of Colophon had traveled from the coast and reached Sogdiana in the summer of 328 and were present at the banquet at which Cleitus was murdered (P*A* 51.4). Nothing else is known about him, but the mere fact of his presence at the King's banquet suggests that he was a man of some importance.

Berve ii.281 no. 575.

Xenophantus (Xenophantos). Greek flute-player, the most celebrated of his time. He performed the funeral hymn for Demetrius Poliorcetes (P*Demetr* 53.5). Sen*de Ira* 2.2 appears to have confused him with Timotheus, and Berve's suggestion (ii.282) that he may have been in Alexander's entourage some forty years earlier is not impossible but highly unlikely.

Berve ii.282 no. 577.

Xenophilus (Xenophilos). Macedonian. In 330, Xenophilus was installed as *phrourarchos* in Susa with 1,000 veterans (C 5.2.16), a position he retained until 317/6.[732] A 3.16.9 says that the garrison commander at Susa was one of the *hetairoi*, a man named Mazarus. This is almost certainly an error: Mazarus was probably the Persian whom Xenophilus replaced. Furthermore, there is a strong likelihood that the man who arranged the surrender of Susa after Gaugamela, Philoxenus, is actually Xenophilus (the two parts of the name have been transposed: see Heckel 2002b). Xenophilus served as *phrourarchos* under the satrap Abulites, then Oropius and Coenus, and eventually Antigenes; the *gazophylax* Xenocles, named by Str 2.1.6 [69], may in fact be Xenophilus, whom D 19.18.1 calls *thesaurophylax*. During the war between Antigonus and Eumenes, he defended Susa against the forces of Seleucus (D 19.17.3, 18.1), and after Eumenes' death and that of Antigenes, he entered into "friendship" with Antigonus. D 19.48.6 makes it clear, however, that Antigonus merely pretended friendship. What became of him is unknown, but it is likely that Antigonus either kept him in honorable detention (as appears to be the case with Peucestas) or eliminated him. Susiana was entrusted to neither Seleucus nor Xenophilus, but rather to the native Aspisas (D 19.55.1), on whom see Billows 376–7 no. 21.

Berve ii.282 no. 578; Billows 440–1 no. 119.

Z

Zariaspes. Noble Persian rebel. He was defeated and captured, along with Ozines (see s.v. **Ordanes**), by Craterus in 325 (C 9.10.19). He was brought to Alexander in Carmania in 324 and executed there (C 10.1.9).

Berve ii.162–3 no. 335.

Zephyrus (Zephyros). A common soldier, Zephyrus is named only in the apocryphal *Letter to Aristotle* 14 as the man who brought Alexander a helmet full of water when the army was suffering greatly from privations in the desert. The famous story of how Alexander poured the water into the ground in front of the army is told by a number of sources, although there is no agreement on the location of the episode: see A 6.26.1–3 (Gedrosia or Parapamisadae); cf. P*A* 42.7–10 (pursuit of Darius); C 7.5.10–12 (Bactria);[733] Fr*Strat* 1.7.7 (Africa: i.e., Egypt); Pol*Strat* 4.3.25 (desert). The story itself may contain an element of truth, but the name Zephyrus appears to have been invented.

Berve ii.163 no. 337.

Zipoetes (Zipoites). Ruler of Bithynia, son of Bas. There is no direct evidence relating to Zipoetes' activities in Alexander's time. He succeeded his father, Bas, in 328/7 and maintained the independence of Bithynia against the Macedonians. Zipoetes ruled for forty-eight years, though he did not assume the title of king until 297, and died in 280 (Memnon, *FGrH* 434 12.4–5). His successor was Nicomedes I. For his career in the age of the Successors see Billows 440–2 no. 121.

Berve ii.163 no. 338.

Zoïlus (Zoïlos). Origins uncertain. Probably Macedonian and perhaps even the father of Mylleas of Beroea (cf. A*Ind* 18.6; Tataki 78 no. 27). Zoïlus met Alexander as he was moving on from Artacoana in 330 BC with 500 allied Greek horsemen (C 6.6.35).[734] Nothing else is known about him.

Berve ii.163–4 no. 339.

Zopyrion. Macedonian. Zopyrion succeeded Memnon as *strategos* of Thrace. He conducted an expedition, allegedly totaling 30,000 (J 12.2.16; 37.3.2), against the Getae, marching to the Borysthenes and besieging Olbia in 325 (thus Beloch iv^2 1.44–5; see also s.v. **Memnon** [3]).[735] The Macedonian force was annihilated, together with their leader, by a combination of the enemy and bad weather (C 10.1.44; cf. J 2.3.4; 12.2.17).[736] News of the disaster encouraged a rebellion by Seuthes (C 10.1.44; cf. Lund 22–4).

Berve ii.164 no. 340.

Anonymous Individuals: Women

a. Women of the Persian Aristocracy

F1. The daughter of Oxyathres, captured at Damascus by Parmenion (C 3.13.13). This may, of course, have been Amastris or Amastrine, or an otherwise unknown sister of hers,[737] but it is also possible that she was the daughter of Oxyathres, son of Darius II (cf. Berve ii.24 n. 2. See also **F2**).

Justi 232; Neuhaus 1902: 619.

F2. The wife of Ochus (Artaxerxes III). She too was captured at Damascus by Parmenion (C 3.13.13). Berve, in his stemma (ii.442), identifies her with the mother of Parysatis and of the three daughters of Ochus captured along with her (C 3.13.12), one of these being, apparently, Parysatis herself. Is this wife of Ochus the daughter of Atossa, the sister whom Ochus murdered after his accession (Val Max 9.2 ext 7)?[738]

F3–4. Two daughters of Ochus (Artaxerxes III) and **F2** above. They were captured at Damascus by Parmenion in 333 (C 3.13.12), along with a third sister, probably Parysatis, the youngest, who married Alexander in Susa in 324 (A 7.4.4). This last identification is, however, far from certain. What became of the other two we do not know.

F5. An earlier wife of Darius III. She was the sister of Pharnaces, who fell in battle at the Granicus River (A 1.16.3; D 17.21.3). On the basis of her brother's name, it appears that this wife of Darius came from the Cappadocian-Pontic nobility. She is, in all probability, the mother of Ariobarzanes, the son of Darius who tried to betray his father and was executed (Aretades of Cnidus, *FGrHist* 285 F1).[739]

F6. The wife of Madates, who ruled the territory of the Uxians and opposed Alexander at the end of 331 BC. The woman herself was a daughter of the sister of Sisygambis, the mother of Darius III (C 5.3.12).

F7. Sister of Sisygambis; mother of **F6** above (C 5.3.12). She was apparently the daughter of Ostanes, a brother of Artaxerxes II.

Neuhaus 1902.

F8. A daughter of Darius III (we do not know by which wife; perhaps **F5**, though her mother could very easily have been one of Darius' concubines); wife of Mithridates, who died at the Granicus, felled by Alexander's own lance (A 1.15.7, 16.3).

F9. A daughter of Darius III, she was the wife of Spithrobates (so D 17.20.2, other sources call him Spithridates), the satrap of Ionia. Diodorus' Spithrobates was killed in battle at the Granicus River by Alexander himself (17.20.5), and it may be that Diodorus has conflated Spithridates and Mithridates, and transferred to the former the position of the King's son-in-law (cf. **F8** above). On the other hand, it may indeed be true that the satrap of Ionia was also a son-in-law of Darius III.

F10. Wife of Hystaspes, granddaughter of Ochus (C 6.2.7). Berve ii.378 identifies her as the daughter of Bisthanes, but this is far from certain (cf. Berve's more cautious stemma, ii.442). She was found among the Persian captives in 330 BC, apparently taken at one of the royal residences. Alexander, upon learning her identity, had her reunited with her husband (C 6.2.6–9).

F11. A woman of a prominent Rhodian family,[740] sister of Memnon and Mentor (Dem 23.154, 157; D 16.52.4), wife of Artabazus. Sometime around 349/8 she accompanied Artabazus to the court of Philip II with her eleven sons and ten daughters (D 16.52.4).[741] These sons seem to have been Pharnabazus and an *anonymus*, also Ariobarzanes, Arsames, Cophen, and six further *anonymi* who surrendered with their father to Alexander in Hyrcania in 330 (C 6.5.4; cf. A 3.23.7). Her daughters included Apame (Artacama), Artonis, and Barsine; to whom we must add seven *anonymae* (**F17–23**). It is doubtful that she was the mother of Ilioneus, and that she is identical with the wife of Artabazus captured at Damascus in 333 BC (**F12** below).

Brunt 1975; Beloch iii^2 2.149–50.

F12. A wife of Artabazus; captured at Damascus together with her son Ilioneus in 333 (C 3.13.13). The fact that Ilioneus was taken at Damascus with his mother suggests that he was still very young. If **F11** had borne all eleven sons before 349/8, then none could have been younger than 16 at the time of the battle of Issus, and it would appear that Ilioneus was a twelfth son of Artabazus and **F12**, a younger wife. But everything depends on the date of Artabazus' flight to Macedonia (D 16.52.4).

F13. Wife of Pharnabazus; mother of his young son, together with whom she was captured at Damascus in 333 (C 3.13.14).

F14–16. Three daughters of Mentor the Rhodian (and of Barsine?); captured at Damascus by Parmenion in late 333 (C 3.13.14). One of these daughters married Nearchus at Susa in 324 (A 7.4.6).

F17–23. Seven daughters of Artabazus and **F11**; D 16.52.4 says that they had ten daughters in 349/8, of whom we know the names of Barsine, Artonis, and Artacama (or Apame).

F24. Daughter of Atropates, she married Perdiccas at Susa in 324 (A 7.4.5; cf. J 13.4.13). Nothing else is known about her, but, in light of Perdiccas' political "marriages" with Nicaea and Cleopatra, it is highly likely that she was repudiated soon after Alexander's death.

b. Aristocratic Women from Bactria-Sogdiana

F25. The wife of Spitamenes, and possibly the mother of Apame, the mother of Antiochus I Soter and wife of Seleucus I Nicator (cf. A 7.4.6; P*Demetr* 31.5); this Apame could have been one of the *tres adulti liberi* mentioned by C 8.3.3.[742] The bizarre account of how, at the beginning of 327, Spitamenes' wife (with the aid of a slave) murdered him in order to win Alexander's favor scarcely flatters Seleucus' mother-in-law (C 8.3.1ff.; *ME* 20–3). Although the woman is doubtless historical, what speaks against the story itself is not only the common folk-motif[743] but also Arrian's report that Spitamenes was killed by the Massagetae, who *sent his head to Alexander* (A 4.17.7; *IA* 87). On the basis of the daughter's name, Apame, it is tempting to regard her as an adherent of the Achaemenid house, but this seems to be ruled out by *ME* 20, which calls her *quaedam Bactrina*.[744] Nothing else is known about her.

Justi 310 (confused); Burstein 1999.

F26. The mother and wife of Sisimithres (C 8.2.19, 28–31; *ME* 19), she bore Sisimithres two sons (C 8.2.19; *ME* 19 adds three daughters). In Curtius' version, she displays more courage than her son, but is finally persuaded to surrender to Alexander (in late autumn 328), who pardoned her and the rest of Sisimithres' family (C 8.2.31).

F27–29. The three daughters of Sisimithres and his mother/wife (**F26** above; *ME* 19). They surrendered to Alexander in late 328 and were pardoned by him (C 8.2.31). Berve ii.354 suggests plausibly that Chorienes was another name for Sisimithres (Brunt i.407 n. 1 thinks it was an official title[745]); if the two are identical, as appears to be the case (*pace* Bosworth 1981: 32ff.), then Sisimithres' three daughters will have been the ones introduced at the banquet where Alexander first met Rhoxane (*ME* 28; they were among the thirty noble maidens[746] mentioned by C 8.4.23; *cohortandus* in 8.4.21 is almost certainly a corruption of Chorienes, but most editions wrongly follow Alde's correction to *Oxyartes*).

Bosworth 1981; Heckel 1986a.

F30. The wife of Oxyartes; mother of Rhoxane and at least two other girls, and of a son named Itanes.[747] She took refuge with her family on the Rock of Sogdiana (A 4.18.4, 19.4) or, as seems more likely, on the Rock of Chorienes/Sisimithres, where she was captured.

F31–32. Sisters (at least two) of Rhoxane. They were captured along with their mother (**F30** above) and Rhoxane on the Rock of Sogdiana (A 4.19.4; cf. 4.20.4) or the Rock of Chorienes/Sisimithres.

c. Women of the Macedonian Aristocracy

F33. A daughter of Parmenion. She married Coenus son of Polemocrates, to whom she bore a son, Perdiccas (Dittenberger, *SIG*^{3} 332, 10; cf. C 6.9.30). She may have been the widow of Attalus, the guardian of Cleopatra-Eurydice.

F34. If not the same woman who married Coenus (**F33** above), then a second, older, daughter of Parmenion, who was married briefly to Attalus (C 6.9.17), the uncle of Cleopatra-Eurydice.[748] But the fact that Coenus belonged to the "newly-weds" (*neogamoi*) in 334/3 (A 1.24.1, 29.4), i.e., shortly after Attalus' death, suggests that Parmenion soon found a new husband for Attalus' widow.

F35. The wife of Meleager son of Neoptolemus, she was undoubtedly the daughter of a prominent Macedonian noble. She married Meleager shortly before the departure of Alexander's Asiatic expedition; Meleager was among the leading "newly-weds" (*neogamoi*) who returned home in the winter of 334/3 (A 1.24.1, 29.4). She never saw her husband again after that reunion: Meleager was executed in 323 (C 10.9.7–21). What became of her is unknown.

F36. The wife of Ptolemy, son of Seleucus, she was undoubtedly the daughter of a prominent Macedonian noble. She married Ptolemy shortly before the departure of Alexander's Asiatic expedition; Ptolemy was among the leading "newly-weds" (*neogamoi*) who returned home in the winter of 334/3 (A 1.24.1, 29.4). But she never saw him again after that reunion, since Ptolemy fell at Issus (A 2.12.2). What became of her is unknown.

F37. Daughter of Antipater (D 17.80.2 wrongly "Antigonus"), wife of Alexander Lyncestes (J 12.14.1; C 7.1.6–7); if she was in fact the mother of Arrhabaeus, the father of Cassander (Habicht 1977b), then she is unlikely to have been identical with any of the known daughters of Antipater: Eurydice, Nicaea, Phila.

F38–39. The daughters of Attalus (presumably only two), captured with Olympias' party at Pydna in 316 (D 19.35.5). Possibly they were the daughters of Attalus son of Andromenes, and Atalante, the sister of Perdiccas.[749] Since both Atalante and her brother were killed in Egypt, and Attalus withdrew to Tyre, Atalante's children may have remained with Rhoxane and Alexander IV, with whom they came to Macedonia and, eventually, into the custody of Olympias. What became of them, we do not know.

d. Indian Women

F40. A daughter of Assacenus (A 4.27.4), captured by Alexander together with her grandmother, Cleophis. C 8.10.35 and *ME* 39, 45 say the child was male. Brunt i.432 n. 1 is confusing: the "queen" in C 8.10.35 *is* Cleophis (cf. 8.10.22), and the son mentioned by Curtius is Cleophis' own (rather than her grandson), and distinct from another son, who was said to have been fathered on her by Alexander himself (C 8.10.36; J 12.7.10).

F41. The mother of Xandrames, the Nanda ruler (D 17.93.3; C 9.2.3, "Aggrammes"); she had been the wife of the previous ruler, whose name is not preserved, but became the lover of Xandrames' father, a barber, who gained the throne when the queen murdered her husband (C 9.2.6–7; D 17.93.3; cf. P*A* 62; see also s.v. **Sandrocottus**).[750]

e. Other Anonymous Women

F42. A Scythian princess (*basilissa*); offered as a bride to Alexander in 329/8 (A 4.15.2). This is possibly the daugther of Carthasis, who had succeeded his dead brother (A 4.15.1; cf. C 7.7.1); Alexander declined the offer (A 4.15.5).

F43. An unnamed Illyrian queen, killed in single combat by the young princess Cynnane, the daughter of Philip II and Audata-Eurydice (Pol*Strat* 8.60). Berve ii.229 dates her death to ca. 344/3, i.e., before Alexander's accession. This seems somewhat early, since Cynnane was born ca. 357, and there is no reason to equate every skirmish with Illyrians with the famous battle of 344/3! But, since Polyaenus mentions Cynnane's exploits before her marriage to Amyntas son of Perdiccas, the battle in question probably occurred late in Philip's reign.

F44. A divinely inspired Syrian woman who protected Alexander at the time of the Pages' conspiracy (Aristobulus, *FGrH* 139 = A 4.13.5–6; cf. C 8.6.16).

F45–47. Three girls sacrificed, along with three boys, by the Taulantians before their battle with Alexander in 335. Their slaughtered bodies were found by the Macedonians when the Taulantians fled (A 1.5.7).

F48–49. Two (or more?) "wives" (*gynaia*) of Greek mercenaries, who were seduced by Damon and Timotheus, soldiers under Parmenion's command (P*A* 22.4). Damon and Timotheus may have been executed.

F50. A native (Babylonian?) woman who gave birth to a freak child, whose body was that of a boy from the head to the loins, whence there grew the foreparts of five different animals (*LM* 90). The story portends the death of Alexander and is pure fiction.

F51–52. Daughters (at least two) of Perilaus. Since they were approaching marriageable age, their father asked Alexander for dowries for them and received fifty talents (P*M* 179f). The anecdote involves the standard *topos* about the generosity of kings, but the existence of Perilaus and his daughters need not be doubted. If Perilaus is identical with the man of the same name who acted as a mediator in Babylon (C 108.15), then he was very likely a Greek *hetairos* of Alexander.

F53. A girl who was brought late one evening to spend the night with Alexander. The King refused to sleep with her when he discovered that she was married (P*M* 179e). Since we cannot put this episode into a historical context, it is virtually impossible to determine whether this woman is fictitious or historical.

F54. A music-girl of Theodorus, the brother of Proteas. Alexander wrote to him and offered to buy her for ten talents on the condition that Theodorus was not in love with her. Alexander appears to be requesting a specific girl, whom he has seen or heard about previously (P*M* 760c).

F55. A harp-girl, whom Antipatrides, one of the King's *hetairoi,* brought to dinner. Alexander was greatly taken by her, but learned to his disappointment that Antipatrides was in love with her. He therefore refrained from touching her (P*M* 760c–d), or ordered her to be taken away (P*M* 180f).

F56. Wife of Archelaus, possibly the son of Theodorus (so Berve ii.85 no. 158), she was painted together with her husband and daughter by Apelles (Pl*NH* 35.96).

F57. Daughter of **F56** and Archelaus, she was painted together with her parents by Apelles (Pl*NH* 35.96).

F58. The daughter of Harpalus and Pythionice. Her mother died ca. 326; the girl, still very young, came to Athens with her father in 324. After his death, she was taken in by Phocion and his son-in-law Charicles, who saw to her upbringing (P*Ph* 22.1, 3).

F59. The daughter of Acuphis, ruler of Nysa, she had a son of military age in 327/6. Alexander required that this son serve with him in India, presumably as a hostage for the good behavior of his grandfather (A 5.2.4).

Anonymous Individuals: Men

a. Members of the Persian Aristocracy

M1. A young son of Pharnabazus, left with other Persians of note in Damascus before the battle of Issus in late 333 (D 17.32.3; cf. C 3.8.12). Soon after the battle, he was captured, along with his mother, by Parmenion (C 3.13.14). He is not mentioned again.

M2. The young son of Memnon and Barsine, left behind at Damascus along with his mother and other notable Persians (D 17.32.3; cf. C 3.8.12). Here he was captured by Parmenion in late 333, soon after the battle of Issus (C 3.13.14).[751]

M3–8. Six unnamed sons of Artabazus and the sister of Memnon and Mentor the Rhodians (see Brunt 1975 for the family); they surrendered to Alexander, along with their father and three other brothers, Ariobarzanes (but see Bosworth i.325), Arsames, and Cophen, in 330 (A 3.23.7). They had earlier spent some time at the court of Philip II (D 16.52.4), and they now received good treatment at Alexander's hands. What became of them is unknown, although it is possible that we do not recognize one or more Persians in the later history of Alexander (or in the age of the Successors) as the son(s) of Artabazus.

M9. A seventh anonymous son of Artabazus. D 16.52.4 says that, in 349/8, Artabazus and the sister of Memnon and Mentor had eleven sons and ten daughters. Nine of the sons are accounted for above (**M3–8**, Ariobarzanes, Arsames, Cophen); we know the names of two others, Pharnabazus and Ilioneus, but the latter was most likely born to a different mother. Ilioneus was captured at Damascus in late 333, apparently still a youth ("im Knabenalter," Berve ii.183), and was presumably born after 349/8. That leaves one more *anonymus* to bring the total of Artabazus' sons by the Rhodian woman to eleven.[752]

M10. The governor of Damascus (*praefectus*: C 3.13.2), that is, probably the commander of the city or citadel. After the battle of Issus, he sent a certain Mardian (**M57** below) to Parmenion, telling him that he was prepared to betray the city and its treasures (C 3.13.2); this he did by leading the Persians, whom Darius III had left with him for safekeeping, and the treasures outside the city-walls (C 3.13.5ff.). He has been wrongly identified (most recently by Atkinson i.257) with Cophen, who had taken the treasures to Damascus before the battle of Issus (A 2.15.1). But this is impossible, since the governor of Damascus was murdered by one of his own men and his head taken to Darius (C 3.13.17; cf. **M11** below). Cophen lived on to surrender to Alexander in 330 and to serve him in Bactria-Sogdiana (cf. the comments of Berve ii.230).

M11. A confidant of the governor of Damascus (**M10**) and, possibly, also a high-ranking Persian; he murdered him and brought his head to Darius (C 3.13.17).

M12. The leader of the Persian cavalry squadron encountered by Alexander after the battle of Gaugamela, once he had broken off his pursuit of Darius (C 4.16.23). Alexander killed him with his spear. As a leader of a cavalry squadron, he doubtless belonged to the Persian nobility. This episode is not mentioned elsewhere, and, since it is just one of a number of duels found in Curtius (cf. 4.6.15–16, 9.25, 15.18; 7.4.33–40; 8.14.35–6; 9.7.16–22),[753] we cannot be certain about the historicity of the event or of **M12** or **M13**.

M13. A Persian cavalryman in the squadron of **M12** above; he too was killed by Alexander (C 4.16.23).

M14. One of the Persian elders who performed *proskynesis* in front of Alexander in Bactria; his style was ridiculed by Leonnatus (A 4.12.2; cf. C 8.2.22–4: Polyperchon; P*A* 74.2–5: Cassander [in Babylon]); for the episode see Heckel 1978c.

b. Members of the Indian Nobility

M15. A son of Porus, who, according to Aristobulus, was sent by his father with sixty chariots to oppose Alexander's crossing of the Hydaspes. He could have prevented the crossing had he attacked, but instead he merely drove by with his chariots, only to be routed by Alexander's *hippotoxotai* (A 5.14.3). Ptolemy records that this son was sent by Porus, but not with sixty chariots (A 5.14.5); he gives the number as 120 chariots and 2,000 cavalry. When he arrived, Alexander had already crossed the river (A 5.14.6), and in the ensuing battle some 400 Indian horsemen fell, including Porus' son (A 5.15.2, 3, Porus learns of his death; cf. 5.18.2 and D 17.89.1). According to a third version, Porus' son gave battle, wounded Alexander himself, and struck Bucephalas (Alexander's horse) a mortal blow (A 5.14.4).

M16. A second son of the Indian king, Porus; he died in battle at the Hydaspes River in 326 (D 17.89.1; A 5.18.2).

M17–18. Two sons of the Indian king, Sophytes (Sopeithes); they surrendered to Alexander along with their father (C 9.1.28). Nothing else is known about them.

M19. A son of the Indian dynast Assacenus; grandson of Cleophis. A 4.27.4 makes this child female, but C 8.10.35 and *ME* 39, 45 agree that it was male.[754]

M20. A brother of Omphis/Taxiles. Alexander sent him to advise Porus to surrender (C 8.14.35), but Porus responded by killing him with a javelin (C 8.14.36).

M21. A brother of Abisares, sent by the latter as a legate to Alexander in 326 (A 5.8.3, 20.5, 29.4; *ME* 55; cf. C 8.13.1; 9.1.7, who speaks only of envoys in general terms).

M22. The king of the Gandaridae (Gangaridae), who lived in the vicinity of the Ganges River. He was murdered by his barber (the father of Xandrames) and his own wife (D 17.93.3; C 9.2.6–7).

M23. The father of Xandrames (or Aggrammes, C 9.2.3), rumored to have been of low birth (cf. P*A* 62.9) and the barber of the king of the Gandaridae (**M22**); he was loved by the queen, whom he married after killing the king and seizing the throne (D 17.93.3 says it was the queen herself who committed the murder; C 9.2.6–7 is ambiguous: *eo interfecto per insidias*).

M24. The commander (*hegemon*) of Massaga; he was killed by a Macedonian catapult missile (A 4.27.2). Certainly he could not have been Assacenus, who had died shortly before Alexander's arrival

(C 8.10.22; *ME* 39; cf. also **M26** below); it is remotely possible, though there is no way of determining, that he is identical with Amminais, a brother of Assacenus, who was responsible for bringing 9,000 mercenaries into the city (*ME* 39). Berve ii.26 thinks that Amminais is the unnamed "brother of Assacenus" who opposed Alexander in the Buner region (A 4.30.5), after the capture of Aornus, but this man appears more likely to have been Aphrices (cf. D 17.86.2; C 8.12.1–3, Erices; *ME* 43, Ariplex). See Anspach i.32; Eggermont 183–4; against Berve ii.97–8.

M25. An Indian *hegemon* or *hyparchos* of the Aspasians, killed by Ptolemy son of Lagus, in single combat in 327/6 (A 4.24.3–4). Lassen ii^2 1.145 n. 2 equates the Aspasians with the Assacenians and makes an argument (accepted by Berve ii.89 no. 172) for the identification of this Indian chieftain with Assacenus, who had died shortly before Alexander reached Massaga. But A 4.30.5, although he mentions Assacenus' brother, daughter (*sic*), and mother (A 4.27.4), is curiously silent about Assacenus himself, suggesting, what might be inferred from C 8.10.22 and *ME* 39, that he died of natural causes.

M26. The Indian *hyparchos* of the Assacenians, whose death at the hands of his rebellious subjects in late spring 326 was reported to Alexander by Sisicottus (A 5.20.7). Berve ii.354 identifies him with the Macedonian *hetairos*, Nicanor (cf. A 4.28.6 and Brunt ii.65 n. 8);[755] but, despite Arrian's notoriously sloppy use of terminology, the *hyparchos* here appears to be a local dynast, perhaps Assagetes or Amminais, if the latter is not identical with **M24** above; possibly, an otherwise unknown tribal chieftain.

M27. An Indian, the ruler of Patala, he surrendered to Alexander in 325 (A 6.17.2). Alexander reinstated him and ordered him to make ready provisions for his Indus expedition. He appears to be the same *hyparchos* of Patala who fled upon Alexander's arrival. Some of the fugitives were captured by Alexanders lightly armed troops, but there is no indication that he was among them (A 6.17.3–6).

M28. Son of the Indian ruler of Nysa, Acuphis. In 327/6, he was required by Alexander to serve with him in India, presumably as a hostage for the good behavior of his father (A 5.2.4).

M29. Son of Acuphis' daughter; he had reached military age in 327/6 and was required by Alexander to serve with him in India, presumably as a hostage for the good behavior of his grandfather. See **M28** above.

c. Other Prominent Barbarians

M30–32. Three adult sons of Spitamenes and the unnamed wife who, in the vulgate tradition, murdered him (C 8.3.3; cf. *ME* 20–3, mentioning only the wife). Of course, these *adulti liberi* need not all have been male, and one of them might have been Apame, who later married Seleucus Nicator. What became of them, if they are not in fact fictitious, we do not know. As brothers of Seleucus' wife, they may have held higher offices in the Seleucid empire.

M33–35. Three sons of Chorienes (C 8.4.21 MSS. *cohortandus*, wrongly emended to *Oxyartes*) = Sisimithres; C 8.2.33 and *ME* 19 say Sisimithres had two sons. When Chorienes/Sisimithres surrendered to Alexander, he was required to give two of his three sons as hostages to serve in the Macedonian army (C 8.4.21). Different primary sources knew the man by different names, and it is likely that one attributed to him three sons, another only two.

M36. The king of the European Scythians; brother of Carthasis (C 7.7.1). He sent Carthasis to the Iaxartes to oppose Alexander (C 7.7.1ff.; *ME* 8; A 4.5.1). The king himself appears to have died shortly afterwards (cf. A 4.15.1).

M37. The leader of the Scythians who plundered the Macedonian baggage at Gaugamela (cf. C 4.15.12ff.); he was killed by Aretes (C 4.15.18).

M38. The champion of the Cadusians; he was killed in single combat in 341/0 (cf. Olmstead 488) by Darius III (D 17.6.1), and, on account of this, Darius was promoted to satrap of the Armenians by Artaxerxes III (J 10.3.3–4).

M39. Son of Azemilcus, king of Tyre, who was with the Persian fleet of Autophradates. He ruled in his father's place and came with an unspecified number of noble Tyrians to submit to Alexander, who was at that time approaching the city (A 2.15.6–7). When the Tyrians refused to admit Alexander into the city and were besieged by the Macedonians, Azemilcus was apparently recalled. Presumably, he was spared along with his father when the city was captured (A 2.24.5).

d. Prominent Macedonians and Greeks

M40. A son of Alexander the Great and Rhoxane; according to *ME* 70, he died at the Acesines River in 326. If this report is true, then it is likely that he died at birth; for no other extant source mentions him.

M41–42. Two sons of Lanice, the sister of Black Cleitus; they died in battle at Miletus in 334 (C 8.2.8; cf. A 4.9.4). Their father's name is unknown, though Carney 1981: 142ff. speculates that he may have been Andronicus.

M43–44. At least two brothers of Polydamas; they served as hostages while Polydamas went on his mission to secure the execution of Parmenion in 330 (C 7.2.13–14; Berve ii.323 prefers to read *filii* instead of *fratres* in Curtius). They may, of course, be fictitious, inserted by Curtius himself for dramatic effect.

M45. A Macedonian Royal Page; although burning incense fell onto his arm and seared his skin, he did not cry out with pain, lest he disturb Alexander's sacrifices (Val Max 3.3 ext 1).

M46. A Macedonian Royal Page, he placed a small table under Alexander's feet, when the latter sat on the throne of the Great King at Susa and could not touch the ground (C 5.2.13; D 17.66.3).

M47–48. At least two sons of Memnon the Rhodian; they fought in the battle at the Granicus River in 334 (A 1.15.2; thus born before 352). Nothing more is known about them.

e. Various *Anonymi*

M49. A Macedonian soldier, who, after Alexander's capture of Persepolis, was leading a mule laden with booty destined for the royal treasury. When the mule's strength gave out, the soldier shouldered the burden himself, and Alexander, upon observing the soldier's dedication, marveled and ordered him to keep carrying the load – right to the latter's own tent (*PA* 39.3).

M50. A common Macedonian soldier who, during the winter storm in Gazaba, warmed himself by the fire, having, unwittingly, seated himself on Alexander's chair; but he was not punished for the error (C 8.4.15–17; cf. Val Max 5.1 ext 1; Fr*Strat* 4.6.3). The episode, if it is not fictitious, served to illustrate how much better off the Macedonians were than the Persians in relation to their king. But the story is also strangely reminiscent of that concerning Dionysius of Mesene, the "Substitute King" (see s.v. **Dionysius** [3]).

M51. A Cretan soldier who delivered to Sisines a letter from Darius' chiliarch,

Nabarzanes (C 3.7.12). This turned out to be a test of Sisines' loyalty and led to his death (perhaps at the hands of the same Cretan; C 3.7.15). The story is told only by Curtius; it and the Cretan himself may very well be fictitious.

M52. An Indian from the town of the Mallians (Sudracae in Curtius), he gave Alexander a near-fatal wound; in the vulgate, he comes to close quarters in order to strike the final blow but is killed by Alexander himself (C 9.5.9–11; D 17.99.3; P*A* 63.6–8).

M53–54. Two Indians (Mallians) killed by Alexander in the engagement mentioned above (C 9.5.8).

M55. Arab soldier of Darius III, who tried to kill Alexander by treachery at the town of Gaza in 331. He was himself slain in the attempt (C 4.6.15–16).

M56–57. Two Arabs killed by Alexander with a dagger as they sat by their campfires. This occurred during the campaign against the Arabs of Anti-Lebanon, at the time when Alexander rescued his old tutor Lysimachus. P*A* 24.13 = Chares, *FGrH* 125 F7.

M58. A Mardian who, when captured by Parmenion's scouts, handed over to him a letter written to Alexander by the governor of Damascus (**M10** above); it contained an offer to betray the city to the Macedonians. The Mardian returned to Damascus with a Macedonian escort, which he eluded, however, as he approached the city (C 3.13.2–4). Nothing further is known about him, and he may have been inserted by Curtius for dramatic effect.

M59. Darius' charioteer in the battle of Gaugamela (331); he was allegedly killed by Alexander's javelin (D 17.60.2; cf. C 4.15.28). The charioteer may in fact have been killed but it is doubtful that his assailant was Alexander.

M60. An ambassador from Sparta, he was present when Alexander speared a lion and killed it with great difficulty; he remarked that Alexander had "fought nobly with the lion for the title of king" (P*A* 40.4). His identity is unknown, and Willrich's attempt (1899: 233) to identify him with Euthycles is rightly rejected by Berve ii.155 n. 1.

M61. An *epistoleus* ("letter-carrier") of Philoxenus (possibly Xenophilus), sent by him to Alexander in 331 to announce the surrender of Susa (A 3.16.6).

M62. A captive brought up by Polystratus, the Macedonian who found the dying Persian King, to translate for Darius (J 11.15.6). The situation itself is almost certainly fictitious, and the captive is brought into the scene for dramatic effect.

M63. A bilingual Lycian who acted as Alexander's guide at the Persian Gates (C 5.4.4, 10–13; 5.7.12; D 17.68.5; cf. P*A* 37.1). He was rewarded for his services with thirty talents (C 5.7.12; cf. Heckel 1980c: 172–4; Zahrnt 1999).

M64. Slave and personal treasurer of Harpalus. After his master's death on Crete, he fled to Rhodes, where he fell into the hands of Philoxenus the Macedonian, who had been sent by Alexander to deal with the Harpalus affair. He was interrogated by him and divulged the names of all who had accepted money from Harpalus, failing to name Demosthenes (Paus 2.33.4). The existence of this slave, and the details of his capture and his information, arouse suspicion – he was perhaps invented by someone (Demochares, for example) to exculpate Demosthenes.

M65. A slave of Seleucus; he ran off to Cilicia and was the object of a full-scale search (P*A* 42.1). We do not know if he was ever caught.

M66. A runaway slave who sought refuge from Megabyxus in a sanctuary in Asia

Minor. Alexander instructed Megabyxus not to violate the sanctity of the place by arresting him there. What became of him we do not know (P*A* 42.1).

M67–68. At least two good-looking slave boys whom Philoxenus wanted to buy for Alexander from Theodorus the Tarentine. Alexander, however, was greatly displeased by even the suggestion (P*A* 22.1–2; cf. Ath 1.22d). The boys were at the time in Ionia, according to P*M* 333a, where only one boy is mentioned.

M69. A captive eunuch; he reported to Alexander that Darius' wife, Stateira, was seriously ill and scarcely breathing. C 4.10.18 makes it clear that this eunuch was distinct from Tyriotes (Teireus), who brought the news of Stateira's death to Darius. (A 4.20.1–3 speaks of another eunuch who, shortly after the battle of Issus, brought Darius information about Alexander's treatment of the captive queens. This is a careless variation on the Teireos episode.)

M70. A captive eunuch of Darius III; he wept to see Alexander place his feet on Darius' table at Susa in 330 (cf. **M46** above; C 5.2.14; D 17.66.4–5).

M71. The eldest of the eighty priests of Amun-Re at Siwah; he addressed Alexander as the "son of Zeus" (C 4.7.25–8).

M72. A Phoenician sailor (thus Aristobulus, *FGrH* 139 F53) who, when Alexander's diadem was blown off his head while he was sailing on the marshes near Babylon, swam after it and recovered it. He placed the diadem on his head in order to keep it dry as he swam. For recovering the diadem, he was given a reward of one talent; but he was flogged (or, some said, executed) for tying the diadem around his head (A 7.22.3–5; this story was told by some about Seleucus: A 7.22.5; App*Syr* 56). In D 17.116.6 he is an oarsman of unspecified nationality.

M73–75. Three boys sacrificed, along with three girls and three rams, by the Taulantians before their battle with Alexander in 335. Their slaughtered bodies were found by the Macedonians when the Taulantians fled (A 1.5.7).

M76–77. Two men from among Alexander's camp-followers, who had become leaders of rival contingents engaged in a mock battle using clods of earth and stones; one took the name Alexander, the other that of Darius. Alexander, when he learned of this, arranged a *monomachia*, arming his namesake, while Philotas armed the one called Darius. The so-called Alexander prevailed, to the King's great pleasure (P*A* 31.2–5 = Eratosthenes, *FGrH* 241 F29).

M78. An unnamed boy, urged by his lover Charon of Chalcis to kiss Alexander at a banquet given in the home of Craterus (Carystius of Pergamum *ap.* Ath 13.603b).

M79. An Indian who had the greatest reputation for marksmanship. He had been taken prisoner by the Macedonians and, when ordered to demonstrate his art, had declined to do so. For this Alexander ordered his execution. But when the King learned that he had preferred execution because he had not practiced for some time and was afraid of falling short of his reputation, he set him free and rewarded him with gifts (P*M* 181b).

Notes

1 See also Heckel 1987a, 1987b, for 176 of them.

2 *PM* 340c wrongly makes him one of the Cinyradae and removes him to Paphos on Cyprus; D 17.46.6 mistakenly places him in Tyre.

3 The story has Near Eastern antecedents (so Drews 1974), but Bosworth 2003a: 182–3 believes that he may indeed have been engaged in gardening, though not in as humble a capacity as the Greek sources suggest.

4 See, for example, Schefold 1968; Stewart 294ff.

5 That is, the Kashmir; C 8.12.13; cf. *ME* 53; see also A*Ind* 4.12. But see now Bosworth ii.177, citing Stein 122–3; Eggermont 1970: 113–14, who identifies Abhisara with Hazara. Megasthenes (*FGrH* 715 F9 = A*Ind* 4.12) mentions the Abissarians, who are mountain-dwellers, in whose territory the Soanus, a tributary of the Indus, rises.

6 Arrian says he sent his own brother with some other envoys bringing money and forty elephants as gifts.

7 Onesicritus (*FGrH* 134 F16b = Ael*NA* 16.39) claimed that Abisares kept two snakes measuring 140 and 80 cubits respectively, and that Alexander was anxious to see them. Onesicritus had seen neither the snakes nor Abisares personally, but took his information from Abisares' ambassadors (*FGrH* 134 F16a = Str 15.1.28 [698]; cf. Brown 76, 95). Cf. also *FGrH* 134 F16c = Tzetz*Chil* 3.940–9.

8 Ps-Call 2.22.1 calls Adoulites (*sic*) an uncle of Darius, but there is nothing to support this claim; Ps-Call is, at any rate, speaking of Persia, not Susiana. The Abulites mentioned in Ctesias' *Persica* (Phot*Bibl* 72 p. 44b) as living in the reign of Artaxerxes II may have been a relative, possibly even his father. The name is Babylonian (hardly surprising since both Darius II and his sister-wife Parysatis were children of Babylonian concubines): see Briant 870; cf. 723–5.

9 Arrian or his source appears to have confused Philoxenus with Xenophilus (see Heckel 2002b and below s.v. **Xenophilus**).

10 His gifts included dromedaries and twelve elephants sent to Darius from India; D 17.65.5 and C 5.2.8 claim that Abulites surrendered in order to buy time for the Great King to mobilize another army by placing distractions in Alexander's path.

11 There is little agreement in the sources about the commanders of this garrison. A 3.16.9 names Mazarus, one of the *hetairoi*, as *phrourarchos* and Archelaus son of Theodorus as *strategos*. Curtius entrusts the city to Archelaus, the citadel to Xenophilus, and the treasury to Callicrates. Bosworth i.319 may be correct in identifying Mazarus with the Persian commandant, whom Xenophilus replaced.

12 Plutarch's anecdote about Alexander throwing the coins to the horses suggests that Abulites may have sent money instead of supplies. A 7.4.1 says only that Abulites was guilty of malfeasance; Badian 1961: 21 sees Abulites as a scapegoat for the Gedrosian disaster.

13 For the name see Justi 12; McCrindle 79 n. 3 suggests the Sanskrit form "Akubhi"; Eggermont links the name with OP Akaufaciya (= mountaineers).

14 The Nysaeans inhabited the area identified as Dionysopolis or *Nagarahara*, near Jalalabad: thus Eggermont 178; cf. McCrindle 338; cf. also Str 15.1.27 [698]; Pl*NH* 6.79; D 1.19.7; A*Ind* 5.9.

15 C 8.10.7–18 and J 12.7.6–8 describe Alexander's dealings with Nysa without reference to Acuphis.

16 Berve ii.11 calls Ada the fourth child of Hecatomnus, but this is far from certain. She was clearly not older than either Mausolus or Artemisia, who as the eldest children formed the first ruling couple; she could, however, have been older than Idrieus or younger than Pixodarus. We have no way of knowing. All that is certain is that Pixodarus was the youngest of the three sons (D 16.74.2; implied also by Str 14.2.17 [656]). If the children were all born to the same mother, a series of births in the 390s seems more likely. The use of the word *gynaion* (D 17.24.2), in this case a term of endearment (cf. Hamilton 57), may also suggest that in 334 Ada was an elderly lady. She appears to have ruled jointly with Idrieus between 351/0 and 344/3: a Milesian dedication of statues of the pair at Delphi (Tod, no. 161B; cf. 161A) probably dates to the last years of their reign (certainly after the end of the Sacred War in 346: thus Tod ii.181). An inscription at Tegea (Tod, no. 161A) identifies Zeus, flanked by Ada and Idrieus, shown in relief below the inscribed names. The relief depicts the two rulers worshipping Zeus Stratius of Labraunda (photo in Roscher, *Lexikon* iv. 1548; Cook ii.503).

17 Brunt i.99 translates γαμβρός in A 1.23.8 as "brother-in-law," but the word refers simply to someone related by marriage and should here be translated as "son-in-law."

18 J 14.5.10 says she and Philip III were both put to death on Olympias' orders, which is, generally speaking, correct, since Olympias forced Adea to commit suicide.

19 For the possibility that Adea-Eurydice and Philip III Arrhidaeus were the occupants of Tomb II at Vergina (Aegae) see Adams 1980; Lehmann 1980, 1982; that it is too late for Philip II is argued by Borza 1987, reiterated in 1999: 69–70; Palagia 2000. Borza 1990: 266 suggests that "Tomb 1 belongs to Philip II, his queen, Cleopatra, and their infant; Tomb 2 belongs to Philip III Arrhidaeus and his queen, Eurydice, and contains as well some of the royal paraphernalia of Alexander the Great; and Tomb 3 belongs to Alexander IV, the last of the Argeadae."

20 Hammond, *HMac* ii.15 n. 3 believes that it is "unlikely on chronological grounds and on the succession of the name, normally from grandfather" that Arrhabaeus II (father of Aëropus) was the son rather than grandson of Arrhabaeus I. The second point is easily dismissed – the operative word in Hammond's sentence is *normally* – and the chronological problems are, in fact, alleviated, especially if Arrhabaeus son of Aëropus was the father of Amyntas and Neoptolemus. Polyaenus' Aëropus could have been born ca. 400 (hence about 62 years old in 338). Arrhabaeus, as father of Amyntas and Neoptolemus, could not have been born much later than 380 and thus in his early forties at the time of his execution.

21 Aeschines' birthdate is based on his own remark at Aes 1.49. For a full discussion of this and related problems see Harris 1988.

22 For details of his family background see Davies 544–7. The family was, however, undistinguished. Dem 18.312–15 compares his career with that of Aeschines, with many unflattering revelations about the latter: he says that Aeschines' mother conducted Phrygian Dionysiac rites, and that Aeschines was with her, that he joined in the Dionysiac march, that he gave out the Bacchic cry! Demosthenes also accused Aeschines of having worked as an actor (cf. Quint 2.17.12) and then as assistant of his father who was a school teacher, *grammatodidaskalos*. See [P]*M* 840a–b; Str 10.3.18 [471], and also

Dem 19.199, 249, 281. For the details of his career as anactor, together with *testimonia*, see O'Connor 74–7, no. 15.

23 A brief life is given by [Plutarch] *Lives of the Ten Orators* 7 = [P]*M* 840a–841a. Full discussion in Harris; see also the introduction in C. D. Adams' Loeb edition of *The Speeches of Aeschines*, no. 106. On Aeschines as an orator see Quint 10.1.77; 11.3.168; 12.10.19, 23.

24 Knaak, *RE* s.v. "Aischrion (7)" identifies him with Aeschrion of Samos (on whom see Ath 7.296f, 8.335c–d), which appears to be ruled out by his Mytilenaean origin.

25 Berve ii.17 cites Ps-Call 2.21 as saying that a certain Aeschylus established the temple of Alexander in Alexandria and served as Alexander's first priest. Kroll's text of Pseudo-Callisthenes A, however, gives the name as Moschylus (*Μόσχυλος*).

26 The story itself is suspect, and there may be some confusion of the popular, but equally fictitious, report that Lysimachus (son of Agathocles!) was exposed to a lion because he pitied Callisthenes and gave him poison (J 15.3.6ff.); furthermore, the "grave" referred to was most likely the lion monument at Ecbatana (on which see Luschey 1968). For the importance of the passage to our understanding of the cults of Hephaestion and Alexander see Habicht[2] 30–3.

27 Including the Paeonians, the Thracian horse numbered 900 (D 17.17.4). Hammond 1980: 83 estimates that Agathon's squadron numbered about 150, assuming that the Thracians were divided into six squadrons of 150. Of the remaining units, the Paeonian *prodromoi* (150 strong) were commanded by Ariston and four squadrons of Lancers were under the lead of Amyntas son of Arrhabaeus. But Berve i.134 thinks that the Thracians were heavily armed horsemen (or at least "mittelschwer gerüstet"), and that some 700 were under Agathon's command, the majority of them Odrysians. Marsden 1964: 71–3 thinks the Odrysian cavalry unit was formed only after Asclepiodorus son of Eunicus brought 500 Thracians as reinforcements to Memphis; Marsden thinks they were 342 strong, counting 171 as the strength of a squadron.

28 D 17.3.4–5 confuses the activities of the Arcadians and Lacedaemonians.

29 8,000 is, however, the number of mercenaries who escaped to Cyprus and eventually to Egypt (A 2.13.2–3), and it is possible that there is some confusion here. D 17.48.2 and C 4.1.27 mention only 4,000 mercenaries who went with Amyntas to Egypt.

30 The names Alcetas and Perdiccas are both attested in the Argead house (Hdt 8.139).

31 C 8.11.1 assigns its capture to Polyperchon.

32 *IG* ii^2.391 records honors for Alcimachus son of Alcimachus of Apollonia, granting him similar honor to those held by his father. If this is the grandson of Agathocles, then our Alcimachus may have been granted property in Apollonia by Philip II (cf. similar grants to Polemocrates, father of Coenus, and the sons of Larichus and Androtimus). Alcimachus would then also have been the father of Lys[ip]pus who is honored as *proxenos* at Ios (*IG* xii.5.1001). See Tataki 66; Osborne ii.102–3 (Alcimachus son of Alcimachus); Tataki 360 (Lysippus).

33 If the name appears as *Ἀλκίμαχον* (accusative), then we are dealing with a local Chian, who is a *philos* of Alexander; if the name is *Ἀλκίμαχος* (nominative), it is the subject of a third person imperative and refers to a Macedonian official (probably the son of Agathocles). Forrest 1969: 204–5, followed by Bosworth i.134, assumes that Alcimachus is a Chian, but Heisserer 106 reads a *sigma* and notes that the earliest editors did as well. Professor Bosworth in private correspondence suggests to me that the tone of the inscription is rather harsh (if we accept the nominative and restored third person imperative), which is certainly true; Alexander may, nevertheless, have been genuinely displeased with Alcimachus' behavior and it is worth noting that Alcimachus is not mentioned again in the Alexander historians.

34 Fr*Strat* 3.4.5 appears to refer to Alexander II, the son of Pyrrhus, who reigned in the 260s.
35 Alexander's departure is generally synchronized with that of his namesake for the East (Gell 17.21.33; J 12.2.1–15). It is likely to have occurred in 334/3, if not in the spring of 334. Certainly, Tauriscus, who had fled with Harpalus before the battle of Issus (late 333), was sent by him to Alexander I and found him in Italy (A 3.6.7).
36 Possibly a corruption of Pandosia. His death is described at length by Livy, who dates it in the same year as the foundation of Alexandria in Egypt (8.24.1, but Livy misdates both events to 326; cf. 8.3.6 where he misdates Alexander's crossing into Italy to 340).
37 If there is any truth that Bruttian, Lucanian, and Etruscan envoys came to Babylon in 323 (A 7.15.4), it may be on account of Alexander I's activities in Italy.
38 The suggestion of Schoder 1982, that Alexander IV and Rhoxane are depicted on the Boscoreale Murals, is supported by no good evidence and is speculation at best. The figure identified as Alexander IV is almost certainly female.
39 For the marriage of Alexander Lyncestes and his descendants see Habicht 1977b; cf. Heckel 1989: 32–3, 37.
40 The King's *consilium* may have expressed doubts about Alexander's suitability at the time, but A 1.25.5 could refer to a retrospective judgment.
41 It is tempting to see in the name Alexander a personification of the "rape of Thebes" by the Macedonians. But it is unlikely that Aristobulus, who was an apologist for the King, would have been the source of such an unflattering depiction.
42 Polyaenus wrongly makes her the mother of Alexander, who was in all probability the son of an Odrysian concubine (Paus 1.10.5). Amastris is accepted as Alexander's mother by Brosius 78 n. 70. Burstein 141–2 n. 17 believes that Lysimachus could have had more than one son named Alexander; but it is surely significant that Lysimachus did not pursue any claims to Heraclea Pontica that Alexander might have been able to make on the basis of his maternity.
43 See also StByz s.v. "Amastris"; Scymnus 962ff. Cf. Scholia to Apollonius, *Argonautica* 2.941–2.
44 I do not see why the evidence of Diodorus, which represents little more than a brief notice, should be preferred to the combined testimony of Justin-Trogus and Satyrus. Furthermore, regencies in Macedonia were frequent (Ptolemy of Alorus had been regent for Perdiccas III, and Antigonus Doson for Philip V, though it is significant that in both cases the regent died, and thus allowed the legitimate king to ascend the throne).
45 For full discussion see Ellis 1971; Errington 1974; Prandi; Worthington 2003.
46 D 17.25.5 puts Neoptolemus on the Macedonian side, and this is accepted by Welles 188 n. 1.
47 Berve's no. 62 comes to mind, though even he must be ruled out if the correct form of the man's name is actually Anemoetas (Dem 18.295).
48 This was normally Parmenion's role, but he had been left behind and would not rejoin the King until spring 333.
49 The battle of Sagalassus occurred after the arrest of Lyncestian Alexander (cf. A 1.25), unless Diodorus' claim that Alexander was arrested shortly before the battle of Issus (D 17.32.1–2; cf. C 7.1.6) is to be taken seriously. The arrest was, however, conducted in secret (A 1.25.9–10), and probably not revealed to Alexander's troops until all detachments reunited at Gordium. With the apparent treason of Alexander, Amyntas' presence became dangerous and his removal a necessity (cf. Heckel 1986b: 299, with n. 22).
50 Amyntas appears to have been overzealous in executing his orders: Gorgias, Gorgatas, and Hecataeus, young men who had found favor with Olympias in Pella, were impressed, against the queen mother's wishes, to serve in Asia, perhaps amongst the fifty Pages who accompanied Amyntas to Susiana (C 7.1.38). D 17.65.1 speaks of Trallians and numbers the

Peloponnesian horse at just under a thousand.

51 C 6.7.15 actually includes a certain Amyntas in the list of conspirators, but it appears that the charges brought against the son of Andromenes afterwards caused his name to be included (mistakenly) in Curtius' list (Badian 1960a: 334 n. 30; Heckel 1975: 394–5).

52 Bosworth i.74 rejects the identification with Anemoetas and argues that Amyntas and Timolaus were "two members of the Macedonian garrison, captured in the lower city during the outbreak of the revolt." A 1.7.1–2, however, indicates that the incitement to rebellion occurred after the murder, and it appears that the victims were deliberately chosen because of their importance; one wonders how Arrian's source would have known, or why he might have preserved, the names of two insignificant members of the garrison who had the misfortune of being caught off guard. One recalls the liberation of Thebes in 379/8, when the leaders of the pro-Spartan party were deliberately targeted.

53 Bosworth i.148–9, suggests that Curtius has confused matters somewhat and that the victors in this contest did not become chiliarchs but rather pentakosiarchs. This argument has a certain attraction, especially since Arrian (4.30.6; 5.23.7) seems to imply that there were at least four chiliarchies of hypaspists; but it must be noted that Curtius does not say that the troops in question *are* hypaspists.

54 Alexander was supposed to have ordered his financial officer to give Anaxarchus as much money as he asked for: he demanded and received 100 talents (P*M* 179f; but in other versions, Alexander's monetary rewards go to Xenocrates, with Anaxarchus receiving only honor: P*A* 8.5; P*M* 331e, though perhaps the text is corrupt, cf. DL 9.60; cf. P*M* 181e). Anaxarchus' reference to Alexander's blood as "ichor of the blessed gods" (DL 9.59) is told elsewhere of Dioxippus (Aristobulus, *FGrH* 139 F47 = Ath 6.251a; cf. P*A* 28.3 for the story in general). On the other hand, Anaxarchus is said to have mocked Alexander's pretensions to divinity (Ael*VH* 9.37). According to Val Max 8.14 ext 2 (cf. P*M* 466d), Alexander, hearing from Anaxarchus that the philosophers believed in numerous worlds, lamented that he had not yet conquered one. In another account he is critical of excessive luxury (P*A* 28.5).

55 Anaximenes was said to have authored a pamphlet abusing the Athenians, Spartans, and Thebans, which he wrote in the style of Theopompus and published under his name. Although the truth became known, the publication created great hostility toward Theopompus (Paus 6.18.5; *Suda* A 1989).

56 The Lampsacenes had sent an envoy to Anaximenes asking him to intervene on their behalf with Alexander. The King replied that he would do the opposite of what Anaximenes asked him. Hence Anaximenes requested that the women and children of Lampsacus be enslaved, their city razed, and the sanctuaries of the gods burned. That Alexander allowed himself to be fooled by such a transparent ploy is hard to believe. The story also suggests that Anaximenes was the benefactor of his state just as Aristotle persuaded Philip II to refound Stageira.

57 Theophr*HP* 4.16.6 says that Androcydes recommended the use of cabbage to counteract the effects of wine (cf. Pl*NH* 17.240).

58 Carney 1981: 157 suggests that he commanded 1,500 mercenaries sent against Spitamenes in 329, but their commander was clearly Menedemus. Andromachus commanded sixty Companions, Caranus the 800 mercenary cavalry; Pharnouches (a Lycian) led the expedition (A 4.3.7). That leaves Menedemus in charge of the infantry, a point which may explain his prominence in the vulgate (C 7.6.24; 7.7.31ff., 39; 7.9.21; cf. *ME* 13). I do not see how Menedemus could be an error for Andronicus; but Curtius (7.6.24) does give Menedemus 3,000 infantry, in addition to 800 cavalry, and it is remotely possible that Andronicus served

under him. Carney 157–8, furthermore, argues that the poem (composed by Pranichus or Pierion) which angered Cleitus and provoked the quarrel with Alexander (P*A* 50.8) dealt with the Polytimetus engagement, in which Cleitus' brother-in-law was (by her theory) killed. Certainly the identification of Proteas as "son of Lanice" creates the impression that his father was already dead in the final years of Alexander's life (Ath 4.129a; Ael*VH* 12.26). That Proteas forgave Alexander for his murder of Cleitus is not unreasonable; despite the apologetic tone of most sources, there is no reason to suppose that Alexander faked his grief. But, it is less likely that Proteas would have remained on intimate terms with a king who condoned the ridiculing of his father; and, indeed, it was not Cleitus but other older Macedonians who first found the poem objectionable. If Andronicus son of Agerrus did perish in the Polytimetus (Zeravshan) fiasco, this episode will not have been the subject of Pranichus' (Pierion's) composition.

59 The names of Mazaeus' sons present a virtually insoluble problem: if Antibelus is identical with Artiboles, then it may be that Arrian has simply misspelled the name in one passage. But since Curtius gives the name of the man who surrended to Alexander as Brochubelus, we would be forced to conclude that (1) Curtius is right about the identity of the son who surrendered to Alexander in 330 and that Arrian not only gave the wrong name but also supplied an incorrect form of the name of the other son as well; or (2) Curtius is wrong about the name of the son who surrendered in 330 and that Arrian also gave the wrong name of Mazaeus' son on one occasion; or (3) there were in fact three sons of Mazaeus – Antibelus, Artiboles, and Brochubelus – and that Brochubelus and Antibelus both surrendered to Alexander in 330, with Curtius naming the former and Arrian the latter. The neatest solution is to assume that the name of the son who surrendered in 330 ended in -belus (either form could be correct) and that Artiboles is a different son altogether.

60 Neither Tauron nor Seleucus was a commander of *pezhetairoi*. General command of those *pezhetairoi* who crossed the Hydaspes with Alexander may have been entrusted to Coenus.

61 Antigenes was certainly old enough and due for retirement. If the Argyraspids are correctly regarded as superannuated hypaspists, we should expect them to be among the 10,000 discharged veterans. And, indeed, Alexander had replaced them with a Persian battalion of Silver Shields (A 7.11.3; cf. J 12.12.3–4).

62 Schachermeyr 1970: 14 n. 10 suggests that Craterus left Antigenes and the 3,000 Argyraspids in Cilicia and, after his death, Antipater picked them up and led them to Syria, whence they were sent in due course to Susiane (320 BC). But Antigenes and the Argyraspids were already in Perdiccas' camp when he invaded Egypt, and Perdiccas' assassination occurred before Craterus' death was known (D 18.37.1; but see 18.33.1, with Hornblower 1981: 51; cf. Errington 1970: 66 n. 127). Furthermore, Antipater arrived in Syria *after* Peithon and Arrhidaeus led the defeated army from Egypt to Triparadeisus (D 18.39.1; cf. A*Succ* 1.30). Thus, Antigenes must have left Cilicia with Perdiccas when he invaded Egypt. It follows that Craterus, when he departed for Macedonia, left behind some of his troops with Cleitus, who took the fleet into the Aegean, and 3,000 Argyraspids under Antigenes. Craterus augmented his army with new recruits, as is clear from Diodorus (18.16.4; cf. Heckel 1982c: 61; Hammond 1989: 65 n. 49, against Brunt ii.489). Hammond, however, thinks the 4,000 veterans left in Cilicia served with Neoptolemus and then Eumenes (1984: 56–7; reiterated in 1989: 65); this is highly improbable.

63 When it was learned that Antigonus was in Media, Antigenes and Eumenes shared the opinion that the army should move back to the coast. But this was rejected by the satraps of central Asia (D 19.21.1).

64 P*Eum* 16.2 claims that, after Paraetacene, Antigenes and Teutamus plotted against Eumenes, but this is inconsistent with the other evidence and can be ascribed either to the tendency to lump the commanders of the Argyraspids together or to a source hostile to Antigenes himself.

65 Antigenes may have had some principles. He plotted against Perdiccas because, like the other generals of note, he had become disillusioned with an arrogant leader (cf. J 13.8.2; D 18.33.3, 5; 18.36.1). In the case of Eumenes, it appears that he remained faithful to him: P*Eum* 17.1–2 makes it clear that Teutamus and his followers led the betrayal. Pol*Strat* 4.6.15 says that Antigonus rewarded Eumenes' captors with gifts, though he punished a large number of the Silver Shields. Clearly, the Argyraspids and their commanders were divided on the matter of Eumenes. Hence, Antigenes was cruelly executed, and Teutamus was apparently rewarded by Antigonus. Antigenes had prevented Teutamus from defecting in Cilicia in 318 (D 18.62.4–7). Antigenes willingly obeyed the orders of Polyperchon the regent (D 18.58.1), allied himself with Eumenes (18.59.3), and resisted the embassies of Ptolemy (D 18.62.1–2), Antigonus (through the agency of Philotas, D 18.62.4–7), and Seleucus and Peithon (D 19.12.2–3, 13.1). Hieronymus would not have praised Antigenes as he does (D 18.62.6), had he regarded him as a traitor.

66 Oikonomides 1989 suggests that the bust of an old one-eyed man in the Ny Carlsberg Glyptothek, I. N. 212, may be Antigonus the One-Eyed. Billows 8 follows Charbonneaux 1952: 219ff. in identifying Antigonus with one of the horsemen, shown (significantly?) in profile (cf. Pl*NH* 35.90; Pollitt 161), on the Alexander Sarcophagus. Apart from the fact that the sarcophagus could be as early as the mid-320s, it should be noted that the battlescene depicts, in all likelihood, the battle of Issus, or perhaps Gaugamela; Antigonus participated in neither of these. Antigonus was also painted by Protogenes (Pl*NH* 35.106; Pollitt 173). Smith 1988 cautiously avoids identifying any surviving portrait as Antigonus I.

67 C 4.5.13 merely elucidates the more compressed observation at 4.1.35. I do not believe that Antigonus won three successives battles before his victory in Lycaonia. Nor am I inclined to accept the view that "Lydia" in C 4.1.35 is anything more than an error on Curtius' part. That Antigonus assumed "overall command in Asia Minor," as Billows 44 n. 80 suggests, can be neither proved nor disproved. In Balacrus' absence, Alexander assigned the military responsibilities in Cilicia to Socrates (apparently the son of Sathon, C 4.5.9).

68 Greater Phrygia, Lycaonia, Pamphylia, and Lycia.

69 Ps-Call 3.19 mentions a hypaspist named Antigonus in the (fictitious) Candace episode (see Berve ii.415 no. 9).

70 The meaning of ἡμιόδιος γενόμενος is unclear. Berve ii.44 n. 2 assumes that it is the title of Antimenes' position as Harpalus' successor.

71 Beloch (iv^2 2.125) regards Antipater as coeval with Philip II, pointing to the relative youth of Cassander, Antipater's eldest attested son. But Antipater would scarcely have been described in a letter of Demades as "an old and rotten thread" (A*Succ* 1.14; P*Dem* 31.5; P*Ph* 30.9) if he had not been well advanced in age in 323/2.

72 *Alexarchus.* Son of Antipater (Str 7, frg 35) and younger brother of Cassander (Ath 3.98d), Alexarchus was born after 350 BC and appears to have remained in Macedonia with his father when Alexander crossed into Asia. His dubious claim to fame was based upon his founding of the city of Uranopolis on Mt. Athos – its circuit was thirty stades (Str 7, frg 35; cf. Pl*NH* 4.37–8) – and his use of elaborate names for simple objects (Ath 3.98d–f). His written work bordered on the incomprehensible. See Berve ii.21 no. 41; Hoffmann 266–8.

73 For Antipater's friendship with Phocion see P*Ph* 26.4–6; 30.3; P*M* 142c–d; cf. 64c; 188f; 533d; P*Agis* 2.2.

74 Cf. Pol*Strat* 4.2.8: a doublet assigning the same ruse to a different context.

75 J 9.4.5; Harpocration s.v. "Alkimachos" = Hyp frag. 19.2.

76 The Spartan alliance now included Elis, Achaea (except for Pellene), and all the Arcadians except Megalopolis (Aes 3.165; Din 1.34; cf. C 6.1.20; cf. also [Dem] 17.7.10; Paus 7.27.7; see also McQueen 1978).

77 D 17.62.5ff. Pol*Strat* 4.4.1 may refer to this campaign, but appears to belong to 347/6; cf. StByz s.v. "Tetrachoriatai."

78 The Spartans, for their part, were forced to send ambassadors to Alexander to beg his forgiveness (Aes 3.133; D 17.73.5–6; C 6.1.20), and it is clear that Antipater was not prepared to make a decision on their future without Alexander's approval. See also s.v. **Eteocles**.

79 J 13.4.5; D 18.3.2; cf. 18.12.1; A*Succ* 1.3. To the areas administered by Antipater were added the lands of the Thracians, Illyrians, Triballians, and Agrianes, as well as Epirus (A*Succ* 1.7; Dexippus, *FGrH* 100 F8 §3; see Kanatsulis 1968: 121 for the view that Antipater was *archon* of Thessaly). Lysimachus, the *strategos* of Thrace, was clearly subject to Antipater's authority.

80 Nicaea was betrothed to Perdiccas, to whose camp she was escorted by Iollas and Archias (A*Succ.* 1.21); later Nicaea married Lysimachus (Str 12.4.7 [565]); Phila married Craterus, who rejected Amastris in her favor (Memnon *FGrH* 434 F4 §4).

81 A fleet of forty quadriremes and 200 triremes was commissioned (D 18.10.2; cf. J 13.5.8) and eventually much of Greece joined the Hellenic War against Macedon. For the members of the anti-Macedonian alliance see D 18.11.1–2; Paus 1.25.3–4; Arcadia remained neutral: Paus 8.6.2; 8.27.10.

82 See also [P]*M* 846d–e; Hyp 6.12; J 13.5.8 has Antipater shut up in Heraclea. The Hellenic War became better known as the Lamian War (see Ashton 1984).

83 In spring 322, Leonnatus brought his satrapal army (spring 322) and enlisted additional troops in Macedonia, finally moving into Thessaly with over 20,000 infantry and 1,500 cavalry (D 18.14.5).

84 In numbers of infantry the armies were roughly equal – the Athenians had some 22,000, for the Aetolians had left previously to deal with some local matter (18.13.4) and were still absent – but in cavalry the Greeks excelled: 2,000 of their total 3,500 were Thessalians under the command of Menon (D 18.15.2, 4).

85 P*Ph* 27–8, 30; P*Dem* 28.1; D 18.18.5; P*M* 188f; cf. Paus 7.10.1; D 20.46.3. The *phrourarchos* was Menyllus (D 18.18.5; P*Ph* 28.1), apparently a Macedonian and friend of Phocion (P*Ph* 18.1), who had served Antipater during Alexander's absence. He ensured that the garrison in no way harmed individual Athenians (P*Ph* 28.7), but is said to have offered Phocion money, which the Athenian declined, as he had earlier rejected an offer from Alexander (P*Ph* 30.1–2). He was replaced after Antipater's death in 319 by Nicanor (P*Ph* 31.1). See Berve ii.259 no. 513.

86 Demosthenes, Hypereides, Himeraeus (brother of Demetrius of Phalerum), and Aristonicus; see also s.v. **Archias** [2]. See also A*Succ* 1.13; P*Ph* 27ff.; P*Dem* 28–9; [P]*M* 849b–c; Paus 1.8.3; 1.25.5; *Suda* A 2704, Δ 456; N*Ph* 2.2; cf. P*Dem* 29–30; [P]*M* 846e–847b; Ath 12.542e.

87 Philoxenus had been appointed by Perdiccas in place of Philotas, who was well disposed toward Craterus. The fact that Philoxenus retained his satrapy at Triparadeisus suggests that he abandoned the Perdiccan cause, probably after receiving news of the defeat in Egypt.

88 The embassy of Demades, who requested that Antipater remove Menyllus' garrison from Munychia, helps to date Antipater's death. The old man was mortally ill when Demades reached him, but the latter did not leave Athens before the end of June 319 (as is clear from *IG* II.[2] 383b); cf. P*Ph* 30.4–6; P*Dem* 31.4–6.

89 Curtius writes Antipater and Asclepiodorus (*Antipatrum Asclepiodorumque*) instead of Antipater son of Asclepiodorus.

90 The garrison commander of Telmissus (Termissus), which Nearchus captured by trickery (Pol*Strat* 5.35).

91 For Antiphilus see also Theon, *Progymnasmata* 1.3; Varro, *de Re rustica* 2.2.

92 Malalas 8.198 Bonn, where her father is called "Pithamenes" and described as Parthian; Str 12.8.15 [578] confuses her with the daughter of Artabazus; Porph Tyr *ap.* Euseb Arm = *FGrH* 260 F32 §5 calls her "Persian" – which may mean that she and her father Spitamenes were of Achaemenid descent (cf. Tarn 1929) – and adds that her son Antiochus was 64 years old at the time of his death and thus conceived very soon after the marriage was consummated in 324. Livy 38.13.5 wrongly calls her Seleucus' sister, perhaps confused by the later Seleucid practice of calling the king's wife his "sister": cf. Macurdy 77).

93 Eggermont 184, arguing for a linguistic connection between the name Aphrices and the territory Udyana (also called Aurdayana), sees Aphrices as the tribal chieftain named by the Greek historians for the place he ruled. But see further Goukowsky 241–2; Benveniste 1966; Litvinsky 1968: 134–5.

94 Hedicke in his edition of Curtius emends the name to *Aphtonius*; "der . . . Name ist sicher verderbt," Hoffmann 180.

95 Perhaps the text of C 5.1.43 should read *regioni Babyloniae ac Cilici<a tenus Mesopotami>ae*; Shackleton-Bailey 1981: 176; cf. D 17.64.5.

96 Engel 1971: 229–30 believes that Diodorus and Plutarch disagree on the fate of Apollonides, the former claiming that he made good his escape to Antigonus, the latter saying that Eumenes, although he had turned in flight, nevertheless arrested and crucified the traitor (P*Eum* 9.3). But Plutarch, as Bosworth 1992: 87 n. 119 recognizes, clearly refers to an earlier incident, in which a certain Perdiccas had betrayed Eumenes, only to be captured by Phoenix of Tenedos and executed in Eumenes' camp (D 18.40.2–4). Nevertheless, the words *ἡττηθεὶς ὑπ' Ἀντιγόνου διὰ προδοσίαν καὶ διωκόμενος* show that Plutarch too has conflated the Perdiccas and Apollonides episodes.

97 It is hard to imagine how Apollophanes, who had been left behind in Ora, could have been deposed at Pura. Those who were charged with neglect of duty had failed to supply the King during his Gedrosian march (for example, Astaspes, Abulites, and Oxyathres). A 6.27.1 appears to have garbled the account of the appointment of Thoas as satrap of Gedrosia, to replace the deceased Apollophanes, and the subsequent removal of Astaspes from Carmania (cf. C 9.10.21, 29). I do not see how Badian 1961: 17, with n. 6, can have Apollophanes both "deposed" and "killed in action," but this seems also to be the view of Seibert 1985: 177: "Möglicherweise haben sich beide Vorfälle zeitlich überlagert."

98 His disappearance may be attributed to his support for Perdiccas. On the other hand, he may, like Archon in Babylon, have been removed by Docimus (A*Succ* 24.3–5).

99 Androsthenes and Hieron of Soli also made unsuccessful attempts at rounding Arabia.

100 Archon's horses had been victorious at the Pythian and Isthmian games (Rhodes & Osborne no. 92, block a §ii).

101 Krüger, followed by Roos/Wirth in the Teubner edition, reads *Ἀρέτην* instead of *Ἀρέτιν* in A 1.15.6.

102 C 7.11.1 says, implausibly, that he had a force of 30,000 and supplies to maintain them for two years.

103 Bosworth ii.131 attempts to reconcile the two versions and suggests that Rhoxane "may have been in Alexander's entourage for several months before the King noticed and married her." This strikes me as implausible because C 7.11.28–9 makes it clear that the leaders associated with Ariamazes (which ought to have included Oxyartes, if his daughter was being kept on the Rock of Sogdiana) were whipped and executed, adding that the captives were sold into

slavery. Oxyartes later acted as a liaison between Alexander and Sisimithres and he may have been induced to do so because his family had taken refuge on Sisimithres' rock.

104 Whether he is the Ariaces who led the Cappadocians at Gaugamela (A 3.8.5) is uncertain.

105 Perhaps also the father of Mithridates (D 19.40.2).

106 The MSS. read Alexander, but this must be an error for Aristander, unless ὁ μὲν θύτης Ἀλέξανδρος should read ὁ μὲν θύτης Ἀλεξάνδρου.

107 The painting was said to have been sold for ten minae per human figure to Mnason, the tyrant of Elatea.

108 Aes 3.162 says this Aristobulus was an apothecary (φαρμακοπώλης).

109 Pearson 151 summarizes the evidence for the possibility that Aristobulus was a Phocian. An inscription from Delphi (*Fouilles de Delphes* III 3, 207; discussed by Pearson 151–2) mentions a certain Sophocles son of Aristobulus, "a Phocian living in Cassandreia." The inscription belongs to the mid-third century (between 263 and 260 or 252/1). The relationship of Sophocles to the historian cannot be proved, but it is at least not impossible chronologically.

110 Tarn ii.42–3 suggests that Aristobulus wrote between 294 and 288, thus placing his birthdate ca. 378, but Tarn wishes to place Aristobulus' *History* before Ptolemy's, and Ptolemy's before that of Cleitarchus in order to discredit Cleitarchus as late and unreliable.

111 Lucian (*How to Write History* 12) claims that Aristobulus depicted Alexander in hand-to-hand combat with Porus and that, when he read the account to the King as they sailed down the Hydaspes, Alexander grabbed the text and threw it overboard, saying that Aristobulus deserved the same treatment. *FGrH* 139 F62 (= A 7.29.4) asserts that Alexander drank to be sociable rather than for love of wine. Aristobulus also placed the blame for Cleitus' death on the victim himself (F29 = A 4.8.9) and claimed that the Pages themselves asserted that Callisthenes had instigated the Hermolaus conspiracy (F31 = A 4.14.1), adding also that Callisthenes died a natural death, albeit in chains (F33 = A 4.14.3).

112 Berve ii.307 no. 611 includes Patraus in his prosopography. I see no personal connection between Patraus and Alexander, apart from his contribution of Paeonian *prodromoi* to Alexander's campaign.

113 See also Atkinson i.384 (cf. Marsden 1964: 31 n. 4), who suggests that Curtius may have misplaced the episode. Unless there really was an earlier engagement at the Tigris, Ariston's *aristeia* may have occurred about three days later, when the Macedonian army encountered some 1,000 stragglers (C 4.10.9–11; cf. A 3.7.7–8.2). Certainly, it is more likely that Alexander should send a single *ile* of Paeonians against them than against a cavalry force of 1,000. It does, however, make Ariston's victory somewhat less heroic. Marsden 1964: 31 goes further and suggests that "he was hauled over the coals by Alexander afterwards" for killing Satropates, who might have given the Macedonians valuable information about enemy numbers and deployments.

114 C 4.5.15, 17 names also a certain Athenagoras.

115 Little is known about his background, but he was an Athenian trierarch and is thus described by Schaefer iii^2 136 n. 1 as "ein wohlhabender Mann."

116 According to Timaeus (codd. Timotheus), Aristotle had a son by Herpyllis, his concubine, whose name was Nicomachus (DL 5.1).

117 Strabo's claim that Hermias was a student of Plato is contradicted by Plato's *Sixth Letter*, although this itself may not be genuine.

118 Against the view that Aristotle's failure to secure the position was caused by his philosophical disagreements with Plato see Guthrie 24–6. The claim (DL 5.2) that he left the Academy before Plato's death and was absent as an Athenian ambassador at Philip's court when Xenocrates

became its head may be an attempt to explain away Aristotle's "failure." DL 5.3 makes it clear that there was some bitterness over Xenocrates' appointment.

119 According to DL Aristotle made the appeal in Pella, and Hamilton 17 suggests plausibly that Alexander may have "interceded with Philip" on Aristotle's behalf. P*A* 7.3 says that the restoration of Stageira was Philip's payment for the education of Alexander. For the various accounts of the restoration see P*M* 1097b, 1126f; Ael*VH* 3.17, 12.54; Dio Chr 2.79; 47.9; Val Max 5.6 ext 5; Pl*NH* 7.109; Tzetz*Chil* 7.140, 441–5.

120 A friendship between Aristotle and Antipater is attested (Paus 6.4.8; DL 5.11, who says that, in the absence of Nicanor, Antipater was to be executor of Aristotle's will; cf. P*A* 74.5) and it is possible that their relationship became closer as that between Aristotle and Alexander deteriorated. DL 5.27 mentions nine books of letters to Antipater. There are also letters to Hephaestion and Olympias from Aristotle, but only one book each.

121 The identification is rejected by Bosworth i.109, 145.

122 Pol*Strat* 4.2.3 speaks of a commander (*hegemon*) in Philip's army named Aëropus who was banished for bringing a female harpist into camp during the Theban campaign (338 BC). If it were possible to identify him with the father of Arrhabaeus and Heromenes, then we might have a motive for their enmity toward Philip and Alexander.

123 Thus Jacoby, *FGrH* iiD, "Kommentar," 563; but Bosworth 2002: 113, with n. 60, accepts Amphimachus as a son of Philine. Arrian, in his *History of the Successors* (*Τὰ μετὰ Ἀλέξανδρον*), appears to have used both Hieronymus and Duris, a combination of sources used also by Trogus (or an intermediary source used by Trogus). I believe that the confusion of Arrhidaeus the satrap with Philip III goes back to Duris (cf. J 13.4.6).

124 Curtius' account of the proceedings in Babylon is sensationalized and full of Roman coloring. Although some of the details may well be correct, the story must be treated with caution. See the discussions in Martin 1983 and Sharples 1994.

125 When Justin writes that Arrhidaeus and Alexander IV were "removed to Cappadocia" he actually means they were taken from Cappadocia into Pisidia (thus D 18.22.1, 25.6).

126 D 18.39.7 omits the intermediate stage, in which Antipater assigned the Kings to Antigonus and then removed them from his possession. This could be either the result of abbreviation or a deliberate omission on the part of Hieronymus of Cardia.

127 Cassander learned of Arrhidaeus' death when he returned from the Peloponnese (D 19.35.1); cf. App*Syr* 54 [275] for another reference to his death.

128 This is apparently the context of Timaeus of Cyzicus' attempt to subvert the constitution of the city with the help of Arrhidaeus (Ath 11.509a). The information comes from Demochares but this passage is not included in Jacoby, *FGrH* 75. It is possible, since Athenaeus is speaking of students of Plato, that he has confused Timolaus of Cyzicus with Timaeus.

129 Whether he is the Arrhidaeus honored with citizenship in Ephesus in 316 (*IEphesos* 5, no. 1451) is unclear. Nor is it possible to determine if the "Arribbaeus" of Pol*Strat* 7.30 refers to Arrhidaeus, or what is the name of the city defended by Mempsis.

130 A 3.25.7: Ἀρσάκην, ἄνδρα Πέρσην.

131 D 17.19.4 calls him *satrapes* and C 3.4.3 writes: *Arsames, qui Ciliciae praeerat*. But Leuze 248–9 argues that Diodorus' usage is imprecise, and that *satrapes* = *hyparchos* (cf. Mithrenes, the *phrourarchos* of Sardis, called *satrapes* by D 17.21.7); Arsames was thus a lieutenant of Mazaeus, who had been satrap of Cilicia under Artaxerxes III and to whose territories Syria was later added.

132 I can find no support for the view of Cook 1983: 226 that "he may have been responsible for the failure to throw the Greek mercenary corps into the fight."

133 C 6.5.3 claims that Artabazus was 94 years old in 330. This is rightly rejected by Berve ii.82. Instead of being in his 95th year, he may however have been in his 59th.

134 See Hornblower 1982 and Weiskopf 1989: *passim*; cf. Krumbholz 73–5; Judeich 204ff.

135 C 7.11.29 says that Artabazus was left in charge of the captured Rock of Ariamazes. This must refer to his role as satrap of Bactria. In 328, when Alexander divided his mobile troops and conducted a sweep of Bactria-Sogdiana, Artabazus was attached to Hephaestion's third of the army (C 8.1.10; cf. 8.1.1); A 4.16.2–3 says there were five sections and that Artabazus joined Coenus, moving against the Scythians who had given refuge to Spitamenes.

136 Tarn 1921: 26 assumes that Artacama is the correct form – observing that "presumably Ptolemy knew his wife's name" – and that the form Apame was mistakenly given by Duris of Samos (whom Tarn regards as the source of P*Eum* 1.7). Aristobulus (*FGrH* 139 F52) appears to have been the source for the marriage of Alexander to Parysatis, but it appears that the list of brides and bridegrooms was certainly taken from Ptolemy, and probably from both of Arrian's primary sources (Kornemann 90; Brunt ii.212–13 n. 4; Hammond 1993: 284 n. 14). Brosius 185 believes that Apame may have been her official name. It is, however, typical of Aristobulus to supply alternative forms of both personal and place names.

137 Berve's rejection of Schubert's view (1898: 109), that Artemius and Xenodochus may have arrived recently from the west with the caravan that brought also fresh fruit from the Mediterranean, as "grotesk" (followed by Hamilton 142) strikes me as less so.

138 In that case, also a relative of the *archihypaspistes* Neoptolemus.

139 Berve ii.87, followed by Badian 1960a: 329 (and consequently many others), identifies Asander son of Philotas as the brother of the great general, Parmenion (Welles 1970: 39, calling him Parmenion's cousin, could be closer to the truth).

140 Adams 1984 argues that this commander is Cassander son of Antipater, but such an appointment would be inconsistent with the rest of his career (see further s.v. **Cassander**). Cartledge 2004: 97 assumes that Asander is the correct reading and describes the man as Parmenion's brother.

141 Tataki 76, referring to an unpublished inscription from Perrhaebian Tripolis.

142 The MSS. consistently write "Casander" and hence [C]asander in D 17.17.4 may also be the son of Agathon. The recurring error of Casander for Asander should not, however, lead us to assume with *RE* s.v. "Asandros (3)" that the claims to Cappadocia (D 19.57.4, 60.2) were Asander's and not Cassander's. Asander is also attested in inscriptions in Asia Minor: *SEG* 26 (1976/77) 1228; *SEG* 33 (1983) 872; *SIG*^{3} 272.

143 For Eupolemus see Billows 1989.

144 A*Ind* 18.3 = Nearchus, *FGrH* 133 F1 should perhaps read: *Λεοννάτος ὁ ⟨Ἀντέου καὶ Ἀσκληπιόδωρος ὁ⟩ Εὐν⟨ίκ⟩ου* (thus Jacoby *FGrH* IIB 681, iiD "Kommentar," 450). This solves the problem of Leonnatus' incorrect patronymic (*Εὔνου*); cf. Heckel 371.

145 If there is indeed a textual corruption involving Asclepiodorus son of Eunicus, it may also have affected the reading *Ἀσκληπιόδωρος ὁ Τιμάνδρου*. Timander may be a corruption of Timanthes, which appears in the following line, or the name of Timander's son (whatever it was) may have dropped out of the text.

146 Caroe 52 locates Massaga (Mazaga in Curtius; Mesoga in Str 15.1.27 [698]) in "the Katgala pass between the valleys of Talash and Adinzai, about eight miles north of Chakdarra on the present road to Dir"; cf. Eggermont 178. Massaga thus lies on the road leading to Bir-Kot (Bazeira) and Udegram (Ora).

147 Berve ii.89: "vgl. V, 20, 7" suggests this (indeed logical) identification. But elsewhere (ii.276) Berve identifies the hyparch of the Assacenians with Nicanor (no. 556). For a lengthy discussion see Bosworth ii.321–2.

148 Thus Rapson, *CHIndia* i.318 (Pushkalavati); but Berve ii.90, following Anspach i.90 n. 36, and Droysen i[2] 2.114 (see now i[3] 326) assumes that Orobatis (A 4.28.5) is the city at which Astis was killed. Anspach points out that Alexander himself captured Peucelaotis, but A 4.28.6 probably refers to the formal surrender to Alexander of the city already subdued by Hephaestion and Perdiccas (cf. Eggermont 1970: 71–4, identifying Orobatis with Shahbazgarhi). For Peucelaotis as the site of Astis' defeat, see now Badian 1987: 123ff. Pushkalavati (Charsadda) had replaced Peshawar as the capital of Gandhara (Caroe 48).

149 According to Din 1.20, the orator Stratocles had also commented on Astylus' susceptibility to bribery.

150 Others released with him were Echecratides the sophist, Demaratus and Sparton the Rhodians.

151 Since the satraps at the Granicus came from as far afield as Cappadocia and Cilicia, we should expect to find Atizyes of Phrygia there as well.

152 The appointment of Orontobates the Mede in Peithon's place will perhaps have made Atropates' bid for independence easier.

153 Attalus was the guardian and uncle of Cleopatra-Eurydice, the last wife of Philip II (P*A* 9.7; Satyrus *ap.* Ath 13.557d; Paus 8.7.7; wrongly Cleopatra's brother, D 17.2.3; J 9.5.9; Ps-Call 1.20.1; or nephew, D 16.93.9); thus also the uncle of Cleopatra's brother, Hippostratus, whom we may identify (tentatively) as the son of Amyntas. Marsyas of Pella (*FGrH* 135/6 F17; cf. Heckel 1980b: 456) singles out Hippostratus son of Amyntas as one of the prominent *hetairoi* of Philip II who perished in the Illyrian campaign of 344/3 BC. The death of Hippostratus in 344/3 would explain why Attalus, and not he, was Cleopatra's guardian in 337; it is self-evident that the father, Amyntas, had died before 337. (For a stemma see Heckel 1982a: 83.)

154 Satyrus, frg. 5; P*A* 9.7ff.; cf. J 9.7.3. Ps-Call (L) 1.20.1 calls him Lysias; but Ps-Call (A) 1.21.1 and Jul Val 1.13–14 distinguish between Attalus and Lysias (see Berve ii.424 no. 47).

155 D 16.93.7; J 9.6.5–6, alleging that he was abused by Attalus himself. For this episode and the sources see Fears 1975. There is no need to identify Pleurias with Pleuratus (Marsyas of Pella, *FGrH* 135/6 F17) or to date the campaign to 344/3. For the date of Pausanias' death see Heckel 1981c: 56.

156 C 6.9.17; she was presumably the same woman who married Coenus son of Polemocrates in 334; cf. C 6.9.30. See **F33**, **34**.

157 D 17.5.1; at 17.2.3 he is called a rival for the throne, though he scarcely had any legal claims to it.

158 D 17.2.4, 5.1; cf. 17.3.2, naming Demosthenes; cf. Judeich 304.

159 Cf. Badian 1963: 249–50. D 17.5.1 says that although he had been in contact with Demosthenes, Attalus sent Demosthenes' letter to Alexander in order to prove that he was not planning to rebel against him.

160 Craterus (A 4.16.1, cf. 17.1; 4.22.1; 5.12.1; 6.17.3), Coenus (A 4.24.1), Polyperchon (A 4.16.1; 4.22.1; implied by J 12.10.1, to be taken with A 6.17.3; cf. Bosworth 1976a: 129 n. 65), Meleager (A 4.16.1; 5.12.1; 6.17.3).

161 Arrian's account does not say that Attalus' fleet actually attacked the Caunians and Cnidians. Either these states joined forces with the Rhodians, with the credit for the victory going to Rhodes and Demaratus, or Attalus' strike against them was preempted by the Rhodian victory.

162 D 18.41.7 says that Antigonus set out against Alcetas and Attalus, "who commanded the entire fleet." What had become of Attalus' fleet, or what remained of it after its defeat by the Rhodians, we do not know; Hauben (22–3) thinks it may have been at anchor in Lycia or Pamphylia.

163 Ramsay 1920: 107 identifies it as Afiom-Kara-Hissar or Leontos-Kephalai.

164 Bosworth ii.114–15 believes that Arrian and Curtius describe two different episodes, pointing out that in A 4.16.4

the Macedonians are taken by surprise whereas in C 8.1.3–4 they made a deliberate sortie. But the element of surprise can be found in both accounts: Curtius calls Attinas *insidiarum, quae parabantur, ignarus*. Furthermore, although the expression *praefectus regionis eius* is often used to designate a satrap or hyparch (C 5.2.8; 5.3.4; 5.8.4; 10.1.20), it cannot mean that in this instance, since the satrap of Bactria-Sogdiana was Artabazus (not Attinas), and the term *praefectus* is also used of those in charge of smaller places (for example, the prefect of Damascus, C 3.13.10 or Gobares the prefect of Parsagadae). Hence I see no reason to believe that Attinas was not a *phrourarchos*. The different accounts will be attributable to the primary sources. Arrian's account derives from Aristobulus, Curtius' from Cleitarchus or perhaps Ptolemy.

165 Cf. P*M* 340c–d, in which Plutarch confused Oarses (Arses) and Darius.

166 Berve ii.98 writes: "Da er am Hydaspes im Herbst 326 unter den Trierarchen der Stromflotte erscheint . . . , muss er im Hoflager eine angesehene Stellung eingenommen haben, wie ja auch sein Vater in hohem Masse Al.s Vertrauen genoss." But the eunuch Bagoas had considerable influence with both Darius and Alexander, and he may have secured for his father Pharnuches the unprecedented command of the troops at the Polytimetus. Of course, it is difficult to explain why the defeat of the Macedonians in that engagement was not explicitly attributed by hostile sources to Bagoas' influence. Bosworth ii.24, 34 identifies Bagoas son of Pharnuches (the trierarch at the Hydaspes) as the son of the Lycian guide on whom the Alexander sources appear to have pinned the blame for the Polytimetus disaster, but stops short of identifying the eunuch and the trierarch. For the nature of eunuch power in the Near East see Grayson 1995. Assyrian and Persian eunuchs must have been similar in many respects to the eunuchs of Imperial China, and it strikes me as not only possible but highly likely that not all eunuchs were captives or slaves but that families derived considerable benefit from handing their sons over to the Imperial service, even if it meant physical mutilation.

167 For his house in the vicinity of Babylon see Ael*VH* 3.23.

168 The epigraphic form Balagros has the support of Antonius Diogenes (*ap.* Phot*Bibl* p. 111a–b) and C 4.13.28 where *Phaligrus* appears to be a corruption of *Philippus Balagri*.

169 Euseb 1.231–2 and Porphyry of Tyre (*FGrH* 260 F3 §2) wrongly make her the daughter of Pharnabazus.

170 Confusion of Baryaxes and Oxydates is highly unlikely. The former is called a Mede, whereas Oxydates is specifically identified as a Persian (A 3.20.3). Furthermore, the charge against Oxydates was that he deliberately shirked battle (A 4.18.3: *ἐθελοκακεῖν*. For the meaning see Powell s.v.), not aspiring to the throne. A 6.29.3 says that he was calling himself "king of the Persians and Medes." Badian 2000a: 93 suggests that he was descended "from the old Median kings." Briant 2003: 740 notes that only three men are specifically identified as Medes in the Alexander historians (see also Atropates and Gobares) but rightly observes that the scarcity of Medes in aristocratic circles may not indicate a decline of their power as much as it reflects the incomplete and uneven nature of the source evidence.

171 I see no good reason for supposing, as Billows 45 (with n. 85) does, that Calas was killed in his battle with Bas. See further s.v. **Calas**.

172 Berve ii.105 wrongly dates this to 324. Alexander had just returned from his winter campaign against the Cossaeans: D 17.112.1.

173 A scholion to Theocritus 17.34 gives her patronymikon as *Βάγα* which is more easily emended to *Μάγα* than *Λάγου*. It is, moreover, supported by the name of the son, Magas (*Pros Ptol* 14533); for we would expect the name of the maternal

grandfather, if the husband (as was the case with Philip) was inferior to the bride. Cf. Macurdy 104.

174 Curtius says that these were mainly Parthians but Arrian speaks of Bactrians. *Parthienorum* in the text of C 5.8.4 should probably be emended to *Bactrianorum* (Atkinson ii.137). In C 4.12.11 the Parthians are named last of the contingents on the left wing, i.e., closest to the center, and this would agree with A 3.16.1 where Darius is accompanied by those who were deployed close to him in battle. But Arrian calls these cavalrymen Bactrians. In A 3.11.4 the Parthians are located on the Persian right.

175 D 17.83.7–8 and C 7.4.8–18 tell of a certain Gobares (Gobryas; D calls him Bagodaras) who escaped from Bessus' camp and received a warm reception from Alexander. This prompted others to expect lenient treatment from the King.

176 There are two versions of Bessus' extradition. One based on Ptolemy himself (A 3.29.7–30.5) claims that Bessus was abandoned by the road by Spitamenes and his fellow-conspirators for Ptolemy to bring to Alexander; the second, recorded also by Aristobulus (A 3.30.5), relates that Spitamenes himself handed Bessus over to the King (cf. C 7.5.36–7).

177 A 3.30.5 has him sent to Bactra (Zariaspa) for execution, but at 4.7.3 Arrian reports that he was mutilated here (his nose and earlobes were cut off) before he was sent to Ecbatana for execution. P*A* 43.6 has Bessus executed – he was torn apart by recoiling trees – on the spot where he was handed over to Alexander; D 17.83.9 also has Bessus mutilated and executed on the spot. *ME* 14 has him killed in Bactria (presumably at Bactra). For a discussion of these accounts and Curtius' attempts to reconcile two primary sources see Heckel 1994: 70.

178 Whether he is identical with the Bianor who was related by marriage to Amadocus of Thrace (Dem 23.10, 17, 180) is impossible to determine. Bosworth i.222 believes he may have belonged to that faction in Acarnania exiled after Chaeronea (Tod ii no. 178; D 17.3.3).

179 Str 16.4.20 [779] cites Ctesias (*FGrH* 688 F66) as mentioning a certain Boxus, but his designation as "Persian" is Casaubon's insertion.

180 The name is attested only in Curtius. According to C 5.13.11, a son of Mazaeus and former satrap of Syria. But the text is almost certainly corrupt and should perhaps read *Brochubelus, Mazaei filius, Syriae quondam praetoris* (see Hamilton 105).

181 Berve ii.110 rightly dismisses the idea that he was the local dynast of Bubacene in Central Asia (cf. C 8.5.2), even though dynasts of the Indian frontier took official regional names. There were no representatives of these regions in the Persian force at Issus.

182 Berve ii.110, following Lehmann-Haupt 115, 142, accepts him as satrap. But it is odd that none of the sources, when describing Mazaeus' surrender of Babylon, mentions Bupares, whether he had fled, died, or been deposed. Bosworth i.291 accepts Leuze's view (410–12) that Bupares was merely acting on behalf of the Babylonian satrap, who may have been unfit to lead the army. But this again fails to explain why there is no mention of Darius' satrap in the account of the city's surrender.

183 In that case, it might be possible to identify him with Cassander's general, sent in 317 to deal with Polyperchon's forces in Perrhaebia (D 19.35.3, 36.6).

184 Aes 3.85 says Demosthenes accepted bribes for this service; cf. 3.103–4.

185 Thus somewhat unusual in that the majority of Athenians with mining interests were anti-Macedonian (Lauffer; cf. the comments of Tritle 125).

186 Hagnonides is said to have favored having Callimedon tortured before he was put to death (P*Ph* 35.2).

187 According to the *Suda* there was a belief that Callisthenes' father was also named Callisthenes.

188 Cf. Simplicius, on Aristotle, *de Coelo* 2.12 = *FGrH* 124 T3.

189 For the rivalry see P*A* 52.8–9; A 4.9.7–11.9; A 4.9.9 names both Agis and Anaxarchus. C 8.5.8–20 mentions Agis

and Cleon in place of Anaxarchus. J 12.6.17 describes Callisthenes' consolation as having the desired effect and says nothing about Anaxarchus. See also Borza 1981.

190 Bosworth ii.141 suggests that Strabo's Cariatae may be a corruption of Zariaspa.

191 Justin's story about the caging of Callisthenes is instructive. Lysimachus was reputed for his cultivation of the philosophers – Onesicritus of Astypalaea, a pupil of Diogenes, was present at Lysimachus' court (PA 46.4) – and already in 324 he had been given the funerary horse of the Indian philosopher Calanus, whose student he had been (A 7.3.4). The story developed that he pitied the philosopher-historian Callisthenes, whom Alexander had caged *like a wild animal* (Tatian *ad Gr* 2, p. 2). Lysimachus, who is said to have been a student of Callisthenes as well (J 15.3.3–6), attempted to give him poison in order to remedy his plight. For this act, according to Justin, he was caged together with a lion, which he killed by tearing out its tongue (15.3.3–8). But Lysimachus was himself guilty of similar cruelty (conduct befitting a tyrant), sometime after 300 BC, when allegedly he mutilated and encaged Telesphorus the Rhodian, merely because he made a tasteless joke about Lysimachus' wife, Arsinoë (Ath 14.616c; Sen*de Ira* 3.17.3–4). As a result, the lion story, now removed from its historical context (it takes place neither in Syria nor in Bazeira), establishes a precedent for Lysimachus' treatment of Telesphorus and is itself explained in terms of Alexander's cruelty to Callisthenes. In fact, Alexander's caging of Lysimachus becomes canonized as one of the three great examples of Alexander's cruelty, together with the murder of Cleitus and the punishment of Callisthenes, in the works of the Roman rhetoricians.

192 Hence probably also the Callisthenes who was involved in the securing of grain from Leucon, king of the Bosporus (Dem 20.33). After the Peace of Philocrates, Callisthenes *may have* proposed a decree to secure Piraeus and bring people in from the countryside (cf. Dem 19.125; but the document linking Callisthenes to this measure is spurious: Dem 18.37–8).

193 Timocles, like the source of Plutarch's *Demosthenes*, links Callisthenes with Demon. Both are absent from the other two lists of politicians whose extradition was demanded after the sack of Thebes. Callisthenes is also ridiculed in a fragment of Antiphanes (Ath 8.338f).

194 "Calanus," as a proper name or nickname, is simply not Macedonian. Understanding the infantry commander's fate depends, in part, on what we make of this name. It was unusual enough to prompt Plutarch to explain how it came to be applied to the Indian philosopher Sphines (PA 65.5). I suspect that we are dealing with a textual error in which Caranus was corrupted to *Cala*nus by a scribe influenced by the repetition of the name *Bala*crus in the same passage (see Heckel 1981d: 64, 69–70).

195 Nothing is known of Alexarchus in Alexander's lifetime. He is said to have founded a city on the Athos peninsula called Uranopolis (Ath 3.98d–e; Str 7, frag. 35; cf. Pl*NH* 4.37) and to have been noted for his obscure language and coining of words.

196 The evidence is late: Euseb 1.231; Syncellus 265a 504 Bonn. Paus 9.7.2 says he died of a disease of worms (see Africa 1982: 6). For tuberculosis (*phthisis*) see Carney 1999.

197 J 13.4.18 (*stipatoribus regiis satellitibusque Cassander, filius Antipater, praeficitur*) appears to mean that Cassander was appointed commander of the *agema* of the hypaspists, in place of Seleucus, who was promoted to chiliarch.

198 For Cassander's dealings with Athens see D 18.64; N*Ph* 2.4–5, 3.1. With ships sent by Antigonus, Cassander seized Aegina and besieged Salamis, but Polyperchon forced him to abandon the latter and to return to Piraeus (D 18.69.1–2; cf. Pol*Strat* 4.11.1, perhaps referring to the same campaign).

199 For Cassander's hostility to Aeacides and his family (on account of Olympias) see *PPyr* 3.2; Paus 1.11.4–5. Cassander is said to have offered Glaucias 200 talents to hand over the child Pyrrhus, but Glaucias refused (*PPyr* 3.5; cf. J 17.3.20).

200 He also eliminated Monimus of Pella and Aristonus, who was guarding Amphipolis (D 19.50.7–51.1).

201 Cassander razed a number of cities on the Thermaic Gulf and transferred their populations to his new metropolis, Thessalonice (Str 7, frg. 21, 24). Potideia was restored and named Cassandreia (D 19.52.2–3; Str 7, frg. 25). In order to please Cassander, Lysippus allegedly designed a new vessel for Mendean wine, which was exported from Cassandreia (Ath 11.784c).

202 Cassander's attack on Elateia (Paus 10.18.7) may belong to this period.

203 Perhaps too much is made of this. The youngest son was called Alexander, but, by the time of his birth, Cassander's own position will have changed dramatically.

204 Ath 4.144e says that Theophrastus wrote a treatise *On Monarchy* for Cassander, although some claim it was the work of Sosibius. *PDemetr* 18.4 claims that Cassander did not use the title king in his letters.

205 Cassander sent Asclepiodorus to invade Cappadocia, and Antigonus sent his nephew Polemaeus against him (D 19.57.4; 19.60.2). Polemaeus also overcame Eupolemus in Caria (D 19.68), who had been sent by Asander, who had briefly joined the opponents of Antigonus.

206 The establishment of Cassandreia was also criticized, since it brought together Olynthians who were traditionally hostile to Macedon (D 19.61.2).

207 The identification of Chaereas and Chares is rejected on chronological grounds by Berve ii.403.

208 The presence of the ethnic may suggest authenticity. If he is not historical, perhaps the name Chaeron was suggested by that of Socrates' emissary to Delphi, Chaerephon (Plato, *Apology* 21). But this is no more than speculation.

209 Ath 11.509b claims that Chaeron gave the property and wives of his enemies to their slaves.

210 Chares was elected *strategos* in 367/6–366/5; 361/0; 358/7–353/2; 349/8–347/6; 341/0–338/7. Ancient sources collected in Develin under each year.

211 Tarn ii.70: "One or two passages apart, like the *proskynesis* matter (which he presumably saw), the fragments only exhibit a trifler, immersed in court ceremonies and dinners, the minutiae of his office; no influence on anybody can be traced" (quoted by Pearson 50 n. 1).

212 Bosworth ii.97 questions whether Charicles' father was the satrap of Lydia, suggesting that "more probably he was the Companion later executed for leaving the command to which he was assigned."

213 For full discussion see Blänsdorff 1971, but the resemblance was noted already by Parke 183 n. 5.

214 The allegation that Cleander raped a virgin of the native aristocracy and gave her to his slave as a concubine (C 10.1.5) may go back to Cleitarchus (for similar charges against Harpalus, cf. D 17.108.4).

215 Thus Berve ii.205, but this implies that Macedonian and Cretan commanders were employed interchangeably.

216 Arrian and Plutarch relate that Cleitus severed Spithridates' arm just as he was about to strike the King; Diodorus, however, records that this man was Rhoesaces, Spithridates' brother. The confusion is inexplicable, the truth indeterminable.

217 Pollitt 162; cf. Berve ii.206. White Cleitus had also been a hipparch and the identity of Apelles' *Cleitus* is not certain.

218 We know nothing of Cleitus' participation in the campaigns of 330–328. Carney 1981: 151 suggests that Alexander "granted Clitus the honor of his position, . . . then . . . prevented him from acquiring much glory through it." A 4.8.1–9.9 and *PA* 50.1–52.4 record Cleitus' death out of chronological context, which may explain their failure to mention him again. There may also have been

further changes in the way the Companions were used; for we hear virtually nothing of Hephaestion as hipparch (see s.v. **Hephaestion**). Schachermeyr 364 suggests that Cleitus' appointment as satrap may be linked with the restructuring of the cavalry commands. Craterus, Coenus, Perdiccas, and others had all joined Hephaestion as hipparchs, and they now may have contributed to Cleitus' demise.

219 The quarrel which precipitated the murder involved the clash of generations and ideologies: Philip against Alexander (A 4.8.4ff.; C 8.1.23ff.; P*A* 50.11; J 12.6.2–3); the Macedonian kingdom versus the new empire (P*A* 51.2–3, 5).

220 But see, for a different picture of the naval activities in the Lamian War, Bosworth 2003b.

221 For the naval battles of the Lamian War see Walek 1924; Ashton 1977; Morrison 1987; Heckel 373–8; Bosworth 2003b.

222 Billows 395 includes a Cleochares son of Pytheas, a Macedonian from Amphipolis honored by the Eretrians in the late fourth century. The likelihood that he is Alexander's envoy in India is extremely remote; nor do the inscriptions that honor him mention service under Alexander (*IG* xii. 9 199; cf. *IG* II.[2] 559 + *IG* xii suppl., p. 178). The Greek form 'Kleochares' is unattested in the Alexander historians.

223 Paus 1.6.3 and [Arist]*Oecon* 2.2.33, 1352[a] 16 call him "satrap"; [Dem] 56.7 is ambiguous. If he did become satrap, it may have been after Hephaestion's death.

224 See also van Groningen 1925; Vogt 1971; Seibert 1972; Hölbl 12–15.

225 Accepted as historical by Berve ii.210 no. 430; Poralla no. 431. For the textual problem see Ziegler 1935: 379; for the identification of the Cleomantis with this Cleomenes see Hamilton 140.

226 Identification with Cleomenes of Naucratis seems impossible (Alexander had written to him from Babylon shortly before his illness: A 7.23.6–8).

227 Accepted by Bosworth 1988b: 170.

228 There is no good reason for following Pearson 78 and identifying Cleon as a poet.

229 P*A* 3.2 may suggest that shortly before losing his eye at Methone, Philip had ceased to have sexual relations with Olympias. *HE* 4 wrongly says that the mother of Cleopatra had the same name.

230 She sent a shipment of grain via Leucas to Corinth in 333/2 (Lyc 1.26); acted as *thearodochos* in 330 (*SEG* xxiii.198); and is named as a recipient of grain from Cyrene (*SEG* ix.2; cf. Kingsley 1986: 169–70).

231 Here she appears to have had a sexual encounter with a handsome young man, news of which reached her brother. He remarked that she ought to get some enjoyment out of her royal status (P*M* 818b–c).

232 Some indication of her earlier support for Eumenes and the Perdiccan party can be found in the fragmentary text of A*Succ* 25, in which we learn also that Perdiccas had taken control of Lydia away from Menander and given it to Cleopatra (25.2).

233 Bosworth 2000 puts the *Last Will and Testament of Alexander*, which offers Cleopatra as bride to Ptolemy (*LM* 117), into this historical context. D 20.37.4 claims that Antigonus, Cassander, and Lysimachus had all at one point sought her hand in marriage.

234 Coenus was one of the "newly-weds" (*neogamoi*) sent home in the winter of 334/3 (A 1.24.1, 29.4).

235 Coenus accompanied Alexander from Awan-i-Kif, through the Caspian Gates – usually identified with Sar-i-Darreh (Seibert 1985: 112; cf. Bosworth i.340, with map opposite) – and gathered provisions in the region of Choarene (mod. Khar).

236 A 4.16.2–3: Hephaestion, Perdiccas, Ptolemy, Coenus (with Artabazus), and Alexander each led one unit; C 8.1.1 says there were only three divisions, led by Alexander, Hephaestion, and Coenus. The heavy infantry (at least four battalions) remained with Craterus in Bactria (A 4.16.1; 4.17.1).

237 Badian 1961 argues that Harpalus fled because he knew that his office would be split between Philoxenus and Coeranus. This is a case of *post hoc, ergo propter hoc* at its worst.

238 Bosworth i.279–80 rejects the view that he was overseer of all these areas and limits him to Phoenicia, but just such a division of power is implied by Arrian's remark that Philoxenus was given charge of the area on the other side of the Taurus (τῆς Ἀσίας τὰ ἐπὶ τάδε τοῦ Ταύρου), and Phoenicia must be used by Arrian in a general (broader) sense.

239 *ME* 17 calls this man Dares, a name otherwise unattested.

240 Willrich 1899 sees Cophen as the intended occupant of the Alexander sarcophagus of Sidon. Although he is right to suggest a Persian "Grabherr," Cophen himself is an unlikely candidate. See s.v. **Mazaeus**.

241 The letter from Craterus to his mother is probably spurious, but may preserve her name correctly.

242 Bosworth i.321–2 assumes that Arrian and the vulgate sources are referring to two different engagements. See also Fuller 226–8; Olmstead 519; Stein 1938: 313ff.; also Str 11.13.6 [524]; 15.3.6 [729].

243 For Craterus' independent commands see *ME* 35, 59, 60; Pol*Strat* 4.13; C 4.3.1; A 3.17.4–5, 18.4–8; C 5.4.14–16, 29, 34; 5.6.11; A 3.21.2; C 6.4.2, 23–4; A 3.25.6, 8; C 6.6.25, 33; A 4.2.2; C 7.6.16, 19; 7.9.20–2; A 4.17.1; C 8.1.6, 5.2; A 4.18.1, 22.1–2, 23.5; C 8.10.4; A 4.24.6–7, 28.7; 5.12.1, 18.1, 21.4; D 17.96.1; A 6.2.2, 4.1, 5.5, 7; A*Ind* 19.1, 3; C 9.8.3, 10.19; A 6.15.5, 7; 6.17.3, 27.3; 7.12.3–4.

244 It is doubtful that Craterus took part in the actual transporting of the treasures to Ecbatana, even though some units of *pezhetairoi* did remain to guard the treasure (A 3.20.1); that task was given to Parmenion (A 3.19.7, but Berve ii.221 assumes that Craterus helped Parmenion).

245 How long this "prolonged espionage" (Badian 1960a: 331) lasted is unknown, though it undoubtedly did not span the years between the disaffection in Egypt and the Dimnus affair; indeed, Antigone's information, which cannot have revealed much that was not already known about Philotas, may well have disappointed Craterus' hopes of building a case against his rival.

246 Alexander's relief of Maracanda: A 4.5.3–6.5; C 7.9.20–1; *IA* 39; *ME* 13. Craterus' arrival: C 7.9.22.

247 A 4.16.1 does not mention Craterus, though his position is clear from A 4.17.1 and corroborated by C 8.1.6.

248 Thus A 4.17.1–2; C 8.1.6 claims that the Massagetae fled but that Craterus slew 1,000 Dahae, perhaps confusing this battle with the one fought by Coenus (A 4.17.6–7).

249 A 4.18.1–2; C 8.4.1 says that when Alexander moved out of winter quarters in spring 327 (cf. A 4.18.4) he had stayed there only a little more than two months: *tertio mense ex hibernis movit exercitum*. Cf. Beloch iii^{2} 2.319.

250 For the division of the forces cf. C 8.10.4: *Cratero cum phalange iusso sequi* refers to a time before Alexander's arrival at Andaca.

251 We are not told about the composition of his force, but it can have included not more than two battalions of *pezhetairoi* (Polyperchon, Alcetas): Alexander had taken the battalions of Attalus and Coenus, while those of Cleitus, Meleager, and Gorgias (formerly Craterus' own) had accompanied Hephaestion and Perdiccas to the Indus (A 4.24.1, cf. 22.7).

252 Arrian records Craterus' departure twice (6.15.5, 17.3), first from Musicanus' kingdom, then from Sind (for textual problems see Bosworth 1976a: 127–9). Craterus had continued south with his troops, not much beyond Pardabathra – he appears not to have participated in the campaign against Oxicanus – where he appears to have remained with the main force while Alexander dealt with Sambus, the defecting satrap of the hill-country to the west of the Indus (A 6.16.3–5; C 9.8.13ff.; D 17.102.6–7). Soon it was learned that Musicanus had rebelled – perhaps massacring the Macedonian garrison. Reprisals were

conducted by Alexander, and Peithon son of Agenor (the new satrap of the region) soon brought Musicanus prisoner to Sind, where he was executed (A 6.17.2; C 9.8.16). At this point, Craterus was sent back to Rohri-Alor to restore order there – in the absence of Peithon, who continued south with Alexander – and also in Arachosia and Drangiana.

253 A 6.17.3 omits Polyperchon, but see J 12.10.1. Polyperchon had accompanied Craterus in the past (A 4.16.1; 4.17.1; cf. C 8.5.2) and was to do so again in 324 (A 7.12.4; J 12.12.8–9, cf. Bosworth 1976a: 129 n. 65). For Polyperchon with Attalus (his relative, so Berve ii.325 and Hoffmann 156 n. 59) see A 4.16.1, where Meleager is also named; with Amyntas, brother of Attalus, C 5.4.20, 30; with Antigenes, J 12.12.8–9. On the other hand, J substitutes the name Polyperchon for Craterus on a number of occasions (13.8.5, 8.7; 15.1.1).

254 Stasanor, satrap of Areia and Drangiana, may very well have been summoned to Carmania by Craterus on the march (A 6.27.3; A 6.29.1 says that he was sent home shortly afterward; cf. Bosworth 1971b: 123 n. 3).

255 Cf. J 12.12.8–9 (Craterus was accompanied by Cleitus, Gorgias, Polydamas, and Antigenes). See C 10.10.15: *credebant etiam Craterum cum veterum militum manu ad interficiendum eum missum*, where *eum* refers to Antipater (wrongly "Alexander" in J. C. Rolfe's Loeb translation, ii.557). According to P*Ph* 18.7, Craterus was to offer Phocion the revenues from one of four Asian towns.

256 That Craterus deliberately disobeyed the King's orders is unlikely. See, however, Badian 1961: 34ff.; Green 460 suspects that Craterus was involved in a conspiracy with Cassander, who was on his way to Babylon. Griffith 1965: 12–17 argues that Craterus was waiting for the new recruits to leave Macedonia before marching on.

257 Thus Badian 1967b: 201–4. This was clearly a ploy on Perdiccas' part to win Antipater's (temporary) support; for he sought to beguile the old regent by feigning cooperation and marrying his daughter Nicaea (see s.v. **Perdiccas** [1]).

258 P*Ph* 26.1 says that the battle of Crannon was fought a short time afterwards, but, since it is dated to 7 Metageitnion (probably August 5; cf. Beloch iv^2 1.74), Craterus will not have reached the Hellespont until late June or early July 322.

259 Over the winter he supplemented his forces; for he had decided to leave Antigenes and the three thousand Argyraspids in Cilicia for security, other troops were given to Cleitus, who was preparing a fleet with which he would sail to the Hellespont. Craterus therefore recruited fresh troops, perhaps from the satrapies of Asia Minor. D 18.16.4 is instructive: *ἦγε δὲ πεζοὺς μὲν τῶν εἰς Ἀσίαν Ἀλεξάνδρῳ συνδιαβεβηκότων ἑξακισχιλίους, τῶν δὲ ἐν παρόδῳ προσειλημμένων τετρακισχιλίους*. . . . This has been taken to mean that Craterus' infantrymen were divided into two units: 6,000 who had campaigned with Alexander since 334 (who had crossed the Hellespont with him at that time), and another 4,000 who had joined Alexander's in the course of his campaigns (e.g., Brunt ii.489; and now Bosworth 2002: 73 n. 31). But this is a curious distinction for the historian to make, and *ἐν παρόδῳ* probably refers to Craterus' own march. The 1,000 Persian archers and slingers, as well as the 1,500 horse, were part of the original force that left Opis (D 18.16.4).

260 It was at this time that Craterus offered Amastris to Dionysius of Heraclea Pontica. The choice of a new husband must have been linked with Dionysius' ability to help secure the crossing of the Hellespont, which was still threatened by the Athenian fleet. By the time Craterus reached the Hellespont, White Cleitus had already won control of the sea, but in the early stages this was far from predictable.

261 Together with the remnants of Leonnatus' army (D 18.14.4–5), the Macedonians numbered 40,000 infantry, 5,000 cavalry, and 3,000 archers and slingers (D 18.16.5).

262 *PPh* 28.2–3; *PDem* 28.1; *PCam* 19.10. Cf. Schaefer iii[3] 391 (Sept. 16); see also Berve ii.259. Cf. D 18.18.5.

263 Peace with the Aetolians: D 18.25.5; J 13.6.9 wrongly speaks of peace with the *Athenians*, adding that Polyperchon was left in charge of Europe; he dealt effectively with the Aetolians (D 18.38). For the decision to go to war with Perdiccas see *ASucc* 1.24; also an alliance was made with Ptolemy (D 18.25.4; cf. 18.14.2). Cf. Seibert 96ff.

264 I do not regard the length of time between Critobulus' service at Methone and his treatment of Alexander in India as an argument against identification. Lengthy service, both in the military and in other spheres, is well attested in this period. Leonidas, Lysimachus the tutor, Philip the physician, and Aristander the seer were all well advanced in years, and in the army we may point not only to veteran officers like Parmenion and Antipater but also to the soldiers who were to form the Argyraspids. Furthermore, it is likely that Alexander's medical staff included men of proven ability.

265 Bosworth 2002: 12 n. 26 argues that the sources do not justify the view that it was Cynnane's intention to marry Adea to Philip Arrhidaeus, but I can see no other purpose for her journey to Asia Minor. See Heckel 1983–4; Carney 29–31.

266 Schaefer iii[2] 313 n. 4 suggests that "Damis" may be a corruption of "Eudamidas," but Berve ii.115 notes the failure of the sources to designate the speaker as a king.

267 *PA* 64–5 fails to distinguish between the Brahmins and the Gymnosophists; cf. *ME* 71–4, 78–84, who locates them among the Mallians. See the comments of Hamilton 178–9; for the difference between Brahmins (who were political advisors) and philosophers see Nearchus, *FGrH* 133 F23 = Str 15.1.66 [716]. See also Stoneman 1994, 1995.

268 Badian 2000b: 254 objects that "if Darius III had begun his reign with an outstanding success, which his predecessors had taken generations to achieve, completing the reconquest of Egypt in a few months, it is inconceivable that none of the Alexander sources would have seized on this opportunity of enhancing the stature of Darius for the greater glory of Alexander." Briant 2002: 820, 860, 1017–18 treats the chronology with caution, but Badian's is an argument from silence and it is pointless to speculate about how the Alexander historians might have treated Darius' achievement. It is, of course, conceivable that they did not know – indeed, did not care – about the recent events in Egypt. But this too is idle speculation.

269 C 3.1.10 says that in the spring Darius had not yet crossed the Euphrates; in fact, C 3.2.1 claims that he did not plan to take the field in person until he received news of Memnon's death, at which time he was still in Babylon. His exact movements are hard to determine, but C 3.7.1–2 says that when he learned of Alexander's illness in Cilicia he "advanced to the Euphrates" and that he crossed this on pontoon bridges in five days, by which time Alexander had already moved on to Soli in Cilicia. The account of his display and enumeration of forces, in the style of Xerxes, is probably nothing more than embellishment, modeled on the Herodotean account (see Blänsdorf 1971). He did not act in time to send help to Celaenae (cf. C 3.1.8).

270 Charidemus and Amyntas son of Antiochus appear to have come with the mercenaries led by Thymondas (C.3.3.1, 8.2–11; cf. A 2.2.1), who numbered about 30,000 (A 2.8.6; D 17.31.2; C 3.2.9, 9.2).

271 Although there may be some truth to the claim that Darius repented this action, there is no truth to the stories of the Great King haunted by dreams of Alexander and Macedonian fighting qualities (D 17.30.6–7); for there is no way that such information could have been brought to the attention of Greek historians. Curtius cleverly reworks this information and casts Charidemus in the role of Demaratus, the Spartan advisor of Xerxes (see Blänsdorf 1971). Note that the

advice of Charidemus was given while Darius was in Babylon, not at Sochi. In other versions it is at Sochi and the advice is given by Amyntas son of Antiochus (P*A* 20.1–4; A 2.6.3).

272 600,000 men (A 2.8.8; P*A* 18.6; *POxy* 1798, col. 4 = *FGrH* 148); 400,000 infantry and 100,000 cavalry (J 11.9.1; D 17.31.2; cf. D 17.39.4, saying that Darius' roughly 1 million troops were about double the number he had at Issus); C 3.2.4–9 has a little over 300,000. The Persian dead at the end of the battle are given as 100,000 infantry and 10,000 cavalry (C 3.11.27; D 17.36.6; but A 2.11.8 says the 100,000 included 10,000 cavalry); 61,000 infantry dead, 40,000 infantry captured, 10,000 cavalry killed (J 11.9.10); 53,000 dead (*POxy* 1798, col. 4). Ptolemy (*FGrH* 138 F6 = A 2.11.8) claimed that Darius and his pursuers could cross a ravine filled in by the bodies of the dead.

273 Chares of Mytilene (*FGrH* 125 F6 = P*A* 20.9; cf. P*M* 341b) says that Darius wounded Alexander on the thigh with his sword. J 11.9.9 claims that both kings were wounded in the engagement but does not mention single combat. Cf. also Callisthenes *ap.* Plb 12.22.

274 Ael*NA* 6.48 says it was a mare that had recently foaled; P*A* 33.8 tells the same story about Gaugamela.

275 D 17.53.1 talks about swords and lances longer than the ones used at Issus. They may be reflected in the *Alexander Mosaic*, which depicts the battle of Gaugamela, and appears to show Persians with *sarissai* (cf. Badian 1999: 80–1). I am, however, inclined to regard them as the *sarissai* of the Macedonians, and their position behind Darius shows how he was in danger of being cut off.

276 Diodorus does not describe the arrival of the news of Stateira's death in Darius' camp. P*A* 30 says she died after the embassy, but C 4.10.18–34 and J 11.12.6–7 place it before. The suggestion that she may have died in childbirth or of complications associated with pregnancy is exploited by the authors who based their account on Cleitarchus. Darius suffers extreme anxiety, believing that his wife has been violated by her captor, but Alexander himself is depicted as a man of great restraint. See further s.v. **Stateira** [1].

277 A 3.15.7 gives the month as Pyanepsion (October/November), but P*Cam* 19.3 dates it to 26 Boedromion (October 1) 331.

278 Whereas at Issus, Darius' flight is said to have caused the collapse of Persian opposition, there is a tradition that Darius did not flee from Gaugamela until his troops were beginning to abandon him. C 4.15.30 says he actually contemplated an honorable death by suicide. See Nylander 1993: 159 n. 86, comparing the accounts of Darius' flight at Issus and at Gaugamela. Furthermore, Darius refused to destroy the bridge over the Lycus (J 11.14.4, wrongly calling it the Cydnus) because the act, while delaying the enemy, would also doom many of his men to death or capture (C 4.16.8–9). At any rate, the description of Darius as lacking spirit and common sense (A 3.22.1) is probably unfair.

279 Darius did not stop in Arbela. He left his treasure and equipment, which he stored there before the battle, behind for Alexander to capture (A 3.15.5; C 5.1.10).

280 C 5.8.3–4 says 30,000 native infantry and 4,000 mercenaries; 4,000 slingers and archers; and 3,300 cavalry. A 3.19.5 gives radically different numbers: 3,000 cavalry and 6,000 infantry; he adds that Darius took 7,000 talents from the treasury at Ecbatana (cf. Str 15.3.9 [731]: 8,000 talents).

281 A 3.21.10 says that Darius was killed by *Satibarzanes* and Barsaentes. The former may be an error for Nabarzanes (cf. Bosworth i.344–5).

282 Perhaps identical with the Deinarchus who served with Timoleon in Sicily (P*Tim* 21.3, 24.4). Demaratus, who is associated with Deinarchus in Sicily, appears to have been the *xenos* of Philip II.

283 Deinarchus had known Polyperchon as a lieutenant of Antipater and wrongly believed that he had some influence with him (P*Ph* 33.5).

284 See also Eusthatius on Homer's *Iliad* 14.229 and Tzetz*Chil* 8.199, lines 408–15; also Lucian, *Imagines* 9 and *How to Write History* 12.

285 The story is told also by C 4.8.6 without naming Deinocrates.

286 Aelian says that, in spite of Demades' prominence in Athens, his father's name was not a matter of common knowledge. Demades' own son, Demeas, was clearly named for the paternal grandfather.

287 The charge that Demosthenes paid Demades five talents to intercede with the King is certainly a fabrication (D 17.15.3). Din 1.104 claims that Demades admitted without shame that he had regularly accepted bribes (but see Williams 1989); cf. also P*M* 188f for Demades' alleged venality, and P*Ph* 20.6, 30.4–5 for his extravagance.

288 Demades' alleged remark that the Macedonian army after the death of Alexander was "like the Cyclops with his one eye put out" (P*M* 181f; cf. P*Galba* 1.4 but P*M* 336f, more plausibly, attributes the remark to Leosthenes) suggests a hostility toward Alexander, as does his famous remark that if Alexander were really dead the world would be filled with the stench of his corpse (P*Ph* 22.5). But he was, after all, a politician and his utterances were intended to please or amuse his audience. Demades proposed honors, proxenies, and citizenship for various Macedonians: Antipater and Alcimachus (Harpocration s.v. "Alkimachos" = Hyp frg. 19.2 [Burtt]; Schwenk no. 4), a son of a certain Andromenes (Schwenk no. 7; even if not the father of Amyntas, Simmias, Attalus, and Polemon, then certainly a prominent *hetairos* of Philip II); Amyntor son of Demetrius, perhaps the father of Hephaestion (*IG* ii[2] 405 = Schwenk no. 24; cf. Heckel 1991); as well as a certain Thessalian from Larissa (*IG* ii[2] 353 = Schwenk no. 51).

289 Ath 13.591f claimed that Demeas was Demades' son by a flute-girl, a charge that he attributes to Hypereides. But the uncorroborated allegations of orators need not be taken seriously.

290 Slanders against him are common enough: Ath 2.44f called Demades a drunkard. Though clearly a man of wit, Demades' alleged reference to Aegina as "the eyesore of Piraeus" (Ath 3.99d) was originally attributed to Pericles.

291 It is highly unlikely that the sources would have been silent about the relationship, considering Demetrius' involvement in Dimnus' conspiracy (A 3.27.5; C 6.7.15), even more so if Curtius is correct in suggesting that Demetrius played a major role in the organization of the plot (C 6.11.37). Furthermore, P*Demetr* 2.1 claims that Demetrius Poliorcetes (born in 337/6) was named for his uncle. Since he was the elder of Antigonus' sons, this suggests strongly that the honor was bestowed upon the elder Demetrius posthumously, that is, that Antigonus' brother died before 336. Plutarch (ibid.) adds that there were rumors that Antigonus married Demetrius' mother Stratonice, who had previously been married to his brother, the father of Poliorcetes. But here too the sources' failure to mention that Poliorcetes' natural father had been executed for conspiring against Alexander creates a deafening silence.

292 Identification with the anti-Macedonian Demo*chares* (Sen*de Ira* 3.23; thus Schaefer ii[2] 381 n. 1) is at best a remote possibility.

293 The word ἀνεψιός can mean either nephew or cousin.

294 This information is not corroborated by the three other lists, and Bosworth i.94 notes that "his is the only name in Plutarch which is at all suspicious." Perhaps his name has been confused with that of Diotimus who appears in both A 1.10.4 and the *Suda*. It is also interesting that the comic poet Timocles, in his play *Delos*, mentions Demon in connection with Callisthenes, who is also unique to the list of P*Dem* 23.4.

295 Despite their political differences, it appears that Demosthenes and Aeschines may have had family connections. See Badian 2000c: 14–15. Aeschines had an uncle named Cleobulus (Aes 2.78). On

the other hand, it is difficult to imagine these orators casting aspersions on relatives that they had in common. Cf. Demosthenes' portrayal of Aeschines' mother: Str 10.3.18 [471]; Dem 18.130, 259. Demochares the historian was a nephew of Demosthenes (Ath 6. 252f–253a), as was Demon (see s.v. **Demon**).

296 His speeches against Aphobus and Onetor, whom he prosecuted when he was 21, have been published with a commentary by Pearson 1972. Of an estate valued at about fourteen talents, Demosthenes received only a little over 7,000 drachmas when, in 366, he reached the age of 18 (see the figures in Davies 126–8).

297 The amount of 300 talents is attested only by the orators Aeschines and Deinarchus. Although the Persian King may have considered distributing such sums to the Greek states in general, there is certainly no possibility that Demosthenes himself received such a sum. Equally questionable is the claim that Arcadia (see s.v. **Astylus**) did not send help to the Thebans in 335 because Demosthenes withheld the promised funds (Aes 3.240; Din 1.18–21). See also the discussion in Worthington 139–43, 160–4.

298 Phocion owed his success to Demosthenes, who supported him against Chares; he defended him against several capital charges and yet it was Phocion who betrayed him and had him exiled (N*Ph* 2.2–3). Cf. P*M* 188a; P*Ph* 9.8, 16.3, 17.1–3 for their rivalry. Polyeuctus was said to have remarked that Demosthenes was the best orator but Phocion was the most effective speaker, and Demosthenes himself allegedly remarked that Phocion was the "cleaver (*kopis*) of my speeches" (P*Ph* 5.5, 9). P*Ph* 7.5 treats Demosthenes as one of those whose contribution was solely in the political/oratorical sphere (and not that of a general).

299 For details and sources see Schaefer iii^2 293–350; Berve ii.138–417; Adams 1901; Will 113–32; Jaschinski; Worthington 41–77; Blackwell 133–44; Worthington 1994, 2000: 101–8.

300 The embassy was actually an intelligence gathering mission. C speaks of Scythians "beyond the Bosphorus," which reflects the mistaken geography of Alexander and his historians, who believed that the Iaxartes was the Tanais (i.e., the Don), which flowed into the Sea of Azov and separated Europe from Asia. See Brunt i.524–5.

301 It is possible that Diodotus was a pseudonym for Eumenes himself (cf. Xenophon's attribution of the *Anabasis* to Themistogenes of Syracuse, Xen*HG* 3.1.2) or that Diodotus was responsible for a later reworking of the *Ephemerides* and not a member of Alexander's expedition.

302 A similar fate befell Magas of Cyrene (Agatharchides *ap*. Ath 12.550c).

303 Dio Chr 4.66 describes a practice during the feast known as the Sacaea in which a prisoner destined to be executed plays out the role of king for a day; Berossus, *FGrH* 680 F2 = Ath 14.639c (cf. Ctesias, *FGrH* 688 F4) depicts this as a Babylonian feast in which for a period of five days servants exchange roles with their masters. Abramenko 2000 sees the episode as part of a genuine conspiracy against Alexander.

304 Pl*NH* 35.139 and Aristobulus, *FGrH* 139 F47 = Ath 6.251a call him a pankratiast; C 9.7.16 is alone in referring to him as a boxer (*pugil*); D 17.100.2, Hyp 2.5–6, and Ael*VH* 12.58 are vague.

305 Cf. P*A* 28.3; P*M* 341b, 190e; DL 9.60; Sen*Ep* 6.7.12; Dio Chr 44.

306 His Macedonian origin is not certain, but I find it highly improbable that Docimus can be identified with the Tarentine of that name whom Philip II deposed from his command (*hegemonia*) because, contrary to Macedonian custom, he bathed in warm water (Pol*Strat* 4.2.1). Griffith 247 n. 1 believes that he may have been a *hegemon* of mercenaries, that is, an infantry commander, from Tarentum. But that would scarcely qualify him for the important commands entrusted to him by Perdiccas, Antigonus, and Lysimachus respectively; nor would it explain his associations with Attalus

son of Andromenes and Alcetas. Perhaps he belonged to the Tarentine horsemen, but these are not attested until the age of the Successors.

307 It is not clear whether Philetaerus was already treasurer of Pergamum under Antigonus or if Lysimachus appointed him after Docimus' defection.

308 Brosius 78 n. 69: "By marrying Drypetis to Hephaistion, Alexander prevented other Macedonian nobles from claiming the right of legitimate succession to the Persian throne through marriage to this royal daughter."

309 Enylus appears as Ainel on his coinage: Hill 1910: 96.

310 At Issus the Peloponnesians are mentioned but their commander is not named; C 4.13.29 wrongly assigns Erigyius' command at Gaugamela to Craterus (cf. Atkinson i.425).

311 See Atkinson ii.107, citing Helmreich 1927: 82–7. Some have accepted the mutilated Greeks as historical (e.g., Radet 1927: 6–8); for a brief discussion of the problem see Yardley & Heckel 173–5. See also Miles 2003.

312 Little of historical value can be gleaned from his *apophthegmata* (*PM* 192a–b, 220d–221a) except that he was a younger contemporary of Xenocrates, that he was king at the time of Alexander's Exiles' Decree, and that he had a realistic view of Macedonian power.

313 Antigonus may have used the charge that Eudamus had murdered Porus to justify his execution.

314 Hammond 1987: 340 reads: τοὺς φρουροὺς [τοὺς μετὰ Εὐ]δραμένους ἀπέ[στειλε]. I suspect, however, that the passage has something to do with the massacre of guards, as the original editors, Clarysse & Schepens 1985, suggested.

315 Hoffmann does not include Eugnostus in his list of Macedonians, and Berve ii.154 suggests that he may be a prominent Greek who was enrolled in the *hetairoi.*

316 Bosworth i.275–6 sees the "mercenaries" as military settlers from the Persian period. He may be right in suggesting that Eugnostus received the position because Lycidas, an Aetolian, might not have been regarded as entirely trustworthy.

317 According to Duris, Philip saw Eumenes exercising and was so impressed by his skill and intelligence that he took him into his following (Duris, *FGrH* 76 F53 = P*Eum* 1.2).

318 P*Eum* 1.4 calls him *archigrammateus*, in part to contrast him with Neoptolemus, who was *archihypaspistes*; cf. *LM* 116: *hypomnematographus*.

319 Whether she is the wife to whom Antigonus returned Eumenes' remains in 315 (P*Eum* 19.2), and hence also the mother of the children mentioned in the same passage, is unclear. If so, then Eumenes, like Seleucus Nicator, will have been unusual in not repudiating his Persian bride.

320 Eumenes' Greek origins must account for the failure of Macedonian officers to serve under him. For Antigonus P*Eum* 3.4; cf. A*Succ* 1.20; D 18.23.3–4; but P*Eum* 3.5 attributes his failure to cooperate to arrogance and ambition. For Alcetas' refusal see D 18.29.2. Alcetas and Eumenes were also divided on the question of whether Perdiccas should marry Nicaea (Alcetas' choice) or Cleopatra (A*Succ* 1.21); after Triparadeisus Alcetas and his colleagues refused to join Eumenes (A*Succ* 1.41). Neoptolemus also resented the Greek commander, but there was a history of personal rivalry (D 18.29.2, 4; P*Eum* 7.7).

321 For Eumenes' death see App*Syr* 53 [267]; App*Mithr* 8; P*Eum* 19.1–3; D 19.44.2–3. Justin refers to his death at 15.1.1 but does not actually mention it in the appropriate context. Paus 1.6.7 argues that Eumenes' lengthy campaigning against Antigonus wore the latter down and was responsible for his ultimate defeat at Ipsus. See also Pol*Strat* 4.6.9–13; 4.6.15, 19; 4.8.1–5; Fr*Strat* 4.7.34; and for Paraetacene and Gabiene see Devine 1985a, 1985b, with ancient sources.

322 Berve ii.160 assumes that these were produced when Philip constituted the League of Corinth in 337.

323 Philadelphus is said to have killed one of Eurydice's sons (Paus 1.7.1).

324 For the textual problem in *PA* 41.10 see Hamilton 109.

325 Ath 13.595e says that the play was produced (a) at the Hydaspes River and (b) *after* Harpalus' flight from Babylonia to the west. Now, if both statements are true, we must assume either that Harpalus' flight occurred sometime in 327/6 or that the Hydaspes River is not the one in India. Droysen i[3] 405 n. 101 suggests that the text should read "Choaspes" rather than "Hydaspes"; Beloch iv[2] 2.434–6 thinks instead of the Medus Hydaspes (cf. Virgil, *Georgics* 4.211); Goukowsky ii.77 and Bosworth 1988a: 149–50 also believe the play was produced in the west, in this case in Carmania in 324. It is not necessary, however, to assume that Glycera came only as far as Tarsus. D 17.108.6 speaks of her being kept in luxury by Harpalus before he mentions Alexander's return from India and Harpalus' flight. It may be possible that Harpalus, in anticipation of the King's return, had already taken up residence in Cilicia.

326 Menander's character Glycera in the *Perikeiromene* may have been inspired by the famous courtesan, but stories of a love relationship between Menander and a certain Glycera are inferences from the text and of little value (see Lefkowitz 1981: 113–14).

327 For the chronology of these events see Heisserer 187–91. Certainly, the services of Gorgus cannot be connected with his crowning of the King at Ecbatana, which must have occurred later in 324.

328 The inscriptions are *IG* iv[2] 616 and 617, the latter preserving the letters ὁπλοφορ-.

329 The patronymic is confirmed by the Ephesian inscription published by Keil 1913: IIp. It might be argued that Nearchus, the source of *AInd* 18 (cf. *FGrH* 133 F1), ought to have known the correct name of the trierarch, but the list contains other errors that are doubtless the scribal errors. These could be attributed to Arrian himself, if not to a later scribe. This would rule out the identification of the trierarch with the *archpeirates* of Pol*Strat* 5.19 (cf. Fr*Strat* 3.3.7: "Mandron"; cf. Berve ii.40).

330 The date of Hagnon's defeat by Thymochares is uncertain. It was originally thought that Hagnon was a supporter of Perdiccas and defeated in the Cypriot campaign of 321/0, but this appears to be refuted by Hagnon's support of the pro-Craterus party in Ephesus. Others have dated the battle to the archonship of Praxibulus (315/4), which is mentioned in *SIG*[3] 409, line 9 (Hauben), but the inscription appears to make a distinction between the time of the naval battle and the archonship of Praxibulus, implying that the battle took place before 315/4. Billows 387 is right to dismiss connections between the sea battle and the events described in D 19.59.1, 62.3–6. The coins minted by the Tean magistrate Hagnon (Poole, *BMC Ionia*, 312, nos. 24, 25) are presumably his.

331 Deinarchus is said to have composed a speech against Hagnonides in the Harpalus affair (Dion Hal *Din* 10 [654]). Hyp 5.40 refers to Hagnonides' impending trial or his upcoming testimony on behalf of Demosthenes (Worthington 279).

332 Hagnonides' chief supporters were Epicurus and Demophilus, who were hunted down and punished by Phocion's son (P*Ph* 38.3).

333 All three versions go back to Pompeius Trogus, but since the information comes from a section that does not deal with Alexander it appears to have been taken from an anecdotal passage in a non-Alexander historian.

334 The family may, however, have had connections with the house of Antigonus the One-Eyed. Tauron may have been in the service of Antigonus (*IG* XII. 9 197, 4), and in the second century we find a prominent Beroean named Harpalus son of Polemaeus (Tataki no. 230); Polemaeus was, of course, the name of Monophthalmus' nephew (and, apparently, his brother; cf. Billows 16–17).

335 Badian 1960b; Bosworth i.284; Carney 1982; Green 222–3; Heckel 1977b;

Jaschinski 10–18; Kingsley 1986; Worthington 1984.

336 Jaschinski 12–18 believes that Harpalus returned to Europe in order to encourage Alexander of Epirus to press his claims to the Macedonian throne; for he was married to Alexander's sister, Cleopatra, and would have had the support of the queen mother, Olympias. This strikes me as highly implausible. For a different interpretation of Harpalus' activities in Greece see Kingsley 1986; cf. Garnsey 1988: 158–62.

337 For his attempts to transplant ivy from Media to Babylon see Theophr*HP* 4.4.1; Pl*NH* 16.144.

338 Cf. Bosworth 1988a: 149; but Worthington 1986: 64 follows Beloch iv^{2} 2.434–6 in dating the production of the play to October 324, at Ecbatana. See also Snell 1964: 99–138; Sutton 1980a; Sutton 1980b: 75–81.

339 Ath 13.595e claims that the play was first performed at the Hydaspes, which Snell 1964: 109ff. takes to mean in India, in 326. Droysen i^{3} 406 n. 101 suggests Choaspes instead of Hydaspes; Beloch iv^{2} 2.434–6 argues that the Medus Hydaspes (Virgil, *Georgics* 4.211, explained by Servius as *fluvius Mediae;* possibly the Karkheh?) is meant. Goukowsky ii.77 thinks it was the Iranian "Hydaspes" (Halil-rud), and that the *Agen* was produced at Salmous in Carmania. Cf. Bosworth 1988a: 149–50.

340 Plutarch details Phocion's involvement with Harpalus. The latter attempted to bribe Phocion with 700 talents; Phocion rejected his bribes, though others accepted (P*Ph* 21.3–4). Harpalus befriended Phocion's son-in-law, Charicles (21.5), who was put on trial for his dealings with Harpalus (22.4). After Harpalus' death, his daughter (by Pythionice) was raised by Charicles and Phocion (22.3).

341 On the chronological problems see, most recently, Worthington 1986; for the political and legal activities in Athens: Will 113ff.

342 Julian, *Epistle* 82 (446a) claims that there was a second, almost certainly incorrect, version that the accident occurred at the Euphrates.

343 I have discussed the family of Hegelochus at length in Heckel 6–11, reiterating the arguments of Heckel 1982a. Berve ii.185 s.v. Ἱππόστρατος stops short of identifying the Hippostratus of the Satyrus fragment with his namesake in Marsyas of Pella, *FGrH* 135/6 F17. I see no serious obstacle to this identification. In fact, it goes a long way toward explaining the so-called conspiracy of Hegelochus mentioned by C 6.11.22–9.

344 Hauben 1972: 57 argues on the basis of C 3.1.19 that Hegelochus commanded the marines, while Amphoterus acted as admiral, but A 3.2.6 speaks of Hegelochus sending Amphoterus to Cos in 332, suggesting that the latter was a subordinate (cf. Berve ii.164 "untergeordnet"). A lower rank for Amphoterus does not rule out the likelihood that his task was to keep an eye on Hegelochus' activities.

345 Here he captured Pharnabazus (who later escaped), along with Aristonicus of Methymna, Apollonides, Phesinus, and Megareus, all of whom he brought to Alexander in Egypt (A 3.2.4–5; cf. C 4.5.14–22).

346 This can be deduced from the fact that Philoxenus demanded the surrender of Hegesias' murderers and imprisoned them in Sardis.

347 We have no firm dates. Polyaenus says that they had been imprisoned "for a long time" in Sardis before making their escape. One of them was crippled in the attempt and sent to Alexander in Babylon.

348 For Alexander's devotion to Hephaestion: C 3.12.16; P*A* 47.9–10; D 17.114.1–3; cf. A 1.12.1; Ael*VH* 12.7 (cf. Bosworth i.103–4); *LDM* 12.4 (397). Craterus: *erat Craterus regi carus in paucis,* C 6.8.2; A 7.12.3; cf. P*A* 47.9–10; P*M* 181d; D 17.114.1–2. Alexander's relationship with Hephaestion has recently been the subject of much discussion and controversy. For a thorough and balanced discussion see Reames-Zimmerman 1999.

349 If Choerilus of Iasos depicted Alexander as Achilles in his third-rate epic poem (Constantius Porphyrogenitus = *FGrH* 153 F10a), he may have compared Hephaestion with Patroclus, but it appears that the stories of Alexander's imitation of Achilles arose after Hephaestion's death (see Perrin 1895). Ps-Call 1.18.5; Jul Val 1.10 relate that Alexander and Hephaestion went to Olympia. This is pure fiction.

350 Aristion's presence at the court is dated by an Athenian embassy, which found him there in 331. Goldstein: 42–3 n. 33 correctly rejects Badian's suggestion that Hephaestion was Demosthenes' "powerful protector at the Court" (1961: 34). *IG* ii[2] 405, a decree of Demades granting Athenian citizenship to Amyntor son of Demetrius and his descendants in 334 BC (cf. Osborne i.69–71, D 21), may refer to Hephaestion's father (Heckel 1991). Perhaps he used his influence (possibly even through his son) to persuade Alexander to treat the Athenians with leniency in 335, or to back down on his demand for the expulsion of the prominent Athenian orators. At any rate, Hephaestion himself was thus, by extension, awarded Athenian citizenship and became the contact for Demosthenes at Alexander's court. It is interesting to note that the ships which conducted the siege-equipment were probably those twenty Athenian vessels retained by Alexander at Miletus (D 17.22.5). Hence Hephaestion may have had other personal Athenian contacts.

351 Perhaps Hephaestion replaced the *somatophylax basilikos* Ptolemy who was killed at Halicarnassus in 334 (A 1.22.4), but this depends on the exact status and identity of that Ptolemy. If Ptolemy was nothing more than the commander of the *agema* of the hypaspists, then his successor in that office would have been Admetus.

352 Hephaestion was of a particularly quarrelsome nature (P*A* 47.11–12; P*M* 337a; P*Eum* 2.1–3; A 7.13.1; 7.14.9; cf. Berve ii.173) and not above maligning others to Alexander (P*A* 55.1). It is hard to believe P*M* 339f that Alexander did not discuss the matter of Philotas with Hephaestion.

353 The other contingents were commanded by Perdiccas, Ptolemy, and Alexander, while Coenus and Artabazus held a joint command; C 8.1.1 speaks of three divisions under Alexander, Hephaestion, and Coenus; C 8.1.10 says Artabazus accompanied Hephaestion. Arrian speaks of *stratia*, implying that the entire force was divided into five parts, but a large portion of the army (the infantry battalions of Polyperchon, Attalus, Gorgias, Meleager, and Craterus, who commanded them, A 4.16.1, 17.1; C 8.1.6) was in Bactria. The main striking force in Sogdiana was the cavalry.

354 Holt 62–3 comments: "It was probably during Hephaestion's mission to colonize the eastern Oxus and its tributaries that Ai Khanoum (Alexandria-Oxiana?) was founded at the strategic juncture of the Oxus and Kochba Rivers."

355 Milns 112 credits Hephaestion with bridging the Euphrates River (in two places) at Thapsacus, which is interesting in view of his later activities (e.g., bridging the Indus), but his role is not documented, as far as I can tell, by the ancient sources (cf. A 3.7.1; C 4.9.12).

356 See Smith[3] 53 and 63, who follows the suggestion of Foucher 1901: 46 that the crossing took place at Ohind or Und, 16 miles north of Attock (Atak), which was formerly thought to be the location of Hephaestion's bridge; see also Eggermont 1970: 102–10. Berve poses the question, who had the *imperium maius* in this venture? Berve ii.171; cf. ii.314, where Berve suggests "dass P. die Fußtruppen, H. die Reiter kommandierte."

357 The claim (D 17.93.1) that Hephaestion returned to Alexander, "having conquered a large part of India," does him more than justice.

358 For this campaign, Alexander devised the following strategy. First the slower troops, Polyperchon's battalion and the elephants, were transferred to the western bank and placed under Craterus'

command, as were the *hippotoxotai* and the force with which Philip son of Machatas had followed the course of the Acesines River (A 6.5.5). Hephaestion and the troops that remained with him were to march five days in advance toward the confluence of the Acesines and Hydraotes. Nearchus was to sail down the Acesines with the fleet, and Ptolemy was to follow Hephaestion's route after a delay of three days. Alexander meanwhile crossed the desert region between the rivers with the intention of taking the Mallians off guard. He hoped that those of the Mallians who escaped southward would be driven into the arms of Hephaestion, while Ptolemy would lie in wait for those who attempted to escape to the west (A 6.5.6). The elaborate strategy proved unnecessary, for Alexander took the Mallians completely by surprise. They had not expected that the enemy would arrive from the west, through the waterless region. Those who retreated to their chief city, where Alexander was critically wounded, were slaughtered, while those of another town, if they did not find refuge in the marshes, were butchered by the forces of Perdiccas (A 6.6.6).

359 Hephaestion appears to have completed this work by the time of Alexander's return, although it is possible that Patala harbor, which became the base for Nearchus' Ocean-fleet, was set in final order by Nearchus himself (A 6.21.3).

360 Whether any of his contemporaries encouraged rumors that Hephaestion was Alexander's minion cannot be determined (Ael*VH* 12.7; J 12.12.11; *LDM* 12.4 (397); D 17.114.3; cf. Tarn ii.319–26, Appendix 18: "Alexander's Attitude to Sex," esp. 321).

361 See Droysen i[3] 312; Berve ii.171; Schachermeyr 383; Hamilton 153; Wilcken 169; Green 375–6. Chares of Mytilene, whom Schachermeyr regards as Alexander's "Chef der Kanzlei," would be a more suitable candidate for such work (Schachermeyr 1970: 17–18, 34).

362 On this point all the sources concur, but there were some who thought it noble that Alexander should display his sorrow, others who found it unfitting for him or for any other king. Those who saw in Alexander's grief an emulation of Achilles reported that he shaved the manes of his horses and his mules, tore down city-walls, and lay upon the corpse of his Patroclus, refusing food and water; the last point is at least typical of Alexander. For Alexander's excessive grief and the agreement of the sources see A 7.14.2; for different attitudes toward the display of emotion, A 7.14.3. The emulation of Achilles: A 7.14.4 (he also cut his own hair); Ael*VH* 7.8; P*Pel* 34.2 (horses' manes, demolished walls), cf. P*A* 72.3. For his refusal of food and drink, A 7.14.8. Cf. Alexander's behavior after Cleitus' death, A 4.9.1ff.; P*A* 51.10–52.1; C 8.2.1ff.

363 Cf. Hamilton 1984: 14. See also McKechnie 1995. D 17.115.6 speaks of the slaughter of 10,000 sacrificial victims; for the cancelation of Hephaestion's monument see D 18.4.2 (who wrongly calls it the pyre, which had already been completed); cf. Badian 1967b: 200–1. According to P*A* 72.5 the work was to be undertaken by Stasicrates (Deinocrates? see Berve, nos. 249, 720), who had offered to shape Mount Athos into a giant likeness of Alexander. See Hamilton 202. For Perdiccas' instructions to take the body to Babylon, D 17.110.8; it is not mentioned by Arrian.

364 Such were the honors accorded the dead Hephaestion. But there were stories of Alexander's anger. Blame was cast on Glaucias the physician and on the healing-god Asclepius: Glaucias was cruelly executed (A 7.14.4; P*A* 72.3), and the temple of Asclepius at Ecbatana razed (Epictetus 2.22.17; but cf. A 7.14.6). On the Cossaeans too, a barbaric people to the west of Ecbatana, Alexander vented his anger (A 7.15.1ff.; D 17.111.4ff.; Pol*Strat* 4.3.31).

365 The hero-cult of Hephaestion is alluded to by Hyp 6.21; cf. Treves 1939 (the cult was in place already in April/May 323); Bickerman 1963; Habicht[2] 28–36. See also Hamilton 200–1, where these views

are summarized; the notion that Alexander sought to introduce his own deification by means of Hephaestion's hero-cult antedates Habicht, see Kornemann 1901: 65. A 7.23.6–8 relates that Alexander was willing to forgive Cleomenes his crimes in Egypt if he saw to a hero's shrine there. For small likenesses of Hephaestion made by the *hetairoi* see D 17.115.1. The lion of Hamadan – 3.56 m long and of brown sandstone (similar in size and style to the lions of Chaeronea and Amphipolis) – may be the one surviving monument of Hephaestion. For this statue, and its history, see Luschey 1968: esp. 121–2; cf. Lane Fox 435.

366 Possibly the man who ruled Media briefly, and, if so, then perhaps from Oropus.

367 It is unlikely that the ethnic Thrax would be applied to him unless his father were Thracian. Thracians with Greek (Macedonian) names in this period normally have non-Greek patronymika. See Besevliev 16–27.

368 For Nearchus' relationship to Heracles see P*Eum* 1.7.

369 J 14.6.2 confuses Heracles with Alexander IV. In a later passage, Demetrius' claim that Antigonus had been guardian of Alexander's children (J 16.1.13) can refer only to the brief period in 320 when he was guardian of Alexander IV (and Philip III Arrhidaeus); cf. A*Succ* 1.38.

370 Somewhat different is Berve's view (ii.168): "Da H. von A III, 26, 3 bei Parmenions Ermordung unter den in Ecbatana anwesenden Strategen nicht genannt wird und später (324) wegen Beraubung eines Heiligtumes in Susa bestraft wurde (A VI, 27, 5), darf man annehmen, dass er Ende 330 mit seinem Kontingent von Parmenion nach Susa beordert ward."

371 Reuss 1 believes "dass der Altersunterschied [i.e., between Hieronymus and Eumenes] kein gar grosser war," and suggests a birthdate for Hieronymus of 361.

372 Demetrius ruled Athens as Cassander's puppet from 317 until 307, when Demetrius Poliorcetes "liberated" the city. He fled the city and came ultimately to Egypt where he died in 283 BC. According to DL 5.75 Demetrius began his career when Harpalus fled to Athens (324 BC). We have no information about any activities of his during Alexander's reign. Hence I have not included him in this collection. See Berve ii.139 no. 259.

373 *LM* 97–8, 103, 106, 109, 111–12, 114, 116, 122; Ps-Call 3.31–3.

374 Berve ii.378 for no good reason makes her a daughter of Bisthanes. Brosius 95 calls her Barsine and identifies her as a daughter of Arses. I do not see any evidence for her name, and the assumption that Arses was her father is based on the claim that he was the only one of Ochus' sons to survive (D 17.5.4). But this ignores two facts: there were sons of concubines who survived (witness Bisthanes, A 3.19.4 with Bosworth i.335) and Hystaspes' wife could have been born to one of the sons whom Bagoas later killed.

375 For an attempt to link [P]*M* 849f with *IG* ii^2 561 see Oikonomides 1987. But the inscription is clearly a decree of Stratocles.

376 The time of his departure and purpose of his mission are not clear. Sealey's attempt to link Iphicrates with Dropides and certain Athenian factions has not gained acceptance (*BICS* 7 [1960]: 33–4).

377 Curtius adds the Athenians Aristogeiton and Dropides, and, instead of Euthycles, names Pasippus, Onomastorides, Onomas, and Callicratidas. But this appears to confuse those captured at Damascus with those taken after Darius' death in 330 (cf. Atkinson i.464–5).

378 C 8.4.22, however, refers to the sons of Chorienes (Sisimithres; the MSS. have *cohortandus*, almost certainly a corruption of Chorienes. Alde's emendation to Oxyartes is implausible; cf. Heckel 1986a: 225).

379 Or possibly from Tereina, unless the text of [P]*M* 845c is corrupt.

380 The story is connected in some way with that of the ring, engraved with the device of an anchor, which Laodice gave to her son (App*Syr* 56 [284–7]).

381 Hence, it is curious that Alexander is said to have sent Leonnatus to the captive Persian queens, and not Laomedon (C 3.12.6–7), and it is possible that the original source of this information (accidentally or deliberately?) substituted the name of Leonnatus for Laomedon. Curtius notes that the man whom Alexander intended to send, Mithrenes, was a Persian speaker.

382 According to the forged will of Alexander, this territory was assigned to Meleager: Jul Val 3.58; Leo 33; Ps-Call 3.33.15; *LM* 117; cf. Heckel 1988: 67; cf. Lehmann-Haupt §26; cf. §§129ff.

383 Judeich's view (1895: 164ff.) that Laomedon was the occupant of the Alexander sarcophagus is incompatible with both the artistic and historical evidence.

384 See Pollitt 90–1 for testimonia; Richter 1950: 284ff.

385 Pearson 254 is perhaps right to comment: "It is useless to spend time on these shadowy figures." The one authentic fragment of the Alexander history adds nothing to our knowledge (*FGrH* F1 = Ath 12.550f).

386 The identity of the Leonnatus of a recently published inscription concerning Philippi (Vatin 1984: 259–70; Missitzis 1985: 3–14; Hammond 1988: 382–91) cannot be determined. The coincidental appearance on the stone of the names Leonnatus and Philotas (without patronymika) has led editors to identify the latter as Parmenion's son (cf. Hammond 1988: 383 n. 2), and to date their mission to Philippi to "either before the Triballian campaign in 335 or before the Persian expedition in 334, when Philotas was available" (Missitzis 1985: 9). Leonnatus could, however, be the son of Antipater of Aegae (cf. A*Ind* 18.3); Philotas is far too common a name to allow a positive identification.

387 C 3.12.6–12 claims that Alexander had intended to send Mithrenes, former satrap of Sardis and a Persian speaker (§§6–7), but sent instead Leonnatus, one of his *hetairoi*. The situation required someone of linguistic skill, and it is unlikely that Leonnatus had such talents. A 6.30.3 says that Peucestas was the only Macedonian to learn the Persian language, but at 3.6.6 he notes that the King placed Laomedon in charge of the captive Persians precisely because he was bilingual (*diglossos*). Hence it may be that Ptolemy, in his *History*, substituted the name of Leonnatus for Laomedon (cf. Heckel 1981b: 272–4). Curtius certainly made use of Ptolemy in his own *History of Alexander*.

388 Berve ii.235 believes that Arrian refers not to Leonnatus the Somatophylax but to the son of Antipater of Aegae, whom Nearchus named as one of the trierarchs at the Hydaspes River (A*Ind* 18.6).

389 Presumably Leonnatus' activities were similar to those of Ptolemy, with whom he shared the rank of Somatophylax and whose earlier military career was somewhat similar (for Ptolemy and Leonnatus together see C 8.1.45–6; A 4.21.4; C 8.6.22; A 4.23.3, 24.10, 25.2–4; C 8.14.15; P*M* 344d; A 6.28.4). But this is of little help, for we know only that the Somatophylakes, Perdiccas, Ptolemy, and Lysimachus, crossed the Hydaspes in the same triakontor as Alexander (A 5.13.1; but cf. Berve ii.172 n. 1); of the other Somatophylakes Arrian says nothing, though Hephaestion, as hipparch, certainly crossed the river at the same time. Curtius, on the other hand, is of little use, for he greatly exaggerates the role and importance of Ptolemy in this battle (C 8.13.17–27).

390 See also P*M* 327b; 341c; 343d; 344c–d; Str 15.1.33 [701]; J 12.9.3–13; Oros 3.19.6–10; *IA* 115–116; *ME* 76–77; cf. Ps-Call 3.4.12–15; Zon 4.13; p.299, 16). There is confusion in the sources over the identities of Alexander's "protectors." One is certain: Peucestas, who was later appointed an eighth Somatophylax for his part in saving the King's life (A 6.28.3–4). The rest are problematic. Aristonus and Ptolemy are named, the former only by Curtius; Ptolemy himself (in conflict with the testimony of Cleitarchus) said that he was not present at the battle (C 9.5.21; cf. A 6.11.8;

6.5.6–7). Three others are mentioned by various sources: Habreas and Limnaeus (= Timaeus), both killed in the skirmish, and Leonnatus, who for his heroism was crowned at Susa by Alexander (A*Ind* 23.6; A 7.5.5): see C 9.5.15, 17 (Leonnatus, Peucestas, Aristonus, Timaeus); P*M* 344d (Leonnatus, Ptolemy, Limnaeus), but P*M* 327b names only Ptolemy and Limnaeus; A*Ind* 19.8 = Nearchus, *FGrH* 133 F1 (Leonnatus, Peucestas); A 6.9.3, 10.1–2 (Leonnatus, Peucestas, Habreas); A 6.11.7 says Leonnatus' role is not attested by all sources.

391 The Alexandria founded by Leonnatus (Pl*NH* 6.97 = Onesicritus, *FGrH* 134 F28) is apparently that amongst the Oreitae (cf. Fraser 165 n. 115).

392 It is usually assumed, but without good evidence, that all the *hetairoi* except Seleucus (e.g., Tarn 1929: 139) repudiated their Susan brides.

393 Phocion was opposed to the Lamian War since he favored a policy of cooperating with the Macedonians (cf. P*M* 546a). At the outbreak of the Lamian War, Phocion likened Leosthenes' words to the cypress tree: beautiful and tall, but bearing no fruit (P*M* 188d). Furthermore, Phocion described Leosthenes' initial success as a good victory in the "short race" but said he feared the "long-distance race of the war" (P*M* 803a–b). Cf. P*Tim* 6.5 for Phocion's opposition. Phocion is said to have lamented the fact that at this time in Athens elected officials were divided between orators (like Eubulus, Aristophon, Demosthenes, Lycurgus, and Hypereides) and *strategoi* (like Diopeithes, Menestheus, Leosthenes, and Chabrias), when what the city needed was someone who served it in both capacities (P*Ph* 7.5; cf. P*M* 486d). For this division of functions see also Plutarch's *Comparison of Demosthenes and Cicero* 3.

394 For Alexander's order to the satraps to disband their mercenaries see D 17.106.3, 111.1; 18.9.1.

395 A full list of the anti-Macedonian allies is given by D 18.11.1–2; Str 9.5.10 [434]; cf. J 13.5.10, where it is wrongly stated that Corinth was persuaded to join.

396 The Boeotians were reluctant to join the Athenian alliance because they had received Theban land when the city was razed by Alexander in 335. Now they were afraid that they would be forced to give it back.

397 A Limnaeus son of Harpalus appears in an inscription from Cassandreia (cf. Henry 1990: 179–80); at Beroea (Tataki 215 nos. 812–14, and p. 423); and at the court of Philip V (cf. Plb 18.34.4).

398 According to Libanius, *ad Dem* 23.768, he was older than Demosthenes. Lycurgus is said to have been a student of Plato (Polemon *ap.* DL 3.46; [P]*M* 841b) and Isocrates (cf. Zosimus, *Life of Isocrates*).

399 D 16.88.1 is mistaken when he says that Lycurgus had already managed the city's finances for twelve years at the time of his prosecution of Lysicles.

400 Immediately preceding this anecdote is a reference to Lynceus of Samos, who attended and described in detail a dinner-party given by Lamia in honor of Demetrius (P*Demetr* 27.2; cf. Ath 3.101e; 4.128a–b). Duris and Lynceus were brothers (Ath 8.337d; *Suda* Λ 776), students of Theophrastus of Eresus (Ath 4.128a–b), and contemporaries of Lysimachus and Demetrius. Of the content of Duris' historical work we are reasonably well informed; Lynceus is more elusive, though it appears that his work was rich in the scandalous gossip of dinner-parties. And dinner-parties, such as the one described by Lynceus, will have been the source of, and the inspiration for, much of the gossip concerning the Diadochoi, and especially the stories about Demetrius, Lamia, and Lysimachus (cf. Ath 6.246e, 261b; 14.614f–615a; P*Demetr* 27.3). Duris of Samos, on the other hand, is known to have written a somewhat sensational *Macedonian History*. Of course, neither may have been the source – perhaps Lysimachus, for an unknown reason, circulated the story himself – but there is a strong probability that the author who invented or, at least, promulgated the story that Lysimachus was caged

with a lion was a contemporary, or near-contemporary, of the Diadoch; Phylarchus, who belongs to the late third century, is not above suspicion.

401 Berve ii.240: "die Rolle, welche man ihm, freilich mit Unrecht, . . . zuschrieb."

402 A similar story regarding Alexander's diadem is told of Seleucus by A 7.22.5, a variant on the version given by Aristobulus (*FGrH* 139 F55).

403 According to Ps-Call 3.32, Lysimachus, Ptolemy, and Perdiccas (*LM* 103 includes the enigmatic Holcias) were summoned to Alexander's deathbed. This may be true, but the claim that Alexander assigned Thrace to Lysimachus (*LM* 111), because he was best qualified to subdue and rule it (J 15.3.15), is fabrication. Similarly, the charge that Alexander envied him his abilities as a commander (so Ael*VH* 12.16; 14.47a) must be rejected: rumors circulated in the years that followed Alexander's death that various Successors had, at one time or another, fallen out of favor with Alexander. Such stories reflected, either favorably or unfavorably, upon the individuals in question and were generated by the propaganda mills of this turbulent age.

404 On a lighter note, it is also reported that Lysippus made a special earthenware drinking vessel for Cassander for his Mendean wine from Cassandreia (Ath 11.784c; see s.v. **Cassander**).

405 C 5.3.13 claims that Alexander not only spared the Uxians but also granted them immunity from taxation. This was, however, merely recognition of the fact that the natives could not be subdued (cf. Cook 1983: 182, 185). The details of the campaign are difficult to reconcile with A 3.17; on which see Bosworth i.321–4 and Speck 2002: 22–37. Arrian adds that the Uxians were required to pay *phoros* (tribute). But we find the Uxians creating difficulties for Antigonus in 317 (D 19.19.3–4, 8). See also Briant 728–9; 1022.

406 The date for the fall of Sidon can be estimated from Isoc*Phil* 102, which speaks of the revolt as still going on in 347, and a Babylonian inscription (*ABC* no. 9) mentioning Sidonian prisoners in Babylon in 345. The date of Mazaeus' assumption of the satrapy of Cilicia is often given as 361, after the Satraps' Revolt (Berve ii.244; Head, HN^2 731), but there is no solid evidence for his holding of the office until 351/0 (D 16.42.1), and even here the date is not certain.

407 Mazaeus was not satrap of Babylon before Gaugamela; for we have the Babylonians commanded by Bupares (A 3.8.5). Briant 846, 848 refers to a Babylonian tablet (*ADRTB* no. –330), which suggests that there had been some communication between Alexander and Babylon after the battle of Gaugamela, either with Mazaeus or with the Babylonians themselves. For the "ritual surrender" of the city see Kuhrt 1987: 48–9.

408 The Medius of Larissa attested as *naopoios* during this period (SIG^3 237, 241, 251 etc.) is the son of Aristophylidas (cf. Berve ii.261 n. 2). Str 11.14.12–14 C531 = *FGrH* 129 T1, F1 suggests that Medius son of Oxythemis was with Alexander in the late 330s.

409 Billows 400 assumes, plausibly, that Medius was a commander of Thessalian cavalry in the period 334–330, but I do not accept his view that after 326 he "becam[e] one of the *hetairoi*." As a member of the Aleuadae, his status as one of the Macedonian King's *hetairoi* will have predated 334.

410 The decree belongs to the archonship of Leostratus and was moved by Philostratus son of Philostratus Cephisieus, and although the archon's name is restored the dating is secured by the name of the *epistates* Stratius son of Philotimus (Bayliss 2002: 90). The first service to Athens, for which he is honored, occurred while he was residing as a *philos* at the court of Antigonus the One-Eyed, but the date and context are unknown. Billows 401 suggests this was with the Athenian embassy that arrived in 307/6 (D 20.46.4), which would force us to postpone his "liberation" (ἐλευθερώσο[ντ]α τ[ήν] τε πόλιν, lines 17–18) to 304/3, which is unlikely. Furthermore, Medius' participation in

the battle of Salamis in 306 suggests that he was probably with Demetrius when he liberated Athens in 307, and Bayliss makes a good case for this as Medius' second service to Athens.

411 It is assumed that Hippostratus was, therefore, a brother of Medius. But it is far less certain that Oxythemis' father was the officer appointed by Antigonus as *strategos* in Media in 316 (D 19.46–7), though the identification is certainly not implausible.

412 *Suda* s.v. *βαβαὶ Μύξος*; cf. Str 14.1.23 [641]. Xen*Anab* 5.3.6: a Megabyzus . . . *neokoros* of Artemis at the end of the fifth century.

413 See also P*M* 58d; 471f; Ael*VH* 2.2; Pl*NH* 35.132.

414 *πολλάκις δὲ λέγει ἀφικέσθαι παρὰ Σανδράκοττον* should be translated "he often speaks of visiting Sandrocottus" and not "he says he often visited Sandrocottus" (Bosworth ii.244; cf. Olshausen 172, who speaks of a single visit).

415 Perhaps the son of Balacrus, or Amyntas?

416 Issus: C 3.9.7; A 2.8.4. Gaugamela: D 17.57.2; A 3.11.9; but Meleager has dropped out of the battle order at C 4.13.28.

417 Whether he took his cue from an *ignotus*, as Curtius (10.7.1–3, 6–7) says, is impossible to determine. J 13.3.2 and D 18.2.2–3 (probably from Hieronymus) say that Meleager was sent by the cavalry to negotiate with the infantry but betrayed the former group. Curtius, however, appears to derive from Cleitarchus (who used eye-witnesses; so Schachermeyr 1970: 85), and the story that Meleager betrayed the cavalry may have been a later invention intended to justify his execution.

418 D 18.4.7 says that Perdiccas used a personal quarrel and the charge that Meleager was plotting against him in order to eliminate him. This may be justification of the execution after the fact. The number of those punished is given in the MSS. of C 10.9.18 as "CCC," but Rolfe, following Bentley, reasons "XXX," which may be preferable. The pamphlet on *The Last Days and Testament of Alexander the Great* names Meleager as one of some fourteen guests at Medeius' dinner-party who were involved in the plot against Alexander, and the forged Testament contained in the pamphlet awards him the satrapy of Coele-Syria and Phoenicia (*LM* 117; Jul Val 3.58; Leo 33; Ps-Call 3.33.15); this satrapy was, in fact, assigned to Laomedon.

419 Curtius' claim (5.11.4) that Darius understood some Greek is doubtless a fiction.

420 Hofstetter 127 supposes he may have been son of Thymondas and a daughter of Artabazus, which I regard as possible, or the son of the famous Memnon and Barsine (perhaps the child captured with his mother at Damascus in 333: C 3.13.14). But, if that is the case, then it would be pointless to identify Mentor, the elder Memnon's brother, as the father of Thymondas. That is, by identifying Mentor as Thymondas' father, the decree makes clear that there was a close relationship between the honorand and Thymondas himself. It has been suggested that the younger Memnon must have been an adult and have done some service for the Athenians (Rhodes & Osborne 508; cf. Schwenk 294), but the Athenians may have taken in the young son of Thymondas just as they had earlier sheltered Tharyps the Molossian (J 17.3.9–11; cf. Hammond 1967: 507).

421 Bosworth ii.97, however, does not accept that Menander the satrap was the father of Charicles and questions also the identity of Hermolaus' father, Sopolis, whom I regard as an ilarch of the Companions.

422 I cannot understand why Berve ii.255 says that Menander died in 321. Billows 403 thinks that Antigonus left Menander behind as *strategos* of Cappadocia, where he may have died ca. 317/6.

423 Tataki 367 no. 37 accepts him as Macedonian.

424 After the death of Nicocreon and until his expulsion from Cyprus, Menelaus is styled BA (that is, *basileus*) on coinage (see Bagnall 41).

425 Pausanias calls him *satrapes* and says explicitly that Menelaus was defeated in a naval engagement, which is what the compressed account of Plutarch also implies. But the evidence of Diodorus is detailed and clear, and Hauben rightly omits Menelaus from his prosopography of fleet commanders.

426 Pol*Strat* 4.7.7 says that "Menelaus, who put out from Salamis in order to bring aid, joined Ptolemy in flight." I see no reason to doubt Justin's (Trogus') claim that Menelaus surrendered to Demetrius and was released by him. It is tempting to assume that Polyaenus has confused Menelaus with Menoitius, but the latter also returned to Salamis after the battle (D 20.52.5).

427 Menes' position is not clear and no explanation is entirely satisfactory. Berve's assumption that he controlled finances, replacing Coeranus of Beroea, is rejected for want of evidence by Brunt i.278 n. 11. Bosworth thinks Menes replaced Balacrus as satrap of Cilicia, assuming control of Syria and Phoenicia as well (i.319; cf. Bosworth 1974: 59–60), but this would place Balacrus' death in 332 or 331 and make Menes' disappearance more difficult to explain. As Bosworth ii.148 notes, the term *hyparchos* refers to someone who ruled *under* a king, but although the terms *hyparchos* and *satrapes* are used synonymously, they are not always the same, and I see no reason why hyparchs cannot have satraps who are in some way subordinate to them.

428 For his trierarchies: *IG* ii^2 1622.199–200, 721–2, 729–30; ii^2 1623.47; ii^2 1629.486–7, and Davies 250–1.

429 A. 3.5.1 records that, in the winter of 332/1, Menoetas son of Hegesander brought 400 mercenaries to Alexander in Memphis. "Menoetas" may, however, be an error for "Menidas" (so Hamilton 1955: 217–18; *contra* Bosworth i.275) and, if so, Menidas will have been the son of Hegesander and commander of 400 mercenary cavalry from 332/1 onwards. It is not specified whether these are cavalry or infantry, but Hamilton 1955: 217–18 comments: "Four hundred seems to me too small a number [i.e., for infantry] and certainly in no other case is so small a number of infantry reinforcements recorded." Identification of the son of Hegesander with Menoetas, the supporter of Peithon, remains a possibility (D 19.47.1).

430 Very different is Curtius' account, which depicts Menidas' skirmish with the enemy as an, apparently unauthorized, attempt to save the baggage. But his efforts were half-hearted, and he abandoned the endeavor (C 4.15.12). In the end, Alexander, reluctantly, sent the *prodromoi* under Aretes to repulse the Scythians who were plundering the camp (C 4.15.13–18). Curtius appears to have based his narrative on an account that sought to vindicate Parmenion and, in the process, depicted Menidas – arguably one of the heroes of Gaugamela who was wounded in action (A 3.15.2; D 17.61.3; C 4.16.32) – as cowardly and inept (Atkinson i.440–1; cf. Devine 1986: 91); he was, of course, destined to become one of Parmenion's assassins (A 3.26.3–4).

431 I do not see why Berve ii.258, with n. 4, following Ausfeld, thinks that Dardanus in the Armenian version of Ps-Call 3.31 is Menidas.

432 Berve ii.259 considers him "anscheinend Grieche aus Ilion," for which there is no support. Instinsky's suggestion (71 n. 1), that *kybernetes* is the corruption of an ethnic, is unnecessary and unhelpful.

433 See Leuze 413–25; Bosworth i.224–5, reiterating the arguments of Bosworth 1974; cf. Brunt i.240 n. 9.

434 This passage appears to be corrupt and one solution is to emend the text to read "he was destroyed." See the Loeb *Strabo*, vol. 5, 329 n. 3.

435 The number is reached by subtracting the 12,000 infantry and 400 cavalry of the departed Aetolians (D 18.38.1) from the total of 25,000 and 1,500 (D 18.38.3).

436 Plutarch says the quarters had been prepared by Eumenes' slaves, and it is possible that Mentor belonged to that number, in which case Eumenes took

him along with him to Alexander to support his claims.

437 Thus Berve ii.260 no. 519; but we may have a parallel case of rapid promotion if Aretis is identical with Aretes.

438 C 6.7.22: *nobili iuveni – Metron erat ei nomen – super armamentarium posito, quod scelus pararetur indicat.* D 17.79.4 speaks of "one of the *paides basilikoi*" but does not name Metron. For his identification as a Page see Berve ii.260; Heckel 293–4.

439 Tataki 374 no. 76 rightly identifies him as Macedonian (cf. Hoffmann 211), against the doubts of Berve ii.264 no. 529. If Micion was not a fleet commander but simply the leader of the troops who landed at Rhamnus, we must ask who Antipater's admiral was in 323.

440 Bosworth 2003b: 21, with nn. 62–3, believes that Micion's raid came at the end of the sailing season in 323, perhaps launched from Chalcis in Euboea. There is, at any rate, no justification for Ferguson's view (18) that the raid occurred after the battle of Amorgos and that Micion was a lieutenant of White Cleitus.

441 D 17.21.7 calls him "satrap," which may be an error, unless Mithrenes became interim satrap of Ionia after the death of Spithridates at the Granicus.

442 Lassen ii^2 189 n. 2, without good reason, emends the form given by Curtius to "Soeris."

443 C 3.13.15 dates his capture to 333, at Damascus: here the MS reading *omaio*, emended to Onomas, should be rendered "Monimus."

444 Aristobulus *ap.* Str 15.1.22 [694] speaks of grain and vines growing in the kingdom of Musicanus.

445 In the *Alexander Romance* (Ps-Call 2.20–1; Jul Val 2.31, 37; cf. Tzetz*Chil* 3.352) he is called Ariobarzanes; *ME* 3 also has Ariobarzanes, but in this case we should emend the text to read "Satibarzanes."

446 StByz s.v. "Lete," but Stephanus thought Nearchus came from Lete in Macedonia.

447 Badian 1975: 150 assumes that Nearchus was recalled from his satrapy because he "had not proved up to expectation in his arduous assignment." I see no evidence for the view that Nearchus himself recruited troops in Greece (Berve ii.269).

448 Against the view that Nearchus himself was a hypaspist commander (Berve ii.269; Billows 407) see Badian 1975: 150–1. Bosworth ii.195, following Hoffmann 191, distinguishes between this Nearchus, a hypaspist commander, and the son of Androtimus. But D 19.19.4–5 mentions a Nearchus serving in a similar role under Antigonus the One-Eyed and in this case it is highly likely that we are dealing with the former admiral.

449 A 6.5.4 places the repair of the ships before Alexander's departure, but Berve ii.270 may be right in seeing the refitting of the fleet as Nearchus' responsibility. Badian 1975: 152–3 sees the damage to the fleet as a sign of Nearchus' incompetence and suggests that Alexander did not allow the fleet to proceed to the junction of the Acesines and Hydraotes "until his own pilot Onesicritus could take charge of the actual navigation" (153). But Alexander's ship fared no better at the confluence of the Acesines and Hydaspes (D 17.97; C 9.4.9–14), and I see no good reason why, in this instance, Alexander should prefer Onesicritus to Nearchus.

450 Calculations based on Aristobulus' own dates for the departure of the fleet and its arrival at Patala result in a voyage of almost nine months. P*A* 66.1 says seven months, Pl*NH* 6.60 only five. But it is not entirely clear what Plutarch and Pliny regard as the starting point of the voyage; they could be counting from Alexander's departure from the junction of the Acesines and the Indus (cf. Hamilton 181–2). For the chronology in general see Beloch iii^2 2.305–7, 320–1.

451 *Suda* N 117 claims that it was Nearchus who lied about being admiral, when he was in fact a steersman. But Onesicritus is sometimes termed *archikybernetes* (Str 15.1.28 [698]; 15.2.4 [721]; P*M* 331e: ἄρχων τῶν κυβερνητῶν) or even leader of the fleet (Pl*NH* 2.185: *dux*; 6.81: *classis praefectus*).

452 Near Gujo; hence east of modern Karachi, if the latter is the Morontobara of *AInd* 22.4. So Brunt ii.371 n. 1; Seibert 1985: 182 identifies "Alexander's Harbor" with Karachi. But see Eggermont 33–4.

453 Capelle speaks of "Rast von zehn Tagen" (*RE* xvi.2, 2133). We do not know how long Nearchus' men remained at Cocala.

454 Mosarna may be modern Pasni. Cf. Brunt ii.384 n. 1; Seibert 1985: 183.

455 Rounding the Ras-al-Kuh headland, the fleet began to sail northwest into the Strait of Hormuz (cf. *AInd* 32.3). Maceta (Ras Musandam, the promontory of Oman) became visible (cf. Str 15.2.14 [726]; Pl*NH* 6.98), and Nearchus rejected Onesicritus' suggestion that they abandon the Carmanian coast and make for it instead (*AInd* 32.7, 9–13).

456 Diodorus (17.106.4) mentions a coastal town named Salmous (C 10.1.10 and Str 15.2.11 [725] are vague, but appear to be following the same source as Diodorus); P*A* 67.7 speaks of the "capital of Gedrosia" (read "Carmania"? thus Badian 1958: 151; cf. Hamilton 186), which could be identical with Salmous. They anchored at the mouth of the Anamis River (*AInd* 33.2; cf. A 6.28.5, on an uninhabited shore of Carmania) in the district of Harmozeia; the King's camp was five days' march inland (*AInd* 33.7), and we are treated in Nearchus' own account to the hazards of the journey.

457 But see Hamilton 211; according to A 7.25.4, Alexander was briefing Nearchus on the details of the upcoming naval expedition to Arabia. For Nearchus' literary achievement see Pearson 112–49; Jacoby, *FGrH* 133, with iiD "Kommentar," 445–68.

458 *Suda* K 240, discussing Callisthenes, wrongly gives the man's name as Nearchus, but adds that he was supposed to have been imprisoned in an iron cage because, together with Callisthenes, he advised Alexander not to demand of the Athenians the title "Lord" (*despotes*).

459 Welles 188 n. 1 argues that Diodorus' version is correct, a view taken up also by Bosworth i.145. But the argument that Alexander would not have trusted Amyntas son of Arrhabaeus if his brother had been a deserter and his father a suspected regicide is all but negated by the case of Alexander Lyncestes, who was actually promoted during the first year of the campaign. If the King had concerns about Amyntas' loyalty, he will not have acted upon them until after the arrest of his uncle. I am inclined to believe that Diodorus, or his source, recognizing Neoptolemus as a prominent Macedonian, wrongly assumed that he was fighting on Alexander's side. The details provided by Arrian put the matter of Neoptolemus' identity beyond doubt. Bosworth's rejection of it forces him to conclude that "[t]he note about his desertion must then be Arrian's own addition."

460 Bosworth 1988a: 104 thinks that Neoptolemus' relationship with Alexander (though somewhat distant) may account for his command of the entire hypaspist corps at a time when the King was eliminating larger commands (e.g., the command of the Companion Cavalry was divided between Hephaestion and Black Cleitus after Philotas' death).

461 *Νεοπτολέμου Καρμανία* is emended by Ausfeld to *Νεοπτολέμου ⟨Ἀρμενία, Τλεπολέμου⟩ Καρμανία*. This does violence to the geographical sequence (i.e., it is doubtful that any source would have placed the administrators of Armenia and Carmania back to back. Furthermore, it is much easier simply to emend *Νεοπτολέμου* to *Τλεπολέμου*.

462 The final struggle between Eumenes and Neoptolemus (it occurred ten days after the initial engagement [P*Eum* 8.1], as reported by P*Eum* 7.7–12, D 18.31 N*Eum* 4.1–2) derives from a single primary source – Hieronymus (Schubert 178–9), who emphasized the long-standing hatred between the two men. That Neoptolemus, who had berated Eumenes as the King's secretary (P*Eum* 1.6), found himself overcome in a bitter hand-to-hand struggle (A*Succ* 1.27) is perhaps Duris' coloring (cf. Hornblower 1981: 196).

463 The metropolis of Bithynia was founded by Antigonus Monophthalmus, but it was refounded by Lysimachus, who renamed it Nicaea for his wife (Str 12.4.7 [565]).

464 Ogden 58 suggests a fourth child, an unnamed daughter who married Dromachaites (Paus 1.9.6).

465 Quoted or paraphrased by Clement of Alexandria (a Christian writer of the late second and early third centuries), *Protrepticus* 4.54.

466 Not to be confused with Baeton the bematist. Baton's remarks are preserved in Ath 7.289c.

467 Cf. Hesychius 1, p. 997; Pollux 1.10. Possibly these included many men from the *agema* who had been trained in horsemanship as Pages of the King.

468 According to Carystius of Pergamum, in the third book of his *Hypomnemata*, when Antipater had Himeraeus put to death, Demetrius of Phalerum (his brother) went to live with Nicanor (Ath 12.543e).

469 Green 1982: 143 puts the liaison (he does not regard her as a legitimate wife; against which see Ogden 18–19) in 352; Carney 60–1 suggests that Philip may have married both Philine and Nicesipolis before Olympias (in 357). I find this highly implausible. The age of Thessalonice at the time of her marriage to Cassander in 315 must be a determining factor.

470 Berve ii.278 n. 1 notes that there is no attested Macedonian bearer of the name. Tataki 57 nos. 95–6 and 140 no. 88 includes an Amphipolitan and Olynthian of that name. These (or their children) may have become naturalized Makedones. Nicias with the ethnic Makedon is first attested in the second century BC (Tataki 385 nos. 54–5, cf. 491 no. 177, first century BC).

471 Apparently the successor of [Cha]ridamus, attested on the coinage of the mid-fourth century (see Head, *HN*[2] 741; cf. Hill 1904: LXXVI). Berve ii.406 no. 822 thinks he is the ruling member of the Cinyradae whom Alexander deposed (P*M* 340d). Since Plutarch gives a garbled version of the story of Straton and Abdalonymus, his comments may have no value for the affairs of Paphos.

472 See also Cic *De natura deorum* 3.82 and *Tusculan Disputations* 2.52.

473 Nevertheless, he issued coins with the legends BA NI and BA NK (*ΒΑΣΙΛΕΩΣ ΝΙΚΟΚΡΕΟΝΤΟΣ*). He was honored at Argos (*IG* iv.583) and made offerings at Delos during his reign (see Bagnall 39, with n. 4).

474 Favorinus *ap.* Jul Val 1.7 (frg. 49) says Olympias' mother was called Anasatia. For the Aeacidae see Paus 1.9.8, 1.11.1; J 12.16.3; P*A* 2; P*Pyr* 1; Hesychius s.v. "Pyrriadai"; D 17.1.5.

475 For the date see P*A* 3.5 with Hamilton 7. See also P*M* 105a–b; Satyrus *ap.* Ath 13.557c; A 4.10.2; J 9.5.9, 9.7.1–2, 11.11.3–5, 12.14.3, 13.6.12, 14.5.8–10; P*A* 3.4–5; Gell 6.1.1, 13.4.1–3; Ath 14.659f–660a; Paus 4.14.7; Lucian, *Alexander* 7; Ael*VH* 12.64, 13.30; A*Succ* 1.21; C 5.2.22, 9.6.26; 10.5.30; *ME* 115–16.

476 Scholars have had a tendency to deride the evidence of Justin but to accept it without qualification when it suits their purposes.

477 The view that Olympias did not return for her daughter's wedding, and that the marriage of Alexander I and Cleopatra was directed against her, is perverse. P*M* 179c is certainly right when he claims that Philip was reconciled with both the son and his mother (διηλλάγη πρὸς αὐτούς).

478 See s.vv. **Gorgatas**, **Gorgias** [2], **Hecataeus** [1]. The fact that this information came up in Amyntas' trial in 330 suggests that Olympias must have written her son a letter critical of Amyntas' actions. For the correspondence between Olympias and her son see Ath 14.659f–660a; A 6.1.4–5; P*M* 332f–333a (Hephaestion was in the habit of reading her letters; cf. P*A* 39.8); P*A* 39.7; *ME* 87 (complaints about Antipater). See also Zumetikos 1894; Pearson 1954/5; Hamilton lix–lx.

479 Livy 8.24.17 says that she was in Epirus to receive her brother's ashes. No doubt she regarded the death of Alexander I

as an opportunity to flex some political muscle and support the claims of her grandchild Neoptolemus against rival factions. For Cleopatra's position see Carney 1987a: 51.

480 Diodorus and Aelian both mention the story that Olympias sent Adea a dagger, a rope, and some poison and told her to choose the instrument of her death. She decided to hang herself with her own girdle. A similar story is told of Eleanor of Aquitaine and her rival Rosamond Clifford (see Kelly 1950: 152–3).

481 Aristonus in Amphipolis and Monimus of Pella were perhaps more loyal to Olympias than to Polyperchon (cf. Phylarchus *ap.* Ath 13. 609c; cf. P*M* 141c–d for Mominus' personal relationship with the queen mother). Both were forced to surrender (D 19.35.4, 50.3, 7; 19.51.1).

482 The figures are problematic. It is hard to imagine that 18,000 Greeks could have been slaughtered with minuscule losses on the Macedonian side (see Parke 180–1; cf. Grote 1913: 18, with n. 1).

483 Bosworth i.302 suspects a textual problem in A 3.12.2 and that *ὧν Βρίσων* is a corruption of *ὧν ⟨Ὀμ⟩βρίων*. The emendation is ingenious, and, although the Cretan origin of Ombrion would seem to weigh against this view, it was in fact another Macedonian whom Ombrion replaced.

484 I do not understand why DL 6.75 writes *Ὀνησίκριτόν τινα*.

485 Pl*NH* 6.81 calls him *classis praefectus*; cf. Pl*NH* 2.185: *dux*. These are, then, only slight exaggerations of Onesicritus' role. Pl*NH* 9.6 refers to *Alexandri Magni classium praefecti*, clearly referring to Nearchus and Onesicritus. See also C 9.10.3; 10.1.10.

486 Onesicritus' connections with Lysimachus reflect a shared interest in philosophy (cf. Lund 8–10, who also cautions that "Justin's emphasis on philosophy as a guiding force in [Lysimachus'] life is at least exaggerated," 10).

487 Xen*Cyr* 8.7 includes what amounts to the Testament of Cyrus, which was no doubt read by Onesicritus, who is known to have recorded the last days of Alexander (*LM* 97 = *FGrH* 134 F37). It may be that the political pamphlet on the *Last Days and Testament* was inspired by Onesicritus' imitation of Xenophon.

488 She later married Demetrius Poliorcetes (P*Demetr* 14.1–2, calling her Eurydice); the marriage produced a son named Corrhagus (P*Demetr* 53.9).

489 Beloch argues that Artaxerxes II (born ca. 428–426; cf. iii^2 2.131) could not have had a daughter of marriageable age before about 390; on the other hand, Deinon, *FGrH* 690 F20a, b, gives Artaxerxes' age at the time of his death (359/8) as 94 (*ap.* [L]*Macrob* 15) or 86 (*ap.* P*Art* 30.9).

490 The name appears in Arrian and Curtius as Orontobates, but coin-legends from Caria give "Roontopates," that is, Orontopates (*BMC Caria* lxxxiv; Head, HN^2 630). Whether the Orontobates of D 19.46.5 (Billows 413–14 no. 85) is a relative cannot be determined.

491 There is some confusion in the sources concerning the troops under the command of Orontopates and Ariobarzanes. A 3.8.5, if the text is not corrupt, reports that these contingents were from the areas bordering on the Red Sea (i.e., Persian Gulf), but C 4.12.7 is probably correct in calling them Mardians, Persians, and Sogdianians, since Orontopates' co-commander Ariobarzanes was satrap of Persis (see s.v. **Ariobarzanes** [2]) and the supreme commander of these troops was Orxines, who claimed descent from the Seven (see s.v. **Orxines**). Curtius' inclusion of the Sogdiani in this force may, however, be an error.

492 The form of the name is attested only in Curtius; cf. Atkinson ii.159. Berve ii.296 has "Orsillus"; this may be a familiar form of the name Orsines/Orxines but there is no compelling reason to identify him with the descendant of the Seven.

493 Berve ii.296 assumes that this occurred in Bactria-Sogdiana between 329 and 327, which is possible and perhaps supported by an earlier reference to Alexander's punishment of the disobedient *phrourarchos* Menander. Numerous garrisons were planted in that area and many served unwillingly. The verb *katatoxeuo* ("to

shoot with an arrow") is unusual since the bow was the weapon of choice of the Persian rather than the Macedonian King. It is possible that the story is a doublet of the one told by *PA* 78.7 that Abulites' son was killed by Alexander's own hand; in that case, Orsodates may be a corruption of the name Oxyathres.

494 Ael*NA* 16.35; Philostratus, *Life of Apollonius* 2.53 p.137; Phot*Bibl* 241 p.327b.

495 Thus rendering highly unlikely Bosworth's attempt (ii.131) to reconcile the accounts by suggesting that Rhoxane was captured on the Rock of Sogdiana (i.e., Ariamazes) but not married to Alexander until he enjoyed the hospitality of Chorienes in 327.

496 The two references are therefore mutually exclusive. Whether Stateira was a full sister of Oxyathres and of her husband Darius is unclear. See further s.v. **Stateira** [1]. Phylarchus, *FGrH* 81 F34 *ap.* Ath 13.609a–b mentions a beautiful woman, Timosa, sent by the king of the Egyptians to Stateira, "the king's wife" (*Στατίρᾳ τῇ βασιλέως γυναικί*), who became the concubine of Stateira's brother Oxyathres. The reference must be to Stateira the wife of Artaxerxes II, who had a brother-in-law named Oxathres (P*Art* 1), and not to the brother and sister of Darius III (*pace* Berve ii.292 n. 2). See also Briant 2003: 680.

497 That is, clearly not one of the Somatophylakes, but perhaps a separate Persian unit similar to the hypaspist guard. The terms *doryphoros* (D 17.77.4) and *custos corporis* (C 7.5.40; *ME* 2) are used also of members of the hypaspists. Pausanias of Orestis, who was a hypaspist, is called *doryphoros* by *PM* 170e–f.

498 The claim by Ps-Call 2.7.8 (cf. Jul Val 2.22–3) that Oxyathres had once been to Macedonia is probably, as Berve ii.292 suggests, the result of confusion with Artabazus.

499 If Arrian uses *ἐθελοκακεῖν* in the Herodotean sense, the word means "to do badly in battle on purpose" (Powell s.v.); cf. Bosworth 1981: 21, who assumes that Oxydates did not aid Phrataphernes against the rebel Arsaces (cf. A 4.7.1).

500 According to the *Last Days and Testament* he was still ruling Media in 323 (*LM* 121: *ex †eis† imperiis omnibus excedat Oxydates, et pro eo Medis imperator sit Craterus* [sc. *Pitho Crateua*]). The forged *Testament* does, in fact, contain numerous (often deliberate) errors, and it may be best to dismiss this as one of them. But the passage does raise the possibility that Atropates took over only Lesser Media, which was later known as Media Atropatene; for there is no indication that Atropates' existing territory was reduced in 323. Also, C 8.3.17 suggests that Oxydates simply went elsewhere: *ut Oxydates inde discederet.*

501 Leugaea appears not to be a Macedonian toponym, and attempts have been made to emend the text (cf. Beloch iii^2 2.326; Berve i.105 n. 3); Bosworth i.211 suggests the name not as "a regional adjective but a native Macedonian title for the squadron."

502 Asander son of Philotas, who was installed as satrap of Lydia, was probably not Parmenion's brother (see s.v. **Asander** [1]). Nevertheless, Parmenion and his sons, the taxiarchs Coenus, Polyperchon, and Amyntas son of Andromenes, along with Polydamas (perhaps commander of the Pharsalian horse), formed a powerful faction in Alexander's army. See Heckel 2003: 202–3.

503 Polyaenus' account, and the figure of 10,000 Macedonian troops (accepted by McCoy 1989: 424), must be treated with caution (cf. Niese i.59 n. 2).

504 Alexander's agent Hecataeus could not have secured Attalus' execution without Parmenion's agreement, and the mission must have been at the same time a test of the latter's loyalty (cf. C 7.1.3).

505 D 17.19.3 says that Alexander attacked at dawn, thus giving the impression that he was following Parmenion's advice. Diodorus may, however, be basing his account on a corrective (pro-Parmenion) version – he does not mention Parmenion's advice, or Alexander's rejection of it – or he may simply have mistakenly translated Parmenion's proposal into action. Beloch iv^2 2.296–7

accepts Diodorus' version as correct; cf. also Bosworth i.114–16, with full discussion of the source problem, with earlier literature on the battle at the Granicus.

506 Both Parmenion and Calas were familiar with the region, having campaigned there in 336 and 335 (D 17.7.10). It appears that Parmenion took with him to Dascylium the Thessalian horse, which he left there for the time to help Calas recover the Troad (A 1.17.8). Arrian curiously separates the appointment of Calas and Parmenion's mission (1.17.1–2) from the instructions given to Calas and Alexander son of Aëropus concerning "Memnon's territory" (1.17.8; did they set out from Sardis?). It would be odd if Alexander made the appointment and then took Calas to Sardis, only to send him back into his satrapy from Ionia. Calas replaced Arsites (A 1.12.8; 1.17.1); for previous rulers of the satrapy see Krumbholz 93.

507 Parmenion drew attention to an omen, an eagle perched on the shore behind Alexander's ships. If the Macedonians won a naval engagement at the beginning of the campaign it would be beneficial to their cause, but a setback would not harm them, since the Persians were already dominant at sea (A 1.18.6). But Alexander responded that he would not fight against a force superior in numbers – 400 Persians (A 1.18.5) to 160 Macedonians under Nicanor (1.18.4) – and in training, and risk good lives to an uncertain element; that a loss would harm Macedonian prestige at a crucial point in the campaign; and that the omen showed that the Macedonians should fight on land, for that was where the eagle was situated, not at sea (A 1.18.7–9).

508 A 1.25.4–10; a different version in D 17.32.1–2; cf. C 7.1.6, and 3.7.11–15 (for the arrest and death of Sisines).

509 Whether this is the result of abbreviation or a deliberate omission by Arrian's source(s), we cannot be sure. The mission invites comparison with Parmenion's capture of Damascus soon after the battle of Issus (below). But Parmenion had up to this point been placed in charge of the less mobile troops, and one suspects that Curtius' source may have written "[Philotas son of] Parmenion."

510 Bosworth i.190 points out that from the Gates to Tarsus it is only about "55 km, a manageable day's stint for the advance column." And it appears more likely that Alexander himself (or possibly Philotas) advanced with the more mobile troops and that Parmenion remained at the Gates, awaiting further instructions from the King. Parmenion had in fact passed through the Gates (A 2.4.4; cf. Atkinson i.155), but this does not rule out the possibility that he stayed behind or followed at a slower pace. A letter from him might be thought to have come from the direction of Cappadocia. D 17.31.4–6 knows nothing about any warning concerning Philip and follows his account of Alexander's illness with the arrest of Alexander Lyncestes (17.32.1–2). This was perhaps the original version given by Cleitarchus; Curtius' account is contaminated by Trogus and/or Ptolemy; I cannot agree with Hammond 1983: 121, who thinks that Trogus and Curtius used a common source (Cleitarchus) for this episode.

511 Parmenion's activities occupied him for the better part of a month, in which he took precautions against Darius' advance. Nevertheless, the Persian King took Parmenion and Alexander by surprise, entering Cilicia from the north (via the Bahche Pass). For a full discussion see Bosworth i.192–3; cf. also Stark 1958: 4, 7; Engels 42–53, esp. 44 n. 97, for a comment on Alexander's alleged ignorance of the Persian position.

512 C 3.12.27; A 2.11.10; P*A* 24.1. Darius had sent most of his baggage and the Persian women (except those of his immediate family) to Damascus before he reached Issus (A 2.11.9; D 17.32.3; C 3.8.12). For Parmenion's capture of the city see A 2.15.1; C 3.13.1ff. is heavily dramatized; cf. Pol*Strat* 4.5.1. Ath 13.607f–608a quotes from what is purportedly a letter of Parmenion to Alexander itemizing the captured spoils,

among them 329 of the Great King's concubines. This letter (if genuine) appears to have reached Alexander at Marathus.

513 Parmenion had earlier advised Alexander to produce an heir before leaving for Asia (D 17.16.2). For Alexander's intimate relations with Barsine see J 11.10.2–3. See also Baynham 1998a.

514 C 4.1.4 (cf. Bosworth 1974: 47–8). It is tempting to see Par*menion* as a corruption of Menon (son of Cerdimmas), on whom see A 2.13.7. But J 11.10.4–5 seems to corroborate some kind of independent command for Parmenion, though *Parmeniona ad occupandam Persicam classem* is clearly corrupt, unless it implies that Parmenion was to secure the coast of Coele-Syria. See also Bosworth i.225.

515 Curtius places the appointment of Andromachus and Parmenion's reunion with Alexander after the fall of Tyre, when the army prepared to move south toward Gaza, the logical time for such an administrative change. Pol*Strat* 4.3.4 gives Parmenion charge of the army at Tyre, while Alexander conducted his Arabian campaign; but Curtius claims that the siege had been entrusted to Craterus and Perdiccas (C 4.3.1; cf. Pol*Strat* 4.13). The story that Parmenion, hard pressed by the Tyrians, had to summon Alexander from Arabia sounds like another attempt to discredit the old general.

516 It is difficult to imagine that these episodes could have been written in Parmenion's lifetime, or even in the King's, when too many influential commanders – to say nothing of the common soldiers – knew the truth of what had happened. Lysimachus' rejection of Onesicritus' story about the Amazon queen shows that fiction was instantly recognizable as such (P*A* 46.4–5); and Cleitus' outrage at the negative portrayal of Macedonian officers demonstrates the kind of hostility that could be generated by such falsehoods (P*A* 50.9). The only thing we can be certain about is that the hostile portrait of Parmenion originated with one of the first Alexander historians. A more positive tradition can be found in Curtius, who in Parmenion's obituary notice says: *multa sine rege prospere, rex sine illo nihil magnae rei gesserat* (7.2.33). Beloch iv² 2.295–6 argues that Philotas was essentially speaking the truth to his mistress when "he declared that the greatest deeds were those accomplished by himself and by his father, and he called Alexander a stripling who reaped on their account the fame of empire" (P*A* 48.5). Passages favorable to Parmenion thus appear to be later inventions: his advice that the army fight in the narrows at Issus (C 3.7.8–10) and that Alexander not read to his soldiers letters from Darius urging them to murder their leader (C 4.10.16–17) is accepted in each case. Curtius himself regards the criticism of Parmenion excessive and directs against Polyperchon Alexander's rejection of the night attack at Gaugamela (4.13.4, 7–10; cf. also 4.12.21).

517 A 15.1 claims that Alexander responded and came to the rescue. Fuller 178 accepts the story; it is rejected by Bosworth 1988a: 82–3; cf. Bosworth i.310; cf. Devine 1975: 381.

518 Parmenion's instructions to invade the land of the Cadusians and Hyrcania (A 3.19.7) were apparently canceled (cf. Bosworth i.337; Seibert 1985: 110–11; cf. Brunt i.529, Appendix 13.5).

519 StByz s.v. "Alexandreiai" names a ninth Alexandria, apparently in Cyprus. Against the existence of Cypriot Alexandria and any connections with Pasicrates of Soli see Fraser 27 n. 56.

520 C 5.12.4 says there were 4,000 mercenaries; A 3.16.2 says only 2,000, adding Glaucus the Aetolian as joint commander.

521 Unless he can be identified with the officer of Antigonus (Billows 414–15 no. 87) who was sent, in 313, in a two-pronged effort, to relieve Callantis, which was being besieged by Lysimachus' forces (D 19.73.6). Pausanias' men were, however, caught off guard by Lysimachus and defeated. Pausanias himself was killed in the engagement; his men were either

ransomed or enrolled in Lysimachus' own army (D 19.73.10). Less likely is Harpalus' murderer, who may have served Thibron in Cyrenaica until his defeat by Ptolemaic forces and then taken refuge with Antigonus. But this is a highly imaginative scenario.

522 At the time of Philip's death Pausanias was a *somatophylax*, that is, a Royal Hypaspist (John of Antioch frg. 40; P*M* 170e–f calls him *doryphoros*; cf. J 9.6.4, *nobilis ex Macedonibus adulescens*; Jos*AJ* 19.1.13 [95] calls him one of Philip's *hetairoi*).

523 For further discussion see Bosworth i.233–4; Atkinson i.261.

524 J 13.4.13; 13.8.10 calls him "Illyrian," perhaps because his source confused his place of origin with Alcomenae in Illyria (so Berve ii.311 n. 3). It is interesting that there was tension between Perdiccas and Peithon in 323, and that another Somatophylax, Aristonus, who remained faithful to Perdiccas and Olympias, was an enemy of Crateuas and his group (19.50.7, 51.1).

525 For doubts concerning the historicity of this event see Grainger: 218–19.

526 Curtius' narrative has a contemporary Roman coloring; cf. Martin 1983, who notes that Peithon's role is suspiciously similar to that of Josephus' Chaerea (164, with n. 5, and 179).

527 J 13.8.10 has Peithon "the Illyrian" declared an outlaw along with Eumenes and Alcetas. Trogus' original almost certainly recorded that Perdiccas was murdered by Peithon.

528 D 19.14.1 calls him Philotas, but in the division of satrapies at Triparadeisus he is listed as Philip (D 18.39.6; A*Succ* 1.35).

529 Hieronymus may have given Peithon a bad press since Peithon had failed to cooperate with Eumenes and was plotting to betray Antigonus.

530 In Peithon's place, Antigonus appointed Orontobates (Billows 413–14 no. 85), a native of the region, under the watchful eye of Hippostratus and a mercenary force. These defeated the remnants of Peithon's army, which had been augmented by some 800 survivors of Eumenes' force at Gabiene (D 19.47.1). Their leaders Meleager (probably the former ilarch of Alexander) and Ocranes the Mede perished in the engagement.

531 Perhaps Peithon led one of the two battalions of infantry that accompanied Hephaestion and Demetrius into the territory of the "cowardly Porus" (A 5.21.5).

532 After the appointment of Agenor's son as satrap, Peithon the taxiarch is not heard of again. Consequently, I do not understand why Berve ii.312 n. 2 believes that the taxiarch was the son of Crateuas, an identification that Bosworth 1988a: 275 considers "highly probable." Nor does Billows 415 no. 88 identify the son of Agenor with the taxiarch. That Peithon shared the satrapy with Oxyartes is highly unlikely and editors are right to emend the text of A 6.15.4: Oxyartes' satrapy is described above (A 6.15.3) as Parapamisadae; perhaps this was extended in a southeasterly direction to the confluence of the Indus and Acesines (Chenab) and was thus adjacent to Peithon's.

533 Peithon's support of Antigonus raises some interesting questions. Did he join him before the battle of Paraetacene? If so, he could have brought with him only a small force of elephants; for Antigonus had a significant number of the beasts at Cretopolis (D 18.45.1; no specific figure is given, but they were clearly a sizeable force) and deployed sixty-five of them at Paraetacene (D 19.27.1) and Gabiene (19.40.1), far short of the 120 brought to Eumenes by Eudamus (cf. D 19.14.8, 15.5, 27.2; cf. P*Eum* 16.3). Furthermore, it will be difficult to explain why Peithon joined Antigonus at this point, when the eastern satraps had uniformly aligned themselves with Eumenes. They had, in fact, assembled to oppose Peithon son of Crateuas (D 19.14.1). Of course, Peithon may have been motivated by strong personal friendship with Antigonus or by fear of Eudamus, who had murdered Porus in the adjacent satrapy (D 19.14.8), but neither of these can be documented. Against the view that he fought with

Eumenes and surrendered to Antigonus are both the silence of the sources and the fact that Antigonus dealt harshly with the prominent subordinates of Eumenes (D 19.44.1).

534 Whether Blitor's authority over Mesopotamia was handed over to Peithon, as Billows 415 speculates, cannot be determined.

535 A 3.15.2, who names the other wounded leaders, omits Perdiccas. Since Perdiccas and Ptolemy became bitter enemies after Alexander's death, certain details concerning Perdiccas were omitted by Ptolemy (Errington 1969; cf. Roisman 1984) in his *History of Alexander*.

536 C 6.8.16 designates Perdiccas as *ex armigeris*; cf. A 3.16.9 for Menes' reassignment.

537 If this is a case of Ptolemy detracting from Perdiccas' reputation, it does not deserve serious consideration, for Ptolemy, by his own admission, was not present at the battle (C 9.5.21; A 6.5.6–7, 11.8).

538 Others attribute the surgery to Critobulus, a doctor from Cos (C 9.5.25). A 6.11.1 calls this man Critodemus.

539 Hence, when the office was later conferred upon Seleucus, J 13.4.17 describes it as *summus castrorum tribunatus*.

540 Eumenes was particularly effective in reconciling the factions (P*Eum* 3.1–2), and, as a Greek, he may have acted as a mediator. The actual liaison between factions was conducted by Pasas the Thessalian, Perilaus, and Damis the Megalopolitan (C 10.8.15). Perdiccas (perhaps through the agency of Eumenes) had also secured the goodwill of the taxiarchs, most notably Attalus son of Andromenes. Their own distrust of Meleager's ambitions will have played no small part in causing them to realign themselves with the Perdiccan party. But Meleager, sensing their opposition, indicated a willingness to relinquish his "control" over Arrhidaeus to the more popular and respected Craterus, though he demanded to be accepted as *tertius dux* (C 10.8.22; J 13.4.5; A*Succ* 1.3).

541 Curtius, portraying Perdiccas as reluctant to accept the crown when it was offered (10.6.18), draws heavily on Roman precedent (Sumner 1961; Devine 1979). Encouraged by the phalanx, Meleager challenged Perdiccas' supremacy with a show of arms. Perdiccas withdrew to the chamber that housed Alexander's body, supported by a mere 600 men, but Meleager had incited the mob, who burst through the barricades and forced the Perdiccan party to quit the city (C 10.7.14–20; J 13.3.3–6; cf. D 18.2.3–4). Leonnatus withdrew the cavalry from Babylon, leaving Perdiccas in the city to reassert his authority over the infantry (C 10.7.21; cf. J 13.3.7–8). Here he survived an assassination attempt, instigated by Meleager in the name of King Philip Arrhidaeus (C 10.8.1–4; J 13.3.7–8, ascribing it to Attalus); Perdiccas now thought it wise to abandon the city and rejoin Leonnatus. Perdiccas appears to win the phalanx over with a passionate appeal and a denunciation of civil war (13.3.9–10); cf. 13.4.1.

542 On the restoration of the Samians see Habicht 1957; Habicht 1975; Errington 1975; Badian 1976.

543 Droysen ii^3 61, Niese i.214, and Vezin 36 all believe that Alcetas acted on Perdiccas' orders. Beloch iv^2 1.83 actually says that Cynnane was murdered by Perdiccas himself; Welles 1970: 53 thinks Perdiccas was incited by Cleopatra. I prefer Macurdy's suggestion that "Perdiccas saw the fatal stupidity of his brother's act" (1932: 50).

544 Cf. A*Succ* 1.25, where Arrhidaeus acts against Perdiccas' wishes. Seibert 110–11 also supposes that there is a contradiction between Pausanias' account and the version given by Diodorus, Justin, and Curtius. For Perdiccas' change of policy see Droysen ii^3 67 n. 2, placing Pausanias' testimony in the proper light. The most thorough discussion is that of Schubert 180–9; see also Badian 1967b: 185–9; Errington 1970: 64–5; Beloch iv^2 1.86–7. Tarn ii.355–6, predictably, disbelieves Alexander's wish to be buried at Siwah, ascribing these reports to Ptolemy's propaganda; less dogmatic is the account given in *CAH*^{2} vi.467.

545 Philotas, a known supporter of Craterus, was deposed from the satrapy of Cilicia (J 13.6.16: his replacement was Philoxenus) as Perdiccas entered that territory; there too provisions were made for the fleet, and Docimus was despatched to Babylon with orders to replace Archon (A*Succ* 24.3–5), suspected of collusion with Arrhidaeus in the highjacking of Alexander's corpse. Eumenes held the western front: his domain was enlarged to include Lycia, Caria, and Phrygia, which had been abandoned by Nearchus, Asander, and Antigonus respectively, and doubtless he kept a watchful eye on Cleopatra in Lydia. Under his command were placed also Neoptolemus and Alcetas (J 13.6.15; D 18.29.2; A*Succ* 1.26; P*Eum* 5.2–3). To White Cleitus, Perdiccas entrusted the defense of the Hellespont (J 13.6.16; cf. A*Succ* 1.26), while another fleet was despatched to Cyprus, under the command of Sosigenes the Rhodian and Aristonus, his most faithful supporter throughout the war, in order to deal with Ptolemy's allies there (A*Succ* 24.6). At the same time, Attalus, who had now married Atalante, was ordered to accompany the army to Egypt with a third fleet. Docimus, meanwhile, secured Babylon without difficulty, defeating in battle Archon, who soon died of his wounds (A*Succ* 24.5).

546 In the west, Neoptolemus, long an enemy of Eumenes (P*Eum* 1.6; 7.7), abandoned the Perdiccan forces and Alcetas, refused to serve under Eumenes, and joined Craterus and Antipater, protesting that his Macedonians would not go into battle with the illustrious Craterus (P*Eum* 5.3; but see Schubert 139–49). Eumenes was, however, victorious, though Perdiccas was never to learn the news. D 18.33.1 says that Perdiccas heard and was encouraged by the news of Eumenes' victory. But this is contradicted by D 18.37.1 (cf. P*Eum* 8.2–3), who says the news arrived in Egypt two days after Perdiccas' murder.

547 The incident is confused by P*Eum* 9.3, leading Engel 1971: 229–30 to suggest that Plutarch refers to the crucifixion of Apollonides (see s.v. **Apollonides** [2]). Plutarch has simply conflated the Perdiccas and Apollonides episodes; cf. Bosworth 1992: 87 n. 119.

548 The troops appear to have been recruited from the Chalcidic peninsula and to have held land they received at the hands of Philip II (see Bosworth i.211).

549 Bosworth i.277 thinks Curtius' figure of 4,000 troops "may be the army of Upper Egypt only"; but for comparable numbers of occupation troops see Atkinson i.366.

550 In his account of the Mallian campaign, Diodorus calls Peucestas *εἷς τῶν ὑπασπιστῶν* (17.99.4). Milns 1982: 123 writes: "Peucestas, the bearer of the Sacred Shield and soon to be appointed as one of the *σωματοφύλακες* . . . and then satrap of the vital satrapy of Persis . . . , was certainly not a junior or middle-ranking hypaspist-officer at the time of the Malli town incident and in all probability was neither the archihypaspist . . . nor a chiliarch. It is thus unlikely that he had any association at all with the hypaspists at this time." But the evidence points to this very thing. P*A* 63.5, 8 agrees with Diodorus (17.99.4) in calling Peucestas a hypaspist; A 6.9.3 claims he carried the Sacred Shield from Ilion, having stated earlier (1.11.7–8) that the arms taken by the Macedonians from the Temple of Athena at Troy were "carried before them by the hypaspists." And Bosworth appears to be on the right track when he writes: "It seems that there was a small group of *hetairoi* who acted as shield-bearers for the king, a body distinct from the corps of hypaspists" (Bosworth i.102). Furthermore, we might ask in what capacity Peucestas accompanied the King into the town of the Mallians. The others who were wounded or killed while defending Alexander were Leonnatus and Aristonus (both members of the Seven), along with Habreas and Limnaeus. But Limnaeus, who is otherwise unknown, appears only in the vulgate and in place of Habreas, and the latter, a "double-pay man" (*dimoirites*),

was apparently a regular hypaspist. Now Alexander normally took with him the Agrianes, the *agema*, and some of the hypaspists, and in this particular incident the most vigorous members of the last two units, climbing different ladders, were the first to enter the city with him. Thus, it seems that Peucestas was the foremost of the Royal Hypaspists; he distinguished himself and won a promotion.

551 A 6.27.6 need not mean that Phrataphernes himself was present.

552 C 4.1.37 speaks of money exacted from the Milesians, which must be an error for the Mytilenaeans.

553 Lycomedes appears to have been succeeded by Chares the Athenian (A 3.2.6; C 4.5.22).

554 Berve ii.380 thinks he accompanied Alexander since 334/3 (cf. Bosworth ii.24) but this strikes me as less plausible. It is more likely that Pharnuches was an Iranian of Lycian origin who had been settled in the Persian heartland. Identification with the unnamed Lycian who led Alexander around the Persian Gates is also unlikely (on this person see Zahrnt 1999).

555 Carney 59 regards her as a daughter of Derdas II; cf. Beloch iii^2 2.75. Worthington 14 wrongly calls her "Illyrian."

556 On the other hand, flatterers of Demetrius, including Adeimantus, set up statues for Phila Aphrodite in Thria, and they called the place where they stood the *Philaion* (Ath 6.255c; cf. Ath 6.254a).

557 A regal outfit and other items that she had sent to Demetrius were intercepted during the siege of Rhodes and sent to Egypt (D 20.93.4; P*Demetr* 22.1).

558 The doubts of Green 1982: 142–4, esp. 143 n. 39 concerning the status of Philine and the nature of Philip's unions with the two Thessalians (cf. Westlake 1935: 168), are unfounded. Ptolemy son of Agesarchus is hardly an unimpeachable source and the language of Satyrus is at best ambiguous. The verb *epaidopoiesato* need not be significant. It lends some variation and it emphasizes the fact that not all Philip's wives produced children. Furthermore, the word *gyne*, like the German *Frau*, can mean "wife" as well as "woman." See Ogden 18–19.

559 Bosworth 2002: 113, with n. 61, accepts Amphimachus as Philine's son.

560 Berve ii.383 no. 775 treats him as a separate individual (cf. Bosworth i.118), and, although I am inclined to regard this Philip as the son of Balacrus, I cannot with certainty deny the existence of a taxiarch named Philip son of Amyntas.

561 Assuming that the patronymikon Ἀμύντου is an error (following the name Amyntas son of Andromenes), then Philip is perhaps the son of Balacrus, named as a taxiarch at Gaugamela in the vulgate.

562 Billows 422 believes that the letter following the name Philippos is "B," i.e., the beginning of the patronymic Balakrou. I believe this letter is "M," if not the first letter of the patronymic then what remains of the ethnic "Makedon" (Heckel 1981f; Heckel 1988: 43).

563 For the Thessalian cavalry at Issus see A 2.8.9, 9.1, 11.2–3; C 3.9.8; 3.11.3, 13–15; D 17.33.2.

564 The city may be the one described by D 17.102.4 and C 9.8.8 (so Welles 413 n. 2); Brunt ii.144 n. 3 thinks C 9.8.8 could refer to the city founded by Alexander near Sogdia (A 6.15.4; cf. Tarn ii.237).

565 Identification with the Philip of *IG* ii^2 561, as suggested by Oikonomides 1987, is impossible for at least three reasons: (1) the decree was almost certainly moved by Stratocles in 307, by which time Iolaus son of Antipater was already dead, and not by Hypereides in 323/2 ([P]*M* 849f); (2) Philip and Iolaus on this inscription appear to have different patronymika; and (3) both were supporters of Demetrius in the years up to and including 307, which would not have been true of the brothers of Cassander.

566 Whether the term *philos* is used in a technical sense here is unclear. C 3.6.1 says that Philip was a companion (*comes*) of the young Alexander, and at the time of Alexander's illness he is already described as φίλτατος Ἀλεξάνδρῳ

ἰατρός (Ps-Call 2.8.4; cf. A 2.4.8). Val Max 3.8 ext 6 calls him *amicus et comes*. Hence, it seems clear that Philip was not promoted to the rank of *hetairos* as a result of the incident. It is interesting to note that Alexander's tutor, Lysimachus, was also an Acarnanian.

567 Schäfer does not comment on the problem in D 19.14.1 (*Πίθων . . . Φιλώταν μὲν τὸν προϋπάρχοντα Παρθυαίας στρατηγὸν ἀπέκτεινε*), but since Diodorus claims that Peithon's actions in Parthia resulted in a coalition of satraps against him (19.14.2), it is unlikely that Philip had already left his satrapy to join forces with Eumenes, leaving Philotas behind as *strategos*. But it would be a desperate solution to assume that Diodorus was wrong about the name (Philotas) of the official, his rank (*strategos* instead of *satrapes*), and his fate (that he was killed rather than driven out). The problem of the ruler of Parthia is explored also by Bosworth 2002: 105–6, who notes (106 n. 32) that "Philotas is surely the *lectio difficilior*." This is undoubtedly true, but it helps establish only the authentic reading of the MSS., not the historical correctness of Diodorus' claim.

568 Billows 421–3 no. 93 identifies the advisor of Demetrius, the commander of Sardis, and the honorand of *IG* ii^{2} 561 with Philip son of Balacrus.

569 Nicanor, one of the *hetairoi* who is left in Alexandria-in-the-Caucasus, that is, in Parapamisadae (A 4.22.5), does not provide a parallel. Brunt's translation (i.415) "to govern the city itself" goes beyond what is necessary. *Kosmein*, although it can mean "to rule," means, first and foremost, "to set in order" (cf. A 6.22.3, where Leonnatus is instructed *ta kata tous Oreitas kosmein*). Whichever translation we adopt, Nicanor should not be regarded as a *phrourarchos*.

570 DL 6.75–6 speaks of an Onesicritus of Aegina, who had two sons named Androsthenes and Philiscus, who became students of Diogenes the Cynic; later Onesicritus himself studied under him. The *Suda* confuses the elder Philiscus with the grandson.

571 Worthington 1986: 71–2 rejects the identification of the *strategos* with the *kosmetes* of the Ephebes (accepted by Davies 540).

572 For Hephaestion's hero-cult see A 7.14.7, 23.6; D 17.115.6; L*Cal* 17.

573 There is no doubt that the demand would not be taken seriously. Nevertheless, it is highly unlikely that Plutarch is referring to Philotas son of Parmenion, since that man will have been too junior to have attracted the attention of the Greeks.

574 It does not follow, however, that once a *phrourarchos* always a *phrourarchos*.

575 But *Augaeus* might be easily emended to *Aegaeus*, i.e., "from Aegae." We know of two other individuals from that city: Leonnatus [1] son of Antipater and Eurylochus [3].

576 Berve ii.393 thinks Philotas accompanied his father to Gordium. A 1.24.3 gives Parmenion a "hipparchy" of Companions. At best, Arrian can be referring to only a few *ilai*, though possibly the term "hipparchy" is wrongly and anachronistically used as a substitute for *ile* (cf. Bosworth i.155; Brunt 1963: 29; Brunt i.lxxv §60; Griffith 1963: 70).

577 Curtius' claim that this was the work of Parmenion may well be a corruption of an original account which gave credit to [Philotas son of] Parmenion.

578 Hegesias *ap.* Dion Hal *de comp verb* 18 p. 123–126R. Hegesias' account is similar, in its main outline, to that given by C 4.6.7–29; both may derive from a common source, most likely Cleitarchus (Hammond 1983: 127–8; more cautious is Pearson 248).

579 Philotas' innocence, at least as far as the Dimnus conspiracy is concerned, is clear enough. The question is whether he deliberately ignored the information in the hope that the plan would succeed or if he was simply guilty of negligence and the victim of a conspiracy concocted either by the King (Badian 1960a, 2000a) or by members of Alexander's inner circle (Heckel 27–33; cf. Heckel 1977a, 2003). For other discussions see Cauer 1894: 8–38; Hamilton 132–8; Rubinsohn 1977;

Bosworth i.359–63; Goukowsky i.38ff.; ii.118–34; Adams 2003; Müller 81–112.

580 Curtius alone names them (6.7.15): Peucolaus, Aphobetus, Theoxenus, Archepolis, Nicanor, Iolaus, Amyntas, Demetrius (cf. A 3.26.3, without names). The instigator, his lover (Nicomachus), and his lover's brother (Cebalinus) are equally undistinguished.

581 C 6.7.6 does not say that Dimnus himself planned it: cf. 6.11.37, where a certain "Calis" (unnamed by C 6.7.15) confesses that he and Demetrius planned the crime.

582 Many scholars have found the view of Badian 1960a, amplified by Goukowsky, that Dimnus' conspiracy was a fabrication designed to "frame" Philotas, difficult to resist. Alexander is portrayed as bent on the destruction of the house of Parmenion, using Philotas, who was "plus vulnérable que son père" (Goukowsky i.39), as a pretext for eliminating the old man. While Philotas attended to the funeral rites of his brother, the plot was hatched: Dimnus' imaginary conspiracy would be divulged to Philotas, who, "comme prévu" (Goukowsky i.39), would then incriminate himself by not bringing the matter to the King's attention. Such a conspiracy *against* Philotas, like the elaborate crimes of Agatha Christie's characters, looks impressive – in retrospect. Because Philotas did not reveal Dimnus' plot to Alexander, it is assumed that he would not have done so under any circumstances. Hamilton 134–5 rightly asks: "how could Alexander *know* that Philotas would fail to pass on the information?" Indeed, it would have been embarrassing to the King had Philotas revealed the conspiracy, if he were then forced to admit to fabricating it in order to test him. And surely one would have to commend the "false conspirators," those "jolly good sports" who out of devotion to their King allowed themselves to be executed for the sake of realism and the success of Alexander's plot.

583 Cebalinus would scarcely have approached Philotas had he known of his involvement, and Philotas could be expected to have taken measures to prevent the conspiracy from coming to light.

584 Later references to his death, which provoked outrage in some sectors of the army and command: A 4.14.2; C 8.1.33, 38, 52; 8.7.4–5; 8.8.5; J 12.6.14.

585 The view of Milns 1966 that the Philotas at the Persian Gates (C 5.4.20, 30; A 3.18.6) commanded a seventh *taxis* of *pezhetairoi* is not compelling. This Philotas was almost certainly the son of Parmenion. But the Philotas who accompanied Lysanias in 336/5 could easily have been a commander of *psiloi* rather than *pezhetairoi*. Four battalions are mentioned in the Aspasian campaign (327/6) – those of Philotas, Attalus, Balacrus, and Philip – of which only Attalus' can have comprised *pezhetairoi*. Perdiccas and Hephaestion, *en route* to the Indus, had taken Gorgias, Cleitus, and Meleager (A 4.22.7). Craterus retained the battalions of Polyperchon and Alcetas, as can be deduced from A 4.23.1, 5; 4.24.1, 25.5–6. Gorgias' battalion was formerly Craterus'; Cleitus' was a new (seventh) unit. Hence Alexander was left with only Coenus and Attalus. Balacrus' men are undoubtedly light infantry (*psiloi*), and it is highly likely that Philip (probably the son of Machatas) and Philotas led similar troops (cf. Bosworth ii.154–5 and Bosworth 1973: 252–3).

586 Heckel 1988: 36–7, though I would now withdraw the tentative identification with Philotas Augaeus, C 5.2.5.

587 Antipater may have used the argument that Philotas had been unable to hold Cilicia and, therefore, did not deserve to be restored (cf. Menander, who abandoned Lydia and was replaced by Cleitus in 320), but his real purpose must have been to offset Antigonus' power in Asia by leaving Cilicia and Lydia in the hands of men more loyal to himself; D 18.50.5 shows that Antigonus wanted to reinstate *his* men in Asia Minor (cf. also 18.62.6–7). See also Heckel 2002a: 90–1.

588 I can find no support for Billows' suggestion (103 n. 27) that Antigenes may

have been killed because "he had caused the execution of Antigonus's friend Philotas."

589 Cf. *PM* 333a: ὕπαρχος τῆς παραλίας.

590 Briant *passim* speaks of the *karanos* as a military official, but I do not think that his powers were restricted to the military sphere.

591 Bosworth i.280–2 argues that the satrap of Caria and the financial official are one and the same, differentiating only between this Philoxenus and the later satrap of Cilicia. This would mean that Philoxenus disappeared from the scene after bringing troops (together with Menander of Lydia, who was confirmed as satrap of Lydia) from the coast to Babylon (A 7.23.1, 24.1). This, at least, solves the difficulty of explaining the disappearance in 323 (in one case permanently, in the other temporarily) of two men named Philoxenus.

592 But Arrian's comments (ἕνα τῶν ἀφανῶν Μακεδόνων, οἷα δὴ ἐν ἡμιολίῳ μισθοφορᾷ ὑπ' Ἀλεξάνδρῳ ἐστρατευμένον) may reflect a bias against Philoxenus on the part of Hieronymus for his betrayal of Eumenes and his apparent opposition to Antigonus the One-Eyed.

593 Φιλόξενός τις Μακεδών. This is hardly how one would describe the *hyparchos* who had exercised power in the coastal region for almost ten years.

594 He had two wives: the first was the sister of Cephisodotus the sculptor and the second known only for her modesty and character (*PPh* 19). It was presumably the second wife who was the mother of Phocus (Davies 559), a son whose lifestyle did not imitate that of his father (*PPh* 20.1–3; 38.3–4), as well as a daughter who married Charicles (*PPh* 21.5).

595 Phocion took Chabrias' son Ctesippus under his wing after the father's death but found him to be stupid and troublesome (*PPh* 7.3–4).

596 Demosthenes had also supported Phocion against his political opponent Chares. For Chares' opposition to Phocion see *PPh* 5.1–2.

597 For his political rivals see *PPh* 4.2, 10.6 (Glaucippus and Hypereides); 5.4, 9–10; 16.3 (Demosthenes); 9.8 (Demosthenes; but *PM* 811a tells the same story about Demades); 10.3–5, 9 (Aristogeiton; cf. *PM* 188b); 17.2–3 (Demosthenes, Hypereides, Charidemus); 20.6 (Demades). For his sayings, many of them concerning Athenian politics and politicians, see *PM* 187f–189b.

598 For Phocion's remark to Antipater that he could not be both flatterer and friend, see *PAgis* 2.2; *PM* 64c, 142b–c, 532f–533a.

599 Although he resisted Athenian appeals that he intervene with Antipater for removal of the Macedonian garrison, Phocion did secure a delay in the payment of the fine imposed after the Lamian War (*PPh* 30.8).

600 Executed with Phocion were Nicocles, Thudippus, Hegemon, and Pythocles. Demetrius of Phalerum, Callimedon, and Charicles were sentenced to death *in absentia* (*PPh* 35.5).

601 Billows 424–5 thinks not, and treats the man who betrayed Sardis as a separate individual (no. 97).

602 Pol*Strat* 4.3.27 mistakenly names Phrasaortes as defender of the Persian Gates instead of Ariobarzanes.

603 Unless Pharismenes is a scribal error for Phradasmenes or vice versa and the two forms refer to the same individual.

604 Arrian refers to Phrataphernes as satrap of Parthia only (A 4.7.1; 4.18.1). Only at A 5.20.7 and 3.23.4 is he called satrap of Parthia and Hyrcania.

605 Bosworth 2002: 105–6 speculates that Phrataphernes may have been removed from office by Philip [10], perhaps for supporting the Perdiccan faction. This is possible but the evidence is lacking. Phrataphernes may simply have died of natural causes.

606 He was apparently the son of the elder Pnytagoras, who perished in 374/3, together with his father Evagoras I, under bizarre circumstances (Theopompus, *FGrH* 115 F103; cf. D 15.47.8; Arist*Pol* 5.1311b). Beloch iii^2 2.99–101 suggests, not implausibly, that the younger Pnytagoras was the son of Nicocreon's daughter (that Pnytagoras the elder was in fact married to the woman with

whom Evagoras was having an affair). Nicocreon son of Pnytagoras thus bears the name of the maternal great-grandfather; see also Hill 1949: 143 n. 3; for the elder Pnytagoras, Isoc 9.62; D 15.4.3. If he was, in fact, the son of the elder Pnytagoras, he could have been born no later than 373/2.

607 Coins of Pnytagoras: Hill 1904: CXff.; Head, HN^2 744; Babelon, *Les Perses Achéménides* CXXV nos. 627–33.

608 C 7.2.4, plausibly, adds that Polemon was carried away by the panic amongst the cavalrymen who had served Philotas: he was not the only one to flee from the camp.

609 Cf. Billows 383, s.v. "Dokimos"; Simpson 1957: 504–5.

610 Demetrius' father-in-law is mentioned in the Armenian version of Eusebius' *Chronicle* (see Jacoby, *FGrH* 128 T1) but Olympias, if she was the mother of Antigonus Doson, must have been born ca. 280 BC, almost certainly too late to be daughter of the Alexander historian. If Eusebius' information is correct, we are dealing with a different Polycleitus. On the other hand, he may have confused the details concerning Phthia, daughter of Olympias II of Epirus, who married both Demetrius II and Antigonus Doson; Olympias II was the great-granddaughter of Menon of Pharsalus. A Thessalian admiral is not unprecedented. Medius of Larissa commanded a portion of Demetrius' fleet at Salamis in 306 BC (D 20.50.3).

611 So Hoffmann 200, followed by Berve ii.322, who tentatively identifies him with the son of Antaeus from Arethusa, SIG^3 269K.

612 Possibly related to the great Polydamas of the second quarter of the fourth century, or indeed one of that man's children, whom Jason of Pherae held hostage (Xen*HG* 6.1.18).

613 According to Str, Polydamas and his Arab guides made the thirty-day trip in only eleven days.

614 That he had young brothers (*fratres*) who were left behind as hostages, when he took the message to Ecbatana, seems unlikely; Berve suggests reading *filii* for *fratres*.

615 Many of the alleged conspirators had connections with Antigonus and/or Antipater. Ath 12.548e (citing a contemporary source, Cephisodorus of Thebes, or possibly Athens; see Jacoby, *FGrH* 112) mentions a doctor from Teos named Polydorus who was said to have dined with Antipater.

616 Plutarch, on three different occasions, quotes Polyeuctus as saying that Demosthenes was the best orator but Phocion the most effective speaker (P*Ph* 5.5; P*Dem* 10.3; P*M* 803e).

617 Polyeuctus was an opponent of Demades. At least, he and Lycurgus opposed honors for Demades introduced by Cephisodotus in 335 (Din 1.101; [P]*M* 820f), despite the fact that both men benefited from Demades' actions (see Will 58–9).

618 The form "Polysperchon" found in some literary sources (P*M* 184c; Ael*VH* 12.43; Ath 4.155c) is etymologically sound (Pape & Benseler 1230), but the epigraphic and papyrological evidence supports Polyperchon, as found in the Latin sources (cf. Polypercon): *IG* ii^2 387 (an Athenian decree of 319/8), line 8; *OGIS* i.4, line 24 (with n. 14); i.5, line 39.

619 Identification of Polyperchon with the mercenary of the same name, who served Callippus at Rhegium and took part in his murder in 351/0 BC (P*Dion* 58.6), should be rejected as implausible. It is unlikely that a member of the Upper Macedonian aristocracy served as a mercenary. Aelian's story (*VH* 12.43) that the son of Simmias was formerly a brigand derives from the propaganda wars of the Successors (cf. Ael*VH* 12.16, 14.47a; cf. J 15.3.3–10; but see Heckel 2007a). The same will be true for the story that he angered Alexander by supporting Parmenion's call for a night attack at Gaugamela (C 4.13.7–10) and that he mocked *proskynesis* (C 8.5.22–6.1).

620 A 4.22.1 says that in 327 Polyperchon, Attalus, and Alcetas were in Sogdiana, under the command of Craterus, completing the subjugation of Paraetacene, while Alexander returned to Bactria. C 8.5.2 records Polyperchon's mission

before the introduction of *proskynesis* at Bactra (8.5.5ff.), and P*A* 55.6 (cf. Hamilton 155) shows that Craterus and his force were still in Sogdiana when the Hermolaus conspiracy was uncovered; for we are told that Alexander informed them of it by letter; Plutarch's failure to mention Polyperchon indicates merely that he was absent from Craterus' camp, probably on a separate mission into the region of Bubacene (C 8.5.2). The story is accepted by Bosworth ii.86–7.

621 Since Alexander left Andaca with only Coenus and Attalus (A 4.24.1), Alcetas and Polyperchon must have remained with Craterus.

622 C 8.11.1 says that it was Polyperchon who was sent to attack Ora; A 4.27.5 names only Attalus, Alcetas, and Demetrius the hipparch.

623 Whether Polyperchon left India with Craterus or continued with Alexander through Gedrosia is uncertain. J 12.10.1 mentions his departure for Babylonia just before Alexander's Gedrosian march. But J regularly substitutes the name of Polyperchon for Craterus (cf. 13.8.5, 7; 15.1.1). It was shortly before Alexander reached the mouth of the Indus that he sent Craterus to Carmania via Arachosia and Drangiana: according to Arrian (6.17.3), Craterus took with him the battalions of Attalus, Meleager, and Antigenes, as well as those *hetairoi* and other Makedones who were unfit for military service. Polyperchon does resurface in the company of Craterus, at Opis in 324, but, unless Arrian has failed to mention him (deliberately or by accident), there is no good reason for preferring the evidence of J, who appears once more to have confused the two marshals (Boerma 199).

624 Polyperchon may, in fact, have replaced Sippas as *strategos* in Macedonia upon his return from Europe, although there is no explicit statement to that effect.

625 Polycles probably spent the years 334–323 in Macedonia, commanding a portion of the army that had been left behind for homeland defense. Of his earlier career nothing is known. See Berve ii.324–5 no. 652.

626 The decision was doubtless made in consultation with Antipater's *consilium* (cf. Hammond, *HMac* iii.130, with n. 3) and not, as Lenschau, *RE XXI.2*: 1800 suggests, by the terms of Antipater's testament.

627 D 18.57.2 does not imply a second invitation. 18.49.4 records the original decision of Polyperchon and his council, 18.57.2 the issuing of the invitation to the queen mother. For her reluctance to come immediately see 18.58.3–4.

628 Lysimachus was, as a result of his marriage to Nicaea, an ally of Cassander. But I see no strong evidence for Engel's characterization of him as "Polyperchons persönlicher Feind" (Engel 98 n. 166). Cf. Will, commenting on Polyperchon's appointment as *epimeletes*: "The illegality of the procedure was not what shocked the new masters of the empire, however, but the fact that the succession to Antipater aroused secret ambitions in some of them. Lysimachus, Macedon's immediate neighbour, would certainly not have disdained the idea of one day restoring for his advantage the union of Macedon and Thrace" (*CAH* vii^2 1.41).

629 A rescue attempt may have misfired (Pol*Strat* 4.11.3); nor was Polyperchon able to bring much-needed relief to Monimus in Pella or Aristonus, both of whom remained loyal to the house of Alexander (D 19.50.7–8).

630 Alexander had blocked the Isthmus, but Cassander was able to land his troops in the Argolid and capture Argos. From there he marched across to Messenia and won over all the towns of the region except Ithome. On his return to the north, he left 2,000 troops with Molyccus at the passes between Megara and the Corinthiad (D 19.54.3–4).

631 Since Polyperchon's support came primarily from the Aetolians, Mendels 1984: 176 reasonably infers that the agreement may have included territorial concessions for the Aetolians as well.

632 See the comments of Bosworth ii.233, 308–9. The estimates of Porus' height may be somewhat exaggerated, but there

is no reason to reject the view that he was exceptionally tall. Nor does this reference (or the rubbish at A 5.4.4) lend support to the view (Tarn ii.169–71) that there was a "short Macedonian cubit," which is wrongly accepted in Yardley & Heckel 245.

633 A 5.20.6 calls him *hyparchos* of the Indians; D 17.91.1 calls him *basileus* (king). In Arrian the term *hyparchos* has a variety of meanings; most often it is used as the equivalent of satrap (cf. Bosworth i.112). The "term" is discussed at length by Bosworth ii.147–9, and I am persuaded by his argument that Alexander and/or his historians regarded the Indian rulers as subjects of the Achaemenid kings. It is, however, unlikely that the word indicates that the second Porus was subordinate to his famous namesake, as Berve ii.345 suggests.

634 Str 15.1.30 (699) says that Porus ruled an area called Gandaris, perhaps (as Bosworth ii.325 suggests) confusing the region to which he fled (i.e., the Nanda kingdom) with the area he ruled.

635 Nor is it clear if he had anything to do with the Rhodian contingent of nine ships and the submission of that island to Alexander. Hauben 1977: 308 n. 7 rightly sees the dating of Rhodes' surrender after the siege of Tyre (thus J 12.11.1; C 4.5.9) as incorrect and due to the fact that the siege of Tyre was already underway when the delegation and the ships came to Sidon. Possibly, Proteas and his *pentekontoros* stopped at Rhodes on the way to the Levant. It is difficult to argue that the ten ships represent only the pro-Macedonian faction: the inclusion in this number of the state trireme seems to weigh against this (A 2.20.2: ἡ περίπολος καλουμένη). On the status of Rhodes at this time see Bosworth i.242–3.

636 Cf. also the discussion in Bosworth i.78–9.

637 But not "als Nachfolger des Hegelochos." Hegelochus may have held a special command over the *prodromoi* and 500 lightly armed troops (A 1.13.1), but this office, reported between Amyntas' scouting mission (A 1.12.7) and the latter's command of the *prodromoi* at the Granicus (1.14.1, 6), looks suspiciously like an error on Arrian's part, ascribable perhaps to the conflicting reports of Ptolemy and Aristobulus (cf. Bosworth i.114). That Hegelochus ever commanded the four squadrons of *prodromoi*, only to be demoted at Gaugamela (A 3.11.8), is highly unlikely.

638 I am no longer inclined to regard him as one of the Seven (see Heckel 259–60) or to see Hephaestion as his successor. If we remove Ptolemy from this list, then we do not know of a single member of the Seven who died in battle in that capacity. Balacrus the former Somatophylax was killed when he was satrap of Cilicia; Arybbas died of illness, as did Hephaestion; and Demetrius was arrested and executed.

639 A 4.7.2 says he was accompanied by Epocillus and Melamnidas; C 7.10.11 mentions only "Maenidas." See s.v. **Menidas**.

640 Arrian calls him *hegemon*, but the term is used loosely.

641 StByz s.v. "Orestia" says he came from Orestis.

642 Volkmann (*RE* xxiii.1607) speculates that, at this time, Ptolemy may have been appointed *edeatros* (the equivalent of the Roman *praegustator*) or "King's Taster" (Ath 4.171b = Chares, *FGrH* 125 F1). Not only would Alexander not risk the life of a Somatophylax for this purpose, but J 12.14.9 indicates that there were others appointed to do this job: the sons of Antipater (who were Pages of Alexander) are described as *praegustare ac temperare potum regis soliti*.

643 Cleitarchus certainly had no reason to diminish Ptolemy's contributions; for there are two later episodes in which the vulgate clearly invents stories that enhance Ptolemy's reputation (C 9.5.21, 8.22–7; D 17.103.6–8). Bosworth i.328 may be correct in suggesting that "he cast himself for the role played by Philotas."

644 Seibert makes a valiant attempt to defend Ptolemy, first (4–7) by rejecting Welles' arguments (1963: 101–16, esp.

107) and then (8–10) by arguing, on the basis of a meticulous study of Arrian's use of Ptolemy's patronymic, that the officer at the Persian Gates was not, in fact, the son of Lagus. But Bosworth i.328–9 is rightly skeptical of Seibert's conclusions; cf. Heckel 1980c: 169 n. 7.

645 His prominence in this undertaking can also be explained by the absence of Craterus, who had taken some 10,000 veterans from Opis to Cilicia (cf. A 7.12.1–4), and the death of Hephaestion (A 7.14; P*A* 72); Perdiccas had been given the task of conveying Hephaestion's corpse to Babylon (D 17.110.8).

646 Thus A*Succ* 1.25: παρὰ γνώμην . . . Περδίκκου. See also s.v. **Perdiccas** [1].

647 Ptolemy further added to his territories by seizing Coele-Syria from Laomedon soon after Triparadeisus and the departure of Antipater (App*Syr* 52 [264–5]; App*Mithr* 9 [27]; D 18.43.2; Paus 1.6.4). See also s.v. **Laomedon** and Wheatley 1995.

648 Berenice had previously been married to an obscure Macedonian named Philip, by whom she had two children, Magas (Paus 1.7.1) and Antigone (P*Pyr* 4.7); the marriage dates to the time before Berenice accompanied Eurydice (daughter of Antipater) to Egypt (P*Pyr* 4.7); hence Philip was probably already dead in 321/0. Magas was later ruler of Cyrene, and Antigone the future wife of Pyrrhus of Epirus (Paus 1.7.1). Philip's low birth is confirmed by the fact that both children bear the names of the maternal grandparents. He may also have been the father of Theoxene, but this is less certain (see Ogden 70, against Beloch iv^2 2.179–80; cf. Seibert 1967: 73). See Berve ii.387–8 no. 787.

649 Berve ii.335 rules this out on the grounds that Ptolemy son of Seleucus was one of those who had recently married (*neogamoi*) in 334. But Macedonian officers did not have to be young in order to take brides.

650 Ath 4.167c has πυμάτωνι, emended by Kaibel to Πυγμαλίωνι.

651 He was supposed to have been criticized for being too young to speak on the issue of Alexander's deification, but pointed out that he was older than the man who was being honored (P*M* 804b); cf. P*M* 784c and P*Ph* 21.2 for Pytheas' relative youth.

652 At some point he and Lycurgus prosecuted a certain Simmias, who was defended by Hypereides (Hyp frg. 62 [Burtt], cited by Harpocration); Dinarchus composed a speech against him *Concerning the Affairs of the Marketplace* (Περὶ τῶν κατὰ τὸ ἐμπόριον. Din frg. 3 [Burtt]).

653 Her name comes up in the comedies of Antiphanes (Ath 8.339a), Alexis (Ath 8.339c–d), who says that the sons of Chaerephilus the fish-seller were among her lovers, and Timocles (Ath 8.339d), adding that Anytus also enjoyed her favors.

654 It is mentioned also by P*Ph* 22.2, who says that it does not merit the thirty talents that Charicles charged Harpalus for the project (see s.v. **Charicles** [2]).

655 Cassander did not participate in the Asiatic campaign but joined Alexander in Babylon in 323. Evius too is not attested before 324 BC.

656 The Spithridates (*fl.* 400) of Xenophon (*HG* 3.4.10; 4.1.3, 20, 26–7), who was active in Hellespontine Phrygia and Paphlagonia, may have belonged to the same family; possibly he was Rhoesaces' grandfather. Berve's view (ii.346; accepted by Hamilton 40) that he held the satrapy around 344/3 (D 16.47.1–2) assumes that Rhoesaces was deposed, for an unspecified reason, and yet fought gallantly at the side of his brother, who had replaced him. Beloch's assumption (iii^2 2.137; followed by Bosworth i.111–12), that the satrap of 344/3 was the father of both Spithridates and the younger Rhoesaces, is preferable. If these assumptions about the family are correct, we may postulate a birthdate ca. 370 for the younger Rhoesaces.

657 C 8.1.20 and D 17.20.1–7 have reversed things somewhat, with Rhoesaces losing his arm and life to Cleitus, though he nevertheless strikes Alexander's helmet (D 17.20.6; he splits the King's helmet and inflicts a scalp wound).

658 The painting by Apelles was described by Lucian, *Imagines* 7; *Herodotus* 4–6 (Pollitt 175–6), a drawing of the scene was made by Raphael, and a painting by "Il Sodoma."

659 Against the view, prevalent in much modern scholarship (see, most recently, Hammond, *HMac* iii.139), that Alexander IV and Rhoxane were left for some time in Epirus, see Macurdy 1932. Also present in Pydna was Deidameia, the daughter of Aeacides and sister of Pyrrhus, to whom Alexander IV was betrothed (P*Pyr* 4.3).

660 At some point she made a dedication to Athena Polias (*IG* ii^2 1492, A, lines 45–57). The dedication is discussed at length by Kosmetatou 2004, but the date remains uncertain, except that we can say with relative certainty that it is unlikely that Rhoxane would have been able to make such a gesture while she was a prisoner in Amphipolis (316–310 BC).

661 Hedicke writes "Sabistamenes"; cf. Schachermeyr 194 n. 206: "Vielleicht hat schon Kleitarch irrtümlich Sabiktamenes statt Sabiktas geschrieben, wie er ja auch einen Arsamenes bot (D 17, 19, 4) anstelle des korrekten Arsames." Possibly Curtius misunderstood and corrupted a Greek passage that read *Σαβίκταν μὲν εἰς Καππαδοκίαν ἔπεμψε* or something similar.

662 This explains Hedicke's curious emendation of the name to "Damaraxus."

663 J 12.10.2, the MSS. have *ambiregi regis* and *ambigeri regis*, which can easily be emended to *Ambi regis*); "Ambira" (Oros), that is *Sambi regis*, "of King Sambus."

664 Eggermont 19–20 notes that Barsaentes and Samaxus came to Alexander with thirty elephants (C 8.13.3–4); Sambus later fled, when he heard of Alexander's favorable treatment of Musicanus, with thirty elephants (D 17.102.7). The case for identifying Samaxus and Sambus is strengthened by the fact that Curtius and Diodorus were almost certainly following the same source (Cleitarchus).

665 C 9.8.13–20 gives a completely different picture of resistance within the territory of Sambus, but it should be noted that Sambus himself is not mentioned. D 17.102.6–103.3 gives a compressed account that shares some details of both Curtius and Arrian, but Diodorus makes it clear that Sambus had fled soon after Alexander's arrival.

666 Berve ii.349 tentatively identifies Josephus' Sanaballetes as grandson of Nehemiah's Sanballat.

667 The story includes another of those famous exchanges between Parmenion and Alexander (Jos*AJ* 11.331ff.), in which Parmenion assumes that Alexander is doing *proskynesis* before the Jewish high priest. For this problem see Schäfer 2003: 1–7; Marcus 1926: 512–32; Bickerman 1988: 3–12. On the assumption that the story is apocryphal, I have omitted Iaddus, Manasses, and Nicaso from my collection.

668 Palimbothra (Str 2.1.9 [70]); Palibothra (Str 15.1.36 [702]).

669 Phylarchus *ap.* Ath 1.18d–e says that Sandrocottus gave Seleucus presents including aphrodisiacs.

670 D 17.78.1 (Chortacana). The town must be in the vicinity of modern Herat, where Alexander founded Alexandria-in-Areia, although the Achaemenid and Alexandrian cities remained separate (Brunt i.497–8; but see the cautious discussion of Fraser 110–15). Engels 89–90 puts Artacoana northeast of Kalat-i-nadiri; rejected by Atkinson ii.207–8.

671 According to Euseb Arm (*ap.* Porphyry of Tyre, *FGrH* 260 F32 §4), he was 75 years old when he died in 281/0. But this dating is suspicious, since it represents the middle ground between the dates of Appian and Justin, and makes Seleucus an exact contemporary of Alexander the Great (cf. Grainger 1). App*Syr* 63 [331], 64 [342] claims that he was 73 years old at the time of his death; J 17.1.10 (cf. Oros 3.23.59) makes him 77 at Corupedium, seven months before he was assassinated by Ptolemaeus Ceraunus (J 17.2.4). Appian's evidence would date Seleucus' birth to 354, which helps to explain why we hear nothing of his military career before 326. But both Appian and J compare Seleucus' age with that of Lysimachus (Appian: Seleucus 73; Lysimachus 70; J: Seleucus 77; Lysimachus 74), and the matter is confounded by

[L]*Macrob* 11, who gives Lysimachus' age at his death as 80 and cites Hieronymus of Cardia as his source. Appian and J agree on one point: Seleucus was three years older than Lysimachus. Pseudo-Lucian may indeed have rounded up Lysimachus' age to include him in a list of octogenarians, but this is more likely to have happened if his true age approached 75 instead of 70. Furthermore, a birthdate of 352/1 would make Lysimachus' career much more difficult to explain. Hence a birthdate ca. 358 for Seleucus appears to be most consistent with all the available evidence.

672 Hence Malalas (p. 203 Bonn) names Pella as Seleucus' birthplace, and Paus 1.16.1 says that he set out from Pella on the Asiatic expedition. App*Syr* 56 [284] mentions Macedonia in general.

673 The omens of Seleucus' future kingship and greatness are collected and discussed by Hadley 1969.

674 D 19.55.7–9 says that Antigonus was disturbed by a Chaldaean prophecy that if Seleucus escaped Antigonus' grasp, he would return to become master of Asia. Seleucus' flight also prompted Antigonus to depose Blitor from Mesopotamia (App*Syr* 53 [269]); in fact, it may have been Seleucus' decision to replace the absent Amphimachus, who had allied himself with Eumenes, with Blitor that formed one of the charges against him.

675 The anecdote is inane and the identity of the individual is of no consequence. Possibly, in its original form, the story mentioned a servant (*ϑεϱάπων* or the participial form *ϑεϱαπεύων*), and this was corrupted into *Σεϱαπίων*.

676 Since Arrian omits all reference to the deposing of Astaspes, which according to C 9.10.21, 29 occurred after Alexander had reached Carmania, it is likely that A 6.27.1 contains a summary of administrative changes, some of them anachronistic. It may be that Alexander appointed Thoas when he reached Gedrosia, after receiving news of Apollophanes' death. He then marched to Carmania, where he deposed Astaspes and replaced him with Sibyrtius. Upon receiving news of the deaths of Thoas and Menon, he sent Sibyrtius to govern Gedrosia and Arachosia and appointed Tlepolemus in Sibyrtius' place.

677 *Phaligrus* in the MSS. of Curtius appears to be a corruption of Philip son of Balacrus (Balagros). Bosworth 1976b: 14 argues that the vulgate is more likely to be correct, that Arrian (Ptolemy) claimed that Simmias commanded his brother's unit "so that he could lay at his door, by implication at least, the break of the Macedonian line and the attack upon the base camp" (ibid.).

678 Note, however, that C 8.4.21–3 has badly conflated Chorienes (his "Cohortandus") and Oxyartes. The sons taken into Alexander's service are those of Chorienes (Sisimithres; cf. 8.2.33), and the thirty maidens introduced at the banquet included Chorienes' own daughters (perhaps all three mentioned by *ME* 19) and Rhoxane, the daughter of Oxyartes. Because both Sisimithres and Chorienes appear in *ME* 19, 28, and because Sisimithres corresponds to Chorienes in A 4.21.1, it is clearly not a case of Curtius' use of Cleitarchus for the name Sisimithres and Ptolemy for Chorienes (*pace* Schachermeyr 353 n. 425). Rather, the failure to reconcile the names Sisimithres and Chorienes probably goes back to Cleitarchus himself, who may have found Chorienes (the father of three sons) in a written source (Onesicritus?) and failed to recognize that he was identical with Sisimithres. Curtius then compressed the episode in such a way that he made it appear that Rhoxane was Chorienes' daughter: *filia ipsius* = *filia Oxyartis* only if "Cohortandus" in 8.2.21 is wrongly emended (as by Alde) to "Oxyartes." But, if Alde's emendation stands, then Curtius is guilty of introducing Oxyartes twice (once under the name Oxartes, a compatriot of Sisimithres, and again as an illustrious satrap), which would in itself not be particularly disconcerting, except that "Cohortandus" in 8.2.21 must be the

Chorienes of *ME* 28–31. Bosworth argues (1981: 32) that Chorienes and Sisimithres are different individuals.

679 D 17.5.5; cf. P*Art* 1.2, 5.5. Thus Neuhaus 1902; followed by Berve ii.356; Hamilton 78; Brosius 67; Briant 772–3. This relationship cannot be disproved, but it is not required by the evidence (Bosworth i.218). Sisygambis would have been one of the few remaining relatives of Artaxerxes III Ochus (see Val Max 9.2 ext 7; J 10.3.1). Brosius 68 rightly observes the failure of the sources to mention a mother–daughter relationship between Sisygambis and the elder Stateira.

680 See C 3.12.13–17; J 11.9.12; *Suda* s.v. "Hephaistion"; D 17.114.2; Val Max 4.7 ext 2; D 17.37.4–6; P*M* 522a; *Fragmentum Sabbaiticum* §5 = *FGrH* 151 F1; *IA* 37 merely says that "one of the women" mistook Hephaestion for Alexander. The scene is depicted in a famous painting by Paolo Veronese, now in the National Gallery, London.

681 Whether she made the arduous journey to Ecbatana to witness the punishment and execution of Bessus (A 4.7.3; C 7.10.10) is unknown. It is not the kind of opportunity her great-grandmother, Parysatis, would have passed up. Also uncertain is whether Sisygambis attended the mass-marriage ceremony in Susa in 334, which saw Alexander marry Stateira and Hephaestion Drypetis (see s.vv. **Stateira** [2], **Drypetis**).

682 Assuming that Sopater was roughly coeval with Alexander and not born during his short reign.

683 Cf. also Stobaeus, *Eclog.* 1.62, p. 421, 15 Wachsmuth.

684 Although we are dealing with Graecisms of an Indian name (perhaps Saubhūti), the form Sophytes appears on coin legends of the early third century (*ΣΩΦΥΤΟΥ*; see Mørkholm 73; cf. Holt 96–7). The dynast who issued the coinage was clearly not the same individual who encountered Alexander. The form Sophites occurs in Curtius, but is restored from *cufites* or *cofites* in J 12.8.10; Oros 3.19.5 has "Cufides."

685 Strabo takes his information from Onesicritus (*FGrH* 134 F21), whose account was probably followed by Cleitarchus (and then Diodorus, Curtius, and Justin). The hunting dogs were discussed also by Aristobulus (*FGrH* 139 F40). Bosworth ii.328 distinguishes between an "eastern" and "western" Sopeithes.

686 Identification with the Sopolis who served Antigonus in the years 312–308 (D 20.27.1–3; Billows 434 no. 108) is highly unlikely.

687 The confusion of ἀδελφός and ἀδελφιδοῦς is easy enough, as is the corruption of the genitive *Σπιτάκου* into *Πιττάκου*. The problem is, however, that A 5.18.2 (cf. 5.14.3–15.2) makes a distinction between Spitaces and the sons of Porus, saying that it was one of Porus' sons who led the force assigned by C 8.14.2 to Porus' brother. To add to the confusion the text of Curtius reads *praemisit Hages*, which has been emended to *praemisit Spitaces*. The emendation is compelling, but it does not solve the basic problem that the lost sources appear to have distinguished between the nomarch Spitaces and a relative (son, nephew, brother) of Porus.

688 I find it difficult to accept Bosworth's suggestion (ii.303–4) that Pittacus was a nephew of the so-called Bad Porus. The sources speak of no resistance by the other Porus (or his relatives) and the campaign against him was conducted by Hephaestion.

689 Perhaps he was, in fact, one of Porus' sons but the confused accounts of the lost sources resulted in a misunderstanding on the part of the extant authors: hence Arrian did not understand that the son of Porus and the Indian nomarch were one and the same person. At some point in the popular tradition the relationship of Spitaces to Porus was also confused.

690 Burstein 1999 believes that the story of Judith may have been influenced by Cleitarchus' account of the death of Spitamenes.

691 Arrian's wording suggests that he was in Alexander's entourage and was sent to Babylonia from Nautaca.

692 Perhaps he was one of those leaders in Eumenes' army whose deaths are alluded to in D 19.44.1. Unlike Stasanor and Tlepolemus, of whom the former was not present and the latter appears to have fled, Stasander was replaced as satrap (D 19.48.2). This suggests that he did not return to his satrapy. It is possible of course that he died in the battle of Gabiene and that the fact went unrecorded. For these events see also Heckel 1980a.

693 Berve ii.361 suggests that he may have been a younger brother of Pasicrates. Although this is far from certain – indeed, it is curious that Nicocles is identified as a son of Pasicrates but no mention is made of Stasanor's family background – there were several members of Cypriot ruling houses enrolled as *hetairoi* of the King. Stasander may have been a relative of Stasanor.

694 Cf. Bosworth ii.38–9. A 4.7.1 says he returned in 329/8 to Alexander in Zariaspa. This is unlikely, and it appears that we are dealing with a failure on Arrian's part to reconcile the information of his sources. D 17.81.3 says that Stasanor and Erigyius were sent to deal with the rebel Satibarzanes. A 3.28.3 and C 7.3.2, 4.32 name Caranus as Erigyius' colleague. Diodorus may have compressed the information about the crushing of Satibarzanes' rebellion and the later appointment of Stasanor. C 8.3.17 muddles things as well, saying that Stasanor replaced "Arsames" and confusing Atropates with Arsaces.

695 According to Aristobulus, *FGrH* 139 F52 = A 7.4.4, this was the name of Darius III's elder daughter, whom other sources call Stateira; it is accepted by several scholars (cf. recently Brosius 77), who have seen in the alleged name change an honoring of Darius' wife or a bid to establish legitimacy. This could be so, but it is more likely that Aristobulus has confused the King's daughter with Alexander's mistress, Barsine. Both came to unhappy ends, and Aristobulus, writing after 301, was presumably no longer clear on the details or concerned about their accuracy.

696 Now, together with her sister Drypetis, in the charge of Sisygambis; for their mother, the elder Stateira, had died before Gaugamela (cf. C 4.10.19, 21, for their grief).

697 Tarn ii.300, predictably, rejects the story in its entirety.

698 But the "name" Tauriscus may be an ethnic, and not an unusual one, if one considers the geographical position of Issus.

699 It is tempting to postulate a family connection between the Antigonids and the royal house of Elimeia: a certain Harpalus appears, perhaps as governor of Beroea, in the mid-third century (Tataki 116 no. 228) in the service of Antigonus Gonatas; a later Harpalus son of Polemaeus (Tataki 116–17 no. 230) was Perseus' ambassador to Rome in 172. Polemaeus was, of course, the name of Antigonus Monophthalmus' nephew (cf. Tataki 255 no. 1082). Furthermore, Tauron is honored along with Myllenas son of Asander (possibly another Beroean; cf. Tataki 231–2 no. 910); Asander son of Agathon, satrap of Caria, is described by *ASucc* 25.1 as welcoming Antigonus, who was a kinsman.

700 For the city see A 5.3.6 and Str 15.1.28 [698] (located between the Indus and the Hydaspes); A 5.8.3; *PA* 59; see also Marshall 1921 and 1951; Dani 1986; Karttunen 1990; cf. Wheeler 1968: 103–6, and Wheeler 1976: 23, 25.

701 A 4.22.6 says that Alexander summoned Taxiles (he does not say whether this was the father or the son) when he reached Parapamisadae.

702 The fact that the report came from Taxiles and Porus suggests that the alliance still held.

703 A 4.20.1–2 tells a similar story, but in the time shortly after Issus, when Stateira was still alive.

704 For the complicated system of checks and balances in the years after Alexander's death see Heckel 2002a. Billows 85 n. 8 suggests that Teutamus may have commanded Eumenes' hypaspists, also 3,000 strong (D 19.28.1, cf. 40.3); D 19.28.1 says that Antigenes and Teutamus

commanded both the Argyraspids and the hypaspists. But Teutamus is regularly described as a commander of the Argyraspids (D 18.59.3, 62.4, 5; cf. 18.58.1 and 62.1; P*Eum* 13.3, 7; 16.2; Pol*Strat* 4.8.2), and Diodorus' references to Antigenes alone constitute a kind of shorthand that can be explained in terms of Antigenes' seniority (D 19.12.1–2, 13.2, 15.2, 21.1, 41.1, 44.1). Eumenes' hypaspists have no early connection with Teutamus, who in 318 and in 315 is still linked with the Argyraspids. Hammond 1978: 135 thinks the hypaspists in Eumenes' army were the "new hypaspists," the successors and "descendants of the hypaspists"; these had failed at Kamelon Teichos, mutinied against Perdiccas, and were assigned by Antipater to Antigenes, in addition to the Argyraspids, at Triparadeisus; see, however, Anson 1988: 131–3.

705 The Greek can mean either Teutamus and his supporters or simply Teutamus himself. Either way the meaning is clear.

706 A 3.18.11–12 and Str 15.3.6 [730] both record the destruction of Persepolis without reference to Thaïs.

707 There is no reason to assume that she was once Alexander's mistress and that Ptolemy took up with her after the King's death. The eldest son, Lagus, must have been born during the campaign: *SIG*^{3} 314 names him as a winner in the chariot race in the Lycaean games in Arcadia in 308/7. Leontiscus was captured in 306 by Demetrius Poliorcetes (J 15.2.7), and Eirene at an unknown date married Eunostus of Soli.

708 Those who reported it as historical were Cleitarchus, Polycleitus, Onesicritus, Antigenes, and Ister; those who rejected it were Ptolemy, Aristobulus, Chares, Anticleides, Philon, Philip of Theangela, Hecataeus of Eretria, Philip the Chalcidian, and Duris of Samos.

709 Theocritus is also mentioned by Stobaeus, *Anthologion* 46 and 123; and Macr*Sat* 7.3.12.

710 Berve believes he may have been Philip II's *hieromnemon* in 341–340 BC (*SIG*^{3} i, pp. 314–15; cf. Ellis 132, Table 3) but the identification is at best tentative.

711 Presumably, Theophilus made several helmets for the King. We know of one iron helmet that was split during the battle of the Granicus (D 17.20.6).

712 Thus Photius' *Life of Theopompus* (Westermann, *Vitarum Scriptores* 204–6).

713 Berve ii.177 rightly sees the quarrel between Theopompus and Theocritus as a political rather than an academic one (cf. Flower 1994: 23–4).

714 There is, however, also a reference to a *Censure of Alexander* (F258). Theopompus had also written an *Encomium of Philip*.

715 Stephanus of Byzantium, citing Lucius of Tarrah, says that Philip gave his daughter to a woman named Nice to raise, hence the name Thessalonice. But this is surely a false etymology and we need not credit the existence of Nice.

716 I do not believe that Diodorus is using the word *philoi* in the technical sense but rather means that Harpalus regarded Thibron (wrongly, as it turned out) as a friend.

717 D 17.108.6: 6,000; D 18.19.2: 7,000. A*Succ* 1.16 says that there were 6,000 mercenaries who accompanied Thibron to Cyrene.

718 Thus Diodorus and Strabo; A*Succ* 1.17–18 has Teucheira.

719 See also P*M* 259d–260d; Zonaras 4.9; also P*M* 1093c = Aristobulus, *FGrH* 139 F2, and P*M* 145e. It is important to note that Alexander did not acquit her on account of the justice of her case (as a victim of rape) but because of her lineage and her noble bearing.

720 His play *The Icarians* featured Pythionice, later Harpalus' mistress: Ath 8.339d.

721 Sen*de Ira* 2.2 confuses him with Xenophantus (Berve ii.282 no. 577). A similar story is told by P*M* 335a of Antigenides, who was no longer alive in Alexander's time (see Berve ii.415 no. 8).

722 The Achaemenid rulers regularly employed eunuchs as *gazophylakes*. Ael*VH* 12.1 mentions a different eunuch of that name in the time of Artaxerxes II.

723 Ps-Call 2.14.11 mentions a Tiridates who is "the first of the archers" or

"commander of archers." The author was perhaps influenced by the historical treasurer but the story in the *Alexander Romance* has no independent value.

724 It is virtually impossible to determine whether Diodorus and Curtius are referring to the same officer by different names, whether a distinction is to be made between satrap and *strategos*, or whether the areas of responsibility (Gedrosia and Ariaspians) should be distinguished.

725 Possibly, we are dealing with Tiridates the *strategos*, who fell out of favor with Alexander and was replaced by Amedines. But this is speculation at best, perhaps even fantasy.

726 Dexippus, *FGrH* 100 F8 §6 makes "Neoptolemus" satrap of Carmania. This is clearly a scribal error and the emendation that makes Neoptolemus satrap of Armenia and Tlepolemus ruler of Carmania is unlikely to represent the original text. He also received the satrapy in the forged will of Alexander: *LM* 121; Ps-Call 3.33.22.

727 The numbers have a suspicious symmetry. There is, however, disagreement concerning how many elephants Xandrames possessed. *ME* 68 has 180; C 9.2.3 gives 3,000; and D 17.93.2 says 4,000.

728 It does not follow from the Greek (*ἄνδρα μακεδονίζοντα τῇ φ[ω]νῇ*) that Xennias was not himself a Macedonian. The author is trying to make the point that the communication took place in the Macedonian tongue. Who better to transmit a message in this language than a Macedonian himself. Indeed, had he not been Macedonian one might expect a comment to that effect. *Contra* Kapetanopoulos 1993; see also Anson 208–9.

729 He is said to have been a teacher of Phocion (P*Ph* 4.2).

730 Val Max 4.3 ext. 3a relates how the courtesan Phryne, for all her beauty, had been unable to seduce Xenocrates at an all-night drinking-party.

731 Not the Somatophylax, as Berve ii.282 suggests, but Arybbas the uncle of Olympias.

732 The city itself was under the control of the *strategos* Archelaus son of Theodorus (see s.v. **Archelaus** [2]).

733 Curtius and Plutarch say that Alexander did not pour out the water but returned it to the men who had brought it, telling them to give it to their sons, for whom they had procured the water in the first place.

734 Zoïlus' contingent was part of a larger group that included 3,000 Illyrians sent by Antipater; 130 Thessalian cavalrymen under Philip son of Menelaus; and 2,600 infantry and 300 cavalry from Lydia.

735 J 12.2.16 calls him "governor of Pontus," but the reference is clearly to the Thracian area bordering on the Black Sea (cf. A*Succ* 1.7; D 18.3.2).

736 Mentioned also by Macr*Sat* 1.11.33.

737 Possibly, though not very likely, a daughter of Timosa (cf. Ath 13.609a–b); this woman was, however, merely a concubine of Darius III's brother.

738 Justi 341, s.v. "Wahuka," reads *Ocha* in Valerius Maximus, instead of Atossa, as proposed by Rumpf. This is rendered more likely by the claim that Atossa, Ochus' sister, contracted leprosy in the lifetime of Artaxerxes II (P*Art* 23.4). Justi 232, and Neuhaus 1902: 619, think that C 3.13.13 (*in eodem grege uxor eiusdem Ochi fuit Oxathrisque – frater hic erat Darei – filia*) refers to the same woman, a daughter of Oxathres, who married Ochus, but who is then not identical with the mother of **F3–4** and Parysatis. But this is not required by the Latin, which appears to indicate that the wife of Ochus and the daughter of Oxathres are two different women.

739 Renault 1975: 184 identifies the brother with the father of Bagoas the trierarch (A*Ind* 18.8, reading "Pharnaces" instead of "Pharnuches"), but this involves needless emendation. This Bagoas is, in all probability, the famous eunuch, and it is tempting to see in his father Pharnuches the Lycian guide who played no small part in the Macedonian disaster at the Polytimetus River. Did Pharnuches receive the command

through Bagoas' influence? Renault confuses the identity of Pharnaces, at any rate, calling him the "brother of Darius' wife and half-sister Stateira" (184).

740 Though she is herself of Greek origin, and although her children appear to have received some Greek education (cf. *PA* 21.9), I have listed her amongst the Persian nobility because of her position in the family of Artabazus.

741 The date of Artabazus' stay at the Macedonian court is uncertain. See Griffith, *HMac* ii.484 n. 5: "It seems safe to think he was with Philip by 344." See, however, Berve ii.83, who dates his arrival to 352; cf. also Beloch iii^2 1.482 n. 2.

742 Despite J. C. Rolfe's translation of *adulti* as "who had now reached manhood" (Loeb), they need not all have been male. Nor can we make anything out of the ages implied by *adulti/adultae*. Apame was of marriageable age in 324, as were the daughters of Darius III, who were in 333 described as *adultae virgines* (C 3.11.25).

743 Cf. Comaetho and Amphitryon, or Scylla and Minos; somewhat similar too is Livy 38.24; Burstein 1999 believes the story of Judith and Holofernes is modeled on the Spitamenes episode.

744 Note that Str 12.8.15 [578] wrongly calls this Apame the daughter of Artabazus. The latter's mother, Apame, *was* Achaemenid (*PArt* 7.4; cf. Xen*HG* 5.1.28); see also Brunt 1975: 25. The name Apame may, however, indicate that Spitamenes himself had Achaemenid blood (cf. Rapson, *CHIndia* i.311, apparently referring to Spitamenes).

745 Perhaps an official name derived from the region he governed, as is suggested by the ending -iene(s).

746 I see no point in listing these among the *anonymae*, since we have the names of no individuals with whom to associate them. Thus they contribute nothing to our understanding.

747 Berve wrongly calls Oxyartes "Vater von drei erwachsenen Söhnen" (ii.292) on the basis of Alde's incorrect emendation of C 8.4.21.

748 I see no reason for thinking that Curtius fabricated the details of Attalus' marriage to a daughter of Parmenion (*pace* Fears 1975: 133 n. 77).

749 Assuming that the marriage was consummated in about spring/summer 322 BC and that Atalante bore two children before her death in May 320. For the marriage and its date see Heckel 381–4.

750 C 9.2.7 (*eo interfecto per insidias*) does not tell us who killed the king, but since Curtius does not contradict Diodorus, we may assume that it was the queen.

751 Berve ii.103, 254 wants to identify him with the Memnon honored at Athens in 327/6 (*IG* ii^2 356). Against this view, see Brunt 1975: 27, who argues that this Memnon is a son of Artabazus and the sister of Mentor and the elder Memnon.

752 Possibly the Memnon of *IG* ii^2 356, according to Brunt 1975: 27.

753 The duel at the Granicus River is lost along with Book 2 (?); it is, however, alluded to at 8.1.20.

754 C 8.10.35 says that he was Cleophis' own son. Perhaps the infant gave rise to the story that Alexander fathered on Cleophis a son bearing his name (C 8.10.36; J 12.7.9–11).

755 Cf. also Bosworth 1983: 38 n. 6.

Appendix

Boeotian Cavalrymen from Orchomenus Who Served Alexander Between 334 and 330 BC

(in the order they appear on *IG* vii.3206)

[. . . . . .] son of [. . .]odoros, *ilarches*
Proppei son of Thiogiton
Mnasidikos son of Athano[doros]
Damostheneis son of Pourrhinos
Thiodotos son of [Po . . . . . .]
[. . .]giton son of Dionysos
Dorkeidas son of Melambi[chos]
[Polo]uxenos son of Xenotimos
Antigenidas son of Simou[los]
Kallikron son of Euryphaon
Echmon son of Echmon
S[im]mias son of Phaollos
Thoinon son of Timogiton
Diod[oro]s son of Telesarchos
Kaphisodoros son of Arxillos
Apollodoros son of Telestas
Thiopompos son of Olympichos
Thiodexiles son of Mnasikles
Kallisthenes son of Menandros
Wanaxion son of Saondas
Pankles son of Dorotheos
Eurybotadas son of Tallos
Hermaios son of Nikios
Argilias son of Laonikos

Trierarchs of the Hydaspes Fleet (326 BC)

(A*Ind* 18.3–8)

Hephaestion son of Amyntor
Leonnatus son of (Eunus)
Lysimachus son of Agathocles
Asclepiodorus son of (Timander)

Archon son of Cleinias
Demonicus son of Athenaeus
Ophellas son of Seilenus
Timanthes son of Pantiades
Nearchus son of Androtimus
Laomedon son of Larichus
Androsthenes son of Callistratus
Craterus son of Alexander
Perdiccas son of Orontes
Ptolemy son of Lagus
Aristonus son of Peisaeus
Metron son of Epicharmus
Nicarchides son of Simos
Attalus son of Andromenes
Peucestas son of Alexander
Peithon son of Crateuas
Leonnatus son of Antipater
Pantauchus son of Nicolaus
Mylleas [possibly Myllenas] son of Zoïlus
Medius son of Oxythemis
Eumenes son of Hieronymus
Critobulus son of Plato
Thoas son of Menodorus [or Mandrodorus A 6.23.2]
Maeander son of Mandrogenes
Andron son of Cabeleus
Nicocles son of Pasicrates
Nithaphon son of Pnytagoras
Bagoas son of Pharnuches

Hieromnemones

Agippus (Agippos): 329/8 BC (*SIG*³ 241c, 150; 251r, col. 1.6). Berve ii.8 no. 14.
Alexarchus (Alexarchos): 329/8 BC (*SIG* ³ 241c, 151, with n. 84). Berve ii.21 no. 42.
Archepolis: several times between 333 and 328 BC (*SIG*³ 241, 251). Berve ii.86 no. 160.
Callixenus (Kallixenos): 329/8 BC (*SIG* ³ 241c). Berve ii.191 no. 407.
Eurylochus (Eurylochos): 342/1 BC (*SIG*³ 242 B6; but the text is uncertain).
Euthycrates (Euthykrates). 335 BC (*SIG*³ 241C n. 84; 251H, col. I. 17, J. 5, K. 7–8). Berve ii.155 no. 314.
Theodorus (Theodoros): 341–340 BC (*SIG*³ I, pp. 314–15; cf. Ellis 132, Table 3)

Athenian Politicians Whose Extradition Was Demanded by Alexander in 335

P*Dem* 23.4	A 1.10.4	*Suda A* 2704	P*Ph* 17.2
Demosthenes	Demosthenes	Demosthenes	Demosthenes
Charidemus	Charidemus	Charidemus	Charidemus
Lycurgus	Lycurgus	Lycurgus	Lycurgus
	Hypereides	Hypereides	Hypereides
Polyeuctus	Polyeuctus	Polyeuctus	
Ephialtes	Ephialtes	Ephialtes	
Moerocles	Moerocles	Patrocles	
Demon			
	Diotimus	Diotimus	
Callisthenes			
	Chares	Chares	
		Thrasybulus	
		Cassander	

Teachers of Alexander the Great*

Ps-Call 1.13.4
Leuconides or Cleonides
Polyneices
Alcippus or Leucippus
Menippus or Melemnus
Aristomenes
Aristotle
Anaximenes

* There is no corroborating evidence that any of the above, apart from Aristotle, actually taught Alexander in his youth. Samuel 1986, however, considers the list an early and historical element of the *Alexander Romance*.

Glossary

agema. The elite guard of the infantry or the cavalry.

Agrianes. Also "Agrianians." A group that lived in the northeastern corner of Paeonia near the source of the Strymon River. Their contingent of peltasts, armed with javelin, was used as an elite force by the King, often in conjunction with the hypaspists.

akontistai. Javelin-men.

Amun, Amun-Re. The Egyptian sun-god, equated by the Greeks with Zeus. Greek and Latin sources give his name as Amon, Ammon, and Hammon.

anaboleus. The individual – probably a member of the Companions (even the *ile basilike*) rather than a Page – who helped the King mount his horse.

apologia. A defense. A sanitized or "whitewashed" account.

apomachoi. Soldiers unfit for battle.

archaioi xenoi. A unit of mercenaries – perhaps soldiers who had served together since the time of Philip II – commanded by Cleander.

archigrammateus. Chief secretary.

archihypaspistes. Commander of the entire corps of hypaspists.

archikybernetes. Chief pilot (e.g., Onesicritus).

archon. Politically, a chief magistrate. Militarily, a commander.

argyraspides. Silver Shields. 3,000 veterans (former hypaspists).

Argyraspids. See *argyraspides*.

asthetairoi. See *pezhetairoi*.

ataktoi. The "undisciplined" or "unruly." A unit of dissenters formed in 330 and placed under the command of Leonidas.

auletes. Flute-player.

bematists. A *bema* is literally a "step" or "stride." Alexander's bematists were those who kept records or distances and conducted surveys. Their works appear to have contained more than mere factual information and not everything they recorded was based on autopsy.

chiliarch. Literally, "commander of a thousand" but in Persian usage the chief executive officer of the King or "second after the King" (*hazarapatish*).

chiliarches. Commander of a thousand men.

chiliarchos. See *chiliarches*.

choregos. A man who assumed the expenses associated with dramatic productions. The service was known as *choregia*.

choreutes. A dancer in the chorus.
consilium. Council, advisory group.
custos corporis. Bodyguard (also *armiger*).
doryphoros (pl. *doryphoroi*). Literally a "spear-bearer," a *doryphoros* was a member of the guard. In the Alexander historians the word is used as a substitute for *somatophylax, armiger*, or *custos corporis* (i.e., a member of the hypaspists).
epimeleia. Guardianship.
epimeletes (pl. *epimeletai*). A guardian or manager of affairs. Used of a regent.
episkopos (pl. *episkopoi*). An overseer.
epistoleus. A letter-carrier (*grammatophoros*), courier.
epitropos (pl. *epitropoi*). Guardian or regent.
erastes. The older "lover" in a homosexual relationship. See *eromenos* below.
eromenos. A homosexual lover, that is, normally the younger partner in the relationship (literally, "the one who is loved").
gazophylax (pl. *gazophylakes*). Treasurer (that is, the guardian of a treasure in one specific place).
gynaion. A "little woman." The term can be used affectionately of an older woman (e.g., Ada or Halicarnassus) or pejoratively of a woman of low standing or of a mistress or common-law wife.
harmostes. A military or garrison commander.
hazarapatish. See chiliarch.
hegemon (pl. *hegemones*). Normally, a military leader or commander. Sometimes used as a substitute for *strategos* but often denoting an officer of lesser rank. Also, the military leader of a league (e.g., the League of Corinth).
Hellenica (Greek: *Hellenika*). Literally, "Greek things or affairs." A history of Greece.
hetaira (pl. *hetairai*). A "female friend," that is, a prostitute or courtesan.
hetairos (pl. *hetairoi*). Companion or friend. A high-ranking individual at court or in the army. Hence a member of a select group of individuals who served as officers, advisors, or administrators.
hieromnemon. A religious official. In the case of the Delphic amphictyony, a state representative.
hippakontistai. Mounted javelin-men.
hipparch. Cavalry commander.
hippeis misthophoroi. Mercenary cavalry.
hippeis prodromoi. Cavalry scouts (also *prodromoi*).
hyparch. See *hyparchos*.
hyparchos. A lieutenant. Often used as the equivalent of satrap.
hypaspistai basilikoi. The Royal Hypaspists.
hypaspists. Elite infantry, selected for their strength and agility rather than on a territorial basis. They were certainly more mobile (hence, perhaps more lightly armed) and provided the link in the Macedonian line between the *pezhetairoi* and the cavalry. There were two types of hypaspists: the regular hypaspists (3,000 in number and commanded by the *archihypaspistes*)

and the Royal Hypaspists, who seem to have been drawn from a higher social class. See Heckel 237–53.

ilarch. See *ilarches*.

ilarches. Cavalry squadron commander.

ile (pl. *ilai*). A cavalry-squadron. In Diodorus, *eile* (pl. *eilai*).

ile basilike. The royal squadron (*eile basilike*, D). Commanded by Black Cleitus.

kitharoidos. One who plays the harp and sings in accompaniment.

logos. A story. In Arrian a report that comes from a primary source other than Ptolemy or Aristobulus (also a *legomenon*).

Macedonica. See *Makedonika*.

Makedones. Native Macedonians. Macedonian citizens.

Makedonika. A history of Macedonia. See s.v. **Marsyas**.

megistoi. The most powerful individuals (in this case, after Alexander's death).

misthophoroi. Mercenaries. Cf. *hippeis misthophoroi*. Also *xenoi*.

nauarchos. Admiral. Fleet commander.

navarch. See *nauarchos*.

neogamoi. Newly weds. Those in Alexander's army in 334/3 who had married before leaving for Asia Minor.

Paeonians. A tribe located in the region between the Strymon and Axius (Vardar) rivers. They served Alexander as cavalrymen.

pais basilikos (pl. *paides basilikoi*). "Royal Boy/Youth," that is, one of the King's Pages.

patronymic (Greek: *patronymikon*). Literally, "father's name." The Greeks had no family (or last) name. Instead a person was identified as "son of x" with the father's name appearing in the genitive case (e.g., Hephaistion Amyntoros = Hephaestion son of Amyntor).

peltasts. Targeteers. Troops, more lightly armed than hoplites, named for their shields (*pelte*, pl. *peltai*).

pentakosiarches. Pentakosiarch. A commander of 500.

pentakosiarchia. A military unit of 500. Half a chiliarchy.

pentekontoros. A fifty-oared ship.

Persica (Greek: *Persika*). Literally, "Persian things or affairs." A history of Persia, of which the most famous examples were written by Ctesias and Dinon.

pezhetairoi (also *pezetairoi*). The "Foot Companions." The core of the Macedonian infantry. Alexander's army included six *taxeis* (1,500 × 6 = 9,000) of *pezhetairoi*. These were territorial levies. Those from Upper Macedonia may have been called *asthetairoi* (thus Bosworth 1973); the term most likely means "close companions" rather than "best (*aristoi*) companions."

Philippica (Greek: *Philippika*). A history of Philip II of Macedon. The most famous example was written by Theopompus of Chios.

Philippeum. A statue-group, showing the family of Philip II, set up at Olympia. Only the base of it survives today.

philos (pl. *philoi*). Friend in the technical sense. See *hetairos*.

phrourarchos. Garrison commander.

presbeis. Envoys, ambassadors.

prodromoi. Scouts. Also *hippeis prodromoi*. Cf. *skopoi*.
prostasia. Guardianship, regency.
prostates. A guardian or regent.
proxenia. An institution that allowed an individual of one state to represent the political and diplomatic interests of another, in lieu of a permanent consul or ambassador. See Marek 1984.
proxenos. An individual who was honored by a foreign state to represent its political interests in his own.
psiloi (sing. *psilos*). Lightly armed troops.
psilokitharistes. A harpist, but one who plays without singing.
sarissa (sometimes *sarisa*). The Macedonian "pike," which in the time of Philip II and Alexander was about 15–18 ft in length. The *sarissophoroi* (below) carried somewhat shorter *sarissai* (ca. 14 ft).
sarissophoroi. Literally, "*sarissa*-bearers." Cavalry armed with the shorter cavalry *sarissa*.
satrap. *Satrapes*. Governor of a province (satrapy). Sometimes called *hyparchos*.
satrapy. *Satrapeia*. Name of a Persian province. The name and the system was taken over by Alexander and his successors.
Seven. In Macedonia, the seven Somatophylakes. See Somatophylax. In Persia, the seven conspirators against the so-called "False Smerdis."
skopoi. Scouts.
somatophylakes. Bodyguards, in the general sense. The term was used of Pages, hypaspists, and the Seven.
Somatophylax. Bodyguard. One of the seven personal guards (staff) of the King.
sphairistes. A ball-player.
Stathmoi. "Stages," title of works written by the bematists (see s.v. above).
strategia. Generalship. In Athens, ten men were elected annually to the *strategia*.
strategos. General. Used of a high-ranking military commander and of a military overseer of a region.
stratiotes. A soldier or, in some cases, a professional soldier.
stromatophylax. Guardian of the household goods, particularly bedding. Apparently a minor official at Alexander's court (see s.v. **Proxenus**).
syngeneis. Greek *συγγενεῖς*. "Kinsmen" of the Great King. An honorific title at the Persian court.
syntrophos. An individual (often a member of the Pages) who was raised at the court in Pella with the King's sons.
taxiarch. See *taxiarches*.
taxiarches. Commander of a *taxis* (see below).
taxis (pl. *taxeis*). An infantry unit, often translated "battalion," sometimes "brigade." The strength of a *taxis* of *pezhetairoi* was 1,500. Chiliarchies (1,000) of hypaspists and lightly armed troops are sometimes referred to as *taxeis* as well.
thearodochos (= *theorodochos*). One who receives *theoroi* (ambassadors sent to consult an oracle).

theoros (pl. *theoroi*). An envoy sent to consult an oracle or to be present at a religious festival.

toxarches. Commander of archers.

toxotai. The archers.

triakontor (*triakontoros*). A thirty-oared ship.

trierarchos (pl. *trierarchoi*). Commander of a trireme or, as in the case of the Hydaspes fleet in 326 (following Athenian practice), the man who paid the cost of fitting out a ship.

trierarchy. A public financial service. Rich men were expected, in Athens, to fund the cost of fitting out a trireme. Alexander adopted this practice at the Hydaspes in 316.

xenagos. Mercenary leader.

xenoi. Mercenary troops. Cf. *misthophoroi*.

xenos. A foreign friend (e.g., Demaratus of Corinth). Also a mercenary (see *xenoi*).

Concordance

Greek/variant forms	*Name in this volume*
Abdalonymos	Abdalonymus
Abdastart	Straton
Abdellonymos	Abdalonymus
Abistamenes	Sabictas
Abouletes	Abulites
Achilleus	Achilles
Adaios	Adaeus
Addaios	Adaeus
Adeia	Adea
Admetos	Admetus
Aegobares	Autobares
Aëropos	Aëropus
Agathokles	Agathocles
Agesilaos	Agesilaus
Aggrammes	Xandrames
Agippos	Agippus
Agonippos	Agonippus
Aiakides	Aeacides
Aigobares	Autobares
Ainel	Enylus
Airikes	Aphrices
Aischines	Aeschines
Aischrion	Aeschrion
Aischylos	Aeschylus
Akouphis	Acuphis
Alacrinis	Lanice
Alexandros	Alexander
Alexarchos	Alexarchus
Alexippos	Alexippus
Alketas	Alcetas
Alkias	Alcias
Alkimachos	Alcimachus
Amadas	Polydamas
Amastrine	Amastris
Ambhi	Taxiles
Ambira	Sambus
Ambus	Sambus
Amestris	Amastris
Amilkas	Hamilcar
Amissos	Damis
Amissus	Damis
Amphimachos	Amphimachus
Amphistratos	Amphistratus
Amphoteros	Amphoterus
Anaxarchos	Anaxarchus
Anaxippos	Anaxippus
Andrakottos	Sandrocottus
Androkles	Androcles
Androkydes	Androcydes
Andromachos	Andromachus
Andronikos	Andronicus
Anemoitas	Anemoetas
Antibelos	Brochubelus
Antibelus	Brochubelus
Antigona	Antigone
Antigonos	Antigonus
Antikles	Anticles
Antiochos	Antiochus
Antipatros	Antipater
Antiphilos	Antiphilus
Apama	Apame
Apeisares	Abisares
Aphobetos	Aphobetus
Aphrikes	Aphrices
Aphthonios	Aphthonius
Apollodoros	Apollodorus
Apollonios	Apollonius
Aposeisares	Abisares
Arboupales	Arbupales
Archelaos	Archelaus
Argaios	Argaeus
Ariakes	Ariaces
Arimases	Ariamazes
Arimazes	Ariamazes

Greek/variant forms	*Name in this volume*
Arimmas	Menon
Ariomazes	Ariamazes
Ariplex	Aphrices
Aristandros	Aristander
Aristarchos	Aristarchus
Aristides	Aristeides
Aristoboulos	Aristobulus
Aristokrates	Aristocrates
Aristokritos	Aristocritus
Aristonikos	Aristonicus
Aristonous	Aristonus
Aristonymos	Aristonymus
Aristophanes	Aristonus
Aristoteles	Aristotle
Aristoxenos	Aristoxenus
Arkesilaos	Arcesilaus
Arrabaeus	Arrhabaeus
Arrhabaios	Arrhabaeus
Arrhidaios	Arrhidaeus
Arridaeus	Arrhidaeus
Arridaios	Arrhidaeus
Arrybas	Arybbas
Arsakes	Arsaces
Arsamenes	Arsames
Artabazos	Artabazus
Artakama	Artacama
Artemios	Artemius
Artone	Artonis
Asandros	Asander
Asklepiades	Asclepiades
Asklepiodoros	Asclepiodorus
Assakanos	Assacenus
Assakenos	Assacenus
Astes	Astis
Astykratidas	Astycratidas
Astylos	Astylus
Atalanta	Atalante
Athenodoros	Athenodorus
Atixyes	Atizyes
Atropatos	Atropates
Attalos	Attalus
Autodikos	Autodicus
Autolycus	Autodicus
Autolykos	Autodicus
Azemilkos	Azemilcus
Bagodaras	Gobares
Baiton	Baeton
Balagros	Balacrus
Balakros	Balacrus
Ballomynos	Abdalonymus
Barzaentes	Barsaentes
Berenike	Berenice
Bessos	Bessus
Betis	Batis
Boubakes	Bubaces
Boupares	Bupares
Boxos	Boxus
Brazanes	Barzanes
Callanus	Calanus
Caranus	Calanus
Casander	Cassander
Chaireas	Chaereas
Chairon	Chaeron
Charidamos	Charidamus
Charidemos	Charidemus
Charikles	Charicles
Charos	Charus
Cheirocrates	Deinocrates
Cheirokrates	Deinocrates
Choirilos	Choerilus
Chorienes	Sisimithres
Chrysippos	Chrysippus
Cleomantis	Cleomenes
Cleonice	Cleodice
Clitarchus	Cleitarchus
Clitus	Cleitus
Cobares	Bagodaras
Cophes	Cophen
Cyna	Cynnane
Damaraxus	Samaxus
Dareios	Darius
Dares	Cophen
Deinarchos	Deinarchus
Deinokrates	Deinocrates
Delios	Delius
Demaratos	Demaratus
Demarchos	Demarchus
Demaretos	Demaratus
Demetrios	Demetrius
Demokrates	Democrates
Demonikos	Demonicus
Dimnos	Dimnus
Dinarchus	Deinarchus
Diodoros	Diodorus
Diodotos	Diodotus
Diognetos	Diognetus
Diokles	Diocles
Dionysios	Dionysius
Dionysodoros	Dionysodorus
Diophantos	Diophantus

Greek/variant forms	*Name in this volume*	*Greek/variant forms*	*Name in this volume*
Diotimos	Diotimus	Hektor	Hector
Dioxenus	Theoxenus	Helene	Helen
Dioxippos	Dioxippus	Hellanice	Lanice
Ditamenes	Stamenes	Hellanikos	Hellanicus
Dokimos	Docimus	Hephaistion	Hephaestion
Dorkeidas	Dorceidas	Heraclides	Heracleides
Draco	Dracon	Heraclitus	Heracleitus
Drakon	Dracon	Herakleides	Heracleides
Echekratidas	Echecratidas	Herakleitos	Heracleitus
Elaptonius	Aphthonius	Herakles	Heracles
Embisares	Abisares	Herakon	Heracon
Enylos	Enylus	Hercules	Heracles
Ephippos	Ephippus	Hermaios	Hermaeus
Ephoros	Ephorus	Hermolaos	Hermolaus
Epokillos	Epocillus	Hiero	Hieron
Erices	Aphrices	Hieronymos	Hieronymus
Erigyios	Erigyius	Himeraios	Himeraeus
Ersilaus	Eurysilaus	Hippokrates	Hippocrates
Eteokles	Eteocles	Hippostratos	Hippostratus
Euagoras	Evagoras	Holkias	Holcias
Eudaemon	Eudamus	Hydrakes	Hydraces
Eudamos	Eudamus	Hyperbolos	Hyperbolus
Eudemus	Eudamus	Hyperides	Hypereides
Eugnostos	Eugnostus	Iolaos	Iolaus
Euios	Evius	Iollas	Iolaus
Euktemon	Euctemon	Iphikrates	Iphicrates
Europe	Europa	Isokrates	Isocrates
Eurydike	Eurydice	Kadmeia	Cadmeia
Eurylochos	Eurylochus	Kalanos	Calanus
Eurysilaos	Eurysilaus	Kalas	Calas
Euthykles	Euthycles	Kallas	Calas
Euthykrates	Euthycrates	Kallias	Callias
Exathres	Oxyathres	Kallikles	Callicles
Gerastratos	Gerastratus	Kallikrates	Callicrates
Gergithios	Gergithius	Kallikratidas	Callicratidas
Glaukias	Glaucias	Kallikron	Callicron
Glaukippos	Glaucippus	Kallimedon	Callimedon
Glaukos	Glaucus	Kallines	Callines
Glykera	Glycera	Kallisthenes	Callisthenes
Gobares	Bagodaras	Kallixeina	Callixeina
Gobryas	Gobares	Kallixenos	Callixenus
Gorgos	Gorgus	Kaphisias	Caphisias
Hamilkas	Hamilcar	Kaphisodoros	Caphisodorus
Harpalos	Harpalus	Karanos	Caranus
Haustanes	Austanes	Kasandros	Cassander
Hegelochos	Hegelochus	Kassandros	Cassander
Hegesimachos	Hegesimachus	Katanes	Catanes
Hegesippos	Hegesippus	Kebalinos	Cebalinus
Hegesistratos	Hegesistratus	Kephisophon	Cephisophon
Hekataios	Hecataeus	Kissos	Cissus

Greek/variant forms	*Name in this volume*	*Greek/variant forms*	*Name in this volume*
Kleadas	Cleadas	Madetes	Madates
Kleandros	Cleander	Maenidas	Menidas
Klearchos	Clearchus	Maiandros	Maeander
Kleitarchos	Cleitarchus	Manapis	Amminapes
Kleitos	Cleitus	Mandanis	Dandamis
Kleochares	Cleochares	Mandron	Andron
Kleodike	Cleodice	Mauakes	Mauaces
Kleomantis	Cleomenes	Mazaios	Mazaeus
Kleomenes	Cleomenes	Mazakes	Mazaces
Kleon	Cleon	Mazaros	Mazarus
Kleonike	Cleodice	Medates	Madates
Kleopatra	Cleopatra	Medeios	Medius
Kodros	Codrus	Medios	Medius
Koinos	Coenus	Megabyxos	Megabyxus
Koiranos	Coeranus	Megakles	Megacles
Kombaphes	Combaphus	Melamnidas	Menidas
Kophaios	Cophaeus	Meleagros	Meleager
Kophen	Cophen	Menandros	Menander
Kophes	Cophen	Menedemos	Menedemus
Korrhagos	Corrhagus	Menelaos	Menelaus
Krateros	Craterus	Menesaichmos	Menesaechmus
Krates	Crates	Meniskos	Meniscus
Krateuas	Crateuas	Menoitas	Menoetas
Kratinos	Cratinus	Menoitios	Menoetius
Kretheus	Cretheus	Menyllos	Menyllus
Krison	Crison	Mikion	Micion
Kritoboulos	Critobulus	Mikkalos	Miccalus
Kritodemos	Critodemus	Minion	Minnion
Krobylos	Crobylus	Minneon	Minnion
Ktesiphon	Ctesiphon	Minythyia	Thalestris
Kyna	Cynnane	Mithracenes	Mithrazenes
Kynane	Cynnane	Mithrines	Mithrenes
Kynnana	Cynnane	Mithrinnes	Mithrenes
Kyrsilos	Cyrsilus	Mithrobaios	Mithrobaeus
Lagos	Lagus	Mithrobouzanes	Mithrobuzanes
Lamachos	Lamachus	Mnasidikos	Mnasidicus
Langaros	Langarus	Mnasikles	Mnasicles
Lanike	Lanice	Mnesitheos	Mnesitheus
Laodike	Laodice	Moirokles	Moerocles
Leonnatos	Leonnatus	Monimos	Monimus
Letodoros	Letodorus	Mousikanos	Musicanus
Leuconides	Leonidas	Mullinus	Myllenas
Leukonides	Leonidas	Nanias	Tiridates
Limnaios	Limnaeus	Nearchos	Nearchus
Lykidas	Lycidas	Neiloxenos	Neiloxenus
Lykomedes	Lycomedes	Neoptolemos	Neoptolemus
Lykon	Lycon	Nicostratus	Sostratus
Lykourgos	Lycurgus	Nikagoras	Nicagoras
Lysimachos	Lysimachus	Nikaia	Nicaea
Lysippos	Lysippus	Nikanor	Nicanor

Greek/variant forms	*Name in this volume*	*Greek/variant forms*	*Name in this volume*
Nikarchides	Nicarchides	Philinna	Philine
Nikasipolis	Nicesipolis	Philippos	Philip
Nikesias	Nicesias	Philippus	Philip
Nikesipolis	Nicesipolis	Philiskos	Philiscus
Nikias	Nicias	Philo	Philon
Nikokles	Nicocles	Philokles	Philocles
Nikokreon	Nicocreon	Philoxenos	Philoxenus
Nikolaos	Nicolaus	Phoinix	Phoenix
Nikomachos	Nicomachus	Phokion	Phocion
Nikomedes	Nicomedes	Phrynichos	Phrynichus
Nikon	Nicon	Pierio	Pierion
Nikostratos	Sostratus	Pitho	Peithon
Ochos	Ochus	Pithon	Peithon
Olcias	Holcias	Pittacus	Spitaces
Olkias	Holcias	Pittacus	Spitaces
Onesikritos	Onesicritus	Pittakos	Spitaces
Ophelas	Ophellas	Pittakos	Spitaces
Orontobates	Orontopates	Pixodaros	Pixodarus
Oropios	Oropius	Pixodoros	Pixodarus
Orsillus	Orsilus	Pizodaros	Pixodarus
Orsilos	Orsilus	Pleistarchos	Pleistarchus
Oxikanos	Oxicanus	Polemaios	Polemaeus
Oxykanos	Oxicanus	Polemo	Polemon
Pakate	Pancaste	Polouxenos	Poluxenus
Pancaspe	Pancaste	Polycritus	Polycleitus
Panegoros	Panegorus	Polydoros	Polydorus
Pankaste	Pancaste	Polyeuktos	Polyeuctus
Pankles	Pancles	Polykleitos	Polycleitus
Pantauchos	Pantauchus	Polykles	Polycles
Pantordanos	Pantordanus	Polykritos	Polycleitus
Parmenio	Parmenion	Polymachos	Pulamachus
Pasikrates	Pasicrates	Polyneikes	Polyneices
Pasippus	Pausippus	Polypercon	Polyperchon
Patraos	Patraus	Polysperchon	Polyperchon
Pausippos	Pausippus	Polystratos	Polystratus
Perdikkas	Perdiccas	Poros	Porus
Perilaos	Perilaus	Portikanos	Porticanus
Perillos	Perilaus	Poseidonios	Poseidonius
Perillus	Perilaus	Poulamachos	Pulamachus
Peroidas	Peroedas	Pranichos	Pranichus
Peucestes	Peucestas	Prokles	Procles
Peukestas	Peucestas	Promachos	Promachus
Peukestes	Peucestas	Protomachos	Protomachus
Peukolaos	Peucolaus	Proxenos	Proxenus
Phaidimos	Phaedimus	Ptolemaeus	Ptolemy
Pharnabazos	Pharnabazus	Ptolemaios	Ptolemy
Pharnakes	Pharnaces	Pulamachos	Pulamachus
Pharnouches	Pharnuches	Pythagoras	Peithagoras
Phasimelos	Phasimelus	Pythionike	Pythionice
Phesinos	Phesinus	Pythonike	Pythionice

Greek/variant forms	*Name in this volume*
Rheboulas	Rhebulas
Rheobulas	Rhebulas
Rhoisakes	Rhoesaces
Rhosaces	Rhoesaces
Rhosakes	Rhoesaces
Roxane	Rhoxane
Sabakes	Sauaces
Sabbas	Sambus
Sabiktas	Sabictas
Sabos	Sambus
Sacrames	Xandrames
Sambos	Sambus
Sanaballetes	Sanballat
Sandrakottos	Sandrocottus
Sandrokottos	Sandrocottus
Sangaios	Sangaeus
Sasibisares	Abisares
Sasigupta	Sisicottus
Sataces	Sauaces
Satrakes	Satraces
Satyros	Satyrus
Sauakes	Sauaces
Seleukos	Seleucus
Sibyrtios	Sibyrtius
Simachus	Hegesimachus
Sisenes	Sisines
Sisikottos	Sisicottus
Sisyngambris	Sisygambis
Sitalkes	Sitalces
Skymnos	Scymnus
Sokrates	Socrates
Sopatros	Sopater
Sopeithes	Sophytes
Sophites	Sophytes
Sostratos	Sostratus
Sphines	Calanus
Spinther	Spithridates
Spitakes	Spitaces
Spithrobates	Spithridates
Stasandros	Stasander
Stasiakes	Sauaces
Stasikrates	Stasicrates
Statira	Stateira
Stephanos	Stephanus
Strato	Straton
Stratonike	Stratonice
Stroibos	Stroebus
Symmachus	Hegesimachus
Syrmios	Syrmus
Syrmos	Syrmus
Tarrhias	Atarrhias
Tasiakes	Sauaces
Tauriskos	Tauriscus
Telephos	Telephus
Teireos	Teireus
Terioltes	Tyriespis
Teutamos	Teutamus
Thallestris	Thalestris
Theaitetos	Theaetetus
Theodoros	Theodorus
Theodotos	Theodotus
Theokritos	Theocritus
Theophilos	Theophilus
Theophrastos	Theophrastus
Theopompos	Theopompus
Thersippos	Thersippus
Thessaliskos	Thessaliscus
Thessalonike	Thessalonice
Thessalos	Thessalus
Thettalonike	Thessalonice
Thettalos	Thessalus
Thimodes	Thymondas
Thiodotos	Thiodotus
Thiopompos	Thiopompus
Thoinon	Thoenon
Thrasyboulos	Thrasybulus
Thrasyboulus	Thrasybulus
Thrasylochos	Thrasylochus
Timandros	Timander
Timarchos	Timarchus
Timoclea	Timocleia
Timokleia	Timocleia
Timokles	Timocles
Timolaos	Timolaus
Timotheos	Timotheus
Tlepolemos	Tlepolemus
Xenodochos	Xenodochus
Xenokles	Xenocles
Xenokrates	Xencrates
Xenophantos	Xenophantus
Xenophilos	Xenophilus
Zephyros	Zephyrus
Zipoites	Zipoetes
Zoïlos	Zoïlus

Bibliography

Abramenko 1992	A. Abramenko, "Die Verschwörung des Alexander Lyncestes und die '*μήτηϱ τοῦ βασιλέως*.' Zu Diodor XVII 32,1," *Tyche* 7: 1–8
Abramenko 2000	A. Abramenko, "Der Fremde auf dem Thron. Die letzte Verschwörung gegen Alexander d. Gr.," *Klio* 82: 361–78
Adams 1901	C. D. Adams, "The Harpalos Case," *TAPA* 32: 121–53
Adams 1980	W. L. Adams, "The Royal Macedonian Tomb at Vergina: An Historical Interpretation," *AncW* 3: 67–72.
Adams 1984	W. L. Adams, "Cassander and the Crossing of the Hellespont: Diodorus 17.17.4," *AncW* 2: 111–15
Adams 1985	W. L. Adams, "Antipater and Cassander: Generalship on Restricted Resources in the Fourth Century," *AncW* 10: 79–88
Adams 1993	W. L. Adams, "Cassander and the Greek City-States (319–317 B.C.)," *Balkan Studies* 34: 197–211
Adams 2003	W. L. Adams, "The Episode of Philotas: An Insight," in W. Heckel and L. A. Tritle (eds.), *Crossroads of History: The Age of Alexander* (Claremont, CA): 113–26
Africa 1982	Thomas W. Africa, "Worms and the Death of Kings: A Cautionary Note on Disease and History," *CA* 1: 1–17
Andréadès 1929	A. Andréadès, "Antimène de Rhodes et Cleomène de Naucratis," *BCH* 53: 1–18
Anson 1980	E. M. Anson, "Discrimination and Eumenes of Cardia," *AncW* 3: 55–9
Anson 1986	E. M. Anson, "Diodorus and the Date of Triparadeisus," *AJP* 107: 208–17
Anson 1988	E. M. Anson, "Antigonus, the Satrap of Phrygia," *Historia* 37: 471–7
Anson 1990	E. M. Anson, "Neoptolemus and Armenia," *AHB* 4: 125–8
Anson 1996	E. M. Anson, "The *Ephemerides* of Alexander the Great," *Historia* 45: 501–4
Ashton 1977	N. G. Ashton, "The *Naumachia* near Amorgos in 322 BC," *ABSA* 72: 1–11
Ashton 1983	N. G. Ashton, "The Lamian War: A False Start?" *Antichthon* 17: 47–63
Ashton 1984	N. G. Ashton, "The Lamian War – *stat magni nominis umbra*," *JHS* 104: 152–7
Atkinson 1988	J. E. Atkinson, "The Military Commissions Awarded by Alexander at the End of 331 BC," in W. Will (ed.), *Zu Alexander dem Grossen* (Amsterdam): 413–35

Auberger 2001 — Janick Auberger, *Historiens d'Alexandre. Textes traduits et annotés* (Paris)

Aulock 1964 — H. von Aulock, "Die Prägung des Balakros in Kilikien," *JNG* 14: 79–82

Ausfeld 1895 — A. Ausfeld, "Das angebliche Testament Alexanders des Grossen," *PhM* 50: 357–66

Ausfeld 1901 — A. Ausfeld, "Das angebliche Testament Alexanders des Grossen," *RhM* 56: 517–42

Babelon 1891 — E. Babelon, "Les monnaies et la chronologie des rois de Sidon," *BCH* 15: 293ff.

Badian 1958 — E. Badian, "The Eunuch Bagoas," *CQ* 8: 144–57

Badian 1960a — E. Badian, "The Murder of Parmenio," *TAPA* 91: 324–38

Badian 1960b — E. Badian, "The First Flight of Harpalus," *Historia* 9: 245–6

Badian 1961 — E. Badian, "Harpalus," *JHS* 81: 16–43

Badian 1963 — E. Badian, "The Death of Philip II," *Phoenix* 17: 244–50

Badian 1965 — E. Badian, "The Administration of the Empire," *G&R* 12: 166–82

Badian 1967a — E. Badian, "Agis III," *Hermes* 95: 170–92

Badian 1967b — E. Badian, "A King's Notebooks," *HSCP* 72: 183–204

Badian 1975 — E. Badian, "Nearchus the Cretan," *YCS* 24: 147–70

Badian 1976 — E. Badian, "A Comma in the History of Samos," *ZPE* 23: 289–94

Badian 1982 — E. Badian, "Eurydice," in E. N. Borza and W. L. Adams (eds.), *Philip II, Alexander the Great and the Macedonian Heritage* (Washington, DC): 99–110

Badian 1987 — E. Badian, "Alexander at Peucelaotis," *CQ* 37: 117–28

Badian 1988 — E. Badian, "Two Postscripts on the Marriage of Phila and Balacrus," *ZPE* 73: 116–18

Badian 1999 — E. Badian, "A Note on the 'Alexander Mosaic,'" in Frances

B. Titchener and Richard F. Moorton, Jr. (eds.), *The Eye Expanded: Life and the Arts in Graeco-Roman Antiquity* (Berkeley): 75–92

Badian 2000a — E. Badian, "Conspiracies," in A. B. Bosworth and E. J. Baynham (eds.), *Alexander the Great in Fact and Fiction* (Oxford): 50–95

Badian 2000b — E. Badian, "Darius III," *HSCP* 100: 241–68

Badian 2000c — E. Badian, "The Road to Prominence," in I. Worthington (ed.), *Demosthenes: Statesman and Orator* (London): 9–44

Barber 1935 — Godfrey L. Barber, *The Historian Ephorus* (Cambridge)

Bayliss 2002 — Andrew J. Bayliss, "A Decree Honouring Medeios of Larissa," *ZPE* 140: 89–92

Baynham 1994 — E. J. Baynham, "Antipater: Manager of Kings," in I. Worthington (ed.), *Ventures into Greek History* (Oxford): 359–92

Baynham 1998a — E. J. Baynham, "Why Didn't Alexander Marry Before Leaving Macedonia?" *RhM* 141: 141–52

Baynham 1998b — E. J. Baynham, "The Treatment of Olympias in the *Liber de Morte* – a Rhodian Retirement," in W. Will (ed.), *Alexander der Grosse: Eine Welteroberung und ihr Hintergrund* (Bonn): 103–15

Baynham 2001 — E. J. Baynham, "Alexander and the Amazons," *CQ* 51: 115–26

Bengtson 1937 — H. Bengtson, "*Φιλόξενος ὁ Μακεδών*," *Philologus* 92: 126–55

Bengtson 1975 — H. Bengtson, *Die Diadochen. Die Nachfolger Alexanders des Grossen* (Munich, 1975)

Benveniste 1966 — E. Benveniste, *Titres et noms propres en iranien ancien* (Paris)

Bernard 1984 — P. Bernard, "Le philosophe Anaxarche et le roi Nicocréon de Salamine," *JS*: 3–49

Bernhardt 1988 — R. Bernhardt, "Zu den Verhandlungen zwischen Dareios und Alexander nach der Schlacht bei Issos," *Chiron* 18: 181–98

Berve 1967 — H. Berve, *Die Tyrannis bei den Griechen*, 2 vols. (Munich)

Bickerman 1963 — E. Bickerman, "Sur un passage d'Hypéride (Epitaphios, col. VIII)," *Athenaeum* 41: 70–85

Bickerman 1988 — E. Bickerman, *The Jews in the Hellenistic Age* (Berkeley and Los Angeles)

Billows 1989 — R. A. Billows, "Anatolian Dynasts: The Case of the Macedonian Eupolemos in Karia," *CA* 8: 173–206

Billows 1993 — R. A. Billows, "*IG* XII 9.22: A Macedonian Officer at Eretria," *ZPE* 96: 249–57

Blänsdorf 1971 — J. Blänsdorf, "Herodot bei Curtius Rufus," *Hermes* 99: 11–24

Bloedow 1995 — E. Bloedow, "Diplomatic Negotiations between Darius and Alexander: Historical Implications of the First Phase at Marathus in Phoenicia, 333/232 BC," *AHB* 9: 93–110

Borza 1981 — E. N. Borza, "Anaxarchus and Callisthenes: Intrigue at Alexander's Court," in H. J. Dell (ed.), *Ancient Macedonian Studies in Honor of Charles F. Edson* (Thessaloniki): 73–86

Borza 1990 — E. N. Borza, *In the Shadow of Olympus: The Emergence of Macedon* (Princeton)

Borza 1994 — E. N. Borza, *Before Alexander: Constructing Early Macedonia*. Papers of The Association of Ancient Historians 6 (Claremont, CA)

Borza 1999 — Eugene N. Borza, *Before Alexander: Constructing Early Macedonia*. Publications of the Association of Ancient Historians 6 (Claremont, CA)

Bosworth 1970 — A. B. Bosworth, "Alexander and Callisthenes," *Historia* 19: 407–13

Bosworth 1971a — A. B. Bosworth, "Philip II and Upper Macedonia," *CQ* 21: 93–105

Bosworth 1971b — A. B. Bosworth, "The Death of Alexander the Great: Rumour and Propaganda," *CQ* 21: 111–36

Bosworth 1973 — A. B. Bosworth, "*ΑΣΘΕΤΑΙΡΟΙ*," *CQ* 23: 245–53

Bosworth 1974 — A. B. Bosworth, "The Government of Syria under Alexander the Great," *CQ* 24: 46–64

Bosworth 1975 — A. B. Bosworth, "The Mission of Amphoterus and the Outbreak of Agis' War," *Phoenix* 29: 27–43

Bosworth 1976a — A. B. Bosworth, "Errors in Arrian," *CQ* 26: 117–39

Bosworth 1976b — A. B. Bosworth, "Arrian and the Alexander Vulgate," in *Entretiens Hardt* 22 (Geneva): 1–46

Bosworth 1978 — A. B. Bosworth, "Eumenes, Neoptolemus and *PSI* XII 1284," *GRBS* 19: 227–37

Bosworth 1980 — A. B. Bosworth, "Alexander and the Iranians," *JHS* 100: 1–21

Bosworth 1981 — A. B. Bosworth, "A Missing Year in the History of Alexander the Great," *JHS* 101: 17–39

Bosworth 1983 — A. B. Bosworth, "The Indian Satrapies under Alexander the Great," *Antichthon* 17: 36–46

Bosworth 1986 A. B. Bosworth, "Alexander the Great and the Decline of Macedon," *JHS* 106: 1–12

Bosworth 1988a A. B. Bosworth, *Conquest and Empire: The Reign of Alexander the Great* (Cambridge)

Bosworth 1988b A. B. Bosworth, *From Arrian to Alexander: Studies in Historical Interpretation* (Oxford)

Bosworth 1992 A. B. Bosworth, "History and Artifice in Plutarch's *Eumenes*," in P. A. Stadter (ed.), *Plutarch and the Historical Tradition* (London): 56–89

Bosworth 1994 A. B. Bosworth, "A Macedonian Prince," *CQ* 44: 57–65

Bosworth 1996a A. B. Bosworth, *Alexander and the East: The Tragedy of Triumph* (Oxford)

Bosworth 1996b A. B. Bosworth, "The Historical Setting of Megasthenes' *Indica*," *CP* 91: 113–27

Bosworth 2000 A. B. Bosworth, "Ptolemy and the Will of Alexander," in A. B. Bosworth and E. J. Baynham (eds.), *Alexander the Great in Fact and Fiction* (Oxford): 207–41

Bosworth 2002 A. B. Bosworth, *The Legacy of Alexander: Politics, Warfare and Propaganda under the Successors* (Oxford)

Bosworth 2003a A. B. Bosworth, "*Plus ça change* . . . Ancient Historians and their Sources," *CA* 22: 167–98

Bosworth 2003b A. B. Bosworth, "Why Did Athens Lose the Lamian War?" in Olga Palagia and Stephen V. Tracy (eds.), *The Macedonians in Athens 322–229 BC* (Oxford): 14–22

Bottéro 1992 Jean Bottéro, *Mesopotamia: Writing, Reasoning, and the Gods* (Chicago)

Bradford 1977 A. S. Bradford, *A Prosopography of the Lacedaemonians from the Death of Alexander the Great, 323 BC to the Sack of the Sparta by Alaric, AD 396* (Munich)

Briant 1973 P. Briant, *Antigone le Borgne* (Paris)

Briant 2003 P. Briant, *Darius dans l'ombre d'Alexandre* (Paris)

Brown 1947 T. S. Brown, "Hieronymus of Cardia," *AHR* 53: 684–96

Brown 1950 T. S. Brown, "Clitarchus," *AJP* 71: 134–55

Brown 1955 T. S. Brown, "The Reliability of Megasthenes," *AJP* 76: 18–33

Brown 1973 T. S. Brown, *The Greek Historians* (Lexington, MA)

Brunt 1963 P. A. Brunt, "Alexander's Macedonian Cavalry," *JHS* 83: 27–46

Brunt 1975 P. A. Brunt, "Alexander, Barsine and Heracles," *RFIC* 103: 22–35

Burkert 2004 Walter Burkert, *Babylon, Memphis, Persepolis: Eastern Contexts of Greek Culture* (Cambridge, MA)

Burstein 1977 S. M. Burstein, "*IG* ii^2 561 and the Court of Alexander IV," *ZPE* 24: 223–5

Burstein 1982 S. M. Burstein, "The Tomb of Philip II and the Succession of Alexander the Great," *EMC* 26: 141–63

Burstein 1999 S. M. Burstein, "Cleitarchus in Jerusalem: A Note on the *Book of Judith*," in Frances B. Titchener and Richard F. Moorton, Jr. (eds.), *The Eye Expanded: Life and the Arts in Greco-Roman Antiquity* (Berkeley): 105–12

Burstein 2000 S. M. Burstein, "Prelude to Alexander: The Reign of Khababash," *AHB* 14: 149–54

Carney 1980 E. D. Carney, "Alexander the Lyncestian: The Disloyal Opposition," *GRBS* 21: 23–33

Carney 1980–1 E. D. Carney, "The Conspiracy of Hermolaus," *CJ* 76: 223–31

Carney 1981 E. D. Carney, "The Death of Clitus," *GRBS* 22: 149–60

Carney 1982 — E. D. Carney, "The First Flight of Harpalus Again," *CJ* 77: 9–11

Carney 1987a — E. D. Carney, "Olympias," *Anc. Soc.* 18: 35–62

Carney 1987b — E. D. Carney, "The Career of Adea-Eurydike," *Historia* 36: 496–502

Carney 1988 — E. D. Carney, "The Sisters of Alexander the Great: Royal Relicts," *Historia* 37: 385–404

Carney 1993 — E. D. Carney, "Olympias and the Image of the Virago," *Phoenix* 47: 29–55

Carney 1999 — E. D. Carney, "The Curious Death of the Antipatrid Dynasty," *AM* 6: 209–16

Carney 2000 — E. D. Carney, "Artifice and Alexander History," in A. B. Bosworth and E. J. Baynham (eds.), *Alexander the Great in Fact and Fiction* (Oxford): 263–85

Cartledge 2004 — P. Cartledge, *Alexander the Great: The Hunt for a New Past* (New York)

Cartledge & Spawforth 1989 — P. Cartledge and A. Spawforth, *Hellenistic and Roman Sparta: A Tale of Two Cities* (London)

Cauer 1894 — F. Cauer, "Philotas, Kleitos, Kallisthenes," *Jahrbücher für classische Philologie*, Suppl. 20

Cawkwell 1963 — G. L. Cawkwell, "Demosthenes' Policy after the Peace of Philocrates," *CQ* 13: 120–38, 200–13

Cawkwell 1978 — G. L. Cawkwell, *Philip of Macedon* (London)

Charbonneaux 1952 — J. Charbonneaux, "Antigone le Borgne et Démétrios Poliorcète sont-ils figurés sur le sarcophage d'Alexandre?" *Revue des Arts* 2: 219–23

Clarysse & Schepens 1985 — W. Clarysse and G. Schepens, "A Ptolemaic Fragment of an Alexander-History," *CE* 60: 30–47

Collins 1997 — N. L. Collins, "The Various Fathers of Ptolemy I," *Mnemosyne* 50: 436–76

Cook 1983 — J. M. Cook, *The Persian Empire* (New York)

Crosby 1950 — Margaret Crosby, "The Leases of the Laureion Mines," *Hesperia* 19: 189–297

Dani 1986 — A. H. Dani, *The Historic City of Taxila* (Paris and Tokyo)

Depuydt 1997 — L. Depuydt, "The Time of Death of Alexander the Great: 11 June 323 BC (–322), ca. 4:00–5:00 PM," *Die Welt des Orients* 28: 117–35

Develin 1981 — R. Develin, "The Murder of Philip II," *Antichthon* 15: 86–99

Devine 1975 — A. M. Devine, "Grand Tactics at Gaugamela," *Phoenix* 29: 374–85

Devine 1979 — A. M. Devine, "The *Parthi*, the Tyranny of Tiberius and the Date of Q. Curtius Rufus," *Phoenix* 33: 142–59

Devine 1985a — A. M. Devine, "Diodorus' Account of the Battle of Paraetacene," *AncW* 12: 75–86

Devine 1985b — A. M. Devine, "Diodorus' Account of the Battle of Gabiene," *AncW* 12: 87–96

Devine 1986 — A. M. Devine, "The Battle of Gaugamela: A Tactical and Source-Critical Study," *AncW* 13: 87–116

Dimitrov & Cicikova 1978 — D. P. Dimitrov and M. Cicikova, *The Thracian City of Seuthopolis* (Oxford), B. A. R. Supplement Series no. 38

Doherty 2004 — P. Doherty, *The Death of Alexander the Great* (New York)

Drews 1974 — R. Drews, "Sargon, Cyrus and Mesopotamian Folk History," *JNES* 33: 387–93

Edson 1934 — C. F. Edson, "The Antigonids, Heracles and Beroea," *HSCP* 45: 213–46

Eggermont 1970	P. H. L. Eggermont, "Alexander's Campaign in Gandhara and Ptolemy's List of Indo-Scythian Towns," *OLP* 1: 63–123
Eissfeldt 1940–1	O. Eissfeldt, "Abdalonymos und 'Lmn,'" *ZAW* 58: 248–51
Ellis 1971	J. R. Ellis, "Amyntas Perdikka, Philip II and Alexander the Great: A Study in Conspiracy," *JHS* 91: 15–24
Ellis 1973	J. R. Ellis, "The Stepbrothers of Philip II," *Historia* 22: 350–4
Ellis & Milns 1970	J. R. Ellis and R. D. Milns, *The Spectre of Philip* (Sydney)
Ellis 1994	W. M. Ellis, *Ptolemy of Egypt* (London)
Engel 1971	R. Engel, "Anmerkungen zur Schlacht von Orkynia," *MusHelv* 28: 227–31
Engel 1972a	R. Engel, "Die Überlieferung der Schlacht bei Kretopolis," *Historia* 21: 501–7
Engel 1972b	R. Engel, "Zur Chronologie von Perdikkas' Massnahmen am Vorabend des ersten Koalitionskrieges 321 v. Chr.," *RhM* 115: 215–19
Engel 1973	R. Engel, "Polyäns Stratagem IV 6, 8 zur 'Seeschlacht am Hellespont,'" *Klio* 55: 141–5
Engels 1978	D. W. Engels, "A Note on Alexander's Death," *CP* 73: 224–8
Errington 1969	R. M. Errington, "Bias in Ptolemy's History of Alexander," *CQ* 19: 233–42
Errington 1970	R. M. Errington, "From Babylon to Triparadeisos: 323–320 BC," *JHS* 90: 49–77
Errington 1974	R. M. Errington, "Macedonian 'Royal Style' and its Historical Significance," *JHS* 94: 20–37
Errington 1975	R. M. Errington, "Arybbas the Molossian," *GRBS* 16: 41–50
Errington 1976	R. M. Errington, "Alexander in the Hellenistic World," in *Fondation Hardt, Entretiens* 22 (Geneva, 1976): 137–79
Errington 1977	R. M. Errington, "Diodorus Siculus and the Chronology of the Early Diadochoi, 320–311 BC," *Hermes* 105: 478–504
Errington 1990	R. M. Errington, *A History of Macedonia* translated by Catherine Errington (Berkeley and Los Angeles)
Erskine 2003	A. Erskine (ed.), *A Companion to the Hellenistic World* (Oxford)
Fears 1975	J. Rufus Fears, "Pausanias, the Assassin of Philip II," *Athenaeum* 53: 111–35
Fedak 1990	J. Fedak, *Monumental Tombs of the Hellenistic Age* (Toronto)
Flower 1994	M. A. Flower, *Theopompus of Chios* (Oxford)
Flower 2000	M. A. Flower, "Alexander the Great and Panhellenism," in A. B. Bosworth and E. J. Baynham (eds.), *Alexander the Great in Fact and Fiction* (Oxford): 96–135
Fornara 1983	C. W. Fornara, *The Nature of History in Ancient Greece and Rome* (Berkeley and Los Angeles)
Forrest 1969	W. G. Forrest, "Alexander's Second Letter to the Chians," *Klio* 51: 201–6
Foucher 1901	M. Foucher, *Sur la frontière Indo-Afghane* (Paris, 1901)
Fraser 1967	P. M. Fraser, "Current Problems Concerning the Early History of the Cult of Serapis," *Opuscula Atheniensia* 7: 23–45
Garnsey 1988	P. Garnsey, *Famine and Food Supply in the Graeco-Roman World* (Cambridge)
Gesche 1974	H. Gesche, "Nikokles von Paphos und Nikokreon von Salamis," *Chiron* 4: 103–25

Gibson 2002 — *Interpreting a Classic: Demosthenes and his Ancient Commentators* (Berkeley and Los Angeles)

Golan 1988 — D. Golan, "The Fate of a Court Historian: Callisthenes," *Athenaeum* 66: 99–120

Graeve 1970 — V. von Graeve, *Der Alexandersarkophag und seiner Werkstatt* (Berlin)

Grainger 1990 — J. D. Grainger, *The Cities of Seleukid Syria* (Oxford)

Grainger 1991 — J. D. Grainger, *Hellenistic Phoenicia* (Oxford)

Grainger 1997 — J. D. Grainger, *A Seleukid Prosopography and Gazetteer* (Leiden)

Grainger 2000 — J. D. Grainger, *Aetolian Prosopographical Studies* (Leiden)

Grayson 1975 — A. K. Grayson, *Babylonian Historical-Literary Texts* (Toronto)

Grayson 1995 — A. K. Grayson, "Eunuchs in Power: Their Role in the Assyrian Bureaucracy," in M. Dietrich and O. Loretz (eds.), *Vom Alten Orient zum Alten Testament* (Neukirchen-Vluyn): 85–98

Green 1982 — P. Green, "The Royal Tombs at Vergina: A Historical Analysis," in W. L. Adams and E. N. Borza (eds.), *Philip II, Alexander the Great and the Macedonian Heritage* (Washington, DC): 129–51

Green 1990 — P. Green, *Alexander to Actium: The Historical Evolution of the Hellenistic Age* (Berkeley and Los Angeles)

Green 2003 — P. Green, "Politics, Philosophy and Propaganda: Hermias of Atarneus and his Friendship with Aristotle," in W. Heckel and L. A. Tritle (eds.), *Crossroads of History: The Age of Alexander* (Claremont, CA): 29–46

Greenwalt 1982 — W. S. Greenwalt, "A Macedonian Mantis," *AncW* 5: 17–25

Greenwalt 1984 — W. S. Greenwalt, "The Search for Arrhidaeus," *AncW* 10: 69–77

Griffith 1963 — G. T. Griffith, "A Note on the Hipparchies of Alexander," *JHS* 83: 68–74

Griffith 1965 — G. T. Griffith, "Alexander and Antipater in 323 BC," *PACA* 8: 12–17

Griffith 1968 — G. T. Griffith, "The Letter of Darius at Arrian 2. 14," *PCPS* 14: 33–48

Grote 1913 — K. Grote, *Das griechische Söldnerwesen der hellenistischen Zeit* (Diss. Jena; publ. Weida i. Th.)

Gutschmid 1882 — A. v. Gutschmid, "Trogus und Timagenes," *RhM* 37: 548–55

Habicht 1957 — C. Habicht, "Samische Volksbeschlüsse der hellenistischer Zeit," *MDAI(A)* 72: 152ff.

Habicht 1975 — C. Habicht, "Der Beitrag Spartas zur Restitution von Samos während des Lamischen Krieges," *Chiron* 5: 45–50

Habicht 1977a — C. Habicht, "Athenisches Ehren-dekret vom Jahre des Koroibos (306/5) für einen königlichen Offizier," *AJAH* 2: 37–9

Habicht 1977b — C. Habicht, "Zwei Angehörige des lynkestischen Königshauses," *AM* 2: 511–16

Habicht 1997 — C. Habicht, *Athens from Alexander to Antony* (Cambridge, MA)

Hadley 1969 — R. A. Hadley, "Hieronymus of Cardia and Early Seleucid Mythology," *Historia* 18: 142–52

Hadley 1974 — R. A. Hadley, "Royal Propaganda of Seleucus I and Lysimachus," *JHS* 94: 50–65

Hamel 1998 — Debra Hamel, *Athenian Generals: Military Authority in the Classical Period* (Leiden)

Hamilton 2000 Bernard Hamilton, *The Leper King and his Heirs: Baldwin IV and the Crusader Kingdom of Jerusalem* (Cambridge)

Hamilton 1955 J. R. Hamilton, "Three Passages in Arrian," *CQ* 5: 217–21

Hamilton 1956 J. R. Hamilton, "The Cavalry Battle at the Hydaspes," *JHS* 76: 26–31

Hamilton 1965 J. R. Hamilton, "Alexander's Early Life," *G&R* 12: 116–25

Hamilton 1972 J. R. Hamilton, "Alexander among the Oreitae," *Historia* 21: 603–8

Hammond 1966 N. G. L. Hammond, "The Kingdoms of Illyria *circa* 400–167 BC," *ABSA* 61: 239–53

Hammond 1967 N. G. L. Hammond, *Epirus* (Oxford)

Hammond 1974 N. G. L. Hammond, "Alexander's Campaign in Illyria," *JHS* 94: 66ff.

Hammond 1978 N. G. L. Hammond, "A Cavalry Unit in the Army of Antigonus Monophthalmus: *Asthippoi*," *CQ* 28: 128–35

Hammond 1980 N. G. L. Hammond, "The Battle of the Granicus River," *JHS* 100: 73–88

Hammond 1983 N. G. L. Hammond, *Three Historians of Alexander the Great* (Cambridge)

Hammond 1984 N. G. L. Hammond, "Alexander's Veterans after his Death," *GRBS* 25: 51–61

Hammond 1987 N. G. L. Hammond, "A Papyrus Commentary on Alexander's Balkan Campaign," *GRBS* 28 (1987): 331–47

Hammond 1988 N. G. L. Hammond, "The King and the Land in the Macedonian Kingdom," *CQ* 38: 382–91

Hammond 1989 N. G. L. Hammond, "Casualties and Reinforcements of Citizen Soldiers in Greece and Macedonia," *JHS* 109: 56–68

Hammond 1992 N. G. L. Hammond, "The Regnal Years of Philip and Alexander," *GRBS* 33: 355–78

Hammond 1993 N. G. L. Hammond, *Sources for Alexander the Great: An Analysis of Plutarch's Life and Arrian's Anabasis Alexandrou* (Cambridge)

Hammond 1994 N. G. L. Hammond, *Philip of Macedon* (Baltimore)

Harris 1988 Edward M. Harris, "When was Aeschines Born?" *CP* 83: 211–14

Hauben 1972 H. Hauben, "The Command Structure in Alexander's Mediterranean Fleets," *Anc. Soc.* 3: 55–65

Hauben 1974 H. Hauben, "An Athenian Naval Victory in 321 BC," *ZPE* 13: 56–67

Hauben 1976 H. Hauben, "The Expansion of Macedonian Sea-Power under Alexander the Great," *Anc. Soc.* 7: 79–105

Hauben 1977 H. Hauben, "Rhodes, Alexander and the Diadochi from 333/332 to 304 B.C.," *Historia* 26: 307–39

Heckel 1975 W. Heckel, "Amyntas, Son of Andromenes," *GRBS* 16: 393–8

Heckel 1977a W. Heckel, "The Conspiracy *against* Philotas," *Phoenix* 31: 9–21

Heckel 1977b W. Heckel, "The Flight of Harpalos and Tauriskos," *CP* 72: 133–5

Heckel 1977c W. Heckel, "Asandros," *AJP* 98: 410–12

Heckel 1978a W. Heckel, "Kleopatra or Eurydike?" *Phoenix* 32: 155–8

Heckel 1978b W. Heckel, "The *Somatophylakes* of Alexander the Great: Some Thoughts," *Historia* 27: 224–8

Heckel 1978c W. Heckel, "Leonnatos, Polyperchon and the Introduction of *Proskynesis*," *AJP* 99: 459–61

Heckel 1978d W. Heckel, "On Attalos and Atalante," *CQ* 28: 377–82

Heckel 1979 W. Heckel, "Philip II, Kleopatra and Karanos," *RFIC* 107: 385–93

Heckel 1980a W. Heckel, "Kelbanos, Kebalos or Kephalon?" *BNf* 15: 43–5

Heckel 1980b W. Heckel, "Marsyas of Pella: Historian of Macedon," *Hermes* 108: 444–62

Heckel 1980c W. Heckel, "Alexander at the Persian Gates," *Athenaeum* 58: 168–74

Heckel 1980d W. Heckel "*IG* ii^2 561 and the Status of Alexander IV," *ZPE* 40: 249–50

Heckel 1981a W. Heckel, "Polyxena, the Mother of Alexander the Great," *Chiron* 11: 79–86

Heckel 1981b W. Heckel, "Leonnatus and the Captive Persian Queens: A Case of Mistaken Identity?" *SIFC* 53: 272–4

Heckel 1981c W. Heckel, "Philip and Olympias (337/6 BC)," in G. S. Shrimpton and D. J. McCargar (eds.), *Classical Contributions: Studies in Honour of Malcolm F. McGregor* (Locust Valley, NY): 51–7

Heckel 1981d W. Heckel, "Some Speculations on the Prosopography of the *Alexanderreich*," *LCM* 6: 63–70

Heckel 1981e W. Heckel, "Two Doctors from Kos?" *Mnemosyne* 34: 396–8

Heckel 1981f W. Heckel, "Honours for Philip and Iolaos: *IG* ii^2 561," *ZPE* 44: 75–7

Heckel 1982a W. Heckel, "Who was Hegelochos?" *RhM* 125: 78–87

Heckel 1982b W. Heckel, "The Early Career of Lysimachus," *Klio* 64: 373–81

Heckel 1982c W. Heckel, "The Career of Antigenes," *SO* 57: 57–67

Heckel 1983 W. Heckel, "Adea-Eurydike," *Glotta* 61: 40–2

Heckel 1983–4 W. Heckel, "Kynnane the Illyrian," *RSA* 13/14: 193–200

Heckel 1986a W. Heckel, "Chorienes and Sisimithres," *Athenaeum* 74: 223–6

Heckel 1986b W. Heckel, "Factions and Macedonian Politics in the Reign of Alexander the Great," *AM* 4: 293–305

Heckel 1987a W. Heckel, "Fifty-Two *Anonymae* in the History of Alexander," *Historia* 36: 114–19

Heckel 1987b W. Heckel, "*Anonymi* in the History of Alexander the Great," *L'Ant. Clas.* 56: 130–47

Heckel 1988 W. Heckel, *The Last Days and Testament of Alexander the Great: A Prosopographic Study*. Historia Einzelschriften, Heft 56 (Stuttgart)

Heckel 1989 W. Heckel, "The Granddaughters of Iolaus," *Classicum* 15: 32–9

Heckel 1991 W. Heckel, "Q. Curtius Rufus and the Date of Cleander's Mission to the Peloponnese," *Hermes* 119: 124–5

Heckel 1994 W. Heckel, "Notes on Q. Curtius Rufus' *History of Alexander*," *Acta Classica* 37: 67–78

Heckel 2002a W. Heckel, "The Politics of Distrust: Alexander and his Successors," in D. Ogden (ed.), *The Hellenistic World* (London): 81–95

Heckel 2002b W. Heckel, "The Case of the Missing Phrourarch: Arrian 3.16.6–9," *AHB* 16: 57–60

Heckel 2003 W. Heckel, "King and 'Companions': Observations on the Nature of Power in the Reign of Alexander the Great," in J. Roisman (ed.), *Brill's Companion to Alexander the Great* (Leiden): 197–225

Heckel 2006 W. Heckel, "Mazaeus, Callisthenes and the Alexander Sarcophagus," *Histoira* 55: 385–96

Heckel 2007a — W. Heckel, "Polyperchon as Brigand: Propaganda or Misunderstanding?" *Mnemosyne* 60: 123–6

Heckel 2007b — W. Heckel, "Nicanor son of Balacrus," *GRBS* 47: 401–12

Helmreich 1927 — F. Helmreich, *Die Reden bei Curtius* (Paderborn)

Henry 1990 — A. Henry, "Bithys Son of Kleon of Lysimacheia," in *"Owls to Athens": Essays on Classical Subjects Presented to Sir Kenneth Dover* (Oxford): 179–80

Heskel 1988 — Julia Heskel, "The Political Background to the Arybbas Decree," *GRBS* 29: 185–96

Higgins 1980 — W. E. Higgins, "Aspects of Alexander's Imperial Administration: Some Modern Methods and Views Reviewed," *Athenaeum* 58: 129–52

Hill 1904 — G. Hill, *Catalogue of Greek Coins in the British Museum: Cyprus* (London)

Hill 1910 — G. Hill, *Catalogue of Greek Coins in the British Museum: Phoenicia* (London)

Hill 1949 — G. Hill, *A History of Cyprus*, vol. 1 (Cambridge)

Hofstetter 1972 — J. Hofstetter, *Zu den griechischen Gesandtschaften nach Persien*. Historia Einzelschriften 18 (Wiesbaden)

Holt 1994 — F. L. Holt, "Spitamenes against Alexander," *Historiogeographika* 4: 51–8

Holt 2000 — F. L. Holt, "The Death of Coenus: Another Study in Method," *AHB* 14: 49–55

Holt 2005 — F. L. Holt, *Into the Land of Bones: Alexander the Great in Afghanistan* (Berkeley and Los Angeles)

Hornblower 1981 — Jane Hornblower, *Hieronymus of Cardia* (Oxford)

Hornblower 1982 — Simon Hornblower, *Mausolus* (Oxford)

Judeich 1895 — W. Judeich, "Der Grabherr des Alexander-sarkophages," *Arch. Jahrb.* 10: 164ff.

Junge 1940 — P. Junge, "Hazarapati-," *Klio* 33: 13–38

Kaiser 1956 — W. B. Kaiser, "Der Brief Alexanders des Grossen an Dareios nach der Schlacht bei Issos" (Diss. Mainz)

Kanatsulis 1942 — D. Kanatsulis, *Antipatros. Ein Beitrag zur Geschichte Makedoniens in der Zeit Philipps, Alexanders und der Diadochen* (Thessaloniki)

Kanatsulis 1958/9 — D. Kanatsulis, "Antipatros als Feldherr und Staatsmann in der Zeit Philipps und Alexanders des Grossen," *Hellenika* 16: 14–64

Kanatsulis 1968 — D. Kanatsulis, "Antipatros als Feldherr und Staatsmann nach dem Tode Alexanders des Grossen," *Makedonika* 8: 121–84

Kapetanopoulos 1993 — E. Kapetanopoulos, "Xennias, *μακεδονίζων τῇ φωνῇ*," *ArchEph*: 13–30

Kapetanopoulos 1994 — E. Kapetanopoulos, "Sirras," *AncW* 25: 9–14

Karttunen 1990 — K. Karttunen, "Taxila: Indian City and a Stronghold of Hellenism," *Arctos* 24: 85–96

Keen 1998 — Antony G. Keen, *Dynastic Lycia: A Political History of the Lycians and their Relations with Foreign Powers c.545–362 BC* Mnemosyne Supplement 178 (Leiden)

Keil 1913 — B. Keil, "Ephesische Bürgerrechts- und Proxeniedekrete aus dem vierten und dritten Jahrhundert v. Chr.," *JÖAI* 16: 231–48

Keller 1904 — Erich Keller, "Alexander der Grosse nach der Schlacht bei Issos bis zu seiner Rückkehr aus Aegypten," *Historische Studien,* Heft 48

Kelly 1950 — Amy Kelly, *Eleanor of Aquitaine and the Four Kings* (Cambridge, MA)

Kelly 1990 D. H. Kelly, "Charidemos's Citizenship: The Problem of *IG* ii² 207," *ZPE* 83: 96–109

Kern 1999 Paul Bentley Kern, *Ancient Siege Warfare* (Bloomington)

Kingsley 1986 B. Kingsley, "Harpalos in the Megarid (333–331 BC) and the Grain Shipments from Cyrene," *ZPE* 66: 165–77

Kleiner 1963 G. Kleiner, *Diadochen-Gräber* (Weisbaden)

Koch 2000 H. Koch, "Todesmonat oder Lebensdauer Alexanders des Großen? Textkritische Bemerkungen zu Iust. 12,16,1," *RhM* 143: 326–37

Kornemann 1901 Ernst Kornemann, "Zur Geschichte der antiken Herrscherkulte," *Klio* 1: 51–146

Kosmetatou 2004 Elizabeth Kosmetatou, "Rhoxane's Dedications to Athena Polias," *ZPE* 146: 75–80

Kuhrt 1987 A. Kuhrt, "Usurpation, Conquest and Ceremonial: From Babylon to Persia," in David Cannadine and Simon Price (eds.), *Rituals of Royalty: Power and Ceremonial in Traditional Societies* (Cambridge): 20–55

Landucci Gattinoni 1992 Franca Landucci Gattinoni, *Lismaco di Tracia*. Milan

Lefkowitz 1981 M. Lefkowitz, *The Lives of the Greek Poets* (London)

Lehmann 1980 Phyllis W. Lehmann, "The So-Called Tomb of Philip II: A Different Interpretation," *AJA* 84: 527–31

Lehmann 1982 Phyllis W. Lehmann, "The So-Called Tomb of Philip II: An Addendum," *AJA* 86: 437–42

Lendering 2005 J. Lendering, *Alexander de Grote. De ondergang van het Perzische rijk* (Amsterdam)

Lenschau 1940 T. Lenschau, "Alexander der Große und Chios," *Klio* 33: 207–14

Lepore 1955 E. Lepore, "Leostene e le origini della guerra lamiaca," *PP* 10: 161ff.

Lévêque 1957 P. Lévêque, *Pyrrhos* (Paris)

Litvinsky 1968 B. A. Litvinsky, "Archaeology in Tadzikistan under Soviet Rule," *East and West* 18: 134–5

Lock 1977 R. A. Lock, "The Origins of the Argyraspids," *Historia* 26: 373–8

Lott 1996 J. B. Lott, "Philip II, Alexander and the Two Tyrannies at Eresos of *IG* XII.2.526," *Phoenix* 50: 26–40

Luschey 1968 H. Luschey, "Der Löwe von Ekbatana," *Arch. Mitt. Iran* 1: 115–22

McCoy 1989 W. J. McCoy, "Memnon of Rhodes at the Granicus," *AJP* 110: 413–33

McKechnie 1995 P. McKechnie, "Diodorus Siculus and Hephaestion's Pyre," *CQ* 45: 418–32

McQueen 1978 E. I. McQueen, "Some Notes on the Anti-Macedonian Movement in the Peloponnese in 331 BC," *Historia* 27: 40–64

Macurdy 1929 G. H. Macurdy, "The Political Activities and the Name of Cratesipolis," *AJP* 50: 273–8

Macurdy 1932 G. H. Macurdy, "Roxane and Alexander IV in Epirus," *JHS* 52: 256–61

Marcus 1926 D. Marcus (ed.) *Josephus, Jewish Antiquities*, Loeb Classical Library, vol. 6 (Cambridge, MA)

Marek 1984 C. Marek, *Die Proxenie* (Frankfurt a. M.)

Marquart 1895 J. Marquart, "Untersuchungen zur Geschichte von Eran," *Philologus* 54: 489–527

Marsden 1964 E. W. Marsden, *The Campaign of Gaugamela* (Liverpool)

Marsden 1977 E. W. Marsden, "Macedonian Military Machinery and its Designers under Philip and Alexander," *AM* 2: 211–23

Marshall 1921 J. Marshall, *A Guide to Taxila* (Calcutta)

Marshall 1951 J. Marshall, *Taxila*, 3 vols. (Cambridge)

Martin 1983 T. R. Martin, "Curtius Rufus' Presentaton of Philip Arrhidaeus and Josephus' Account of the Accession of Claudius," *AJAH* 8: 161–90

Mendels 1984 D. Mendels, "Aetolia 331–301: Frustration, Political Power and Survival," *Historia* 33: 129–80

Merkelbach 1954 R. Merkelbach, *Die Quellen des griechischen Alexanderromans*. Zetemata, Heft 9 (Munich)

Merkelbach 1977 R. Merkelbach, *Die Quellen des griechischen Alexanderromans*, 2nd edition, revised and enlarged (Munich)

Merker 1964 I. L. Merker, "Notes on Abdalonymos and the Dated Coinage of Sidon and Ake," *ANSMusN* 11: 13–20

Merker 1965 I. L. Merker, "The Ancient Kingdom of Paionia," *Balkan Studies* 6 (Thessaloniki): 35–46

Merker 1970 I. L. Merker, "The Ptolemaic Officials and the League of the Islanders," *Historia* 19: 141–60

Merker 1979 I. L. Merker, "Lysimachos – Thessalian or Macedonian?" *Chiron* 9: 31–6

Meyer 1879 Eduard Meyer, *Geschichte des Koenigreichs Pontos* (Leipzig)

Miles 2003 M. Miles, "Segregated We Stand? The Mutilated Greeks' Debate at Persepolis, 330 BC," *Disability and Society* 18: 865–79

Milns 1966 R. D. Milns, "Alexander's Seventh Phalanx Battalion," *GRBS* 7: 159ff.

Milns 1982 R. D. Milns, "A Note on Diodorus and Macedonian Military Terminology in Book XVII," *Historia* 31: 123ff.

Missitzis 1985 L. Missitzis, "A Royal Decree of Alexander the Great on the Lands of Philippi," *AncW* 12: 3–14

Momigliano 1931 A. Momigliano, "Peucesta," *RFIC* 59: 245–6

Morrison 1987 J. S. Morrison, "Athenian Sea-Power in 323/2 BC: Dream and Reality," *JHS* 107: 88–97

Mortensen 1991 K. Mortensen, "The Career of Bardylis," *AncW* 22: 49–59

Mortensen 1992 K. Mortensen, "Eurydice: Demonic or Devoted Mother?" *AHB* 6: 156–71

Mosley 1971 D. Mosley, "Greeks, Barbarians, Language and Contact," *Anc. Soc.* 2: 1–6

Neuhaus 1902 O. Neuhaus, "Der Vater des Sisygambis und das Verwandschaftsverhältniss des Dareios III Kodomannos zu Artaxerxes II und III," *RhM* 57: 610–23

Nylander 1993 C. Nylander, "Darius III – the Coward King: Points and Counterpoints," in J. Carlsen et al. (eds.), *Alexander the Great: Reality and Myth* (Rome): 145–59

O'Brien 1992 J. M. O'Brien, *Alexander the Great: The Invisible Enemy* (London)

Ogden 1996 Daniel Ogden, "Homosexuality and Warfare in Ancient Greece," in A. B. Lloyd (ed.), *Battle in Antiquity* (London)

Oikonomides 1987 A. N. Oikonomides, "The Decree of the Athenian Orator Hyperides Honoring the Macedonians Iolaos and Medios," *Praktika B* (Athens): 169–82

Oikonomides 1989 A. N. Oikonomides, "The Elusive Portrait of Antigonus I, the 'One-Eyed,' King of Macedonia," *AncW* 20: 17–20

O'Neil 1999 J. O'Neil, "Olympias: 'The Macedonians will never let themselves be ruled by a woman,'" *Prudentia* 31: 1–14

O'Neil 2002 J. O'Neil, "Iranian Wives and their Roles in Macedonian Royal Courts," *Prudentia* 34: 159–77

Ormerod 1924	Henry A. Ormerod, *Piracy in the Ancient World: An Essay in Mediterranean History* (Liverpool)
Osborne 1973	M. J. Osborne, "Orontes," *Historia* 22: 515–51
Özet 1994	M. A. Özet, "The Tomb of a Noble Woman from the Hekatomnid Royal Period," in J. Isager (ed.), *Hekatomnid Caria and the Ionian Renaissance* (Odense): 88–96
Palagia 1980	O. Palagia, *Euphranor* (Leiden)
Palagia 2000	O. Palagia, "Hephaestion's Pyre and the Royal Hunt of Alexander," in A. B. Bosworth and E. J. Baynham (eds.), *Alexander the Great in Fact and Fiction* (Oxford): 136–206
Parke 1928	H. W. Parke, "When Was Charidemus Made an Athenian Citizen?" *CR* 42: 170
Pearson 1954/5	L. Pearson, "The Diary and Letters of Alexander the Great," *Historia* 3: 429–39
Pearson 1972	L. Pearson, *Demosthenes: Six Private Speeches* (Norman, Oklahoma)
Pekridou 1986	A. Pekridou, *Das Alketas-Grab in Termessos* (Tübingen)
Perdrizet 1899	P. Perdrizet, "Venatio Alexandri," *JHS* 19: 273–9
Perrin 1895	Perrin, B., "Genesis and Growth of an Alexander-Myth," *TAPA* 26: 56–68
Peters 1941	C. Peters, "Zum Namen Abdalonymos," *OLZ* 44: 265ff.
Pfister 1961	F. Pfister, review of P. H. Thomas, *Die Überlieferung der Metzer Alexander-Epitome* (Cologne, 1959), in *Deutsche Literaturzeitung* 82: 893
Phillips 2004	David D. Phillips, *Athenian Political Oratory: 16 Key Speeches* (London)
Picard 1964	C. Picard, "Sépultures des compagnons de guerre ou successeurs macédoniens d'Alexandre," *Journal des Savants*: 298ff.
Poddighe 2001	E. Poddighe, "Il decreto dell'isola di Nesos in onore di Tersippo: ancora una nota sulla politica greca di Poliperconte nel 319 AC," *AHB* 15: 95–101
Pollitt 1986	J. J. Pollitt, *Art in the Hellenistic Age* (Cambridge)
Prag, Musgrave, & Neave 1984	A. J. N. W. Prag, J. H. Musgrave, and R. A. H. Neave, "The Skull from Tomb II at Vergina: King Philip II of Macedon," *JHS* 104: 60–78
Radet 1927	G. Radet, "Notes sur l'histoire d'Alexandre, VII: la prise de Persépolis," *REA* 29: 5–34
Ramsay 1920	W. M. Ramsay, "Military Operations on the North Front of Mount Taurus, III: The Imprisonment and Escape of Dokimos (Diod. XIX 16)," *JHS* 40: 107–12
Ramsay 1923	W. M. Ramsay, "Military Operations on the North Front of Mount Taurus, IV: The Campaigns of 320 and 319 BC," *JHS* 43: 1–10
Rawlinson 1889	H. G. Rawlinson, *History of Phoenicia* (London)
Rawlinson 1912	H. G. Rawlinson, *Bactria* (London)
Reames-Zimmerman 1998	Jeanne Reames-Zimmerman, "Hephaistion Amyntoros: Éminence Grise at the Court of Alexander the Great," Diss. Pennsylvania State University
Reames-Zimmerman 1999	Jeanne Reames-Zimmerman, "An Atypical Affair? Alexander the Great, Hephaistion Amyntoros and the Nature of their Relationship," *AHB* 13: 81–96
Renard and Servais 1955	M. Renard and J. Servais, "A propos du mariage d'Alexandre et de Roxane," *L'Ant. Clas.* 24: 29–50
Renault 1975	Mary Renault, *The Nature of Alexander* (London)
Reuss 1881	F. Reuss, "König Arybbas von Epirus," *RhM* 36: 161ff.

Rice 1993 E. E. Rice, "The Glorious Dead: Commemoration of the Fallen and Portrayal of Victory in the Late Classical and Hellenistic World," in John Rich and Graham Shipley (eds.), *War and Society in the Greek World* (London): 224–57

Richter 1950 G. M. A. Richter, *The Sculpture and Sculptors of the Greeks* (New Haven)

Riginos 1994 Alice S. Riginos, "The Wounding of Philip II of Macedon: Fact and Fabrication," *JHS* 114: 103–9

Robert 1934 "Étude d'épigraphie grecque XXXIV," *RPh* 8: 267–92

Robinson 1929 C. A. Robinson, Jr., "The Seer Aristander," *AJP* 50: 195–7

Roebuck 1948 C. Roebuck, "The Settlements of Philip II with the Greek States in 338 BC," *CP* 43: 73–92

Roisman 1984 J. Roisman, "Ptolemy and his Rivals in the History of Alexander," *CQ* 34: 373–85

Roisman 2003 J. Roisman (ed.), *Brill's Companion to Alexander the Great* (Leiden)

Rosen 1967 K. Rosen, "Political Documents in Hieronymus of Cardia," *Acta Classica* 10: 101ff.

Rubinsohn 1977 Z. Rubinsohn, "The 'Philotas Affair' – A Reconsideration," *AM* 2: 409–20

Samuel 1986 A. E. Samuel, "The Earliest Elements in the Alexander Romance," *Historia* 35: 427–37

Schachermeyr 1920 F. Schachermeyr, "Das Ende des makedonischen Königshauses," *Klio* 16: 332–7

Schachermeyr 1970 F. Schachermeyr, *Alexander in Babylon und die Reichsordnung nach seinem Tode* (Vienna)

Schäfer 2002 C. Schäfer, *Eumenes von Kardia und der Kampf um die Macht im Alexanderreich* (Frankfurt)

Schäfer 2003 P. Schäfer, *The History of the Jews in the Graeco-Roman World* (London)

Schefold 1968 K. Schefold, *Der Alexander-Sarkophag* (Berlin)

Schoder 1982 R. V. Schoder, "Alexander's Son and Roxane in the Boscoreale Murals," *AncW* 5: 27–32

Schreiber 1903 T. Schreiber, *Studien ueber das Bildnis Alexanders des Grossen: Ein Beitrag zur alexandrinischen Kunstgeschichte.* Koeniglich sachsischen Gesellschaft der Wissenschaften, Philologisch-historische Klasse, Abhandlungen 21 (Leipzig)

Schubert 1898 R. Schubert, "Der Tod des Kleitos," *RhM* 53: 99–117

Schubert 1901 R. Schubert, "Die Porusschlacht," *RhM* 56: 543–62

Sealey 1960 R. Sealey, "Who was Aristogeiton?" *BICS* 7: 33–43

Seel 1972 O. Seel, *Eine römische Weltgeschichte* (Nürnberg)

Seibert 1967 J. Seibert, *Historische Beiträge zu den dynastischen Verbindungen in hellenistischer Zeit.* Historia Einzelschriften, Heft 10 (Wiesbaden)

Seibert 1970 J. Seibert, "Philokles, Sohn des Apollodoros . . . ," *Historia* 19: 337–51

Seibert 1972 J. Seibert, "Nochmals zu Kleomenes von Naukratis," *Chiron* 2: 99–102

Seibert 1979 J. Seibert, *Die politischen Flüchtlinge und Verbannten in der griechischen Geschichte* (Darmstadt, 1979)

Seibert 1985 J. Seibert, *Die Eroberung des Perserreiches durch Alexander den Grossen auf kartographischer Grundlage* (Wiesbaden)

Seibert 1987 J. Seibert, "Dareios III," in W. Will (ed.), *Zu Alexander d. Gr.* Amsterdam: 1. 437–56

Shackleton-Bailey 1981 D. R. Shackleton-Bailey, "Curtiana," *CQ* 31: 175–80

Sharples 1994 — I. Sharples, "Curtius' Treatment of Arrhidaeus," *MedArch* 7: 53–60

Sherwin-White 1978 — Susan Sherwin-White, *Ancient Cos*. Hypomnemata, Heft 51 (Göttingen)

Shoemaker 1968 — G. Shoemaker, "Dinarchus: Traditions of his Life and Speeches," Diss. Columbia University

Shrimpton 1991 — G. S. Shrimpton, *Theopompus the Historian* (Montreal and Kingston 1991)

Simpson 1957 — R. H. Simpson, "A Possible Case of Misrepresentation in Diodorus XIX," *Historia* 6: 504–5

Smith 1988 — R. R. R. Smith, *Hellenistic Royal Portraits* (Oxford)

Snell 1964 — B. Snell, *Scenes from Greek Drama* (Berkeley and Los Angeles)

Sofman & Tsibukidis 1987 — A. S. Sofman and D. I. Tsibukidis, "Nearchus and Alexander," *AncW* 16: 71–7

Sohlberg 1972 — D. Sohlberg, "Zu Kleitarch," *Historia* 21: 758–9

Speck 2002 — H. Speck, "Alexander at the Persian Gates: A Study in Historiography and Topography," *AJAH* n.s. 1: 1–234

Spencer 2002 — Diana Spencer, *The Roman Alexander: Reading a Cultural Myth* (Exeter)

Stadter 1965 — Philip A. Stadter, *Plutarch's Historical Methods: An Analysis of the Mulierum Virtutes* (Cambridge, MA)

Stark 1958 — Freya Stark, *Alexander's Path from Caria to Cilicia* (New York)

Stein 1937 — A. Stein, *Archaeological Reconnaissances in North-West India and South-East Iran* (London)

Stein 1938 — A. Stein, "An Archaeological Journey in Western Iran," *Geog. Journal* 92: 313–42

Stoneman 1994 — R. Stoneman, "Who were the Brahmans?" *CQ* 44: 500–10

Stoneman 1995 — R. Stoneman, "Naked Philosophers: The Brahmans in the Alexander Historians and the Alexander Romance," *JHS* 115: 99–114

Stylianou 1998 — P. J. Stylianou, *A Historical Commentary on Diodorus Siculus, Book 15* (Oxford)

Sumner 1961 — G. V. Sumner, "Curtius Rufus and the *Historiae Alexandri*," *AUMLA* 15: 30–9

Sutton 1980a — D. F. Sutton, "Harpalus as Pallides," *RhM* 123: 96

Sutton 1980b — D. F. Sutton, *The Greek Satyr Play* (Meisenheim am Glan)

Tarn 1921 — W. W. Tarn, "Heracles son of Barsine," *JHS* 41: 18–28

Tarn 1929 — W. W. Tarn, "Queen Ptolemais and Apama," *CQ* 23: 138–41

Tarn 1933 — W. W. Tarn, "Two Notes on Ptolemaic History," *JHS* 53: 57–61

Tarn 1951 — W. W. Tarn, *The Greeks in Bactria and India* (Cambridge)

Teodorsson 1990 — S.-T. Teodorsson, "Theocritus the Sophist, Antigonus the One-Eyed and the Limits of Clemency," *Hermes* 118: 380–2

Treves 1939 — P. Treves, "Hyperides and the Cult of Hephaestion," *CR* 53: 56–7

Tritle 2003 — Lawrence Tritle, "Alexander the Great and the Killing of Cleitus the Black," in W. Heckel and L. A. Tritle (eds.), *Crossroads of History: The Age of Alexander* (Claremont, CA): 127–46

van Groningen 1925 — B. A. van Groningen, "De Cleomene Naucratita," *Mnemosyne* 53: 101–30

Vatin 1984 C. Vatin, "Lettre adressée à la cité de Philippes par les ambassadeurs auprès d'Alexandre," in *Praktika B* (Athens): 259–70

Vogelsang 1985 W. Vogelsang, "Early Historical Arachosia in South-East Afghanistan," *Iranica Antiqua* 20: 55–99

Vogt 1971 J. Vogt, "Kleomenes von Naukratis: Herr von Ägypten," *Chiron* 1: 153–7

Walek 1924 T. Walek, "Les opérations navales pendant la guerre lamiaque," *RPh* 48: 22–30

Wehrli 1964 C. Wehrli, "Phila, fille d'Antipater et épouse de Démétrius, roi des Macédoniens," *Historia* 13: 140–6

Wehrli 1968 C. Wehrli, *Antigone et Démétrios* (Geneva)

Weippert 1972 O. Weippert, *Alexander-imitatio und römische Politik in republikanischer Zeit* (Würzburg)

Weiskopf 1989 M. Weiskopf, *The So-Called "Great Satraps' Revolt," 366–360 BC: Concerning Local Instability in the Achaemenid Far West* (Stuttgart)

Welles 1963 C. B. Welles, "The Reliability of Ptolemy as an Historian," in *Miscellanea di studi alessandri in memoria di Augusto Rostagni* (Turin): 101–16.

Welles 1970 C. Bradford Welles, *Alexander and the Hellenistic World* (Toronto)

Westlake 1935 H. D. Westlake, *Thessaly in the Fourth Century BC* (London)

Wheatley 1995 P. V. Wheatley, "Ptolemy Soter's Annexation of Syria 320 BC" *CQ* 45: 433–40

Wheatley 1997a P. V. Wheatley, "The Lifespan of Demetrius Poliorcetes," *Historia* 46: 19–27

Wheatley 1997b P. V. Wheatley, "Problems in Analysing Source Documents in Ancient History: The Case of Philip, Adviser to Demetrius Poliorcetes, 314–312 BC, and *IG* ii^2 561," *Limina* 3: 61–70

Wheatley 1998 P. V. Wheatley, "The Date of Polyperchon's Invasion of Macedonia and the Murder of Heracles," *Antichthon* 32: 12–23

Wheatley 1999 P. V. Wheatley, "Young Demetrius Poliorcetes," *AHB* 13: 1–13

Wheeler 1968 M. Wheeler, *Flames over Persepolis* (New York)

Wheeler 1976 M. Wheeler, *My Archaeological Mission to India and Pakistan* (London)

Whitby 2004 Michael Whitby, "Four Notes on Alexander," *Electrum: Studies in Ancient History* 8: 35–48

Wilcken 1901 U. Wilcken, "Zu den Pseudo-Aristotelischen Oeconomica," *Hermes* 36: 187–200

Wilhelm 1943 A. Wilhelm, "Alexander der Große an die Chier," in *Griechische Königsbriefe*. Klio-Beiheft 48: 1–16

Williams 1984 J. M. Williams, "A Note on Athenian Chronology, 319/8–318/7 BC," *Hermes* 112: 300–5

Williams 1989 J. M. Williams, "Demades' Last Years, 323/2–319 BC: A 'Revisionist' Interpretation," *AncW* 19: 19–30

Willrich 1899 H. Willrich, "Krateros und der Grabherr des Alexandersarkophags," *Hermes* 34: 231–50

Winter 1912 F. Winter, *Der Alexandersarkophag aus Sidon* (Strassburg)

Wirth 1965 G. Wirth, "Zur grossen Schlacht des Eumenes 322 (*PSI* 1284)," *Klio* 46: 283–8

Wirth 1967 G. Wirth, "Zur Politik des Perdikkas 323," *Helikon* 7: 281–322

Wirth 1971a	G. Wirth, "Alexander zwischen Gaugamela und Persepolis," *Historia* 20: 617–32
Wirth 1971b	G. Wirth, "Dareios und Alexander," *Chiron* 1: 133–52
Wirth 1972	G. Wirth, "Nearchos der Flottenchef," in *Acta Conventus "Eirene,"* reprinted in *Studien zur Alexandergeschichte* (Wiesbaden): 51–75
Wirth 1985	G. Wirth, *Philipp II* (Stuttgart)
Wirth 1988	G. Wirth, "Nearch, Alexander und die Diadochen. Spekulationen über einen Zusammenhang," *Tyche* 3: 241–59
Wirth 1989	G. Wirth, *Der Kampfverband des Proteas. Spekulationen zu den Begleitumständen der Laufbahn Alexanders* (Amsterdam)
Wood 1997	Michael Wood, *In the Footsteps of Alexander the Great* (Berkeley and Los Angeles, 1997)
Worthington 1984	I. Worthington, "The First Flight of Harpalus Reconsidered," *G&R* 31: 161–9
Worthington 1986	I. Worthington, "The Chronology of the Harpalus Affair," *SO* 61: 63–76
Worthington 1994	I. Worthington, "The Harpalus Affair and the Greek Response to Macedonian Hegemony," in I. Worthington (ed.), *Ventures into Greek History* (Oxford): 307–30
Worthington 2000	I. Worthington (ed.), *Demosthenes: Statesman and Orator* (London)
Worthington 2003	I. Worthington, "Alexander's Destruction of Thebes," in W. Heckel and L. A. Tritle (eds.), *Crossroads of History: The Age of Alexander* (Claremont, CA): 65–86
Xirotiris & Langenscheidt 1981	N. I. Xirotiris and F. Langenscheidt, "The Cremations from the Royal Macedonian Tombs of Vergina," *AE*: 142–60
Ziegler 1935	K. Ziegler, "Plutarchstudien," *RhM* 84: 379–80
Zahrnt 1999	M. Zahrnt, "Alexander der Grosse und der lykische Hirt. Bemerkungen zu Propaganda während des Rachekrieges (334–330 v. Chr.)," *AM* 6: 1381–7
Zumetikos 1894	A. M. Zumetikos, *De Alexandri Olympiadisque Epistularum fontibus et reliquiis* (Berlin)

Stemmata

Key to the Stemmata

= (1) Phila (2)	Indicates the first and second marriages
Wife =	The name of the wife is unknown
Husband =	The name of the husband is unknown
Daughter, Son	The name of the daughter or son is unknown
x	The name and sex of the individual are both unknown
F1	Anonymous female discussed in the *Who's Who*
M3	Anonymous male discussed in the *Who's Who*
~	mistress, lover
=	marriage
—(b)—	betrothal
(?)	The name of the individual is not certain but can be guessed at
----------	The relationship is not certain
I, II, III, IV	First, second, third, fourth king (or "queen") of that name

Stemma I The Macedonian royal house

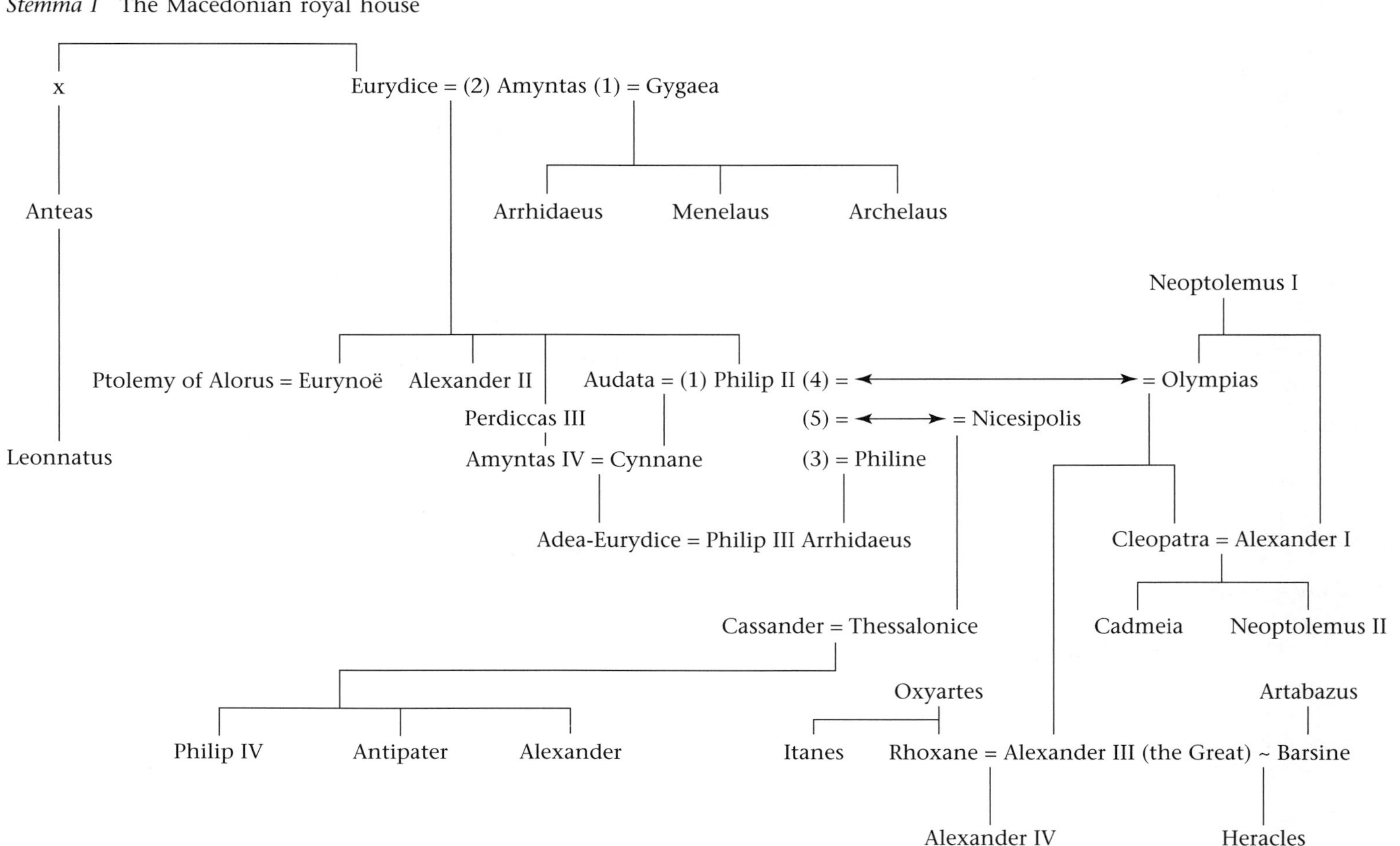

Stemma II The royal house of Epirus

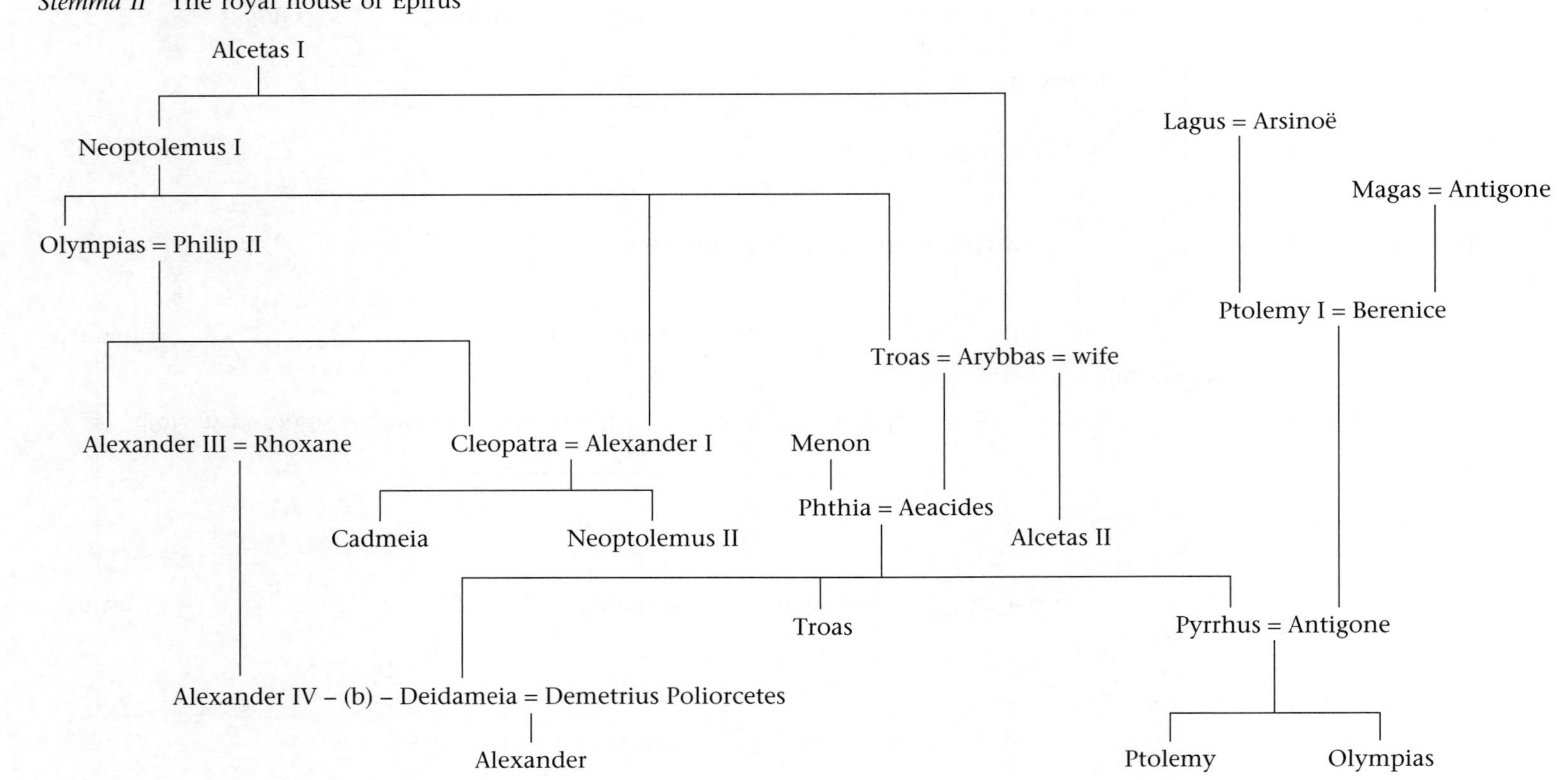

Stemma III The last Achaemenids

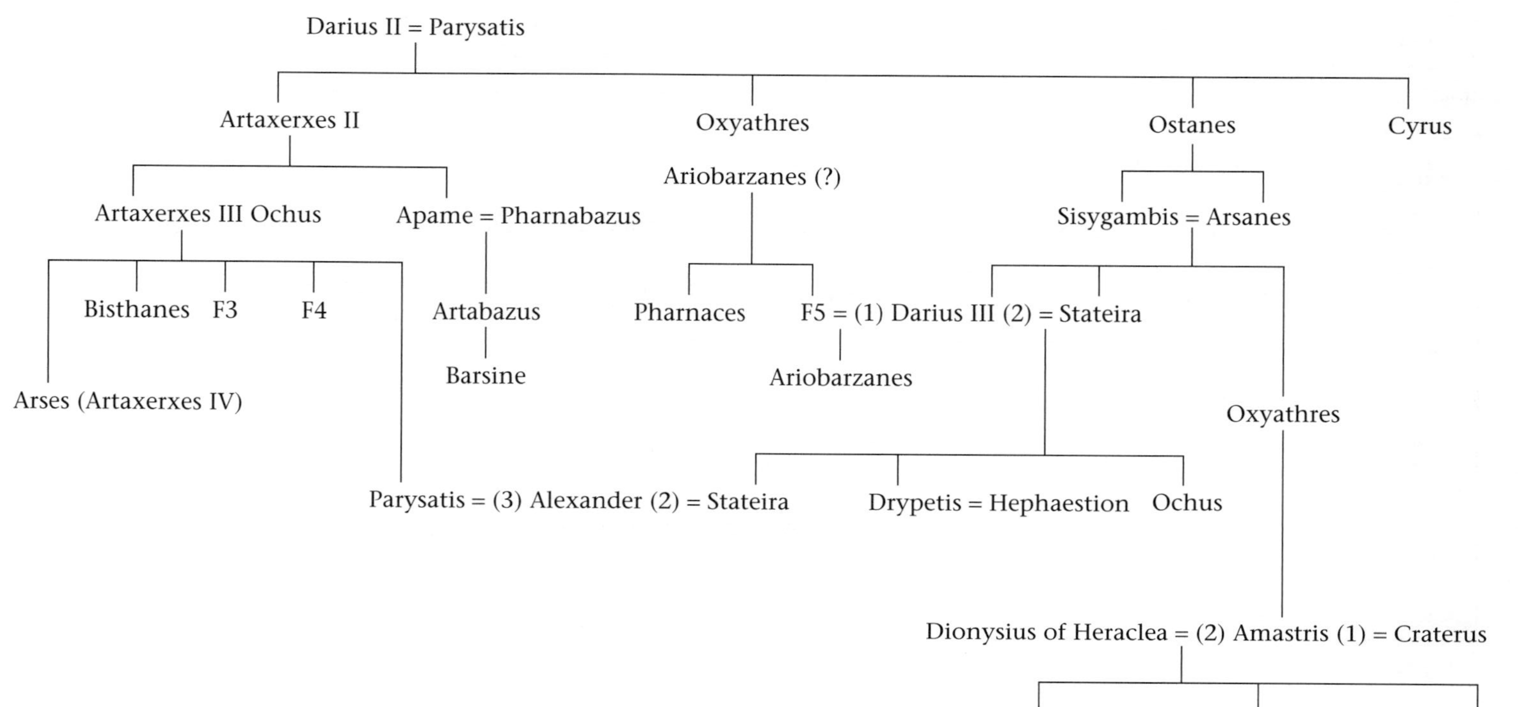

Stemma IV The house of Pharnabazus

Stemma V The house of Iolaus

Iolaus

Cassander

Antipater

Antigone = Magas

Ptolemy I = (2) Berenice (1) = Philip

Antigone = Pyrrhus

Magas

Philip

Nicanor

Pleistarchus

Alexarchus

Iolaus

Perilaus

Balacrus = (1) Phila (2) = Craterus

Alexander Lyncestes = F37

Arrhabaeus

Cassander = Thessalonice

Antipater

Craterus

Cassander

(3) = Demetrius Poliorcetes

Philip IV

Antipater

Alexander

Perdiccas = (1) Nicaea (2) = Lysimachus

Ptolemy I = Eurydice

Antigonus Gonatas

Stratonice

Arsinoë II = (2) Ptolemy II (1) = Arsinoë I

Agathocles = Lysandra

Ptolemy Ceraunus

Stemma VI The family of Antigonus

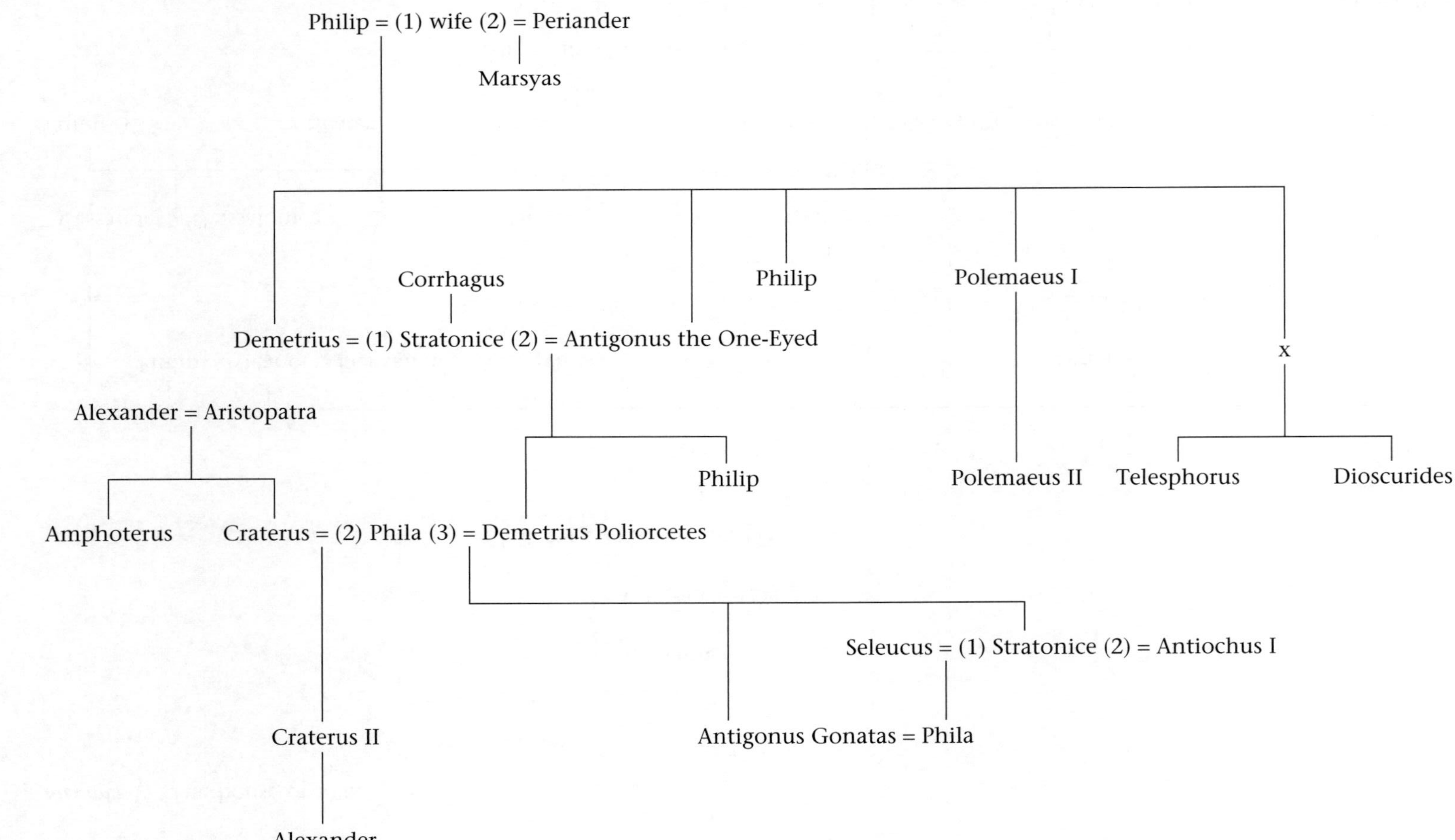

Stemma VII The house of Parmenion

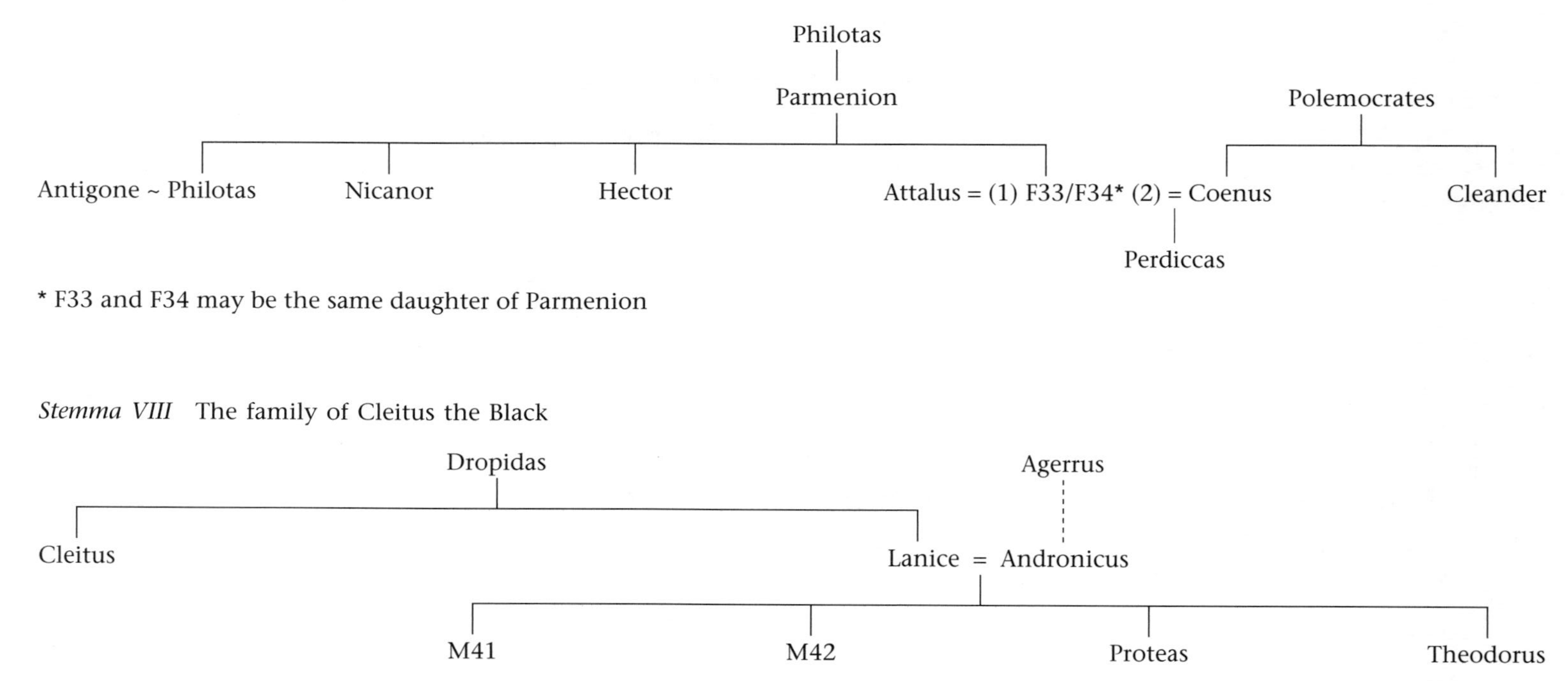

* F33 and F34 may be the same daughter of Parmenion

Stemma VIII The family of Cleitus the Black

Stemma IX The house of Agathocles

Agathocles

Alcimachus

Philip

Autodicus = Adeia

Antipater

Berenice = (2) Ptolemy I Soter (1) = Eurydice

Nicaea = (1) Lysimachus

Lysandra = Agathocles

= (4)

Ptolemy Philadelphus (1) = Arsinoë I

(2) = (3) Arsinoë II Philadelphus (1) =

Ptolemy

Lysimachus

Philip

Stemma X The house of Ptolemy

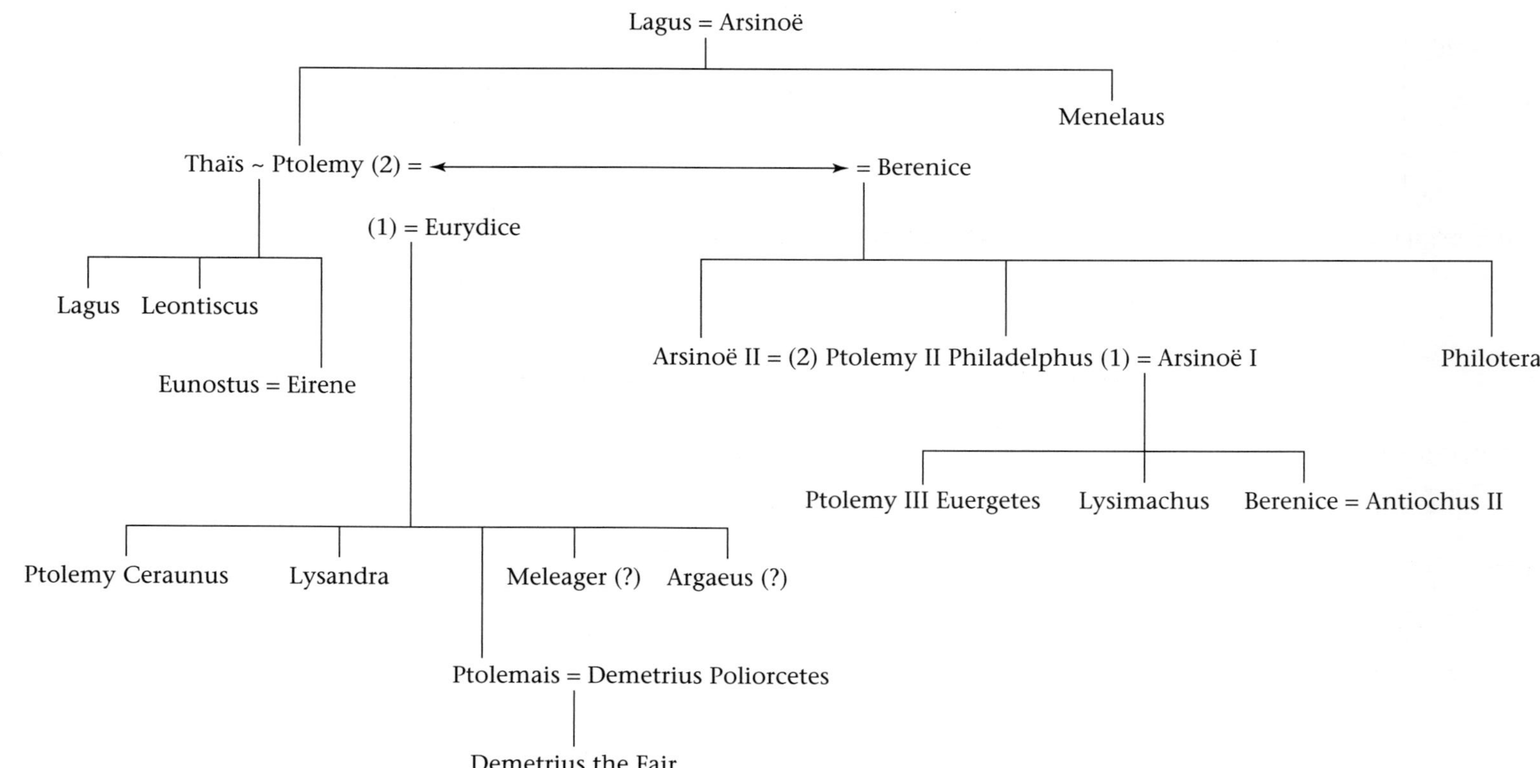

Stemma XI The house of Seleucus

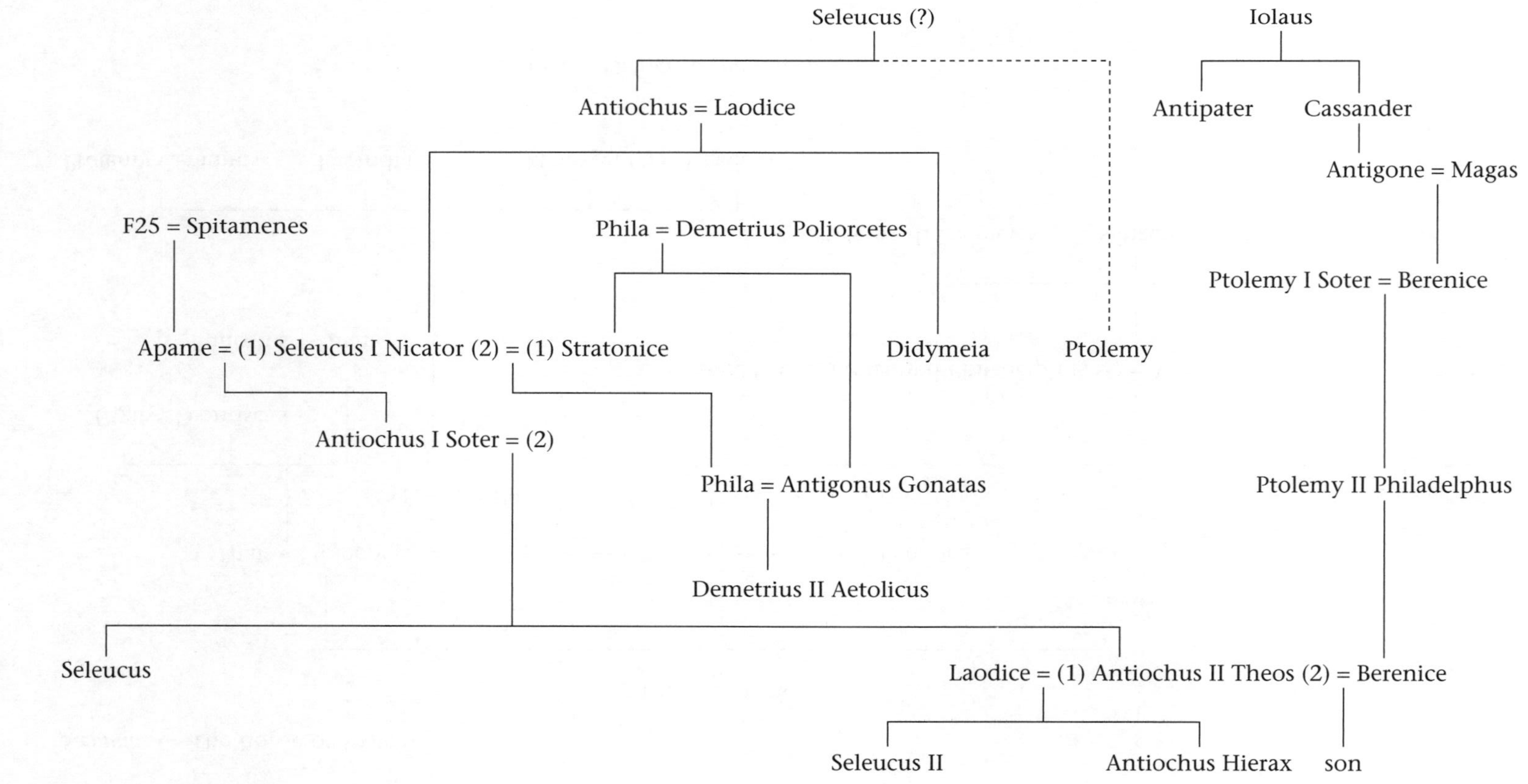

Stemma XII The relatives of Simmias and Andromenes of Tymphaea

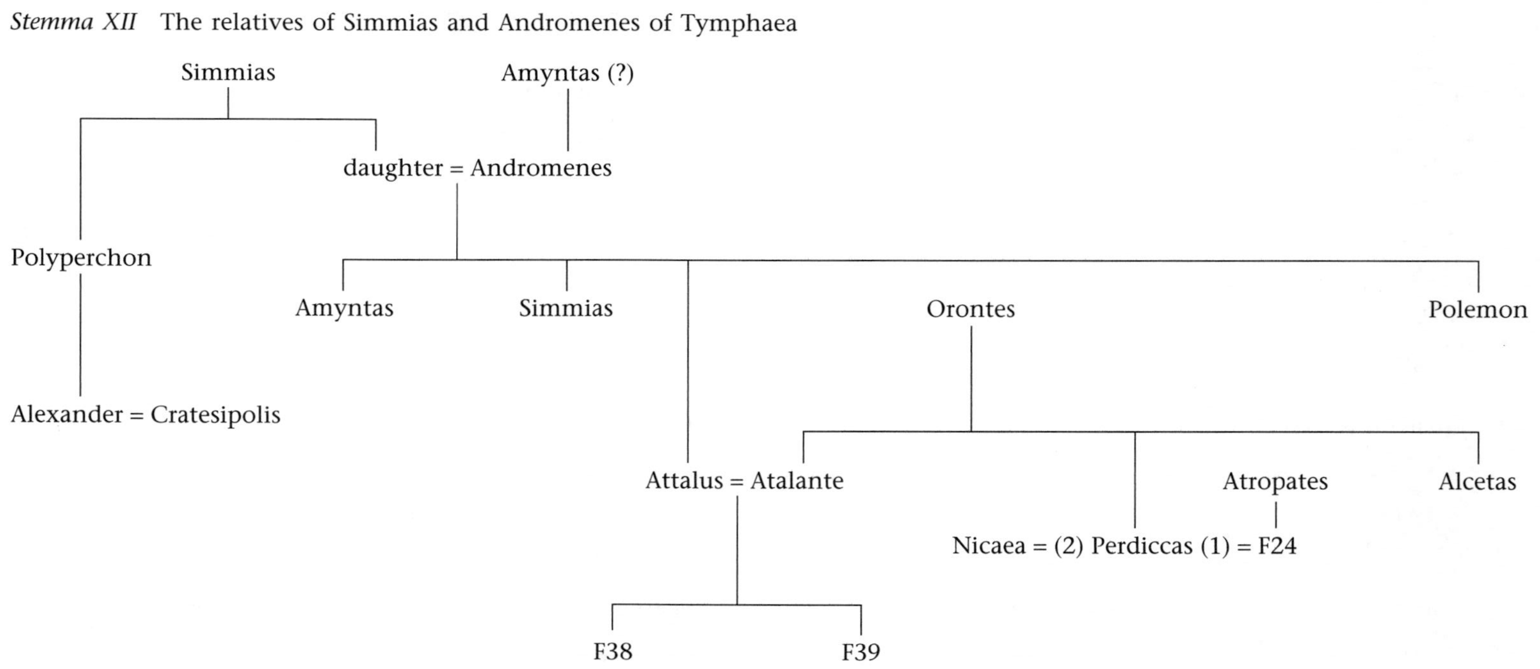

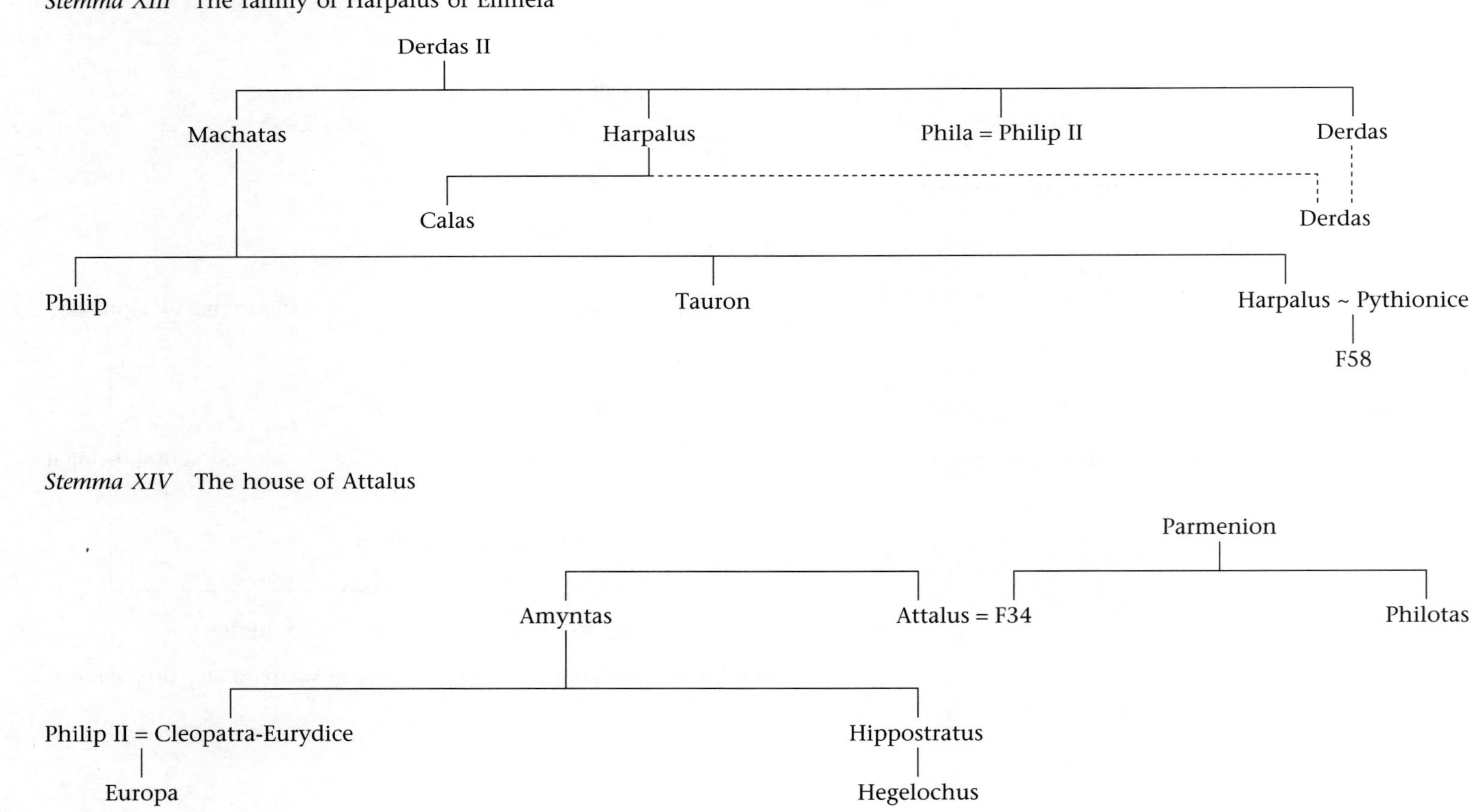

Stemma XIII The family of Harpalus of Elimeia

Stemma XIV The house of Attalus

Stemma XV The house of Aëropus of Lyncestis

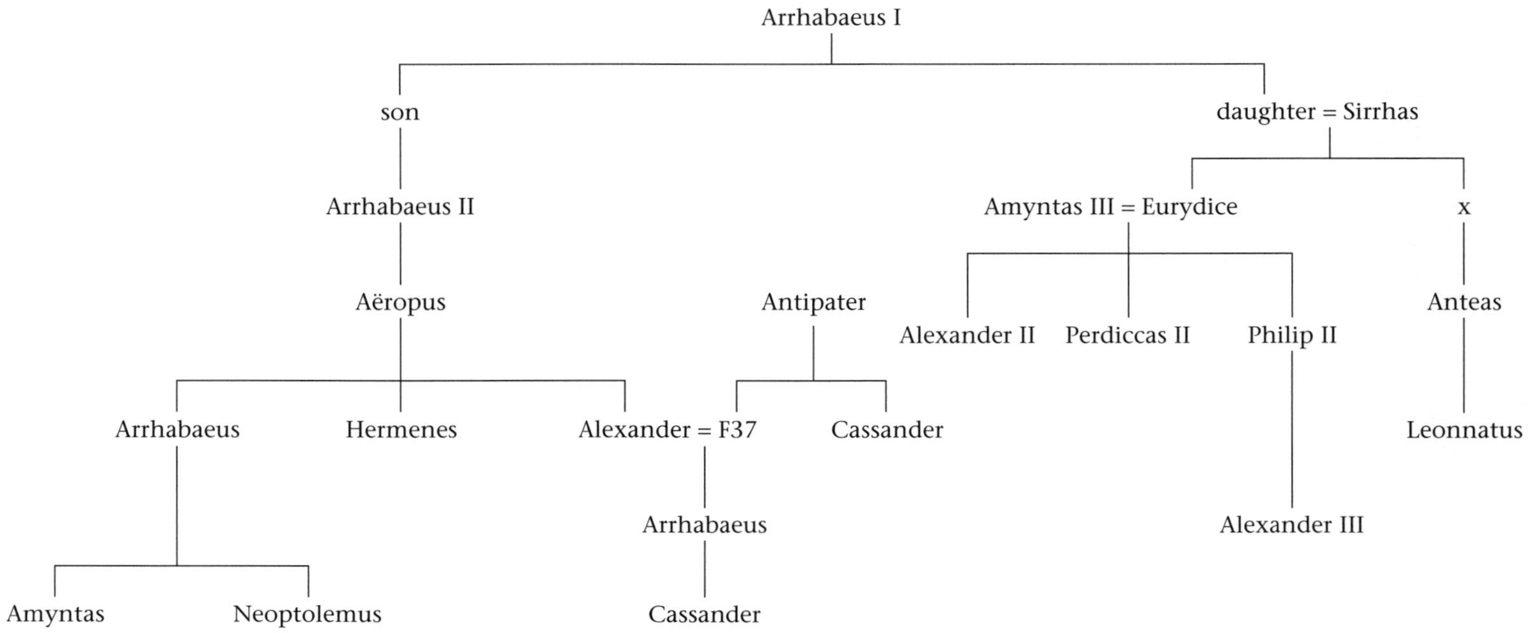

Arrhabaeus I
son
daughter = Sirrhas
Arrhabaeus II
Amyntas III = Eurydice
x
Aëropus
Antipater
Alexander II
Perdiccas II
Philip II
Anteas
Arrhabaeus
Hermenes
Alexander = F37
Cassander
Leonnatus
Arrhabaeus
Alexander III
Amyntas
Neoptolemus
Cassander

Stemma XVI The Hecatomnids of Caria

Hecatomnus = wife
Mausolus = Artemisia
Idrieus = Ada
Pixodarus = Aphneis
Ada = Orontopates

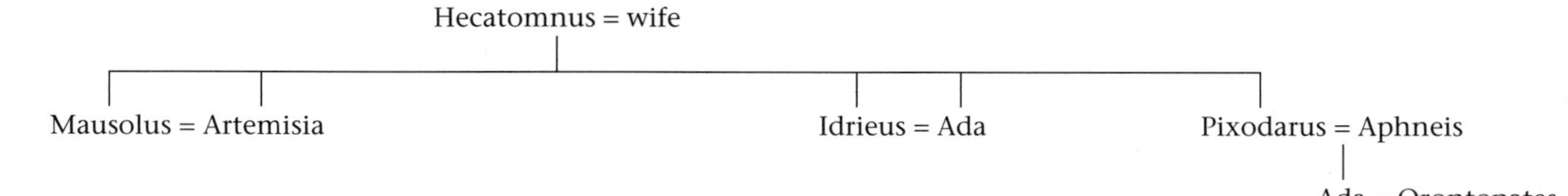